Zambia

THE BRADT TRAVEL GUIDE

The Bradt Story

In 1974, my former husband George Bradt and I spent three days sitting on a river barge in Bolivia writing our first guide for like-minded travellers: *Backpacking along Ancient Ways in Peru and Bolivia*. The 'little yellow book', as it became known, is now in its seventh edition and continues to sell to travellers throughout the world.

Since 1980, with the establishment of Bradt Publications, I have continued to publish guides for the discerning traveller, covering more than 100 countries and all six continents; in 1997 we won *The Sunday Times* Small Publisher of the Year Award. *Zambia* is the 163rd Bradt title or new edition to be published.

The company continues to develop new titles and new series, but in the forefront of my mind there remains our original ethos – responsible travel with an emphasis on the culture and natural history of the region. I hope that you will get the most out of your trip, and perhaps have the opportunity to give something in return.

Travel guides are by their nature continuously evolving. If you experience anything which you would like to share with us, or if you have any amendments to make to this guide, please write; all your letters are read and passed on to the author. Most importantly, do remember to travel with an open mind and to respect the customs of your hosts – it will add immeasurably to your enjoyment.

Happy travelling!

Hilary Bradt

Hilary Bradt

19 High Street, Chalfont St Peter, Bucks SL9 9QE, England
Tel: 01753 893444 Fax: 01753 892333 Email: bradtpublications@compuserve.com

Zambia

THE BRADT TRAVEL GUIDE
Second Edition

Chris McIntyre

Bradt Publications, UK
The Globe Pequot Press Inc, USA

First published in 1996 by Bradt Publications.
This second edition published 1999 by Bradt Publications,
19 High Street, Chalfont St Peter, Bucks, SL9 9QE, England
Published in the USA by The Globe Pequot Press Inc, 6 Business Park Road,
PO Box 833, Old Saybrook, Connecticut 06475-0833

British Library Cataloguing in Publication Data
A catalogue record for this book is available in the British Library
ISBN 1 898323 99 2

Library of Congress Cataloging-in-Publication Data
applied for

Photographs
Front cover A walking safari from Kakuli Bushcamp, South Luangwa
Text Peter Dolby (PD), Sir Peter Holmes (PH),
Chris McIntyre (CM), Paul Mount (PM)
Illustrations Edwina Hannam, Annabel Milne
Maps Steve Munns

Typeset by Linden Sheffield
Printed and bound in Italy by LegoPrint S.p.A. - Trento

Author

Chris McIntyre went to Africa in 1987, after reading physics at Queen's College, Oxford. He taught with VSO in Zimbabwe for almost three years and travelled around extensively. In 1990 he co-authored the UK's first *Guide to Namibia and Botswana*, before spending three years as a business analyst in London.

Since 1994 Chris has concentrated on what he enjoys: Africa. He is now managing director of Sunvil Discovery – a specialist African division of one of the UK's top independent tour operators – which organises individual trips to Southern Africa. In 1996 he wrote the first edition of this Guide to Zambia – then the first overseas guidebook to Zambia – and in '98, Bradt's acclaimed *Namibia* guide. He can be contacted by email on africa@sunvil.co.uk

He is a Fellow of the Royal Geographical Society and contributes to various magazines, including *Wanderlust, BBC Wildlife* and *Travel Africa*. Based in London, he spends two or three months each year travelling and researching in Southern Africa.

MAJOR CONTRIBUTORS

Judi Helmholz counts travel consultant, entrepreneur, safari guide, chicken farmer and 'facilitator' amongst her occupations. She lives beside the Zambezi with her husband, Arthur, several rottweilers and 4,000 chickens. She has explored many of Zambia's wild places, and is active in conservation and tourism – serving as one of Zambia's first female Honorary Wildlife Police and with Livingstone's Tourism Association and Chamber of Commerce. She provided anecdotes and information on Livingstone, the Western Provinces, and Zambia's languages.

Gerard Zytkow has lived in Zambia for 35 years, and travelled extensively in the wilds. He provided vital news and information on the Copperbelt and northern Zambia, and helped greatly with communications in these areas.

THE NEXT EDITION

Our readers play a vital role in updating books for the next edition. If you have found changes, or new and exciting places, or have a story to share, do write. The most helpful contributions will receive a free book. Email the author on chris@sunvil.co.uk or write to:

'Zambia', Bradt Publications, 19 High St, Chalfont St Peter, Bucks, SL9 9QE, UK. Tel: 01753 893444 Fax: 01753 892333

Contents

Introduction   IX

PART ONE   THE COUNTRY   I

Chapter I   **Facts and Figures**   3

Chapter 2   **History and Economy**   7
                  History 7, Economy 17

Chapter 3   **People and Culture**   21
                  People 21, Culture 27

Chapter 4   **The Natural Environment**   35
                  Physical environment 35, Flora and fauna 36, Conservation 40

Chapter 5   **Planning and Preparations**   45
                  Getting there 45, Entry requirements 47, When to go 49,
                  Money 55, What to take 56, Maps and navigation 58, Photography
                  and optics 59, Vehicle hire 60, Organising a safari 61, Suggested
                  intineraries 64

Chapter 6   **Health and Safety**   65
                  Health 65, Safety 75

Chapter 7   **In the Wilds**   79
                  Driving 79, Bush camping 82, Walking in the bush 86,
                  Canoeing 89, Minimum impact 91

Chapter 8   **Zambia Today**   93
                  Cost of living 93, Getting around 94, Accommodation 98,
                  Food and drink 99, What to buy 101, Organising and booking
                  103, Communications and media 104, Miscellaneous 107

PART TWO   THE GUIDE   III

Chapter 9   **Lusaka**   I13
                  Getting there and away 113, Orientation 117, Where to
                  stay 117, Where to eat 131, Getting around 134, Banks and
                  money 134, What to see and do 135, Shopping 139,
                  Information and addresses 141

Chapter 10   **Livingstone and Victoria Falls**   145
                  Livingstone 149, Victoria Falls 171, What to see
                  and do 177, Useful information 190

Chapter 11   **Lake Kariba and the Lower Zambezi**   195
                  From Livingstone to Lusaka 195, Lake Kariba 199, From Lusaka
                  to Chirundu 207, Lower Zambezi National Park 211

Chapter 12	**The Luangwa Valley**	219
	From Lusaka to the Luangwa 219, South Luangwa National Park 225, North Luangwa National Park 251, Luambe National Park 255, Lukusuzi National Park 256, Luangwa Valley safari operators 256	
Chapter 13	**Bangweulu Area**	259
	Mkushi 259, Serenje 261, Kasanka National Park 263, Lavushi Manda National Park 269, Lake Bangweulu and Swamps 270, Mpika 276	
Chapter 14	**Northern Zambia**	283
	The Great North Road 283, Lake Tanganyika 292, Kalambo Falls 294, Sumbu National Park 295, The road to Mweru Wantipa 301, Nyika Plateau National Park 307	
Chapter 15	**The Copperbelt**	313
	Kapiri Mposhi 315, Kabwe 317, Ndola 319, Kitwe 321, Chingola 327	
Chapter 16	**The Kafue River Basin**	329
	Mumbwa 329, Kafue National Park 329, Lochinvar and Blue Lagoon National Parks 346	
Chapter 17	**The Western Provinces**	353
	Northwestern Zambia 353, Barotseland 358, Southwestern Zambia 370	
Appendix 1	**Wildlife Guide**	377
Appendix 2	**Languages**	395
Appendix 3	**Further Reading**	397
Index		401

LIST OF MAPS

Chipata	222
Copperbelt, The	314
Eclipse map	52
Kabwe	316
Kafue River Basin	330
Kafue, Northern	334
Kafue, Southern	340
Kariba and the Lower Zambezi	194
Kasanka National Park	264
Kitwe	322
Lake Bangweulu area	258
Languages	22
Livingstone	150
Livingstone and Victoria Falls	148
Lochinvar National Park	348
Lower Zambezi	210
Luangwa Valley	220
Lukulu	364
Lusaka Central	118
Lusaka: Cairo Road area	132
Lusaka, Overview	112
Mfuwe area	230
Mpika Town	276
Mpulungu	288
Mpulungu, The lake around	290
Ndola	318
North Luangwa area	252
Northern Zambia	282
Nsefu Sector, Around the	234
Nyika Plateau	306
Rainfall	38
South Luangwa National Park	224
Southern Wetlands	272
Southern Zambia	146
Sumbu National Park	296
Topography	34
Victoria Falls	170
Western Zambia	352
Zambia	front cover

Acknowledgements

Writing this book has been a team effort. Firstly, my endless love and thanks to Purba for her help and good company. Purba's patience and tolerance of my Africa obsession have been immense – both whilst researching in Zambia, when it would have been lovely just to relax, and also back in London whilst I'm tied to the word-processor. Without her, I'd be lost!

Whilst researching, I've been helped by many people who have made researching a pleasure and this book possible. Thanks to my colleagues at Sunvil Discovery, especially Rob McDowell and Heather Tyrrell (both veteran Africa travellers) for their help, support, information and advice, and to Noel Josephides and John der Parthog. I am very grateful to Peter Dolby, Paul Mount and Sir Peter Holmes for use of their photographs. Kiran Bhatarah of BA, Donald Pelekamoyo of ZNTB, and Laura Boardman of UNICEF, all made valuable contributions.

Many of Sunvil Discovery's travellers helped with feedback – and I'm especially grateful for extensive comments from Sue Grainger, Val and Bob Leyland, Harvey Linehan and Roger Marston.

In Zambia, many went far out of their way to contribute, including: Rose-Marie Baldry of Lusaka Lowdown; Philip Briggs, for the kind use of his writings on Nyika; Bernie & Adrienne Esterhuyse, for their boundless hospitality and help; Lisa Harmer, for timely advice on charities; for Colin Louw, for help on a vital day; Edmund Farmer, for valuable communications; Ilse Mwanza, for many pertinent points; Hazell and Ewart Powell, despite the email problems; Arthur Sonnenberg, for hospitality and good company; Karun Thanjavuvr, for news from Lukulu; Anne Butler, Pippa Turner, Peter and their team; David, else he forgets his kindness; and Philip, for his economical help.

Everyone in 'the Valley' was tremendous and pulled out the stops to help me. Nick, Craig and team from Kapani stand out; as do Jo, Robin, Margaret, Beth and Sara; also Carol, Rod and Bryan; Andrea, Rob and their team; and Anke and Georgina. Miranda Carr and John Coppinger deserve special mentions, not only for their help and good company whilst I was there, but also for answering obscure questions after I'd left.

Valuable help also came from Angelina of Proflight, Jeanne and Chris Blignaut, Simon Burgess, Fr. Ivo Burkhardt, Michelle Cantley, Nickson Chilangwa, Grant, Kevin and Jenny Cummings, Jane Dennyson, Pete and Lynn Fisher, David Foot, Di Flynn, Rob Fynn, Tong Green, Adam Haines, Fil Hide, Ros Kearney, Liesl Nel, Fr. Kessel of Lundazi, Steve McCormack, Robin Miller, Helen Mills, Jake da Motta, Victoria Nash, Beryl Neilson, Map Patel, Gene Pecker and Samantha, Ron and Lyn Ringrose, Mwape Sichilongo, Oscar and Andrew Sardanis from Chaminuka, Sheila Siddle, Alistair Tough, Gwen Wawn, Derek White and Beatrice Wienand.

Bradt's team who've worked with me on this have been superb – Hilary Bradt, Janice Booth, Steve Munns, Linden Sheffield and especially Tricia Hayne. That which is good and correct owes much to their care and attention; errors and omissions are my own.

Introduction

Stalking lion on foot certainly focuses your attention. You think about where you walk; you see every movement; and your ears are aware of every sound. Not everyone's idea of fun, but Zambia isn't for everyone.

It's now several years since I wrote the first edition of this guide – the first English guidebook to Zambia – and walking safaris still inspire me. I've been back to Zambia often, but no two walks are alike. One thing always reoccurs: the realisation that the more you learn of the bush, the more you realise you don't know.

It is the same with the country. The more you delve into it, the more fascinating it becomes. The old tourist board slogan, 'Zambia: the real Africa', still stands. Zambia is still 'real'. It's unsanitised, unpackaged, and still largely unvisited. Zambia offers the best of wild Africa, in a country with very few visitors. It gives an authentic taste of what the whole continent was like: wild, beautiful and slightly unpredictable.

For the cognoscenti, it remains *the* place for walking safaris. Zambia's premier national park, South Luangwa, is the main name to conjure with. It has top camps, Africa's best game, and many of its best guides. Throughout Africa there are khaki-uniformed chauffeurs who drive through the bush, but in South Luangwa you find expert guides to trust with your life. Further, projects are gathering momentum here to give visitors an option of really interacting with the local communities. This has long been an omission from traditional safaris and may sound less interesting than leopards – but once you've glimpsed an African culture from the inside, and recognised your own ways as foreign, you'll understand the fascination and be back for more.

Zambia is gradually becoming better known, but still 'South Luangwa' and 'wildlife' are all that many people know of it. The rest of this huge country (twice the size of Zimbabwe) remains undiscovered, its smaller camps unknown, its people unmentioned.

Zambia's attractions are legion, if you seek them out – and the following chapters will try to show you how. Whether you are arriving inside a private plane, or travelling with a backpack, I've written this book to try to guide you to some of Zambia's lesser-known areas and to help you understand more about them. Many are gems.

A classic example is the Kafue National Park. This is just becoming better known – and about time too. It's a wilderness area the size of Wales! When uncovered by receding floodwaters, its remarkable Busanga Plains flush green with grass and fill with game. This leaves an area of great beauty and stupendous wildlife. Yet only now are a few people seeing it (and returning with the most amazing tales). In the rest of Kafue you'll also find walking safaris, remarkable leopard viewing, few other visitors – and a handful of small safari camps.

Zambia's Lower Zambezi National Park isn't so seasonal. At any time of year large herds of elephant and buffalo can be appreciated from a leisurely canoe trip along the Zambezi. When it's dry a few small camps open here, offering canoeing and even fishing as well as walking and driving safaris. Again, this park is remarkably empty of people, but full of game.

In the centre of Zambia lies the huge Lake Bangweulu, surrounded by the swamp that defeated Livingstone – his heart was buried nearby. This land of islands and waterways is a permanent wetland, home to the rare shoebill stork and an endemic species of antelope, the black lechwe. Traditional communities have lived here for centuries and now they guide visitors around as part of a World Wide Fund for Nature project.

Far to the west, Liuwa Plain National Park is the venue for one of Africa's last great wildlife migrations: blue wildebeest in their thousands, plus zebra, tsessebe and buffalo, all converging on the plains for the rains. Liuwa is remote and getting there needs planning, but the rewards are spectacular. A plain of honey-coloured grass, covered in animals, stretches as far as you can see, with no other visitors to spoil the view.

Nor is wildlife Zambia's only attraction. In the ancient Lozi kingdom of Barotseland, for example, the landscape has changed little since Livingstone's day. The rich cultural heritage of a monarch and his people survived colonialism almost unscathed. Their seasonal rhythm is still followed, as the whole kingdom still moves by boat from the rich floodplains to higher ground in February or March, making one great, grand traditional flotilla.

In the north, Shiwa N'gandu still stands as one of the subcontinent's most fascinating memorials to British colonial rule. There's simply nowhere else like it in Southern Africa. Here an English aristocrat built a Tuscan-style manor house and richly furnished it from Europe. He tried to carve out a utopian estate from the untamed bush, whilst helping Zambia to achieve its own independence. But Africa gradually defeated his dream and he died – to be buried with the full honours of an African chief, and a knighthood from the King of England. Shiwa's great manor still offers a fascinating insight into colonial attitudes and exudes a palpable sense of history.

The fascination goes on. Zambia is a wonderful country if you can get to its heart. Its government encourages tourism, and foreign exchange is desperately needed to alleviate the poverty of many of its people. But for such logic, this guide might have remained unwritten, as many would prefer Zambia to stay as it is – a favourite place to visit, with superb wildlife, fascinating culture, few other visitors, and Zambians who still treat travellers with kindness and hospitality.

Now, having committed more of Zambia's secrets to paper, I again ask those who use this guide to do so with respect. Zambia's wild areas need great care to preserve them. Local cultures are easily eroded by a visitor's lack of sensitivity, and hospitality once abused is seldom offered again. Enjoy – but be a thoughtful visitor, for the country's sake.

Part One

The Country

Facts and Figures

Location

Zambia is landlocked in the tropics of southern Africa, distant from both the Atlantic and the Pacific Oceans. It is at the northern edge of the region referred to as 'Southern Africa', while sharing many similarities with its neighbours in East and Central Africa.

Size

Zambia is shaped like a giant butterfly, and covers about 752,610km^2. That is slightly smaller than the UK and France combined, and slightly larger than California plus Nevada. In comparison with its neighbours, it is almost double the size of Zimbabwe, but only two-thirds that of South Africa.

Topography

Most of Zambia is part of the high, undulating plateau that forms the backbone of Africa. The plateau's altitude is typically 1,000–1,600m above sea level. It is deeply incised by great valleys: the Zambezi, the Kafue, the Luangwa and the Luapula.

There are several large lakes on Zambia's borders: Tanganyika and Mweru in the north, and the man-made Kariba in the south. Lake Bangweulu, and its swamps and floodplain, dominate a large area of the interior.

Climate

Zambia's climate can be split into three periods. From December to April it is hot and wet, with torrential downpours often in the late afternoon. From May to August it is dry, and fairly cool. From September to November it remains dry, but gets progressively hotter. Zambia's climate is generally moderate; only in the great valleys does it feel oppressive.

Flora and fauna

Zambia is a large country, with many large national parks, and game management areas (GMAs) where conservation and sustainable utilisation of the native wildlife is encouraged.

Miombo woodland – a mixture of grassland dotted with trees and shrubs – makes up about 70% of Zambia's natural environment, with mopane woodland dominating the lower-lying areas. The native fauna is classic big game found throughout East and Southern Africa. Amongst the predators, leopard do exceptionally well here; lion are common but cheetah are not. Wild dog are as rare as they are anywhere else in the continent, and there are many smaller predators. Zambia's antelope are especially interesting for the range of subspecies that have evolved. Giraffe, wildebeest, waterbuck and, especially, lechwe are notable for this – each having subspecies endemic to the country.

With rich vegetation and lots of water, Zambia has a great variety of both resident and migrant birds: over 700 species in total. Wetland and swamp areas attract some specialised waterfowl, and Zambia is on the edge of the range for both Southern African and East African species.

Population

Zambia has a population of about ten million. The vast majority are of black African (Bantu) descent, though there are significant communities whose ancestors came from Europe and India.

Zambia is a large country, so its population density – around 13 people per km^2 – is about half that of Zimbabwe, a third that of South Africa, or about a quarter the population density of Kenya. Like much of subSaharan Africa, Zambia's population growth rate is high, at around 3% per annum.

The capital, Lusaka, is home to about 10% of the country's population, whilst the four main towns of the Copperbelt, Kitwe, Ndola, Kabwe and Mufulira, have almost 1.5 million people between them. Thus the rural areas have a generally low density, and the country retains large tracts of wilderness.

Zambia's urban population is about 42% of the total, which has reduced in the last few years due to a 'return migration' of people moving back to the land. The difficulty of life in the cities is often cited as one root cause of this.

Language

English is the official language in Zambia, and most urban Zambians speak it fluently. In the rural areas it is used less, though only in truly remote settlements would there be problems communicating in English.

The main vernacular languages are Bemba, Kaonde, Lozi, Lunda, Luvale, Nyanja and Tonga – though more than 72 different languages and dialects are spoken in the country.

Religion

The majority of Zambians are Christian, having been gradually converted since the first missionaries arrived in the 19th century. There is also a significant proportion of both Muslims and Hindus, originating in the Asian communities who settled whilst Zambia was under British rule. At the same time, traditional African beliefs are widely adhered to – even by Zambia's Christians.

History

Zambia's first Stone-Age, hunter-gatherer inhabitants were supplanted by Bantu groups from the north, who arrived with their Iron-Age culture in the first few centuries AD. Cecil Rhodes' powerful British South Africa Company took these groups under British rule in around 1890.

In 1924, the British colonial office took over the territory officially. In 1953 Northern Rhodesia, as Zambia was known, was joined to Nyasaland (Malawi) and Southern Rhodesia (Zimbabwe) to form the Central African Federation – though much administration still relied on the British.

Largely peaceful internal pressure, including the voices of several influential British residents, eventually led to Zambia gaining its independence in 1964, when it joined the Commonwealth.

Economy

The economy is currently in a poor state, with a huge national debt and no practical means to pay this off. Copper exports account for around 90% of the country's foreign exchange, which makes Zambia highly dependent upon the price of copper on the world's markets. Zambia's inflation rate is now around 28%, and is projected to fall to around 15% by the end of 1999.

Currency

The currency here is the Zambian kwacha (Kw), which is subdivided into 100 ngwee. This has been devaluing steadily, in line with the country's inflation rate. In the few months that this guide has taken to research and publish, the exchange rate for US$1 has risen from around Kw2,000 to about Kw2,500. (For £1 from Kw3,200 to Kw4,000.) Thus most of the prices in this guide are in US$ and, for those which are in kwacha, I have assume a notional rate of around US$1 for Kw2,500 and converted them accordingly for ease of reference. (See *Currency and inflation* in *Chapter 8* for further comments.)

Government

The chief of state and the head of government is the president, who appoints cabinet ministers from members of the National Assembly, a chamber of 150 elected representatives.

Zambian citizens of 18 years and over are eligible to vote, and the country is split up into nine provinces for administration purposes: Central, Copperbelt, Eastern, Luapulu, Lusaka, Northern, Northwestern, Southern and Western.

The judicial system was set up according to a British model, based on English common law and customary law. Legislative acts receive judicial review in an *ad hoc* constitutional council.

Politics

Since November 1991 President Frederick Chiluba has led a government dominated by the Movement for Multiparty Democracy (MMD) XE "Movement for Multiparty Democracy (MMD)" . He has been liberalising the economy and conforming to a plan agreed with the IMF, which is widely appreciated as good, though some of the economic measures are difficult, especially for more impoverished Zambians.

In October 1996 the MMD won a second resounding election victory. The losers, the United National Independence Party (UNIP), partially boycotted the vote as the candidacy of their leader, the former president Kenneth Kaunda, had been excluded on a technicality. Increasingly the MMDís commitment to democracy is questioned.

Now, at the turn of the millennium, elections are in sight for 2001. The constitution limits any president to two terms in office. Democrats of all parties wait to see if the MMD will try to change this, to allow Chiluba to stand for another term. If changed, they fear that the autocracy of Robert Mugabeís Zimbabwe could be repeated here. Meanwhile, Kenneth Kaunda (who promised not to run for president again) is also manoeuvring for the race.

Natural resources

Copper is easily the country's most important natural resource, with cobalt second. Amethyst, fluorite, feldspar, gypsum, lead, zinc, tin and gold also occur in small quantities, as well as a variety of gemstones.

Other, less traditional, exports are now on the increase, including timber, fresh vegetables and cut flowers. In the UK it's now quite normal to find mangetout and other vegetables from Zambia in the larger supermarkets.

Tourism

Zambia has never had many tourists: it currently receives only about 10% of the number who visit Zimbabwe. Many of these just come across the border for a day-trip, to see the Zambian side of the Victoria Falls. Others travel through Zambia as quickly as possible in overland trucks, from Malawi or Tanzania to Zimbabwe.

Few stay for long in Zambia itself, because it is perceived as expensive and/or difficult. Zambia's visitors are counted in only thousands per year, and they come mostly for the wildlife and the experience of staying in remote bush camps, tracking game with top guides. These numbers are growing steadily, as people seek out more remote corners of the continent, and realise that good wildlife guides are few and far between.

Independent budget travellers in Zambia are rare. Those who do come should be well prepared. Once in the country, they will realise that their novelty value in the rural areas ensures them a warm welcome; this alone makes Zambia a fascinating destination.

History and Economy

2

HISTORY
Zambia's earliest inhabitants

Palaeontologists looking for evidence of the first ancestors of the human race have excavated a number of sites in Zambia. The earliest remains yet identified are stone-age tools dated at about 200,000 years old, which have been recovered in gravel deposits around what is now the Victoria Falls. It is thought that these probably belong to the *Homo erectus* species, whose hand-axes have been dated in Tanzania to half a million years old. These were hunter-gatherer people, who could use fire, make tools, and had probably developed some simple speech.

Experts divide the Stone Age into the middle, early, and late Stone Ages. The transition from early to middle stone-age technology – which is indicated by a larger range of stone tools often adapted for particular uses, and signs that these people had a greater mastery of their environment – was probably in progress around 125,000 years ago in Zambia.

The famous 'Broken Hill Man' lived around this time. His skull was unearthed from about 80m underground during mining operations near Kabwe in 1921. He was from a species called *Homo rhodesiensis*, which may have been a late survivor of *Homo erectus*, or an early ancestor of us – *Homo sapiens*. (Kabwe's old name was Broken Hill, explaining the origin of this name.)

The late Stone Age is normally characterised by the use of composite tools, those made of wood and/or bone and/or stone used together, and by the presence of a revolutionary invention: the bow and arrow. This first appeared in Zambia, and throughout the world, about 15,000 years ago. Skeletons found around the Kafue Flats area indicate that some of these late stone-age hunters had a close physical resemblance to the modern San/bushmen people, whose culture, relying on a late stone-age level of technology, survived intact in the Kalahari Desert until the middle of the 20th century.

The Iron Age

Around 3,000BC, late stone-age hunter-gatherer groups in Ethiopia, and elsewhere in north and west Africa, started to keep domestic animals, sow seeds, and harvest the produce: they became the world's first farmers.

By around 1,000BC these new pastoral practices had spread south into the equatorial forests of what is now the Democratic Republic of Congo, to around Lake Victoria, and into the northern area of the Great Rift Valley, in northern Tanzania. However, agriculture did not spread south into the rest of central/Southern Africa immediately. Only when the technology, and the tools, of iron-working became known did the practices start their relentless expansion southwards.

The spread of agriculture and iron-age culture seems to have been a rapid move. It was brought south by Africans who were taller and heavier than the existing small inhabitants. The ancestors of the San/bushmen people, with their simple stone-age technology and hunter-gatherer existence, just could not compete with these iron-age farmers, who became the ancestors of virtually all the modern black Africans in Southern Africa.

This major migration occurred around the first few centuries AD, and since then the San/bushmen of Southern Africa have gradually been either assimilated into the migrant groups, or effectively pushed into the areas which could not be farmed. Thus the older iron-age cultures persisted in the forests of the north and east of Zambia – which were more difficult to cultivate – much longer than they survived in the south of the country.

More immigrants

By the 4th or 5th century AD, iron-age farmers had settled throughout much of southern Africa. As well as iron-working technology, they brought with them pottery, the remains of which are used by archaeologists to work out the migrations of various different groups of these Bantu settlers. These migrations continued, and the distribution of pottery styles suggests that the groups moved around within the subcontinent: this was much more complex than a simple north-south influx.

The origins of trade

In burial sites dating from the latter half of the first millennium, occasional 'foreign' objects start to occur: the odd cowrie shell, or copper bangles in an area where there is no copper. This indicates that some small-scale bartering with neighbouring villages was beginning to take place.

In the first half of the second millennium, the pace and extent of this trade increased significantly. Gold objects appear (as well as the more common copper, iron and ivory) and shells from the Indian Ocean. The frequency of these indicates that trade was gradually developing. We know from European historical sources that Muslim traders (of Arab or possibly African origin) were venturing into the heart of Africa by around AD1400, and thus trade routes were being established.

As trade started, so the second millennium also saw the development of wealth and social structures within the tribes. The evidence for this is a number of burial sites that stand out for the quantity and quality of the goods that were buried with the dead person. One famous site, at Ingombe Ilede, near the confluence of the Lusitu and Zambezi rivers, was occupied regularly over many centuries. There is evidence that its inhabitants traded from the 14th century with people further south, in Zimbabwe, exporting gold down the Zambezi via traders coming from the Indian Ocean. Indications of cotton-weaving have also been found there, and several copper crosses unearthed are so similar that they may have been used as a simple form of currency – valuable to both the local people and the traders from outside.

By the middle of the second millennium, a number of separate cultures seem to have formed in Zambia. Many practised trade, and a few clearly excelled at it. Most were starting to develop social structures within the group, with some enjoying more status and wealth than others.

The chiefs

From around the middle of the second millennium, there is little good archaeological evidence that can be accurately dated. However, sources for the events of this period in Zambia's history are the oral histories of Zambia's people, as well as their current languages and social traditions. The similarities and differences between the modern Zambian languages can be extrapolated by linguistic experts to point to the existence of about nine different root languages, which probably existed in Zambia in the 15th century AD.

The latter half of the second millennium AD saw the first chiefs, and hence kingdoms, emerge from Zambia's dispersed clans. The title 'chief' can be applied to anyone from a village headman to a god-like king. However, this was an era of increasing trade, when the groups with the largest resources and armies dominated local disputes. Thus it made sense for various clans to group together into tribes, under the rule of a single individual, or chief.

One of the oldest groups is thought to have been that of the *Chewa* people, led by the *Undi*, who came to the Luangwa area from the southern side of Lake Malawi in the 16th century. By the end of that century the *N'gandu* clan (clan of the crocodile) established a kingdom amongst the Bemba people. These lived mostly in woodland areas, practising simple slash-and-burn types of agriculture. Perhaps because of the poverty of their lifestyle, they later earned a reputation as warriors for their raids on neighbouring tribes.

In the latter part of the 17th century the first recorded *Lozi* king (or Litunga, as he is known) is thought to have settled near Kalabo, in the west of Zambia, starting a powerful dynasty which lasts to the present day. Early in the 18th century Mwata Kazemba established a kingdom around the southern end of Lake Mweru in the Luapula Valley.

The growth of trade

As various cohesive kingdoms developed, their courts served as centres of trade, and their chiefs had the resources to initiate trade with other communities. Foodstuffs, iron, copper, salt, cotton, cloth, tobacco, baskets, pottery and many other items were traded within Zambia, between the various tribes.

From around the 14th century, Zambia had a trickle of trade with non-Africans: mostly Muslims exporting gold through the east coast of Africa. (This trade had started as early as the 10th century on the Limpopo River, south of Zimbabwe's gold-fields.) However, by the early 17th century the Muslims had been supplanted by the Portuguese, and by the latter half of the 17th century these Portuguese traders were operating out of Mozambique, trading gold, ivory and copper with Zambia.

Trade with the outside world escalated during the 18th century, as more and more tribes became involved, and more foreigners came to trade. Some chiefs started to barter their commodities for weapons, in attempts to gain advantage over their neighbours. Those vanquished in local conflicts were certainly used as sources of slaves – an increasingly valuable trading commodity. These and other factors increased the pressure on Zambians to trade, and the influx of foreign traders made the picture more complex still.

By the early 19th century, both traders and slavers were visiting Zambia with increasing frequency. These were responding to the increasing consumer demands of newly industrialised Europe and America. More trade routes were opening up, not just through Mozambique and Angola, but also to the north and south. Internal conflicts were increasing, as both the means to conduct these, and the incentives for victory, grew.

Western requirements

During the 19th century, the West (western Europe and North America) had traded with the native Africans to obtain what they wanted – commodities and slave labour – without having to go to the trouble of ruling parts of the continent.

However, as the century progressed, and the West became more industrialised, it needed these things in greater quantities than the existing tribal structures in Africa could supply. Further, there was demand for materials that could be produced in Africa, like cotton and rubber, but which required Western production methods.

Given that the West wanted a wider range and greater quantity of cheaper raw materials, the obvious solution was to control the means of supply. African political organisation was widely regarded as primitive, and not capable of providing complex and sustained trade. Inward investment would also be needed, but would be forthcoming only if white enterprises were safe from African interference. Hence the solution to Western requirements was to bring Africa, and the Africans, under European rule.

Another reason for considering the acquisition of African territory was that the world was shrinking. There were no inhabitable continents left to discover. Staking a nation's claim to large chunks of Africa seemed prudent to most of the Western powers of the time, and growing competition for these areas meant they could always be traded for one another at a later date.

Livingstone's contribution

David Livingstone's *Missionary Travels and Researches in South Africa* excited great interest in England. This account of his journeys across southern Africa in the 1840s and 50s had all the appeal that undersea or space exploration has for us now. Further, it captured the imagination of the British public, allowing them to take pride in their country's exploration of Africa, based on the exploits of an explorer who seemed to be the epitome of bravery and righteous religious zeal.

Livingstone had set out with the conviction that if Africans could see their material and physical well-being improved – probably by learning European ways, and earning a living from export crops – then they would be ripe for conversion to Christianity. He was strongly opposed to slavery, but sure that this would disappear when Africans became more self-sufficient through trade.

In fact Livingstone was almost totally unsuccessful in his own aims, failing to set up any successful trading missions, or even to convert many Africans permanently to Christianity. However, his travels opened up areas north of the Limpopo for later British missionaries, and by 1887 British mission stations were established in Zambia and southern Malawi.

The scramble for Africa

British foreign policy in Southern Africa had always revolved around the Cape Colony, which was seen as vital to British interests in India and the Indian Ocean. Africa to the north of the Cape Colony had largely been ignored. The Boers were on the whole left to their farming in the Transvaal area, and posed no threat to the colony.

However, Germany annexed South West Africa (now Namibia) in 1884, prompting British fears that they might try to link up with the Boers. Thus, to drive a wedge through the middle of these territories, the British negotiated an alliance with Khama, a powerful *Tswana* king, and proclaimed as theirs the Protectorate of Bechuanaland – the forerunner of modern Botswana.

Soon after, in 1886, the Boers discovered large gold deposits in the Witwatersrand (around Johannesburg). The influx of money from this boosted the Boer farmers, who expanded their interests to the north, making a treaty with Khama's enemy, the powerful Lobengula. This in turn prompted the British to look beyond the Limpopo, and to back the territorial aspirations of a millionaire British businessman, Cecil Rhodes. By 1888 Rhodes, a partner in the De Beers consortium, had control of the lucrative diamond-mining industry in Kimberley, South Africa. He was hungry for power, and dreamt of linking the Cape to Cairo with land under British control.

His wealth enabled Rhodes to buy sole rights to mine minerals in Lobengula's territory. Thence he persuaded the British government to grant his company – the British South Africa Company – the licence to stake claims to African territory with the authority of the British government. In 1889 Rhodes sent out several expeditions to the chiefs in the area now comprising Zimbabwe, Zambia and Malawi, to make treaties. These granted British 'protection and aid' in return for sole rights to minerals in the chiefs' territories, and assurances that they would not make treaties with any other foreign powers. This effective strategy was greatly helped by the existing British influence from the missions, which were already established in many of the regions. By 1891 the British had secured these areas (through Rhodes' British South Africa Company) from the other European powers, and confirmed their boundaries in treaties with the neighbouring colonial powers.

By the closing years of the 19th century, Zambia – or Northern Rhodesia as it was called – was clearly under British rule. However, this had little impact until local administrations were set up, and taxes started to be collected.

The mines

In the early years of the 20th century, the Rhodes' British South Africa Company did little in Northern Rhodesia. Its minerals were not nearly as accessible or valuable as those in Southern Rhodesia, and little protection or aid actually materialised. It became viewed by the colonials as a source of cheap labour for the mines of South Africa and Southern Rhodesia.

To facilitate this, taxes were introduced for the local people, which effectively forced them to come into the cash economy. Virtually the only way for them to do this was to find work in one of the mines further south. By 1910 a railway linked the mine at Kimberley, in South Africa, with Victoria Falls and beyond, making long-distance travel in the subcontinent more practical.

Meanwhile the cost of administering and defending the company's interests was rising, and in 1923 Southern Rhodesia became self-governing. In 1924 the British colonial office took over administration of Northern Rhodesia from the British South Africa Company, though the mining rights remained with the Company. The Colonial Office then set up a legislative council to advise on the government of the province, though only a few of its members came from outside the administration.

Shortly afterwards, in 1928, huge deposits of copper were located below the basin of the upper Kafue, under what is now known as the Copperbelt. Over the next decade or so these were developed into a number of large copper mines, working rich, deep deposits of copper. World War II demanded increased production of base metals, and by 1945 Northern Rhodesia was producing 12% of the non-communist world's copper. This scale of production required large labour forces. The skilled workers were mostly of European origin, often from South Africa's mines, whilst the unskilled workers came from all over Northern Rhodesia.

Wages and conditions were very poor for the unskilled miners, who were treated as migrant workers and expected to go home to their permanent villages every year or so to 'recover'. Death rates among them were high. Further, the drain of men to work the mines inevitably destabilised the villages, and poverty and malnutrition were common in the rural areas.

Welfare associations

As early as 1929 welfare associations had formed in several of the territory's southern towns, aimed at giving black Africans a voice and trying to defend their interests. These associations were often started by teachers or clerks: the more educated members of the communities. They were small at first, far too small to mount any effective challenge to the establishment, but they did succeed in raising awareness amongst the Africans, all of whom were being exploited.

In 1935 the African mineworkers first organised themselves to strike over their pay and conditions. By 1942 the towns of the African labourers in the Copperbelt were forming their own welfare associations, and by 1949 some of these had joined together as the Northern Rhodesian African Mineworkers' Union. This had been officially recognised by the colonial government as being the equal of any union for white workers.

In 1952 the union showed its muscle with a successful and peaceful three-week strike, resulting in substantial wage increases.

Central African Federation

The tiny European population in Northern Rhodesia was, on the whole, worried by the growth of the power of black African mineworkers. Most of the white people wanted to break free from colonial rule, so that they could control the pace and direction of political change. They also resented the loss of vast revenues from the mines, which went directly to the British government and the British South Africa Company, without much benefit for Northern Rhodesia.

During the 1930s and 1940s the settlers' representation on Northern Rhodesia's Legislative Council was gradually increased, and calls for self-rule became more insistent. As early as 1936 Stewart Gore-Browne (founder of *Shiwa N'gandu*; see *Chapter 13*) had proposed a scheme for a Central African Federation, with an eye to Britain's future (or lack of one) in Africa. This view gained ground in London, where the government was increasingly anxious to distance itself from African problems.

In 1948 the South African Nationalist Party came to power in South Africa, on a tide of Afrikaner support. The historical enmity between the Afrikaners and the British in South Africa led the British colonials in Southern and Northern Rhodesia to look to themselves for their own future, rather than their neighbours in South Africa. In 1953 their pressure was rewarded and Southern and Northern Rhodesia were formally joined with Nyasaland (which is now Malawi), to become the independent Central African Federation.

The formation of the Federation did little to help the whites in Northern Rhodesia, though it was so strongly opposed by the blacks, who feared that they would then lose more of their land to white settlers. Earlier, in 1948, the Federation of African Societies – an umbrella group of welfare associations – changed its name at an annual general meeting into an overtly political 'Northern Rhodesian Congress'. This had branches in the mining towns and the rural areas, and provided a base upon which a black political culture could be based. A few years later, it was renamed as the Northern Rhodesia African National Congress.

Independence

Despite the Federation, Northern Rhodesia actually remained under the control of the Colonial Office. Further, the administration of the Federation was so biased towards Southern Rhodesia that the revenues from its mines simply flowed there, instead of to Britain. Thus though the Federation promised much, it delivered few of the settlers' wishes in Northern Rhodesia.

A small core of increasingly skilled African mineworkers gained better pay and conditions, whilst poverty was rife in the rest of the country. By the 1950s small improvements were being made in the provision of education for black Zambians, but widespread neglect had demonstrated to most that whites did not want blacks as their political or social equals. Thus black politics began to focus on another goal: independence.

In 1958 elections were held, and about 25,000 blacks were allowed to vote. The Northern Rhodesia African National Congress was divided about whether to participate or not, and eventually this issue split the party. Kenneth Kaunda, the radical Secretary General, and others founded the Zambia African National Congress (ZANC). This was soon banned, and Kaunda was jailed during a state of emergency.

Finally, in 1960, Kaunda was released from jail, and greeted as a national hero. He took control of a splinter party, the United National Independence Party (UNIP), and after a short campaign of civil disobedience forced the colonial office to hold universal elections. In October of 1962, these confirmed a large majority for UNIP. In 1963 the Federation broke up, and in 1964 elections based on universal adult suffrage gave UNIP a commanding majority. On October 24 1964 Zambia became independent, with Kenneth Kaunda as its president.

Zambia under Kaunda

President Kenneth Kaunda (usually known as just 'KK') took over a country whose income was controlled by the state of the world copper market, and whose trade routes were entirely dependent upon Southern Rhodesia, South Africa, and Mozambique. He also inherited a Kw50,000,000 national debt from the colonial era, and a populace which was largely unskilled and uneducated. (At independence, there were fewer than one hundred Zambians with university degrees, and fewer than a thousand who had completed secondary school.)

In 1965, shortly after Zambia's independence, Southern Rhodesia made a Unilateral Declaration of Independence (UDI). This propelled Zambia's southern neighbour further along the path of white rule that South Africa had adopted. Sanctions were then applied to Rhodesia from the rest of the world. Given that most of Zambia's trade passed through Rhodesia, these had very negative effects on the country's economy.

As the black people of Rhodesia, South Africa and South West Africa (Namibia) started their liberation struggles, Kaunda naturally wanted to support them. Zambia became a haven for political refugees, and a base for black independence movements. However ideologically sound this approach was, it was costly and did not endear Zambia to its economically dominant white-ruled neighbours. As the apartheid government in South Africa began a policy of destabilising the black-ruled countries around the subcontinent, so civil wars and unrest became the norm in Mozambique and Angola, squeezing Zambia's trade routes further.

The late 1960s and early 1970s saw Zambia try to drastically reduce its trade with the south. Simultaneously it worked to increase its links with Tanzania – which was largely beyond the reach of South Africa's efforts to destabilise. With the help of China, Tanzania and Zambia built excellent road and rail links from the heart of Zambia to Dar es Salaam, on the Indian Ocean. However, Tanzania was no match as a trading partner for the efficiency of South Africa, and Zambia's economy remained sluggish.

During these difficult years Zambia's debt did not reduce, but grew steadily. The government's large revenues from copper were used in efforts to reduce the country's dependence on its southern neighbours, and to improve standards of living for the majority of Zambians. Education was expanded on a large scale, government departments were enlarged to provide employment, and food subsidies maintained the peace of the large urban population. Kaunda followed Julius Nyerere's example in Tanzania in many ways, with a number of socialist policies woven into his own (much promoted) philosophy of 'humanism'.

In retrospect, perhaps Kaunda's biggest mistake was that he failed to use the large revenues from copper either to reduce the national debt, or to diversify Zambia's export base – but his choices were not easy.

By 1969, the Zambian government was receiving about three-quarters of the profits made by the mining industries in taxes and duties. Because of this, they were reluctant to invest further. With the aim of encouraging expansion in the industry and investment in new mines, the government started to reform the ownership of the copper mines. A referendum was held on the subject and the government took control of mining rights throughout the country. It then bought a 51% share in each of the mines, which was paid for out of the government's own dividends in the companies over the coming years. Thus began ZCCM (Zambia Consolidated Copper Mines), which is today in the throes of privatisation.

In the early 1970s, the world copper price fell dramatically. Simultaneously the cost of imports (especially oil) rose, the world economy slumped and the interest rates on Zambia's debt increased. These factors highlighted the fundamental weaknesses of Zambia's economy, which had been established to suit the colonial powers rather than the country's citizens.

The drop in the price of copper crippled Zambia's economy. Efforts to stabilise the world copper price – through a cartel of copper-producing countries, similar to the oil-producing OPEC countries – failed. The government borrowed more money, betting on a recovery in copper prices that never materialised.

In the 1970s and 1980s Kaunda's government became increasingly intertwined with the International Monetary Fund (IMF) in the search for a solution to the country's debt. None was found. Short-term fixes just made things worse, and the country's finances deteriorated. The West did give Zambia aid, but mostly for specific projects that usually had strings attached. What Zambia most needed (and still does) was help with the enormous interest payments that it was required to make to the West.

Various recovery plans, often instituted by the IMF, were tried. In 1986 food subsidies were sharply withdrawn, starting with breakfast meal, one of the country's staple foods. This hit the poor hardest, and major riots broke out before subsidies were hastily reintroduced to restore calm. In 1988 Zambia applied to the United Nations for the status of 'least developed nation' in the hope of obtaining greater international assistance. It was rejected. By the end of the decade Zambia's economy was in tatters. The official exchange rate bore little relation to the currency's actual worth, and inflation was rampant.

Despite Kaunda's many failures with the economy, his policies did encourage the development of some home-grown industries to produce goods which could replace previously imported items. It created systems for mass education, which were almost entirely absent when he came to power: there are now primary and secondary schools for everyone, and two universities (one in Lusaka and another in Kitwe).

Since the late 1980s, Zambia has been one of the world's poorest countries, with a chronic debt problem, a weak currency and at times very high inflation. A reputation for corruption, reaching to the highest levels of the government, did little to encourage help from richer nations.

The early 1990s

These economic problems, and the lack of obvious material benefits for the majority of Zambians, gradually fomented opposition. UNIP's tendency to become authoritarian in its demands for unity also led to unrest. Kaunda's rule was finally challenged successfully by the capitalist Movement for Multiparty Democracy (MMD) led by Frederick Chiluba. This received widespread support during the late 1980s, on a platform of liberalisation and anti-corruption measures.

Kaunda agreed to an election, apparently certain that he would win. In the event, UNIP was resoundingly defeated by the MMD (16% to 84%), and Chiluba became Zambia's second elected president, in November 1991. Kaunda accepted the results, at least on face value. However, he is said to believe that the elections were unfair because many of Zambia's older people, whom he regarded as his natural constituency, didn't vote. Apparently he still believes that the majority of Zambians want him as president. He has continued to live in Zambia and to head UNIP – which, in itself, is a rare and encouraging co-existence in the volatile world of modern African politics.

When elected, Frederick Chiluba faced enormous economic problems, which he has attempted to tackle. He has succeeded in liberalising and privatising much of the economy. There is now a freely floating market for the kwacha, and policies to attract inward investment. However, the country's debt has not reduced. In 1995 this stood at US$6.25 billion, and debt service payments were some 40% of the gross national product – equivalent to about US$600/£400 per capita per annum. One of Chiluba's highest priorities has, necessarily, been to try to get the major industrialised nations to write off large chunks of this. Zambia owes US$3.1 billion to the World Bank and the IMF alone.

So, Zambia's economy remains unbalanced by its dependence upon copper and severely weakened by debt. Initially Chiluba gained the confidence of Western donors when he came to power in 1991. However, his reforms are long-term, and much of their success depends on the continued willingness of international donors to help him.

Certainly the general attitude towards visitors has changed under Chiluba: Zambia is a more welcoming country now than it was under Kaunda's reign. Tourism is recognised as a very direct and helpful source of jobs and foreign currency, and the climate of suspicion prevailing in Kaunda's Zambia has been replaced with a warmer welcome.

Chiluba's attention has, necessarily, been focused on the country's unbalanced economy and the huge debt burden. Observers have noted that Zambia's absence from the world's headlines in most of the 1990s was an example of 'no news being good news'.

The late 1990s

Presidential elections were held in 1996. However, using his enormous majority, Chiluba changed the constitution to include a clause that 'no person born of non-Zambian parents can be president'. Kenneth Kaunda, as is well known, was born of Malawian parents, and so this was a clear move to exclude him from running for the office. It was not the only such move, and caused endless furore.

KK was head of UNIP and so he called for all UNIP candidates to boycott the elections, believing that they could not be fair. In the event, several UNIP candidates split off and stood as independent candidates, but the overall result was another resounding win for Chiluba. (MMD won about 132 of 150 seats.) It's widely thought that he would have won anyhow, even in a fair election, so it seems a pity that he resorted to dubious tactics to achieve the victory.

With poetic justice, it now transpires that Chiluba himself is of illegitimate birth and uncertain national origin. *The Post* newspaper claimed to have researched and verified that his own parents were of DRC/Zairean descent, which has led to a long-running persecution of the paper by the government for 'being disrespectful' and 'insulting' the president – all of which are punishable offences in Zambia. (Travellers take note!)

The coup

Later, at the end of October 1997 a small group of soldiers briefly took over the state-run radio station. They were led by one 'Captain Solo', who claimed to represent the 'National Redemption Council'. (Neither had been heard of before.) He announced that the group had launched 'Operation Born-again' and ousted the MMD government and Chiluba, saying later in the short broadcast that he had seen 'an angel and the message was that the Government had to be overthrown'.

Although this group transpired to have been little more than a few drunken soldiers, Chiluba used the incident as an excuse to institute a state of emergency for five months. He detained more than 70 civilians and soldiers, including opposition leaders and the former President, KK. Some detainees claimed torture was used during interrogations, allegations which were later substantiated by the government's own human rights commission headed by Supreme Court judge, Lombe Chibesakunda.

A year later the case against many had to be dropped for lack of evidence. Many are now suing the state for wrongful arrest. Others remain in jail, still awaiting trail.

This clampdown by the state attracted heavy criticism from human rights groups and affected the international donor community's willingness to release funds for debt relief.

Conclusion

Overall, many regard President Chiluba's presidency as a disappointment; although, looking at conditions in neighbouring Zaire and Zimbabwe, most agree that the situation in Zambia could be worse.

Chiluba has continued KK's habit of regularly reshuffling ministers (thus ensuring that none develop their own power base), he's been slow to take decisions, and has proved unable to control corruption effectively. Critics claim that events rather than politicians control the country and look forward to the next elections when the constitution dictates a new president. However, possible candidates within MMD have been slow to surface, and many opposition leaders are still in jail, awaiting trials for treason in the wake of the failed coup.

Chiluba has repeatedly vowed that he will stand by the constitution and not in the 2001 elections. However the opposition fears that he will emulate Namibia's Sam Nujoma, who is attempting to change Namibia's constitution 'at the will of the people' to allow him to remain president. KK also plans to stand again, despite his promises that he had retired from politics.

On a positive note, Chiluba has showed determination not to be drawn into the conflict in neighbouring Democratic Republic of Congo (DRC). This has already sucked Zimbabwe, Angola, Namibia and Chad in on the side of President Laurent Kabila, against Uganda and Rwanda who have taken the side of the anti-Kabila rebels. He has avoided any military involvement in this war and has played a high-profile role in brokering various peace talks. Given Zambia's position between DRC, Angola and Zimbabwe, and the porous nature of its borders, this war continues to be a cause for concern in Zambia.

On a less consequential note, keep your eye open for political slogans when you travel. I recently saw one in Livingstone encouraging people to vote for women with the slogan: 'A government without women is like a pot on one stone.' Which is, of course, immediately intelligible to any Zambian who cooks on an open fire.

ECONOMY
Overview
Zambia remains one of the world's poorest countries, with a major national debt, corruption and a weak currency.

In the mid-1990s, even until 1997, its prospects looked good. GDP growth was about 6.5%; inflation had been reduced to 24% (down from 187% in 1993); a prolonged decline in manufacturing was being reversed; non-traditional exports were expanding at a rate of 33% a year; and the privatisation programme was being hailed as one of Africa's most successful. Even the kwacha had been stabilised and a surge in foreign investment was being reported.

By 1998, the reversal of Zambia's economic fortunes had been stark. GDP growth was minimal, manufacturing output was again in a downturn, and inflation was slowly rising. While the breakdown in the ZCCM privatisation was a major cause of this reversal (see *Copper*, under *Zambia's mining industry*, below), part of the problem stems from reactions to the government's actions after the coup attempt in late '97. On both counts, western donors withheld aid to Zambia.

Finally, in 1999, it seems that the aid and debt relief are again forthcoming. Again there is optimism that Zambia's economy can continue to improve. The international community's increasing willingness to look at more radical schemes for debt relief is a real source of hope, though the problems with selling off the mines continue to haunt the government.

The burden of debt
Zambia is a country visibly crippled by its debt burden. According to UNICEF, over two-thirds of all Zambians live in poverty; other sources put this figure higher, with 98% of the population living on less than US$2 a day. This burden is borne out by statistics: outstanding external debts are estimated at more than US$6.3 billion. At over US$600 per person, Zambia has the highest level of per capita debt in the world. With a GDP of $3.9 billion, Zambia's debt, as a percentage of GDP, is almost 200%.

Zambia's annual debt repayments total $132 million, which is 35% of the value of exports of goods and services. Its interest payments alone equal 13% of these exports. To put this into perspective, Zambia spends five times more on its interest repayments than it does on education and three times as much as on healthcare.

The consequences of this are clear: literacy is declining and the percentage of infant deaths has doubled in the past seven years. Despite this, Zambia has managed to remain current on its debt-service payments and even to clear some of its arrears. However, these commitments are clearly a major constraint on economic development.

Zambia relies on foreign donors for 35% of its budget, which means that for every dollar Zambia receives in aid, it repays US$3 to service its debt. At the Paris Club meeting of western donors in 1998, funds were promised to alleviate this, but were withheld pending the sale of the copper mines (ZCCM). This had a very real affect on the country, and there was concern amongst the donors that it could seriously threaten Zambia's debt-service ability.

Structural adjustment programme
For most of Chiluba's presidency, Zambia has been following a programme of economic reforms dictated, in part, by the IMF. This scheme, known as the

Enhanced Structural Adjustment Facility (ESAF), allows the world's poorest nations to pay lower interest rates on the money that they owe. Zambia has joined this, though it is criticised by experts as being of more benefit to the IMF than to Zambia, as Zambia will first have to repay all its arrears to date.

In December 1995, Zambia qualified for assistance under ESAF and embarked on a series of far-reaching reforms. These centred on trade liberalisation, deregulation and exchange rate reform. Pivotal to the whole programme was a greater role for the private sector, and the sale of state-owned enterprises. The main aim of the scheme was to encourage foreign direct investment.

Having met these requirements, Zambia is now in the IMF's 'good books'. However the social consequences don't always get mentioned: rising unemployment, increased prices for basic necessities (including the staple mealie-meal) and cuts in health care and education. All of these have tended to foster an increase in crime and social unrest. The message to the ordinary Zambian looking for his next meal is that it's going to get worse before it gets better, which can't be easy to swallow.

Privatisation

As part of the structural adjustment programme, the Zambia Privatisation Agency (ZPA) was set up to oversee privatisation. To date it has sold over 200 companies, of which Zambians bought about 70%. A few have failed, but the majority seem to be viable. This trend may start to slow down as many of the remaining companies are large, and will require more protracted negotiations. However, the ZPA hopes to be finished by about 2001. (It is interesting that the ZPA is not involved in the selling of the mines, though it did advise the government to accept Kafue's offer.)

Latest developments

In mid-February 1999, the Finnish Government announced that it was writing off US$7.5 million of Zambia's debt. Later, at the end of March, the IMF decided to give Zambia a much-needed boost with US$14 million of its new US$349 million Enhanced Structural Adjustment Facility (ESAF) loan. Also, the World Bank gave US$65 million, despite the continuing problems in selling the mines. These were crucial signals to other donors, and on April 16 of the same year the Paris Club agreed to write off US$670 million of Zambian debt, and restructure the repayments of about US$330 million of the rest.

Optimists hope that these payments will mark the start of concerted efforts by the international community to alleviate Zambia's crippling debt of over US$6 billion. One step towards this, taken early in 1999, has been to confer on Zambia the status of highly indebted poor country (HIPC status). This is facilitating the World Bank and other donors to relieve more of the debt.

Structure of the economy

Zambia relies on its mining sector for the vast majority of its export earnings and about 7% of its GDP. Aside from that, Zambia's other industries are small. They include construction, chemicals, textiles and fertiliser production.

Agriculture accounts for only 20% of Zambia's GDP, but by far the majority of its workforce. Tourism remains tiny as yet, but has tremendous potential in the long term.

Zambia's high, well-watered plateau means that it has about 40% of Southern Africa's water resources. Hydroelectric schemes, which provide most of the country's power, make it self-sufficient in energy. Zambia already exports power to neighbouring countries.

Zambia's mining industry

Zambia's economy is totally dependent upon its mining sector, and particularly its copper mines. Mining contributes about 7% of the country's GDP and about 68% of its export earnings. It employs perhaps 11% of the country's workforce.

Copper

Zambia is the world's fourth largest copper-producer. It has large, high-quality deposits of copper ore. Output from these declined from around 700,000 tons in the late 1970s, to 259,000 tons in 1998. This is expected to recover to 300,000 tons in 1999, though the average price of the copper is likely to drop by about 10%.

All the mines are controlled by Zambia Consolidated Copper Mines (ZCCM), which has long been viewed as the jewel of Zambia's economic crown. Of these, Nchanga and Nkana mines alone account for 65% of Zambia's total copper production. However, disuse and mismanagement have caused Zambia's mines to lapse into an almost irreparable degenerative state. They are currently recording losses of around US$15–20 million per month.

As part of the government's ongoing privatisation programme, ZCCM was to be sold off – thus stemming the losses and offering the mines some chance of survival. In June 1998, the government rejected an offer by the 'Kafue consortium', which was the only viable bid for them. They maintained that the price was too low.

In retrospect, it seems that Kafue's offer was the best the government could have hoped for, and the rejection is now seen as equivalent to economic suicide. Zambia's economy remains on the edge of bankruptcy, and its future prosperity is partly dependent upon the speedy sale of these mines.

Anglo American, the South African mining giant, offered about US$73 million for the Nkana, Nchanga and Kongola Deep mines and in April '99 the government signed a memorandum of understanding for this sale. However, one of Anglo's preconditions to the deal is that it must find a 'substantial' mining partner to assist it. So far only Chile's state-owned mining corporation, Codelco, has shown any interest and the deal looks far from completion. The irony of the situation is that the mines originally belonged to Anglo American, before KK nationalised them.

As yet there are no major secondary industries that use copper, and so the metal is exported as copper ingots to the USA, UK, Japan, Malaysia, Thailand, Indonesia and Europe.

Cobalt

Zambia is the world's largest producer of cobalt, producing around 5,000 tons per annum of this valuable, strategic metal: around 20% of the world's total production. In one deal, a private mining company was granted rights to extract cobalt and copper from Nkana's slag heap. This company estimates that this still has about 56,000 tons of cobalt and 86,000 tons of copper within it, so Zambia's output is expected to remain high.

Coal

Zambia has only one coal mine, at Maamba, where production has been declining for some time. It is currently running at about 300,000 tons per annum, though it is thought that this could increase by 60% if modern machinery and more efficient practices were introduced. This has recently been privatised.

Other mineral resources

Zambia has natural resources of amethyst, fluorite, feldspar, gypsum, aquamarine, lead, zinc, tin and gold – as well as a variety of gemstones. All are on a small scale, and few are being commercially exploited. An exception is emeralds, which are said to be among the highest quality in the world. These are being mined to the order of about US$200 million per year. However, about half of them are thought to be smuggled out of the country, so the real amounts remain uncertain.

Agriculture

Agriculture accounts for only 20% of Zambia's GDP, but employs perhaps 85% of its workforce. Zambia's varied topography encourages a wide diversity in the crops cultivated. Most farming is still done by small-scale subsistence farmers, although large commercial farms are gradually appearing, often financed by private investors. There remain many fertile areas that are not being exploited, largely because of the lack of infrastructure in rural parts of the country.

Zambia's main crops and agricultural products are maize (the staple food for most people), sorghum, rice, peanuts, soya beans, sunflowers, tobacco, cotton, sugarcane, cassava, cattle, goats, beef and eggs.

More recently, the 'floricultural' sector has started to bloom for export. That consists of roses, vegetables, fruit, coffee and tea. Poor communications mean that many of these need to be located near Lusaka's main airport, to ensure that flowers and vegetables are freshly delivered. (Export growers regularly charter cargo planes to Europe now.) Processing and packaging companies are developing in parallel with this, with some companies supplying packaged vegetables to British supermarkets.

Other industrial sectors

Zambia's manufacturing industry accounts for about 30% of its GDP, but its costs are high and so it isn't very competitive regionally. The domestic market is small, therefore most small industries need to develop larger economies of scale before they can compete with, say, South African companies. Areas with potential for this include food, cement, tobacco and textiles.

Tourism

Tourism remains one of Zambia's least developed sectors, and yet arguably holds the greatest potential. The praises of its national parks are sung elsewhere in the book, but here it's worth noting that Zambia's best camps command prices (and standards) to match their equivalents in Tanzania, Zimbabwe or Botswana. What's more, Zambia still has vast tracts of pristine wilderness, which is exactly what's needed for new safari destinations.

Zambia has the (arguable) benefit of a late-developing tourism industry, which should allow it to learn from the mistakes of others. Hopes for the development of tourism lie firmly with the private sector, and the government is proving happy for private investors to buy into the industry. It is expanding slowly – which is by far the best way for a tourism industry to move if it is to stay on a sustainable basis.

People and Culture

PEOPLE
The population
Recent statistics suggest that Zambia's population stands at about ten million, and this is increasing by around 3% per year. About 49% of Zambia's population are under 15 years of age, whilst some 73% of those above age 15 are literate. About 10% of Zambians live in Lusaka.

Statistics indicate that the average life expectancy for a Zambian is 42 years. Around 99% of the population are black African in origin, and the remaining 1% are mostly people of European or Indian origin.

However, the statistics say nothing of the warmth that the sensitive visitor can encounter. If you venture into the rural areas, take a local bus, or try to hitchhike with the locals, you will often find that Zambians are curious about you. Chat to them openly, as fellow travellers, and you will find most Zambians to be delightful. They will be pleased to assist you where they can, and as keen to help you learn about them and their country as they are interested in your lifestyle and what brings you to Zambia.

A note on 'tribes'
The people of Africa are often viewed, from abroad, as belonging to a multitude of culturally and linguistically distinct tribes – which are often portrayed as being at odds with each other. Whilst there is certainly an enormous variety of different ethnic groups in Africa, most are closely related to their neighbours in terms of language, beliefs and way of life. Modern historians eschew the simplistic tags of 'tribes', noting that such groupings change with time.

Sometimes the word tribe is used to describe a group of people who all speak the same language; it may be used to mean those who follow a particular leader or to refer to all the inhabitants of a certain area at a given time. In any case, tribe is a vague word which is used differently for different purposes. The term 'clan' (blood relations) is a smaller, more precisely defined, unit – though rather too precise for our broad discussions here.

Certainly, at any given time, groups of people or clans who share similar language and cultural beliefs do band together and often, in time, develop 'tribal' identities. However, it is wrong to then extrapolate and assume that their ancestors will have had the same groupings and allegiances centuries ago.

In Africa, as elsewhere in the world, history is recorded by the winners. Here the winners, the ruling class, may be the descendants of a small group of intruders who achieved dominance over a larger, long-established community. Over the years, the history of that ruling class (the winners) usually becomes regarded as the history of the whole community, or tribe. Two 'tribes' have thus become one, with one history – which will reflect the origins of that small group of intruders, and not the ancestors of the majority of the current tribe.

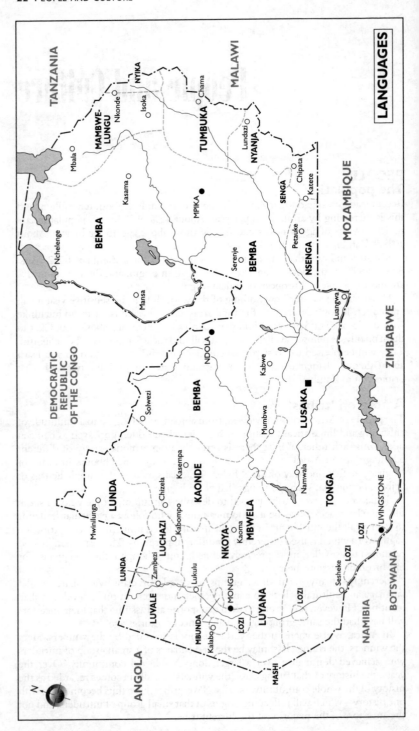

RICH LANGUAGES

Judi Helmholz

When considering where languages are at their richest and most descriptive, it is often noted that Eskimos have many ways of saying 'snow'. Each of their words describes a slightly different type of snow – the differences being too subtle to express so concisely in English. In a similar vein, Bantu languages have areas where they are more descriptive and colourful than plain English. For example, in Lozi no fewer than 40 words are used to mean 'woman'. All have slightly different implications. These include:

Liombe	tall, beautiful woman
Cebucebu	crafty, old woman
Katubaminzi	woman who destroys village life by bad behaviour
Likula	woman with many husbands
Kamundendule	woman who speaks loudly and carelessly
Mumbulu	doddering old woman
Namukuka	woman not at present married
Njakati	woman with a voracious appetite
Licenkenene	small, stout woman
Muketa	thin, old woman.
Mubala	newlywed, just arrived in her husband's village
Mushuwi	woman fishing with a basket net
Njimikati	woman who cultivates a lot

Zambia is typical of a large African country. Currently historians and linguistics experts can identify at least 16 major cultural groupings, and more than 72 different dialects are spoken in the country. As you will see, there are cultural differences between the people in different parts of the country. However, these are no more pronounced than those between the states of the USA, or the different regions of the (relatively tiny) UK.

There continues to be lots of inter-marriage and mixing of these peoples and cultures – perhaps more so than there has ever been, due to the efficiency of modern transport systems. Generally, there is very little friction between these communities (whose boundaries, as we have said, are indistinct) and Zambia's various peoples live peacefully together.

African language groups

Below are detailed some of the major language groups, arranged alphabetically. This is only a rough guide to the many languages and dialects of Zambia's people. Although these different language groupings do loosely correspond to what many describe as Zambia's tribes, the distinctions are blurred further by the natural linguistic ability of most Zambians. Whilst it is normal to speak English plus one local language, many Zambians will speak a number of local languages fluently.

When the colonial powers carved up Africa, the divisions between the countries bore only a passing resemblance to the traditional areas of these various ethnic groups. Thus many of the groups here are split between several countries. Note that the estimates of populations quoted below are based on surveys done during the 1980s, and average estimated population growth rates since then.

A COW FOR CARELESSNESS
Judi Helmholz

As with most African countries, Zambia has a complex tribal system for administering justice, righting wrongs and ensuring that compensation is paid for any misdoing. Marimbi, a young employee of friends, Chad and Tracy, had damaged a young schoolgirl. 'Damaged' in this case meant getting the girl pregnant.

It is a serious matter, though not because she is pregnant or is young or was a virgin; there is little shame associated with pre-marital sex or pregnancy in Zambia. It is serious mainly in terms of ensuring appropriate compensation is paid to the girl's family.

The fathers of the boy and girl generally meet to negotiate these 'damages' which are paid in the form of cattle and/or cash, varying by local custom and circumstances. If the fathers can't come to some sort of agreement, the matter goes to court.

Damages could cost somewhere between one and six cows or the cash equivalent. A six-cow offence might be getting a schoolgirl pregnant, resulting in her leaving school, and thereby losing her future employment potential. Marimbi had a six-cow offence.

Oddly enough, compensation isn't paid out until the girl actually delivers the child. At 2am one night, Marimbi frantically pounded on the door to the house shouting, 'Mami, come quickly! The baby is coming!' Lynn, Chad's mother visiting from South Africa, ran outside to find Marimbi's girlfriend heavily in labour.

Time was of the essence. Lynn grabbed her car keys, yelled at the couple to get into the car and set out, although as a visitor to Livingstone, she had no idea where the hospital was. Marimbi was desperately trying to give her directions, while his girlfriend was labouring in the back seat.

'Mami, the baby is coming!' He yelled. 'Ahhhhh, the head is coming! Ahhhhh the baby is here!' Suddenly the sound of a wailing infant erupted from the back seat. Marimbi's girlfriend had just given birth in Lynn's brand new BMW.

Marimbi, girlfriend and baby made it to the hospital safely. The next week, Marimbi reported the baby was sick. A day later, he mentioned that the baby had died. When asked how, Marimbi stated quite matter-of-factly that the baby had died because it had come in contact with a pregnant woman. According to local beliefs, a new-born child will die if it comes into contact with a pregnant woman.

But Marimbi was not distressed. You see, his six-cow offence had now been reduced to a one-cow offence. His girlfriend could go back to school and life could continue as it was.

Bemba

Bemba is the first language of about two and a quarter million Zambians: almost a quarter of the country's population. It is spoken in the rural areas of northern Zambia, from the Luapula River eastwards to Mpika, Kasama and beyond. Because people from these areas were the original workers in the mines of the Copperbelt, Bemba has subsequently achieved the status of *lingua franca* in the major urban areas of the Copperbelt and Lusaka.

It is recognised for administration and educational purposes within Zambia, whilst outside its borders Bemba is also spoken by over 150,000 people in the Democratic Republic of Congo, and around 37,000 in Tanzania.

Kaonde

Kaonde-speakers live mostly around the northern side of Kafue National Park, centring on the area around Kasempa, and extending southeast as far as Mumbwa. They are one of Zambia's larger language groups, and probably number about 200,000.

Lozi

There are about 500,000 Lozi-speakers in Zambia, concentrated in the western and southern provinces, around Barotseland and Livingstone. The centre of Lozi culture is the rich agricultural floodplain around the upper Zambezi River – and it is here that the Ku-omboka (see *Festivals*, page 27) takes place each year.

Luchazi

This language has only a small number of speakers, perhaps 70,000 in the west of Zambia – less than 1% of the country's population. There are thought to be a similar number of Luchazi-speaking people in Angola.

Lunda

Not to be confused with Luunda, which is a dialect of Bemba, Lunda is the first language of about 230,000 Zambians and is spoken in areas of the Copperbelt, as well as nearby DRC and Angola. It is officially taught in primary schools, and can occasionally be heard on radio or seen in newspapers in the area.

Luvale

Luvale is an important language in Angola, where it is spoken by almost one million people. In Zambia there are only about 215,000 people whose first language is Luvale, and they live in the northwestern and western provinces of Zambia.

Luyana

The Luyana-speaking people are a small group, perhaps numbering 130,000 in total. Their language has not been well documented, though it is spoken in Zambia, Angola, Namibia and also Botswana. In Zambia it is found almost exclusively in the Western Province.

Mambwe-Lungu

These are other languages that need further study – so far they appear to differ from each other only slightly, as dialects would. In total about 280,000 Zambians count them as their first language – about 3% of the population. Their stronghold is in the northeast of the northern province, south of Lake Tanganyika. As you might expect, they are also spoken in Tanzania.

Mashi

Mashi seems to be spoken by only a tiny number of Zambians, perhaps only 25,000 people, who are often nomadic within a southwestern area of the western province. Little has been documented about this language – though it has been noted that virtually all the native speakers of Mashi follow traditional religious practices, rather than the more recently introduced Christian beliefs.

Mbunda

The first language of about 130,000 Zambians, Mbunda is spoken in the north of Barotseland and the northern side of western Zambia – as well as in Angola.

Nkoya-Mbwela

Nkoya and Mbwela are two closely related languages. Mbwela is often referred to as a dialect of Nkoya, though here we have grouped them together as equals. They also have only a tiny number of speakers – around 80,000 people – who are found around the Mankoya area, in Zambia's western and southern provinces.

Nsenga

There are thought to be over 330,000 people speaking Nsenga as their first language, of whom the vast majority live in Zambia. These are clustered around the area of Petauke – near to the borders with Zimbabwe and Mozambique, across which the language is also spoken.

Nyanja

Nyanja is the Bantu language most often encountered by visitors in Zambia. It is widely used in much of the country, including the key cities of Lusaka and Livingstone. Nyanja is sometimes described as not being a language *per se*, but rather a common skill enabling people of varying tribes living in eastern, central and southern parts of Zambia and Malawi to communicate without following the strict grammar of specific local languages. In other words, like Swahili and other 'universal' languages, Nyanja is something of a *lingua franca* for Zambia.

Nyanja is certainly the official language of the police, and is widely used for administrative and educational purposes. About a million Zambians use Nyanja as their first language – mostly in the eastern and central areas of the country – and there may be double that number using the language in Malawi. Then there are around 330,000 Nyanja-speakers in Zimbabwe, and perhaps 500,000 in Mozambique. A total of approaching four million people in the subcontinent speak Nyanja as a first language.

Nyika

Also known as Nyiha, or more precisely as Chi-Nyika, Nyika is spoken most widely in Tanzania, and also in Malawi. In Zambia it is used around the Isoka and Chama areas, across to the Malawi border. (It is closely related to the language known as Ichi-Lambya in Tanzania and Malawi.)

Tonga

Tonga is the language of a small minority of Zimbabweans, many of whom were displaced south by the creation of Lake Kariba (see page 199). However, in Zambia it is the first language of around one million people, about 11% of the country's population, and is widely used in the media. Tonga is distributed throughout the south of the country, with its highest concentration in the middle Zambezi valley.

Tumbuka

Zambia has about 430,000 people who speak Tumbuka as a first language, mostly living on the eastern side of the country. Outside Zambia many Tumbuka-speakers live in Malawi and Tanzania, bringing the total number to about two million.

Other ethnic groups
White Zambians
There are a small number of white Zambians, very different from the expat community (see below) who are often white but simply working in the country on a temporary basis. Many white Zambians will trace their families back to colonial immigrants who came over during British rule, but most will regard themselves as Zambian rather than, say, British. This is generally an affluent group of people, and many of the country's businesses, and the vast majority of the safari companies, are owned and run by white Zambians.

Asian Zambians
Like the white Zambians, many people of Asian origin came here during the colonial period. When the British ruled African colonies like Zambia as well as India, there was movement of labour from Asia to Africa. Now, like the white Zambians, this is generally an affluent group. On the whole, Zambians of Asian descent retain a very strong sense of Asian identity and culture, and many are traders or own small shops.

Expatriates
Distinct from Zambians, there is a large 'expat' community in Zambia. These foreigners usually come to Zambia for two or three years, to work on short-term contracts, often for either multi-national companies or aid agencies. Most are highly skilled individuals who come to share their knowledge with Zambian colleagues – often teaching skills that are in short supply in Zambia.

In recent years there has been a migration of trained Zambian teachers and lecturers to neighbouring countries, where they are paid better. (The University of Zambia, for example, has lost more than 350 lecturers in the last five years. Most are now teaching in Botswana, Lesotho, Swaziland or South Africa.)

CULTURE
Festivals
Zambia has several major cultural festivals which, on the whole, are rarely seen by visitors. If you can get to one, then you will find them to be very genuine occasions, where ceremonies are performed for the benefit of the local people and the participants, and not for the odd tourist who is watching.

Cultural celebrations were strongly encouraged during Kenneth Kaunda's reign, as he favoured people being aware of their cultural origins. 'A country without culture is like a body without a head', was one of his phrases. Thus during the 1980s one group after another 'discovered' old traditional festivals. Most are now large local events, partly cultural but also part political rally, religious gathering, and sports event.

Bear in mind that, like most celebrations worldwide, these are often accompanied by the large-scale consumption of alcohol. To see these festivals properly, and to appreciate them, you will need a good guide: someone who understands the rituals, can explain their significance, and can instruct you on how you should behave. After all, how would you feel about a passing Zambian traveller who arrives, with curiosity, at your sibling's wedding (a small festival), in the hope of being invited to the private reception?

Photographers will find superb opportunities at such colourful events, but should behave with sensitivity. *Before* you brandish your camera, remember to ask permission from anyone who might take offence.

The Ku-omboka

This is the most famous of the ceremonies, and takes place in the Western Province. It used to be around February or March, often on a Thursday, just before full moon. The precise date would only be known a week or so in advance, as it was decided upon by the Lozi king. Now that the ceremony attracts more visitors, it is usually held at Easter; though if water levels are not high enough, it will not take place at all.

The Lozi Kingdom is closely associated with the fertile plains around the Upper Zambezi River. When dry, this well-defined area affords good grazing for livestock, and its rich alluvial soil is ideal for cultivation. It contrasts with the sparse surrounding woodland, growing on poor soil typical of the rest of western Zambia. So for much of the year, these plains support a dense population of subsistence farms.

However, towards the end of the rains, the Zambezi's water levels rise. The plains then become floodplains, and the settlements gradually become islands. The people must leave them for the higher ground, at the margins of the floodplain. This retreat from the advancing waters – known as the Ku-omboka – is traditionally led by the king himself, the Litunga, from his dry-season abode at Lealui, in the middle of the plain. He retreats with his court to his high-water residence, at Limulunga, on the eastern margins of the floodplain.

The Litunga's departure is heralded by the beating of three huge old royal war drums – Mundili, Munanga, and Kanaono. These continue to summon the people from miles around until the drums themselves are loaded above the royal barge, the *nalikwanda*, a very large wooden canoe built around the turn of the century and painted with vertical black-and-white stripes. The royal barge is then paddled and punted along by 96 polers, each sporting a skirt of animal skins and a white vest. Their scarlet hats are surmounted by tufts of fur taken from the mane of unfortunate lions.

The royal barge is guided by a couple of 'scout' barges, painted white, which search out the right channels for the royal barge. Behind it comes the Litunga's wife, the Moyo, in her own barge, followed by local dignitaries, various attendants, many of the Litunga's subjects, and the odd visitor lucky enough to be in the area at the right time. The journey takes most of the day, and the flotilla is accompanied by an impromptu orchestra of local musicians.

John Reader's excellent book, *Africa: A Biography of the Continent* (see *Further Reading*), comments:

> 'When the Litunga boards the nalikwanda at Lealui he customarily wears a light European-style suit, a pearl-grey frock coat and a trilby hat; when he leaves the barge at Limulunga he is dressed in a splendid uniform of dark-blue serge ornately embroidered with gold braid, with matching cockade hat complete with a white plume of egret feathers.'

In fact, Chapter 47 of this book contains the fascinating story of some of the first Europeans to see the original Ku-omboka, and the sad narration of the gradual European subjugation of the Lozi kingdom. It also includes details of the Litunga's trip to London, in 1902, for the coronation of King Edward VII. It was here that the problem arose of what the Litunga should wear. Reader reports:

> 'By happy coincidence, the king [Edward VII] took a particular interest in uniforms; he was an expert on the subject and is even said to have made a hobby of designing uniforms. Doubtless the king had approved the design of the new uniforms with which Britain's ambassadors had recently been issued. Certainly he was aware that the introduction of these new outfits

had created a redundant stock of the old style, which were richly adorned with gold braid. Lewanika [the Litunga] should be attired in one of those, the king ordained. And thus the Litunga acquired the uniform which has become part of the Kuomboka tradition. Not an admiral's uniform, as is often reported, but a surplus dress uniform of a Victorian ambassador; not a gift from Queen Victoria, but the suggestion of her son...'

When the royal barge finally arrives at Limulunga, the Litunga steps ashore in the ambassador's uniform to spend an evening of feasting and celebrations, with much eating, drinking, music and traditional dancing.

Likumbi Lya Mize
The Luvale people of western Zambia have an annual 'fair' type of celebration, which takes place for four or five days towards the end of August. 'Likumbi Lya Mize' means 'Mize day' and the event is held at the palace of the senior chief – at Mize, about 7km west of Zambezi.

This provides an opportunity for the people to see their senior chief, watch the popular Makishi dancers, and generally have a good time. As you might expect, there is also lots of eating and drinking, plus people in traditional dress, displays of local crafts, and singing.

Umutomboko
This is nothing to do with the Ku-omboka, described above. It is an annual two-day celebration, performed in the last weekend of July, whereby the Paramount Chief Mwata Kazeme celebrates the arrival of the Luunda people, the 'crossing of the river'. It is held in a specially prepared arena, close to the Ng'ona River, at Mwansabombwe.

On the first day the chief, covered in white powder, receives tributes of food and drink from his subjects – the cause for much feasting and celebration by all. On the second an animal (often a goat) is slaughtered and the highlight is the chief's dance with his sword.

Shimunenga
This traditional gathering is held on the weekend of a full moon, in September or October, at Maala on the Kafue Flats – about 40km west of Namwala. Then the Ila people (whose language is closely related to Tonga) gather together, driving cattle across the Kafue River to higher ground. It used to be a lechwe hunt, but that is now forbidden!

The Nc'wala
On 24 February there is a festival to celebrate the first fruit, at Mutenguleni village, near Chipata. This large celebration was recently revived, after 80 years of not being practised. It consists of two parts. Firstly Chief Mpezeni tastes the first fruit of the land – usually sugarcane, maize and pumpkins. Secondly there is the ritual rebirth of the king (involving the king being locked up in his house) and the blessing of the fruit – which consists of a fairly gory spearing of a black bull whose blood the king has to drink. It's all accompanied by traditional dancing and beer-drinking.

Other festivals
The above list of festivals is by no means exhaustive, and a few others which are known include:

Kufukwila A May celebration led by Chief Mokumbi of the Kaonde people, held in the Solwezi area of northwestern Zambia.

Kulamba Also a thanksgiving ceremony for the Chewa people, held in August. It's held in the Katete Province, in eastern Zambia, and here you'll be able to see lots of fascinating Nyao (secret society) dancers.

Lukuni Luzwa Buuka A celebration of past conquests by the Toka people in the Southern Province, usually held in August.

Lwiinda A ceremony celebrated by Chief Mokuni, of the Toka-Leya people near Livingstone, around February. The people honour their ancestors and offer sacrifices for rain.

Malaila A ceremony to honour past chiefs, held in July by the Kunda people. (This is currently celebrated by Chieftainess Nsefu, near Mfuwe in the Luangwa Valley.)

Tuwimba A thanksgiving festival, in October, for the Nsenga people.

Cultural guidelines

Comments here are intended to be a general guide, just a few examples of how to travel more sensitively. They should not be viewed as blueprints for perfect Zambian etiquette. Cultural sensitivity is really a state of mind, not a checklist of behaviour – so here we can only hope to give the sensitive traveller a few pointers in the right direction.

When we travel, we are all in danger of leaving negative impressions with local people that we meet. It is easily done – by snapping that picture quickly, whilst the subject is not looking; by dressing scantily, offending local sensitivities; by just brushing aside the feelings of local people, with the high-handed superiority of a rich Westerner. These things are easy to do, in the click of a shutter, or flash of a dollar bill.

However, you will get the most representative view of Zambia if you cause as little disturbance to the local people as possible. You will never blend in perfectly when you travel – your mere presence there, as an observer, will always change the local events slightly. However, if you try to fit in and show respect for local culture and attitudes, then you may manage to leave positive feelings behind you.

One of the easiest, and most important, ways to do this is with greetings. African societies are rarely as rushed as Western ones. When you first talk to someone, you should greet them leisurely. So, for example, if you enter a bus station and want some help, do not just ask outright, 'Where is the bus to ...' That would be rude. Instead you will have a better reception (and better chance of good advice) by saying:

Traveller:	'Good afternoon.'
Zambian:	'Good afternoon.'
Traveller:	'How are you?'
Zambian:	'I am fine, how are you?'
Traveller:	'I am fine, thank you. *(pause)* Do you know where the bus to ...'

This goes for approaching anyone – always greet them first. For a better reception still, learn these phrases of greeting in the local language (see pages 395–6). English-speakers are often lazy about learning languages, and, whilst most Zambians understand English, a greeting given in an appropriate local language will be received with delight. It implies that you are making an effort to learn a little of their language and culture, which is always appreciated.

Occasionally, in the town or city, you may be approached by someone who doesn't greet you. Instead s/he tries immediately to sell you something, or even hassle you in some way. These people have learned that foreigners aren't used to greetings, and so have adapted their approach accordingly. An effective way to dodge their attentions is to reply to their questions with a formal greeting, and then

INEXPLICABLE ZAMBIA
Judi Helmholz
There are always challenges to be overcome when living, working or travelling in a foreign country. One day we asked an old colonial farmer for advice. He was 60 years old, born and raised here. 'How long do you have to be here before you can truly understand this country?' we queried, hoping for some words of wisdom. 'I can't answer that, you'll have to ask someone who has been here longer,' he replied in a matter-of-fact tone.

politely – but firmly – refuse their offer. This is surprisingly effective.

Another part of the normal greeting ritual is handshaking. As elsewhere, you would not normally shake a shop-owner's hand, but you would shake hands with someone to whom you are introduced. Get some practice when you arrive, as there is a gentle, three-part handshake used in Southern Africa which is easily learnt.

Your clothing is an area that can easily give offence. Most Zambians frown upon skimpy or revealing clothing, especially when worn by women. Shorts are fine for walking safaris, otherwise dress conservatively and avoid short shorts, especially in the more rural areas. Respectable locals will wear long trousers (men) or long skirts (women).

Photography is a tricky business. Most Zambians will be only too happy to be photographed – provided you ask their permission first. Sign language is fine for this question: just point at your camera, shrug your shoulders, and look quizzical. The problem is that then everyone will smile for you, producing the type of 'posed' photograph that you may not want. However, stay around and chat for five or ten minutes more, and people will get used to your presence, stop posing and you will get more natural shots of them (a camera with a quiet shutter is a help).

Note that special care is needed with photography near government buildings, bridges, and similar sites of strategic importance. You must ask permission before photographing anything here, or you risk people thinking that you are a spy.

If you're travelling, and seeking directions to somewhere, don't be afraid to stop and ask. Most people will be polite and keen to help – so keen that some will answer yes to questions if they think that this is what you want to hear. So try to avoid asking leading questions. For example, 'Yes' would often be the typical answer to the question, 'Does this road lead to…' And in a sense the respondent is probably correct – it will get you there. It's just that it may not be the quickest or shortest way.

To avoid misunderstandings, it is often better to ask open-ended questions like, 'Where does this road go to?' or 'How do I drive to …'

The specific examples above can only be taken so far – they are general by their very nature. But wherever you find yourself, if you are polite and considerate to the Zambians you meet, then you will rarely encounter any cultural problems. Watch how they behave and, if you have any doubts about how you should act, then ask someone quietly. They will seldom tell you outright that you are being rude, but they will usually give you good advice on how to make your behaviour more acceptable.

Helping Zambia's poorer communities
Visiting Zambia, especially the rural agricultural areas and the towns, many visitors are struck by the poverty and wish to help. Giving to beggars and those in need on

EDUCATION FOR THE POOR

Lisa Harmer

I am a VSO (Voluntary Services Overseas) volunteer in Lusaka, Zambia. My placement as a fundraiser for a Zambian Non-Governmental Organisation evoked 'Fundraising? In Africa?' when I told people what I was going to do. However, if you have a good cause, people will support you.

The NGO in question is Zambia Open Community Schools (ZOCS), which provides children excluded from government schools with a free basic four-year education.

Education in Zambia is not free. The average Zambian family has six children, and for each child attending school the family must buy a uniform, pay school and examination fees, and buy books and other school requirements. These expenses are unaffordable for a large proportion of the population; and there are not enough government school places anyway. Consequently, over 660,000 school-aged children, the majority of them girls and orphans, are not in school. Organisations such as ZOCS have developed to address this need.

ZOCS has 22 schools, based mainly in the compound areas around Lusaka. They are in the heart of the communities they serve, and each school involves many people on the Parent-Community Committees. The community is responsible for the management of the school and contributes to the overall development of ZOCS. Therefore, each school reflects the needs and environment of its community.

The schools are housed wherever is available: in a church hall, under an outside shelter or beneath a tree. A few communities have secured land and, with the help of donors who have provided materials, have built their own school building. Our teachers also live in these communities; they are untrained and so receive in-service training throughout the school year.

Part of my job is to work with the Parent–Community Committees on fundraising and income-generating activities. This increases community participation in the school, developing a level of financial independence and a long-term goal of self-sustainability.

Our schools provide these children with an opportunity to learn. This education enables them to contribute positively to the society in which they live, and gives them hope for their future.

If you would like to know more about the work of ZOCS or how you can help, please contact us at: Zambia Open Community Schools, Box 50429, Lusaka, Zambia; tel: 01 227084; email: zocs@zamnet.zm

the street is one way. It will alleviate your feelings of guilt, and perhaps some of the immediate suffering, but it is not a long-term solution.

There *are* ways in which you can make a positive contribution, but they require more effort than throwing a few coins to someone on the street. My favourite is the ZOCS project, mentioned in the box above, which provides a basic education to some of the young Zambian, who could not otherwise afford school at all. Education is vital for Zambia's future, while in the present it gives children some hope. Deaths from AIDS have left increasing numbers of orphans, many of whom end up on the streets. This project is making a difference on a local level, helping communities to organise their own schools.

There are many other charities equally worthy of your help, trying to provide sustainable solutions at a local level. Some are part of Chin – a network of non-governmental organisations, community-based groups, and government departments working with children in need. Their website is www.chin.org.zm, and it will give you some idea of the scale of the help required. All welcome donations – so make a resolution now to help at least one of them as an integral part of the cost of your trip.

Local charities working in Zambia

Disacare Wheelchair Centre Plot 11305 Libala (off Chilimbulu Rd), Behind Libala Secondary School, Lusaka. Tel/fax: 01 261712; email: disacare@zamnet.zm
Working with the less able-bodied staff in their workshop, Disacare make wheelchairs – the only producer in Zambia – that suits the terrain and can be repaired using parts from Zambia. They also make items of carpentry, tailoring, sculptures, and produce grill doors. They don't have a postal address.

Appropriate Paper Technology (APTERS) P.Bag 232x RW, Lusaka.
Set up by two men who had polio, APTERS now employs disabled people to make papier-mâché aides (eg: standing frames and feeding chairs) for children with cerebral palsy, using from recycled paper and cardboard. They hold clinics for parents to learn how to use these, and also make commercial products (eg: children's tables, chairs, dolls' houses) to help finance the project. They are based in the old polio department at university teaching hospital.

Bauleni Special Needs School PO Box 320080, Woodlands, Lusaka. Tel: 01 263073; fax: 01 262540.
This is a school for children with learning and physical disabilities who live in Bauleni area and the surrounding farms. They promote a Christian ethos and provide free education for disabled children with particular emphasis on mutual caring and independence in daily life.

Habitat for Humanity P.Bag 461X, Ridgeway, Lusaka. Tel: 01 232246; fax: 01232250; email: hfhzam@zamnet.zm
This is a non-profitmaking, Christian NGO trying to solve the housing problems of the poor. Since 1984 they have built over 720 houses in four different projects. Families pay back the loan over a period of 10 years into a revolving fund, enabling more houses to be built in the same community. Volunteers provide most of the labour.

Zambia National Association for the Physically Handicapped (ZNAPH) PO Box 72908, Ndola.
Based on Buteko Avenue in Ndola, ZNAPH runs a carpentry workshop for physically handicapped people. It trains them to be carpenters and to produce furniture that is sold to raise funds for the workshop.

Zambili d'Afrique PO Box 30369, Lusaka. Tel: 01 237745/231307; fax: 01 220691; email: zcrafts@zambili.co.zm
This is an NGO working with Traidcraft Exchange, a UK-based organisation which promotes ethical and effective business in support of fair trade. Zambili helps small and medium-sized businesses to start exporting their goods.

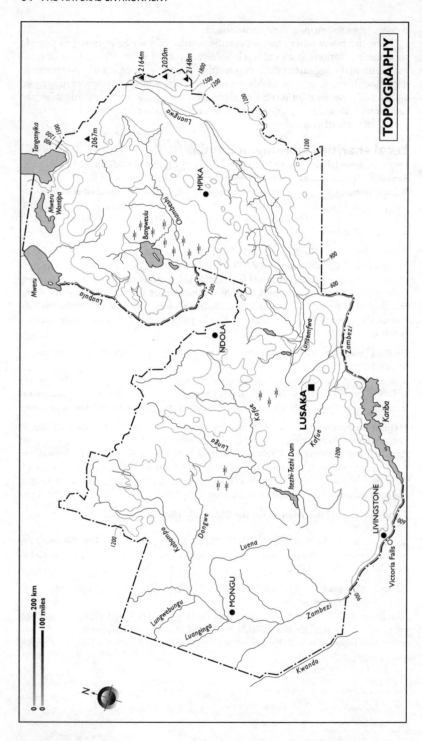

TOPOGRAPHY

The Natural Environment

PHYSICAL ENVIRONMENT
Geology and topology
Zambia lies landlocked between the Tropic of Capricorn and the Equator, shaped like a giant butterfly and covering about 752,610km². Most of this is part of the high, undulating plateau that forms the backbone of the African continent. Much of Zambia has an altitude of between 1,000m and 1,600m, whilst only a few of the low-lying rift valleys lie below 500m.

Zambia's oldest rocks, known as the Basement Complex, were laid down at an early stage in the pre-Cambrian era – as long as 2,000 million years ago. These were extensively eroded and covered by sediments which now form the Katanga system of rocks, dating from around 1,000 to 620 million years ago. These are what we now see near the surface in most of northeast and central Zambia, and they contain the important mineral deposits of the Copperbelt. Later still, from about 300 to 150 million years ago, the karoo system of sedimentary rocks was deposited: sandstones, mudstones, conglomerates and even coal. Towards the end of this era, molten rock seeped up through cracks in the crust, and covered areas of western Zambia in layers of basalt – the rock that is seen cut away by the Zambezi River in the gorges below Victoria Falls.

About 150 million years ago, during the Jurassic era of the dinosaurs, Africa was still part of Gondwana – a super-continent which included South America, India, Australasia and Antarctica. Since then Zambia's highlands have been eroded down from an original altitude of over 1,800m (Nyika Plateau is still at this altitude) to their present lower levels.

Very recently, perhaps only a few million years ago, the subcontinent had a dry phase. Then the sands from the Kalahari Desert blew far across southern Africa. Much of western Zambia now lies beneath a covering of Kalahari sand, as becomes abundantly clear the moment you try to drive in western Zambia.

Climate
Situated squarely in the tropics, Zambia gets a lot of strong sunlight, though the intense heat normally associated with the tropics is moderated in most places by the country's altitude and its rainfall.

Zambia's climate follows a similar pattern to that in most of Southern Africa, with rainfall when the sun is near its zenith from November to April. The precise timing and duration of this is determined by the interplay of three air-streams: the moist 'Congo' air-mass, the northeastern monsoon winds, and the southeastern trade winds. The water-bearing air is the Congo air-mass, which normally brings rain when it moves south into Zambia from Central Africa. This means that the northern areas, around Lakes Tanganyika and Mweru, receive the first rainfall – often in late October or November. This belt of rain will then work south, arriving in southern Zambia by the end of November or the start of December.

As the sun's intensity reduces, the Congo air-mass moves back north, leaving southern Zambia dry by around late March, and the north by late April or May. Most areas receive their heaviest rainfall in January, though some of the most northern areas have two peaks: one in December and one in March. This twin-peak cycle is more characteristic of central and eastern Africa. The heaviest total rainfall is found in the north, and the lightest in the south.

Lusaka's climate statistics are typical of the pleasant climate found in the higher areas of southern and central Zambia:

| | Temp °C | | Temp °F | | Humidity % | | Rainfall |
	max	min	max	min	am	pm	mm
Jan	26	17	78	62	84	71	231
Feb	26	17	78	62	85	80	191
Mar	26	17	78	62	83	56	142
Apr	26	15	78	59	71	47	18
May	25	12	77	52	59	37	3
Jun	23	10	73	50	56	32	0
Jul	23	9	73	48	54	28	0
Aug	25	12	77	53	46	26	0
Sep	29	15	84	59	41	19	0
Oct	31	18	87	64	39	23	15
Nov	29	18	84	64	57	46	91
Dec	27	17	80	62	76	61	150

The lower-lying valleys, including the Luangwa and Lower Zambezi, follow the same broad pattern but are considerably hotter throughout the year. In October, which is universally the hottest month, temperatures there often reach over 45°C in the shade.

FLORA AND FAUNA
Flora
Vegetation types
As with animals, each species of plant has its favourite conditions. External factors determine where each species thrives, and where it will perish. These include temperature, light, water, soil type, nutrients, and what other species of plants and animals live in the same area. Species with similar needs are often found together, in communities which are characteristic of that particular environment. Zambia has a number of different such communities, or typical 'vegetation types', within its borders – each of which is distinct from the others. The more common include:

Mopane woodland
The dominant tree here is the remarkably adaptable mopane, *Colophospermum mopane*, which is sometimes known as the butterfly tree because of the shape of its leaves. It is very tolerant of poorly drained or alkaline soils, and those with a high clay content. This tolerance results in the mopane having a wide range of distribution throughout southern Africa; in Zambia it occurs mainly in the hotter, drier, lower parts of the country, including the Luangwa and Zambezi valleys.

Mopane trees can attain a height of 25m, especially if growing on rich, alluvial soils. These are often called cathedral mopane, for their height and the graceful arch of their branches. However, shorter trees are more common in areas that are poor in nutrients, or have suffered extensive fire damage. Stunted mopane will form a low scrub, perhaps only 5m tall. All mopane trees are deciduous, and the leaves turn beautiful shades of yellow and red before falling in September and October.

Ground cover in mopane woodland is usually sparse; just thin grasses, herbs and the occasional bush. The trees themselves are an important source of food for game, as the leaves have a high nutritional value – rich in protein and phosphorus – which is favoured by browsers and is retained even after they have fallen from the trees. Mopane forests support large populations of rodents, including tree squirrels, *Peraxerus cepapi*, which are so typical of these areas that they are known as 'mopane squirrels'.

Miombo woodland
Without human intervention, the natural vegetation of most of Zambia (about 70%) is miombo woodland and its associated *dambos* (see below). This exists on Zambia's main plateau and its adjacent escarpments, where the acid soils are not particularly fertile and have often been leached of minerals by the water run-off.

Miombo woodland consists of a mosaic of large wooded areas and smaller, more open spaces dotted with clumps of trees and shrubs. The woodland is broadleafed and deciduous (though just how deciduous depends on the available water), and the tree canopies generally don't interlock. The dominant trees are *Brachystegia*, *Julbernardia* and *Isoberlinia* species – most of which are at least partially fire-resistant. There is more variation of species in miombo than in mopane woodland, but despite this it is often known simply as 'Brachystegia woodland'. The ground cover is also generally less sparse here than in mopane areas.

Munga woodland
The word 'munga' means thorn, and this is the thorny woodland which occurs when open grassland has been invaded by trees and shrubs – normally because of some disturbance like cultivation, fire or overgrazing. *Acacia*, *Terminalia* (bearing single-winged seeds) and *Combretum* (bearing seeds with four or five wings) are the dominant species, but many others can be present. Munga occurs mainly in the southern parts of Zambia.

Teak forest
In a few areas of southwestern Zambia (including the southern part of Kafue National Park), the Zambezi teak, *Baikaea plurijuga*, forms dry semi-evergreen forests on a base of Kalahari sand. This species is not fire-resistant, so these stands occur only where slash-and-burn type cultivation methods have never been used. Below the tall teak is normally a dense, deciduous thicket of vegetation, interspersed with sparse grasses and herbs in the shadier spots of the forest floor.

Moist evergreen forest
In the areas of higher rainfall (mostly in the north of Zambia), and near rivers, streams, lakes and swamps, where a tree's roots will have permanent access to water, dense evergreen forests are found. Many species occur, and this lush vegetation is characterised by having three levels: a canopy of tall trees, a sub-level of smaller trees and bushes, and a variety of ground-level vegetation. In effect, the environment is so good for plants that they have adapted to exploit the light from every sunbeam.

This type of forest is prevalent in the far north of the country, especially in the Mwinilunga area. However, three more localised environments can give rise to moist evergreen forests in other areas of the country.

Riparian forests (often called riverine forests) are very common. They line

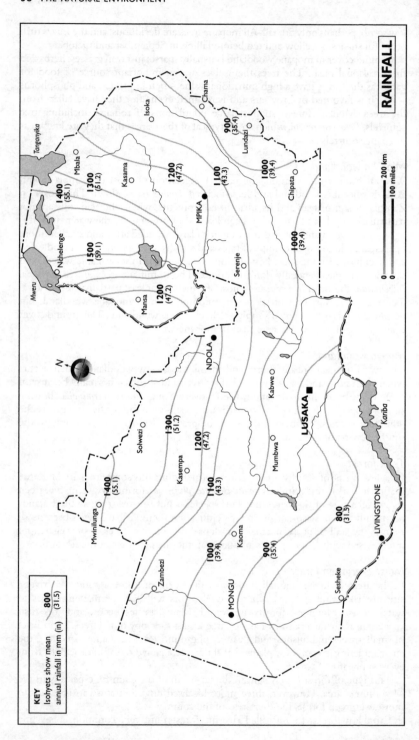

KEY
Isohyets show mean
annual rainfall in mm (in)
800
(31.5)

RAINFALL

Tanganyika

Mbala ○
1400 (55.1)
1300 (51.2)
Isoka ○
Kasama ○
1200 (47.2)
Chama ○
900 (35.4)
Lundazi ○
1000 (39.4)

Mweru
Nchelenge ○
1500 (59.1)
● MPIKA
1100 (43.3)
Chipata ○

Mansa ○
1200 (47.2)
Serenje ○
1000 (39.4)

N

● NDOLA
Kabwe ○
■ LUSAKA
Kariba

Solwezi ○
1300 (51.2)
1200 (47.2)
Kasempa ○
1100 (43.3)
Mumbwa ○

Mwinilunga ○
1400 (55.1)

Kaoma ○
1000 (39.4)
900 (35.4)
800 (31.5)
LIVINGSTONE ●

Zambezi ○
● MONGU
Sesheke ○

0   200 km
0   100 miles

many of Zambia's major rivers and are found in most of the national parks. Typical trees and shrubs here include ebony (*Diospyros mespiliformis*), mangosteen (*Garcinia livingstonei*), wild gardenia (*Gardenia volkensii*), sausage tree (*Kigelia africana*), Natal mahogany (*Trichilia emetica*), and various species of figs. But walk away from the river, and you'll find riparian species thinning out rapidly.

Montane forests are found on the lower slopes of mountains, where the rainfall is high. The Zambian slopes of Nyika Plateau are probably the best example of this kind of vegetation.

Finally **swamp** forest occurs near to some of Zambia's permanent swamps. Kasanka National Park probably has the country's best, and most accessible, examples of this.

Dambo

A dambo is a shallow grass depression, or small valley, that is either permanently or seasonally waterlogged. It corresponds closely to what is known as a 'vlei' in other parts of the subcontinent. These open, verdant dips in the landscape often appear in the midst of miombo woodlands and support no bushes or trees. In higher valleys amongst hills, they sometimes form the sources of streams and rivers. Because of their permanent dampness, they are rich in species of grasses, herbs and flowering plants, like orchids – and are excellent grazing (if a little exposed) for antelope. Their margins are usually thickly vegetated by grasses, herbs and smaller shrubs.

Pan

Though not an environment for rich vegetation, a pan is a shallow, seasonal pool of water with no permanent streams leading into or out of it. The bush is full of small pans in the rainy season, most of which will dry up soon after the rains cease. Sometimes there's only a fine distinction between a pan and a dambo.

Floodplain

Floodplains are the low-lying grasslands on the edges of rivers, streams, lakes and swamps that are seasonally inundated by floods. Zambia has some huge areas of floodplain, most obviously beside the Kafue River, in the Barotseland area around the Zambezi, and south of the permanent Bangweulu Swamps. These often contain no trees or bushes, just a low carpet of grass species that can tolerate being submerged for part of the year. In the midst of some floodplains, like the Busanga Plains, you'll find isolated small 'islands' of trees and bushes, slightly raised above the surrounding grasslands.

Montane grassland

More common in other areas of Africa, montane grassland occurs on mountain slopes at higher altitudes where the precipitation is heavy and the climate cool. Zambia's best examples of this are on Nyika Plateau, and here you'll find many species of flora and fauna that occur nowhere else in Zambia.

Fauna (see also *Appendix 1, Wildlife Guide*)
Mammals

Zambia's large mammals are typical of the savannah areas of east and (especially) southern Africa. The large predators are here: lion, leopard, cheetah, wild dog and spotted hyena, although cheetah and wild dog are relatively uncommon.

Elephant and buffalo occur in large herds in protected national parks, and in small, furtive family groups where poaching is a problem. Black rhino are probably, sadly, extinct in Zambia, though there are white rhino in the small, well-protected, Mosi-Oa-Tunya National Park at Livingstone.

Antelope are well represented, with puku and impala numerically dominant in the drier areas. There are several interesting, endemic sub-species found in Zambia, including the Angolan and Thornicroft's giraffe, Cookson's wildebeest, Crawshay's zebra, and two unusual subspecies of lechwe – the black and the Kafue lechwe – occurring in very large numbers in some of the country's larger marshy areas.

Because Zambia is a wet country, with numerous marshy areas, its natural vegetation is lush and capable of supporting a high density of game. The country has a natural advantage over drier areas, and this accounts for the sheer volume of big game to be found in its better parks.

Birdlife
Much of Zambia is still covered by original, undisturbed natural vegetation, and hunting is not a significant factor for most of Zambia's 733 recorded species of birds. Thus, with a range of verdant and natural habitats, Zambia is a superb birding destination.

Whilst the animal species differ only occasionally from the 'normal' species found in southern Africa, the birds are a much more varied mix of those species found in southern, eastern and even central Africa. The obvious celebrity is the ungainly shoebill stork – which breeds in the Bangweulu Swamps, and only one or two other places in central Africa. A lesser-known attraction is Chaplin's barbet, Zambia's only endemic bird species, found in southern Zambia around the south side of Kafue National Park. However, there are many other unusual, rare and beautifully coloured species that attract enthusiasts to Zambia.

In addition to its resident bird species, Zambia receives many migrants. In September and October the Palaearctic migrants appear (ie: those that come from the Northern Hemisphere – normally Europe), and they remain until around April or May. This is also the peak time to see the intra-African migrants, which come from further north in Africa.

The rains from December to around April see an explosion in the availability of most birds' food: seeds, fruits and insects. Hence this is the prime time for birds to nest, even if it is also the most difficult time to visit the more remote areas of the country.

Field guides
Finding good, detailed field guides to plants, animals and birds in Zambia is becoming much easier. There are now very comprehensive guides on the flora and fauna of Southern Africa, which remain invaluable in Zambia. However, for total coverage there are now many smaller guides, published in Zambia, covering snakes, trees, wild flowers, birds and the like. There's even a comprehensive guide to the Zambian bird species that have been excluded from the Southern Africa guides. (See *Further Reading* for more details.)

The traveller is recommended to seek out some of the excellent books now being produced by the Wildlife and Environmental Conservation Society of Zambia (see page 104), which are ideal for general game viewing and birdwatching. Again see *Further Reading* for recommendations and details.

CONSERVATION
A great deal has been written about the conservation of animals in Africa; much of it is over-simplistic and intentionally emotive. As an informed visitor you are in the

unique position of being able to see some of the issues at first hand, and to appreciate the perspectives of local people. So abandon your preconceptions, and start by appreciating the complexities of the issues involved. Here I shall try to develop a few ideas common to most current thinking on conservation; ideas to which the text in the rest of the book only briefly alludes.

Firstly, *conservation* must be taken within its widest sense if it is to have meaning. Saving animals is of minimal use if the whole environment is degraded, so we must consider conserving whole areas and ecosystems, not just the odd isolated species.

Observe that land is regarded as an asset by most societies, in Africa as it is elsewhere. To 'save' the land for the animals, and use it merely for the recreation of a few privileged foreign tourists, is a recipe for huge social problems – especially if the local people remain excluded from benefit and in poverty. Local people have hunted animals for food for centuries. They have always killed game that threatened them, or ruined their crops. If we now try to protect animals in populated areas without addressing the concerns of the people, then our efforts will fail.

The only pragmatic way to conserve Zambia's wild areas is to see the development of the local people, and the conservation of the animals and the environment, as inter-linked goals.

In the long term, one will not work without the other. Conservation without development leads to resentful locals who will happily, and frequently, shoot, trap and kill animals. Development without conservation will simply repeat the mistakes that most developed countries have already made: it will lay waste a beautiful land and kill off its natural heritage. Look at the tiny areas of undisturbed natural vegetation that survive in the UK, the USA, or Japan. See how unsuccessful we in the Northern Hemisphere have been at long-term conservation over the past 500 years.

As an aside, the local people in Zambia are sometimes wrongly accused of being the only agents of degradation. Many would like to see 'poachers' shot on sight, and slash-and-burn agriculture banned. But observe the importation of tropical hardwoods by the West to see the problems that our demands place on the natural environment in the developing world.

In conserving some of Zambia's natural areas and assisting the development of her people, the international community has a vital role to play. It could effectively encourage the Zambian government to practise sustainable long-term strategies, rather than grasping for the short-term fixes which politicians seem universally to prefer. But such solutions must have the backing of the people themselves, or they will fall apart when the foreign aid budgets eventually wane.

In practice, to get this backing from the local communities it is not enough for a conservation strategy to be compatible with development. Most Zambians are more concerned about where they live, what they can eat, and how they will survive, than they are about the lives of small, obscure species of antelope that taste good when roasted.

To succeed in Africa, conservation must not only be *compatible* with development, it must actually *promote* it. It must actively help the local people to improve their own standard of living. If that situation can be reached, then local communities can be mobilised behind long-term conservation initiatives.

Governments are the same. As Luangwa's late conservationist Norman Carr once commented, 'governments won't conserve an impala just because it is pretty'. But they will work to save it *if* they can see that it is worth more to them alive than dead.

The best strategies tried so far on the continent attempt to find lucrative and sustainable ways to use the land. They then plough much of the revenue back into the surrounding local communities. Once the local communities see revenue from conservation being used to help them improve their lives – to build houses, clinics and schools, and to offer paid employment – then such schemes rapidly get their backing and support.

Carefully planned, sustainable tourism is one solution that can work effectively. For success, the local communities must see that the visitors pay because they want the wildlife. Thus, they reason that the existence of wildlife directly improves their income, and they will strive to conserve it.

It isn't enough for people to see that the wildlife helps the government to get richer; that won't dissuade a local hunter from shooting a duiker for dinner. However, if he is directly benefiting from the visitors, who come to see the animals, then he has a vested interest in saving that duiker.

It matters little to the Zambian people, or ultimately to the wildlife, whether these visitors come to shoot the wildlife with a camera or with a gun. The vital issue is whether the hunting is done on a sustainable basis (ie: only a few of the oldest 'trophy' animals are shot each year, so that the size of the animal population remains largely unaffected).

Photographers may claim the moral high-ground, but should remember that hunters pay far more for their privileges. Hunting operations generate large revenues from few guests, who demand minimal infrastructure and so cause little impact on the land. Photographic operations need more visitors to generate the same revenue, and so generally cause greater negative effects on the country.

Tourism

Zambia lies in the heart of subSaharan Africa. To the northeast lie the 'original' safari areas of East Africa: Kenya and Tanzania. Some of their best parks are now rather crowded, though their wildlife spectacles are still on a grand scale. South of Zambia are the more subtle attractions of Zimbabwe, Botswana and Namibia. Each country draws its own type of wildlife enthusiasts, and all have an element of wilderness that can seem difficult to find in East Africa today.

All have embraced tourism in different ways. Zambia is fortunate in having addressed this question later than the others, with the chance to learn from the mistakes of its neighbours. It is hoped that sustainable tourism can be a saviour of Zambia's economy as well as its wildlife, though there is a long way to go before tourism contributes a sizeable slice of the country's revenue.

Tourism is helping Zambia – both in economic terms and with conservation. It is providing employment and bringing foreign exchange into the country, which gives the politicians a reason to support the preservation of the parks. That said, most Zambian safari operators have yet to really mobilise themselves behind the development objectives of the local people. There are many innovative models for tourism aiding development and sustainable land use, in and out of national parks, in the rest of Southern Africa. They show how things could be developed. Zambia would be wise to learn fast.

The visitor on an expensive safari is generally, by his or her mere presence, making a financial contribution to development and conservation in Zambia. See page 33 for ways in which you can support small local charities which directly help the people of Zambia. When on safari, one very simple thing that you can do to help is to question your safari operator, in the most penetrating of terms:

- Besides employment, how do local people benefit from this camp?
- How much of this camp's revenue goes directly back to the local people?
- What are you doing to help the people living near this reserve?

- How much control do the local people have in what goes on in the area in which these safaris are operated?

If more visitors did this, it would make a huge difference. If safari operators felt that their clients wanted them to be involved with community development, then they would rapidly get involved.

At present most operators make some form of small 'charity' donation to the local communities, but few get locals involved in any meaningful way beyond employment as camp workers, guides and scouts. If they looked to the rest of Southern Africa, they would realise that the local people *must* benefit more (and more directly) from tourism if conservation is going to be successful in Zambia.

Hunting

Big game hunting, where visiting hunters pay large amounts to kill trophy animals, is practised on a number of private ranches and hunting areas. It is also a valuable source of revenue in the long term for people living in the country's Game Management Areas (GMAs). In some this is already working, whilst in others development agencies, including the World Wide Fund for Nature (WWF), are working to start up sustainable schemes.

National parks and GMAs

In practice, there is room for both types of visitors in Zambia: the photographer and the hunter. The national parks are designated for photographic visitors; here no hunting is allowed. Around these are large areas designated as Game Management Areas (GMAs). GMAs contain villages and local people, and hence small-scale farms, but hunting is (at least in theory) controlled and practised sustainably. Both local and overseas hunters use these, and the latter usually pay handsomely for the privilege.

Integral to this model is that the GMAs provide a buffer between the pristine national park and the land outside where uncontrolled hunting is allowed. This should serve to protect the national park's animals from incursions by poachers, whilst the park acts as a large gene pool and species reservoir for the GMA.

Currently over 20 of Zambia's 34 GMAs have been allocated to safari outfitters for hunting, and the USA supplies the largest number of hunters. The theory of GMAs is very good, but their administration has many practical difficulties. In some of them hunting by the local people has been uncontrolled, and in a few much of the game has been wiped out – resulting in no income from the wildlife, and so more pressure to hunt unsustainably. Many have projects that aim to reverse this trend, to regenerate their game resources and then set the communities off on a sustainable path. However, much more work needs to be done if there is to be a long-term effect felt across the country.

Zambia Wildlife Authority

As part of the government's drive to liberalise the economy, government departments with the potential for self-sufficiency are being reformed. At the time of writing, the National Parks and Wildlife Service (NPWS) is being disbanded and replaced by the Zambia Wildlife Authority (ZWA). This should have more autonomy and greater financial independence.

The funding for the early stages of this is coming from the European Development Fund through the European Commission. It is hoped that the parks can become financially self-sustaining, and then be able to use more of their revenue for wildlife protection and community development schemes.

This move follows a study of Zambia's parks by the European Commission.

The idea is that certain parks (those judged 'viable' for wildlife by the study) will be directly funded by the European Development Fund, through the EU, to enable them to become self-sustaining.

Poaching

After tales of government corruption and complicity with poachers, those travellers who have not ventured into Zambia can be forgiven for asking, 'Is there any game left in Zambia?' The answer is a definitive 'yes'.

The 1970s and especially the 1980s saw rampant hunting in the GMAs, and considerable poaching of Zambia's national parks – partly small-scale hunting for food by local people, and partly large commercial poaching operations. The government reaction to this was a mixture of indifference and, allegedly, complicity. The only national park with an appreciable number of foreign visitors, South Luangwa, was effectively defended from all but the persistent infiltrations of specialist rhino-poachers. Other parks were, to various extents, neglected. Most still suffer from the results of that past neglect even now.

However, various parks and GMAs are now, once again, being developed for visitors. With that development comes a reason to protect the parks (as well as a financial motivation – see page 41). Kafue's game populations are almost back to normal, as are those in the Lower Zambezi National Park. Both Kasanka and North Luangwa are being effectively protected with the help of two very different private conservation initiatives, and the WWF is working hard to help the local people earn an income from the sustainable utilisation of wildlife around the Bangweulu Swamps. Camps are opening up along the upper reaches of the Zambezi, and the remote parks of Sumbu and Liuwa Plain still have very viable populations of game.

So the message from Zambia is upbeat. The main parks have excellent game populations and many more are gradually recovering. Unlike much of Africa, Zambia has not generally been ravaged by overgrazing, and so even the parks that have suffered from poaching have usually retained their natural vegetation in pristine condition. This gives hope that good game populations can be re-established, and that large tracts of Zambia will once again be returned to their natural state.

Planning and Preparations

GETTING THERE
By air

However you get to the subcontinent, if you don't fly directly to Lusaka then do book your flight to Africa and any internal flights at the same time. Booking the whole trip together is almost certain to save you money. Sometimes the airline taking you to Africa will have cheap regional flights within Africa, for example Harare–Victoria Falls is usually free with a London–Harare flight on Air Zimbabwe. At other times the tour operator you book through will have special deals if you book all the flights with them. And most importantly, if you book all your flights together then you'll be sure to get connecting ones, so you have the best schedule possible.

From Europe

Since Zambia Airways went into liquidation in December 1994, direct flights to Zambia from Europe have been very straightforward: BA runs them three times per week. There are few alternatives.

Various other airlines have connecting flights to Lusaka, usually either through Nairobi (like KLM) or Johannesburg, but only BA flies direct. Unfortunately even BA's flights are not usually non-stop, as they often fly via Harare.

These routes are mainly for business traffic and pre-booked holidays; finding cheap 'bucket-shop' tickets is usually difficult (if not impossible). Expect to pay about £600/US$960 for a return flight. Tour operators usually have access to slightly cheaper seats, but you will only be able to buy these if you are buying a complete holiday from them. (This often makes sense; see *Tour operators* on page 62.)

If you want a cheap flight, but don't mind spending longer travelling, then consider using one of the nearby regional centres and connecting through to Zambia. Harare is easily reached using various carriers including Air Zimbabwe, KLM, British Airways and Lufthansa. Expect London–Harare prices from about £500/US$800. There are frequent flights from Harare to Victoria Falls, as well as Lusaka – or you can easily travel overland by bus.

Similarly, Windhoek, in Namibia, has international connections with Air Namibia to London and Frankfurt. A regional service links that to Victoria Falls (sometimes quite cheaply).

Johannesburg is certainly the busiest airport on the subcontinent, and most of the world's larger airlines have flights there, or at least connections. From Johannesburg, South African Airways (SAA) has flights to Zambia about 4 times per week. Nairobi is also an important African gateway, and Kenya Airways flies from Nairobi to Lusaka 4 times weekly.

If you're visiting the Luangwa Valley during your trip, then consider using Lilongwe as a gateway, and taking one of the frequent flights operated by Air Malawi between there and Mfuwe, in Zambia's Luangwa Valley.

From North America

If you are coming from the US then you will probably need to stop at London or Johannesburg to make connections to Zambia. There are no direct flights. Booking everything in the US may not save you money; investigate the flight prices in comparison with those available in London. Increasingly visitors from America are discovering that UK operators offer better-value safaris than their competitors in America. So consider buying a cheap ticket across the Atlantic, and then organising your Zambian trip through a reliable UK operator.

Note that there is a US$2 departure tax for all international flights from Lusaka or Livingstone, and that this is always payable at departure by you. It cannot be pre-paid on your ticket, so you must have a few dollars left at the airport before you leave.

Overland

Most overland border posts open from about 06.00 to 18.00, although this is less rigidly adhered to at the smaller, more remote posts.

To/from Zimbabwe

Zambia's greatest flow of visitors comes from Zimbabwe, over the Livingstone-Victoria Falls border. Many come over for just a day trip, so this is usually a very relaxed and swift border crossing. The crossings over the Kariba Dam and at Chirundu are also straightforward, and the latter is especially good for hitchhiking on long-distance lorries, which ply the route from Harare to Lusaka.

To/from Botswana

Despite their territories only meeting at a point, Botswana does have one border crossing with Zambia: a reliable ferry across the Zambezi linking Kazungula with the corner of Botswana, which costs about US$25/£17 per vehicle.

To/from Namibia

There is a ferry crossing, again costing about US$25/£17 per vehicle, between Zambia and Katima Mulilo in Namibia. This can be linked with the Kazungula ferry by a relatively smooth drive through Namibia and Botswana, to provide an alternative route between Sesheke and Kazungula. Though it takes much longer, and involves several border crossings, using the ferries does avoid the terrible road on the Zambian side of the Zambezi. See *Driving west*, page 153, for more details.

To/from Angola

Angola is, at the time of writing, still not regarded as a safe country to visit. The easiest border post with Angola is near Chavuma, northwest of Zambezi town. Elsewhere in western Zambia there is a danger of accidentally wandering into Angola, as the border has few markings.

To/from Democratic Republic of Congo (Zaire)

There are numerous crossings between Zambia and DRC, especially around the Copperbelt. Otherwise there is a good track leading into DRC reached via Mwinilunga and Ikelenge.

To/from Tanzania

Many visitors from Tanzania (and a few from Burundi or DRC) enter Zambia by ferryboat across Lake Tanganyika, into Mpulungu. The main alternative is the land border, either by road crossing or by TAZARA train, crossing east of Tunduma.

See *Chapter 15*, and the section on *Kapiri Mposhi* (page 315), for more details of TAZARA's important rail link between Zambia and Dar es Salaam.

To/from Malawi
The main crossing between Zambia and Malawi is east of Chipata. This would also be the swiftest way to reach the Nyika Plateau, as the roads in Malawi are better than those to Nyika in Zambia.

To/from Mozambique
There is a land crossing between Zambia and Mozambique south of Katete, west of Chipata, though this is not often used. A more common route would be via Malawi or Zimbabwe.

ENTRY REQUIREMENTS
Visas
Zambia's visa rules appear, on reading them, to be very complex. In practice, it's certainly best and probably essential to ask at your nearest Zambian embassy or high commission – as only they will know the latest news and how the rules are generally being interpreted.

All visitors to Zambia need a visa, except those from Ireland or Commonwealth countries (with the exception of citizens of Britain, Cyprus, Ghana, India, Bangladesh, Nigeria, Sri Lanka and Pakistan – who *do* need them). US citizens need visas, whilst most citizens of neighbouring Southern African countries (including South Africa) do not.

Costs for visas vary, but most are US$25/£16 for a single-entry visa, US$25/£16 for a transit visa, US$40/£26 for a double or multiple-entry entry visa. Most can be obtained either overseas at your local Zambian diplomatic mission, or at border posts (including the international airports). They are generally valid for use up to three months from date of issue, and for a maximum stay of 90 days. You may be asked to show an onward ticket, or at least demonstrate that you can support yourself as you pass through the country (credit cards are invaluable), but this is unusual.

The main exception to these changes is the Finns, whose visas are free, the Norwegians who pay just 150 Kroner, and the British who pay a huge £33 for a single-entry or £45 for a double or multiple-entry visa. (The latter is apparently in response to the UK making similar regulations for visiting Zambians.)

Having said this, UK citizens who have pre-arranged trips, booked using an overseas operator in conjunction with a local Zambian operator, are exempt from any charges. Check with your overseas tour operator, as most will make arrangements so that you do not have to pay for a visa.

Similarly, if you're crossing into Zambia for the day from Zimbabwe, and have your name put on a list compiled by local Zambian tour operators at least 24 hours in advance, you'll avoid any fee at the border.

Visa extensions
Visas can be extended, by personal application to the Immigration Office, Box 50300, 2nd Floor, Memaco House, Cairo Road, Lusaka. Tel: 01 251725; fax: 01 252659.

You'll need two completed application forms (each with a passport photo), a valid passport and proof of sufficient funds to cover your stay. If it's a business application then you'll also need an explanatory letter with some good reasons. Your application will take at least three working days to process.

In the 1980s, during KK's rule, Zambia effectively discouraged visitors. The government fostered paranoia about foreign press and spies, and so visitors were routinely treated with suspicion – especially those with cameras. Fortunately this distrust has now vanished, and the prevailing attitude amongst both the government and the people is very welcoming. Visitors are seen as good for the country because they spend valuable foreign currency – so if you look respectable then you will not find any difficulties in entering Zambia.

Given this logic, and the conservative nature of local Zambian customs, the converse is also true. If you dress very untidily, looking as if you've no money, when entering via an overland border, then you may be questioned as to how you will be funding your trip. Dressing respectably in Zambia is not only courteous, but will also make your life easier.

Zambia's diplomatic missions abroad

Angola Zambian Embassy, PO Box 1496, Luanda. Tel: 02 30162; fax: 02 393483

Australia Zambian High Commission, Box 517, Canberra Rex Hotel, Canberra City Act 2601, Canberra

Belgium Zambian Embassy, 469 Av Molière, 1060 Brussels. Tel: 02 343 5649; fax: 02 347 4333

Botswana Zambian High Commission, Zambia House, Plot 1118, The Mall, Box 362, Gaborone. Tel: 351951; fax: 353952

Canada Zambian High Commission, 130 Albert St, STL, 1610 Ottawa, Ontario K1P 5G4

China Zambian Embassy, Dongsijie, San-Li-Tun, Beijing. Tel: 6532 1554; fax: 6532 1778/1891

Democratic Republic of Congo Zambian Embassy, BP 1144, Kinshasa. Tel: 243 12 23 038

Egypt Zambian Embassy, 10 El-Gumhuriya Muttahada Square, PO Box 253, Mohandessine, Cairo 12311. Tel: 02 361 0282; fax: 02 361 0283/0833

Ethiopia Zambian Embassy, Old Airport Area, PO Box 1909, Addis Ababa. Tel: 01 711302

France Zambian Embassy, 76 Av O'Jena, 75116 Paris

Germany Zambian Embassy, Bad Godesberg, Mittelstr 39, 5300 Bonn 2. Tel: 0228 376811/813; fax: 0228 379536

India Zambian High Commission, F-8/22 Vasant Vihar, New Delhi 110057. Tel: 011 687 7681/7848/7862; fax: 011 687 7928

Japan Zambian Embassy, 9-19 Ebisu 3-Chrome, Shibuya-Ku, CPO Box 1738, Tokyo

Kenya Zambian High Commission, City Hall Annex, Box 48741, Nairobi. Tel: 02 724 850/796/799; fax: 02 718 494

Malawi Zambian High Commission, Box 30138, Capital Hill, Lilongwe 3. Tel: 731911

Mozambique Zambian Embassy, Avenida Kenneth Kaunda 1286, Maputo. Tel: 01 492 452

Namibia Zambian High Commission, 22 Curt von François (Corner of Republic Rd), PO Box 22882, Windhoek. Tel: 061 237610/237611; fax: 061 228162

Nigeria Zambian High Commission, PO Box 6119, 11 Keffi St, South West Ikoyi, Lagos. Tel: 02 269 0426–7

Russian Federation Zambian Embassy, Prospect Mira 52, Moscow. Tel: 095 288 5001; fax: 095 975 2056

South Africa Zambian High Commission, 353 Sanlam Building, Festival St, PO Box 12234, Hatsfield, Pretoria. Tel: 012 342 1541 or 012 326 1487/1854/1859; fax: 012 342 4963

Sweden Zambian Embassy, Engelbrektsgatan 7, Box 26013, Stockholm. Tel: 08 679 9040; fax: 08 679 6850

Switzerland Permanent Mission of Zambia to the UN, 17–19 Chemin du Champs-d'Anier, 1209 Le Petit Sacconneux, Geneva. Tel: 022 788 5330–1; fax: 022 788 5340

Tanzania Zambian High Commission, Box 2525, Plots 5 and 9, Ohio St, Sokoine Street Junction, Dar es Salaam. Tel: 051 27261/27262; fax: 051 46389
Uganda Zambian High Commission, 20 Philip Rd, Kololo, Kampala. Tel: 041 233777
UK Zambian High Commission, 2 Palace Gate, London W8 5NG. Tel: 020 7589 6655; fax: 020 7581 1353
USA Zambian Embassy, 2419 Massachusetts Av NW, Washington DC 20008. Tel: 202 265 9717–9; fax: 202 332 0826; email: zambia@tmn.com
Zimbabwe Zambian High Commission, Zambia House, 48 Union Av, Box 4698, Harare. Tel: 04 790851–5; fax: 04 790856

Zambia National Tourist Board offices
Australia c/o Orbitair International, Level 10, 36 Clarence St, Sydney, NSW 2000. Tel: 02 9299 5300; fax: 02 9290 2665
Italy c/o Relazioni Turishche, Via Mauro Macchi 42, 20124 Milan. Tel: 02 6690341; fax: 02 66987381
Hungary c/o CRS International, Radnoti Miklos V.40 111/16, H-1137 Budapest. Tel: 01 269 5092; fax: 01 131 3960
South Africa 1st Floor, Finance House, Ernest Oppenheimer Rd, Bruma Lake, Office Park, Bruma 2198. PO Box 591232, Kengray 2100, South Africa. Tel: 011 622 9206/7; fax: 011 622 7424
UK 2 Palace Gate, Kensington, London W8 5NG. Tel: 020 7589 6343; fax: 020 7225 3221
USA 237 East 52nd St, New York, NY 10022. Tel: 212 308 2155; fax: 212 758 1319

WHEN TO GO
Weather – the dry or wet season?
See the section on *Climate*, page 35, for a detailed description of the weather that can be expected, and note that Zambia's rainy season occurs between around December and April (slightly different every year).

The **dry season** (May to November) is the easiest time to travel, as then you are unlikely to meet rain and can expect clear blue skies. This is ideal if this is your first trip to Africa, or if seeing lots of big game is top of your wish-list.

Within this, you'll find June–August the coolest, and then from September onwards the heat gradually builds up. Note that where the altitude is relatively low – like the Luangwa, the Lower Zambezi valley or Lake Tanganyika – the temperature is always higher. These places, especially, can get very hot towards the end of October, and occasions of over 40°C in the shade in the middle of the day have earned October the tag of 'suicide month' amongst the locals.

November is a variable month, but many days can be cooler than October, as the gathering clouds shield the earth from the sun. Sometimes these bring welcome showers; sometimes they simply build, and with them come tension and humidity.

The **wet season**, December to March, is totally different, and the days can vary enormously from one to the next. Even within a day, skies will often change from sunny to cloudy within minutes and then back again. Downpours are usually heavy and short. Even in the lower valleys, temperatures are pleasant, rising to only around 30°C, and the nights moderately cool (typically down to perhaps 10°C). You will need a good waterproof for the rainy season, but it seldom rains for long enough to really stop you doing anything. Except travelling on bush roads...

Travelling
Travelling around Zambia in the dry season often has its challenges – but in the wet season it's a totally different game. Most untarred roads become quagmires;

many are completely impassable. The rivers swell to bursting, often beyond, as their surging brown waters undermine trees and carry them downstream like pooh-sticks. Streams that were ankle-deep in October become potential rafting challenges. Many rural areas are cut off for a few months, so getting anywhere away from the main routes can be tricky.

However, if you are planning to fly into a national park for a safari, then the South Luangwa remains a possibility. Flights there are less frequent, but still run. It is the only one of Zambia's national parks to remain open. A few camps also welcome visitors and use the park's network of all-weather roads for driving safaris. One camp, based inside the park and up-river, runs canoeing and boating safaris. If you've often been to Africa in the dry season, then this is a fascinating time to visit – like being introduced to a different side of an old friend.

Vegetation

During the wet season, the foliage runs wild. The distinctive oxbow lagoons of the Luangwa and Lower Zambezi fill, while trees everywhere are deeply green. The open sandy plains become verdant meadows, often with shallow pools of water. It's a time of renewal, when a gentler light dapples Zambia's huge forests and areas of bush.

When the rains end, the leaves gradually dry and many eventually drop. More greys and browns appear, and good shade becomes harder to find. Eventually, by late September and October, most plants look dry and parched, coloured from straw-yellow to shrivelled brown.

Game

From the point of view of most herbivores, the wet season is a much more pleasant time. Those in national parks live in enormous salad bowls, with convenient pools of water nearby. It's a good time to have their young and eat themselves into good condition. Val and Bob Leyland were the first visitors for whom I ever organised a trip during the rains. On returning, they commented that 'having [previously] visited Africa last dry season, there's something special about seeing all the animals when they aren't struggling with thirst and a lack of vegetation… It gives a sense of luxuriance which isn't there in the dry season.'

Visiting South Luangwa in the wet season you will see game, but probably less of it. Last trip during the rains I went on two night drives. On the first we saw a good range of antelope (including some wonderful sightings of young animals), a few elephant and buffalo and a leopard at the end of the evening. The next we found a hyena on a kill, and later followed three lionesses hunting for several hours. The birding was consistently phenomenal, far better than during the dry season.

However, if game viewing is your priority, or this is one of your first trips to Africa, then the animals are much easier to spot when it's dry, as no thick vegetation obscures the view. Further, they are forced to congregate at well-known water points, like rivers, where they can be observed. Many more tracks are navigable in the bush, and so more areas can be explored by vehicle. So if you want to see large numbers of animals, then do come to Zambia in the dry season – and later rather than earlier if possible.

A few specific animal highlights include:

Feb–May Most of the herbivores are in their best condition, having fed well on the lush vegetation.

May–Aug Leopard are generally easier to see, as they come out more during the twilight hours. Later in the year they often come out later in the evening, waiting until it is cool.

Sept–Oct Buffalo groups tend to amalgamate into larger, more spectacular herds. (They splinter again just before the rains.) Lion sights become more frequent, as they spend more time near the limited remaining water sources.

Oct–Dec Crocodiles are nesting, and so found on or near exposed sandbanks.

Nov The great wildebeest migration reaches Liuwa Plains, in western Zambia. However, you'll need a small expedition to witness it.

Nov–Mar Baby warthogs and impala start to appear in November, followed by most of the mammals that calve sometime during the rainy season.

Birdlife

The birdlife in Zambia is certainly best when the foliage is most dense, and the insects are thriving: in the wet season. Then many resident birds are nesting and in their bright, breeding plumage. This coincides to a large extent with the 'summer' period, from around October to March, when the Palaearctic migrants from the Northern Hemisphere are seen.

Certainly in terms of waterbirds – storks, herons, ducks, geese and the smaller waders – the rainy season (and just after) is an infinitely better time to visit. The birding calendar's highlights include:

Mar–July Large breeding colonies of storks and herons gather to breed. The only sites I know are in the Nsefu sector of the South Luangwa National Park.

Aug–Oct 'Fishing parties' of herons, egrets and storks will arrive at pools as they dry up, to feed on the stranded fish.

Sept–Nov Carmine bee-eaters form large nesting colonies in the soft sand of vertical riverbanks.

Oct–Nov Pennant-winged nightjars are in resplendent breeding plumage

Nov–April Most of the weavers are in breeding plumage

Feb–April Fire-crowned bishop birds, yellow-billed storks and the spectacular paradise whydahs have their breeding plumage on display.

Apr–June Resident African skimmers are nesting.

Photography

I find the light clearest and most spectacular during the rainy season. Then the rains have washed the dust from the air, and the bright sunlight can contrast wonderfully with dark storm clouds. The vegetation's also greener and brighter, and the animals and birds often in better condition.

However, it will rain occasionally when you're trying to take shots, and the long periods of flat, grey light through clouds can be very disappointing. Sometimes it can seem as if you're waiting for the gods to grant you just a few minutes of stunning light, between the clouds. A more practical time is probably just after the rains, around April to June, when at least you are less likely to be interrupted by a shower.

The dry season's light is reliably good, if not quite as inspirational as that found during the rains. You are unlikely to encounter any clouds, and will get better sightings of game to photograph. Do try to shoot in the first and last few hours of the day, when the sun is low in the sky. During the rest of the day use a filter (perhaps a polariser) to guard against the sheer strength of the light leaving you with a film full of washed-out shots.

Other visitors

Virtually all of Zambia's tourists come during the dry season, and mostly from August to October. Zambia's small camps and lodges ensure that it never feels

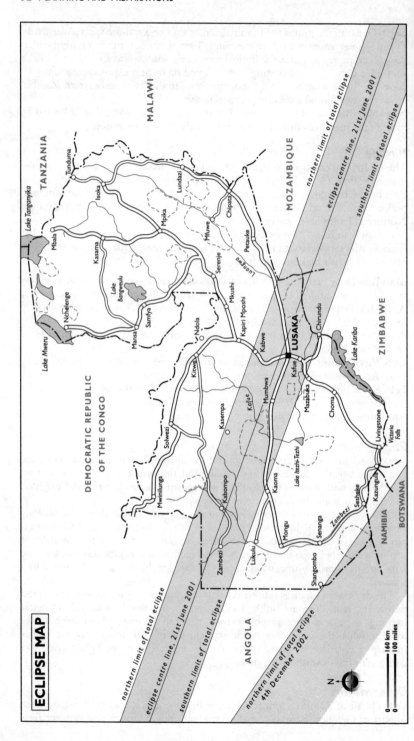

busy, even when everywhere is full. (In fact, the country's capacity for tourism remains tiny compared with that of anywhere else in East or Southern Africa.)

Most of those visiting outside of this season are *cognoscenti*, who visit early or late in the season – May to July or November – when the camps are quieter and often costs are lower. Meanwhile, only a handful of visitors come during the rains, from December to April. The camps that do open then will often be quiet for days. Their rates can be much lower, and they're often far more flexible about bringing children on safari.

Much of the blame for this 'glut or famine' of visitors lies with overseas tour operators. Many who advertise trips here just don't know Zambia well enough to organise trips in the rainy season, when there are fewer internal flights, and the connections can be less easy. It's much easier for them to make blanket generalisations like 'it's not possible' or 'not interesting' or that 'you won't see any game' if you visit in the wet season. None of which is true – but most people don't know this in advance.

While the rains are not the ideal time for everybody's trip, they are a fascinating time to visit and should not be dismissed without serious thought.

Walking safaris

For safe and interesting walking, you need the foliage to be low so that you can see through the surrounding bush as easily as possible. This means that the dry season is certainly the best time for walking. Walking in the wet season, through shoulder-high grass, is possible – but I'd only go with a very experienced guide and it is harder than during the dry season. The best months for walking are June to September, as October can get hot on longer walks.

Solar eclipses

Two major solar eclipses are predicted to be visible from Zambia in the first few years of the millennium. The first of these, on **Thursday 21 June 2001**, is the better one to go and see. Its duration is about double that experienced from the UK during the 1999 eclipse. This total eclipse is expected to be visible in a band as follows:

Time	Northern limit		Southern limit		Centre line		Duration
(GMT)	*Latitude*	*Longitude*	*Latitude*	*Longitude*	*Latitude*	*Longitude*	*at centre*
13.00	12°11'S	22°14'E	13°58'S	22°32'E	13°5'S	22°22'E	4m 1s
13.02	12°29'S	23°11'E	14°16'S	23°29'E	13°22'S	23°19'E	3m 57s
13.04	12°48'S	24°10'E	14°35'S	24°29'E	13°41'S	24°19'E	3m 52s
13.06	13°9'S	25°12'E	14°56'S	25°32'E	14°2'S	25°21'E	3m 48s
13.08	13°32'S	26°17'E	15°19'S	26°38'E	14°25'S	26°27'E	3m 43s
13.10	13°57'S	27°25'E	15°43'S	27°48'E	14°50'S	27°36'E	3m 38s
13.12	14°24'S	28°37'E	16°11'S	29°2'E	15°17'S	28°49'E	3m 33s
13.14	14°54'S	29°54'E	16°41'S	30°21'E	15°47'S	30°7'E	3m 27s
13.16	15°26'S	31°16'E	17°14'S	31°47'E	16°20'S	31°31'E	3m 22s

This area covers Lusaka, the north of Kafue National Park, the whole of the Lower Zambezi area and a large swathe of central Zambia. The eclipse will pass across in the middle of the afternoon, as Zambia is two hours ahead of Greenwich Mean Time (GMT), and the weather is likely to be fine with few, if any, clouds around.

The solar eclipse on **Wednesday 4 December 2002** covers a small and remote corner of Zambia, between Shangombo and the southwestern half of Sioma

Ngwezi National Park. The band of totality is expected to be as follows:

Time (GMT)	Northern limit Latitude	Longitude	Southern limit Latitude	Longitude	Centre line Latitude	Longitude	Duration at centre
06.02	14°58'S	19°56'E	15°10'S	19°13'E	15°4'S	19°35'E	1m 1s
06.04	15°58'S	21°31'E	16°13'S	20°49'E	16°5'S	21°10'E	1m 4s
06.06	16°55'S	22°58'E	17°11'S	22°17'E	17°3'S	22°37'E	1m 7s
06.08	17°49'S	24°19'E	18°6'S	23°38'E	17°57'S	23°59'E	1m 10s
06.10	18°40'S	25°35'E	18°58'S	24°54'E	18°49'S	25°14'E	1m 12s

It will occur in the morning, at a time of the year when clouds are more likely. Namibia's Caprivi Strip, or the Kasane area in Botswana, will probably be easier places to get to than the extremes of southwestern Zambia.

Eclipse Predictions by kind permission of Fred Espenak, NASA/ GSFC. Fred's website is one of the best sources for information – http://sunearth.gsfc.nasa.gov/eclipse

Trips to see the eclipse

As early as September 1999, virtually all of Zambia's safari lodges and camps in the Lower Zambezi and Kafue were booked up over the period of the June 2001 eclipse. Most were booked by leading UK and US tour operators, who are now

TYPES OF ECLIPSE

Eclipses happen when the sun, moon and earth are in direct alignment. They occur in two varieties: lunar and solar. A lunar eclipse can be seen on rare nights when the full moon is shielded from the sun by the earth's shadow. Then the sun and the moon are on opposite sides of the earth. Watching a lunar eclipse you'll see a bright, full moon darkened for an hour or so.

A total solar eclipse happens when the new moon passes directly between the sun and the earth, so that parts of its shadow falls on the earth and blocks the sun completely. This shadow will sweep across the globe in a narrow path, where day briefly turns to night and observers see a halo around the sun, the corona. Outside this 'path of totality', a larger area of the earth will be covered by a partial shadow (known as the penumbra). Here some of the sun remains visible during the eclipse.

Similar effects are observed during a partial solar eclipse. Then only the penumbra touches the earth; its umbra misses it completely. This happens when the alignment between the sun and the planets is not quite complete, or when the moon is far away from the earth in its orbit.

Sometimes the moon's umbra passes across the earth, but doesn't touch its surface. This happens when the moon is farthest out in its orbit, and the cone of the moon's shadow diminishes before touching the earth. This is called an annular eclipse, and it appears to earthbound observers as the moon obscuring the centre of the sun, but leaving a bright ring of sunlight around the edge.

Of all the eclipses, total eclipses are by far the most spectacular. Fewer than 70 total eclipses are said to occur every century, and the path of totality only ever covers a tiny fraction of the earth's surface - so they really are once-in-a-lifetime events.

offering small groups trips to see the eclipse. The added bonus of an eclipse is a great excuse for people to visit Zambia for a safari holiday.

Your choice in planning a visit is either to secure a place from a tour operator on one of these, or to travel independently and prepare to camp. Demand for space on organised trips is very strong indeed - book now if you want one. All of Lusaka's main hotels will be full; the lodges outside the city are already.

If you have your own vehicle, then consider seeing the eclipse in the Western Province, which few other visitors will be able to reach.

MONEY
Black market

Until recently there was a 'black market' in foreign currency in Zambia, with US dollars worth much more if changed surreptitiously with a shady (and illegal) street dealer rather than at a bank. This was a result of the official (government decreed) exchange rate for the kwacha not corresponding to the true market value of the currency.

Now this has changed. The government's financial reforms have enabled the kwacha to float at a free-market rate, wiping out the black market. Now the shady characters on the street who hiss 'change money' as you pass are more likely to be con-men relying on sleights of hand than genuine money-changers.

Budgeting

Zambia is not a cheap country to visit, especially if you want to see some of the national parks. This isn't because of high park fees: on the contrary, US$15–20/£10–12 per day is reasonable by African standards. Rather, costs are high because most safari camps are small and seasonal, and their supply logistics are difficult and costly. However, you do generally get what you pay for: camps in remote locations and pristine environments.

To make up a trip using such camps, which are the only practical way for most visitors to Zambia, budget for an all-inclusive cost of about US$260–320/£160–200 per person per day when staying in a camp. Internal flights cost varying amounts, but US$160/£100 per leg would be a good approximation.

If you have your own rugged 4WD with equipment *and* the experience to use it, then you will be able to camp and cook for yourself which can dramatically cut costs: down to US$10–30/£7–18 per person per day for both park fees and camping fees. However, to hire such a vehicle and supply it with fuel would cost another US$150–300/£95–190 per day.

The cost of food depends heavily on where you buy it, as well as what you buy. If you can shop in Lusaka for your camping supplies then you will save money and have a wider choice than elsewhere. Imported foods are inevitably more expensive than locally produced items. If you are sensible, then US$10–16/£7–10 per day would provide the supplies for a good, varied diet, including the odd treat. In any event, it will be cheaper than eating out.

If you are staying in Lusaka, or one of the main cities, then the bigger hotels are about US$70–90/£45–55 per person sharing, whilst a nice small guesthouse will cost around US$20–40/£12–25. (These are only practical provided you get around under your own steam, and don't need airport transfers.)

Camping at organised sites on the outskirts of the cities is, again, a good bet if you have the equipment and transport. It will cost an almost universal US$5/£3 per person per night.

Restaurant meals in the towns are cheap compared with Europe or America: expect to pay US$10–20/£7–12 for a good evening meal, including a local beer or two. Imported beers are more expensive than local beer (which is perfectly adequate), and South African wines are more costly again. European wines and spirits, as you might expect, are ridiculously priced (and so make excellent gifts if you are visiting someone here). You will pay well over US$100/£65 for a bottle of champagne in Lusaka!

How to take your money

If you are changing money at one of the main banks, in a major town, then there is no difference in the rates between presenting a travellers' cheque, or presenting pounds sterling or US dollars in cash. This perhaps makes travellers' cheques preferable from a security point of view, as they are refundable if stolen. (AMEX travellers' cheques are probably the most widely recognised.)

However, if you are likely to need to use a bureau de change at any time, then you will need cash. They will often not even consider taking travellers' cheques. If you are bringing cash then carry it in convenient denominations of US dollars, or pounds sterling: perhaps US$5, US$10 and US$20; and £10 or £20 notes. Because of the risk of forgeries, people are suspicious of larger denomination notes. US$100 and even US$50 bills are often rejected in shops and even banks.

South African rand are also accepted, though not as widely as dollars or pounds. Sometimes you can pay for hotels and services in US dollars directly, as you would with kwacha; however this gets less common away from the bigger towns. The western provinces are perhaps an exception to this rule, as rand are more commonly acceptable there than further east or north.

Note that, although some safari camps accept credit cards, if park fees are not included then they will usually need to be paid directly at the park gate, in US$ cash. Often travellers' cheques will not be accepted for this.

Around Livingstone there is a market for buying/selling Zimbabwean dollars and selling/buying kwacha. The relative premium over the official rate depends on the availability of consumables in the shops in Victoria Falls, versus those in Livingstone.

However, the money-changers near the border are notorious for their dishonesty. Finding a way to change money safely is difficult; these con-men rip off even street-wise locals. It is better to try changing money in Livingstone town, at the banks, or even at one of the shops (often those run by the Asian community are the most approachable in this regard).

WHAT TO TAKE

This is an impossible question to answer fully, as it depends on how you intend to travel and exactly where you are going. If you are flying in for a short safari holiday then you need not pack too ruthlessly – provided that you stay within your weight allowance. However, note that smaller, privately chartered planes may specify a maximum weight of 10–12kg for hold luggage, which *must* be packed in a soft, squashable bag. Once you see the stowage spaces in a small charter plane, you'll understand the importance of not bringing along large or solid suitcases.

If you are backpacking then weight becomes much more important, and minimising it becomes an art form. Each extra item must be questioned: is its benefit worth its weight?

If you have your own vehicle then neither weight nor bulk will be so vital, and you will have a lot more freedom to bring what you like. Here are some general guidelines:

Clothing

For most days all you will want is light, loose-fitting cotton clothing. Pure cotton, or at least a cotton-rich mix, is cooler and more absorbent than synthetic materials, making it more comfortable in the heat.

For men shorts (not too short) are fine in the bush, but long trousers are more socially acceptable in the towns and rural villages. (You will rarely see a respectable black Zambian man wearing shorts outside a safari camp.) For women a knee-length skirt or culottes is ideal. Zambia's dress code is generally conservative: a woman wearing revealing clothing in town implies that she is a woman of ill repute, whilst untidy clothing suggests a poor person, of low social standing.

These rules are redundant at safari camps, where dress is casual, and designed to keep you cool and protect skin from the sun. Green, khaki and dust-brown cotton is *de rigueur* at the more serious camps (especially those offering walking trips) and amongst visitors out to demonstrate how well they know the ropes.

At the less-serious camps you'll see a smattering of brighter coloured clothes amongst many dull bush colours, the former usually worn by first-time visitors who are less familiar with the bush. Note that washing is done daily at virtually all camps, so few changes of clothes are necessary. A squashable hat and a robust pair of sunglasses with a high UV-absorption are essential.

Finally avoid anything which looks military. Leave all your camouflage patterns at home. Wearing camouflage is asking for trouble anywhere in Africa. You are very likely to be stopped and questioned by the genuine military, or at least the police, who will assume that you are a member of some militia – and question exactly what you are doing in Zambia. Few will believe that this is a fashion statement elsewhere in the world.

Footwear

If you plan to do much walking, either on safari or with a backpack, then lightweight walking boots (with ankle support if possible) are essential. This is mainly because the bush is not always smooth and even, and anything that minimises the chance of a twisted ankle is worthwhile. Secondly, for the nervous, it will reduce still further the minute chance of being bitten by a snake, or other creepy-crawly, whilst walking.

Because of the heat, bring the lightest pair of boots you can find – preferably go for canvas, or a breathable Gore-tex-type material. Leather boots are too hot for wearing in October, but thin single-skin leather is bearable for walking in July and August. *Never* bring a new pair, or boots that aren't completely worn in. Always bring several pairs of thin socks – two thin pairs of socks are more comfortable than one thick pair, and will help to prevent blisters.

Camping equipment

If you are coming on an organised safari, then even a simple bushcamp will mean walk-in chalets with linen, mosquito nets and probably an en-suite shower and toilet. However, if you're planning on doing any camping, then note that little equipment is available in Zambia, and see *Camping equipment* on page 84 for ideas of what you should bring.

Other useful items

Obviously no list is comprehensive, and only travelling will teach you what you need, and what you can do without. Here are a few of my own favourites and essentials, just to jog your memory. For visitors embarking on an organised safari, camps will have most things but useful items include:

- Sunblock and lipsalve – for vital protection from the sun
- Binoculars – totally essential for game-viewing
- A small pocket torch (see *Camping equipment*, page 84)

- 'Leatherman' tool – never go into the bush without one
- A small water bottle, especially on flights (see *Camping equipment*)
- Electrical insulating tape – remarkably useful for general repairs
- Camera – long lenses are vital for good shots of animals
- Basic sewing kit – with at least some really strong thread for repairs
- Cheap waterproof watch (leave expensive ones, and jewellery, at home)
- Couple of paperback novels
- Large plastic 'bin-liner' (garbage) bags, for protecting luggage from dust
- Simple medical kit and insect repellent

And for those driving or backpacking, useful extras are:

- Concentrated, biodegradable washing powder
- Long-life candles – as Zambian candles are often soft, and burn quickly
- Nylon 'paracord' – bring at least 20m for emergencies and washing lines
- Hand-held GPS navigation system, for expeditions to remote areas
- Good compass and a whistle
- More comprehensive medical kit

MAPS AND NAVIGATION

Zambia has an excellent range of detailed 'Ordnance Survey' type maps available cheaply in Lusaka, from the basement office of Mulungushi House. See *Lusaka*, page 117, for details. There are also a few maps of the parks, aimed at tourists, which are useful to supplement these – including an excellent 1989 map of South Luangwa's landscape and vegetation. If you are driving yourself around, then go there to buy all the maps for your trip at the start.

Outside of Zambia, two commercially produced maps are commonly available. One (ISBN 0921 463839) is produced by International Travel Maps, 345 West Broadway, Vancouver, BC, Canada, V5Y 1P8; and the other (ISBN 0-333-63819-0) by Macmillan, which is based in the UK but represented in Zambia.

The **International Travel Map** is printed only on one side, a 1:1,500,000 scale map with contours, roads, and the park. Around this are printed boxes of general-interest text, from words on the wildlife to Zambia's history and geography. The cartographers have worked hard on the roads, carefully marking many of the pontoons, though their coverage of the main points of interest to tourists has been less detailed. This is just a jazzed up version of the main country map, of the same scale, available in Zambia.

Macmillan's map has a less-detailed 1:2,200,000 scale, and hasn't even tried to include the same details of contours or smaller tracks. However, it has been more successful at marking the points of interest for visitors, and on the reverse side are many excellent 'inset' maps of the main parks, plus plans of Lusaka and Livingstone. It's worth getting hold of for an overview of the country before you go.

Navigation by any of these maps becomes more difficult as your location becomes more remote. Expecting any of them to be accurate is unrealistic. Thus if you're heading into the wilds, get what maps you can and compare them with reality as you go. They'll often be very close, but seldom spot on.

GPS systems

If you are heading into one of the more remote parks in your own vehicle, then consider investing in a hand-held GPS: a Global Positioning System. Under an open, unobstructed sky, these can fix your latitude, longitude and elevation to within about 100m, using 24 American military satellites which constantly pass in the skies overhead. They will work anywhere on the globe.

Commercial units now cost from around US$160/£100 in Europe or the USA. As is usual with high-tech equipment, their prices are falling and their features are expanding as time progresses.

I have used one of the older, less expensive models, the Garmin GPS 38, for some time. It enables you to store 'waypoints' and build a simple electronic picture of an area, as well as working out basic latitude, longitude and elevation. So, for example, you can store the position of your campsite and the nearest road, making it much easier to be reasonably sure of navigating back without simply re-tracing your steps. This kind of function can be invaluable in remote areas with lots of bush and no signposts.

Although a GPS may help you to recognise your minor errors before they are amplified into major problems, note that such a gadget is no substitute for good map work and navigation. They're great fun to use, but shouldn't be relied upon as a sole means of navigation.

Most of these units use *lots* of battery power, so bring plenty of spares with you. Do try not to rely on them too much – or you will be unable to cope if your GPS fails.

PHOTOGRAPHY AND OPTICS

Don't expect to find any reasonably priced or reasonably available optical equipment in Zambia – so bring everything that you will need with you.

Cameras

35mm SLR cameras with interchangeable lenses offer you the greatest flexibility. For general photography, a mid-range zoom lens (eg: 28–70mm) is best – much more useful than the standard (50mm) lens. For wildlife photography you will need at least a 200mm zoom lens, otherwise most animals and birds will look like mere dots on the horizon.

Compact cameras are fine for shots of people and landscapes, but of little use for pictures of the wildlife.

Auto-focus zoom lenses are a godsend for capturing animals and birds that move in the time that it takes to focus manually, but they need extra care to ensure that they remain dust-free. A few grains of sand or dust in the wrong place will render some such lenses useless.

Binoculars

For a safari holiday, especially if you are doing much walking, a good pair of binoculars is essential. They will bring you far more enjoyment than a camera, as they make the difference between merely seeing an animal or bird at a distance, and being able to observe its markings, movements and moods closely. Do bring one pair per person; one between two is just not enough.

There are two styles: the small 'pocket' binoculars, perhaps 10–12cm long, which account for most popular modern sales – and have only been in production since the 1980s. These were popularised by the makers of compact and auto-focus cameras, and are now often made in the Far East. Then there are larger, heavier styles, double or triple that size, which have been manufactured for years. Many of the remaining manufacturers of these are in the CIS, Germany or Austria.

The small ones are now mass-produced at around US$160/£100, whilst the larger ones vary widely in cost and quality. If you are buying a pair, then consider getting the larger style. The smaller ones are fine for spotting animals; but are difficult to hold steady, and very tiring to use for extensive periods. You will only realise this when you are out on safari, by which time it is too late.

Around 8 x 30 is an ideal size for field observations, as most people need some form of rest, or tripod, to hold the larger 10 x 50 models steady. Get the best-quality ones you can for your money. The cheapest will be about US$60/£40, but to get a decent level of quality spend at least US$300/£200. You will be able to see the difference when you use them.

Accessories

The bush is very dusty, so bring plenty of lens-cleaning cloths, and a blow-brush. Take great care not to get dust into the back of any camera, as a single grain on the back-plate can be enough to make a long scratch which ruins every frame taken.

Tripods are very useful if you're serious, though they are inconvenient to lug around. A small bean-bag is very useful for resting the camera on the window-sill of a vehicle.

Film

Film is expensive in Zambia, and outside of the main centres supplies are very limited – so bring a large stock of anything that you will want to use. The range of film speeds should be dependent upon the type of photography that most interests you. For most landscape shots, where you will have plenty of light, a slow film (100ASA or less) will give the highest quality of results. For wildlife photography, you will probably need a faster film – 200 or even 400ASA – unless you're using very fast lenses.

Pictures taken around dawn and dusk will have the richest, deepest colours, whilst those taken in the middle of the day, when the sun is high, will seem pale and washed-out by comparison. Beware of the very deep shadows and high contrast which are typical of tropical countries – film just cannot capture the range of colours and shades that our eyes can. If you want to take pictures in full daylight, and capture details in the shadows, then you will need a good camera, and to spend some time learning how to use it fully. By restricting your photography to mornings, evenings and simple shots you will encounter fewer problems.

Especially after exposure, film deteriorates rapidly in the heat. Aim to keep all your film away from direct sunlight, somewhere shady and cool.

VEHICLE HIRE

With difficult roads, which seem to vanish completely in some of the more remote areas, driving around Zambia is not easy. The big car-hire firms do have franchises in Lusaka, but they concentrate their efforts on business-people who need transport around the city. They often insist that foreigners hiring cars also hire a chauffeur. Basically, they're just not geared up for visitors in search of recreation.

A basic model like a Toyota Corolla from, say, AVIS will cost around US$80/£50 per day, with 50km 'free' per day, and an 80¢/50p charge per kilometre after that. Just add up the distances on a map and you'll realise that this isn't viable for most trips. Further, a vehicle like these Toyota Corollas just wouldn't stand up to the potholes found on most of the main highways – never mind the state of the dirt tracks beyond.

See *Car hire* in the chapters on *Lusaka* and *Livingstone* for the relevant contact details. Until recently, it hasn't been possible to hire reliable 4WD vehicles in Zambia. This is changing, but slowly, so the only option is to bring them in from outside, or arrange for a safari company to take you around on a mobile safari.

Hiring a 4WD

If you want to explore Zambia in your own 4WD, then it's best to use a long-standing and reliable company with a base in Victoria Falls: Safari Drive. They have probably the region's best-equipped 4WD vehicles and also other bases in Maun (Botswana) and Windhoek (Namibia). Contact their main office in the UK at Wessex House, 127 High Street, Hungerford, Berks, RG17 0DL. Tel: 01488 681611; fax: 01488 685055.

They have a small fleet of high-quality Land Rover 110 Tdi which usually come fully equipped with everything that you'll need for comfortable bush camping, including long range fuel tanks, roof tents, and even portable fridges.

They can arrange insurance for their vehicles inside Zambia – which many less experienced companies outside Zambia cannot. There are other 4x4 hire companies, but Safari Drive have an enviable reputation for quality, which is what you need most when you rely so heavily on a vehicle.

Alternatively a new company, Foley Hire Ltd, has recently set up in Livingstone, offering Land Rovers as well; see *Chapter 10*. However, I don't have any personal experience of them, so would welcome comments from anyone who has used their vehicles.

ORGANISING A SAFARI

Most visitors who come to Zambia for few weeks' safari stay at some of the small safari camps. Combinations of time in Kafue, the Luangwa Valley, the Lower Zambezi and a few days around the Falls would be typical.

When to book

These trips are not cheap, but nor should they be difficult for a knowledgeable operator to arrange. If you have favourite camps, or a tight schedule, then book as far ahead as you can. Eight to ten months in advance is perfect. Bear in mind that most camps are small, and thus easily filled. They organise their logistics with military precision and so finding space at short notice, especially in the busier months, can be tricky. (The exception to this rule is usually the rainy season.)

If you are looking to travel in the next few months, then one or two of your chosen camps may be full; you'll have to accept alternatives.

How much?

Safaris in Zambia are not cheap. Expect to pay US$1,600–3,000/£1,000–1,900 per person sharing per week, plus international airfares. This would include a few of your internal transfers or flights, camp transfers, meals, activities, laundry, park fees and even drinks. This isn't cheap, so you can expect a good level of service from the operator who is arranging it for you. If you don't get it, go elsewhere.

How to book

It's best to arrange everything together, using a reliable, independent tour operator. Many operators sell trips to Zambia, but few know the country well. Insist on dealing directly with someone who does. Zambia is changing fast, so up-to-date local knowledge is vital in putting together a trip that runs smoothly and suits you. Make sure that whoever you book with is bonded, so your money is protected if they go broke. If you're unsure, pay with a credit card. Never book a trip from someone who hasn't spent time there – you are asking for problems.

Booking directly with the Zambian camps is possible, but communications are difficult. The camps are the easy bit. Once they are organised, you need to piece together the jigsaw puzzle of complex transfers, internal flights and stop-overs to link them into your trip. Local agents in Lusaka can help, but most offer no advantages over good operators overseas – and you will have little recourse if anything goes wrong. At present they're no cheaper.

European, US and local operators usually work on commission for the trips that they sell, which is deducted from the basic cost that the visitor pays. Thus you should end up paying the same whether you book through an overseas operator or talk directly to a camp in Zambia.

Perhaps because of the UK's historical links, or the high number of British safari-goers, there seems to be more competition amongst UK tour operators than elsewhere. Hence they've a reputation for being generally cheaper than US operators for the same trips.

Which tour operator?

Zambia is something of a touchstone for tour operators to Southern Africa: those who know Zambia well are the small core of Africa specialists. Most operators can send you to Cape Town with ease. But ask them where to visit in Zambia, and you'll rapidly sort those that know Southern Africa from those that haven't got a clue.

Don't let anyone convince you that there are only three first-class safari camps in Zambia, as it's rubbish. If your operator doesn't know most of the camps in this book – and offer a wide choice to suit you – then use one that does.

Here I must, as the author, admit a personal interest in the tour operating business. I organise and personally run the Southern African operations of the UK operator **Sunvil Discovery** (tel: 020 8232 9777; fax: 020 8568 8330; email: africa@sunvil.co.uk). We are currently the leading operator from the UK to Zambia, and also organise trips for travellers to Africa from all over the world (especially America). Booking your trip with us will always cost you the same or less than if you contacted Zambia's camps directly – plus you have our independent advice, full financial protection, and experts to make all the arrangements for you.

Sunvil Discovery has probably the most comprehensive choice of the best Zambian lodges, camps and destinations available anywhere. In Zambia our safaris are completely flexible, depending on where you want to go. They start at about US$2,480/£1,550 per person for a week, including flights from London, accommodation, meals and game activities. I also believe that Sunvil Discovery has the best value programme to Zambia – and will happily send you a detailed colour brochure to demonstrate this. Just call us.

For a fair comparison, the best African tour operators include:

In the UK

Abercrombie & Kent Sloane Square House, Holbein Place, London SW1W 8NS. Tel: 020 7730 9600; fax: 020 7730 9376

Acacia Expeditions 23a Craven Terrace, London W2 3QH. Tel: 020 7706 4700; fax: 020 7706 4686; email: acacia@afrika.demon.co.uk

Africa Archipelago 6 Redgrave Road, London SW15 1PX. Tel: 020 8780 5838; fax: 020 8780 9482; email: worldarc@compuserve.com

Art of Travel 21 The Bakehouse, 119 Altenberg Gardens, London, SW11 1JQ. Tel: 020 7738 2038; fax: 020 7738 1893

Cazenove & Lloyd 3 Alice Court, 116 Putney Bridge Rd, London SW15 2NQ. Tel: 020 8875 9666; fax: 020 8875 9444

Crusader 57 Church St, Twickenham TW1 3NR. Tel: 020 8892 7606; fax: 020 8744 0574; email: naturalworld@crusadertravel.com

Gane & Marshall 98 Crescent Rd, New Barnet, Herts EN4 9RJ. Tel: 020 8441 9592; fax: 020 8441 7376; email: holidays@ganeandmarshall.co.uk
Grenadier Safaris 11/12 West Stockwell St, Colchester, CO1 1HN. Tel: 01206 549585; fax: 01206 561337
Hartley Safaris The Old Chapel, Chapel Lane, Hackthorn, Lincs LN2 3PN. Tel: 01673 861600; fax: 01673 861666; email: infor@hartleys-safaris.co.uk
Nomad Africa Travel Smugglers Cottage, Church Rd, Westbourne, Emsworth, Hants PO10 8UA. Tel/fax: 01243 373929
Okavango Tours and Safaris Marlborough House, 298 Regents Park Road, London N3 2TJ. Tel: 020 8343 3283; fax: 020 8343 3287
Scott Dunn World 12 Noyna Rd, London SW17 7PH. Tel: 020 8672 1234; fax: 020 8767 2026
Sunvil Discovery Upper Square, Old Isleworth, Middlesex, TW7 7BJ. Tel: 020 8232 9777; fax: 020 8568 8330
Wildlife Discovery 29 Bell St, Reigate, Surrey RH2 7AD. Tel: 01737 223903; fax: 01737 241102

In the USA
Adventure Center 1311 63rd St, Suite 200, Emeryville, California 94608. Tel: 510 654 1879; fax: 510 654 4200
Adventure Travel Desk (ATD) 308 Commonwealth Rd, Wayland, MA 01778. Tel: 800 552 0300 or 508 653 4600; fax: 508 655 5672
David Anderson Safaris 4635 Via Vistosa, Santa Barbara, CA 93110. Tel: 800 733 1789 or 805 967 1712; fax: 805 964 8285

In Australia
The Classic Safari Company Town Hall House, Level 11/456 Kent St, Sydney NSW 2000. Tel: 01 800 351 088 or 02 9264 5710; fax 02 9267 3047
African Wildlife Safaris 1st Floor, 259 Coventry St, South Melbourne, Victoria 3205. Tel: 03 9696 2899; fax: 03 9696 4937

Warning There are just one or two rather slippery overseas operators which offer surprisingly inexpensive small group trips to Zambia. In their glossy sales literature, they avoid specifying exactly which of the camps they will use for the trip. They refer simply to 'remote bushcamps' or 'nice comfortable lodges' – without actually specifying their names. (Despite the fact that *all* Luangwa's camps, without exception, do have names.)

They do this to retain the flexibility to swap around your trip at the last minute. Then, they can force down the price of the camp that they have booked for your group's trip (by threatening to send you elsewhere). Or they can send you to another camp that's willing to open for a lower price. It's a shoddy way to do business.

Either way, it means that the camp your group visits has been forced to offer the operator an unusually cheap rate. So they tend to cut corners. You won't get the quality of guiding, or service, or catering that they'd usually give to full-paying clients. For you, the visitor, this invariably means that you'll be staying in one of the poorer camps, perhaps with an inexperienced guide or in one of the less interesting areas of the valley.

Usually the operator pockets a large proportion of these savings, and you're left with a poorer trip because of it. It's best to avoid any company which doesn't specify (*in writing* to you) exactly which camps are included in your trip, and how long you are going to stay at each. There's never a good reason why they can't do this.

SUGGESTED ITINERARIES

Those backpacking and driving themselves around Zambia need time but have great flexibility, and part of the adventure of such a trip is having no itinerary. However, most visitors have a much shorter time. In this case, getting your itinerary right and arranging it carefully in advance is important.

For most people, the three main areas of attraction in Zambia are the Luangwa Valley, Kafue National Park and the Lower Zambezi Valley. All are worth visiting for a week; less than three nights in either is really too short.

Most visitors use light aircraft to get between the parks. Because of this, a week in any two of these three parks makes a very good combination. Keen walkers would always include the Luangwa. Those who are on less leisurely itineraries might opt for seven nights in Kafue, four in Luangwa and three in Lower Zambezi – though more time in both parks would be ideal.

Looking in more detail at the Luangwa, the choice is bewildering. It's probably best to start with a few days near Mfuwe (Mfuwe Lodge, Kapani, Chinzombo, Nkwali, Kafunta, etc) and then spend time further into the park. If you like walking, you'll then choose bushcamps. There's often a slight saving if you spend at least a week exclusively with one operator.

If you want to visit North Luangwa National Park, then first spend a few days in the South Park before perhaps four in North Luangwa.

If you've longer, then consider a week in the south or centre of South Luangwa, followed by three nights in the north of South Luangwa (perhaps at Tafika), then four nights in the North Park at Mwaleshi. Alternatively the set walking safaris organised by Robin Pope Safaris are excellent.

In the north of Kafue, most overseas visitors go to Lunga River Lodge and its Busanga Bushcamp; or to Lufupa Lodge and Shumba Camp, run by Busanga Trails. Mixing these two operations doesn't generally help.

On the south side of Kafue, the Nanzhila Camps are often used for three or four days from Livingstone, while the other camps attract more regional tourists who arrive with their own vehicles.

Lusaka tends to be an entry or exit point, and often a transit point, but seldom a destination. Livingstone and Victoria Falls are usually added on for three or four days at the end of a trip, after which your return flight can be arranged easily from Victoria Falls' busy airport.

Kasanka, Bangweulu and Shiwa N'Gandu are most frequently visited as part of guided 4WD itineraries lasting a week to ten days, which often start in Lusaka and end in North Luangwa, or vice versa. Liuwa Plain is difficult to get to; you need to join a small expedition. Sumbu can be reached by scheduled airlines, which needs careful planning, or from Mpulungu. And as for the rest of Zambia – it's visited so infrequently that there is no 'normal' way to link it all together – so go and explore it!

Health and Safety

There is always great danger in writing about health and safety for the uninitiated visitor. It is all too easy to become paranoid about exotic diseases that you may catch, and all too easy to start distrusting everybody you meet as a potential thief – falling into an unjustified us-and-them attitude toward the people of the country you are visiting.

As a comparison, imagine an equivalent section in a guidebook to a Western country – there would be a list of possible diseases and advice on the risk of theft and mugging. Many Western cities are very dangerous, but with time we learn how to assess the risks, accepting almost subconsciously what we can and cannot do.

It is important to strike the right balance: to avoid being either excessively cautious or too relaxed about your health and your safety. With experience, you will find the balance that best fits you and the country you are visiting.

HEALTH
Before you go
Travel insurance
Visitors to Zambia must take out a comprehensive **medical insurance policy** to cover them for emergencies, including the cost of evacuation to another country within the region. Such policies come with an emergency number (often on a reverse-charge/call-collect basis). You would be wise to memorise this – or indelibly tattoo it in as many places as possible on your baggage.

Personal effects insurance is also a sensible precaution, but check the policy's fine print before you leave home. Often, in even the best policies, you will find a limit per item, or per claim – which can be well below the cost of a replacement. If you need to list your valuables separately, then do so comprehensively. Check that receipts are not required for claims if you do not have them, and that the excess that you have to pay on every claim is reasonable.

Annual travel policies can be excellent value if you travel a lot, and some of the larger credit card companies offer excellent policies. That said, often it is better to get your valuables named and insured for travel using your home contents insurance. These year-round policies will try harder to settle your claim fairly as they want your business in the long term.

Immunisations
Having a full set of immunisations takes time, normally at least six weeks, although visiting your doctor as late as a few days before you travel can offer some protection. Ideally, see your doctor early on to establish an inoculation timetable.

Legal requirements
No immunisations are required by law for entry into Zambia, unless you are coming from an area where yellow fever is endemic (eg: Democratic Republic of

Congo). In that case, a vaccination certificate may be required.

Recommended precautions

Preparations to ensure a healthy trip to Zambia require checks on your immunisation status: it is wise to be up-to-date on tetanus (10-yearly), polio (10-yearly) and diphtheria (10-yearly). Most travellers are advised to have Hepatitis A immunisation with Havrix, which costs about £80 but protects for 10 years. (Note that complete protection requires two injections several months apart.)

Typhoid immunisation is rather ineffective; it needs boosting every three years unless you are over the age of 35 and have had four or more courses; such travellers do not need further immunisations. Immunisation against cholera is no longer required anywhere in Africa.

Vaccination against rabies is unnecessary for most visitors, but would be wise for those who plan to travel (or live) for extended periods in rural areas.

Travel clinics

UK

Note that getting vaccinations (see *Immunisations*) at these specialist centres can be more costly than using your GP, but often their specialists will be more up-to-date on the latest advice.

British Airways Travel Clinics There are 32 throughout the country. Call 01276 685040 to find your nearest. Apart from providing inoculations and malaria prophylaxis, they sell a variety of health-related travel goods.

Hospital for Tropical Diseases 4 St Pancras Way, London NW1 0PE. This also has a touch-tone advice line, with information prepared by the Malaria Reference Laboratory; tel: 0891 600350.

MASTA (Medical Advisory Service for Travellers Abroad) working with the London School of Hygiene and Tropical Medicine (Keppel St, London WC1 7HT) has a touch-tone advice line (0891 224 100). It is a premium line number, charged at 50p per minute. You can get information about your particular trip, and be sent further written advice. There is no clinic here.

Nomad Traveller's Store and Medical Centre 3–4 Wellington Terrace, Turnpike Lane, London N8 0PX; tel: 020 8889 7014. This private pharmacy, specialising in travel medicine, is linked to the next-door centre selling travel equipment.

Trailfinders Travel Clinic 194 Kensington High St, London W8 7RG; tel: 020 7938 3999. This centre has a doctor on site and most vaccinations are available immediately.

Tropical Medicine Bureau This Irish-run organisation has a useful website with general guidance on subSaharan African destinations: www.tmb.ie

USA

Centers for Disease Control This Atlanta-based organisation is the central source of travel health information in North America, with a touch-tone phone line and fax service. Traveller's Hot Line: 404 332 4559. Each summer they publish the invaluable *Health Information for International Travel* which is available from the Center for Prevention Services, Division of Quarantine, Atlanta, GA 30333.

IAMAT (International Association for Medical Assistance to Travellers) 736 Center St, Lewiston, NY 14092, USA. Tel: 716 754 4883. Also at Gotthardstr 17, 6300 Zug, Switzerland. A non-profit organisation that provides health information and lists English-speaking doctors abroad.

Australia
TMVC Tel: 1300 65 88 44; website: www.tmvc.com.au. TMVC has 20 clinics in Australia, New Zealand and Thailand, including:

Brisbane Dr Deborah Mills, Qantas Domestic Building, 6th floor, 247 Adelaide St, Brisbane, QLD 4000; tel: 7 3221 9066; fax: 7 3321 7076

Melbourne Dr Sonny Lau, 393 Little Bourke St, 2nd floor, Melbourne, VIC 3000; tel: 3 9602 5788; fax: 3 9670 8394.

Sydney Dr Mandy Hu, Dymocks Building, 7th floor, 428 George St, Sydney, NSW 2000; tel: 2 221 7133; fax: 2 221 8401.

South Africa
There are four **British Airways travel clinics** in South Africa: *Johannesburg,* tel: (011) 807 3132; *Cape Town,* tel: (021) 419 3172; *Knysna,* tel: (044) 382 6366; *East London,* tel: (0431) 43 2359.

Malaria prophylaxis (prevention)
Malaria is the most dangerous disease in Africa, and the greatest risk to the traveller. It is common throughout Zambia, and so it is essential that you take all possible precautions against it.

Prophylaxis regimes aim to infuse your bloodstream with drugs that inhibit and kill the malaria parasites which are injected into you by a biting mosquito. This is why you must start to take the drugs *before* you arrive in a malarial area – so that they are established in your bloodstream from day one. Unfortunately, the malaria parasites continually adapt to the drugs used to combat them, so the recommended regimes must adapt and change in order to remain effective. None is 100% effective, and all require time to kill the parasites – so keeping up the prophylaxis regime for some weeks after you leave the infected area is usually recommended.

It is vital that you seek current advice on the best antimalarials to take. If *mefloquine* (Lariam) is suggested, start this two weeks before departure to check that it suits you; stop it immediately if it seems to cause vivid and unpleasant dreams, mood swings or other changes in the way you feel. Anyone who is pregnant, has been treated for psychiatric problems, is epileptic, has suffered fits in the past, or has a close blood relative who is epileptic should avoid *mefloquine.* The usual alternative is *chloroquine* (Nivaquine) weekly plus *proguanil* (Paludrine) daily.

Prophylaxis does not stop you catching malaria; however it significantly reduces your chances of fully developing the disease and will lessen its severity. Falciparum (cerebral) malaria is the most common in Africa, and usually fatal if untreated, so it is worth your while trying to avoid it.

It is unwise to travel in malarious parts of Africa whilst pregnant or with young children: the risk of malaria in many areas is considerable and such travellers are likely to succumb rapidly.

Because the strains of malaria, and the drugs used to combat them, change frequently, it is important to get the latest advice before you travel. Normally it is better to obtain this from a specialist malaria laboratory than from your local doctor, who may not be up-to-date with the latest drugs and developments. In the UK, call the recorded message at the Malaria Reference Laboratory in London (tel: 0891 600350). In the USA call the Center for Disease Control in Atlanta, Georgia (tel: 404 332 4559).

Medical kit
Pharmacies in Zambia often lack medicines and general supplies, and you will find very little in the rural areas. So you must take with you anything that you expect to need. If you are on an organised trip, an overlanding truck, or staying at hotels,

lodges or safari camps, then you will not need much as these establishments normally have comprehensive emergency kits. In that case, just a small personal medical kit might include:

- Antihistamine tablets
- Antiseptic
- Aspirins or paracetamol
- Condoms and contraceptive pills
- Lip-salve (ideally containing a sunscreen)
- Malaria prophylaxis
- Insect repellent
- Micropore tape (for closing small cuts – and invaluable for blisters)
- Moisturising cream
- Sticking plaster (a roll is more versatile than pre-shaped plasters)
- Sunscreen

However, if you are likely to end up in very remote situations, then you should also consider taking the following:

- Burn dressings (burns are a common problem for campers)
- Injection swabs, sterile needles and syringes
- Lint, sterile bandage and safety pins
- Oral rehydration sachets
- Steristrips or butterfly closures
- Strong painkiller (codeine phosphate – also use for bad diarrhoea)
- Tweezers (perhaps those on a Swiss army knife)
- Water purification equipment (2% tincture of iodine and dropper is ideal)
- Several different malaria treatment courses and broad-spectrum antibiotics – plus a good medical manual (see *Further Reading*).

If you wear glasses, bring a spare pair. Similarly those who wear contact lenses should bring spare ones, also a pair of glasses in case the dust proves too much for the lenses. If you take regular medication (including contraceptive pills) then bring a large supply with you – much easier than hunting for your usual brand in Namibia. Equally, it's worth having a dental check-up before you go, as you could be several painful days from the nearest dentist.

Hospitals, dentists and pharmacies

Should you need one, Lusaka, Livingstone and the Copperbelt have reasonable private hospitals. These are well above the standards of local hospitals, which should be avoided where possible. Provided you have medical insurance, there should be no problem getting treatment at any of these. Pharmacies in these same towns stock a good range of medicine, whilst that available in the smaller towns is often very limited. Bring with you a repeat prescription for anything you may lose or run out of.

Staying healthy

Rural Zambia is often not a healthy place to be. However, visitors using the better hotels, lodges and camps are unlikely to encounter any serious problems. The standards of hygiene in even the most remote bushcamps are generally at least as good as you will find at home.

Major dangers in Zambia are car accidents (especially likely if you drive at night) and sunburn. Both can also be very serious, yet both are within the power of the visitor to avoid.

The following is general advice, applicable to travelling anywhere, including Zambia:

Food and storage

Throughout the world, most health problems encountered by travellers are contracted by eating contaminated food or drinking unclean water. If you are staying in safari camps or lodges that rely on overseas visitors, then you are very unlikely to have problems. However, if you are backpacking and cooking for yourself, or relying on local food, then you need to take more care.

Tins, packets, and fresh green vegetables (when you can find them) are least likely to cause problems – provided that clean water has been used for washing the vegetables and preparing the meal. In Zambia's warm climate, keeping meat or animal products unrefrigerated for more than a few hours is asking for trouble.

Water and purification

Whilst piped water in the major towns is unlikely to harbour any serious pathogens, it will almost certainly cause upset stomachs for overseas visitors. In more rural areas, the water will generally have had less treatment, and therefore will be even more likely to cause problems. Hence, as a general rule, ensure that all water used for drinking or washing food in Zambia is purified.

To purify water yourself, first filter out any suspended solids – perhaps passing the water through a piece of closely woven cloth, or something similar. Then either vigorously boil it for a minimum of two minutes, or sterilise it chemically. Boiling is much more effective, provided that you have the fuel available.

Tablets sold for purification are based on either chlorine, iodine or silver, and normally adequate. Just follow the manufacturer's instructions carefully. Iodine is most effective, especially against the resilient amoebic cysts that cause amoebic dysentery and other prolonged forms of diarrhoea.

A cheaper alternative to tablets sold over the counter is to travel with a small bottle of medical-quality tincture of iodine (2% solution) and an eye dropper. Add four drops to one litre of water, shake well, and leave to stand for ten minutes. If the water is very cloudy – even after filtering – or very cold, then either double the iodine dose, or leave to stand for twice as long.

Note that this tincture of iodine can also be used as a general external antiseptic, but it will stain things deep purple if spilt – so seal and pack its container exceedingly well.

Heat and sun

Heat stroke, heat exhaustion and sunburn are often problems for travellers to Africa, despite being easy to prevent. To avoid them, you need to remember that your body is under stress and make allowances for it. First, take things gently – you are on holiday after all. Next, keep your fluid and salt levels high: lots of water and soft drinks but go easy on the caffeine and alcohol. Thirdly, dress to keep cool with loose fitting, thin garments, preferably of cotton, linen or silk. Finally, beware of the sun. Hats and long-sleeved shirts are essential. If you must expose your skin to the sun, then use sun-blocks and high factor sun-screens (the sun is so strong that you will still get a tan).

Avoiding insect bites

The most dangerous biting insects in Africa are mosquitoes, because they can transmit malaria, yellow fever, and a host of other diseases. Research has shown that using a mosquito net over your bed, and covering up exposed skin (by wearing long-sleeved shirts, and tucking trousers into socks) in the evening, are the most effective steps towards preventing bites. Bed-net treatment kits are available from travel clinics; these prevent mosquitoes biting through a net if you roll against it in your sleep, and also make old and holy nets protective. Mosquito coils and chemical insect repellents will help, and sleeping in a stream of moving air, such as under a fan, or in an air-conditioned room, will help to reduce your chances of being bitten.

Visitors on safari are also exposed to bites during the day from tsetse flies. These large dark flies (bigger than house flies) bite during the day and are especially attracted both to the scent of cattle and to dark colours. Dark blue seems to be their favourite, so avoid wearing that and don't forget your insect repellents even during the day. (See *Sleeping sickness,* page 74.)

DEET (diethyltoluamide) is the active ingredient in almost all repellents, so the greater the percentage of DEET, the stronger the effect. However, DEET is a strong chemical. Just 30% is regarded as an effective, non-toxic concentration. It will dissolve some plastics and synthetic materials, and may irritate sensitive skin. Because of this, many people use concentrated DEET to impregnate materials, rather than applying it to themselves. Mosquito nets, socks, and even cravats can be impregnated and used to deter insects from biting. Eating large quantities of garlic, or cream of tartar, or taking yeast tablets, are said to deter some biting insects, although the evidence is anecdotal – and the garlic may affect your social life.

Snakes, spiders and scorpions...

Encounters with aggressive snakes, angry spiders or vindictive scorpions are more common in horror films than in Africa. Most snakes will flee at the mere vibrations of a human footstep whilst spiders are far more interested in flies than people. You will have to seek out scorpions if you wish to see one. If you are careful about where you place your hands and feet, especially after dark, then there should be no problems. You are less likely to get bitten or stung if you wear stout shoes and long trousers. Simple precautions include not putting on boots without shaking them empty first, and always checking the back of your backpack before putting it on.

Snakes do bite occasionally, and you ought to know the standard first-aid treatment. First, and most importantly, *don't panic.* Most snakes are harmless and even venomous species will only dispense venom in about half of their bites. If bitten, you are unlikely to have received venom; keeping this fact in mind may help you to stay calm.

Even in the worst of these cases, the victim has hours or days to get to help, and not a matter of minutes. He/she should be kept calm, with no exertions to pump venom around the blood system, whilst being taken rapidly to the nearest medical help. The area of the bite should be washed to remove any venom from the skin, and the bitten limb should be immobilised. Paracetamol may be used as a painkiller, but never use aspirin because it may cause internal bleeding.

Most first-aid techniques do more harm than good; cutting into the wound is harmful and tourniquets are dangerous; suction and electrical inactivation devices do not work; the only treatment is antivenom. In case of a bite which you fear may be both serious and venomous then:

- Try to keep calm. It is likely that no venom has been dispensed
- Stop movement of the bitten limb by applying a splint
- If you have a crepe bandage, firmly bind up as much of the bitten limb as you

can. Release the bandage for a few minutes every half-hour
- Keep the bitten limb *below* heart height to slow spread of any venom
- Evacuate the victim to a hospital that has antivenom
- *Never* give aspirin. You may offer paracetamol, which is safe
- *Do not* apply ice packs
- *Do not* apply potassium permanganate

If the offending snake can be captured without any risk of someone else being bitten, take it to show the doctor. But beware, since even a decapitated head is able to dispense venom in a reflex bite.

When deep in the bush, heading for the nearest large farm or camp may be quicker than going to a town: it may know how to get a supply of antivenom, and probably will have the facilities to radio for help by plane.

Diseases and when to see a doctor
Travellers' diarrhoea
There are almost as many names for this as there are travellers' tales on the subject. Firstly, do resist the temptation to reach for the medical kit as soon as your stomach turns a little fluid. Most cases of travellers' diarrhoea will resolve themselves within 24–48 hours with no treatment at all. To speed up this process of acclimatisation, eat well but simply: avoid fats in favour of starches, and keep your fluid intake high. Bananas and papaya fruit are often claimed to be helpful. If you urgently need to stop the symptoms, for a long journey for example, then Lomotil, Imodium or another of the commercial anti-diarrhoea preparations will do the trick. They stop the symptoms, by paralysing the bowel, but will not cure the problem. (If you do decide to take these, they are best taken in conjunction with an antibiotic like ciprofloxacin – 500mg twice a day for three days.)

When severe diarrhoea gets continually worse, or the stools contain blood, pus or slime, or it lasts for more than three or four days, you must seek medical advice. There are as many possible treatments as there are causes, and a proper diagnosis involves microscopic analysis of a stool sample, so go straight to your nearest hospital. The most important thing, especially in Zambia's hot climate, is to keep your fluid intake up.

The body's absorption of fluids is assisted by adding small amounts of dissolved sugars, salts and minerals to the water. Sachets of oral rehydration salts give the perfect biochemical mix you need to replace what is pouring out of your bottom but they do not taste so nice. Any dilute mixture of sugar and salt in water will do you good so, if you like Coke or orange squash, drink that with a three-finger pinch of salt added to each glass. The ideal ratio is eight level teaspoons of sugar and one level teaspoon of salt dissolved in one litre of water. Palm syrup or honey make good substitutes for sugar, and including fresh citrus juice will not only improve the taste of these solutions, but also add valuable potassium.

Drink two large glasses after every bowel action, and more if you are thirsty. If you are not eating you need to drink three litres a day *plus* whatever you are sweating *and* the equivalent of what's going into the toilet. If you feel like eating, take a bland diet; heavy greasy foods will give you cramps.

If you are likely to be more than a few days from qualified medical help, then come equipped with a good health manual and the selection of antibiotics which it recommends. *Bugs, Bites & Bowels* by Dr Jane Wilson-Howarth (see *Further Reading*, page 398) is excellent for this purpose.

Malaria

You can still catch malaria even if you are taking anti-malarial drugs. Classic symptoms include headaches, chills and sweating, abdominal pains, aching joints and fever – some or all of which may come in waves. It varies tremendously, but often starts like a bad case of flu. If anything like this happens, you should suspect malaria and seek immediate medical help. A definite diagnosis of malaria is normally only possible by examining a blood sample under the microscope. It is best to get the problem properly diagnosed if possible, so don't treat yourself if you can easily reach a hospital.

If (and only if) medical help is unavailable, then self-treatment is fairly safe, except for people who are pregnant or under twelve years of age. Fansidar, mefloquine, high-dose chloroquine (preferably intravenous) and quinine can all be used to treat malaria. In Zambia you will often be able to get experienced local advice to tell you which will be the most effective.

Quinine is very strong, but often proves to be an effective last defence against malaria. Include it in your medical kit, as occasionally rural clinics will have the expertise to treat you, but not the drugs. Treatment consists of taking two quinine tablets (600mg) every eight hours for up to seven days, until the fever abates. Quinine's side effects are disorientating and unpleasant (nausea and a constant buzzing in the ears), so administering this whilst on your own is not advisable.

Sexually transmitted diseases

AIDS is spread in exactly the same way in Africa as it is at home, through body secretions, blood, and blood products. The same goes for the dangerous Hepatitis B. Both can be spread through sex.

Remember the risks of sexually transmitted disease are high, whether you sleep with fellow travellers or with locals. About 40% of HIV infections in British people are acquired abroad. Using condoms or femidoms will reduce this risk considerably, but not eliminate it. Conservative estimates suggest HIV infection rates in Zambia of 30%, although the infection rate of high-risk groups, like prostitutes, is far greater. If you notice any genital ulcers or discharge get treatment promptly.

Hepatitis

This is a group of viral diseases that generally start with Coca-Cola-coloured urine and light-coloured stools. It progresses to fevers, weakness, jaundice (yellow skin and eyeballs) and abdominal pains caused by a severe inflammation of the liver. There are several forms, of which the two most common are typical of the rest: Hepatitis A (or infectious hepatitis) and Hepatitis B (or serum hepatitis).

Hepatitis A, and the newly-discovered Hepatitis E, are spread by the faecal-oral route, that is by ingesting food or drink contaminated by excrement. They are avoided in the same ways you normally avoid stomach problems: by careful preparation of food and by only drinking clean water. There is now an excellent vaccine against Hepatitis A, Havrix, which lasts for ten years and is certainly worth getting before you travel. See *Recommended precautions* on page 66.

In contrast, the more serious but rarer Hepatitis B is spread in the same way as AIDS (by blood or body secretions), and is avoided the same way as one avoids AIDS. There is a vaccine that protects against Hepatitis B, but this is expensive. It is usually only considered necessary for medical workers and others with a high risk of exposure, including expatriates.

There are no cures for hepatitis, but with lots of bed rest and a good low-fat, no-alcohol diet most people recover within six months. If you are unlucky enough to contract hepatitis of any form, use your travel insurance to fly straight home.

Rabies

Rabies is contracted when broken skin comes into contact with saliva from an infected animal. The disease is almost always fatal when fully developed, but fortunately there are excellent post-exposure vaccines. It is possible, albeit expensive, to be immunised against rabies before you travel, but not really worthwhile unless your risk of exposure to it is high (eg: if you are working with animals). Even if you have been immunised, it is standard practice to treat all cases of possible exposure with two post-exposure jabs.

Rabies is rarely a problem for visitors, but the small risk is further minimised by avoiding small mammals. This is especially true of any animals acting strangely. Both mad dogs in town and friendly jackals in the bush should be given a very wide berth.

If you are bitten, clean and disinfect the wound thoroughly by scrubbing it with soap under running water for five minutes, and then flood it with local spirit or diluted iodine. Then seek medical advice. A post-bite rabies injection is needed even in immunised people, and those who are unimmunised need a course of injections.

These should be given within a week if the bites are to the face. The incubation period for rabies is the time taken for the virus to travel from the area of bite to the brain. This varies with the distance of the bite from the head – from a week or so, to many months. If the bites are further from the brain the incubation period is longer and you probably have more time; make sure you get the injections even if you are a very long way from civilisation.

Never say that it is too late to bother. The later stages of the disease are horrendous – spasms, personality changes and hydrophobia (fear of water). Death from rabies is probably one of the worst ways to go.

Bilharzia

Bilharzia is an insidious disease, contracted by coming into contact with infected water. It is caused by an infestation of parasitic worms which damage the bladder and/or intestine. Often the parasites are present in the local population who have built up a measure of immunity over time, but the visitor who becomes infected may develop a severe fever for weeks afterwards. A common indication of an infection is a localised itchy rash – where the parasites have burrowed through the skin – and symptoms of a more advanced infection will probably include passing bloody urine. Bilharzia is readily treated by medication, and only serious if it remains undetected (the symptoms may be confused with malaria) and untreated.

The life-cycle of the parasites starts when they are urinated into a body of water. Here they infect particular species of water-snails. They grow, multiply, and finally become free-swimming. Then they leave the snails to look for a human, or primate, host. After burrowing through the skin of someone coming into contact with the water, they migrate to the person's bladder or intestine where they remain – producing a large number of eggs which are passed every day in the urine, so continuing the cycle.

The only way to avoid bilharzia infection completely is to stay away from any bodies of fresh water. Obviously this is restrictive, and would make your trip less enjoyable. More pragmatic advice is to avoid slow-moving or sluggish water, and ask local opinion on the bilharzia risk, as not all water is infected. Generally these snails do not inhabit fast-flowing water, and hence rivers are free from infection.

However, dams and standing water, especially in populated areas, are usually heavily infected. If you think you have been infected, don't worry about it – just get a test done on your return.

Sleeping sickness or trypanosomiasis

This is really a cattle disease, which is occasionally caught by people. It is spread by bites from the distinctive tsetse fly – which is slightly larger than a housefly, and has pointed mouth-parts designed for sucking blood. These flies are easily spotted as they bite during the day, and have distinctive wings that cross into a scissors shape when they are resting.

Prevention is easier than cure, so avoid being bitten by covering up. Chemical insect repellents are also helpful. Dark colours, especially blue, are favoured by the flies, so avoid wearing these if possible.

Tsetse bites are nasty, so expect them to swell up and turn red – that is a normal allergic reaction to any bite. The vast majority of tsetse bites will just do this. However, if the bite develops into a boil-like swelling after five or more days, and a fever two or three weeks later, then seek immediate medical treatment to avert permanent damage to your central nervous system. The name 'sleeping sickness' refers to a daytime drowsiness which is characteristic of the later stages of the disease.

Because this is a rare complaint, most doctors in the West are unfamiliar with it. If you think that you may have been infected – draw their attention to the possibility. Treatment is straightforward, once a correct diagnosis has been made.

Some Africans view the fly positively, referring to it as a guardian of wild Africa, because fear of the disease's effect on cattle has prevented farming, and hence settlement, encroaching on many areas of wild bush. In recent years the tsetse fly has been subject to relentless spraying programmes in much of the sub-continent, designed to remove the last natural barrier to cattle farming. Then material screens, impregnated with a chemical attractant derived from cattle and an insecticide, are hung in shady areas under trees in order to attract and kill any remaining flies.

Tsetse flies are common in many areas of Zambia – including most of the national parks – although cases of sleeping sickness are exceedingly rare.

Returning home

Many tropical diseases have a long incubation period, and it is possible to develop symptoms weeks after returning home (this is why it is important to keep taking anti-malaria prophylaxis for at least four weeks after you leave a malarial zone). If you do get ill after you return home, be certain to tell your doctor where you have been. Alert him/her to any diseases that you may have been exposed to. Several people die from malaria in the UK every year because victims do not seek medical help promptly or their doctors are not familiar with the symptoms, and so are slow to make a correct diagnosis. Milder forms of malaria may take up to a year to reveal themselves, but serious (falciparum) malaria will become apparent within four months.

If problems persist, get a check-up at one of the hospitals that specialise in tropical diseases. Note that to visit such a hospital in the UK, you need a letter of referral from your doctor.

For further advice or help in the UK, ask your local doctor to refer you to the London Hospital for Tropical Diseases, 4 St Pancras Way, London NW1 (tel: 020 7387 4411).

SAFETY

Zambia is not a dangerous country. If you are travelling on an all-inclusive trip and staying at lodges and hotels, then problems of personal safety are exceedingly rare. There will always be someone on hand to help you.

Even if you are travelling on local transport, perhaps on a low budget, you will not be attacked randomly just for the sake of it. A difficult situation is most likely to occur if you have made yourself an obvious target for thieves, perhaps by walking around, or driving an expensive 4WD, in town at night. The answer then is to capitulate completely and give them what they want, and cash in on your travel insurance. Heroics are not a good idea.

For women travellers, especially those travelling alone, it is doubly important to learn the local attitudes, and how to behave acceptably. This takes some practice, and a certain confidence. You will often be the centre of attention but, by developing conversational techniques to avert over-enthusiastic male attention, you should be perfectly safe. Making friends of the local women is one way to help avoid such problems.

Theft

Theft is a problem in Zambia's urban areas. Given that a large section of the population is living below the poverty line and without any paid work, it is surprising that the problem is not worse. Despite Lusaka's reputation, in my experience theft is no more of a problem here than it is in Harare – while the centre of Johannesburg is significantly more dangerous than either.

How to avoid it

Thieves in the bigger cities usually work in groups – choosing their targets carefully. These will be people who look vulnerable and who have items worth stealing. To avoid being robbed, try not to fit into either category – and certainly not into both. Observing a few basic rules, especially during your first few weeks in Zambia's cities, will drastically reduce your chances of becoming a target. After that you should have learnt your own way of assessing the risks, and avoiding thefts. Until then:

- Try not to carry anything of value around with you.
- If you must carry cash, then use a concealed money-belt for your main supply – keeping smaller change separately and to hand.
- Try not to walk around alone. Move in groups. Take taxis instead.
- Try not to look too foreign. Blend in to the local scene as well as you can. Act like a street-wise expat rather than a tourist, if you can. (Conspicuously carrying a local newspaper may help with this.)
- Rucksacks and large, new bags are bad. If you must carry a bag, choose an old battered one. Around town, a local plastic carrier bag is ideal.
- Move confidently and look as if you know exactly what you are doing, and where you are going. Lost foreigners make the easiest targets.
- Never walk around at night – that is asking for trouble.

If you have a vehicle then don't leave anything in it, and avoid leaving it parked outside in a city. One person should always stay with it, as vehicle thefts are common, even in broad daylight. Armed gangs doing American-style vehicle hijacks are much rarer, but not unknown – and their most likely targets are new 4WD vehicles. If you are held up then just surrender: you have little choice if you want to live.

SAFETY FOR WOMEN TRAVELLERS
Janice Booth

When attention becomes intrusive, it can help if you are wearing a wedding ring and have photos of 'your' husband and children, even if they are someone else's. A good reason to give for not being with them is that you have to travel in connection with your job – biology, zoology, geography, or whatever. (But not journalism – that's risky.)

Pay attention to local etiquette, and to speaking, dressing and moving reasonably decorously. Look at how the local women dress, and try not to expose parts of yourself that they keep covered. Think about body language. In much of Southern Africa direct eye-contact with a man will be seen as a 'come-on'; sunglasses are helpful here.

Don't be afraid to explain clearly – but pleasantly rather than as a put-down – that you aren't in the market for whatever distractions are on offer. Remember that you are probably as much of a novelty to the local people as they are to you; and the fact that you are travelling abroad alone gives them the message that you are free and adventurous. But don't imagine that a Lothario lurks under every bush: many approaches stem from genuine friendliness or curiosity, and a brush-off in such cases doesn't do much for the image of travellers in general.

Take sensible precautions against theft and attack – try to cover all the risks before you encounter them – and then relax and enjoy your trip. You'll meet far more kindness than villainy.

Reporting thefts to the police

If you are the victim of a theft then report it to the police – they ought to know. Also try to get a copy of the report, or at least a reference number on an official-looking piece of paper, as this will help you to claim on your insurance policy when you return home. Some insurance companies won't act without it. But remember that reporting anything in a police station can take a long time, and do not expect any speedy arrests for a small case of pick-pocketing.

Arrest

To get arrested in Zambia, a foreigner will normally have to try quite hard. During the Kaunda regime, when the state was paranoid about spies, every tourist's camera became a reason for suspicion and arrest. Fortunately that attitude has now vanished, though as a precaution you should still ask for permission to photograph near bridges or military installations. This simple courtesy costs you nothing, and may avoid a problem later.

One excellent way to get arrested in Zambia is to try to smuggle drugs across its borders, or to try to buy them from 'pushers'. Drug offences carry penalties at least as stiff as those you will find at home – and the jails are a lot less pleasant. Zambia's police are not forbidden to use entrapment techniques or 'sting' operations to catch criminals. Buying, selling or using drugs in Zambia is just not worth the risk.

Failing this, arguing with any policeman or army official – and getting angry into the bargain – is a sure way to get arrested. It is *essential* to control your temper and stay relaxed when dealing with Zambia's officials. Not only will you gain respect, and hence help your cause, but also you will avoid being forced to cool off for a night in the cells.

If you are careless enough to be arrested, you will often only be asked a few questions. If the police are suspicious of you, then how you handle the situation will determine whether you are kept for a matter of hours or for days. Be patient, helpful, good-humoured, and as truthful as possible. Never lose your temper; it will only aggravate the situation. Avoid any hint of arrogance. If things are going badly after half a day or so, then start firmly, but politely, to insist on seeing someone in higher authority. As a last resort you do, at least in theory, have the right to contact your embassy or consulate, though the finer points of your civil liberties may be overlooked by an irate local police chief.

Bribery

Bribery is a fact of life in Zambia, though it is a difficult subject to write about. If you're visiting on an organised holiday, then it's unlikely to become an issue – you'll not come across any expectation of bribes. However, independent travellers ought to think about the issue before they arrive, as they are more likely to encounter the problem, and there are many different points of view on how to deal with it.

Some argue that it is present already, as an unavoidable way of life, and so must be accepted by the practical traveller. They view using bribery as simply practising one of the local customs. Others regard paying bribes as an unacceptable step towards condoning an immoral practice, thus any bribe should be flatly refused, and requests to make them never acceded to.

Whichever school of thought you favour, bribery is an issue in Zambia that you may need to consider. It is not as widespread, or on the same scale, as countries further north – but on a low level is not uncommon. A large 'tip' is often expected for a favour, and acceptance of small fines from police for traffic offences often avoids proceedings which may appear deliberately time-consuming. Many pragmatic travellers will only use a bribe as a very last resort, and only then when it has been asked for repeatedly.

Never attempt to bribe someone unsubtly, or use the word 'bribe'. If the person involved hasn't already dropped numerous broad hints to you that money is required, then offering it would be a great insult. Further, even if bribes are being asked for, an eagerness to offer will encourage any person you are dealing with to increase their price.

Never simply say 'here's some dollars, now will you do it?' Better is to agree, reluctantly, to pay the 'on-the-spot-fine' that was requested; or to gradually accept the need for the extra 'administration fee' that was demanded; or to finally agree to help to cover the 'time and trouble' involved... provided that the problem can be overcome.

BUSH CAMPING - E.H

In the Wilds

DRIVING

Driving around Zambia isn't for the novice, or the unprepared. Long stretches of the tarred roads are extensively potholed, most of the secondary gravel roads are in very poor repair, and many areas rely on bush tracks maintained only by the passage of vehicles. If you plan on exploring in the more rural areas, and remote parks, then you will need at least two sturdy, fully equipped 4WD vehicles. It is interesting to note that several of Zambia's car hire companies only rent vehicles (saloons for use only in the towns) if you take a local driver – it says something of the roads in general.

Equipment and preparations
Fuel

Petrol and diesel are available in most of the towns, and shortages are now rare. However, for travel into the bush you will need long-range fuel tanks, and/or a large stock of filled jerrycans. It is essential to plan your fuel requirements well in advance, and to carry more than you expect to need.

Remember that using the vehicle's 4WD capability, especially in low ratio gears, will significantly increase your fuel consumption. Similarly, the cool comfort of a vehicle's air conditioning will burn your fuel reserves swiftly. In April '99 the price in Lusaka for diesel was Kw1,108 per litre, and petrol Kw1,194 per litre. The further you go away from the major centres, the more these prices will increase.

Spares

Zambia's garages do not generally have a comprehensive stock of vehicle spares – though bush mechanics can effect the most amazing short-term repairs, with remarkably basic tools and raw materials. Spares for the more common makes are easiest to find, so most basic Land Rover and Toyota 4WD parts are available somewhere in Lusaka, at a price. If you are arriving in Zambia with a foreign vehicle, it is best to bring as many spares as you can.

Navigation

See the section on *Maps and navigation* in *Chapter 5* for detailed comments, but there are good maps available – and for this there's no alternative to visiting the Surveyor General's office in Mulungushi House, in Lusaka. You should seriously consider taking a GPS system if you are heading off the main roads in the more remote areas of the country.

Coping with Zambia's roads
Tar roads

Many of Zambia's tar roads are excellent, and a programme of tarring is gradually extending these good sections. However, within them there are occasional patches of potholes. These often occur in small groups, making some short stretches of tar very slow going indeed. If you are unlucky, or foolish, enough to hit one of these sections after speeding along a smooth stretch of tar, then you are likely to blow at least one tyre and in danger of a serious accident. For this reason, if for no other, even tar roads that look good are worth treating with caution. It is wiser never to exceed about 80kph.

Strip roads

Occasionally there are roads where the sealed tar surface is only wide enough for one vehicle. This becomes a problem when you meet another vehicle travelling in the opposite direction...on the same stretch of tar. Then local practice is to wait until the last possible moment before you steer left, driving with two wheels on the gravel adjacent to the tar, and two on the tar. Usually, the vehicle coming in the opposite direction will do the same, and after passing each other both vehicles veer back on to the tar. If you are unused to this, then slow right down before you steer on to the gravel.

Gravel roads

Gravel roads can be very deceptive. Even when they appear smooth, flat and fast (which is not often), they still do not give vehicles much traction. You will frequently put the car into small skids, and with practice at slower speeds you will learn how to deal with them. Gravel is a less forgiving surface on which to drive than tar. The rules and techniques for driving well are the same for both, but on tar you can get away with sloppy braking and cornering which would prove fatal on gravel.

Further, in Zambia you must always be prepared for the unexpected: an animal wandering on to the road, a rash of huge potholes, or an unexpected corner. So it is verging on insane to drive over about 60kph on any of Zambia's gravel roads. Other basic driving hints include:

Slowing down If in any doubt about what lies ahead, always slow down. Road surfaces can vary enormously, so keep a constant lookout for potholes, ruts or patches of soft sand which could put you into an unexpected slide.

Passing vehicles When passing other vehicles travelling in the opposite direction, always slow down to minimise both the damage that stone chippings will do to your windscreen, and the danger in driving through the other vehicle's dust cloud.

Using your gears In normal driving, a lower gear will give you more control over the car – so keep out of high 'cruising' gears. Rather stick with third or fourth, and accept that your revs will be slightly higher than they normally are.

Cornering and braking Under ideal conditions, the brakes should only be applied when the car is travelling in a straight line. Braking whilst negotiating a corner is dangerous, so it is vital to slow down before you reach corners. Equally, it is better to slow down gradually, using a combination of gears and brakes, than to use the brakes alone. You are less likely to skid.

Driving at night

Never drive at night unless you have to. Both wild and domestic animals frequently spend the night by the side of busy roads, and will actually sleep on quieter ones. Tar roads are especially bad as the surface absorbs all the sun's heat by day, and then radiates it at night – making it a warm bed for passing animals. A high-speed collision with any animal, even a small one like a goat, will not only kill the animal, but will cause very severe damage to a vehicle, with potentially fatal consequences.

4WD driving techniques

You will need a high-clearance 4WD to get anywhere in Zambia that's away from the main arteries. However, no vehicle can make up for an inexperienced driver – so ensure that you are confident of your vehicle's capabilities *before* you venture into the wilds with it. You really need extensive practice, with an expert on hand to advise you, before you'll have the first idea how to handle such a vehicle in difficult terrain. Finally, driving in convoy is an *essential* precaution in the more remote areas, in case one vehicle gets stuck or breaks down. Some of the more relevant techniques include:

Driving in sand

If you start to lose traction in deep sand, then stop on the next piece of solid ground that you come to. Lower your tyre pressure until there is a distinct bulge in the tyre walls (having first made sure that you have the means to re-inflate them when you reach solid roads again). A lower pressure will help your traction greatly, but increase the wear on your tyres. Pump them up again before you drive on a hard surface at speed, or the tyres will be badly damaged.

Where there are clear, deep-rutted tracks in the sand, don't fight the steering wheel – just relax and let your vehicle steer itself. Driving in the cool of the morning is easier than later in the day because when sand is cool it compacts better and is firmer. (When hot, the pockets of air between the sand grains expand and the sand becomes looser.)

If you do get stuck, despite these precautions, don't panic. Don't just rev the engine and spin the wheels – you'll only dig deeper. Instead stop. Relax and assess the situation. Now dig shallow ramps in front of all the wheels, reinforcing them with pieces of wood, vegetation, stones, material or anything else which will give the wheels better traction. Lighten the vehicle load (passengers out) and push. Don't let the engine revs die as you engage your lowest ratio gear, and use the clutch to ensure that the wheels don't spin wildly and dig themselves further into the sand.

Sometimes rocking the vehicle backwards and forwards will build up momentum to break you free. This can be done by intermittently applying the clutch and/or by getting helpers who can push and pull the vehicle at the same frequency. Once the vehicle is moving, the golden rule of sand driving is to keep up the momentum: if you pause, you will sink and stop.

Driving in mud

This is difficult, though the theory is the same as for sand: keep going and don't stop. That said, even the most experienced drivers get stuck. Many areas of Zambia (like large stretches of the Kafue, Luangwa and Lower Zambezi valleys) have very fine soil known as 'black-cotton' soil, which becomes impassable when wet. This is why many of the camps close down for the rains, as the only way to get there would be to walk.

Push-starting when stuck

If you are unlucky enough to need to push-start your vehicle whilst it is stuck in sand or mud, there is a remedy. Raise up the drive wheels, and take off one of the tyres. Then wrap a length of rope around the hub and treat it like a spinning top: one person (or more) pulls the rope to make the axle spin, whilst the driver lifts the clutch, turns the ignition on, and engages a low gear to turn the engine over. This is a very difficult equivalent of a push start, but it may be your only option.

Rocky terrain

Have your tyre pressure higher than normal and move very slowly. If necessary, passengers should get out and guide you along the track to avoid scraping the undercarriage on the ground. This can be a very slow business, and often applies in some of Zambia's mountainous areas.

Crossing rivers

The first thing to do is to stop and check the river. You must assess its depth, its substrate (type of riverbed) and its current flow; and determine the best route to drive across it. This is best done by wading across the river (whilst watching for hippos and crocodiles, if necessary). Beware of water that's too deep for your vehicle, or the very real possibility of being swept away by a fast current and a slippery substrate.

If everything is OK then select your lowest gear ratio and drive through the water at a slow but steady rate. Your vehicle's air intake must be above the level of the water to avoid your engine filling with water. It's not worth taking risks, so remember that a flooded river may subside to safer levels by the next morning.

Many rivers in Zambia have hand-operated pontoons – usually wooden platforms tied on top of buoyant empty oil cans and kept in line by steel cables stretched across the river. There are often, but not always, local people around who man these, for either a large official charge or a handsome tip. You need to take great care (everybody out, use first gear) when driving on and off these, and make sure that the pontoon is held tightly next to the bank on both occasions.

Overheating

If the engine has overheated then the only option is to stop and turn it off. Don't open the radiator cap to refill it until the radiator is no longer hot to the touch. Even then, keep the engine running and the water circulating while you refill the radiator – otherwise you run the risk of cracking the hot metal by suddenly cooling it. Flicking droplets of water on to the outside of a running engine will cool it.

In areas of tall grass keep a close watch on the water temperature gauge. Grass stems and seeds will get caught in the radiator grill and block the flow of air, causing the engine to overheat and the grass to catch fire. You should stop and remove the grass seeds every few kilometres or so, depending on the conditions.

Driving near big game

The only animals which are likely to pose a threat to vehicles are elephants – and generally only elephants which are familiar with vehicles. So, treat them with the greatest respect and don't 'push' them by trying to move ever closer. Letting them approach you is much safer, and they will feel far less threatened and more relaxed. Then, if the animals are calm, you can safely turn the engine off, sit quietly, and watch as they pass you by.

If you are unlucky, or foolish, enough to unexpectedly drive into the middle of a herd, then don't panic. Keep your movements, and those of the vehicle, slow and measured. Back off steadily. Don't be panicked, or overly intimidated, by a mock charge – this is just their way of frightening you away. Professionals will sometimes switch their engines off, but this is not for the faint-hearted.

BUSH CAMPING

Many 'boy scout' type manuals have been written on survival in the bush, usually by military veterans. If you are stranded with a convenient multi-purpose knife, then these useful tomes will describe how you can build a shelter from branches, catch passing animals for food, and signal to the inevitable rescue planes which are combing the globe looking for you – whilst avoiding the attentions of hostile forces.

In Zambia, bush camping is usually less about survival than comfort. You're likely to have much more than the knife: probably at least a bulging backpack, if not a loaded 4WD. Thus the challenge is not to camp and survive, it is to camp and be as comfortable as possible. With practice you'll learn how, but a few hints may be useful for the less experienced:

Where you can camp
In frequently-visited national parks, there are designated campsites that you should use, as directed by the local game scouts. Elsewhere the rules are less obvious, though it is normal to ask the scouts, and get their permission, for any site that you have in mind.

Outside of the parks, you should ask the local landowner, or village head, if they are happy for you to camp on their property. If you explain patiently and politely what you want, then you are unlikely to meet anything but warm hospitality from most rural Zambians. They will normally be as fascinated with your way of life as you are with theirs. Company by your campfire is virtually assured.

Choosing a site
Only experience will teach you how to choose a good site for pitching a tent, but a few points may help you avoid a lot of problems:

- Avoid camping on what looks like a path through the bush, however indistinct. It may be a well-used game trail.
- Beware of camping in dry riverbeds: dangerous flash floods can arrive with little or no warning.
- In marshy areas camp on higher ground to avoid cold, damp mists in the morning and evening.
- Camp a reasonable distance from water: near enough to walk to it, but far enough to avoid animals which arrive to drink.
- If a lightning storm is likely, make sure that your tent is not the highest thing around.
- Finally, choose a site which is as flat as possible – you will find sleeping much easier.

Camp fires
Camp fires can create a great atmosphere and warm you on a cold evening, but they can also be damaging to the environment and leave unsightly piles of ash and blackened stones. Deforestation is a major concern in much of the developing world, including parts of Zambia, so if you do light a fire then use wood as the locals do: sparingly. If you have a vehicle, consider buying firewood in advance from people who sell it at the roadside.

If you collect it yourself, then take only dead wood, nothing living. Never just pick up a log: always roll it over first, checking carefully for snakes or scorpions.

Experienced campers build small, highly efficient fires by using a few large stones to absorb, contain and reflect the heat, and gradually feeding just a few thick logs into the centre to burn. Cooking pots can be balanced on the stones, or the point where the logs meet and burn. Others will use a small trench, lined with rocks, to similar effect. Either technique takes practice, but is worth perfecting. Whichever you do, bury the ashes, take any rubbish with you when you leave, and make the site look as if you had never been there. (See *Further Reading* for details of Christina Dodwell's excellent *Travel, Survival and Bush Cookery*.)

Don't expect an unattended fire to frighten away wild animals – that works in Hollywood, but not in Africa. A campfire may help your feelings of insecurity, but lion and hyena will disregard it with stupefying nonchalance.

Finally, do be hospitable to any locals who appear – despite your efforts to seek permission for your camp, you may effectively be staying in their back gardens.

Using a tent (or not)

Whether to use a tent or to sleep in the open is a personal choice, dependent upon where you are. In an area where there are predators around (specifically lion and hyena) then you should use a tent – and sleep *completely* inside it, as a protruding leg may seem like a tasty take-away to a hungry hyena. This is especially true at organised campsites, where the local animals are so used to humans that they have lost much of their inherent fear of man.

Outside game areas, you will be fine sleeping in the open, or preferably under a mosquito net, with just the stars of the African sky above you. On the practical side, sleeping under a tree will reduce the morning dew that settles on your sleeping bag. If your vehicle has a large, flat roof then sleeping on this will provide you with peace of mind, and a star-filled outlook. (Hiring a vehicle with a built-in roof-tent would seem like a perfect solution, until you want to take a drive whilst leaving your camp intact.)

Camping equipment

If you are taking an organised safari, you will not need any camping equipment at all. However, for those travelling independently very little kit is available in Zambia. So buy high-quality equipment beforehand as it will save you a lot of time and trouble once you arrive. Here are a few comments on various essentials:

Tent During the rains a good tent is essential in order to stay dry. Even during the dry season one is useful if there are lion or hyena around. If backpacking, invest in a high-quality, lightweight tent. Mosquito-netting ventilation panels, allowing a good flow of air, are essential. (Just a corner of mesh at the top of the tent is *not* enough for comfort.) Don't go for a tent that's small; it may feel cosy at home, but will be hot and claustrophobic in the heat.

I have been using the same *Spacepacker* tent (manufactured by Robert Saunders Ltd, Five Oaks Lane, Chigwell, Essex IG7 4QP, UK) for over ten years. It's a dome tent with fine mesh doors on either side which allow a through draft, making all the difference when temperatures are high. The alternative to a good tent is a mosquito net, which is fine unless it is raining or you are in a big game area.

Sleeping bag A lightweight, 'three-season' sleeping bag is ideal for Zambia, unless you are heading up to the Nyika Plateau in winter where the nights freeze. Down is preferable to synthetic fillings for most of the year, as it packs smaller, is lighter, and feels more luxurious to sleep in. That said, when down gets wet it loses its efficiency, so bring a good synthetic bag if you are likely to encounter much rain.

Ground mat A ground mat of some sort is essential. It keeps you warm and comfortable, and it protects the tent's ground sheet from rough or stony ground. (Do put it underneath the tent!) Closed cell foam mats are widely available outside Zambia, so buy one before you arrive. The better mats cost double or treble the cheaper ones, but are stronger, thicker and warmer – well worth the investment. Therm-a-Rests, the combination air-mattress and foam mats, are strong, durable and also worth the investment – but take a puncture repair kit with you just in case of problems.

Sheet sleeping bag Thin pure-cotton sheet sleeping bags (eg: YHA design) are small, light and very useful. They are easily washed and so are normally used like a sheet, inside a sleeping bag, to keep it clean. They can, of course, be used on their own when your main sleeping bag is too hot.

Stove 'Trangia'-type stoves, which burn methylated spirits, are simple to use, light, and cheap to run. They come complete with a set of light aluminium pans and a very useful all-purpose handle. Often you'll be able to cook on a fire with the pans, but it's nice to have the option of making a brew in a few minutes while you set up camp. Methylated spirits is cheap and widely available, even in the rural areas, but bring a tough (purpose made) fuel container with you as the bottles in which it is sold will soon crack and spill all over your belongings.

Petrol- and kerosene-burning stoves are undoubtedly efficient on fuel and powerful – but invariably temperamental and messy. Gas stoves use pressurised canisters, which are not allowed on aircraft, and difficult to buy in Zambia.

Torch (flashlight) This should be on every visitor's packing list. Find one that's small and tough, preferably water- and dust-proof. Head-mounted torches leave your hands free (useful when cooking or mending the car) but some people find them bulky and uncomfortable to wear. The small, strong and super-bright torches (such as Maglites) are excellent, but their bulbs are difficult to buy in Zambia. Bring several spares with you.

Those with vehicles will find a strong spotlight, powered by the car's battery (perhaps through the socket for the cigarette lighter), is invaluable for impromptu lighting (and game drives at night).

Water containers For everyday use, a small two-litre water bottle is invaluable, however you are travelling. If you're thinking of camping, you should also consider a strong, collapsible water-bag – perhaps 5–10 litres in size – which will reduce the number of trips that you need to make from your camp to the water source. (Ten litres of water weighs 10kg.) Drivers will want to carry a number of large containers of water, especially if venturing into the Kalahari sand in western Zambia, where good surface water is not common.

See *Planning and preparations*, page 57, for a memory-jogging list of other useful items to pack.

Animal dangers for campers

Camping in Africa is really *very* safe, though you may not think so from reading this. If you have a major problem whilst camping, it will probably be because you did something stupid, or because you forgot to take a few simple precautions. Here are a few general basics, applicable to anywhere in Africa and not just Zambia

Large animals

Big game will not bother you if you are in a tent – provided that you do not attract its attention, or panic it. Elephants will gently tip-toe through your guy ropes whilst you sleep, without even nudging your tent. However, if you wake up and make a noise, startling them, they are far more likely to panic and step on your tent. Similarly, scavengers will quietly wander round, smelling your evening meal in the air, without any intention of harming you.

- Remember to use the toilet before going to bed, and avoid getting up in the night if possible.
- Scrupulously clean everything used for food that might smell good to scavengers. Put these utensils in a vehicle if possible, suspend them from a tree, or pack them away in a rucksack inside the tent.

- Do not keep any smelly foodstuffs, like meat or citrus fruit, in your tent. Their smells may attract unwanted attention.
- Do not leave anything outside that could be picked up – like bags, pots, pans, etc. Hyenas, amongst others, will take anything. (They have been known to crunch a camera's lens, and eat it.)
- If you are likely to wake in the night, then leave the tent's zips a few centimetres open at the top, enabling you to take a quiet peek outside.

Creepy crawlies

As you set up camp, clear stones or logs out of your way with great caution: underneath will be great hiding places for snakes and scorpions. Long moist grass is ideal territory for snakes, and dry, dusty, rocky places are classic sites for scorpions.

If you are sleeping in the open, it is not unknown to wake and find a snake lying next to you in the morning. Don't panic, your warmth has just attracted it to you. You will not be bitten if you gently edge away without making any sudden movements. (This is one good argument for using at least a mosquito net!)

Before you put on your shoes, shake them out. Similarly, check the back of your backpack before you slip it on. Just a curious spider, in either, could inflict a painful bite.

WALKING IN THE BUSH

Walking in the African bush is a totally different sensation to driving through it. You may start off a little unready – perhaps even sleepy for an early morning walk – but swiftly your mind will awake. There are no noises except the wildlife, and you. So every noise that isn't caused by you must be an animal; or a bird; or an insect. Every smell and every rustle has a story to tell, *if* you can understand it.

With time, patience, and a good guide you can learn to smell the presence of elephants, and hear when a predator alarms impala. You can use ox-peckers to lead you to buffalo, or vultures to help you locate a kill. Tracks will record the passage of animals in the sand, telling what passed by, how long ago, and in which direction.

Eventually your gaze becomes alert to the slightest movement; your ears aware of every sound. This is safari at its best: a live, sharp, spine-tingling experience that's hard to beat and very addictive. Be careful: watching game from a vehicle will never be the same again for you.

Walking trails and safaris

One of Zambia's biggest attractions is its walking safaris, which can justly claim to be amongst the best in Africa. The concept was pioneered here, in the Luangwa Valley, by the late Norman Carr. He also founded Nsefu Camp and Kapani Lodge, and trained several of the valley's best guides. It was he who first operated walking safaris for photographic guests, as opposed to hunters. The Luangwa still has a strong tradition of walking – which, in itself, fosters excellent walking guides. Several of the camps are dedicated to walking safaris, and guiding standards are generally very high.

One of the reasons behind the valley's success is the stringent tests that a guide must pass before he, or she, will be allowed to take clients into the bush. Walking guides have the hardest tests to pass; there is a less demanding exam for guides who conduct safaris from vehicles.

The second major reason for excellence is Zambia's policy of having a safari

Above Lion relaxing on the Busanga Plains (PM)
Below Leopard spotlit on a night-drive in South Luangwa (PH)

Above Hippos – perhaps Africa's most dangerous animals – in Kafue (PM)

Below Elephant and zebra under a sausage tree (*Kigelia africana*) beside Mfuwe Lagoon, South Luangwa (CM)

Above Female impala jumping (PM)

Above right Puku, one of Zambia's most common antelope, beside the Luangwa River in October (CM)

Left Thornicroft's giraffe on a drying lagoon in South Luangwa (CM)

Below Zebra in the Luangwa Valley (PM)

Above Old Manor at Shiwa
N'gandu (CM)

Right Thatching a bush
lodge near Livingstone (CM)

Below Curio sellers at
Kabwata Cultural Centre
in Lusaka (CM)

guide and an armed game scout accompany every walking safari. These groups are limited (by park rules) to a maximum of seven guests, and there's normally a tea-bearer (carrying drinks and refreshments) as well as the guide and armed scout.

If a problem arises with an aggressive animal, then the guide looks after the visitors – telling them exactly what to do – whilst the scout keeps his sights trained on the animal, just in case a shot is necessary. Fortunately such drastic measures are needed only rarely. This system of two guides means that Zambia's walks are very safe. Few shots are ever fired, and I can't remember hearing of an animal (or a person) ever being injured.

Contrast this with other African countries where a single guide (who may, or may not, be armed) watches out for the game *and* takes care of the visitors at the same time. The Zambian way is far better.

Etiquette for walking safaris

If you plan to walk then avoid wearing any bright, unnatural colours, especially white. Dark, muted shades are best; greens, browns and khaki are ideal. Hats are essential, as is sun-block. Even a short walk will last for two hours, and there's no vehicle to which you can retreat if you get too hot.

Binoculars should be immediately accessible – one pair per person – ideally in dust-proof cases strapped to your belt. Cameras too, if you decide to bring any, as they are of little use buried at the bottom of a camera bag. Heavy tripods or long lenses are a nightmare to lug around, so leave them behind if you can (and accept, philosophically, that you may miss shots).

Walkers see the most when walking in silent single file. This doesn't mean that you can't stop to whisper a question to the guide; just that idle chatter will reduce your powers of observation, and make you even more visible to the animals (who will usually flee when they sense you).

With regard to safety, your guide will always brief you in detail before you set off. S/he will outline possible dangers, and what to do in the unlikely event of them materialising. Listen carefully: this is vital.

Face-to-face animal encounters

Whether you are on an organised walking safari, on your own hike, or just walking from the car to your tent in the bush, it is not unlikely that you will come across some of Africa's larger animals at close quarters. Invariably, the danger is much less than you imagine, and a few basic guidelines will enable you to cope effectively with most situations.

Firstly, don't panic. Console yourself with the fact that animals are not normally interested in people. You are not their normal food, or their predator. If you do not annoy or threaten them, you will be left alone.

If you are walking to look for animals, then remember that this is their environment not yours. Animals have been designed for the bush, and their senses are far better attuned to it than yours. To be on less unequal terms, remain alert and try to spot them from a distance. This gives you the option of approaching carefully, or staying well clear.

Finally, the advice of a good guide is far more valuable than the simplistic comments noted here. Animals, like people, are all different. So whilst we can generalise here and say how the 'average' animal will behave – the one that's glaring at you over a small bush may have had a *really* bad day, and be feeling much grumpier than normal.

That said, here are a few general comments on how to deal with some potentially dangerous situations:

Buffalo

This is probably the continent's most dangerous animal to hikers, but there is a difference between the old males, often encountered on their own or in small groups, and large breeding herds.

The former are easily surprised. If they hear or smell something amiss, they will charge without provocation – motivated by a fear that something is sneaking up on them. Buffalo have an excellent sense of smell, but fortunately they are short-sighted. Avoid a charge by quickly climbing the nearest tree, or by side-stepping at the last minute. If adopting the latter, more risky, technique then stand motionless until the last possible moment, as the buffalo may well miss you anyhow.

The large breeding herds can be treated in a totally different manner. If you approach them in the open, they will often flee. Sometimes though, in areas often used for walking safaris, they will stand and watch, moving aside to allow you to pass through the middle of the herd.

Neither encounter is for the faint-hearted or inexperienced, so steer clear of these dangerous animals wherever possible.

Black rhino

Unfortunately there are few, if any, black rhino left in Zambia. However, if you are both exceptionally lucky enough to find one, and then unlucky enough to be charged by it, use the same tactics as you would for a buffalo: tree climbing or dodging at the last second. (It is amazing how even the least athletic walker will swiftly scale the nearest tree when faced with a charging rhino.)

Elephant

Normally elephants are only a problem if you disturb a mother with a calf, or approach a male in musth (state of arousal). So keep well away from these. Lone bulls can usually be approached quite closely when feeding. If you get too close to any elephant it will scare you off with a 'mock charge': head up, perhaps shaking – ears flapping – trumpeting. Lots of sound and fury. This is intended to be frightening, and it is. But it is just a warning and no cause for panic. Just freeze to assess the elephant's intentions, then back off slowly.

When elephants really mean business, they will put their ears back, their head down, and charge directly at you without stopping. This is known as a 'full charge'. There is no easy way to avoid the charge of an angry elephant, so take a hint from the warning and back off very slowly as soon as you encounter a mock charge. Don't run. If you are the object of a full charge, then you have no choice but to run – preferably round an anthill, up a tall tree, or wherever.

Lion

Tracking lion can be one of the most exhilarating parts of a walking safari. Sadly, they will normally flee before you even get close to them. However, it can be a problem if you come across a large pride unexpectedly. Lion are well camouflaged; it is easy to find yourself next to one before you realise it. If you had been listening, you would probably have heard a warning growl about twenty metres ago. Now it is too late.

The best plan is to stop, and back off slowly, but confidently. If you are in a small group, then stick together. *Never* run from a big cat. First, they are always faster than you are. Secondly, running will just convince them that you are frightened prey, and worth chasing. As a last resort, if they seem too inquisitive and follow as you back off, then stop. Call their bluff. Pretend that you are not afraid and make loud, deep, confident noises: shout at them, bang something. But do not run.

John Coppinger, one of Luangwa's most experienced guides, adds that every single compromising experience that he has had with lion on foot has been either with a female with cubs, or with a mating pair, when the males can get very aggressive. You have been warned.

Leopard

Leopard are very seldom seen, and would normally flee from the most timid of lone hikers. However, if injured, or surprised, then they are very powerful, dangerous cats. Conventional wisdom is scarce, but never stare straight into the leopard's eyes, or it will regard this as a threat display. (The same is said, by some, to be true with lion.) Better to look away slightly, at a nearby bush, or even at its tail. Then back off slowly, facing the direction of the cat and showing as little terror as you can. As with lion – loud, deep, confident noises are a last line of defence. Never run from a leopard.

Hippo

Hippo are fabled to account for more deaths in Africa than any other animal (ignoring the mosquito). Having been attacked and capsized by a hippo whilst in a dugout canoe, I find this very easy to believe, but see *Wildlife Guide* for an alternative comment on this. Visitors are most likely to encounter hippo in the water, when paddling a canoe (see *Canoeing*, below), or fishing. However, as they spend half their time grazing on land, they will sometimes be encountered out of the water. Away from the water, out of their comforting lagoons, hippos are even more dangerous. If they see you, they will flee towards the water – so the golden rule is never to get between a hippo and its escape route to deep water. Given that a hippo will outrun you on land, standing motionless is probably your best line of defence.

Snakes

These are really not the great danger that people imagine. Most flee when they feel the vibrations of footsteps; only a few will stay still. The puff adder is responsible for more cases of snakebite than any other venomous snake in Zambia because, when approached, it will simply puff itself up and hiss as a warning, rather than slither away. This makes it essential to always watch where you place your feet when walking in the bush.

Similarly, there are a couple of arboreal (tree dwelling) species which may be taken by surprise if you carelessly grab vegetation as you walk. So don't.

Spitting cobras are also encountered occasionally, which will aim for your eyes and spit with accuracy. If one of these rears up in front of you, then turn away and avert your eyes. If the spittle reaches your eyes, you must wash them out *immediately* and thoroughly with whatever liquid comes to hand: water, milk, even urine if that's the only liquid that you can quickly produce.

CANOEING

The Zambezi – both above the Falls and from Kariba to Mozambique – is in constant use for canoeing trips. One good operator, Remote Africa Safaris (see page 257), even features canoeing on the Luangwa whilst it is high and in flood. Canoeing along beautiful, tropical rivers is as much a part of Zambia's safari scene in the Lower Zambezi as are open-top Land Rovers. Generally you either canoe along the river for a set number of days, stopping each night at a different place, or canoe for a short stretch as an activity at one of the camps – as an alternative to a walk or a game drive.

Most operators use large, two- or three-person Canadian-style fibreglass canoes. Three-person canoes usually have a guide in the back of each, while two-person canoes are often paddled in 'convoy' with a guide in just one of the boats. Less confident (or lazier) paddlers might prefer to have a guide in their own canoe, while the more energetic usually want to have the boat to themselves.

Zambezi canoe guides

Most of the Zambezi's specialist canoeing operations are run by large companies on a very commercial basis. On these you can expect to join a party of about seven canoes, one of which will contain a guide. S/he should know the stretch of river well and will canoe along it regularly. The actual distances completed on the two/three night trips are quite short. All the trips run downstream and a day's canoeing could actually be completed in just three hours with a modicum of fitness and technique.

Like other guides, there is a professional licence that the 'river guides' must possess in order to be allowed to take paying guests canoeing. Note that only a few of the best river guides also hold licences as general professional guides (ie: are licensed to lead walking safaris). These all-rounders generally have a far deeper understanding of the environment and the game than those who are only 'river guides'.

However, their greater skill commands a higher wage – and so they are usually found in the smaller, more upmarket operations. Given the inexperience of some of the river guides, I would always be willing to pay the extra. Although the safety record of river trips is good, accidents do happen occasionally.

The main dangers
Hippo

Hippos are strictly vegetarians, and will usually only attack a canoe if they feel threatened. The standard avoidance technique is first of all to let them know that you are there. If in doubt, bang your paddle on the side of the canoe a few times (most novice canoeists will do this constantly anyhow).

During the day, hippopotami will congregate in the deeper areas of the river. The odd ones in shallow water – where they feel less secure – will head for the deeper places as soon as they are aware of a nearby canoe. Avoiding hippos then becomes a fairly simple case of steering around the deeper areas, where the pods will make their presence obvious. This is where experience, and knowing every bend of the river, becomes useful.

Problems arise when canoes inadvertently stray over a pod of hippos, or when a canoe cuts a hippo off from its path of retreat into deeper water. Either is dangerous, as hippos will overturn canoes without a second thought, biting them and their occupants. Once in this situation, there are no easy remedies. So – avoid it in the first place.

Crocodiles

Crocodiles may have sharp teeth and look prehistoric, but are of little danger to a canoeist...unless you are in the water. Then the more you struggle and the more waves you create, the more you will attract their unwelcome attentions. There is a major problem when canoes are overturned by hippos – then you must get out of the water as soon as possible, either into another canoe or on to the bank.

When a crocodile attacks an animal, it will try to disable it, normally by getting a firm, biting grip, submerging, and performing a long, fast barrel-roll. This will disorient the prey, drown it, and probably twist off the limb that has been bitten.

In this dire situation, your best line of defence is probably to stab the reptile in its eyes with anything sharp that you have. Alternatively, if you can lift up its tongue and let the water into its lungs whilst it is underwater, then a crocodile will start to drown and will release its prey.

Jo Pope reports that a man survived an attack in the Zambezi recently when a crocodile grabbed his arm and started to spin backwards into deep water. The man wrapped his legs around the crocodile, to spin with it and avoid having his arm twisted off. As this happened, he tried to poke his thumb into its eyes, but with no effect. Finally he put his free arm into the crocodile's mouth, and opened up the beast's throat. This worked. The crocodile left him and he survived with only a damaged arm. Understandably, anecdotes about tried and tested methods of escape are rare.

MINIMUM IMPACT

When you visit, drive through, or camp in an area and have 'minimum impact' this means that that area is left in the same condition as – or better than – when you entered it. Whilst most visitors view minimum impact as being desirable, spend time to consider the ways in which we contribute to environmental degradation, and how these can be avoided.

Driving

Use your vehicle responsibly. If there's a road, or a track, then don't go off it – the environment will suffer. Driving off-road can leave a multitude of tracks that detract from the 'wilderness' feeling for subsequent visitors. Equally, don't speed through towns or villages: remember the danger to local children, and the amount of dust you'll cause.

Hygiene

Use toilets if they are provided, even if they are basic longdrop loos with questionable cleanliness. If there are no toilets, then human excrement should always be buried well away from paths, or groundwater, and any tissue used should be burnt and then buried.

If you use rivers or lakes to wash, then soap yourself near the bank, using a pan for scooping water from the river – making sure that no soap finds its way back into the water. Use biodegradable soap. Sand makes an excellent pan-scrub, even if you have no water to spare.

Rubbish

Biodegradable rubbish can be burnt and buried with the campfire ashes. Don't just leave it lying around: it will look very unsightly and spoil the place for those who come after you.

Bring along some plastic bags with which to remove the rest of your rubbish, and dump it at the next town. Items that will not burn, like tin cans, are best cleaned and squashed for easy carrying. If there are bins, then use them, but also consider when they will next be emptied, and if local animals will rummage through them first. Carrying out all your own rubbish may still be the sensible option.

Host communities

Whilst the rules for reducing impact on the environment have been understood and followed by responsible travellers for years, the effects of tourism on local people have only recently been considered. Many tourists believe it is their right, for example, to take intrusive photos of local people – and even become angry if the local people object. They refer to higher prices being charged to tourists as a rip-off, without considering the hand-to-mouth existence of those selling these products or services. They deplore child beggars, then hand out sweets or pens to local children with outstretched hands.

Our behaviour towards 'the locals' needs to be considered in terms of their culture, with the knowledge that we are the uninvited visitors. We visit to enjoy ourselves, but this should not be at the expense of local people. Read *Cultural guidelines*, pages 30, and aim to leave the local communities better off after your visit.

Local payments

If you spend time with any of Zambia's poorer local people, perhaps camping in the bush or getting involved with one of the community-run projects, then take great care with any payments that you make.

Firstly, note that most people like to spend their earnings on what *they* choose. This means that trying to pay for services with beads, food, old clothes or anything else instead of money isn't appreciated. Ask yourself how you'd like to be paid, and you'll understand this point.

Secondly, find out the normal cost of what you are buying. Most community campsites will have a standard price for a pitch and, if applicable, an hour's guided activity, or whatever. Find this out before you sleep there, or accept the offer of a walk. It is then important that you pay about that amount for the service rendered – no less, and not too much more.

As most people realise, if you try to pay less you'll get into trouble – as you would at home. However, many do not realise that if they generously pay a lot *more*, this can be equally damaging. Local rates of pay in rural areas can be very low, and a careless visitor can easily pay disproportionately large sums. Where this happens, local jobs can lose their value overnight. (Imagine working hard to become a game scout, only to learn that a tourist has given your friend the equivalent of your whole month's wages for just a few hours guiding. What incentive is there for you to carry on with your regular job?)

If you want to give more – for good service, a super guide, or just because you want to help – then either buy some locally made produce (at the going rate), or donate money to one the organisations working to improve the lot of Namibia's most disadvantaged (see page 32). ZOCS is one such charity, working for some of Zambia's poorest children, but if you ask locally you'll often find projects that need your support. Some lodges and camps will assist with community projects, and be able to suggest a good use for donations.

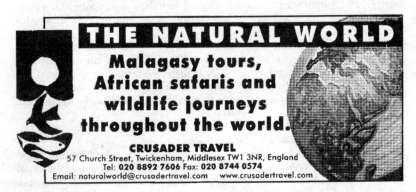

Zambia Today

Tourists still come to Zambia in small numbers, and largely restrict themselves to a few of the main towns and national parks. Away from these centres, visitors are regarded with mild curiosity and often shown great warmth and hospitality. Zambia is a genuinely friendly country which (perhaps Lusaka excepted) has not yet had sufficient bad experiences of visitors to lower its opinion of them.

Zambia's attitude to tourism has changed considerably over the past few years, and visitors are now generally seen as good for the country because they spend valuable foreign currency and create employment. Tourism is helping Zambia's economy and its conservation policy, by making a major contribution to the preservation of the national parks.

COST OF LIVING

Like anywhere else, the cost of visiting Zambia varies with the style in which you travel, and the places where you spend your time. However, unlike many countries, Zambia's lack of infrastructure leads to a polarisation of travelling styles.

If you plan a couple of weeks to visit the parks, staying at small private safari camps, then it's not a cheap destination. You will probably need the odd small charter flight, and an average US$225–375/£150–250 per day, including basically everything, would be expected. This is actually quite good value for an exclusive safari in a pristine and remote corner of Africa – the kind of trip at which Zambia excels.

At the other end of the spectrum, if you travel through Zambia on local buses, camping and staying in the odd local (sometimes seedy) resthouse, then Zambia is not expensive. A budget of US$30–50/£20–30 per day for food, accommodation and transport would suffice. However, most backpackers who undertake such trips are simply 'in transit' between Malawi and Zimbabwe. They see little of Zambia's wildlife or its national parks, missing out on even its cheaper attractions.

Finding a trip of medium expenditure, between these two extremes, is difficult. One possibility is to make use of the odd medium-priced safari camp. Lufupa/Shumba in northern Kafue, and the Wildlife Camp in South Luangwa, are obvious options, as is Kasanka – especially if four or five people are travelling together.

Hiring a vehicle is another possibility, as then you can buy food, camp and drive yourself around. However it requires driving expertise and lots of planning; it isn't something to undertake lightly.

Creatively using these options, being prepared to pay where necessary, you might spend only US$160/£100 per day whilst seeing some of the very best that the country has to offer.

Currency and inflation

Zambia's unit of currency is the kwacha. Theoretically each kwacha is divided into 100 ngwee, although one ngwee is now worth so little that these subdivisions are never used. The old practices of strict exchange control and unrealistic exchange rates have now gone – as has the black market for currency that these policies created.

As the result of the present free market, US dollars and UK pounds sterling are easily changed, and it is sometimes possible to spend US dollars (in small denomination notes) directly.

On 7 July 1999 the exchange rates were £1=Kw4,000; US$1=Kw2,500. I've used this as a convenient value for converting kwacha prices in the book into US dollars – basically for ease of use.

Inflation has varied enormously since at least 1989. It now seems to be slowing down, and was recently (June '99) quoted as being 28%, but projected to drop to around 15% by the end of the year.

Though it seems to have stabilised a little in recent months, its rates against the US dollar and UK pound have varied greatly in the last four years. The rough trends have been as follows:

		Rate of exchange/Kw	
Date	To US$	To British £	To SA Rand
1995: Jan/July	700 / 925	1,100 / 1,480	195 / 255
1996: Jan/July	975 / 1,270	1,500 / 1,970	267 / 289
1997: Jan/July	1,290 / 1,310	2,100 / 2,180	278 / 287
1998: Jan/July	1,450 / 1,945	2,380 / 3,200	295 / 310
1999: Jan/July	2,425 / 2,500	3,980 / 4,000	410 / 415

This constant movement of the currency and large inflation makes thinking and calculating in US dollars the easiest way to plan. It explains why we have used US$ for most of the prices in this guide, and even converted kwacha prices into dollars for reference.

Banks

If you need to change foreign currency, receive bank drafts, or do any other relatively complex financial transactions, then banks in the larger cities (ideally Lusaka) are your best option. They open as early as 08.15–08.30, and close around 14.45–15.30 from Monday to Friday. Some work a shorter day on Thursday, from 09.00 to 11.00. A few of the bigger banks in Lusaka also open 09.00–11.00 on Saturdays. Cashpoint (ATM) machines do not exist yet in Zambia.

GETTING AROUND
By air

If you want to fly internally in Zambia then there are a few possibilities. Several local companies use the routes vacated by Zambia Airways; some are good but all are still finding their feet commercially. Most are reliable, but all change their schedules periodically. None are yet featured on any of the global flight reservations systems. You are strongly advised to book your internal flights through an experienced tour operator, who uses them regularly. (As an aside, this means that if the airline goes bust the tour operator loses money; you don't.)

The services that I have encountered are high-quality operations, so you need have few worries about safety. On the whole, the smaller charter operations are more reliable, and more flexible for individual passengers, than the larger airlines with higher profiles in the country and more fixed schedules.

However, if you book an internal flight a long time in advance, be aware that its timings (and indeed existence) may change. Cancellation at short notice is unlikely, though taking a philosophical attitude towards this possibility would be wise. A good operator will always be able to make a back-up plan for you.

Air companies

Aero Zambia Zambia Insurance Brokers House, Dedan Kimathi Rd, P Bag 8717, Lusaka. Tel: 01 226111 or 225848; fax: 226147. This is one of the larger airlines, but it's in the news a lot lately and has been grounded several times recently. Use with caution, and take reliable advice before doing so.

Air Malawi at Pamodzi Hotel. Tel: 01 254455. Flights linking Lusaka and Lilongwe (on Thurs, Fri and Sun) have recently started stopping at Mfuwe on Sundays – thus connecting with BA's weekly flights into and out of Lilongwe

Airwaves Air Charters Tel: 01 223952/224334; cell: 752304/755640; fax: 223504

Avocet Air Charters Tel: 01 233422 (airport) or 264866 (after hours); cell: 702056; fax: 229261/2

Eastern Air c/o Steve Blagus Travel, Nkwazi Rd, PO Box 31530. Tel: 01 227739/40 or 227285; fax: 223724; tlx: ZA 43320. This is one of Zambia's larger small airlines and works with regular shuttle flights between some of the more outlying areas and places. Current schedule is:

    Lusaka–Ndola–Kasama–Kasaba Bay–Kasama–Ndola–Lusaka: Mondays/Thursdays
    Lusaka–Mongu–L'stone–Lusaka–Mfuwe–Chipata–Lusaka: Tuesdays
    Lusaka–Mfuwe–Chipata–Lusaka: Fridays
    Lusaka–Ndola–Mansa–Ndola–Lusaka: Saturdays
    Lusaka–Chipata–Mfuwe–Lusaka–L'stone–Mongu–Lusaka: Sundays

However, these will probably have changed by the time you need them …

Proflight PO Box 30536, Lusaka. Tel: 01 264439 or 263686 or 263687; airport tel: 271437; fax: 222888/262379. Five flights per week between Lusaka and Mfuwe during the dry season, plus a couple to Livingstone. This super little airline also organises a lot of charters

Zambian Airways PO Box 310277, Lusaka International Airport. Tel: 01 271066 or 271230; tlx: ZA 40410. This has no connection with the old Zambia Airways (which went bust in the early '90s). Instead this is the good small company which was called Roan Air until September 1999. Until then it used shiny new 19-seater planes, running regular hops to and from the Copperbelt and, during the dry season, also flights from the Copperbelt and Lusaka to Mfuwe.

Now, as Zambian Airways, they plan to expand, possibly including an agreement to connect with Air Namibia to run London–Lusaka–Windhoek flights. This will be an exciting development if it becomes established.

Stabo Air Charters Tel: 01 235976 (24-hour); cell: 771822; fax: 233481

Staravia PO Box 34273, Lusaka. Tel: 01 291962; airport tel: 01 271332/3

If you want to fly into, or out of, Mfuwe International Airport, then you can normally find a scheduled way. However, getting anywhere else is often a matter of chartering your own plane. This isn't for the backpacker's budget, but if you plan to stay at private safari camps then it will be within your price range.

If you decide to arrange your own plane, then expect a five-seater to cost around US$1.10/£0.70 per kilometre, including any mileage to/from its base. Thus rough round-trip mileages would be:

Lusaka – Mfuwe	880km
Lusaka – Livingstone	810km
Lusaka – Kafue	500km

By rail

There are two totally separate rail systems in Zambia: ordinary trains and TAZARA trains. Zambia's ordinary trains have a limited network and are slow and uninteresting, so few travellers use them as a means of transport.

In contrast the TAZARA service is very popular with backpackers and runs from Kapiri Mposhi to the Indian Ocean, at Dar es Salaam in Tanzania. This is a reliable international transport link which normally runs to time and is by far the fastest way between Zambia and Tanzania with the exception of flying. See *Chapter 15*'s section on *Kapiri Mposhi* for more details of this useful service.

By bus

Zambia's local buses are cheap, frequent and a great way to meet local people, although they can also be crowded, uncomfortable and noisy. In other words they are similar to any other local buses in Africa, and travel on them has both its joys and its frustrations.

In the main bus stations, there are two different kinds: the smaller minibuses, and the longer, larger 'normal' buses. Both will serve the same destinations, but the smaller ones go faster and stop less. They may also be a little more comfortable. Their larger relatives will take longer to fill up before they leave the bus station (because few buses ever leave before they are full), and then go slower and stop at more places. For the smaller, faster buses there is a premium of about 20% on top of the price.

Then there are a few 'postbuses' which operate between the post offices in the main towns, taking both mailbags and passengers as they go. These conform to a more fixed schedule, and tickets are booked in advance – thus restricting passenger numbers. They can be booked in advance from the post offices involved, or by telephoning Ndola (02) 615864, Kitwe (02) 223396, or Lusaka (01) 225795.

By coach

There are always one or two luxury coach services that connect Lusaka to Livingstone, often one service to Harare and usually one to Johannesburg. However, they seem to open and close with alarming regularity, so ask locally for the latest news on what's operating. See the *Lusaka* and *Livingstone* chapters for details of the *Trans-Zambezi Intercape* and *Euro-Africa* coaches that are running at the time of writing.

By taxi

Taxis are common and very convenient in Lusaka, Livingstone and the main towns of the Copperbelt. (Elsewhere they are uncommon or don't formally exist.) They can be hailed down in the street, and never have meters. They all have typed sheets of the 'minimum' rates to and from various local places, though charges can be higher if their customers appear affluent. Rates should always be agreed before getting into the vehicle. If you are unsure of the route then rates per kilometre, or per hour, are easy to negotiate.

By postboat

Rather like the postbuses, postboats operate on the Upper Zambezi and the waters of Lake Bangweulu during the rainy season, transporting cargo, passengers and even vehicles. Contact them by telephoning Samfya (02) 830254, Ndola (02) 617740, or Mongu (07) 221175.

Driving

Driving in Zambia is on the left, based on the UK's model. However, the standard of driving is generally poor, matched only by the quality of the roads. Most roads in the cities, and the major arteries connecting these, are tar. These vary from silky-smooth recently laid roads, to potholed routes that test the driver's skill at negotiating a 'slalom course' of deep holes, whilst avoiding the oncoming traffic that's doing the same.

Inconveniently, the smooth kind of road often changes into the holed variety without warning, so speeding on even the good tar is a dangerous occupation. Hitting a pothole at 40–60km/h will probably just blow a tyre; any faster and you risk damaging the suspension, or even rolling the vehicle.

Away from the main arteries the roads are gravel or just dirt and usually badly maintained. During the dry season these will often need a high-clearance vehicle: a 4WD is welcome here, but not vital. (The exceptions are areas of western Zambia standing on Kalahari sand, which always requires 4WD.) During the wet season Zambia's gravel roads are less forgiving, and they vary from being strictly for 4WDs to being impassable for any form of vehicle. Travel on anything except the tar roads is very difficult during the rains.

Hitchhiking

Hitchhiking around Zambia is a practical way to get around – especially in the more remote areas. Most of Zambia's poorer citizens hitchhike, and view buses as just a different form of vehicle. Either way, lifts are normally paid for.

Hitching has the great advantage of allowing you to talk one-to-one with a whole variety of people, from local business-people and expats, to truck-drivers and farmers. Sometimes you will be crammed in the back of a windy pick-up with a dozen people and as many animals, while occasionally you will be comfortably seated in the back of a plush Mercedes, satisfying the driver's curiosity as to why you are in Zambia at all. It is simply the best way to get to know the country, through the eyes of its people, though it is not for the lazy or those pressed for time.

Waiting times can be long, even on the main routes, and getting a good lift can take six or eight hours. Generally, on such occasions, the problem is not that lots of potential vehicles refuse to take you. The truth is that there are sometimes very few people going your way with space to spare. If you are in a hurry then combining hitchhiking with taking the odd bus can be a quicker and more pragmatic way to travel.

The essentials for successful hitching in Zambia include a relatively neat set of clothes, without which you will be ignored by some of the more comfortable lifts available. A good ear for listening and a relaxed line in conversation are also assets, which spring naturally from taking an interest in the lives of the people that you meet. Finally, you must always carry a few litres of water and some food with you, both for standing beside the road, and for lifts where you can't stop for food.

Dangers of drink driving

Unfortunately, drinking and driving is common in Zambia. It is more frequent in the afternoon/evening, and towards the end of the month when people are paid. Accepting a lift with someone who is drunk, or drinking and (simultaneously) driving, is foolish. Occasionally your driver will start drinking on the way, in which case you would be wise to start working out how to disembark politely.

An excuse for an exit, which I used on one occasion, was to claim that some close family member was killed whilst being driven by someone who had been drinking. Thus I had a real problem with the whole idea, and had even promised a surviving relative that I would never do the same... hence my overriding need to leave at the next reasonable town/village/stop. This gave me an opportunity to encourage the driver not to drink any more; and when that failed (which it did), it provided an excuse for me to disembark swiftly. Putting the blame on my own psychological problems avoided blaming the driver too much, which might have caused a difficult scene.

Safety of hitchhiking
Not withstanding the occasional drunk driver, Zambia is generally a safe place to hitchhike for a robust male traveller, or a couple travelling together. Dressing neatly and conservatively is a very good idea. It is safer than the UK, and considerably safer than the USA; but hitchhiking still cannot be recommended for single women, or even two women travelling together. This is not because of any known horror stories, but because non-Zambian women, especially white women, hitching would evoke intense curiosity amongst the local people. Local people might view their hitching as asking for trouble, whilst some would associate them with the 'promiscuous' behaviour of white women seen on imported films and TV programmes. The risk seems too high. Stick to buses.

ACCOMMODATION
Hotels
Hotels in Zambia tend to be large concrete blocks with pretensions to an 'international' standard, or small, run-down places catering to Zambians who are not very particular about quality.

The large hotels are restricted to Lusaka and the Copperbelt. They generally have clean modern rooms, good communications, and all the facilities that international business people expect. Their prices reflect this, at around US$70–90/£45–55 per person sharing, or US$120–140/£75–90 for a single. These generally have little to distinguish them from each other, and are pretty soulless. The only alternatives are a few game-lodge-cum-hotels which are within reach of Lusaka – like Lilayi, Chisamba, Chaminuka and Lechwe Lodge. These have more character and make more interesting places to stay than the international hotels – but they're further away from town and take time to get to.

Zambia's smaller and cheaper hotels vary tremendously, but very few are good and many seem over-priced. Zambian hotels are a very uninspiring bunch on the whole, so most visitors spend as little time in them as possible.

Guesthouses
In the last few years Zambia's larger towns, and especially Lusaka, have seen large numbers of small, pleasant guesthouses beginning to spring up throughout the more spacious suburbs. These are not very practical if you need a courtesy bus to the airport, room service, or a telephone beside your bed – but they are often full of character and very good value. Expect them to cost US$20–40/£12–25 per person sharing, or US$30–60/£20–40 for a single.

Government resthouses
These are dotted around the country in virtually every small town: a very useful option for the stranded backpacker. The town or district council usually runs them and, although a few have degenerated into brothels, others are adequate for a brief overnight stop. The sheets are usually clean, and most have rooms with private facilities. These are normally clean, though rarely spotless or in mint condition.

Lodges and bushcamps

Zambia's lodges and bushcamps are a match for the best in Africa. As befits a destination for visitors who take their game viewing and birdwatching seriously, the camps are very comfortable but concentrate on good guiding rather than luxury *per se*. En-suite showers and toilets are almost universal, the accommodation is fairly spacious, the organisation smooth and food invariably good to excellent. However, few forget that their reputations are won and lost by the standards of their individual guides.

Aside from larger operations like Mfuwe and Chichele Lodge (which are different in emphasis), expect a maximum of ten to eighteen guests, and close personal care. But beware: if you seek a safari for its image, wanting to sleep late and then be pampered in the bush; or expect to dine from silverware and sip from cut-glass goblets... then perhaps Zambia isn't for you after all.

FOOD AND DRINK
Food

Zambia's native cuisine is based on *nshima,* a cooked porridge made from ground maize. This is usually made thin, perhaps with sugar, for breakfast, then eaten thicker – the consistency of mashed potatoes – for lunch and dinner. For these main meals it will normally be accompanied by some tasty relish, perhaps made of meat and tomatoes, or dried fish. (In Zimbabwe this is *sadza*, in South Africa *mealie-pap*.)

You should taste this at some stage when visiting. Safari camps will often prepare it if requested, and it is always available in small restaurants in the towns. Often these will have only three items on the menu: nshima and chicken; nshima and meat; and nshima and fish – and they can be very good.

Camps, hotels and lodges that cater to overseas visitors will serve a very international fare, and the quality of food prepared in the most remote bushcamps amazes visitors. Coming to Zambia on safari your biggest problem with food is likely to be the temptation to eat too much.

RECIPE FOR FRIED TERMITES
Judi Helmholz

November typically marks the beginning of the rainy season in Zambia. The first rains bring vast swarms of termites out of their nests to find mates and reproduce. Termites are a once-a-year delicacy not to be missed for culinary adventurers. And capturing them is half the fun!

Termites are attracted to light, so it's easiest to catch them when they are swarming around one in the evening. Get a large bowl and fill it with water. Catch live termites with your hand as they fly around and drop them into the water (which keeps them from flying or crawling out). Or you can wait until the morning and collect them off the ground after they have dropped their wings (then you don't have to pull the wings off yourself). Gather as many as you need, live ones only.

Preparation Remove any wings from termites and throw wings away. Place wingless termites in a colander or bowl to rinse. Rinse them under running water. Heat a frying pan and a dash of cooking oil until sizzling temperature. Drop in live termites and sauté until they are crisp and golden brown (about one minute). Add salt to taste. Serve in a bowl as you would peanuts. *Bon appétit!*

If you are driving yourself around and plan to cook, then get most of your supplies in Lusaka or the larger towns. Shoprite stores have revolutionised what's available, and really have all that you will need. Away from Shoprite, in the smaller towns, availability is limited to products which are popular locally. These include bread, flour, rice, soups and various tinned vegetables, meats, and fish. This is fine for nutrition, but you may get bored with the selection in a week or two.

Alcohol

Like most countries in the region, Zambia has two distinct beer types: clear and opaque. Most visitors and more affluent Zambians drink the **clear beers**, which are similar to European lagers and always served chilled. Mosi, Castle and Rhino are the lagers brewed by South African Breweries' Zambian subsidiaries. They are widely available and usually good. There is one craft brewery in Zambia which makes Dr. Livingstone's Lager, Zikomo Copper Ale, Safari Stout and Baobab White, which is brewed with the fruit from the baobab tree.

Note that all beer produced in Zambia has a deposit on its bottles, like those of soft drinks. The contents will cost about US$0.50/Kw1,100 from a shop, or about US$1.30/Kw3,000 in a hotel bar. Imported lagers such as Windhoek, Holsten and Amstel will cost almost double this.

Less affluent Zambians usually opt for some form of the **opaque beer** (sometimes called Chibuku, after the market-leading brand). This is a commercial version of traditional beer, usually brewed from maize and/or sorghum. It's a sour, porridge-like brew, an acquired taste. Costing around Kw1,000 for a litre carton, it is much cheaper than lager. Locals will sometimes buy a bucket of it, and then pass this around a circle of drinkers. It would be unusual for a visitor to drink this, so try some and amuse your Zambian companions.

Remember that traditional opaque beer changes flavour as it ferments and you

ABOUT CIGARETTES AND BEER
Willard Nakutonga and Judi Helmholz

There are several types of beer or Mooba (meaning 'beer' in Nyanja) produced in Zambia, including the following brews:

Mosi Lager is a bottled beer reflecting the local name for Victoria Falls – '*Mosi Oa Tunya*', meaning the 'Smoke that Thunders'. It is one of the most popular beers in Zambia. **Rhino Lager** is another bottled beer, produced and distributed throughout Zambia. You can ask for it by saying *Nifuna mooba wa* Rhino – I want rhino beer.

Chibuku or **Shake-Shake** is a much cheaper, opaque beer. Resembling an alcoholic milkshake, it is an acquired taste and a favourite amongst more traditional and less affluent Zambians.

Kachusu is the name for the main illicit beer – akin to 'moonshine'. It is brewed in villages or at shebeens, and it is wise never to agree to drink this. Not only is it illegal, so you may be arrested for just drinking it, but it may also damage your liver and kidneys.

Cigarettes, or *fwaka* in Nyanja, can be purchased almost anywhere. In local markets, you can find big bins of raw tobacco, or tobacco shavings, on sale for those who like to roll their own. The most popular brand available in Zambia is Peter Stuyvesant, affectionately referred to as 'Peters'. Don't even think about trying *mbanje* or *dagga* (marijuana); if you're arrested there is no bail, and the penalty is five years in prison with hard labour.

can often ask for 'fresh beer' or 'strong beer'. If you aren't sure about the bar's hygiene standards, stick to the pre-packaged brands of opaque beer like Chibuku, Chinika, Golden, Chipolopolo or Mukango.

Soft drinks

Soft drinks are available everywhere, which is fortunate when the temperatures are high. Choices are often limited, though the ubiquitous Coca-Cola is usually there and the price is usually around US$0.75/Kw1,000. Diet drinks are rarely seen in the rural areas – which is no surprise for a country where malnutrition is a problem.

Try to buy up at least one actual bottle (per person) in a city before you go travelling: it will be invaluable. Because of the cost of bottle production, and the 'deposit' system (a standard US$0.25/Kw600 per bottle), you will often be unable to buy full bottles of soft drinks in the rural areas without swapping them for empty ones in return. The alternative is to stand and drink the contents where you buy a drink, and leave the empty behind you. This is fine, but can be inconvenient if you have just dashed in for a drink while your bus stops for a few minutes.

Water

Water in the main towns is usually purified, provided there are no shortages of chlorine, breakdowns, or other mishaps. The locals drink it, and are used to the relatively innocuous bugs that it may harbour. If you are in the country for a long time, then it may be worth acclimatising yourself to it – though be prepared for some days spent near a toilet. However, if you are in Zambia for just a few weeks, then try to drink only bottled, boiled, or treated water in town – otherwise you will get stomach upsets.

Out in the bush, most of the camps and lodges use water from bore-holes. These underground sources vary in quality, but are normally free from bugs so the water is perfectly safe to drink. Sometimes it is sweet, at other times a little alkaline or salty. Ask the locals if it is suitable for an unacclimatised visitor to drink, then take their advice.

Tipping

Tipping is (I'm told) illegal, but is used widely and often expected, though the amounts are small. Helpers with baggage might expect US$0.50 equivalent, whilst sorting out a problematic reservation would be US$2–3. Restaurants will often add an automatic service charge to the bill, in which case a tip is not obligatory. If they do not do this, 10% would certainly be appreciated if the service was good.

A tip is seen, by some, as a polite way to reward someone for a favour, and thus can sometimes be used as a bribe for services rendered. See the general comments on *Bribery*, at the end of *Chapter 6*.

WHAT TO BUY
Curios

Zambia's best bargains are handicrafts: carvings and baskets made locally. The curio stall near the border to the Falls has an excellent selection, but prices are lower if you buy within Zambia, in Lusaka or at some of the roadside stalls.

Kabwata Cultural Centre, page 136, is an obvious place to do some shopping. Wherever you buy handicrafts, don't be afraid to bargain gently. Expect an eventual reduction of about one quarter of the original asking price and always be polite and good-humoured. After all, a few cents will probably make more difference to the person with whom you are bargaining than it will mean to you.

Note that you will often see carvings on sale in the larger stalls which have been imported from Kenya, Tanzania, DRC and Zimbabwe. Assume that they would be cheaper if purchased in their countries of origin, and try to buy something Zambian as a memento of your trip.

Occasionally you will be offered 'precious' stones to buy – rough diamonds, emeralds and the like. Expert geologists may spot the occasional genuine article amongst hoards of fakes, but most mere mortals will end up being conned. Stick to the carvings if you want a bargain.

Supplies

In the past four years Zambia's shops have emerged from a retailing time-warp, where cramped corner-shops had the monopoly. Until a few years ago, most of the country's residents were innocent of consumer-friendly hypermarkets where wide, ergonomically designed aisles are lined with endless choice.

Then, in 1996, Shoprite/Checkers arrived promoting a largely alien practice of high volume, low margin superstores using good levels of pay to reward honest employees. This rocked Lusaka's existing, mainly Asian, shop-owning community – who had always gone for the high-margin corner-shop approach. Rumours were rife of the ways in which Shoprite's arrival was resisted, and even blocked by the capital's existing business community.

However, now Shoprite has now found a very solid footing. Within just a few years, it has opened stores in most of Zambia's major towns, and these are normally the best and cheapest places to shop for supplies. Increasingly you'll also find the chain's fast food subsidiary, Hungry Lion, next door, selling chips, burgers and similar hygienic (sanitised?) bites.

However, all is not rosy. To many it seems that while the state is dismantling many of its own monopolies, the private sector is being allowed to generate new ones. Many aggressive South African companies, from Shoprite to Supreme, and HI-FI to Electric City, are starting to move into Zambia and dominate it, causing resentment from local businesspeople.

Critics say the success of these is down to South Africa's policy of lucrative tax breaks which effectively subsidise exports. They fear that by allowing these new companies to build monopolies, local entrepreneurs are losing out. They point to the import bills generated by such stores, which often source more of their stock from outside Zambia than from inside.

Whatever the arguments, you can now buy most things in Zambia (and in

SIGN OF THE TIMES
Judi Helmholz

When it comes to creativity and marketing, Zambian entrepreneurs are unsurpassed. Take the 'Just Imagine Grocery Store & Bottle Shop'. Unfortunately customers often have to do just that, as there are often no groceries or bottles to be found there. Similarly, the 'Good Neighbour Grocery Store & Bottle Shop' doesn't always live up to its name, as its assistants are no strangers to price disputes.

Catchy slogans like 'We Admit We Are The Best' or 'Choice Restaurant – For All Your Super Feeding Requirements' adorn stores and shop fronts. 'No Sweat, No Sweet', the Zambian equivalent of 'no work - no reward', appears to be popular for everything from roadside stalls to school mottos to butchers' shops.

kwacha) at a price. Perhaps the best advice for the careful visitor is to try to buy Zambian products wherever possible, for the sake of the local economy.

ORGANISING AND BOOKING
Public holidays

New Year's Day	January 1
Youth Day	around March 11–13
Good Friday	
Holy Saturday	
Labour Day	May 1
Africa Freedom Day	May 25
Heroes' Day	first Monday of July
Unity Day	first Tuesday of July
Farmers' Day	first Monday of August
Independence Day	October 24
Christmas Day	December 25
Boxing Day	December 26

National parks
Head office
Currently all of Zambia's national parks fall under the control of the National Parks and Wildlife Service – known simply as the NPWS – which is a department of the Ministry of Tourism. They set the rules and administer the parks from their head office near Chilanga, about 20km south of Lusaka. However, this is currently changing into the Zambia Wildlife Authority; see *Chapter 4*, page 43, for details.

Until then, address written requests to the Chief Warden, Private Bag 1, Chilanga – though telephoning (01 278366) or calling in person will be much more effective. If you want to do anything unusual, or to go to any of the more remote parks, then it will make your trip easier if you buy your permits in advance from Chilanga. Clear your trip with them, and get some written permission that looks official: a letter from Chilanga and the appropriate permits work wonders at even the most remote scout camps.

The next best option is to try to get permission at the regional NPWS offices – which will probably be easier than negotiating with the scouts on the gate.

Entry permits
Most organised trips will include park entry fees in their costs, but if you are travelling on your own then you must pay these directly, either at NPWS offices or in the parks. There is a scale of entry fees, and separate charges for camping in the parks. Currently South Luangwa costs US$20/£13 per person per day, whilst Kafue, Lower Zambezi, Lochinvar and Sumbu are US$10/£7. The rest cost US$5/£3.50 per person per day. On top of these, vehicles are charged US$5/£3.50 per entry, and camping within the park is another US$15/£10 per person per night.

Guides
For more adventurous trips to remote parks, hire a game scout from the nearest camp to act as your guide. This will save wasted driving time, and probably personal anguish over navigational puzzles. You may have to feed the scout, but even then this can be an inexpensive way to get a local guide who may be able to add a whole new dimension to your trip.

Wildlife and Environmental Conservation Society of Zambia (WECSZ)

Until 1998 this was called the Wildlife Conservation Society of Zambia, and universally known as the WCSZ. Now the society is keen to emphasise its broader remit for the environment in its widest sense. (This goes along with the global shift in thinking from just protecting parks and animals, to looking after the whole environment and the local people as well.)

Its work remains similar, supporting environmental education and awareness in Zambia. It sponsors various conservation activities; runs innovative children's conservation clubs, like the Chongololo clubs; publishes a number of good, inexpensive field guides specific to Zambia (see *Further Reading*).

It also owns several very simple camps in the National Parks – Kafwala and David Shepherd camps in Kafue, and the Wildlife Camp at Mfuwe – and although these are managed by others, some of the revenue still comes back to the WECSZ. Bookings for these camps can be made in person or by post, through the WECSZ, PO Box 30255, Lusaka; tel: 254226 or 251630; email: wcsz@zamnet.zm.

To find out more, visit the WECSZ offices off Los Angeles Boulevard, near Longacres Lodge. Many of their books are also stocked by the bookshops in town, or even by Magenge Crafts, beside Mfuwe airport.

Membership for non-Zambians costs US$35 per person per year, or US$100 for supporter.

COMMUNICATIONS AND MEDIA
Post

The post is neither cheap nor fast, though it is fairly reliable for letters and postcards. The charges are increased to keep pace with devaluations of the kwacha, but currently it costs around Kw700 to send a postcard and Kw900 for a letter.

Couriers are a very reliable way of sending things safely, but they are expensive. See under *Lusaka*, page 142, for contact details. A more affordable alternative is Mercury Mail, below.

Mercury Mail

Mercury is an international courier company, like DHL or UPS. As well as offering a normal courier service, they offer a much cheaper international mail service. It works by couriering post along with their normal courier shipments to 'hubs' in other countries. From there they are posted by reliable first-class mail. Thus they avoid the Zambian postal service, but do use the (normally reliable) post in the UK, for example.

So far, this is set up to send mail from anywhere via London to Zambia, and from Zambia to Johannesburg, Harare or anywhere in the world (via the London hub). Note that there is no track-and-trace facility, and so valuable or urgent documents are better couriered using their full, more expensive service, which is proving generally fast and reliable. In Zambia, their posting/collection points are:

Lusaka Mercury Couriers Head Office PO Box 33333, 47 Joseph Mwilwa Rd, Rhodes Park. Tel: 01 231137 or 239872; fax: 01 239872
Ndola NEI Building, Lufunsa Av. Tel/fax: 02 620187
Kitwe Foyer of Hotel Edinburgh. Tel: 02 230172; fax: 02 230173
Livingstone John Hunt Way (beside Living Inn). Tel: 03 321571
Mfuwe c/o Moondogs Café at the airport
Kasama c/o Kasama Service Station

Sending mail from the UK to Zambia

From the UK (or anywhere else in the world), you address your letter clearly to the recipient, including the name of the closest Mercury office. Then you write their phone number on the outside of the envelope. Eg: *Mr A Zambian, c/o Mercury Mail (Lusaka), Mr A's address, Lusaka. Mr A's telephone at work: 01 123456; at home 01 234567.*

Then you place this inside another envelope addressed to *Mercury Couriers – Lusaka (or whichever Mercury office), Trans-Africa Air Express, Unit 15, Britannia Industrial Estate, Poyle Road, Colnbrook, Slough SL3 0ER.* To check that this service still operates, telephone 01753 749090 in the UK. (Note there is no 'trace' facility here, so there's no point in asking them about mail you have sent.)

You pay for just the stamp to send the envelope to Mercury's UK office. When the package arrives at the relevant Zambian office, the recipient is called and told about the package. S/he then pays the freight costs from London to Zambia (which are a lot less than courier fees) when collecting it from the office.

Because of this, don't send unsolicited mail through the system without first checking with the Zambian companies that they are prepared to pay to receive it. Also note that if the recipient isn't on the phone, then this system won't work unless they are prepared to regularly drop into the Mercury office.

Sending mail from Zambia

You can send mail outward to basically anywhere. It'll be sent out of Zambia with the normal courier shipments, and then put in the hands of the local postal service at the destination country. Simply take it to one of the Mercury offices. A 100g letter currently costs US$2.20 to the UK, South Africa or Zimbabwe, US$2.80 to the rest of Europe, and US$4.20 to anywhere else in the world. The maximum weight that you can send is 2kg, which would cost US$21.10 to the UK, South Africa or Zimbabwe, US$27.70 to the rest of Europe, or US$40.30 to anywhere else.

Telephone

The Zambian telephone system is overloaded and has difficulty coping. Getting through to anywhere can be hard, and this difficulty generally increases in proportion to the remoteness of the place that you are trying to contact. If you must use the phone, then persistence is the key – just keep on trying and eventually you should get a line that works.

To dial into the country from abroad, the international access code for Zambia is 260. From inside Zambia, you dial 00 to get an international line, then the country's access code (eg: 44 for the UK, or 1 for the USA).

New lines are difficult to acquire from the state-owned company that has a monopoly over the phone system, and old ones can take time to repair. Thus for local people or companies to have four or five different numbers is very common. Just try them all until one works for you.

The old payphones used to be always out of order, but recently cardphones have been springing up. You can dial internationally from these, and you buy cards containing credits for various different amounts.

Regional codes in Zambia

There are only 12 regional codes in Zambia, most of which cover large regions of the country. The main towns associated with these codes are:

01 Chilanga; Chirundu; Chisamba; Chongwe; Kafue; Luangwa; Lusaka; Mumbwa; Namalundu Gorge; Nampundwe; Siavonga

02 Chambishi; Chililabombwe; Chingola; Itimpi; Kalulushi; Kawambwa; Kitwe;
Luanshya; Mansa; Masaiti; Mufulira; Mwense; Nchelenge; Ndola; Samfya
03 Livingstone
032 Choma; Gwembe; Itezhi-Tezhi; Kalomo; Maamba; Mazabuka; Monze; Namwala; Pemba
04 Chinsali; Isoka; Kasama; Luwingu; Mbala; Mpika; Mporokoso; Mpulungu; Mungwi;
Nakonde
05 Chibombo; Kabwe; Kapiri Mposhi; Mkushi; Serenje
062 Chadiza; Chipata; Katete; Mfuwe; Sinda
063 Nyimba; Petauke
064 Chama; Lundazi
07 Kalabo; Kaoma; Lukulu; Mongu; Senanga
08 Kabompo; Kasempa; Mufumbwe; Mwinilunga; Solwezi; Zambezi

Fax

If you are trying to send a fax to, or within, Zambia then *always* use a manual setting
to dial (and redial, and redial...) the number. Listen for a fax tone on the line
yourself. Only when you finally hear one should you press the 'start' button on
your machine to send the fax.

Telex

Telex machines are becoming less and less common in Zambia, but where they do
exist they provide communication which you can instantly verify. You need not
worry if your message has arrived, as the answer-back code will confirm that for you.

Email and the internet

Contrary to what you may have expected, the email community in Zambia is quite
large. Initially, virtually all websites and addresses were accessed through the
Zamnet Server, which was associated with the University of Zambia. This has split
from the university to become a separate company, but not before users
encountered numerous problems using it, earning it a wide variety of nicknames.
'Damnet' was one of the less offensive.

Now Zamnet is located near the south end of Cairo Road, by the roundabout,
in the USIS Building (which used to be the Meridian Bank). Short-term users can
drop in and use the computers and email for about US$3.50 per half-hour.

Because of the problems with Zamnet, many email subscribers are in the
process of changing their addresses, some to alternative service providers within
Zambia and others to providers outside (usually linked by satellite telephone
systems, in order to avoid the telephone problems).

Note that although increasing numbers of people and businesses in Zambia are
getting email, far fewer have access to the internet.

For information on travel to/in Zambia, there are two obvious sites on the web.
Firstly this book, and later updates to it, will be appearing on Sunvil Discovery's
website – www.sunvil.co.uk/africa/ – along with my other guidebooks and
considerable information on Sunvil Discovery's trips to Southern Africa.

Secondly, there is an extensive site produced by African Insites – www.africa-
insites.com/zambia/ – which has a lot of pictures and advertising from Zambian
companies, as well as general descriptions of areas and travel information.

Media
The press

The main daily papers are *The Post*, which is privately owned and fairly
independent, and the *Times of Zambia* and the *Daily Mail*, both of which are owned

by the government. The *Financial Mail* is part of the *Daily Mail*, as are the *Sunday Mail* and the *Sunday Times*. On the whole, *The Post* is the most outspoken and interesting paper.

There are also several weekly papers, including the *National Mirror* and several which are very political. There are also a few good monthlies, including *The Farmer*, *Profit* and the indispensable *Lusaka Lowdown*.

Zambia claims to have a free press, and most issues are debated openly. However, when the more sensitive ones are skirted around, only *The Post* tries to take a more investigative approach. Often this is respected, but see Zambia's most recent history in *The late 1990s*, page 15, for an example of an incident when the authorities were less than respectful in their approach.

You can find the very the latest news from *The Post* in Zambia on the web at www.zamnet.zm/zamnet/post/post.html, or from the *Times of Zambia* at www.zamnet.zm/zamnet/times/times.html. Some of the stories can be fascinating, so it's well worth having a look before you go.

Radio and TV

Radio is limited, as Zambia National Broadcasting Corporation, ZNBC, runs three channels which are all used as government communication tools: Radio 1, Home Service and Radio 4. (Radio 4 used to be the rather fun Radio Mulungushi, until it was swallowed up.)

There is some good news though, as in the cities – especially Lusaka – you'll find smaller commercial stations. The obvious is probably Phoenix Radio, which broadcasts popular music and Zambian news, though it's worth scanning the airwaves. Outside of the large cities, you'll find little, although those with short-wave radios can always seek the BBC World Service, the Voice of America, and Radio Canada.

The public TV stations are also run by ZNBC. They broadcast only in the evenings, from about 17.00 to 23.00, and stick to the official party line on most issues. That said, do tune in – some of their panel debates can be fascinating! Many of the larger hotels with TVs in rooms will also subscribe to satellite TV channels, often including BBC World, CNN, and/or the South African cable network, Mnet, with its multitude of sports and movie channels.

MISCELLANEOUS
Electricity

The local voltage is 220V, delivered at 50Hz. Sockets fit plugs with three square pins, like the current design in the UK.

Embassies

There's often a list of Lusaka's diplomatic missions, including those in neighbouring countries when necessary, in the front of the telephone directory.

Angolan Embassy 6660 Mumana Rd, Olympia Rd Ext, PO Box 31598, Lusaka. Tel: 01 290346/291142; fax: 292592/5

Australian Embassy Australian High Commission, Memaco House, Cairo Rd, Lusaka

Belgian Embassy Anglo American Building, 3rd Floor, 74 Independence Av, Woodlands, PO Box 31204, Lusaka 10101. Tel: 01 252344/252512/252909; fax: 01 250075; telex: ZA 40000 amgel

Botswana High Commission 5201 Pandit Nehru Rd, Diplomatic Triangle, PO Box 31910, Lusaka. Tel: 01 250555/250019/252058; fax: 253895; tlx: ZA 41710

Brazilian Embassy Anglo American Building, 74 Independence Av, Woodlands, PO Box 34470, Lusaka. Tel: 01 250400; fax: 251652; tlx: ZA 40102

British High Commission Diplomatic Triangle, 5210 Independence Av, PO Box 50050, Lusaka. Tel: 01 251133; fax: 253798; tlx: ZA 41150 UKREP

Bulgarian Embassy 4045 Lusaka Rd, Sunningdale, PO Box 32896, Lusaka. Tel: 01 263295

Canadian High Commission 5199 United Nations Av, PO Box 31313, Lusaka. Tel: 01 250833; fax: 254176; email lsaka@paris03.x400.gc.ca

Chinese Embassy 7430 United Nations Av (corner of Haile Selassie), PO Box 31975, Lusaka. Tel: 01 253770/252410/251169; fax: 251157

Cuban Embassy 5574 Magoye Rd, Kalundu, PO Box 33132, Lusaka. Tel: 01 291308/80; 291586

Danish Embassy 2nd Floor, Ndeke House Annex, Haile Selassie Av, PO Box 50299, Lusaka. Tel :01 254277/254182/253750; fax: 254618; tlx: ZA 43580

DRC (Zaire) Embassy 1124 Perirenyatwa Rd, PO Box 31287, Lusaka. Tel: 01 213343/229044/5. (There is also a Consulate at Mpelembe House, Broadway Rd, Ndola. Tel: 02 614247.)

Egyptian Embassy Plot No. 5206, United Nations Av, Longacres, PO Box 32428, Lusaka 10101. Tel: 01 254149; tlx: ZA 40021

Finnish Embassy Anglo American Building, 6th Floor, 74 Independence Av, PO Box 50819, Lusaka. Tel: 01 251988/250213/250211/251234/252026; fax: 254981/253783; tlx: ZA 43460; email: finemb@zamnet.zm

French Embassy 4th Floor, Anglo American Building, 74 Independence Av, PO Box 30062, Lusaka. Tel: 01 251322/251340; fax: 254475; tlx: ZA 41430

German Embassy 5209 United Nations Av, PO Box 50120, Lusaka. Tel: 01 250644/251259/251262; fax: 254014; tlx: ZA 41410

Indian High Commission 1 Pandit Nehru Rd, PO Box 32111, Lusaka. Tel: 01 253159/253160/253152; fax: 254118; email: indiazam@zamnet.zm; tlx: ZA 41420

Irish Embassy 6663 Katima Mulilo Rd, Olympia Park Extension, PO Box 34923, Lusaka. Tel: 01 290650/291124/292288482; fax: 290482; tlx: ZA 43110

Italian Embassy 5211 Embassy Park, Diplomatic Triangle, PO Box 31046, Lusaka 10101. Tel: 01 250755/250781/250783; fax: 254929; email: italyzam@zamnet.zm; tlx: ZA 43380 ITALDI

Japanese Embassy 5218 Haile Selassie Av, PO Box 34190, Lusaka. Tel: 01 291693/251555; fax: 224421; tlx: ZA 41470

Kenyan High Commission 5207 United Nations Av, PO Box 50298; Lusaka. Tel: 01 250722/250742/250751; fax: 253829; tlx: ZA 42470

Korean Embassy 8237 Nangwenya Rd, Rhodes Park, PO Box 34030, Lusaka. Tel: 01 252978/252994; fax: 261476

Malawian High Commission 5th Floor, Woodgate House, Cairo Rd, PO Box 50425, Lusaka. Tel: 01 228296–8; fax: 223352; tlx: ZA 41840

Mozambique Embassy Plot 9592, Kacha Rd, Northmead, PO Box 34877, Lusaka. Tel: 01 220333/217671; fax: 220345; tlx: ZA 45900

Namibian High Commission 6968 Kabanga Rd, Rhodes Park, Lusaka. Tel: 01 252250/250968; fax: 252497

Netherlands Embassy Plot 5208, United Nations Av, PO Box 31905, Lusaka. Tel: 01 253590/253994/253819; fax: 253733/250220; tlx: ZA 42690

Nigerian High Commission 5203 Haile Selassie Av, PO Box 32598, Lusaka. Tel: 01 253177/253365/253268; fax: 253560; tlx: ZA 41280

Norwegian High Commission 65 Birdcage Walk, Haile Selassie Av, PO Box 34570, Lusaka. Tel: 01 252188/252625; fax: 253915; tlx: ZA 40100

Portuguese Embassy 23 Yotam Muleya Rd, Woodlands, PO Box 33871, Lusaka. Tel: 01 260296; fax: 253893/6; tlx: ZA 40010

Russian Embassy Plot No 6407, Diplomatic Triangle, PO Box 32355, Lusaka.

Tel: 01 252120/252128/252183; fax: 253582; tlx: ZA 40341
Saudi Arabian Embassy 4896 Los Angeles Bd, PO Box 33441, Lusaka.
Tel: 01 253266/253325; fax: 253449; tlx; ZA 40341
Somalian Embassy 377A Kabulonga Rd, PO Box 34051, Lusaka. Tel: 01 262119/263944; tlx: ZA 40270
South African High Commission 4th Floor, Bata House, Cairo Rd, P bag W369, Lusaka. Tel: 01 228443/9; fax: 223268
Swedish Embassy Haile Selassie Av (opposite Ndeke House), PO Box 30788, Lusaka. Tel: 01 251711; fax: 254049; tlx: ZA 41820
Tanzanian High Commission Ujaama House, 5200 United Nations Av, PO Box 31219, Lusaka. Tel: 01 253320/23/24 or 253222; fax: 254861
United Kingdom – see *British High Commission*, above
United States Embassy Independence Av (corner of United Nations Av), PO Box 31617, Lusaka. Tel: 01 250955; fax: 252225; tlx: ZA 41970
Zimbabwean High Commission 4th Floor, Memaco House, Cairo Rd (south end, next to Findeco House), Lusaka. Tel: 01 229382/3

Hospitals and dentists

Should you need one, there are good hospitals in Zambia. However, the public health system is over-stretched and under-funded – so unless your illness is critical, it will take time for you to be attended to and treated at the public hospitals. Also a large number of patients in the public hospitals have serious infectious diseases, so there's a risk of coming away from these with something worse than you had when you arrived.

In the main cities – Lusaka, Livingstone and the Copperbelt – there are better-funded private hospitals that cater for both affluent Zambians and expats/diplomatic staff. These are much better, and will accept payment from genuine travel health insurance schemes.

Pharmacies in Lusaka have a basic range of medicines, though specific brands are often unavailable. So bring with you all that you will need, as well as a repeat prescription for anything that you might run out of. Outside of Lusaka, Livingstone, and perhaps the larger cities of the Copperbelt, you will be lucky to find anything other than very basic medical supplies. Thus you should carry a very comprehensive medical kit if you are planning to head off independently into the wilds.

Imports and exports

There is no problem in exporting normal curios, but you will need an official export permit from the Department of National Parks to take out any game trophies. Visitors are urged to support the letter and the spirit of the CITES bans on endangered species, including the ban on the international trade in ivory. This has certainly helped to reduce ivory poaching, so don't undermine it by buying ivory souvenirs here. In any case, you will probably have big problems when you try to import them back into your home country.

Maps

Excellent maps covering the whole of Zambia are available in Lusaka and the major cities, if you can find them. By far the best place for maps is the main government map office at the Ministry of Lands, in the basement of Mulungushi House (very close to the junction between United Nations and Independence Avenue; see page 119).

There are several different series kept here, including the useful 1:250,000 series, a number of town plans, some 'tourist' maps of the parks and many more detailed maps of selected areas. Some are always out of print – but you can usually find at least some sort of map to cover most areas.

Part Two

The Guide

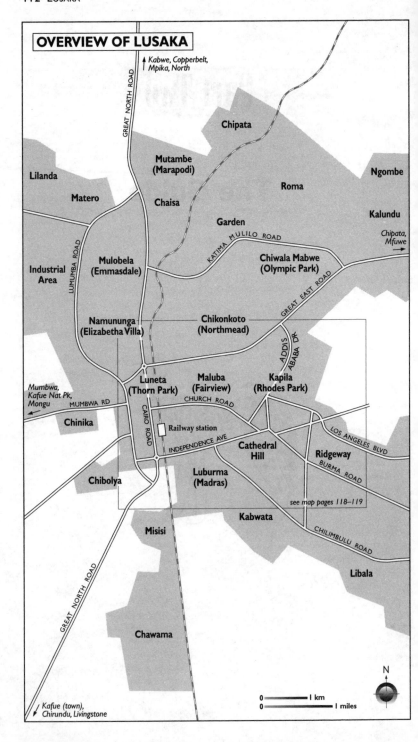

OVERVIEW OF LUSAKA

Lusaka

Despite the assertions of the tourist board, Lusaka is still not high on Zambia's list of major attractions. Its wide tree-lined boulevards can be pleasant, but the traffic is chaotic and many of the suburbs are sprawling and dirty. However, Lusaka is no worse than London, New York, or any number of other big cities. Like them, it has a fascination because it is unmistakably cosmopolitan, alive and kicking. As home to one-tenth of Zambia's people, it has a discernible heartbeat which smaller or more sanitised cities lack. So if you go to Zambia with an interest in meeting a cross-section of its people, Lusaka should figure on your itinerary.

In my experience, the city's bad reputation for crime is exaggerated. It is certainly unsafe for the unwary – but less so than Nairobi or Johannesburg. Walking around at night is stupid, and during the day pickpockets will strike if you keep valuables obvious or accessible. However, visitors to Lusaka who allow their paranoia to elevate the city's dangers to the dizzy heights of Lagos are deluding themselves. It isn't *that* dangerous, if you are careful.

The rest of this chapter aims to provide you with some useful contact details, help you find places to stay and eat that will suit your budget, and suggest options for spending your spare time.

GETTING THERE AND AWAY
By air

Lusaka is well served by international flights, though regional flights catering to overseas visitors sometimes by-pass the city to serve Livingstone and/or Mfuwe instead. Currently British Airways is the main intercontinental carrier from Europe direct to Zambia, but other carriers are possible if you use neighbouring African capitals as gateways to the region. See *Planning and Preparations,* page 45, for more details of the best fares to Zambia, and *Zambia Today,* page 94, for general comments on getting around the country by air. International airlines represented in Lusaka include:

Air Angola PO Box 37731, Lusaka. Tel: 01 222401/221684; fax: 238633; tlx: ZA 40550
Air Botswana c/o Steve Blagus Travel, Nkwazi Rd, PO Box 31530.
Tel: 01 227739/40 or 227285; fax: 223724; tlx: ZA 43320
Air France Chindo Rd, Woodlands. Tel: 01 264930/36; airport tel: 271212; fax: 264950; tlx: ZA 41390
Air India 1st Floor, Shop 4, Findeco House, Cairo Rd, PO Box 34471.
Tel: 01 223128 or 226349; fax: 228124
Air Malawi ZNIB House, PO Box 36384, Cairo Rd. Tel: 01 228120/21; fax 228124
Air Namibia c/o Premier Travel and Tours. Tel: 01 226568; fax: 222710
Air Tanzania 5300 Pandit Nehru Rd, PO Box 32635. Tel: 01 251189

Air Zimbabwe 2 Kalidas Building (next to Society House), Cairo Rd, PO Box 35191.
Tel: 01 225431 or 225540
British Airways Holiday Inn, PO Box 22006. Tel: 01 254444/53/73; fax: 250623
Kenya Airways Findeco House, PO Box 31856. Tel: 01 228484-6; tlx: ZA 40460
South African Airways Ground Floor, Hotel Intercontinental.
Tel: 01 254350/352/357/369/394 or 253953.

The charter companies and local airlines based in Lusaka have had a chequered
past, with companies forming and disappearing with monotonous regularity. Since
the national carrier, Zambia Airways, went down nothing has successfully replaced
it. Zambia Express looked promising, but then disappeared in mid-'98, taking with
it the cash from many advance bookings.

The current contenders are wisely sticking to domestic routes. Aero Zambia is
included here because, despite its recent problems, it may still survive. Of the
others, Zambian Airways (formerly Roan Air) has the best planes. Their 19-seaters
are so shiny and new they make you wonder who found the money to buy them.
Proflight are consistently reliable, but really a large charter company with a few
scheduled routes. They've a long way to go before they compete on a larger scale.

Outside of Zambia (and even inside sometimes), most travel agents won't have
a clue about the intricacies of Zambia's internal flights. So make sure that you
arrange flights through a specialist tour operator that knows and understands the
situation here. If you need to arrange something whilst you are in Zambia, or need
to contact an airlines in a hurry, then try the following:

Aero Zambia Zambia Insurance Brokers House, Dedan Kimathi Road, P Bag 8717,
Lusaka. Tel: 01 226111 or 225848; fax: 226147
Avocet Air Charters Tel: 01 233422 (airport) or 264866 (after hours); cell: 702056;
fax: 229261/2
Eastern Air c/o Steve Blagus Travel, Nkwazi Rd, PO Box 31530. Tel: 01 227739/40 or
227285; fax: 223724; tlx: ZA 43320
Proflight PO Box 30536, Lusaka. Tel: 01 264439 or 263686 or 263687; airport tel: 271437;
fax: 222888/262379
Zambian Airways (formerly Roan Air) PO Box 310277, Lusaka International Airport.
Tel: 01 271066 or 271230; tlx: ZA 40410
Stabo Air Charters Tel: 01 235976 (24-hour); cell: 771822; fax: 233481
Staravia PO Box 34273, Lusaka. Tel: 01 291962; airport tel: 01 271332/3

Lusaka Airport

The airport is well signposted, if isolated, at 25km from the centre, off the Great
East Road. Transport there is either by the courtesy buses of the big hotels
(Intercontinental, Holiday Inn or Taj Pamodzi), or by private taxi. A taxi should
cost around Kw50,000/US$20 between the airport and the city, though this is the
route for which the drivers will charge most imaginatively.

As you approach the airport, the road splits into two. The left fork goes to the
private hangars of the smaller airlines, Aero Zambia, Zambian Airways (formerly
Roan Air), Eastern Air, Proflight and Star Avia. If you are taking one of these
flights, then you will usually go directly to the relevant hangar. Most courtesy
buses will drop you at the right place, if you ask the driver.

Otherwise, head for the main terminal on the right, which services the larger
airlines and the international flights.

If you are arriving into the main terminal and connecting to one of the smaller
airlines for an internal flight, say Proflight, then there will normally be someone
from Proflight to meet you in the main terminal, and transfer you through to their

hangar. If in doubt, ask at the helpful information desk in the airport's main hall.

By bus
Local buses
The Intercity Bus Terminal is a noisy, bustling station sheltering under a large purpose-built roof, on the western side of Dedan Kimathi Road. It is not a place to go idly strolling at night, or to display your valuables, but it is the obvious place to catch a bus to virtually any of Zambia's main towns. Locals are paranoid about thieves who frequent the area, so expect warnings about safety. However, if you keep your belongings with you and are careful, then you should have no problems. Despite the apparent confusion that greets you, there is some order to the Terminal's chaos. The buses sitting in bays are grouped roughly by their eventual destinations, as indicated by the white boards displayed next to the driver. If you can't see the name you want, then ask someone – most people will go out of their way to help.

Generally there are two different prices for any given place: a higher one to travel in a smaller, faster minibus, and a lower rate for the larger, slower normal buses. Expect about a 20% premium for a minibus.

Most buses (big or small) will not leave until they are full, which can take hours. If possible, it is better not to pay until the bus has started on its way, as you may want to swap buses if another appears to be filling faster and hence is likely to depart earlier. Buses to some destinations leave frequently, others weekly – dependent upon demand. The only way to find out is to go there and ask. Just a few of the many options include:

To Livingstone Four or five buses per day, leaving between 07.00 and 11.00; costs Kw16,500 for a minibus or Kw15,000/US$6 for an ordinary bus.
To Kitwe Numerous departures, mostly in the morning and early afternoon; costs Kw12,000/US$4.80 for a minibus or Kw10,000/US$4 for an ordinary bus.
To Kapiri Mposhi Numerous departures throughout the day; costs Kw9,000/US$3.60 for a minibus or Kw7,000 for an ordinary bus.
To Chipata About three buses per day, costing around Kw16,500/US$6.60 per person.
To Mongu Normally two buses per day, on in the early morning, and another in the afternoon; costs Kw18,000/US$7.20 for a minibus or Kw13,500/US$5.40 for an ordinary bus.

A few international buses also leave from here to Zimbabwe, including:

To Harare Run by Dzimiri Special Buses, departing once a day, Mon–Sun, between about 09.00 and 10.00; costs Kw18,000/US$7.20 (Z$300).
To Lilongwe Departs Tuesday, Fridays and Sundays around 08.00; costs Kw25,000/US$10.
To Dar es Salaam Departs every day; takes about two days to reach destination. Costs around Kw35,000/US$14.

Postbuses
The post office runs a very limited number of scheduled buses for mail, which only stop at post offices. Seats can be booked in advance for passengers. These are quicker and less crowded than the normal local buses (they claim to run to a timetable), though not more comfortable.

The booking office for postbuses is at their depot, behind the main post office, off Cairo Road and Dar-es-Salaam Place. Book three days before departure for either of their three routes:

To Kasama Costs Kw15,500/US$6.20 and stops at Kabwe, Kapiri Mposhi, Mkushi, Serenje, Mpika and Kanona. Departs Wednesday at 07.00.

To Mongu Costs Kw12,000US\$4.80 and stops at Mumbwa and Kaoma. Departs Saturday at 07.00.

To Chipata Costs Kw12,500/US\$5 and stops at Nyimba, Petauke, Sinda and Katete. Departs Monday at 07.30.

The above costs reduce proportionately if you alight at a town en route. These buses return to Lusaka on the day following their outward journey. Tickets can be booked at local post offices where they stop, but note that these buses cannot be hailed from the roadside.

Luxury coaches

Coach operators seem to come and go, so ask around Cairo Road's travel agents for the latest news.

To/from South Africa

Trans-Zambezi Intercape (tel: 251369/58; fax: 254917), under the Intercontinental Hotel (see page 120) on Haile Selassie Avenue, runs a luxury, express coach service to Johannesburg, complete with videos and music. This is booked in advance from them.

The coach departs from the side of the Intercontinental Hotel on Sundays, Wednesdays and Fridays at 13.30. At 21.00 it normally stops for a break at the Holiday Inn Hotel in Harare, and passes through Petersberg in South Africa at 10.00 the following morning. It arrives at Park Station (the Transit Centre) in Johannesburg at about 13.30 the following day. The cost is US\$80 oneway.

It returns on Tuesdays, Thursdays and Sundays, departing from Jo'burg at 09.00 and arriving in Lusaka at 11–12.00 the following day. Note that even if you want to get off in Harare, you'll probably have to pay the whole fare.

To/from Livingstone

There is usually at least one operator running fast air-conditioned coaches between Livingstone and Lusaka. However, these operators seem to change regularly, so do re-check locally before you travel.

Currently try Euro-Africa Coaches: their office is behind Findeco House, on Cairo Road. There are departures from here daily, at about 07.30–08.00, using modern, fast coaches which run to time and can be booked and paid for in advance. The journey takes about six hours, and a ticket costs about US\$15.

By train

Few travellers use Zambia's ordinary trains for transport, but if you have lots of patience, and a few good books, then try them. Lines link Lusaka with Livingstone and the Copperbelt. Express trains to Livingstone leave at 19.30 every Monday, Wednesday and Friday, taking about 12 hours. Slower trains, which stop even more frequently, leave every morning.

The regular, efficient TAZARA trains to Tanzania are different. They leave from Kapiri Mposhi, not Lusaka, so see page 315 for details. Despite this, their main office is in Lusaka. Take Independence Avenue from the south end of Kafue Road, over the bridge across the railway line. The main TAZARA office is in the building on your left, known as Tazara House. This usually displays the current timetable on a notice board outside, on the left of the door, and inside you buy tickets for TAZARA in advance. It opens Mon–Fri: 08.30–13.30 and 14.00–15.30.

ORIENTATION

Lusaka is very spread out, so get hold of a good map when you first arrive (see *Maps* section, below). Its focus is the axis of Cairo Road, which runs roughly north–south. This is about six lanes of traffic wide, 4km long, and has a useful pedestrian island which runs like a spine down its centre. Parallel to Cairo Road, to the west, is Chachacha road – a terminus for numerous local minibuses, and home to a lively market. Cairo Road is the city's commercial centre and the location for most large shops, so it bustles with people during the day.

Completely separate, about 2km to the east, is the much larger, more diffuse 'Government Area'. It is linked to Cairo Road by Independence Avenue, and centres on the areas of Cathedral Hill and Ridgeway. Here you will find the big international-standard hotels, government departments and embassies set in a lot more space. It has a different atmosphere from the bustle of Cairo Road: the quiet and official air that you often find in diplomatic or administrative corners of capitals around the world.

Maps

Excellent, detailed maps covering the whole of Zambia can be bought cheaply from the main government map office at the Ministry of Lands. This is in the basement of Mulungushi House, by the corner of Independence Avenue and Nationalist Road. Prices are very good, at around Kw5–10,000 per map. Aside from the normal 'Ordnance Survey' type maps, there are several special tourist maps available. To see what's in stock, browse through the maps on the right of the door before finally choosing. Include in your purchase the detailed street map of Lusaka. This is essential for navigating around the capital, and comes complete with an alphabetical street index.

For trips venturing off the main roads, you'll simply have to come here and buy up a selection of the 1:250,000 series. They're generally very good, though their information is inevitably dated.

A limited selection of Zambia's most commonly used maps can also be found at The Book House (used to be called the Wildlife Shop), on the east side of Cairo Road, just north of the main post office, and at shops in the lobbies of the larger hotels. These are more convenient than Mulungushi House, but the choice is much more limited and the same maps cost more.

WHERE TO STAY

There is little to choose between Lusaka's international-standard hotels – which are functional and efficient, if often soulless. You might ask yourself if you need to be near the centre, or can afford to stay beyond the suburbs, at somewhere like Lilayi, Chisamba or even Lechwe Lodge (see page 208). These are more pleasant than being in town, but transport can be a costly issue.

Those on a budget should choose their lodgings with care. Price is often a poor guide and the quality of the budget hotels varies considerably. Ask around if you can, as new places are opening all the time. If your budget is very tight then head for a backpacker's dorm or a camping site. Lusaka's cheap hostels are often seedy.

A warning: if you plan to make international phone calls from any hotel, find out their charges first. Bills can run into hundreds of dollars for just a few minutes. An international calling card, organised outside Zambia and billed abroad, is usually a much cheaper alternative – though some of these are blocked by the exchanges.

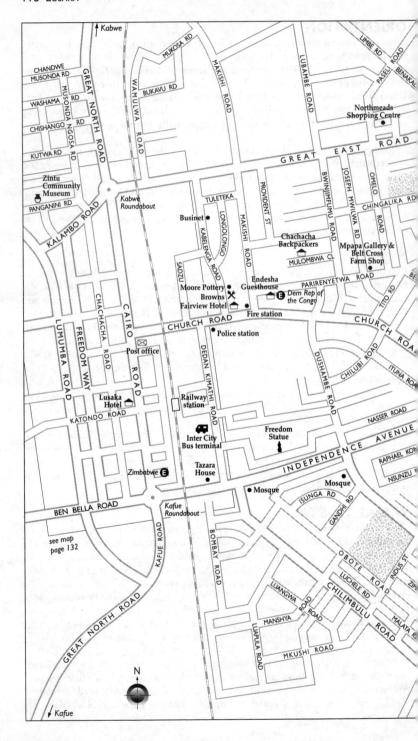

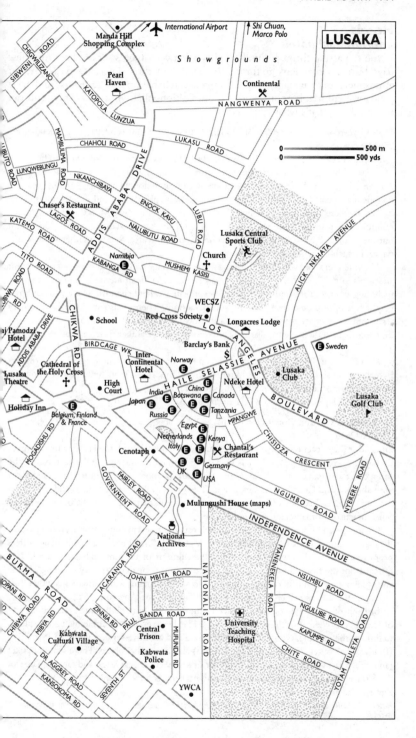

Hotels
International hotels
If you're passing through Lusaka, perhaps between flights, or are here for a few days' business, then look no further. None of these three hotels deserves prizes for atmosphere or originality, but all organise reliable airport transfers, and have pleasant comfortable rooms and communications that work efficiently. You can rely on them; that's what you need.

Hotel Intercontinental (200 rooms) Haile Selassie Av, PO Box 32201. Tel: 250600-1 or 250148; fax: 251880
On the north side of Haile Selassie Avenue, this is Lusaka's most imposing hotel. The rooms are reasonably big, so you can expect an en-suite bath/shower, TV with M-Net (a South African cable channel), fridge and telephone. Rooms with double beds have enough space to include both a couch and a desk, and the decor is always plain, clear, and slightly uninspiring. For meals there's a restaurant which changes style on some days. Mondays it's Italian, for example. (Keep an eye on the notices in the lifts for the latest restaurant news!) You can eat outside or in, and it overlooks a large swimming pool. Nearby there's a rather soulless bar, typical of such large hotels.

The Intercon's lobby is a good meeting place, with huge windows looking out to the front and a piano that's sometimes played. Nearby there is a small arcade of upmarket shops, including an office for South African Airlines and an excellent chemist, where you can buy a good range of imported cosmetics and sun-tan lotions. There is also an expensive jewellery shop, and some smart gift shops (some of the town's best quality T-shirts in town are found here, starting at US$25 each), also an office for the Trans-Zambezi Intercape buses (see page 116).

However, you should note that the Intercon has recently been bought and the new owners have extensive and ambitious plans to refurbish and modernise it, including the creation of a business centre and shopping mall on the ground floor.
Rates: US$130 single, US$150 double, including breakfast

Holiday Inn Garden Court (155 rooms) PO Box 30666. Tel: 251666; fax: 253529; tlx: ZA 42510
Situated at the corner of Independence Avenue and Church Road, the Holiday Inn occupies the site of the old Ridgeway Hotel. Its air-conditioned rooms are similar to those of the Intercon or the Pamodzi, and show little more imagination. They are functional and clean with showers and baths, telephones, colour TVs (with M-Net), razor plugs, and tea/coffee-making facilities. Beds are queen-size double or twin. For a pampering, the beautician at Le Soleil practises aromatherapy and massage here.

On the ground floor there's the main hotel restaurant, serving buffet meals from breakfast through to dinner (at Kw20,000/US$8), and McGinty's Traditional Irish Pub, which offers promising pub lunches while maintaining the calm air of the Emerald Isle. A cool, dark retreat from the heat! However, instead of gazing into your pint here, try stepping outside and studying the beautiful colony of masked weavers nesting over the ornamental pond. Just watch for the three small crocs that share the pond with a few nervous goldfish.

In front of either side of the entrance to the Holiday Inn you'll find several shops and offices. The Golden Spur Restaurant (see page 131) here succeeds in attracting non-residents to dine in the evening, with straightforward food and attentive service, while AVIS and BA (PO Box 22006; tel: 254444/53/73; fax: 250623) also have offices here. There's an upmarket (and, when last visited, un-named) purveyor of lovely curios, carvings, and fabrics. The slot for a travel agency, which used to be Bushwhackers, is now occupied by a branch of the Zambian Safari Company.
Rates: US$140 single, US$160 double, including full breakfast and airport transfers to international flights

Taj Pamodzi Hotel (204 rooms) PO Box 35450. Tel: 254455; fax: 224005 or 250995; tlx: ZA 44720 PAMHO; email: pamodzi@zamnet.zm

Opposite the Holiday Inn, at the corner of Church Road and Addis Ababa Drive, the Pamodzi is a member of the Taj group of hotels, but despite this has a number of excellent individual touches. Its rooms are good, with air-conditioning, a bath/shower, satellite TV (with Mnet, BBC, CNN, etc), fridge and direct-dial telephone, and the level of service is impressive. All rooms have a proper balcony, and the higher of the Pamodzi's nine floors have some fine views.

There's a comfortable lobby downstairs, a pleasant restaurant and a bar. Adjacent to the hotel is an affiliated fitness centre with two squash courts, a gym, aerobics and a sauna. This is one of the best gyms in town, and it is popular with many of Lusaka's more affluent residents. Outside, lawns surround a good swimming pool.

The restaurant serves a good and varied buffet breakfast, and for dinner there's often a choice. Menus change regularly and various 'special' nights come and go throughout the week, ensuring that if you're here for a while you shouldn't get too bored. I've often stayed here, and always found the staff to be courteous and helpful.

Rates: US$130 single, US$150 double, including breakfast

Lodges outside town

If you've more than a night and want somewhere to relax away from the city, then try one of these. All have lots of space and are set in large areas of greenery, often stocked with game. Because of this, all are out of the centre, so communications can be less easy. Also, because they are smaller, most of them organise transfers to/from the airport (or the city) on an individual basis, and this is reflected in their rates or in transfer charges. However, for an extended stay all are very pleasant and worth seeking out. Listing them alphabetically:

Chaminuka Lodge (8 twin rooms) PO Box 35370, Lusaka. Tel: 233303/4; fax: 233305

Chaminuka is 28km north of the international airport (about 50km northeast of town) and signposted down a small turning (beside which there is usually a police roadblock on the main road). This is about 30 minutes' drive, though the gravel road can take longer during the rains, when you would certainly want a 4WD for the journey. However, the lodge usually provides transfers for its guests.

The main lodge stands atop a small rise overlooking the Chitoka Lake, one of four small lakes in the reserve. Highest is the main lounge, which is large, spacious and adorned with original art, sculptures, animal skins, hunting trophies and comfy leather sofas. Its walls are large sliding glass doors, often left open. It's all very grand, reflecting its origins as the private home of one of Lusaka's most affluent citizens.

Dotted around this main building are eight large suites, all with en-suite facilities and lots of space. Some are doubles, some twins, and some interconnect to make family rooms. All have their own music systems, solid wooden beds and patio-doors on to the lawns which surround the lodge. There are a few small lounges spread around, plus a sunken TV lounge, a dining room, a sauna, a small library, a snooker room (with full-size table), and an office where a laptop is on hand in case you can't completely ignore the rest of the world. Outside are two swimming pools, with adjacent terrace, a tennis court and a jacuzzi.

Surrounding all of this is 35km^2 of Chaminuka Nature Reserve, a nature reserve dating from 1978 that has been augmented over time with decommissioned farmland. This has a variety of different woodland and savannah habitats, lots of wetlands (at least when visited in March!), and about 2,400 head of game. Cheetah, lion and hyena are kept in their own fenced enclosures, though the lodge has plans to release some of these in due course.

The lodge's activities are flexible. In addition to 4WD game drives, walks, and fishing sorties on the lakes, there is riding available at the lodge's stable, which currently has about a dozen horses and equipment. If you stay for a while at Chaminuka, then consider a day or two in their bushcamp. Chaminuka is very comfortable, conveniently close to the airport, and notable for its good food and friendly team of staff. However, its plethora of hunting trophies or high costs may discourage some visitors.

Rates: US$600/US$400 for a twin/single including full board and all drinks, activities and transfers to/from town or airport

Chaminuka Bushcamp (4 twin chalets) PO Box 35370, Lusaka. Tel: 233303/4; fax: 233305

A short drive from the lodge, within Chaminuka Nature Reserve, Chaminuka Bushcamp is a lot more basic. The simple thatched chalets have mosquito nets and an en-suite shower and toilet. Outside there's usually a campfire, a raised lookout mound and a dining area under thatch, with open sides. It's very much like a small Luangwa bushcamp, and activities are as flexible as for the main lodge.

Rates: US$400/US$275, including full board and all drinks, activities and transfers to/from town or airport. This is usually combined with a stay at the main Chaminuka Lodge

Chisamba Safari Lodge (20 rooms) PO Box 51018, Lusaka. Tel: 704600–3; fax: 704800/221175

Opened at the end of '99, Chisamaba stands in 12km^2 of rolling bush about 45km north of Lusaka. To get there take the Great North Road for about 38km, and then turn right and follow the signs for a further 7km. Note that during the rainy season this road can be uneven and very wet in places, barely suitable for a low-clearance saloon vehicle.

Its lounge, bar and dining room are all set beneath a large, curved thatched roof that's been cleverly constructed. Inside the main thatched area are lots of separate nooks and crannies. Some contain tables and dining chairs, others more comfy sofas. Perfect to hide away and relax. Chisamba's food is very good, gaining it a reputation amongst the more affluent residents of Lusaka as an excellent venue for Sunday lunch. In one corner you'll find the 'Trading Post', a well-stocked shop for books and curios.

The bedrooms are stunning: high, thatched ceilings and lots of style and space. All have en-suite bathrooms with marble tops, bath and separate (powerful) shower. Mossie nets cover the king-size doubles (or twins). All have direct-dial telephones using cellular links (reliable but expensive), tea/coffee makers, and TV with MNet cable channels.

Outside, beautiful herbaceous borders surround a figure-of-eight swimming pool and a network of lawns. Beyond lies a wilderness area, including a lake, which is home to a wide range of wildlife. The author can testify to watching a memorable flock of Abdim's stork during the wet season here, but the grass was too high (and lunch too good) to go out

MPHAMVU'S STORY

Christine Coppinger (age 10) and Jenny Coppinger (age 9)

When we got Imphamvu she was an aufan her mother had died from antharax. We found her on the way to North Luangwa quite close to Chibembe. She was standing on her own too weak to runaway. Our friends Dup and Rambo put her in the car and took her back to Chibembe, with the help from the guests. We had an elephant called Moto and a zebra called Ebba.

Imphamvu made friends for a while but after a time they caught antharax from Imphamvu and died. After that we got another pet zebra but she also died. After many years at Chibembe we left to make our own camp called Tafika. Impamvu came with us. She lived many happy years with us but she started raiding the local villagers fields and drinking their beer. Now she had to go to a game ranch outside Lusaka and that's where she still is today.

searching for game. You'd expect to find zebra, warthogs, reedbuck, puku, kudu and impala here, amongst other common game. More surprising is the presence of Lichtenstein's hartebeest, tsessebe, oribi, Kafue lechwe, eland and sitatunga. Clearly it's worth exploring during the dry season, either driving or on one of two short marked trails.

Finally, there is a nine-year-old elephant named Mphanvu, whom you may occasionally see on drives. If she seems friendly it's because she was rescued in the Luangwa by John Coppinger (of Remote Africa Safaris) and brought up there. After attempts to release her back into elephant groups in South Luangwa, she was walked up to North Luangwa National Park, in the hope of re-introducing her there, further from people. That failed and she ended up at Shiwa Ngandu, before finally coming to Chisamba. Now she's friendly but very heavy and strong, and so treat her with great respect and keep your distance.

Rates: US$160 for a double/twin, US$128 for a single, including breakfast. Transfers to/from town cost US$20 per person per trip, US$25 for the airport

Lechwe Lodge (6 rondavels) PO Box 37940, Lusaka. Tel: 032 30128; fax: 032 30707; cell: 01 704803; email: kflechwe@zamnet.zm
Though 90 minutes' drive south of Lusaka, Lechwe is a super spot if you've two or three days to relax and don't need to come into town at all. It's very simple, natural and unpretentious. See page 208 for more details.

Rates: US$120 per person, including all activities, meals, drinks and laundry. Road transfers to/from Lusaka are US$40 per vehicle (max 4 people) per journey. Air transfers to the lodge are also possible at around US$150 per plane (max 5 people) per trip

Lilayi Lodge (12 rooms & 5 suites) PO Box 30093. Tel: 279022/5; fax: 279026; tlx: ZA 40536 LILAYI
If you can arrange the transport, then Lilayi is the most pleasant, and the best value, of the upmarket options in Lusaka. It is on a game farm about 20 minutes' drive from the centre of town off the Kafue Road.

To get there head south on Cairo Road and continue over the Independence Avenue roundabout. Turn left after about 11km, then right at the T-junction, where the police training college is in front of you. Take the next left turn and continue straight to the Lodge. It is about 10km off the main road.

Lilayi's accommodation is in very comfortable, well-furnished brick rondavels spread out over green lawns. Five of the rondavels are suites, which have a bedroom, spacious lounge, and en-suite bath, shower and toilet. The other six rondavels have two bedrooms in them, with en-suite showers and toilets, and they share a lounge. (If the hotel is not full, then they may give you a suite for the price of a room.)

The main building has a large bar and dining area overlooking a large pool, plus another upstairs lounge and an excellent small library for reference. The restaurant is excellent, and often complemented by a popular outdoor braai.

Lilayi is set on a large farm criss-crossed by game-viewing roads. It has been well stocked with most of Zambia's antelope – including some of the less common species – like roan, sable, Defassa waterbuck, tsessebe and giraffe. So if you failed to sight something in one of the parks, walk around here for a few hours before you leave. Horse riding is also possible here, for experienced riders, at about US$20 per person. There are also facilities for badminton and volleyball.

Rates: US$80/US$120 standard/deluxe single, US$90/130 double, bed & breakfast

Budget hotels
Even 'budget' hotels aren't that cheap in Lusaka, but if you have Kw50–100,000 (US$20–40) per night to spend then there is a choice of smaller hotels. However, many are used extensively for conferences and few shine. Most visitors prefer the city's smaller guesthouses, which are often much friendlier for the same kind of

price. However, in case you need one, the budget hotels include:

Andrews Motel (95 rooms) PO Box 30475. Tel: 272101/2 or 273535; fax: 274798 or 272532

Andrews Motel is about 8km from the Independence Avenue roundabout on the Kafue Road. Despite the impression of a fading motel being neglected by over-relaxed staff, Andrews remains popular with locals – perhaps because its facilities include two tennis courts and a spacious pool, with adjacent bar and snack area.

Being out of the centre, it has the space for a layout typical of a motel, with a security guard on the gate and parking bays in front of rooms. This should reassure those concerned about the safety of vehicles. The rooms are a little dingy, but all have air-con units, twin beds and baths, though no showers. There's a campsite just to the right of the main hotel.

Rates: Kw85,000/US$34 per twin; Kw130,000/US$52 for a family room for 4 persons, including a basic breakfast of cereals and fruit

Barn Motel Great East Rd (50 rooms) Tel: 282890/1/2 or 233163; fax: 228949

On the Great East Road beyond the airport turn-off, about 20km from the city, the Barn has little to recommend it.

Rates: about Kw50–60,000/US$20–24 double, including breakfast

Belvedere Lodge Tel: 263079

On the east side of the city, close to Kabulonga shopping centre, Belvedere stands at the corner of Leopard's Hill Road and Chindo Road. The rooms are small, uninspiring and outdated – though fairly clean. Each has a fan, and an en-suite toilet and bathroom. It is often booked up by visiting officials, so if you plan to stay here ring ahead to see if there is space before you arrive.

Rates: Kw46–59,000/US$18–24 for a twin room, Kw10–16,000/US$4–6 for a single, including dinner, bed & breakfast. There is no bed & breakfast tariff here

Chainama Hotel (28 rooms) PO Box 51033. Tel: 292451–6; fax: 290809

On the south side of the Great East Road, about 7km from the centre of town, Chainama Hotel has quite spacious rooms. These have tables and chairs, plenty of space, telephones, fans, and remote-control TVs with M-net and CNN. A picture window takes up one wall of most of the rooms, and the en-suite bathrooms have showers but not baths.

Rates: Kw90,000 for a single or a twin; non-Zambians pay US$60

Fairview Hotel (30 rooms) P Bag E186, Lusaka 10101. Tel: 222604/5; fax: 237222; email: fairview@zamnet.zm

The Fairview is just out of the centre of town on Church Road, on the left past the fire station. It is a hotel training centre, as well as the centre for a number of small high-tech services.

Rates: Kw70,000 per twin, including a basic breakfast

Garden House Hotel (50 rooms) Mumbwa Road, PO Box 30815. Tel: 01 287337 or 233004; fax: 01 233264

About 6km from the city on the Mumbwa road, the Garden House is ideal if you arrive late from Kafue. All the rooms have an en-suite shower or bath, and toilet, and the decor (or at least the art dotted around) tries hard to be original and Zambian. There is a pool and tennis court, and the Garden House is perhaps notable as the place where the MMD (the party currently in government) was started in 1990.

Rates: about Kw50–70,000 double, including breakfast

Hillview Hotel (10 rooms) Makeni PO Box 30815. Tel: 278554; fax 229074

About 15km from the city, take the Kafue road and turn right shortly after Andrews Motel. The Hillview is about 5km down the tar road, and has an airy, almost colonial atmosphere.

Rates: about Kw70–90,000 double, including breakfast

Kafue Road Garden Hotel (16 rooms) Kafue Road, PO Box 30815. Tel: 274646/7; fax: 233264

On the edge of town, opposite the Castle Shopping Centre and fuel station, this has quite pleasant rooms set in its own gardens. All the rooms have an en-suite shower or bath, and toilet.

Rates: US$45 double, US$30 single, including breakfast

Longacres Lodge (58 rooms) c/o Hostels Board of Management, PO Box 50100 Tel: 251761

This government-run lodge is unique for its labyrinth of long corridors, sometimes open at one side. To find it go 100m north of Los Angeles Boulevard, on Haile Selassie Avenue. That's about 600m past the Intercontinental Hotel if you approach from town.

It is sparsely furnished though reasonably clean, and often used for government conferences. The carpeted rooms have a basic twin beds, or a double, and perhaps a dressing table or wardrobe. Some have fridges; some have TVs (local stations only). Each also has a simple en-suite tiled bathroom with a toilet, a bath and a basin.

Rates: Kw65,000 for a double bed, Kw79,000 for twin, and larger suites for Kw90,000, including a basic continental breakfast

Lusaka Hotel (70 rooms) PO Box 30044. Tel: 229049 or 221833; fax: 225726; tlx: ZA 41921

Some decades ago the Lusaka Hotel was the only hotel in Lusaka, right at the centre of town (just a few metres from Cairo Road) on the bustling Katondo Road. Now the area around the hotel's entrance is always busy with people loitering suspiciously, and if you stay here you should be careful with your belongings.

Inside, the hotel feels old, small and noisy, but clean. The standard rooms have tea/coffee makers, M-net television, a telephone, a fan and an en-suite toilet/shower room. The deluxe rooms are a little larger with baths as well as showers, and air-conditioning instead of fans.

Rates: Kw65,000/80,000 standard/deluxe singles; Kw83,000/99,000 standard/deluxe doubles, including a basic continental breakfast

Ndeke Hotel (46 rooms) Chisidza Crescent, PO Box 30815. Tel: 251734 or 250050; fax: 233264

Near the roundabout of Haile Selassie Avenue and Los Angeles Boulevard, the Ndeke opened in '81. It is an old hotel with a slightly offbeat, dingy atmosphere, despite its general cleanliness and highly polished floors.

The rooms all have en-suite toilets and baths, and the double rooms have TVs. At the front is a slightly sunken lounge adorned with apparently new art, and at the back there's a pool table outside in the courtyard.

Rates: US$45 double, US$30 single, including breakfast

Small guesthouses

The last few years have seen a real boom in the numbers, and the quality, of small guesthouses throughout Zambia, but especially in Lusaka. Some are simply restaurants that offer a few rooms for guests as a legal convenience, others are dedicated entirely to their guests. A few are old favourites, but beware of the speed with which these open up and then close down again.

I've listed them alphabetically, and those with no (or few) details here have started up too recently to be inspected for this edition.

Arabian Nights (7 rooms) Tel: 750102; fax: 295613

In Kalundu, Arabian Nights is really a restaurant (see page 131), but it also has a few rooms above. To get there, take the Great East Road several kilometres east of Addis Ababa Drive and watch for signs to turn north, on to Lufubu Road. Then take the first right turn on to Kabompo Close. Arabian Nights will be on your right.

The rooms are large and all different. Most are named and there's a loose theme of Tudor England with a few eastern touches thrown in. The King's Privy Chamber is the largest, and all have double beds and en-suite facilities. Residents have use of the large pool outside. Arabian Nights is better suited to a long stay than a one- or two-night stop as, though the accommodation is good, it seems an afterthought when compared to the restaurant.

Rates: US$45 single, US$65 double, including a full breakfast

Chasers (2 rooms) 9 Lagos Rd, off Addis Ababa. Tel: 752659
Chasers is mainly a pub/restaurant (see page 133), but it does have safe parking and rooms for overnight guests. Note that it stays open until midnight most evenings, and 02.00 on Fridays and Saturdays, so do ask for a quiet room unless you intend to be one of the revellers downstairs.

Rates: US$45 single, US$65 double, including a full breakfast

Anina's Guesthouse Plot 29, Lilayi Road, Off Kafue Rd, PO Box 50987, Lusaka. Tel/fax: 223373; cell: 704831
This has four rooms, one of which one is self-contained.

Blue Crest Executive Guesthouse 15 Sable Rd, Lusaka. Tel/fax: 260536
On the site of the old Ingandu Inn, the Blue Crest is very new (June '99). It has three twin rooms, with en-suite facilities, and also three 3-bedroom flats which come complete with a dining room and kitchen each. Clearly this aims to cater more for those who will stay for extended periods than casual visitors.

Rates: US$40 single, US$35 per person sharing, for the rooms – US$70/45 for the flats – including light breakfast

Chantal's Guesthouse (3 rooms) United Nations Avenue opposite the Netherlands Embassy, PO Box 51042, Lusaka. Tel: 252163
This is primarily a restaurant, but also has a few rooms for guests.

Endesha Guest House (5 rooms) Parirenyetwa Rd, PO Box 32372. Tel: 225780/1; fax: 225781
Very close to the Cairo Road area, Endesha opened early in 1999 and is clearly marked. Leave town on Church Road, take a left on to Makishi Road, just after the fire station, and then turn first right on Parirenyetwa Road. Endesha is on your right.

All its rooms have the luxury of a double and a single bed, though their decor is simple, and perhaps a little stark, with just the odd picture. Each room has a TV, a small fridge and a fan. The more expensive rooms have en-suite facilities, whilst the others have private toilets and showers, but these are sometimes a short walk across a corridor. All the toilets and bathrooms are all small and clean.

Endesha's communal areas are less stark than the rooms, and the lounge area even has a big goldfish tank in it. Outside, the private parking area is protected by high walls and a sliding security gate, and within sight of the outside thatched bar, which is used by residents and guests only. Its owner is Mohamed Ali Hanslot, who also runs a couple of similar guesthouses in Ndola.

Rates: US$50 per room en suite, US$40 per room with private but separate shower/toilet, excluding breakfast

Gringos (8 rooms) Plot 214B, Zambezi Rd (corner of Lukanga), Roma, P Bag E353. Tel: 295190/292984
Again, Gringos is mainly a bar/restaurant (see page 133) serving lunch and dinner, sometimes in its lovely garden at the back. But down a maze of corridors, it also has a few deluxe rooms – large carpeted double rooms with en-suite shower, bath and toilet. Nearby standard rooms have twin beds and share toilets and showers. All have fans, but none is in pristine condition. They are fairly priced.

Rates: Kw60,000 deluxe double, Kw45,000 twin double, including breakfast

Jul's Guesthouse (4 rooms) Plot 5508 Lusiwasi Rd (off Libala Rd), Kalundu, PO Box 32863, Lusaka. Tel: 292979 or 293972; fax: 291246

Jul's has four double rooms with en-suite facilities in a quiet, residential area and has a tennis court, a swimming pool, and a lounge with satellite TV. Self-catering is possible, or meals can be arranged in advance.

Rates: US$40 per person sharing, US$80 single

Kaingo Executive Guest House (6 rooms) 35D Leopard's Lane (off Leopard's Hill Rd), Kabulonga, PO Box 31402. Tel: 263231

To reach Kaingo, take Leopard's Hill Road out of town from the roundabout on Los Angeles Boulevard. After St. Mary's, but before Lake Road Primary School, take a right turn on to Leopard's Hill Lane, which bisects it. A little way down here there's an alley on the right, and Kaingo is the first gate on the right.

This small, well-kept guesthouse has been open since around '94, deep in the suburbs. It is run by Winnie Kwesha, who clearly aims mainly for business visitors and NGO personnel sent to Zambia for short postings. The rooms are all different, but all are en suite and 'rustic' in their use of potted plants, stone, wooden floors, nice fabrics and rugs. All have double beds (except the singles). The communal areas are relaxed; there's a comfy TV lounge/bar and all meals can be provided if requested. Outside is a small swimming pool.

Rates: US$75–90 double, US$55 single, including breakfast. Discounts for long stays

Laughing Waters Lodge (12 rooms) Mungwi Rd (After Zambian Breweries Plc), Lusaka West. Tel: 227546; fax: 224829; email: lwlodge@zamnet.zm

Laughing Waters is a new lodge run by Reggie and Chi-Chi Muzariri, and Gerry Louverdis, a little out of town. To get there, go to the north end of Cairo Road and turn left at the roundabout on to Kalambo, then right at the T-junction on to Lumumba Road. Continue for about 1km, then take a left at the second set of traffic lights into Mungwi road (the same road as Zambia Breweries). Continue for about 8km on this road (past Palmgreen Service Station), and then the lodge is signposted clearly on the right-hand side of the road.

The lodge has a variety of different rooms. Two rondavels (they call these the honeymoon suites) which sleep two people each; two hotel-room style chalets, each sleeping two; four self-catering chalets, which each can sleep four; two executive chalets, which also sleep up to four people each; and two family chalets, one of which has six beds, the other enough for up to twelve people.

All these are slightly different in layout or style. The self-catering and executive chalets all have television sets, and satellite TV should be installed before this book is published. In addition, the self-catering chalets have stoves and mini-bar/ fridges. There's a small restaurant with bar here, plus an outside bar that's handy for the swimming pool. It's in its own small game area, where ostriches currently roam, and there are plans to introduce impala and kudu, and even small elephants (if elephants are ever small!).

Rates: US$70 per person for rondavels, hotel-room chalets and family chalets, US$75 per person for self-catering chalets, and US$80 per person for executive chalets. Including breakfast

Margaret's Guest House (6 rooms) Plot 62, Luwato Rd, Roma, PO Box 51121. Tel: 295356

Leaving Lukanga Road, Luwato Road seemed to be more in need of repair than most when last visited. On the right is Roma's small shopping centre, a Kwik Save supermarket, a pharmacy, a clinic, a public telephone and a hair and beauty salon. Margaret's itself is on the left, looking a little rundown, and is run by Magrate Sambi.

The deluxe room has a king-size bed, TV, en-suite toilet and bath, and even a cot! Other rooms have twin beds and share communal toilets and baths. (Look out for the wonderful old enamel bath.) There's a comfortable TV room with MNET and a stereo for guests to use. Despite its rundown exterior and fairly simple rooms, Margaret's seems clean and well run.

Its communal areas are comfortable and its atmosphere very friendly and helpful.
Rates: Kw65,000 deluxe double, Kw45,000 twin double. Continental/full breakfast Kw4,000/Kw9,500. Lunch and dinner are available, if requested in advance

Millenium Lodge House number 5, off Reedbuck Rd, Kabulonga, Lusaka.

Palmwood Lodge (5 rooms) Chudleigh, PO Box 35256, Lusaka. Tel/fax: 286570

Pearl Haven Inn (4 rooms) Twikatane Rd, off Addis Ababa Drive, Rhodes Park, PO Box 50109, Lusaka. Tel: 252412/252455; fax: 251126; cell: 773202; email: ejhala@zamtel.zm
Run by Malcolm Jhala, Pearl Haven is a new (April '99) guesthouse in a commercial residential area, conveniently located for Chasers, the Polo Grill, and Marco Polo. It is five minutes' walk from the new Manda Hill complex. It has two double rooms and two twins, each with en-suite toilet and shower, TV with satellite channels, and a direct-dial phone. It's surrounded by its own gardens and has a small bar, swimming pool and restaurant for residents.
Rates: US$35 single, US$50 double, US$60 twin, including full English breakfast

Vineyard Guest House (11 rooms) Mumana Rd, Chilwa Mabwe, PO Box 34993. Tel: 292361; fax: 291204
Having opened in '96, the Vineyard is a well-established little guesthouse with a good reputation. It stands behind high walls on Mumana Road (between Bende and Chianama Roads), on the outer edge of Chilwa Mabwe residential area. Once inside, and past the security guard, you'll find carefully tended green lawns and an outside sitting area, under thatch, reminiscent of a bush lodge's bar.

Inside the 11 rooms are all different, and priced as such. The smallest are pleasant and simple, with en-suite facilities and fans. The largest, room one, has two king-size beds (one is a waterbed) and an upright piano!

The Vineyard has a small gym with machines for running, weights and cycling; the owner lives next door and residents are free to use the swimming pool there.

Dinner can be cooked on request (about Kw19,000 for three courses). This is a super place to stay if you're in Lusaka for a few weeks or months.
Rates: Kw44–77,000 per room, including continental breakfast

Wayside B&B (7 rooms) Plot 40, Makeni Rd, PO Box 30453 Tel: 274444; tel/fax: 273439
Run by Beverley and John, this is out of town. Take the Kafue Road past the Castle Service Station, and then take a left on to Makeni (may be McKenny) Road. The Wayside is signposted about 2km from the main road. I haven't visited this, but reports of it say that the owners are welcoming and very hospitable.
Rates: Kw40,000 single, Kw50,000 double, if one night stayed. Reduction of Kw5,000 per night for durations of 2–6 nights. Reductions of Kw10,000 per night for longer

Zamearth Lodge (7 rooms) Plot 5520, Magoye Rd, Kalundu, P Bag 107, Woodlands. Tel/fax: 294680
Run by Ms Marjorie Munachonga, Zamearth opened in 1992. It still has only seven rooms, which are often full with long-term visitors working for aid agencies. Two rooms (the suite and the deluxe) have en-suite facilities, the others share toilets and showers. All are serviced daily and are comfortable, with clean carpets and soft furnishings. There is one telephone for guests, and the main complaint is the expense of the Lodge's laundry service.

The Lodge is well signposted in side streets to the north of the Great East Road, after the showgrounds but before the University of Zambia. It is probably the best-value accommodation in town.
Rates: Kw45,000 single, Kw60,000 double, including a full breakfast. Other meals available, including dinner for Kw11,500

Hostels and camping

If you're really visiting on a tight budget, then look towards one of the camping sites on the edge of town, or one of the backpackers' dorms in the centre.

Chachacha Backpackers' 161 Mulombwa Close. Tel: 222257

Off Bwinjimfumo Road, which runs between the Great East Road and Church Road, Chachacha is two-thirds of the way down Mulombwa Close on the right hand side (useful to know if you arrive after dark).

Its clean and well-kept dorms have eight bunk beds, while for a little more privacy get one of the private rooms, or the A-frame chalet in the garden (this has just one double bed). All showers, toilets, and the kitchen facilities are communal, and the atmosphere is buzzy and friendly.

A set meal is usually available for around Kw7,000–7,500 each evening, as is breakfast each morning. If you wish to cook for yourself then head for the 'campers' kitchen' at the back, where hotplates, a fridge and various cooking utensils are supplied. If you're feeling decadent, there's a laundry service available.

Inside, one wall has a large street map of Lusaka on it, while upon another (near the bar) is writ the collected wit of former inmates. To contact the outside world, use the payphone (the managers will sell you a phonecard), or rent the computer for a while. This will cost you Kw5,000 per half hour, plus Kw2,000 per email sent or received (cha@zamtel.zm).

To get around Lusaka, bikes can be hired at US$2 per hour or US$8 for a full day. For further afield, Chachacha will store your backpack free of charge, and rent you a tent to help you on your travels. Chachacha is run by Mildred, and certainly the liveliest place in Lusaka for independent backpackers.

Rates: US$3 per person camping, US$6 for a dorm bed; rooms are US$12/14 for a single/double room and US$18 for the double A-frame chalet in the garden

Eureka PO Box 30370. Tel/fax: 272351 or tel: 278110; email: eureka@zamnet.zm

Lusaka's best campsite is on a private farm, owned and run by Henry and Doreen van Blerk. It is on the eastern side of Kafue Road, about 10km from the Independence Avenue roundabout, and was started in 1992 with the aim of attracting budget travellers. It now has a large area of beautiful lawn under trees for camping on, protected by an electric fence and within a game area. Expect to be woken by antelope at breakfast!

Until the (planned) kitchen and dining room are complete, most people bring their own food and cook on one of the outside barbecues. However, steaks and pies are available from a thatched bar that is central to the campground. Here you'll also find easy chairs, a darts board and a pool table.

As well as camping there are a number of simple thatched A-frame chalets for hire, each with two or three beds, whose occupants share well-kept toilets and showers with the campers. For more privacy, get one of the three 2-bed chalets, each with en-suite shower and toilet. Chalets are worth booking in advance, if possible.

Eureka has maintained its position as the city's best place for budget travellers with their own transport, and is a very safe, pleasant spot. It even has a swimming pool and a volleyball court.

Without a vehicle, get here from town by going to Kulima Tower bus stop (on south side of Lusaka on Freedom way between Katunjila road and Ben Bella Road) and taking the Chilanga bus. Ask to be dropped at Eureka; the fare is about Kw800. Similarly, picking up lifts from minibuses into town is fairly easy, by just waiting outside the gates. However, some travellers without vehicles do prefer to stay nearer the centre of town.

Rates: US$5 per person per night camping (or US$2.50 for overlanders and backpackers). US$22/20 for a 3-bed/2-bed A-frame, US$30 for a 2-bed en-suite chalet

Fringilla B&B Tel/fax: 611199; fax: 611213

Situated about 50km north of Lusaka on the Great North Road (look out for the sign on the east side of the road), Fringilla makes a good base if you have transport, though it is far if you want to spend much time in Lusaka itself. It's part of a large, working farm which has expanded now to include a butchery (which also makes processed meats), a dairy, a clinic, a post office and even a small ZNCB bank.

Amidst these is the small B&B run by Alan and Julie Fringilla. A restaurant, lounge and kitchen now occupy the old farm building, around which is a large veranda and lawn dotted with tables and chairs. The chalets are arranged around the main farmhouse; all have en-suite facilities and are simple but pleasant.

Meals are a big focus here and the cooking is excellent. 'Wholesome country cuisine' is supplemented with 'themed' dinners (eg Indian, Thai, etc) from around the world. Horse riding is possible and there are pleasant walks around the farm. Game drives can be arranged (in advance) on a nearby game farm.

Alternatively, separate from the main house, there is a shady campsite complete with an ablution block (with baths and showers) and a small field kitchen where you can cook. If you don't want to camp then there are also a few simple huts here, sharing the campers' facilities. *Rates: US$35 twin/double, US$28 single, US$48 for a family room. Alternatively, camping is US$4 per tent, and the huts are US$9*

Pioneer Campsite PO Box CH29, Lusaka. Cell: 771936; email: pioneer@zamnet.zm
Owned by Chris and Beatrice Wienand (who also run a game ranch in the Luangwa and have started Chamafumbu Camp on the Kafue), Pioneer is about 20 minutes' drive from the centre of Lusaka or 15 from the airport. To get there, drive out east on Great East Road, and then turn right 3km past turn-off to the airport. It's a further 5km (3.5 of tar, 1.5 of gravel) and clearly signposted from there. If you haven't got transport, then they pick up travellers daily (Mon–Fri) at 16.30 at Businet (see page 143), the Internet Café, on Kabelenga Road, off Church Road. There's no charge for this. They can also arrange transfers to/from town or the airport on request, costing Kw10,000 for one person, plus Kw5,000 for every additional person.

Pioneer has beds in dorms, two-bed thatched chalets and a large grassy camping site with plenty of shade and a clean ablution block – all in about 26 acres of woodland surrounded by an electric fence. The chalets share the campers' ablutions at the moment, but may shortly have en-suite showers and toilets added. The owners plan to stock the grounds with some antelope, and also build a dam wall to make a lake for fishing.

Barbecue packs are available, as is a fridge/freezer space, ice and laundry facilities, if you need them. The large, thatched, 'clubhouse' bar has comfy chairs, a darts board and satellite TV. It serves snacks, but will also provide meals on request. Expect a full breakfast to be about Kw5,000, a light lunch around Kw3,000, and dinner Kw10–12,000. (Try the home-made ice-cream at Kw2,000.)
Rates: US$5 camping per person (US$2.50 for registered overland companies), US$8 for a bed in a dorm, US$20 for a 2-bed chalet

Sikh Temple
On a bend on the northeast side of the quiet Mumbwa Road, behind gates with clear yellow-and-gold insignia, lies the calm of a Sikh Temple. Whilst it is meant for pilgrims, travellers are welcomed provided that they do not smoke, drink alcohol or cook meat whilst here. There are twin rooms for which there is no charge, but it is customary to leave a donation.

YWCA Tel: 252726
South of Ridgeway, on the main Nationalist Road opposite the teaching hospital, between Chire Close and Dama Close, the YWCA is easy to find. It accepts both men and women to stay. However, the rooms are small and very basic. The cooking, washing and toilet facilities are all shared, and none too clean.

Every Tuesday morning (about 07.30–14.00) there's a vegetable market here, held partly in aid of the YWCA's work. You'll find lots of clean, fresh fruit and spices, and a very local, natural atmosphere. The prices are very low and fair, so if you need to stock up on fresh vegetables this is a good place to do so.

Rates: Kw18,000 per person per night. Bring your own food

WHERE TO EAT

In the past few years fast-food places have sprouted up all over Cairo Road, so there's no longer any need to search for eateries. However, for something good you'll still have to look hard.

If you're on a tight budget, then you will want to buy supplies from the shopping centres and cater for yourself. See the *Shopping: food and drink* section (page 140) for details of these. Equally there are street-food stalls and people selling snacks from baskets around the markets and bus stations – though judge their standards of hygiene carefully: food cooked as you watch is by far the best, but not very common. (In mid-'99 a controversial policy was started of banning all vendors from the streets of the city. You can judge for yourself if it has been a success.)

If you've more to spend, Lusaka has an increasing number of restaurants, and a high turnover of new ones. Fortunately, the rate of new ones opening seems to slightly outstrip the rate at which others close. Inevitably my recommendations are soon obsolete, so do ask around for what's new, or at least buy a copy of *Lusaka Lowdown*, for the best of the latest restaurants.

Yuppies with withdrawal symptoms might head for the designer beverages of **Chit Chat Café**, on 5A Omelo Mumbwa Road (marked as Omela Road on some maps, between the Great East and Church Roads). It serves a trendy choice of coffees, teas, fruit-juices and milkshakes on its L-shaped veranda, plus substantial breakfasts, light salady lunches and even burgers (albeit not greasy ones). There are a selection of overseas magazines for sale, and Chit Chat caters very well for children. If you're wondering about the prices… don't go! It closes on Mondays, but opens 09.00–19.00 Tuesday–Thursday, 09.00–11.00 on Friday and 10.00–19.00 at the weekend.

For competent but unimaginative food, the big hotels – the **Intercon**, **Pamodzi** and **Holiday Inn** – all have their own restaurants. The **Golden Spur** steak house at the Holiday Inn is very popular, and its charges are typical of the genre. The menu's huge, but expect around Kw6–15,000 for a starter, Kw12–19,000 for a steak main course, or Kw9–13,000 for a pizza or a burger. This is expensive compared with the fast food on Cairo Road, but it's a safer venue at night and never lacks helpful, willing staff. Both the Intercon and the Pamodzi have 'themed' evenings in their hotel restaurant, allowing quips like, 'if this is Thursday, it must be Italian.' These vary from quite good to totally dreadful.

If you seek a better meal, then you need to be mobile. Most other restaurants occupy obscure locations in the suburbs, so visitors who don't have their own transport end up resigned to dining in their own hotel.

Arabian Nights (tel: 750102, fax: 295613), in Kalundu (also see page 125), is typical. It is signposted off the Great East Road, several kilometres east of Addis Ababa Drive, and virtually all of its diners will drive there in the evening. Nobody walks. The restaurant itself is large and serves high-quality Pakistani cuisine, plus a few Cajun specialities and more universal dishes. Starters are around Kw7,500–8,500, main courses Kw19–23,000. There's a special vegetarian menu with five separate dishes at Kw16,000. Groups use a separate room (called the Tudor Lodge), upstairs, for medieval-style banquets.

The Showgrounds area, beside the Great East Road, is one popular place to hunt for eateries. On the edge of this, the **Marco Polo Restaurant** (tel: 250111) at the

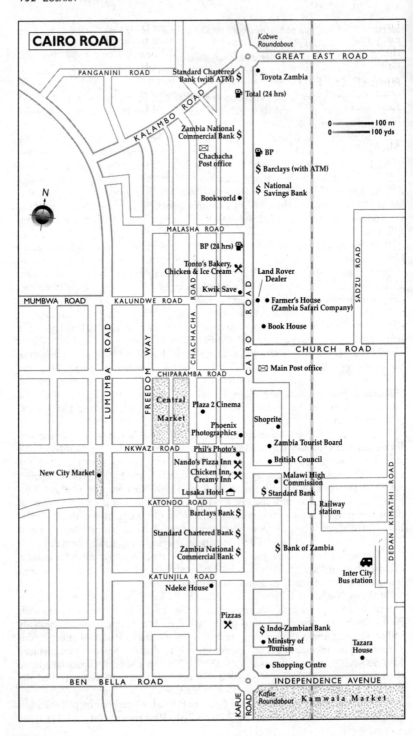

CAIRO ROAD

Lusaka Polo Club has been an enduring favourite for fairly elaborate fare. It's most easily reached from the Nangwenya Road entrance to the Showgrounds, and is closed on Mondays. Simpler eats are found at the nearby **Continental** (ex Polo Grill), which is altogether more lively. This is popular amongst the young-and-privileged crowd, serving a range of bites with a better selection of drinks and even occasional live music. Inside the Showgrounds, the **Shi Chuan Chinese Restaurant** (tel: 253842) has opened where the old Calabash Restaurant used to be, and serves good Chinese food.

Near the east gate of the grounds the **Spitfire Grill** (tel: 252333) was new in March '99, replacing the old Oasis Restaurant. It is very big and trying hard to impress. Expect starters at around Kw4,000, burgers and pizzas at around Kw10,000, and good, large steaks at Kw18,000. Wines are around Kw20,000 per bottle, or Kw3,000 corkage if you bring your own. In fact, the Showgrounds area as a whole is worth an evening visit when its restaurants and bars come to life.

Away from there, **Mike's Car Wash Centre**, on the left about 5km out of town on the Kafue Road, is the venue for **Mike's Restaurant & Take-away**, which is also a popular spot for an evening of drinking and eating. Expect a bill of around Kw15–25,000 for a good meal with a few beers. Also on the way out of town, **Pizza Island** (open 08.00–23.00) is at the Castle Shopping Centre on Kafue Road. The *sharwamas* from here come highly recommended (rolled chapatis with various tasty fillings), as do the pizzas.

If you'd like a good bar which also serves food, and has regular functions, then try **Brown's** on Kabelenga Road, between the Great East Road and Church Road, near Moore Pottery. It's a 'happening' twenty-to-thirty-somethings' place, relaxed and mixed. You'll find a variety of good beer on tap and some tasty light meals on the menu.

In a similar vein, **Chasers** (tel: 752659) is found at 9 Lagos Road (off Addis Ababa) in the leafy suburbs of Kapila (Rhodes' Park). It has safe parking and a garden outside, for when the bar's too busy. Inside it's rather like a friendly pub and serves simple, inexpensive food (sandwiches Kw5–8,000, steaks Kw10,000). Chasers remains open until around 02.00 on Friday and Saturday evenings.

Gringos (tel: 295190/292984), on the corner of Lukanga and Zambezi Roads in Roma has a few guestrooms (see page 126) but is mainly a restaurant. It serves lunch 12.00–14.30 and dinner 19.00–22.00, while its bar stays open longer: 18.00–23.00. At the back there's an open garden area that sometimes hosts a barbecue. Here you'll find starters at Kw1–5,000, steaks, Mexican dishes and fish main courses at Kw9–12,000 and desserts about Kw3,500. It's not a good idea to just drop in here unannounced; try to book at least a few hours in advance.

If you're looking for somewhere really special, then a consensus of informed opinion gives Lusaka's top three spots for foodies as:

Jaylin Restaurant (in the Lusaka Club at Longacres) tel: 252206
This is an old favourite, based in the Lusaka Club, near the corner of Los Angeles Boulevard and Haile Selassie Avenue. The atmosphere of this old sports club is colonial and almost seedy. Walk past the doorman, and towards the back of the club house you'll find what seems like an uninspiring café. However, it serves some of the best (and best value) food in town. The menu isn't fancy, but the food is good quality. The sizeable pepper steaks are a renowned, and consistently good, speciality. Don't miss them. Their salads are always good, as are their chow meins and stir-fried dishes – and the proprietor is invariably around to keep an eye on things. Expect to pay about US$15–20 per head for a meal with a few beers or glasses of wine.

Dil Restaurant 153 Ibex Hill Road. Tel: 262391; fax: 224515
East of Kabulonga, this is sometimes cited as Lusaka's best restaurant for its consistently high-quality Indian cuisine. The chef's from Bombay and, at about US$25 for a meal, the food is very good, but not cheap.

Hibiscus 40 Central Rd, Jesmondine. Tel: 01 295011
For something a little more dramatic, the Hibiscus is run by a fiery French-Canadian woman, Ms Paule Cadou, who goes to great lengths to import fresh seafood from Mozambique. So expect stylish sauces, top-class European food, and a bill of around US$30–40 per head. It's closed on Tuesdays.

GETTING AROUND

Lusaka is very spread out, so if you don't have your own vehicle you'll probably want to use taxis, and/or the small minibuses that ply between the outer suburbs/townships and the centre. If you are careful, then these are very useful and quite safe. The other possibility is to note that car hire firms usually supply their cars with a driver – who can act as a convenient guide for a short business trip.

Taxis

Lusaka's taxis are mostly small, decrepit Datsun 120Y or 1200 models, held together by remarkable roadside mechanics and lots of improvisation. The licensed ones will have a large number painted on their side, and even these will have no fare meter. When taking a taxi, you should agree a rate for the journey before you get into the vehicle. If you know roughly what it should cost, then most drivers recognise this and don't try to overcharge. As a last resort when bargaining, all licensed taxis should have a rate-sheet, giving the 'standard' prices for waiting time and various common journeys – though drivers will not admit to having one if the bargaining is going their way. Typical fares are:

Kw7,000	between Ridgeway (big hotels) and Cairo Road
Kw40,000	between the airport and town
Kw15–25,000	between the centre of town and the inner suburbs
Kw12,000	per hour of additional waiting time

If you need a vehicle all day, then consider hiring a taxi with its driver. Start by making a clear deal to pay by the hour or the kilometre, and record the time or the mileage reading. Around Kw10,000 per hour, or Kw1,000 per kilometre, is fair, though a tough negotiator would pay less.

Minibuses

These are the packed transport that the city's poorer commuters use to travel between the outer, satellite suburbs and the centre of town. There are many different routes, so if you want to find out which to use then go down to Chachacha Road, which is the unofficial terminus for most of them. These are an especially good way to reach the farther flung suburbs, or to get a lift along one of the main routes out to a good hitching spot. Fares are not normally dependent upon distance, and you can expect to pay less than Kw2,500 per journey. Minibuses usually have regular stops, but can sometimes just be flagged down if they're not full and you are lucky.

BANKS AND MONEY
American Express

Steve Blagus Travel is Zambia's official AMEX representative. Their office is at 24C Nkwazi Road, Lusaka 10101. Tel: 238889. They are open Mon–Fri 08.00–16.30 and Sat 08.30–11.30.

Banks

The main banks generally have their head offices along Cairo Road. These are the best ones to use if you are dealing with foreign currency or transfers. Their contact details are:

Barclays Bank of Zambia Kafue House, Cairo Rd. Tel: 228858/66 or 227859/63; fax: 222519
Citibank CitiBank House, Chachacha Rd. Tel: 229025; fax: 226254
Credit Africa Bank Anchor House, Cairo Rd. Tel: 220201; fax: 220196
Finance Bank Chanik House, Lusaka Square, Cairo Rd. Tel: 229733/39/40; fax: 224450
Prudence Bank 11th Floor, Society House, Cairo Rd. Tel: 220506; fax: 223691
Standard Chartered Bank Standard House, Cairo Rd. Tel: 229242; fax: 222092

Bureaux de change

These can be found along Cairo Road, but usually only deal with cash and will not exchange travellers' cheques. Many seem to do little to safeguard the privacy of transactions and hence the security of their customers. Alternatively most of the larger hotels will change money, including travellers' cheques, though they generally offer poor rates, or charge steep commissions – *and* may insist that you are a guest of the hotel.

Changing money on the street is of no advantage, as the rates are the same, but opens you to a much greater risk of being ripped off. Use a bank if you can, or a hotel if you cannot.

WHAT TO SEE AND DO

Perhaps the most fun to be had around town is simply people-watching, and talking with those who live here. From the poor street-vendors (if they're still allowed on the streets!) to taxi drivers and the aid-agency expats in the larger hotels, you'll find that people are usually happy to chat. They will comment freely on politics and the issues of the day, and probably ask you how you view things as a foreigner.

These conversations can be fascinating, but be mindful that there aren't debating points to be earned, just new points of view to learn. Try not to expound your prejudices, or to jump to hasty conclusions on issues with which you are not familiar, and you'll have much longer and more interesting conversations. Other ways to spend your time in Lusaka include:

Local markets

Several of the markets are fascinating to wander around, but pay attention to your safety and don't take anything valuable with you. Think twice before wandering around with a backpack, which is inviting theft, and if you have a safe place to leave your money belt, then don't bring that either.

The more relaxed of the two main markets to visit is about 500m east of the south end of Cairo Road. Walk over the railway on the Independence Avenue bridge, and you can't miss it on your right. Here is the country's centre for the sale of clothing donated by charities from the west. This trade, known as *salaula*, has badly affected Zambia's indigenous clothes industry – which previously thrived on the production and sale of printed cotton fabrics, like the common *chitenjes*. This is why *salaula*'s long-term value as a form of aid is hotly debated.

On the western side of Cairo Road, the old 'Soweto' market (which was between Katondo and Nkwazi roads) has been replaced with the **New City Market**, which is now along Lumumba Road. This is the city's biggest market, lively and interesting – it's even popular with adventurous expats on Saturday mornings. However, it is a place to be wary of, not well suited to single or less confident foreign travellers. Again, dress down for a visit and don't even think of taking those valuables with you.

There are two other large markets in the centre, though both are smaller than the New City Market. The **Central Market** is on on Chachacha Road, and **Kamwala Market** is off Independence Avenue near the Kafue Road fly-over bridge.

Bazaars

Somewhat different in character to the markets are a couple of genteel, upmarket bazaars, although their atmosphere is equally interesting.

The **Dutch Reformed Church** has a bazaar (entry Kw1,000 per person) on the last Saturday of each month from 09.00. Find it about 4km east of Ridgeway on Kabulonga Road, past Bishop's Road and towards Ibex Hill. It's quite a focal point for Zambia's growing Africaans community, whilst also attracting a large number of local expats. Expect gifts and crafts, from jewellery to hand-made clothing, as well as good biltong, furniture and even cosmetics. It's friendly and relaxed so do sit down for coffee and cakes. You can watch the people go by, and try a *koeksuster* – a delicious and traditional sweet twisted pastry.

There are occasional indoor flea markets held at the **National Sports Development Centre**. They normally have about 50 stalls with a variety of handmade crafts and open between 09.00 and 13.00 on a Saturday. There is secure parking, refreshments are always available, and entry is a nominal Kw1,000 per adult. At other times you'll find Lusaka's cheapest and best squash courts (glass-backed) here, as well as tennis courts and a bar.

Places to visit
Kabwata Cultural Centre

On Burma Road, just west of Jacaranda Road, are the rondavels of the Kabwata Cultural Village. These are all that remain of 300 similar huts, which were built in the 1930s and '40s by the colonial government to house Lusaka's black labour force. They were designed with just one room, to house single men, whose families were expected to remain in the rural areas and permanent urban settlements.

Between '71 and '73 the government demolished most of them to construct the flats now seen nearby. Fortunately, in 1974, 43 rondavels were saved and turned into a 'cultural centre' – a base where artists from all over Zambia could live and work. The aim was to preserve the country's cultural heritage.

Sadly, with little money spent on it, the centre has gradually crumbled. It probably remains the city's best spot for buying hand-carved crafts and curios. Many of the rondavels, set back a little from the road, shelter stone- and wood-carvers. Large wooden hippos (around Kw45,000) are cheaper than equivalent carvings near Livingstone's bridge over the Zambezi. The prices and quality of the carvings are good, and sometimes tribal dances are held here at 15.00 on Sundays during the winter. But the centre is in a poor state of repair.

Recently the German Agency for Technical Co operation (GTZ) has got together with the country's Tourism Council and hatched plans to upgrade and revitalise the centre. These include various new homesteads to represent the country's diverse ethnic groups, plus a craft shop, a restaurant serving traditional and other food, and even a 500-seater amphitheatre where visitors can watch traditional dances. Ideas of accommodation for visitors to stay overnight have even been mooted. Let's hope it all happens.

Kalimba Reptile Park

Kalimba is gradually becoming worth the journey. It now has good displays of crocodiles, snakes, chameleons and tortoises, including the rare African slender-nosed crocodile, *Crocodilus cataphractus*.

These occur throughout the DRC to West Africa, but are endangered because of the degradation of their habitat and because they are hunted for food in the DRC! In Zambia, *cataphractus* are found only in the Luapula River system, where they were (erroneously) thought to be extinct until recently.

Kalimba also has fishing ponds for anglers, crazy golf, a children's playground and volleyball court. Drinks and snacks are available, and I'm sad to record that Kalimba's fastest-selling burgers are croc-burgers. Chalets and a camping site are planned for the future.

To get there, head out of town on the Great East Road, then take a left on to District Road at the Caltex station, about 1km before the Chelstone Water Tower. This heads towards the east side of Ngwerere. Follow this road, the D564, about 11km to a T-junction, turn right and park about 1km later on the right.

Open: daily, 09.00–18.00. Rates: adults US$2.50, children US$1.25

Moore Pottery Factory

On the eastern side of Kabelenga Road, between the Great East Road and Church Road, Moore Pottery (PO Box 31277, tel: 235976 or 221814; fax: 237417) is well worth the 15-minute walk from Cairo Road for its excellent selection of beautiful ceramics.

It was founded in 1961 by Major Moore, but changed hands several times before being rescued by Christopher Mutale in 1991. The plan was to demolish the building, but instead he restored some of the original machinery and re-employed skilled workers who'd left.

The factory now has its own truck that collects most of its materials from Zambia: feldspar from Kapiri Mposhi, kaolin (China clay) from Serenje, and chalata ball clay from the Mkushi River. These are milled, mixed with water, sieved and purified on site. The resulting mix is then sieved to form hard clay cakes, and finally squeezed to produce solid cylinders of clay, the raw material for the pots. This turns out too heavy for bone china, but perfect for traditional African pottery.

Some of the finished products are authentic African pots, decorated with soft browns, fiery reds and brilliant white using natural additives mined in Zambia, like copper oxides, carbonates, malachite, manganese, copper ash and cobalt. Their inspiration is taken from various African tribes, and the work is beautiful. Some are just pure clay sculpture, created by the artists there. Other products are more mundane: terracotta floor tiles (using a different recipe of clays), and electrical insulators for ZESCO, the Zambian power utility. Most are for sale and, although expensive, they are top quality and make super gifts if you can carry them home safely.

Munda Wanga Zoo and Botanical Gardens

On Kafue Road, about 15km from the centre (in the Chilanga area), just after the turn-off for Lilayi Lodge, Munda Wanga was once the showpiece of Lusaka. Sadly, in recent years, the zoo's caged collection of unfortunate animals has been sad to the point of depressing. Fortunately, it was privatised in late '98, and there are ambitious, and hopefully realistic, plans to revitalise the zoo and botanical gardens, and also to open a theme park with water-game and adventure playgrounds here. These are being done with the close involvement of the team at Kalimba (see above), and so there's scope for optimism that it will eventually be a showcase once again.

The plan is for the zoo to specialise in native Zambian species, housed in humane open enclosures with specific Zambian themes. For visitors who have no time to travel to one of the national parks, this could be an easy way to see the wide variety of Zambian fauna.

The botanical gardens are being redeveloped and extended to include an indigenous forest. This will all take some time, but the first phase is scheduled to open in late '99 – when it is hoped that the Botanical Gardens will once again be a super venue for a picnic or a laze in the sun.
Open: daily, 09.00–18.00. Rates: adults US$2.50, children US$1.25

National Archives
A good library on Africa, and also an exhibition of photographs. Drop in if you're passing; they are found on Government Road. Maps are also for sale here.
Open: daily, 08.00–17.00

Namwandwe Art Gallery
Those interested in Zambian painting and sculpture might also try the Namwandwe Art Gallery, which is about 15km from the centre of Lusaka on Leopard's Hill Road, just past the American School. Expect oil paintings by prominent Zambian artists as well as watercolours, wood and stone carvings, and some delicate ceramics by over 150 Zambian artists. There are also pieces from other African artists.
Open: Tues–Fri 09.00–16.30; Sat and Sun 09.00–12.00; closed Mon

National Museum
This is off Independence Avenue, and has a large, popular witchcraft display.

Parliament buildings
Guided tours are organised around the National Assembly, on Nangwenya Road (off Addis Ababa Drive), on the last Thursday of the month.
Open: normally Friday afternoons only

Political Museum
Situated at the Mulungushi International Conference Centre, this displays some interesting, if slightly unimaginative, exhibits on the country's struggle for independence. Tel: 228805.
Open: daily, Mon–Fri 09.00–16.30. Admission free

The Showgrounds
Known more formally as the Agricultural Society Showgrounds, this is an enclosed area on the south side of the Great East Road, just past the new Manda Hill Complex.

This area has its own network of little roads which, once a year, fill to overflowing with visitors to stalls and displays for an annual exhibition of many aspects of Zambian industry and commerce. For most of the rest of the year it's quieter and reduces to an eclectic mix of restaurants, bars and businesses from Barclays Bank to a canine vet and a primary school to fast food outlets. Note that many of its entrances and exits close around sunset.

Zintu Community Museum
Houses a good cultural exhibition containing arts and crafts from all over the country in its building on Panganini Road. Tel: 223183.
Open: daily, Mon–Fri 10.00–15.00. Admission free

Nightlife
The period that a nightclub remains in fashion, and hence remains in business, is even shorter than the life of most restaurants. So recommendations in this section will, by their very nature, be out of date quickly. Better to ask the locals about the best places, and follow their recommendations. You should always be mindful of your safety, not take much cash to a club with you, and not linger anywhere that feels uncomfortable.

Current favourites include **Chez Ntemba**, behind the Kamwala market, which has a small cover charge and plays mainly rumba. The bar is good and on Friday and Saturday nights partying continues until dawn – but there's no food available. Elsewhere the **Cosmo Club** (tel: 273020) on Kafue Road is somewhat more chic – described by one clubber as 'where the rich go'.

Other possibilities include **Versus Café Inn,** again on Kafue Road, **Go Bananas** on Panganini Road and **Mr. Pete's Steakhouse** on Panganini Road (tel: 223428 or 291192).

At the other end of the scale, the **Theatre Club**, opposite the Pamodzi, is a fascinating place to chat to the locals if it's open. Its *raison d'être* is amateur dramatics, but it's been going downhill for several years. Recently an ambitious committee has started to try to turn the place around. Contact Nick Montgomerie (tel: 239408) or Siri Pelchen (tel: 253639) for the latest news on this.

Browns (see also page 133) on Kabelenga Road, near Moore Pottery, now has live jazz and blues music every Thursday and Friday evening.

SHOPPING
Lusaka's main shopping centre used to be Cairo Road where, before 1996, it was very difficult to find the right place to buy what you wanted. It was full of small, cramped private trader's shops. Then Shoprite opened its flagship store in the centre, and shopping immediately became easier (see *Shopping* in *Zambia Today* for more comments on this).

Now that the city's retailing horizons have widened, more large stores are gradually opening up. As I write, the city is eagerly awaiting the new **Manda Hill Shopping Complex**, on the corner of the Great East Road and Manchichi Road. It promises to be the biggest and best that Lusaka has yet seen. It's due to open in October '99 covering 81,420m2 at a cost of US$22.5 million. There will be about 55 shops, secure parking for 800 cars, a modern cinema complex and several acres of landscaped recreational ground. Expect restaurants, fast food outlets, pavement cafés and even a pub in this mall. Its main tenants will be Shoprite and Game, big South African retailers – and if this idea is a success here, then there's a similar development planned for Kitwe!

If you're buying in bulk, then don't forget the new **Shoprite Wholesale Outlet**. It's on the Kafue Road, about 2–3km after the Cairo Road roundabout, on the left hand side. You do not need to purchase vast quantities, though buying just one or two of something is not usually allowed. It's certainly the cheapest place to shop.

Food and drink

If you need food and supplies, then there are several obvious places – apart from the Manda Hill complex, mentioned above. The first is the original **Shoprite**, beside Lusaka Square, on the eastern side of Cairo Road. This was Shoprite's pioneering store in Zambia. It is huge and very successful. Inside you'll find a wide range of fresh vegetables and all kinds of food plus clothes and tupperware – very much like what you'd find in a large supermarket in Europe or America. There's an in-store bakery, a deli counter, a butchery, etc. Perhaps more surprising, it also stocks a basic range of tools, some bicycle parts, engine oil and a few basic motor spares including a very limited range of car tyres!

Outside of Lusaka's centre, there are a couple of smaller (but still sizeable) supermarkets, supplying good-quality produce. **Melissa Minimarket** is one of the best, situated just off the Great East Road in Northmead, behind the Mobil petrol station. It isn't cheap, but several delis and a bakery or two have sprung up around it (*Jimmy's Deli* has a good choice of yoghurts) and opposite it is a small craft market selling some good malachite bracelets, necklaces and a wide selection of carvings.

Kabulonga Shopping Centre is similar, though not quite as upmarket. Found at the corner of Kabulonga and Chindo Roads, it is very convenient if you have to stay at Belvedere Lodge. Next to it, on Chindo Road, is a large and impressive **Melissa Supermarket**, flanked on the other side of the road by an informal gathering of local vendors of fruit and vegetables.

Fresh vegetables can also be picked up from various street-sellers, like the excellent stall at the BP station on the south side of the Great East Road. (Though note there is a new move to ban street-vendors from the nation's streets. It's just being implemented at time of press.)

BC Farms, on Joseph Mwilwa Road, a few blocks northwest of the Pamodzi, has excellent fresh farm produce and an interesting notice-board if you want to buy/sell something from/to the expat or UN residents.

Cascades is equally good for fresh vegetables (it's on Sable Road, where the El Toro Coffee Shop is). If you're shopping on a Saturday morning, then the **Lusaka Garden Club** will be open in the Showgrounds. It's a popular and quite genteel social affair, where you can have tea and cakes as well as buy your vegetables!

For an atmosphere more typical of rural Zambia, try the vegetable market at the **YWCA**, on Nationalist Street (see page 130), every Tuesday morning. Great fresh vegetables and some money goes to a good cause.

Other supplies

For **cosmetics**, **toiletries** or **sun creams**, try the pharmacies and curio shops in the Holiday Inn, Pamodzi, and (especially) Intercontinental Hotels. Don't expect bargain prices, but you should find something close to what you are seeking.

For **books** on Zambia or wildlife, try The Book House, which is in a small row of shops near the junction of Cairo and Church Roads. (It used to be known as the Wildlife Bookshop, and was associated with the WCSZ, the forerunner of the Wildlife and Environmental Conservation Society.) For a wider range of literary interests, try Bookworld, either at the north end of Cairo Road or in Kabulonga shopping centre. Alternatively, Wed–Fri 09.30–17.00 or Saturday 09.30–12.30, Mary's Book Shop opens on Leopard's Hill Road, 1km beyond the end of the tarmac. The Video Shop, on Bishop's Road in Kabulonga, also stocks a small selection of second-hand books – which tends to be a more interesting and eclectic range than the new books which are available.

Exclusive Books (tel/fax: 264969) also has a good range; find it in Bancroft Garden Centre beside the Dutch Reformed Church east of Ridgeway on Kabulonga Road, past Bishop's Road and towards Ibex Hill. The garden centre here also offers toasties and snacks as well as a wide variety of vegetation.

Basic **camera supplies** can be found at Phoenix Photographics and Royal Art Studios, which are adjacent on Cairo Road, near Society House. Alternatively try Fine Art Studios, on Chachacha Road. Don't expect to find a great range of anything at any of these, though they do stock a good range of Fuji film, and even the slow *Velvia* slide film on which many of the photographs in this book are taken.

Car repairs used to be difficult to arrange as spare parts were in poor supply. However, in the last few years this has changed considerably as (particularly) Toyota have moved into Zambia. Their main centre, for parts, sales and service, is towards the north end of Cairo Road (PO Box 33438. Tel: 229109/13 or 221635, fax: 223846).

Alternatively, for other makes, garages include the Impala Service Station (PO Box 31407; tel: 238275 or 238284; fax: 238285) on the Great North Road just past the roundabout at the end of Cairo Road, which now specialises in tyres and wheel-balancing, and AutoWorld (PO Box 31407; tel: 223207 or 237716/9; fax: 223323) on Freedom Way, near the corner with Ben Bella Road.

Souvenirs and curios

For typical **African carvings, basketware and curios**, you probably won't get better value or a wider selection than at Kabwata Cultural Centre, on Burma Road (see *What to see and do* above). However, you could also try African Relics, at the airport; The Gift Box, on Chachacha Road; the outdoor market at Northmead opposite Melissa Minimarket; and Desert Gold (PO Box 34086; tel: 255329/251255).

Aside from these, Lusaka is not a shopper's paradise, though if you want pirate music cassettes then the stalls on Chachacha Road have some cheap buys.

If you can transport it safely, there is good value (if not actually cheap) **pottery** to be had at Moore Pottery (see page 137) on Kabulonga Road, or Bente Lorentz Pottery, off Los Angeles Boulevard behind Longacres Market.

Gems and jewellery can be found in expensive shops at the Intercontinental, Pamodzi or Holiday Inn, though don't expect any bargains. More original (but alas, not cheaper) creations in silver can be found at Kalipinde, on Panganini Road.

For a more practical and much cheaper souvenir get a *chitenje* for about Kw5–10,000 – there are shops in the smallest of towns. You will see these 2m-long sections of brightly patterned cotton cloth everywhere, often wrapped around local women. Whilst travelling use them as towels, sarongs, picnic mats or – as the locals do – simply swathed over your normal clothes to keep them clean. When back home, you can cut the material into clothes, or use them as coverings. Either way, you will have brought a splash of truly African colour back home with you.

INFORMATION AND ADDRESSES
British Council

If you are in Lusaka for any length of time then the British Council runs a good library, with lending and reference sections, from its offices in Heroes Place off Cairo Road. Joining fee is £4 (US$6) for books, and £10 (US$15) for videos.

Car hire

See *Vehicle hire* in *Chapter 5* for advice and a guide to typical rates. Lusaka's car hire companies cater more for business people visiting the city than for tourists. Consequently they may insist upon foreign drivers using a chauffeur, and will usually only have time-and-mileage rates rather than the 'unlimited-mileage' rates normally expected by those hiring cars for fly-drive trips. (Which makes sense as you'd have to be insane to hire a 2WD for a fly-drive trip around Zambia.) The larger companies are:

AVIS PO Box 38645, Holiday Inn, Lusaka. Tel: 251642 or 251652 or 251666; fax: 252201
Jul's Car Hire Plot 5508 Lusiwasi Rd, (off Libala Rd), Kalundu, PO Box 32863, Lusaka, Zambia. Tel: 292979 or 293972; fax: 01 291246
New Ace Car Hire Zimco House, Ground Floor, Cairo Rd, Lusaka. Tel: 232654; cell 704368
Zungulila Zambia PO Box 31475, TAZ House Annex, corner of Chiparamba Rd & Chachacha Rd. Tel: 227730 or 223234 or 220251; fax: 227729

Couriers

If you need to send something valuable then do not trust the postal service. A courier is by far the best way. Alternatively, if you just need something sending rapidly then look towards Mercury's excellent 'mercury mail' service (see *Chapter 8*, page 105, for comprehensive details). Three of the main couriers in Lusaka are:

DHL (Zambia) Tel: 229768
Mercury Couriers Tel: 231137; fax: 239872
Skynet Couriers Tel: 227125

To make sure that your post and packages arrive within Zambia, Mercury mail or one of the above is also the best way.

Emergencies

For a serious medical condition, see *Chapter 6, Health and Safety*, and don't hesitate to use the emergency number given with your medical insurance. As a failsafe, many adventure/safari companies, lodges and camps also subscribe to an emergency medical evacuation service. Good travel insurances will also cover you for use of their service, although authorisation for this in an emergency can take time. Their regional offices are:

Health International/Medical Air Rescue Service (MARS) Cairo Rd North End (next to Barclays Bank), P O Box 35999, Lusaka. Tel: 01 236644 or 702664 for emergencies, or 231175/6 for general enquiries; fax: 231081 or 224833; email: himrsz@zamnet.zm

Specialty Emergency Services The Grove, P O Box 31500, Kafue Rd, Lusaka. Tel: 01 273302–7; fax: 273181/273301; email: mcd@zamnet.zm

For less life-threatening conditions, your embassy or hotel can be of help, as both will be able to recommend a doctor. A sick foreign traveller will usually be accepted by one of the well-equipped clinics used by the city's more affluent residents without too many questions being asked at first. Proof of comprehensive medical insurance will make this all the more speedy, so try:

Corpmed Clinic on Cairo Road (north end, behind Barclays Bank) Tel: 01 222612 or 226983. This is probably Lusaka's best equipped hospital with a very modern trauma centre, its own ambulance service, and a laboratory. This is managed by MARS (see above). There's a doctor on duty here 24-hours, though the clinic routinely opens for non-emergencies Mon–Fri 08.00–16.00, and Sat 09.00–11.00

Primary Care Services Ltd Katopola Road and the Great East Road. Tel: 01 253858. This also has a dental surgery, tel: 01 261247

Monica Chiumya Memorial Clinic off Buluwe Road, near Lake Road, Kabulonga. Tel: 260491

Alternatively, the University Teaching Hospital has a department for emergencies (tel: 01 254113), though it is now sadly overstretched and best avoided if possible.

Internet cafés
Before 1999 there were no internet cafés in Lusaka. Now there are two, and I'm sure that by the time you read this there'll be lots more.

Lusaka City Library Internet Café
Situated in the front of the City Library, in Katondo Street, opposite the Development Bank, this was just setting up in the middle of '99 as this book goes to press. So far it has four computers, a telephone, fax, secretarial services and a Mercury Courier Agency. After hours the premises are available for computer training and chess courses. For more info call Rieke on 01 773993.

Businet Internet Café Plot 4974 Kabelenga Road (on top of Lewis Construction's offices, between Church Road and the Great East Road), PO Box 32056, Lusaka. Tel: 01 229261; fax 229262; email: admin@businet.co.zm

Here you can pick up your mail, browse the web on the 'latest large-screen multi-media computers with a high-speed connection to the Internet', or use their more standard fax and secretarial services. They serve fresh coffee too.

Post and communications
Lusaka's busy main post office is in the centre of Cairo Road, on the corner with Church Road. The main hall on the ground floor has a row of assistants in cubicles – above which the occupant's responsibilities are detailed.

Upstairs on the first floor, you will find the telegraph office (open Mon–Fri 08.30–16.30, Sat 08.00–12.00). Here you can send a telex or a fax, or even make an international phone call. It is often crowded and conversations are anything but private, but they can be accomplished surprisingly fast. Time is metered in three-minute units, and a call will be cut off automatically unless you instruct the operators otherwise.

Travel agents
Cairo Road seems lined by travel agents, as if the capital's residents do little but travel. At the last count, there were 35 different agencies in Lusaka's yellow pages telephone directory. However, attentive and efficient service isn't so common, and at present only a few are used to the demands of overseas clients.

Most safari arrangements are best made as far in advance as possible. Unless you are travelling totally independently (driving or hiking and camping everywhere), you should book with a good specialist tour operator before you leave (see page 62). This will also give you added consumer protection, recourse from home if things go wrong – and most importantly it'll get you into the places you want to visit.

If you are in Lusaka and need to arrange something urgently, then try to get a personal recommendation of a good local agent. Many have their own favourite properties, or trips, and will recommend those, regardless of what would suit you best. You will certainly have to accept that there is little choice in the camps that are left.

However, if you are stuck then your best bet would be to contact one of Lusaka's better travel agents:

African Tour Designers PO Box 31802, Castle Shopping Centre, on Kafue Road. Tel: 01 224616/223641/225386; fax: 224915
Kachelo Travel Plot 31H, Sable Rd, Kabulonga, PO Box 30946, 10101. Tel: 01 263973 or 260817 or 26 5569; fax: 265560
Steve Blagus Travel 24C Nkwazi Rd, P.O. Box 31530. Tel: 01 227739/40 or 227285; fax: 225178; tlx: ZA 43320
Voyages PO Box 37609. Tel: 0\1 253082/3/4; fax 253048. On Suez Road, just past Danny's Restaurant, Voyages is barely 100m from the Holiday Inn Hotel.
Zambian Safari Company Farmers House, Cairo Rd. Tel: 01 228682; fax: 222906

Further information

There are few really useful sources of information about Lusaka, except for the excellent monthly *Lusaka Lowdown*. These super booklets approach 100 pages in length and have independent reviews of restaurants, lots of topical articles and letters, and a fair sprinkling of humour. At only about Kw1,000 per copy, you can't afford *not* to buy a copy if you see one – even if you're only passing through the capital. Seek them out at hotels, larger supermarkets, service stations, bookshops in Lusaka and Shoprite outlets across the country. From outside Zambia, you can check out their website at www.lowdown.co.zm. Other than this, reliable, up-to-date information on Lusaka is difficult to find.

Livingstone and Victoria Falls

Livingstone is probably better oriented towards visitors than any other corner of Zambia. However, visitors travelling north from Zimbabwe are attracted simply by the Victoria Falls, and Livingstone often remains unseen. Some even view it with suspicion, being bigger and less well known than the small Zimbabwean town which shares the name of the waterfall.

This chapter aims to give details of both sides of the river: Zambian and Zimbabwean. Both have different views of the waterfall, as both have different attractions for visitors. Just as it is worth seeing both sides of the Falls to appreciate the whole waterfall, you will almost certainly find attractions that interest you in both Livingstone and Victoria Falls.

Tourism on the Zambian side of the Falls still lags behind that on the Zimbabwe side, but this is changing as Livingstone becomes popular in its own right. Historians might note that most of the adventure activities like rafting, bungee jumping, and microlighting originated on the Zambian side of the Falls, before being taken over by the larger commercial interests of Zimbabwean companies. While Livingstone's infrastructure may not be as developed, this means that it also feels pleasantly less commercial.

History

We can be sure that the Falls were well known to the native peoples of Southern Africa well before any European 'discovered' them. After the San/bushmen hunter-gatherers, the Tokaleya people inhabited the area, and it was probably they who christened the Falls 'Shongwe'. Later, the Ndebele knew the Falls as the 'aManza Thunqayo', and after that the Makololo referred to them as 'Mosi-oa-Tunya'.

However, their first written description comes to us from Dr David Livingstone, who approached them in November 1855 from the west – from Linyanti, along the Chobe and Zambezi rivers. Livingstone already knew of their existence from the locals, and wrote:

> 'I resolved on the following day to visit the falls of Victoria, called by the natives Mosioatunya, or more anciently Shongwe. Of these we had often heard since we came into the country: indeed one of the questions asked by Sebituane [the chief of the Makololo tribe] travelling was, "Have you the smoke that sounds in your country?" They did not go near enough to examine them, but, viewing them with awe at a distance, said, in reference to the vapour and noise, "'Mosi oa tunya" (smoke does sound there). It was previously called Shongwe, the meaning of which I could not ascertain. The

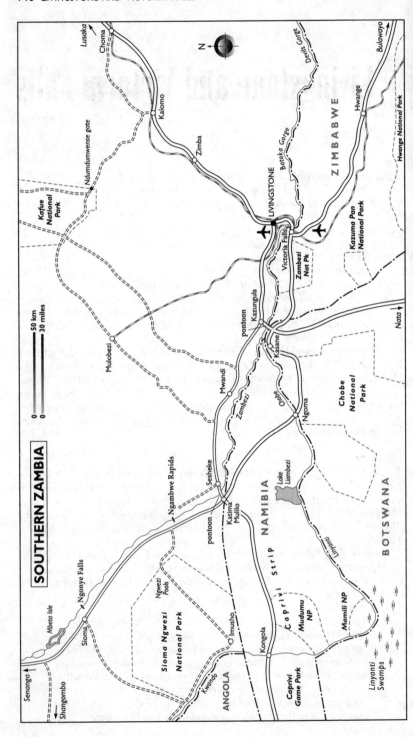

word for a "pot" resembles this, and it may mean a seething caldron; but I am not certain of it.'

Livingstone continues to describe the river above the Falls, its islands and their lush vegetation, before making his most famous comment about sightseeing angels, now abused and misquoted by those who write tourist brochures to the area:

'Some trees resemble the great spreading oak, others assume the character of our own elms and chestnuts; but no one can imagine the beauty of the view from anything witnessed in England. It had never been seen before by European eyes; but scenes so lovely must have been gazed upon by angels in their flight. The only want felt is that of mountains in the background. The falls are bounded on three sides by ridges 300 or 400 feet in height, which are covered in forest, with the red soil appearing amongst the trees. When about half a mile from the falls, I left the canoe by which we had come down this far, and embarked in a lighter one, with men well acquainted with the rapids, who, by passing down the centre of the stream in the eddies and still places caused by many jutting rocks, brought me to an island situated in the middle of the river, on the edge of the lip over which the water rolls.'

from the autobiographical *Journeys in Southern Africa*

Those who bemoan the area's emphasis on tourism should note that there must have been sightseeing boat trips ever since David Livingstone came this way.

Being the most eastern point reachable by boat from the Chobe or Upper Zambezi rivers, the area of the Falls was a natural place for European settlement. Soon more traders, hunters and missionaries came into the area, and by the late 1800s a small European settlement had formed around a ferry crossing called the Old Drift, about 10km upstream from the Falls. However, this was built on low-lying marshy ground near the river, buzzing with mosquitoes, so malaria took many lives.

By 1905 the spectacular Victoria Falls bridge had been completed, linking the copper deposits of the Copperbelt and the coal deposits at Wankie (now Hwange) with a railway line. This, and the malaria, encouraged the settlers to transfer to a site on higher ground, next to the railway line at a place called Constitution Hill. It became the centre of present-day Livingstone, and many of its original buildings are still standing. A small cemetery, the poignant remains of Old Drift, can still be seen on the northern bank of the Zambezi within the Mosi-oa-Tunya National Park.

In 1911 Livingstone became the capital of Northern Rhodesia (now Zambia), which it remained until 1935, when the administration was transferred to Lusaka.

Geology

The Falls are, geologically speaking, probably a very recent formation. About a million years ago, the Zambezi's course is thought to have been down a wide valley over a plateau dating from the karoo period, until it met the Middle Zambezi rift – where the Matetsi River mouth is now.

Here it fell about 250m over an escarpment. However, that fast-falling water would have eroded the lip of the waterfall and gouged out a deeper channel within the basalt rock of the escarpment plateau – and so the original falls steadily retreated upstream. These channels tended to follow some existing fissure – a crack

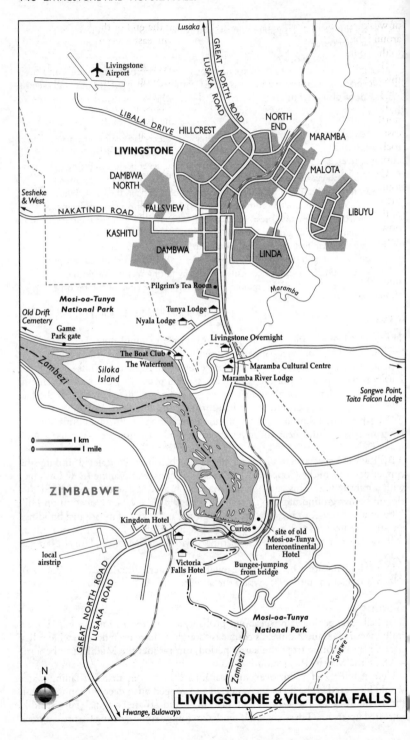

LIVINGSTONE & VICTORIA FALLS

or weakness, formed when the lava first cooled at the end of the karoo period. At around the Batoka Gorge these fissures naturally run east–west in the rock, parallel to the course of the valley.

By around the Middle Pleistocene period, between 35,000 and 40,000 years ago, this process had formed the Batoka Gorge, carving it out to within about 90km of the present falls.

However, as water eroded away the lip of the falls, its valley gradually turned north, until it was almost at right-angles to the basalt fault lines which run east–west. Then the water began to erode the fissures and turn them into walls of rock stretching across the valley, perpendicular to it, over which gushed broad curtains of water.

Once such a wall had formed, the water would wear down the rock until it found a fault line behind the wall, along which the water would erode and cause the rock subsequently to collapse. Thus the new fault line would become the wall of the new falls, behind the old one. This process resulted in the eight gorges that now form the river's slalom course after it has passed over the present Falls. Each gorge was once a great waterfall.

Today, on the eastern side of the Devil's Cataract, you can see this pattern starting again. The water is eroding away the rock of another fault line, behind the line of the present falls, which geologists expect will form a new waterfall a few thousand years from now.

LIVINGSTONE
Orientation
Livingstone town itself is compact, and surrounded by several small township suburbs just a few kilometres from its centre. Navigation is easy, even without a map, though signposts are often missing.

Livingstone's main street is the important Mosi-oa-Tunya Road. Sections of this are lined with classic colonial buildings – corrugated iron roofs and wide wooden verandas. Drive north on the main street out of the city, and it becomes Lusaka Road leading to the capital.

Head south for about 10km and you reach the Zambezi River and Victoria Falls themselves. There are some places to stay around here, a border post to cross the Zambezi into Zimbabwe, a small museum, and an excellent curio stand selling locally produced souvenirs.

Travel west from town on Nakatindi/Kazungula Road and you soon find yourself parallel to the Zambezi, following its north bank upstream towards Kazungula and the ferry to Botswana. Signposts point left, to small, exclusive lodges, perched at picturesque spots on the river's bank.

Getting there and away
By air
Livingstone's international airport is just 5km northwest of the town centre on Libala Drive. It has only basic facilities: a bar serving drinks and snacks, and a few small shops selling post cards, curios and crafts.

It is served by two domestic carriers, Eastern Air and Zambian Airways (formerly Roan Air), who offer scheduled flights. Eastern Air flies Lusaka-Livingstone-Mongu-Lusaka on Wednesdays and Saturdays. Zambian Airways flies Lusaka-Livingstone-Lusaka on Fridays and Sundays. Flights to Lusaka cost about US$160 one way. Book through their Lusaka offices (see page 114), or via one of the travel agents in Livingstone.

The only charter company based here is Del Air (see page 191), who offer flight

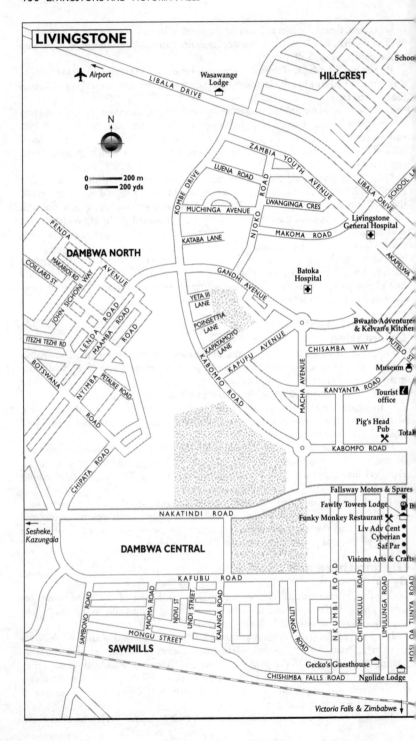

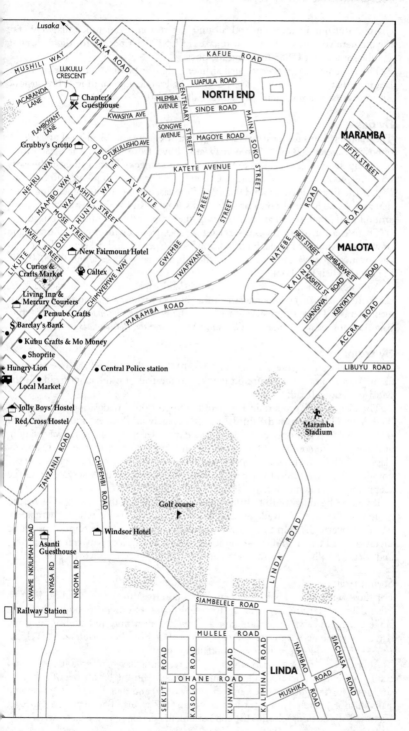

charters to/from Livingstone and around the region. Remember that if you're leaving here you must pay departure taxes of US$20 per person for flights leaving Zambia, and about US$5 for domestic ones

There are no major international airlines calling at Livingstone at the moment. But note that if you are trying to fly into the Falls area, then landing at Livingstone Airport is just as convenient as Victoria Falls Airport.

By bus

The main terminus for local buses is Akapelwa Street, just on Mosi-oa-Tunya Road, opposite Barclay's Bank. (Some may also leave from around the post office, including the popular post bus to Lusaka.) Here a range of buses gather in the early morning. Most head towards Lusaka, though one or two will go west to Sesheke. Expect the first to leave around 06.30, and the last around 11.00, depending upon demand. A seat to Lusaka on a large bus costs around Kw14,000, on a small minibus around Kw17,000. If you are backpacking, then expect the attentions of bus touts.

There is a EuroAfrica coach service that goes from Livingstone to Lusaka and onwards to Kitwe or Ndola. It costs around US$6 per leg and tickets can be bought (in advance) at Bwaato Adventure's office. It normally leaves about 07.00–07.30, but check when you book.

Although often more like cut-down overland trips, and aimed at backpackers, there are usually several operators running buses or trucks to Windhoek, Maun or even Harare. These often stop at parks on the way. See *Backpackers' overland trips*, page 190, for examples like the *Okavango Mama* and *the Botswana Bus*.

By train

The railway station (reservations: tel: 03 321001 ext 336) is well signposted and is about 1km south of the centre on the way to the Falls, on the eastern side of the Mosi-oa-Tunya Road.

The Zambezi Express train is scheduled to go from Livingstone to Lusaka on Tuesdays, Thursdays, and Saturdays at 18.30, arriving the next morning around 07.00. Bookings can only be made on the day of departure at the railway station, and can only be confirmed by payment – thus you must go in person. Economy class is US$5, first class US$10 and two- or four-berth first-class sleeper compartments are US$14 per person. There is an onward train service up to the Copperbelt or down to Johannesburg from Lusaka.

If you are heading south to Bulawayo or Johannesburg, then it would be best to go across the border (walk or taxi) to Victoria Falls, from where there is an excellent overnight train to Bulawayo. (This makes much more sense than a long diversion via Lusaka.) There are no longer any train services between Livingstone and Victoria Falls.

Steam train

For those with more flexible budgets, Train de Luxe offers the 'Zambezi Express Steam Train' service between Victoria Falls and Hwange, in both directions three times weekly. Departure times allow for morning and afternoon game drives at Hwange. Contact: Railway Safaris, PO Box 2536, Bulawayo. Tel/fax: (2639) 75575/64466; email: res@traindeluxe .co.zw.

Alternatively, the Victoria Falls Safari Express runs day-trips on a luxury steam train. These leave Victoria Falls heading north, stop on the bridge over the border for lunch (or a sundowner, depending on the time) and then head back to Victoria Falls. Unfortunately, you can't join the train in Zambia. They have an office in Victoria Falls station, tel: (26313) 4682 or email: fallsexp@mail.pci.co.zw.

Driving west

If you have a vehicle and intend to head west, into Namibia's Caprivi Strip, Botswana, or Western Zambia, then Nakatindi Road continues past the lodges by the river and, after about 60km, to Kazungula – where Namibia, Botswana, Zimbabwe and Zambia all meet at a notional point. Here you can continue northwest, within Zambia to Sesheke, or take the ferry across the Zambezi into Botswana, near Kasane. The road from Kazungula to Sesheke is about 130km, and has been in a very bad state of repair for years, with large, frequent potholes making the drive very slow and uncomfortable. (See *The Western Provinces*, pages 375–6, for more on Sesheke.)

As an aside, Kazungula is said to take its name from the tree known locally as the Muzungula tree (aka sausage tree, *Kigelia africana*) on which David Livingstone is reported to have carved his name when he passed.

The less bumpy option is to cross the Zambezi into Botswana, drive through Kasane and on to an excellent gravel road to the Namibian border at Ngoma, where you cross the Chobe River into Namibia. From there the good gravel road to Katima Mulilo is now being tarred, and from Katima you can drive across into Zambia. There is a small village on the Zambian side of the border, also called Katima Mulilo, and a ferry across the Zambezi to Sesheke. This is a longer drive, and has half-a-dozen border posts at which you must complete border formalities – which means lots of time standing around and filling in forms. However, the driving is much more comfortable, and both Kasane and Katima have good supplies and communications.

This route also involves purchasing a Botswana road insurance, for about 20 Botswana pula or 25 South African rand (US$ or UK£ are not accepted) on entry into Botswana. As a deterrent to car thieves, if you have a South African registered vehicle then you may also need to obtain police clearance at Katima Mulilo to take the vehicle out of Namibia.

Where to stay

There is no lack of accommodation in Livingstone, or across the river in Victoria Falls. In both there's a very wide range of options from campsites and backpackers' hostels to guesthouses, hotels and luxury lodges. The choice is overwhelming, though knowing the options in advance will make finding good value much easier. The Zambian side of the Falls is quieter, but has many bush lodges with lovely situations on the Zambezi River, a short distance from town. Zimbabwe has very few equivalents. Most have a true 'bush' location, whilst being close enough to enjoy the attractions and activities of the Falls.

In town

In alphabetical order:

Asanti Guesthouse (6 rooms)

Signposted from the main Mosi-oa-Tunya Road, opposite Nakatindi Road, Asanti Guesthouse is actually at the intersection in the middle of Nyasa Road. It has six very basic rooms, linked by nicely painted (but rather dark and gloomy) corridors. Five share a couple of separate showers, bathrooms and toilets. The sixth has an en-suite shower and toilet, as well as a more secure lock on the door than the others. It is clean but its atmosphere was less than welcoming when the author last visited, despite the presence of two helpful staff.
Rates: Kw30,000 per en-suite room, Kw20,000 for the other. Breakfast not included

Chanter's Guesthouse (3 rooms) Lukulu Crescent, PO Box 60623. Tel: 03 323412. (Manager tel: 323850)

Run by former Lusaka hotelier, Richard Chanter, this is more of a restaurant (see page 165) than a dedicated guesthouse. However, it has three guest rooms and plans to expand to a total of seven. It stands in a leafy residential area on the northern side of Livingstone, perhaps 2km from the centre. To reach it leave the centre on Mosi-oa-Tunya Road, towards Lusaka, and turn left on to Obote Avenue, just before the road bends to the left. Chanter's is on Lukulu Crescent, the fourth right turn. This is not named on some maps.

All three rooms have wooden parquet floors, twin beds, satellite TV (all showing the same station) and a bath with shower attachment in the tiled, en-suite bathroom. Two rooms have ceiling fans and one is air-conditioned. They're pleasant but unremarkable. Its public rooms are more stylish, the tables and chairs extending on to a patio and garden at the back. Meals are served all day at this popular local dining spot, and the food is excellent.

Rates: US$40 per room per night, including basic continental breakfast. A la carte options for breakfast are available, but cost extra

Fawlty Towers Lodge & International Backpackers 216 Mosi-oa-Tunya Road, Livingstone. Tel/fax: 03 323432; email: ahorizon@zamnet.zm

Located on the Mosi-oa-Tunya Road, just south of the turn-off to Nakatindi/Kazungula Road, you can't miss this popular international backpackers' place. Look for the colourful wrought-iron burglar bars shaped like African faces. Enter through the large gates covered by straw mats, and you come to the lively bar, which has a pool table, comfortable sitting areas... and also serves as reception.

Upstairs, in the main building, are four dorms, each sleeping six, and one separate double room. The rooms are basic, but do have colourful curtains and (a very welcome rarity) air conditioning. There are two comfortable lounges with a TV/video each, and a kitchen, a large dining room, toilets and showers.

Behind this you'll find a spacious private garden area with an inviting swimming pool surrounded by lawns. Campers here on the lawns have toilets and showers, all clean with hot and cold running water. Also in the garden area is a bungalow housing two double rooms and a dorm (which sleeps six). This has a communal lounge, two showers and toilets, and a shared kitchen (all accessories provided). Everything is neat and clean and showers have both hot and cold running water. There are plans to build a further nine (en-suite) chalets in this garden area.

Bed linen and mosquito nets are provided free of charge, as is unlimited coffee and tea. Barbecues are held on Monday nights in the garden area, otherwise the excellent 'Funky Monkey' restaurant stands just at the back of the garden. There is also a comprehensive workshop in the back of the garden, where you can service your vehicle, if necessary.

Also here is a booking office where you can book any activities or one of African Horizons' trips (see page 190) on the 'Botswana Bus' (around US$350 for a week). Phone, fax and internet service are also available here, and you can rent a mountain bike for US$8 per day, or US$5 for a half-day.

If you're backpacking without your own transport, then Fawlty Towers is clean, well run and tremendously convenient for the centre of Livingstone. Vibrant colours and ethnic touches help to give it fun atmosphere and it runs daily transfers to and from Victoria Falls.

Rates: US$10 per person for the bungalows, US$6 for a dorm bed. Camping is US$3 per person. At 24 hours' notice, the 'Backpacker's Special' transfers you from the Falls, gives you a dorm bed for the night, a drink in the bar and a meal at the Funky Monkey – all for US$10.

Gecko's Guesthouse PO Box 60007. Tel/fax: 03 322267; email: gecko@ zamnet.zm

Run by Dave Lewis, and the base for Livingstone Safaris (see page 192), Gecko's is on the south side of Livingstone, on Limulunga Road. Travelling from Livingstone to the Falls, passing the railways station on your left, take a right turn beside Ngolide Lodge and then first right again. Gecko's is then on the left, perhaps 10 minutes' walk from the centre. Recognise it by its green gates and white walls with railings.

It's a lovely residential place to stay, a little quieter than the backpackers' places in the centre of town. It has one dorm sleeping six, which is airy and light. There are also four private rooms for two people each and endless space for camping. All guests share well-kept showers and toilets. There's a kitchen for cooking (implements provided), as well as a comfy lounge and lots of useful notice boards. A cook comes in daily and will prepare an evening meal for you, on request. Bedding and fans are provided free, as is tea and coffee. There's secure parking, a safe place to leave luggage and Dave's team will arrange any activities for you during your stay.

Rates: US$6 for a dorm bed, US$10 per person sharing a private room, US$12 for a single room. Camping is US$4 per tent

Grubby's Grotto Tel: 03 324024; tel/fax: 322370
Run by the indomitable Grubby, this is used only by overland trucks. It can be difficult to find, as most maps don't show the section of road it is on. The easiest way to get there is to turn north from Mosi-oa-Tunya Road for three blocks, and then turn right on to Maambo Way (some maps still show a very old name of Northway for this road). Follow this past Kashitu Street, and Grubby's is behind a large set of gates on the left, just before Obote Avenue.

Once inside you'll find a huge old colonial house, which is largely empty. The lawns around the house are used for camping; there's a large swimming pool and a bar at the front which opens on to the veranda. Food isn't normally provided, though with advance notice, a sheep on a spit can be arranged for large truck parties. The overland groups staying here form the basis of the trips for Raft Extreme (see page 192).

Rates: US$3 per person camping, except the crew who get free rooms

Jolly Boys' Hostel PO Box 61088, Plot No. 559 Mokambo Way. Tel/fax: 03 324299; email: jboys@zamnet.zm
Mokambo Way (or *Road*, on some maps) runs parallel to Mosi-oa-Tunya Road, on its eastern side, and Jolly Boys' is easy to find just south of Mutelo Street. This is a quintessential backpackers' lodge, run by the friendly Paul Quinn (with occasional help from his Mum, Val) in a large old residential building with a substantial garden.

It has a total of 24 beds, including two in a private room. All share toilets and showers. The dorms each have 6 beds (3 bunks) and are clean and well kept. A cook organises a simple set menu for breakfast and evening meals, costing Kw4,500 for English breakfast (Kw3,000 for the veggie option), and Kw5,000 for dinner. Friday nights are often sociable affairs with dinner outside from a barbecue. As usual, there's a bar at the back for drinks.

Jolly Boys' facilities are good, with a telephone, fax, pool, fridge, and kitchen. The atmosphere is relaxed and unpretentious, though sometimes too busy to allow much peace and quiet. Paul and the staff arrange activities for you in the Falls, and know the area well.

Rates: Dorm beds are US$6, camping US$3 per person per night

Living Inn PO Box 60853, 25 John Hunt Way. Tel: 03 324203-5 or 324182/3; fax: 324206; tlx: 24380 SHAR ZA
This is a small, basic hostel with a central open-air quadrangle surrounded by two storeys of small rooms. Those upstairs are slightly different from those below. All have air-conditioning, a fan and TV with Mnet. They are carpeted and each has a couple of easy chairs, a table, a double bed and a bathroom with a shower.

Downstairs the rooms have no TV and are tiled, not carpeted, but they do have both double and single beds. All have telephones, though none is direct dial (all rely on an operator). Living Inn seems to do well from hosting small workshops and conferences for Zambians, but few visitors stay here. If you are stuck for somewhere in the centre of town, then it might be worth trying.

Rates: Kw60,000 for a twin, Kw45,000 for a single

Livingstone Overnight PO Box 60443. Tel/fax: 03 320371; email: overnight@ outpost.co.zm

Run by the friendly Anita and Allan Goodyear, Livingstone Overnight started in October '97 on a site not far from the Maramba Cultural Centre. It's perhaps 500m off the main road, signposted by a large orange warthog.

It's an impressively beautiful campsite – aiming to attract upmarket overlanding companies (if that's not a contradiction in terms) and campers who have their own vehicles and want peace and quiet. The green lawns of the campground are dotted with shady trees and bushes (even the odd banana plant), and there's a comfortable, partially open, lounge/reading room and a pool with loungers.

Slightly separate from the campsite, there are three A-frame chalets with en-suite facilities. One sleeps two people, the others can take four. All are spartan, but very nicely done. Four large Meru-style tents, again with en-suite facilities, are also being built, and will probably be very comfortable and cost about the same. If you want to camp somewhere civilised and safe, this could be for you.

Rates: US$65 per person per night in an A-frame, including dinner and breakfast. US$5 per person camping

Maramba River Lodge (5 chalets, tree platform and camping) PO Box 60957.
Tel: 03 324189; fax: 324266
Between the border post and Livingstone town, about 5km from each, lies this well established campsite just off Mosi-oa-Tunya Road. It's open and grassy with occasional thickets and trees. Near the river are a good swimming pool and a large bar that's open all day. Firewood and braai (barbecue) packs are available.

Maramba River has five A-frame chalets for rent, all with ceiling fans and en-suite shower and toilet. Three of them take two people, and the other two will accommodate four (two single beds and two bunk beds). Windows are made of netting, with reed mats for blinds. Chalets feel new and basic, and probably get very hot in the summer, but they're very good value. Even simpler (and an old favourite of the author) is a wooden platform in one of the trees. Activities and excursions can be booked from the lodge.

The showers and toilets are clean and security guards patrol during the night. The site is within the Mosi-oa-Tunya National Park, so expect hippos, crocodiles, antelope and the occasional elephant to be around. It's a good campsite, and the chalets are very good value when compared with rooms in town or Victoria Falls.

Rates: US$25 for a 2-bed chalet. The larger chalets are US$35 for 3 people, US$45 for 4 people. US$5 per person camping

New Fairmount Hotel (73 twin rooms) PO Box 60096. Tel: 03 320723-8; fax: 321490;
email: nfhc@zamnet.zm
In the centre of town, on Mosi-oa-Tunya Road between Mose and Mwela Streets, the New Fairmount is a large, old hotel that was once the town's focal point. Its rooms have en-suite facilities and air-conditioning and are clean, but all are ordinary and lacklustre. They are in need of updating and refurbishing. All are set around white-painted concrete courtyards at the back, where there's a good swimming pool and plenty of shady sitting places.

A desk for Bwaato Adventures occupies a corner of the New Fairmount's cavernous entrance lobby, while a small shopping arcade hides in a courtyard behind. There you'll discover a video library, a clothes shop, a hair salon and even an office where you can send emails (if you are a hotel resident!).

Rates: Kw103,400 for a twin, Kw84,100 for a single, including breakfast

Ngolide Lodge (16 rooms) 110 Mosi-oa-Tunya Road. Tel: 03 321092; fax: 321113.
Opened in October '98, this is found on the south side of town, as Mosi-oa-Tunya Road leaves Livingstone for the Falls. It has a large thatch roof and small gardens in front. It's more of a hotel than a lodge, well-built and compact, yet somewhat lacking in atmosphere when I last visited.

Its rooms all lead off a central quadrangle. Each has a high thatched ceiling, polished floors, and twin or double beds with mossie nets. The stone bathrooms should keep you cool in the heat, aided by a free-standing fan. Rooms are very comfortable, and each has its own tea/coffee maker and satellite TV.

Rates: Kw90,000 for a twin/double, Kw80,000 for a single, including full breakfast

Nyala Lodge (10 tented chalets plus camping) PO Box 60774. Tel: 03 322446; fax: 321248 email: nyala@zamnet.zm

Nyala Lodge is new and about 5km from town near the entrance to the Mosi-oa-Tunya National Park. From town, head toward the border and look for the well-signposted turn on the right (beside Tunya Lodge). Nyala is run by Moyra and Matthew Wayte and has ten nicely appointed, Meru-style tents under thatched roofs.

All have en-suite showers and toilets, and individual verandas. They are comfortably furnished complete with curtains, cement-tiled floors and nice linen. The roomy bathrooms are uniquely designed – the shower is surrounded by potted plants and rock walls, from where water cascades off a small ledge that serves as the shower tap.

The main lodge area is well designed and maintained, and has satellite TV, a lovely swimming pool, large bar/lounge and a restaurant. Breakfast, lunch, and dinner are served daily with lots of choices on the menu. Snacks are always available.

Nyala also has about ten acres for campers in designated sites with braai stands and separate ablutions. There is another swimming pool and bar under construction, which will cater solely to campers when complete.

Approaching Nyala it would be easy to be discouraged by the ominous electric fence surrounding the property. But once inside, Nyala has a bush-like feel with many indigenous trees, shrubs and small gardens, and it's very good value.

Rates: US$30 per person sharing, US$60 single, including breakfast. Camping US$5 per person

Red Cross Hostel Mokambo Road. Tel: 03 322473

Next to Jolly Boys', on its right, this basic hostel charges the same as Jolly Boys' for a bed. It is slightly run down but is convenient if next door is full.

Rates: Beds in the hostel dormitories are US$5 per night

Tunya Lodge (32 twin rooms) PO Box 60700. Tel/fax: 03 321511

Just south of Livingstone, on the way to Victoria Falls, this used to be called the Zambezi Motel. It's well located on the Mosi-oa-Tunya Road and is reasonably priced, but hasn't changed in years and is in serious need of refurbishment. Motel-style rooms are laid out in small blocks, with parking spaces dotted around. It does have a restaurant and a bar, but with so many new and interesting places to stay, this uninspiring motel with its pale green exterior and depressing rooms has little to recommend it.

Rates: Kw25,000 single, Kw40,000 double, including a light breakfast

Thompson's Guest House (5 rooms) Lusaka Road, Livingstone. Tel: 03 320565/324100; fax: 322122

Thompson's is beside the main road as you approach Livingstone from Lusaka. It has three double rooms and two singles, a lounge where you can watch videos and self-catering facilities. This basic guesthouse is away from the centre of town, but it is an inexpensive alternative for budget travellers if other places are full.

Rates: Double rooms are US$12, singles $8

Wasawange Lodge (19 rooms) PO Box 60278. Tel: 03 324066 or 324077/8; fax: 324067

Situated 3km along Libala Road – the way to the airport – just on the edge of town, Wasawange Lodge is a comfortable small hotel with a few ethnic touches. Its rooms are individual rondavels with en-suite facilities, air-conditioning, a fridge/mini-bar and satellite TV. The rooms are well cleaned and serviced, with high wooden ceilings, large mirrors and rugs to cover nice stone floors. Wasawange's popular with business visitors and has a good restaurant, a pool, sauna and jacuzzi, and even a small conference room. Because of its popularity and small size, you will often need to book in advance to get a room.

Rates: US$85 single, US$105 double, bed and breakfast

Windsor Hotel (22 rooms)
Marked on many maps on Chipembi Road (opposite the golf course), this looks as if it were once a lovely hotel … but now it's empty and dilapidated. Theoretically you can still stay or camp here, but it would be inadvisable given its advanced state of decay.

Beside the Zambezi

For many years, there have been two properties in prime sites beside the river, within a short walking distance of the Falls. The largest, the 100-room Mosi-O-Tunya Intercontinental Hotel, was just behind the small field museum and curio sellers and affectionately known as the 'Intercon'. Even those who came from Zimbabwe for the day, and couldn't venture farther, would stop here for a drink beside the pool. Next door was the Rainbow Lodge. The government ran this for years, and it had become dilapidated.

The Rainbow's site was put up for 'tender' as long ago as 1995. Then, in 1998, a solution was found. Sun International, the large South African hotel chain (owners of much of Sun City), planned to take over the Intercon and Rainbow sites.

Plans were hatched to flatten both and build afresh. There would be a top-quality hotel, superior to Zimbabwe's flagship Victoria Falls Hotel, a cheaper hotel for families, and a few very posh self-contained apartments, complete with butlers and chefs. Improvements in Livingstone's infrastructure (specifically its airport) would follow in the wake.

It's taken some time to finalise the negotiations, but they now seem to be almost concluded and it's likely that building will start soon. When finished this will be the biggest project in the Livingstone area for years, as well as a first-class place.

Aside from this, the lodges by the river, going from west (up-river) to east (below the Falls), are:

Jungle Junction (10 huts plus camping) Tel: 03 324127; email: jungle@zamnet.zm
Jungle Junction stands on a small, lush island on the Zambezi. Transfers to the island are arranged by Jungle Junction's office in Livingstone, but the launch site is reached via the same turn-off as Zambezi Royal Chundu. It's about an hour's drive from Livingstone, near the Kazungula/Botswana border.

The island facilities are rustic and basic, but the setting is splendid with palm trees and beaches. Jungle Junction has a well-earned reputation for its alternative and hippie atmosphere, attracting visitors wishing to 'party' in paradise, away from watchful eyes in town, and to experience a riverside setting at low cost.

Visitors can camp or stay in one of the ten Fisherman's Huts – tents with mosquito-screening, encircled by reeds – which are dotted around the island. All have mattresses, bedding, linen and mosquito nets. The open-air, bush-style ablutions are shared and include flush toilets and bucket showers, many cleverly constructed around trees and natural features.

Facilities include a large kitchen, a bar, a fire area, a restaurant, several small tables and a shop. The shop is stocked with dry goods, vegetables and basic essentials but you should bring your own perishables if you plan to cook for yourself. Alternatively, the restaurant serves breakfast, lunch and dinner for about US$3–4 per meal, from a set menu.

Activities include fishing, boat trips, sunset/booze cruises and nature walks, though many visitors just 'hang out' in one of the many hammocks strung up around the island. Transfers to/from the island, and some activities, use *mokoros* (dugout canoes) – which are fun but perilous. The river has plenty of crocodiles and some have become habituated to the island's activity, and so venturing too near to the river can be dangerous. It's claimed that there are places to swim, but you would need to be totally out of your mind before this seemed like a safe idea.

Rates: US$50 is the 'cover charge', including transfers to and from Livingstone and all island-based *activities. Fisherman's huts are US$10 per person sharing, or US$15 for singles. Camping is US$5 per person. Meals are extra.*

Zambezi Royal Chundu Safari & Fishing Lodge (6 chalets) PO Box 60889, Livingstone. Tel/fax: 03 321772; email: chundu@icon.co.za. Alternatively book with their South African agents on tel/fax: (2711) 953 3224.

Zambezi Royal Chundu is the furthest lodge from Livingstone on the river bank (a little further than Kubu), and is about 11km off the main road. Owned by Adam and Lynne Morze, and opened in 1996, in some ways Royal Chundu still feels new. Adam grew up in the area, speaks the local language, and has a good relationship with the local Toka-Leya people (a sub-group of the Lozi people).

Most activities are included when you stay here. You can drive to the Falls and take a tour around, visit the Mosi-oa-Tunya game park or one of the local villages, or go walking or horse riding around the local area. On the river you can take a guided *mokoro* or canoe trip, or try your luck at tiger or bream fishing. Even day trips to Chobe in Botswana are included (and using the ferry at Kazungula, Royal Chundu is only 22km from Botswana).

Royal Chundu has just six brick-under-thatch chalets, all set back from the river next to one another, with a lawn in front of them. These are solidly and compactly built, with four-poster twin beds under mossie netting and en-suite bathroom. Each chalet has gauze windows, electricity and nice fabrics.

The main building of the lodge has plenty of space, comfy chairs and tables. In one direction there's a walkway out on to a deck overlooking the river, in the other lies the swimming pool. Royal Chundu is a comfortable lodge, where no effort will be spared to look after you. It's perfect for visitors who just want to fish, but too far from the Falls for a short stop.

Rates: US$250 per person per night, including all meals, excursions and laundry for the brick chalets. Transfers to/from Livingstone are free. Those to/from Vic. Falls or Kasane are free if you stay three or more nights at Royal Chundu.

Treetops (3 twin-bed chalets) Contact via Zambezi Royal Chundu, above.

Treetops is immediately adjacent to its sister-property, Zambezi Royal Chundu, and is also run by the Morze Family. It shares facilities like the pool, bar, restaurant, boats, etc with Chundu. Here you'll find three private chalets, built on wooden decks raised on stilts above the Zambezi under an enormous canopy of waterberry trees. Walkways link the chalets to their land-locked bathrooms. Treetops offers a full range of activities, like Royal Chundu, though all are at extra cost.

These chalets aim to be a simpler and more economical alternative to the luxury lodge for visitors who are driving themselves, fishing or simply relaxing by the river.

Rates: US$55 per person, including breakfast

Mawala Lodge (2 rondavels) PO Box 60273, Livingstone. Tel/fax: 03 324455; email: mawala@zamnet.zm

Opened in July 1999, the lodge stands on the Zambezi, about 30km from Livingstone. To get here, follow the directions to the Kubu Cabins turn-off from the main Kazungula Road, and look for Mawala's signpost there. It shares the same driveway towards the river as Kubu. That takes roughly ten minutes from the main road, down a winding sandy track through the bush.

Mawala is run by Mike and Susan Walsh, long-time residents of the area. It has a small dam for fishing, and a swimming pool surrounded by nice green lawns, but set slightly away from the river. A playground for children is also planned. The main building is solidly constructed of poles and thatch with some beautiful hardwoods. There is an upstairs bar and restaurant, with a lovely view of the river and Zambezi National Park beyond. Mawala's bar and restaurant is open to the public, offering a nice place to have a riverside meal, if a bit far from town. However, some guests may find a flow of outside visitors intrusive.

Accommodation is in one of two thatched rondavels. One is beside the river and the other is right next to the main building. The riverfront rondavel, or honeymoon chalet, is reached across a small footbridge. It has a bedroom with a small double bed, a dressing area, en-suite shower and toilet and a river view. The other rondavel is larger, double-storey and better for families. Downstairs is a small lounge/sitting area, a double room and a small bathroom painted in blue; upstairs are two twins. Both rondavels are basic, but lack decorative flare or charm. The bright, off-white paint used on the lodge's exterior walls doesn't help at all. Activities like sunset/booze cruises, fishing, and vehicle tours into town are all inclusive. Other excursions can be booked at extra cost.

Rates: US$140 per person sharing, US$150 single, including full board, transfers and activities. Children under 5 are free; those aged 6–12 years cost US$45; 13–17 years cost US$85. Overnight stay (dinner, bed and breakfast) cost US$70 per person.

Kubu Cabins – The Livingstone Explorers' Club (5 chalets, 6 tents and a campsite) PO Box 60748. Tel/fax: 03 324091
Usually known simply as 'Kubu Cabins', this is well signposted. Leave town on the Nakatindi Road and continue for about 25km, until the camp is indicated off to the left. Follow the signs, and the lodge will appear after a further 5km of sandy track. (This last 5km needs careful driving with a low-slung car.)

The cabins have a beautiful site, opposite the Zambezi National Park in Zimbabwe. Kubu's bar-lounge area is friendly and comfortable – built under thatch, on a wooden deck overlooking the river. 'Kubu' means hippo, which are common here, and there is an extensive collection of drums and xylophones if you wish to accompany their nocturnal grunts.

Kubu's chalets are solid wood-and-thatch structures, thoroughly mosquito-proofed, with twin beds, en-suite facilities, mains lights and electricity. There is also a more spacious honeymoon suite that has a double bed, sunken bath and one side open to the river. The Meru-style tents are further from the main lodge, near the riverbank in a thicket of vegetation. Each has its own en-suite shower and toilet.

As well as its chalets and tents, downstream Kubu has a good grass campsite set under false ebony, marula and teak trees by the river. There is a kitchen area, clean toilets and hot showers.

Activities cost extra, apart from a complementary birding walk along the bank. Kubu run their own sunset and birdwatching boat trips, and short mountain bike trails, but organise other activities with the local operators. Canoeing is usually with Makora Quest (see page 192), who are less than a kilometre downstream, and horse riding is available through nearby Chundukwa. Kubu is a good place to relax and the food is delicious, however if you wish to make a lot of trips into the falls, for sightseeing or activities, then the transfer costs can begin to add up.

Rates: US$96 per person sharing for dinner, bed and breakfast (US$135 in the honeymoon suite). Transfers to Livingstone Airport are free, to/from town they cost US$15 per vehicle plus US$5 per person. To/from Vic. Falls they cost US$25 per vehicle, plus US$5 per person. Camping is US$10 per person, including firewood.

Chundukwa River Camp (4 chalets) PO Box 61160. Tel/fax: 03 324452 at the camp. (Town office is tel/fax: 324006.)
Owned and run by Doug and Dee Evans, who also run two bushcamps in southern Kafue, this is the base for Chundukwa Adventure Trails (also see page 191 for details). It is perfect if you want to do some activities, but not the right place if you just want a place to sleep for a few nights.

The camp is roughly 22km out of Livingstone, on the Kazungula Road, before Kubu Cabins. It has three twin-bedded chalets, and one larger for honeymoon or family use. Each is divided in two: the thatched, wooden bedroom with balcony perches on stilts amongst the waterberry trees above the river, whilst the private toilets and showers are just a few yards away (over a wooden walkway) on the riverbank. A novel design; using rustic beams and branches, it's simple but well done.

There is a small thatch *boma* and lounge area next to the river where meals are served, a peaceful spot to relax and enjoy the atmosphere and a swimming pool overlooking the river.

Activities include canoeing (using 2-man kayak-type canoes, accompanied by a guide in a single kayak), horse riding (using McLelen-type, American saddles and a stable of 12 horses), boat trips and island excursions. Doug is an experienced guide of some repute, so the activities that Chundukwa offers are done well.

Rates: US$170 per person sharing, US$215 single, including all meals, bar, boat trips, canoeing, horse trails, transfers (on the Zambian side) and trips to see the Falls.

Tongabezi (5 twin-bed tents and 3 double houses) P Bag 31. Tel: 03 323235; fax: 323224; email: tonga@zamnet.zm
Set on a sweeping bend of the Zambezi, Tongabezi has set the region's standard for innovative camp design since it opened over a decade ago. It remains one of the most exclusive places to stay on the north side of the Zambezi, but some of its temporary staff from overseas have been widely criticised for their arrogance and haughtiness.

Like Livingstone, it is now said to be changing for the better. There's talk of investing more in the local Zambian staff, supporting local communities and funding nearby school projects. If this happens, then Tongabezi will be a stunning place to stay, oozing style and quality with first-class food and accommodation.

Choose between tented twin-bedded chalets or one of the four suites (or houses): the Bird House, the Tree House, the Dog House or the Honeymoon Suite (once cited as 'worth getting married for'). Each suite is well designed, with a large double bed, impressive bath, and one side completely open on to the river. This is more private than it might appear.

There is a lovely riverside thatched bar and spacious lounge area. The swimming pool is set against a rock wall, under a tumbling waterfall, while sun-loungers wait on a large wooden deck over the Zambezi.

Guided sunrise and sunset boat trips, canoeing, birdwatching trips, fishing, game drives (to Mosi-oa-Tunya National Park), museum tours, transfers (in Zambia) and even tennis are included. Very few of the guests here are local, so it is best to arrange your stay from overseas before you arrive. There are also options to sleep on Sindabezi, one of the islands in the river, and have a champagne breakfast on Livingstone Island (see page 187), beside the falls. These should also be booked well in advance.

Rates: US$285 per person per night for a tent, US$355 for a house, including drinks, transfers and most activities

Sindabezi Island (3 twin-bed and one double tents) contact via Tongabezi
Sindabezi Island is a short boat trip downstream from its parent lodge, Tongabezi. This small island has just four thatched chalets, each accommodating two people. It's all wonderfully private and designed as an island hideaway from which you can explore the river and surrounding islands. Elephants and hippos are frequent visitors to the island, and activities include canoeing, boating, walking, fishing, birdwatching and also the use of a vehicle on the Zambian side.

Rates: US$285 per person per night, including drinks, transfers and most activities

The River Club (10 luxury chalets including Honeymoon Suite) Book through Wilderness Safaris, PO Box 288, Victoria Falls, Zimbabwe. Tel: (26313) 3371/2/3; fax: 4224/2020
Designed to reflect the colonial era, the River Club was opened in 1998, perched on a rise beside the Zambezi, next to Tongabezi. Guests are usually driven from town to a launch site, and then brought up-river by boat to the lodge, a short ten-minute ride. If you are driving, then the turn-off from the Nakatindi/Kazungula road is signposted for the River Club, and the same as the turn for Tongabezi.

The lodge has ten thatched, en-suite chalets which are cleverly designed and constructed on stilts, amidst indigenous riverside trees. All are high up with their entirely open fronts, facing over the Zambezi below. Two chalets, including the more secluded Honeymoon

Suite, have double beds. The other eight have two singles. All are large with good decoration, quality fabrics and many nice touches (like the claw-foot bathtubs). Each is also named after an explorer or colonial figure, like Stanley and Livingstone.

The main lodge building is also constructed in the colonial style with tin roof and wide verandas (which looks better than it sounds). Inside is the reception, a small gift shop, a formal dining room (with a magnificent teak table), a comfortable lounge, a massive double-sided fireplace and a well-stocked library. Antiques, colonial pictures and many decorator touches add to the lodge's ambience.

Meals are elegant affairs of a high standard. The general manager, Peter Jones, is a charming and affable host, and a raconteur of note. The entire atmosphere, decor and service are all reminiscent of the colonial era. Even the staff dress in white uniforms, red sashes and matching fezes to pamper the guests (perhaps reminding some that the 'good old colonial days' were not so good for most black Africans!?).

Overlooking the river is also a large swimming pool, with sweeping lawns. Croquet is an optional activity, but there's also the choice of fishing, canoeing, sundowner boat trips, game park drives, museum visits, and trips to local villages, stone-age sites and Livingstone town.
Rates: US$285 per person per night, including drinks, transfers and most activities

Thorn Tree Lodge (7 twin-bed tents, 2 honeymoon suites) PO Box 60403, Livingstone. Tel: 03 324480; fax: 321320 or contact Safari Par Excellence (page 193)
For many years, Thorn Tree Lodge was synonymous with *Across Africa Overland* (see page 191). Now it is owned and run by Safari Par Excellence, who have offices in Livingstone and Victoria Falls. To drive there take the main Nakatindi Road, and turn left at the signpost (also indicating to Melrose Farm). This is well before Chundukwa, so if you get that far, turn back.

Thorn Tree's accommodation is in large Meru-style tents – built on a brick base under a thatched roof, with en-suite electricity and showers. Two are honeymoon suites, raised up on teak decking with open sides overlooking the river. All have well furnished interiors, and their hot water is heated by traditional Rhodesian boilers.

There's a very comfortable bar and dining area, from which you can watch elephants hopping between the islands in the Zambezi. Also a figure-of-eight swimming pool, one end of which is under thatch for shade. Watch for a barman serving drinks in the centre. On the other side of camp is a shaded sitting area that overlooks a waterhole. Buffalo, elephants, hippo, waterbuck and bushbuck are regular visitors.
Rates: US$260 per person, including full board, activities, drinks and transfers. This reduces to US$210 from mid-January to mid-June.

The Waterfront (20 tents on platforms, 24 rooms in chalets, plus camping) near the Boat Club. Contact Safari Par Excellence, tel/fax: 03 321320, or via Victoria Falls tel: (26313) 2051/2054; fax: (26313) 4510; email: zambezi@africaonline .co.zw
This is a large riverside complex, incorporating a 'camping village' and 'adventure centre', which was built in '99 by Safari Par Excellence (see page 193) on a beautiful spot, formerly known as the Makumbi launch site. To get here leave Livingstone towards the Falls, on the Mosi-oa-Tunya Road, then turn right at Tunya Lodge towards the river and Mosi-oa-Tunya Game Park. The Waterfront is adjacent to the old Zambezi Boat Club, and you'll see a sign to it pointing left as you approach the boat club.

The Waterfront isn't a super-luxury development. Rather it's aiming to offer affordable riverside accommodation very close to the Falls and also caters for overland trucks. It has a stunning setting within the Mosi-oa-Tunya National Park – which was one of the best places to view spectacular Zambezi sunsets and enjoy the hippos and birdlife before this development.

The main thatch-and-pole building has a lovely view over the river and contains the reception and booking office, a spacious bar, a lounge and the restaurant on the ground floor. Upstairs an internet café is planned. Outside, amongst palm trees, are sitting areas and a large pool which seems (clever design) to flow into the Zambezi.

Sprawling to the left of the main building are 20 permanent tents perched on wooden platforms along the river. These each have two beds; all bedding and linen is supplied. Nearby ablutions are clean and spacious and contain flush toilets and hot and cold showers. A separate grassed camping area can take about 60 campers, and this also has similar toilets and showers.

There are plans to add eight large A-frame style chalets, each containing three separate double rooms (with their own en-suite showers and toilets). This is planned to be on the right of the main building, separate from the tents or camping area.

The Waterfront is intended by Saf Par as a one-stop-shop, where their own 'Adventure Centre' will offer a full range of activities and excursions – many of which will doubtless be operated by themselves (see page 193). Among these will be two boats offering sunset cruises directly from the Waterfront's own jetty. The *Makumbi*, currently being refurbished, is a larger boat and will offer upmarket cruises. The smaller *Jambezi* will offer a more normal booze cruise.

Rates: Tents are US$20 per person, rooms in chalets US$50 per person, camping US$5 per person

Songwe Point Village (8 rustic huts) Contact via Victoria Falls Safari Lodge, Zimbabwe. Tel: (26313) 3211; fax: 3205/3207; email: saflodge@saflodge.co.zw
Songwe Point Village is a joint venture between the local community and Victoria Falls Safari Lodge. It promises the cultural experience of staying in an African village-style setting with local people and an enhanced high level of comfort. The 'village' is poised on the edge of one of the gorges downstream of the Falls, 100m above the Zambezi. It's a breathtaking location.

As the crow flies, it's only 5km downstream from the Falls, but the road winding through the bush, small villages and out to the gorge is a 30-minute drive. (See the directions to Taita Falcon Lodge, below.) Accommodation is in rustic, but comfortable, thatched huts. Each has its own bathroom (toilet and wash basin). Showers and baths, positioned on the edge of the gorge, are memorable.

The hosts welcome visitors into the 'village family' and explain local customs and beliefs. Meals are served in the traditional style and in a central thatched enclosure, called a 'Ntantaala'. There is traditional singing and dancing in the evenings and guests are encouraged to participate if the mood strikes them. Everything tries hard to be authentic, right down to an ox-wagon journey to a small field museum displaying stone-age artefacts, some more than 700,000 years old.

The area is seeped in archaeological history (see *Zambia's earliest inhabitants* at the start of *Chapter 2*) and the emphasis is on sharing African culture with visitors. Guided visits are offered to early stone-age sites, the 700-year old Mukuni Village, the tree where David Livingstone first met the local Chief, and various other local historical and cultural sites.

Rates: US$145 per person sharing, including full board, activities, drinks and transfers

Taita Falcon Lodge (6 chalets) PO Box 60012, Livingstone. Tel/fax: 03 321850; cell: (26311) 208387
This lodge, opened in 1996, is perched overlooking rapid number 17 in the Batoka Gorge, downstream of the Falls. It is a 45-minute drive from Livingstone, along the road normally used to bring rafters back from the river. To get there, take the main road from town towards the Falls, and then take the well-signposted left just before you arrive. From here it's about 11km of long, winding track through the Mokuni Village area. Near the end, you'll pass a turn on the right to Songwe Point. You'll want a 4WD for this trip during the rains.

The lodge is named after a rare falcon which frequents cliffs and gorges, especially in the Zambezi Valley. (Look for these especially in the evenings, perhaps trying to catch swallows or bats on the wing. Taita falcons are small (less than 30cm long) with cream to brown underparts – no bars or markings – and a strong, fast style of flight. This area is one of the best in Africa for spotting them.)

Run by Faan and Anna-Marie Fourie, the lodge is a pleasant, friendly place. Its six chalets use stone, reeds and local furnishings throughout. All have en-suite facilities, but are rustic and quite simple – thatched ceiling with beams, the odd stone wall, and spaces between the walls and roof for light and flow-through ventilation. Most are doubles/twins, but one is larger, having four beds.

The camp's particularly notable for a lovely deck beside the bar, overlooking the gorges and river below. It's a great place to watch rafters from a very safe distance. Despite the fact that the chalets have been set back from the precipice, I'd be very wary of bringing children here because of the cliffs nearby. The lodge's electricity is from a generator, and there's a nice small pool for a dip.

Taita Falcon's a good place if you want a remote spot away from it all, at which to relax and rest. However, if you want to pop in and out of the Falls for activities, then Taita can feel cut off from the epicentre of things

Rates: US$95 per person sharing, US$120 single, including full board and airport transfers on arrival and departure

Where to eat
Take-aways
There are several take-aways in town, including Megabite, Shambas, Eat Rite and the large Hungry Lion. For a few thousand kwacha, these serve the usual fare of pre-packaged chips, burgers, somosas, sandwiches and soft drinks. They are all in the centre of town, along Mosi-oa-Tunya Road. The intersection of Kapondo Street and Mosi-oa-Tunya Road is also particularly good; here you'll find the marvellously titled 'Rave Stone Pub and Nightclub' as well as the more palatable offerings from Eat Rite – a clean and efficient (if generic) fast-food joint – and Bakerite. Just down Kapondo Street is Livingstone's Shoprite/Checkers, the town's outpost of the large South African supermarket chain. Its bakery counter is a good place to look for a quick bite to eat.

If you prefer to sit down, then the Insaka Bar & Restaurant is inside Bwaato Adventures, to the right of the main post office. This offers basic lunches and dinners.

If you're travelling between the border and town, then try **Pilgrim's Tearoom,** on the west side of the road just south of town (1.2km south of the railway station). It's open daily from 07.30 to 17.00, and very occasionally in the evening for special events. It's large, airy, and serves great food, often on individual wooden boards with a side salad. Note that this place sometimes caters to large coach groups, in which case the service can be outrageously slow.

Restaurants
For a long time most of Livingstone's better places to eat were the in-house restaurants of the better lodges and hotels. For example, if you have a vehicle, the food at Kubu Cabins is worth the drive (you must book in advance). However, recently more dedicated restaurants have opened up, some with small guesthouses attached. Here's a small selection of the current favourites:

Funky Monkey
This modern little bar and restaurant is situated behind Mosi-oa-Tunya Road and shares the same site as Fawlty Towers. It can be accessed through the gardens of Fawlty Towers, or by going around the corner to the road behind. Just follow the signs at the corner of the Mosi-oa-Tunya and Kazungula Roads to get to the front of the restaurant.

Funky Monkey is open for lunches and evening meals every day, except Monday, and it is proving popular amongst both residents and visitors. The tables are scattered in a walled courtyard and the setting is lovely and peaceful. There is a thatched roof bar, and some seating inside and upstairs on a small deck. It serves great food in a friendly, relaxed atmosphere and they play good music at the bar. The menu includes choices like seafood crêpes, quiche, steaks, salads and deep-fried brie. Expect a meal with a few drinks to cost around US$12 per person.

Pig's Head Pub Tel: 03 320758
Another popular local dining spot is the Pig's Head Pub, located off Mosi-oa-Tunya Road, across the road from the Total fuel station, next to the Livingstone Fire Brigade. Look for the sign indicating where to turn off the main road.

The Pig's Head has been designed in the mould of an English pub, complete with a snooker table. They offer lunch and dinner daily, except Sundays. It's a little dark inside, but on sunny days meals and drinks can be taken in the courtyard outside. They have good hamburgers and other 'standard' pub-grub like chicken pies, pizzas and chips – costing around US$7–10 per meal.

Chanter's Guesthouse PO Box 60623. Tel: 03 323412. (Manager tel: 323850)
Run by Richard Chanter, this is also a small guesthouse (see page 153), though the restaurant comes first. It's about 2km from the centre, so take Mosi-oa-Tunya Road towards Lusaka until, just before the road bends to the left, you turn left on to Obote Avenue. Chanter's is on Lukulu Crescent, the fourth right turn, which is unnamed on some maps.

Inside, the main restaurant is wooden-panelled and slightly formal, yet lovely and airy as it extends outside on to a patio and beyond across an enclosed lawn. The friendly staff serve food from the menu all day, from breakfast to evening dinner, and there's a 'specials' board worth studying. Costs are Kw2,500 for a light continental breakfast, and around Kw12,000 for a full one. Chanter's offers one of Livingstone's most comprehensive menus, where main courses, for lunch or dinner, are mostly around Kw10,000, though steaks can be up to Kw13,000. There's a good selection of vegetarian options (apparently to suit a sizeable local Indian community) for around Kw8–10,000. It's certainly worth seeking out, though off the beaten track.

Nightlife
Local Livingstone nightlife centres largely around dancing and drinking, although the bars at various restaurants offer a nice atmosphere if one simply wants to relax and chat. Those wishing to dance should try Eat Rite on Kapondo Street, which moonlights as a night-club – Steprite Sounds – on Fridays and Saturdays. Dress code is 'no shorts, no tropicals and no vests' and entry is free.

Rave Stone, across the street, can also be a fun night-spot. The New Fairmount Hotel has a popular disco/dance club, generally jam-packed on weekend nights. In all of these places, you can dance until you drop and, because they can become rowdy later in the evenings, it's probably advisable to venture out in a group.

Getting around
By taxi
Livingstone town is small enough to walk around, as is the Falls area. However if you are travelling between the two, or going to the airport, or in a hurry, then use one of the plentiful taxis. A taxi between town and either the border or the airport will cost around Kw5,000/US$2 per person depending upon number of passengers. From the airport to the border is about Kw12,500/US$5 or more.

You can also negotiate to hire a taxi for the day to take you around town, to the Falls and into the game park, but for a more informative trip it's better to go with the licensed, more knowledgeable tour operators. Most drivers are unfamiliar with the riverside lodges, and will be reluctant to take you there cheaply, as they will not find a passenger for the return journey.

Banks and money
Livingstone has several major banks and various Bureaux de Change. There are also freelance 'money changers' around Eat Rite and at the border. Unless you are *very* savvy or desperate, avoid the money changers. They always take advantage of unsuspecting (and even suspicious) tourists by short-changing them somehow.

Banks generally offer a better exchange rate than bureaux de change, but can take more time and hassle. You can also often change money at many of the lodges and hotels. This is the least favourable exchange rate, but most convenient method.

The major banks are situated around the post office area, parallel to the main road. Most open Mon–Fri 08.00–14.00, but get there early if you want to avoid long queues. The main ones include:

Barclay's Bank Tel: 03 32114; fax: 322317
Zambia National Commercial Bank Tel: 03 321901
Union Bank Tel: 03 321385; fax: 320695
Finance Bank Tel: 03 323305 (next to Liso House, opposite Pemube Crafts)

Alternatively the larger bureaux de change include:

Falls Bureau de Change Tel: 03 322088
In post office complex, next to Zamtel Telecom Centre, this is open Mon–Fri, 09.00–13.00 and 14.00–17.00, Sat 09.00–13.00
Mo Money situated on the main road between Kubu Crafts and Capital Theatre
Southend Bureau de Change Tel: 03 320241/320773; fax: 322128
In Liso House, almost opposite Pemube Crafts.

Shopping
Food and drink
There is no shortage of grocers and shops in Livingstone and you can find most things, although imported gourmet items might be hard to come by. Mini Market and RiteShop, across the corner from each other, stock the best supply of fresh fruits and vegetables in addition to all the basics like eggs, milk, cheese, chickens, meats and dry goods.

Shoprite Checkers, on Kapondo Street, is a large South African supermarket chain with a wider variety of goods, but at generally higher prices. They have a good meat section. The fruits and vegetables at Checkers are not very fresh since most have travelled up from South Africa via Lusaka and down to Livingstone. Zambian open-air markets and wheel-barrow marketeers, positioned around town, also have fresh tomatoes, onions and other basic fruits and vegetables, generally at less cost.

Other supplies

For cosmetics, toiletries or medicines Livingstone has several well-stocked **chemists/pharmacies.** Both those below have an excellent selection of of items as well as insect repellents, sun creams, medical supplies, batteries, film and more. Each has a trained pharmacist, who can also offer advice on medications and fill prescriptions if on duty.

LF Moore Chemists Tel/fax: 03 321640
Located on Akapelwa Street, across from the High Court and bus depot, LF Moore was established in 1936 and remains the best stocked chemist in town. It is open every day: Mon–Fri 08.00–12.30 and 14.00–18.00, Sat 08.00–13.00, and Sun/Public Holidays 09.30–12.30

LM Pharmacy Tel: 03 324486
Next to Zambia National Commercial Bank, near the post office, this pharmacy is also open every day: Mon–Fri 08.00–13.00 and 14.00–17.30, Sat 08.00–14.00, Sun/Public Holidays: 08.30–12.00.

For **books** try Pemube on the main road. See page 168. They have probably the best selection of wildlife reference books and regional travel guides as well as a book exchange and new paperback novels.

Basic **camera supplies** can be found at either LF Moore Chemists (see above), on Akapelwa Street, or better still at the Konica Film Centre on the main road. Konica does one-hour photo processing and stocks film, photo albums and related supplies.

For **cassette tapes of popular music** including many African selections, try the open-air local market down at the bottom of Kapondo Street. They have a wide selection of cheap (probably bootlegged!) cassette tapes. Follow your ears for blaring music and you'll find a kiosk selling tapes!

Chitenje, the colourful lengths of traditional African cloth, can be found at most of the small Indian shops on the main road and on Kuta Way, one block down, parallel to the main road. These make lovely souvenirs and nice sarongs.

If you need **car repairs**, try Fallsway Motors (tel: 03 321049) at the corner of Nakatindi Road or Channa's Motors (tel: 03 320468) on the main road just across the railway line. Their facilities are somewhat limited, but they should be able to get you on the road again at least temporarily.

The best workshop in town is Foley's Africa (PO Box 60525, tel/fax: 03 320888), but they cater mainly for Land Rovers. In an emergency they might be able to help, or at least advise on who could repair your vehicle. They are located on the Mosi-oa-Tunya Road, next to BP and across from the Total fuel station; you can't miss their big sign. For **punctures and tyre repairs** try the Total fuel station.

Souvenirs and curios

If you like bargaining and have lots of patience, try the **Curio and Craft Centre** in Mukuni Park where local artisans, craftsmen and carvers sell their wares. They have great selection of wooden carvings and crafts, but expect to be bombarded with vendors vying for your attention and business.

Similarly, there is the **curio village** at the Zambian side of the Falls (beside the Falls Museum) with a wider selection of items and even more aggressive salesmen! It can be fun if you have time and enjoy haggling over prices, but frustrating if you are in a hurry. Failing those, one of the following might suit you much better:

Kubu Crafts Tel: 03 324093
On left of the old Capitol Cinema is this lovely shop, which is really geared more towards

interior design than passing visitors. It stocks teak furniture, jewellery, pottery, plates, paintings by local artists, glasses and beautiful hand-made cards amongst other things. In case you're wondering, it's owned and run by Lucy and Roelf, from Kubu Cabins!

Livingstone Museum
The museum has a small craft shop in the back with generally a nice selection of locally produced baskets, carvings and other curios. They tend to have the lowest prices in town, but whether it's well stocked or not is hit or miss. You don't need to pay museum entry to visit the curio shop, just tell them where you are going.

African Visions
Located on Mosi-oa-Tunya Road, in the Livingstone Adventure Centre complex, you'll recognise this shop by its distinctive burglar bars of African faces. It is the best stocked (and most expensive) curio shop in town. Visions is a lovely shop with a wide selection of textiles, baskets, carvings, artefacts and many Zambian-produced souvenirs. Worth a visit (see *Magenge* in *Mfuwe*, page 232, for more comments).

Tabawa Trading Tel/fax: 03 324454; email: judi@zamnet.zm
If you are a serious collector of or interested in textiles or artefacts from the DRC and Zambia, then you should contact this company. They specialise in upmarket items and export them overseas. They also design and make high-quality soft interior furnishings, like pillows, and utilise traditional African textiles and artefacts in their products. They don't have a shop in town, but serious buyers can make an appointment to view their wide selection of merchandise.

Pemube Crafts 116a Mosi-oa-Tunya Road. Tel: 03 320044
This large shop on the main road in town stretches back and covers quite an area, though it isn't densely stocked. You'll find Zairean masks, malachite carvings and jewellery as well as local wooden curios and a good selection of creations of wire. There's also a small selection of books, some fabrics, a few simple safari-type clothes and the odd accessory (cloth-covered water-bottles).

On the right of the shop are a few noticeboards listing the various activities and accommodation available, and the shops also acts as a booking agent for local activities. It's an interesting place ... but one is left wishing that they'd specialise in just one or two things and have a more comprehensive selection of them.

Information and addresses
Car hire
If you don't have a vehicle and wish to explore the area at your own pace, you can hire a car with or without a driver. Alternatively, you can hire a 4WD with full kit if you wish to do self-drive safaris.

Foley Hire Limited Tel/fax: 03 320888
Newly established, Foley Hire is a sister-company of Foley Africa, Livingstone's local Land Rover specialist. They offer all sorts of options, from vehicles just for the day to fully-kitted-out expedition-ready multi-day hires. All vehicles are Land Rovers with choice ranging from basic 110 Defenders to fully equipped 110 and 130 Defenders. Other models are planned to follow, including Land Rover Discoverys.

A fully outfitted vehicle could include: roof and ground tents, awning, table and chairs, additional fuel and water tanks, sand ladders, hi-lift jack, jerry cans, gas cooker, fridge, power winch, water filtration unit and shower, ropes, shovel, axe, camp lights, bedding (duvets and pillows), cooler box, kitchen equipment, books, maps, etc. The list goes on and on!

One-way drop-offs are sometimes possible, at a cost. A basic 110 Defender, without extras, costs around US$100 per day, inclusive of insurance and with unlimited mileage. An equipped vehicle is more like US$200 per day.

AJ Car Hire & Tours PO Box 60192, Tel/fax: 03 322090. Located in Liso House (room 306), on Mosi-oa-Tunya Road
This small local hire company has vehicles for self-drive or chauffeured hire as well as transfers, tours and activity bookings. They have two 5-seater Toyota Saloon cars (US$40/day plus 50¢/km), one 8-seater Toyota Hiace mini van (US$55/day plus 50¢/km) and one 26-seater Mitsubishi bus (US$100/day plus US$1/km). These current prices are subject to various taxes and possible extra charges. All vehicles have an air-conditioning unit.

Emergencies
Medical facilities are limited in Livingstone and there are no European-standard hospitals. It is probably not advisable to go to the Livingstone Hospital for any medical treatment or emergencies, as the facilities and care provided are far below acceptable standard.

However, there are a couple of very good doctors who maintain small medical clinics in town. They can do malaria and other routine tests and also make house-calls:

Dr Shanks, Southern Medical Centre cell: 01 777 017
Located in the post office complex, next to Shamba's takeaway, the clinic is open Mon–Fri 08.00–17.00, Sat 09.00–12.00, Sun 11.00–12.00, public holidays 10.00–12.00. The doctor makes house calls after hours as needed.

Dr P J Tidgi, Health Care Lab & Clinic Tel: 03 322038
On the corner of Mutelo and an unnamed street (near Hindu Hall), down the street behind Mosi-O-Tunya House, the highest building in town. The clinic is open similar hours to the above and the doctor also makes housecalls.

Internet cafés
There's only one internet café in Livingstone so far, although residents of Fawlty Towers can use their facilities, for a price.

Cyberian Outpost PO Box 60352. Tel/fax: 03 324440; email: cyberian@ outpost.co.zm
Unlikely though it may seem, there's an internet café in the heart of Livingstone, between the Livingstone Adventure Centre and Safari Par Excellence, on Mosi-ao-Tunya Road, just south of the turn-off to Nakatindi Road.

This was started in November '98 by the helpful Jen Cowie. Ten minutes at the terminal for internet access (eg: accessing hotmail accounts!), including sending or receiving emails, costs US$2. If you don't have your own email address, then friends can send messages to you at traveller@outpost.co.zm. This costs just US$0.50 per email. You can also make international calls cheaply here (US and UK, for example, are both US$3.70 per minute to call), and sending faxes costs the call time plus US$1. The outpost is also a convenient agent for Mercury Mail (see page 105), which is a reliable way to send things abroad. They've also a useful notice board and make great filter coffee. So drop in and log on!

Post and communications
You can't miss the **Livingstone Post Office** (tel: 03 321400) in the centre of town in a sprawling complex of banks and shops, adjacent to the main road. It's open Mon–Fri 08.00–17.00, Sat 08.00–13.00, and closed Sun.

Zambia has some lovely stamps for sale, a favourite of stamp collectors. The best way to send mail quickly within Zambia is via EMS (Expedited Mail Service). It is a reasonably priced service where letters are hand delivered. It is also available to overseas destinations and is generally less expensive than a courier company.

One reliable courier is **DHL** (Tel: 03 320044), located inside Pemube on Mosi-oa-Tunya Road. Here you can send letters, parcels and small packets via this

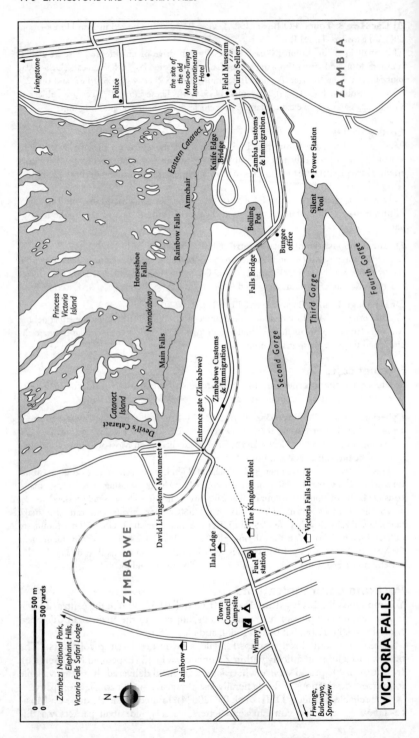

VICTORIA FALLS

international express mail service to destinations within Zambia and worldwide. This is costly but reliable. If you need important documents sent from overseas, DHL is one of the quickest ways to be assured of them reaching you safely. It takes about a week from Europe or the USA.

Another good alternative is to use the **Mercury Mail** service. See page 105 for full details; you'll find their office just next to Living Inn.

If you need to make phone calls or send/receive faxes, and can't do so where you are staying, then there are several places in town.

The **Zamtel Public Telecommunications Centre** is conveniently next to the post office. It opens Mon–Fri 08.00–13.00 and 14.00–17.30; Sat 08.00–12.30. Phone calls within Livingstone are about US20¢ per minute, but about US$1.20 per minute to elsewhere in Zambia.

International calls to Europe, USA and Australia average US$12 for three minutes. Incoming faxes cost about US15¢ per page and should be marked to your attention and faxed to tel: 03 320068. Strangely, Zamtel has no incoming public telephone line to inquire about faxes or other information, so you need to go there personally. (I wouldn't rely on this route for any vital faxes.)

Nearby, upstairs in the Zambia State Insurance Building, are the **Moono Secretarial Services** (tel: 03 320517) who offer the same telecom services at comparable rates to Zamtel (keeping the same hours as Zamtel) as well as typing. Also there are **Timeroll Enterprises** (tel: 03 321609) who offer the same but also telegrams and telex. Timeroll are open all day on Sunday but closed on Saturday. The offices are rather run down and the building poorly maintained, but the facilities are there if you need them.

VICTORIA FALLS (THE ZIMBABWEAN SIDE)
Orientation
The buzzing town of Victoria Falls is less than 2km south of the Zambezi, the border with Zambia. It feels smaller than Livingstone, but is a major tourist centre with a bewildering variety of activities and options on offer. The heart of the town is small, comprising shops, offices and a campsite within a few metres of the landmark Wimpy restaurant on the corner. Those buildings that are not either travel agencies/tour operators or take-aways seem to sell souvenirs, camping equipment or at least T-shirts. Few remain oblivious to the potential of the tourist dollar, so the strolling visitor is usually bombarded with people touting for every possible service.

Between the town and the Falls, the railway station stands opposite the old, and still gracious, Victoria Falls Hotel – now adjoined by the towering Kingdom, on the former Makasa Sun site.

Head south from the Wimpy, away from the Falls, and you soon pass the main township on the left. Later, some 25km from the centre, comes Victoria Falls airport, as you begin the long road south to Bulawayo.

Go northeast, following the Zambezi upstream, and the scenery rapidly opens out to bush. You pass several hotels before reaching the National Park's riverside restcamp and campsite, on your right, and then entering the Zambezi National Park.

Getting there and away
By air
Victoria Falls airport is much busier than Livingstone's and is well-serviced by many airlines. Two of these – Air Zimbabwe and Zimbabwe Express – have daily scheduled flights to Hwange, Kariba, Harare and onwards. International airlines

like British Airways/Comair, South African Airways, Air Namibia and Air Botswana have regularly scheduled services linking neighbouring countries. It is easy to fly in and out of Victoria Falls to both domestic and regional destinations.

The airport contains a small bar and restaurant serving snacks, a bank, bureau de change and several small curio/newspaper stands. There is a new bar/restaurant and duty-free shop in the international departure lounge. (Remember you'll need US$20 departure tax here, in dollar notes.)

If you arrive by air without having pre-booked an airport transfer (about US$14 per person, or US$50 for a whole vehicle), then you can usually get a taxi. Alternatively, if arriving on Air Zimbabwe, take their inexpensively priced airport bus (about US$5) to town which leaves you in front of their office. Prices for taxis to and from the airport are negotiable, but expect to pay somewhere between US$10 and US$20 per taxi. Airlines with offices/agents in town include:

Air Zimbabwe Tel: (26313) 4136/7; fax: (26313) 4318
You can't miss their office, next to the post office, on Livingstone Way, opposite Avis. Air Zimbabwe also offers a cheap and convenient airport bus to and from town for their scheduled flights. They also serve as agent for South African Airways and can sometimes help with bookings for other regional carriers.

Zimbabwe Express Tel/fax: (26313) 5992
Their office is located inside the Elephant Walk Shopping Complex, behind the post office.

British Airways/Comair Tel: (26313) 2053; fax: 5825; Zimbabwe cell: 011 405 282; email: bamnvfa@pci.co.zm
There is a booking office for British Airways, and their partner Comair, situated in Flame Lily Court, a small complex behind the Pink Baobab. Sheila and Kathy, who run the office, are exceptionally helpful.

By bus
Victoria Falls is well connected to the town of Hwange, Hwange Safari Lodge (near Hwange National Park's Main Camp), and Bulawayo by good bus services. Several normal local buses, run by Hwange Special Expresses, depart daily from the car park behind the main shopping arcade. The swifter, plusher Ajay Express (tel: Bulawayo 62521) buses go once a day from the Kingdom Hotel. Ask at the hotel reception about booking tickets in advance.

By train
For those in search of nostalgia, a classic overnight steam train service links Bulawayo with Victoria Falls. This is easily Zimbabwe's best train journey, and a great way to arrive at (or perhaps to leave) the Falls. First class, with four berths per cabin, costs US$30 per person – a bargain worth booking well in advance. Second class has six berths per cabin and costs US$17 per person. Third class has only (uncomfortable) wooden benches costing US$8 per person. Treat yourself: book the best available and sleep whilst you travel in style.

Where to stay
Victoria Falls has many hotels, catering for a very international crowd. None is cheap and most are very busy – as basically the demand for staying here still outstrips the supply of beds (despite the large number of beds!).

If your budget is limited, don't forget your camping kit. Also remember that having a vehicle opens up possibilities on the outskirts of town, giving you more options than just the town council's crowded campsite in the centre.

Hotels

Whereas Zambia has a number of excellent bush lodges along the Zambezi river-front, the hotels near the Falls on the south side of the river are more conventional. Most are quite large, but their atmosphere differs widely. None are really bush lodges – despite the claims of one or two. Included here are a few of my favourites, the more famous, and even the more notorious within about 10km of the Falls:

A'Zambezi Rainbow Hotel (95 rooms) PO Box 130, Victoria Falls. Tel: (26313) 4561/4; fax: (26313) 4536

About 5km out of town on Park Way, the A'Zambezi is a few hundred yards outside the gates to the Zambezi National Park. The rooms all overlook the river from within a large, semi-circular thatched building. There is the usual pool, bars and restaurant, and a convenient courtesy bus to whisk you in and out of town. Consider taking the more adventurous walk into town via the path by the river (see *Victoria Falls National Park*, page 187).

Rates: US$180 single, US$138 per person sharing, including breakfast

Elephant Hills Hotel (276 rooms) Tel: (26313) 4793; fax: (26313) 4655/6

Elephant Hills is a large brick complex of very modern design. It has superb facilities and a view over the Zambezi in the distance a few kilometres east of the Falls – just follow the road to the Zambezi National Park. Elephant Hills has risen, phoenix-like, from the ashes of a hotel that was burned down during the struggle for Zimbabwe's independence. The facilities include three restaurants, several bars, a casino, an 18-hole golf course and several swimming pools. Each room has fans, air-con, local and CNN TV, lots of space, and a balcony. It is all very impressive, though too big and modern to be charming.

Rates: US$283 single, US$157 per person sharing, including breakfast

Ilala Lodge (16 rooms) Livingstone Way, PO Box 18. Tel: (26313) 4203

A good small lodge in the heart of Victoria Falls, on Livingstone Way opposite the Avis garage and the Kingdom. They have recently expanded from the original 16 rooms and built an entire new wing. There is a swimming pool and the property is surrounded by cool green lawns frequented by warthogs and other small game. The lodge has a small casino and popular nightclub, called Downtime. This excellent small lodge offers an intimate atmosphere, is in a very convenient position and invariably needs to be booked in advance.

Rates: US$200 single, US$143 per person sharing, including breakfast

The Kingdom (296 rooms) PO Box 90, Victoria Falls. Tel: (26313) 4275; fax: 4782

Adjacent to the Victoria Falls Hotel, the Kingdom is a large new hotel mirroring the Great Zimbabwe ruins. It is located on the site of the former Makasa Sun and is reminiscent of a small version of Sun City – a fun, fantasy hotel.

Expect dramatic architecture as you walk in: a large water feature mirroring the Falls. The rooms and entertainment areas surround a large artificial lake, complete with vegetation and waterfowl. The rooms all have en-suite facilities, with a view of the lake or the adjacent parkland. The central living area is divided into a 'Casino Wing' – which includes the (glitzy) casino, a food court and shops – and the 'Reception Wing', which incorporates an upstairs reception and conference room, and a downstairs open-plan breakfast area, overlooking two large swimming pools and an outside bar area.

The rooms are either lake-facing, which face inside, on to the bars and restaurants; or forest-facing, with a view outside the hotel. The lake-facing rooms are probably less peaceful, as they have a window on the evening's action below.

There are no hotel dining rooms, except for the breakfast hall. All your other meals can be eaten in the many familiar food-chain restaurants, which are located in the food court. The hotel design is very open plan with high ceilings, wrought iron work and a feeling of African outdoors. It's very impressive, and more than a little overwhelming.

Rates: US$114 single, US$114 per person sharing, including breakfast

Rainbow Hotel (44 rooms) PO Box 150, Victoria Falls. Tel: (26313) 4583/5; fax: 4516/4654
On the corner of Park Way and Courtney Selous Drive, the Rainbow has been built, it is claimed, in Moorish style. Hence the architect's fondness for arches. That aside, it has pleasant gardens and a large pool boasting a bar to which you can swim.
Rates: US$130 single, US$98 per person sharing, including breakfast

Sprayview Hotel (45 rooms) PO Box 70, Victoria Falls. Tel: (26313) 4344/6; fax: 4713
The Sprayview used to be by far the cheapest of the hotels in the Falls. It was efficient, inexpensive and always full. It was upgraded and refurbished a few years ago, with a new marble reception and a few shops and booking agents at the front. The prices went up a little, but the rooms remained basically the same, and it's still remarkable value. Do book well in advance to get in there though, as it's got one of the highest occupancies (% of rooms that are, on average, full) on the subcontinent.
Rates: US$77 single, US$53 per person sharing, including breakfast

Victoria Falls Hotel (141 rooms) PO Box 10, Victoria Falls. Tel: (026313) 4203/4
Started in 1905, with its back facing the train station, the Victoria Falls Hotel has a stunning position overlooking the second cataract and the railway bridge. It has recently been completely refurbished and has a new wing built. The almost Edwardian ambience of the town's oldest and most famous hotel retains a strong colonial hint – as close to Singapore's old Raffles Hotel as you can find in Africa. In the 1950s Laurens van der Post wrote:

> '... this hotel in the bush on one of the great rivers of the world has been like a second home to me. I have known it since boyhood and seen it grow into one of the most remarkable establishments in Africa. Before many a long expedition I have spent the night there, and enjoyed celebrating the successful end of many another with a hot bath, dinner jacket, and civilised dinner.'
>
> from *The Lost World of the Kalahari*

It remains the most prestigious place to stay south of the river, and the *Livingstone Room* restaurant is easily the most stylish venue in town for dinner. If you cannot afford to stay here, it is worth dressing up in your finest and at least having lunch, enjoying the delicious food and distant view of the bridge and Falls. The Victoria Falls Hotel is either absolutely charming, or far too colonial, depending upon your taste.
Rates: US$347 single, US$193 per person sharing, including breakfast

Victoria Falls Safari Lodge (141 rooms) PO Box 29, Victoria Falls. Tel: (26313) 3201–4; fax: 3205/7
The Victoria Falls Safari Lodge aims for the thatch-and-wood feel of a traditional bush lodge, yet within reach of the Falls. It is too big to achieve the intimacy of such lodges, but does have a relaxed, rural atmosphere away from the bustle of town. It is very comfortable, and if you don't want to venture out then the rooms overlook a water-hole which attracts game from the nearby Zambezi National Park. Its restaurant has a good reputation, and the bar is quite a meeting place.
Rates: US$269 single, US$179 per person sharing, including breakfast

Guesthouses

Many residents of Victoria Falls are capitalising on the tourist boom by offering accommodation in newly built guesthouses in the residential areas. This is quite a new phenomenon in the last few years. Some are very comfortable and cozy, complete with swimming pools and lovely gardens. I have not yet checked all of these out myself yet, though a selection worth investigating would include:

Gertie's Lodge 597 Nguhuma Crescent, PO Box 66, Victoria Falls. Tel/fax: (26313) 2002
About 2km from the town centre in a quiet residential neighbourhood, Gertie's has four brick-under-thatch chalets. Two sleep four people each, and the other two sleep six (upstairs master bedroom has a fold-out couch as well, which accommodates the extra two). The

chalets all have toilet and shower facilities, a living area and tea/coffee-making facilities. Shared facilities include a swimming pool and lounge with satellite TV and reading area.

Hunter's Lodge PO Box 132, Victoria Falls. Tel/fax: (26313) 5977
Located 2km from town in a residential area, this thatched lodge offers bed and a full English breakfast. Each room has its own mini-bar/fridge and tea/coffee-making facilities. There is a swimming pool, lounge (with satellite TV) and a barbecue area. There is also a cottage, containing three bedrooms (sleeping 6 to 8 people) equipped for self-catering.

Moira's Place 357 Gibson Road, Victoria Falls. Tel: (26313) 2179
Located on a quite road near town, Moira's Place offers self-catering accommodation in A-frame chalets/cottages. Facilities include a swimming pool, shared kitchen and dining area, hot and cold ablutions and a tropical garden setting. Rates are US$10 per person per night.

Mosi-oa-Tunya Lodge Stand 609, PO Box 165, Victoria Falls. Tel: (26313) 4336/4639; fax: (26313) 4639
This is a self-catering lodge with two double-storey, thatched brick chalets set in a well-kept garden. One chalet has four bedrooms and the other has six; all have their own en-suite bathrooms. Both have a fully-equipped kitchen and a lounge with dining area, and there's a shared swimming pool and barbecue area.

Penny Wise Cottages Stand 248, Kings Way, PO Box 49, Victoria Falls. Tel: (26313) 5912; fax: (26313) 4555
This small bed-and-breakfast has twin-bedded rooms with en-suite showers and toilets. Shared facilities include a swimming pool, a fully-equipped kitchen and lounge with TV.

Reynard Cottages 403 Reynard Road, Victoria Falls. Tel: (26313) 2103/4418; fax: (26313) 2103
Within walking distance of town, this B&B is reasonably priced and has a swimming pool, barbecue facilities, a lounge with TV/video and laundry service. It has a number of separate twin bedrooms, some with en-suite facilities, and some family rooms within the owner's main house.

Tranquillity Tel/fax: (26313) 5903
This self-catering lodge in the main residential area offers en-suite accommodation and caters to families, couples and business travellers. Rooms have air-conditioning and queen-sized beds. Facilities include a pool and lovely garden. Airport transfers can be arranged.

Villa d'Afrique P Bag 5951, Victoria Falls. Tel/fax: (26313) 5945
A five-minute drive from the centre brings you to this upmarket stand of small villas in the residential area near the Sprayview Hotel, off Reynard Road. There are four self-contained units, each with a lounge, kitchen, bathroom and two twin bedrooms. The villas are well furnished, tastefully designed and fully serviced. They share a garden, a swimming pool, and an open-air thatch sitting area for outdoor dining. With advance notice, a chef is available who can prepare meals for you.

Camping
In many ways the Zambian sites are better – at Maramba River, Livingstone Overnight, Nyala Lodge, The Waterfront, Kubu Cabins, etc – but if you must be south of the river then there are two obvious options:

Victoria Falls Town Council Campsite
As befits the attractions of Victoria Falls, this is probably the busiest campsite in Southern Africa. This makes it great for meeting other budget travellers, but lousy if you seek any space to yourself, peace and quiet, or even sleep. Large numbers of people, often disgorged from enormous trucks, seem to arrive and depart at perplexing hours of the night, often causing the maximum possible noise and disturbance. That said, it is very central and hence convenient.
Rates: US$12 per person camping, US$30 in dormitories

Zambezi National Park Restcamp

For those with a vehicle, this is about 6km out of town, on Park Way, which leads to the Zambezi National Park. There is a caravan and camping park, on the right of the road, next to the river. Then a kilometre or so later is the site for the chalets next to the entry gate to the national park.

The chalets have four beds in each – excellent value for small groups – and have self-catering facilities and braais. Their lawns lead down to the river, so keep a careful watch for the local wildlife. You can book these in advance either in Harare or in the National Parks office on Livingstone Way.

The campsite is slightly nearer to town, but still too far away to be convenient if you are walking. With a vehicle this is a good place to camp, being much quieter than the campsite in town.

Rates: US$40 per chalet, US$10 per person camping

Where to eat

If you're looking to splash out on an expensive meal, then the best restaurants are all in the hotels. More frugal travellers should seek a take-away in town, or cook for themselves.

Take-away

There is a great choice of take-aways, and most are within two minutes' walk of the Wimpy and around the shopping arcade beside Shearwaters. Some travellers never get beyond Wimpy, but Naran's take-away is definitely worth a try, as is the excellent ice-cream bar between the supermarket and Wimpy. Some of the restaurants around here, listed below, also do take-away food. If you've time for a leisurely breakfast, then consider the Victoria Falls Hotel, or The Kingdom – both do all-you-can-eat buffets for about US$12.

Restaurants

There are now a huge variety of places to eat on the Zimbabwe side, which come in and out of fashion equally quickly. There are places for all tastes and budgets, new ones springing up all the time. Popular and reasonably priced restaurants/take-aways include Wimpy, The Pink Baobab, Explorers, The Bisto, Cattlemen's, Subway, the Croc & Paddle (in Elephant Walk Shopping Complex); and the new Kingdom has a wide selection of everything from a Spur's (steaks, burgers, salads, etc) to a pizzeria.

The most impressive hotel restaurant is the Livingstone Room at the Victoria Falls Hotel, which serves classic European dishes, à la carte, in a formal jacket-and-tie atmosphere. You'll understand why Laurens van der Post donned his dinner jacket here. Lunches, outside on the terrace, are exceptional, and more affordable for a similar level of luxury.

Further out of town, the Elephant Hills and the Safari Lodge both have good restaurants, both in keeping with their different styles. The Safari Lodge's bar is the best place for a drink at sundown, as the animals all come to the waterhole.

Getting around

Victoria Falls is quite small: walking from the Wimpy corner to the Falls entry gate takes only about ten minutes. The hotels that are further away all have courtesy bus services; check the precise details with their receptions.

If you are in a rush, then hail a taxi. These are inexpensive and convenient, despite their usual poor state of repair. Bargain before getting into the vehicle, and expect a fare around Z$10 per kilometre.

Car hire

This is expensive, working out at about US$90 per day for a short hire. It is the best way if you want to visit Hwange National Park independently, but isn't worthwhile for just getting around town. Note that Zimbabwean car hire firms will not yet let their cars into Zambia, Botswana or South Africa. (Although firms from South Africa and Botswana will sometimes let their vehicles into Zimbabwe.)

Contact Avis (tel: 26313 4532), situated in the garage opposite the Makasa Sun, or Hertz (tel: 26313 4267 or 4268) through UTC in the shopping centre next to the Wimpy. If you are planning a trip from the UK, then Sunvil Discovery in the UK (tel: 020 8232 9777; fax: 020 8568 8330; email: africa@sunvil.co.uk) offer a unique 100% Collision Damage Waiver (CDW) insurance as part of their fly-drive trips around Zimbabwe.

Bicycle hire

This is an excellent, practical option for getting around and is highly recommended. It will cost around US$10 per day, and bicycles can be taken across the border into Livingstone.

Several companies rent bicycles, including the Avis garage, opposite the Kingdom, or Michael's in Park Way.

WHAT TO SEE AND DO

The Falls area has been a major crossroads for travellers for the past hundred years. From the early missionaries and traders, to the backpackers, overland trucks and package tourists of the last few decades – virtually everyone passing through the region from overseas has stopped here. Recently this has created a thriving tourism industry, mostly based south of the river. Apart from simply marvelling at one of the world's greatest waterfalls, there are now lots of ways to occupy yourself. Some are easily booked after you arrive; one or two are better pre-arranged.

The last decade has witnessed a gradual shift in the town's atmosphere. Visitors used to be from Southern Africa, with perhaps the odd intrepid backpacker and the fortunate few who could afford an upmarket safari. Now the sheer volume of visitors to the Falls has increased massively. This increase, especially noticeable in the proportion of younger visitors, has fuelled the rise of more active, adventurous pursuits like white-water rafting, bungee-jumping, and other thrill-based pastimes.

A genteel cocktail at the Victoria Falls Hotel is no longer the high point of a visit for most people. You are more likely to return home with vivid memories of the adrenaline rush of shooting rapids in a raft, or the buzz of accelerating head-first towards the Zambezi with only a piece of elastic to save you.

The Falls

The Falls are 1,688m wide and average just over 100m in height. Around 550 million litres (750 at peak) cascades over the lip every minute, making this one of the world's greatest waterfalls.

Closer inspection shows that this immense curtain of water is interrupted by gaps, where small islands stand on the lip of the falls. These effectively split the Falls into smaller waterfalls, which are known as (from west to east) the Devil's Cataract, the Main Falls, the Horseshoe Falls, the Rainbow Falls and the Eastern Cataract.

Around the Falls is a genuinely important and interesting rainforest, with plant species (especially ferns) rarely found elsewhere in Zimbabwe or Zambia. These are sustained by the clouds of spray, which blanket the immediate vicinity of the Falls. You'll also find various small antelope, monkeys and baboons here, whilst the lush canopy shelters Livingstone's lourie amongst other birds.

The flow, and hence the spray, is greatest just after the end of the rainy season – around March or April, depending upon the rains. It then decreases gradually until about December, when the rains in western Zambia will start to replenish the river. During low water, a light raincoat (available for rent!) is very useful for wandering between the viewpoints. However, in high water a raincoat is largely ineffective as the spray blows all around and soaks you in seconds. Anything that you want to keep dry must be wrapped in several layers of plastic or, even better, zip-lock plastic bags.

The Falls never seem the same twice, so try to visit several times, under different light conditions. At sunrise, both Danger Point and Knife-edge Point are fascinating – position yourself carefully to see your shadow in the mists, with three concentric rainbows appearing as halos. (Photographers will find polarising filters invaluable in capturing the rainbows on film – as the light from the rainbows at any time of day is polarised.)

Moonlight is another fascinating time, when the Falls take on an ethereal glow and the waters blend into one smooth mass which seems frozen over the rocks.

On the Zambian side, viewing the Falls could not be easier. Simply follow the signs and your nose along the paths from in front of the field museum and curio stalls. One track leads upstream for a while. This is best explored in the late afternoon (take your own snacks and drinks) and you may catch a stunning sunset.

If you visit when the river is at its lowest, towards the end of the dry season, then the channels on the Zambian side may have dried up. Whilst the Falls will be less spectacular then, you can sometimes walk across the bed of the Zambezi as far as Livingstone Island, before you are stopped by a channel which is actually flowing. Looking down on the Falls from their lip does afford a totally different perspective – just don't slip!

The main path leads along the cliff opposite the Falls, then across the swaying knife-edge bridge, via scenic points, photo stops and a good vantage point from which to watch bungee-jumpers. This finishes at the farthest west of the Zambian viewpoints.

A third path descends right down to the water's edge at the Boiling Pot, which is often used as a raft launch-site. It is a beautiful (but steep) hike down through palm-fringed forest – well worth the long, hot climb back. Take a picnic and relax by the river if you've time.

Viewing the Falls by moonlight is not restricted, though elephants wander about occasionally and it is best not to go alone. If you can visit during a full moon then watch for a lunar rainbow, an amazing sight.

From the Zimbabwean side, viewing the Falls is more regulated. There is now a small ticket booth and display at the entrance gate to the Falls, which is a few hundred yards from the Zimbabwean border post. A ticket costs US$20 per person, and you can return for no extra cost during the same day.

Technically this area is within the Victoria Falls National Park – and you will find a map of the paths at the entrance. Start at the western end, by Livingstone's statue – inscribed with 'Explorer, Missionary and Liberator', and overlooking the Devil's Cataract.

Visiting the viewpoints in order, next is the Cataract View. If water levels are low, and the spray not too strong, after clambering down quite a steep stairway you will be greeted by views along the canyon of the Falls. Climbing back up, wander from one viewpoint to the next, eastwards, and you will eventually reach the slippery-smooth rocks at Danger Point.

Few of these viewpoints have anything more than brushwood fences and low railings to guard the edges – so going close to the edge is not for those with vertigo. Viewing the Falls by moonlight is possible by special arrangement.

Birding

Birdwatching isn't normally regarded as an adrenaline sport, but with the outstanding avifauna to be found in and around the Falls, serious 'twitchers' (as keen bird-watchers are known) might disagree.

Even the casual visitor with little interest will often see fish eagles, Egyptian geese, lots of kingfishers, numerous different bee-eaters, ibis (including sacred), and various other storks, egrets and herons. Meanwhile, avid twitchers will be seeking the more elusive rarities like Taita falcon, as they occur only rarely and this is certainly one of the best sites to look for them. Rock pratincoles have almost as restricted a distribution (just following the Zambezi), but can often be seen here balancing on boulders by the water's edge and hawking for insects. Look in the riverine forest around the Falls and you may spot a collared palmthrush rummaging around, and again these are really quite rare birds recorded in only a few areas.

In contrast, African finfoot occur throughout the subcontinent, but are always shy. They prefer slow water, overhung with leafy branches, and they find the upper sections of the Zambezi perfect, so are often seen there if you look when it's quiet.

Museums

Given its history, it is no surprise that Livingstone has several good museums. The main Livingstone Museum is the most important of these, and certainly one of the best in the country.

Livingstone Museum

In a prime position on the crest of Mosi-oa-Tunya Road, in the middle of town, this museum is worth exploring for a few hours. There are exhibits on the Stone Age, and features on more recent history, animals and traditional village life in the area. There is also a unique collection of Livingstone's personal possessions and the museum often has special exhibits.

The staff are friendly and knowledgeable and guided tours are included. It is worth a visit, if only to familiarise yourself with the area and culture.

Rates: entry fee US$2, (US$1 for a child)

Railway Museum

This specialist museum (PO Box 60927; tel: 321820; fax: 324509) is situated about 1km along Chishimba Falls Road, towards the southwest side of town. There's a collection of old steam locomotives and memorabilia, and displays on railway history – appropriate for a town where the railway was built in 1905. However, if you're not a railway enthusiast, give it a miss.

Rates: entry fee US$5. Open: 08.30–16.30 every day

Field Museum

Much smaller than the main museum in town, this is next to the curio stands by the border and concentrates on the origin of the Falls, and the development of man in the area.

Rates: entry fee US$2, (US$1 for a child)

Local culture

On the Zimbabwean side, you will find practised (and very commercial) tribal dances held, usually just before dinner, at various venues including Elephant Hills

Hotel, the Boma (at Victoria Falls Safari Lodge) and the Falls Craft Village. If you want something more sensitive to the local cultures, not to mention authentic, then look north, to Livingstone.

Cultural day trips

There are several companies offering tours around Livingstone and its environs, often including visits to traditional villages, the Mosi-oa-Tunya National Park, Livingstone's museums and historical sites around the Falls. Makora Quest and Shungu Mufu are the two best operators of these trips on the Livingstone side. These are small companies, both are run by people who have lived in Livingstone for years. They understand the place well and its nuances, far better than a new guide from one of the larger companies who has learnt to give a handful of set speeches from a training manual.

A typical trip may begin with a guided walk around the Zambian side of the Falls, followed by a fascinating visit to the Nakatindi village just east of the Falls. This typical Zambian settlement is home to 6–7,000 people and a guide who lives here will take you around. This is probably the closest you will get to an insight into the life of normal Zambians – an excellent chance to see how the local people live, and to talk with them.

Lunch is offered, followed by a short safari around the Mosi-oa-Tunya National Park. These tours have been run for years, and part of their beauty is that a small percentage of their cost is automatically paid to the Nakatindi village. Thus the villagers are happy to see strangers strolling around, accompanied by a local guide, and you will not encounter any begging or hassle.

Rates: roughly US$80 per person for a full day, or US$50 for a half day

Maramba Cultural Centre

This normally deserted kraal stands beside the main road between the border and Livingstone town, about 5km from each. Don't be put off by the structure's poor repair; this is caused by elephants looking for tasty seedpods from the tall winterthorn trees, *Acacia albida*, in and around the facility.

Each Saturday and Sunday, between about 15.00 and 17.00, traditional cultural dances are performed by the Maramba Cultural Dance Troupe for the public. Usually this involves about 20 dancers and five drummers, all wearing traditional costumes, demonstrating authentic dances from all around Zambia. It is well attended by local Zambians and you will find a much more authentic atmosphere here than in the more 'staged' shows. Simultaneously, demonstrations of village life are held in rondavels around the centre. Beers and soft drinks are available, as are toilets.

Entry: About US$1 per person, plus US$1 per camera and US$2 per video camera

Curio stalls

Just inside the Zambian border, next to the field museum, is an outstanding curio stand. The carvers and traders come mostly from Mukuni village, though the goods come from as far afield as Zaire and Malawi. Mukuni Park in the centre of town (see page 167) has a similar area of curio vendors, but not as wide a selection of goods.

Both are excellent places to buy wooden and stone carvings, chess boards, drums, malachite bangles and the like. Similar carvings are for sale in Zimbabwe, but often at twice the price, so visitors to Zimbabwe who just cross the border to shop here are common enough for this to have become known as 'the best place in Zimbabwe for curios'.

There are usually about 20 or 30 separate traders, laying their wares out separately. All compete with one another and vie for your business. The best buys are heavy wooden carvings: hippos, rhinos and smaller statues, often made out of excellent quality, heavy wood. However, you should consider the ethics of encouraging *any* further exploitation of hardwoods.

This is a place to bargain hard and expect to hear all sorts of pre-fabricated stories as to why you should pay more. When you start to pay, you will realise how sophisticated the traders are about their currency conversions, reminding you to double-check any exchange rates. Traders will accept most currencies and sometimes credit cards.

Victoria Falls Craft Village
Behind the main post office on Livingstone Way, this is Zimbabwe's more regulated answer to Zambia's curio stalls. Amongst this complex are well-built curio shops as well as traders on the surrounding ground. Within the shops you'll find some excellent pieces and if you are shopping for high quality pieces of art, then this may be the place for you. Alternatively, try the new Elephant's Walk Shopping Complex.

But if you're simply seeking good-value curios then look to the carvers and vendors outside, who will bargain hard for your business. Zimbabwe's currency regulations means that they can only accept Zimbabwe dollars for payment, but there are several bureaux de change nearby.

Thrills and spills
The Falls has become the adventure capital of Southern Africa in the last few years. There is an amazing variety of ways to get your shot of adrenaline: white-water rafting, canoeing, bungee-jumping, abseiling, river boarding or simply a flight over the Falls.

None comes cheaply. Most are in the US$50–150 range per activity. There are also choices of operator for most of these – so if you book locally, shop around to find something that suits you before you decide. Prices won't vary much – but you will find the true range of what's available. Whatever you plan, expect to sign an indemnity form before your activity starts.

Flight of Angels
Named after Livingstone's famous comments, the 'Flight of Angels' is a sightseeing trip over the Falls by small aircraft, microlight, helicopter or ultra-light aircraft. This is a good way to get a feel for the geography of the area, and is surprisingly worthwhile if you want to really appreciate the Falls. Any of these can be readily booked from agents in the area, including:

Light aircraft
Del Air offers daily scenic flights over the Falls, departing from Livingstone Airport. They use a Cessna 206; every seat is a window seat and the high mounted wing allows maximum photo opportunities. The flight offers stunning views of the Falls and gorges and takes visitors upstream over the Mosi-oa-Tunya National Park for game viewing. Tour operators in Victoria Falls offer comparable flights using the small runway near the town (not the main airport).
Rates: US$50 per person for 25 minutes, US$70 per person for 40 minutes, including transfers to/from your accommodation on either side of the border

Microlight

This is a totally different experience from a light aircraft: essentially sightseeing from a propeller-powered armchair 500m above the ground. It is only available on the Zambian side and is operated by Batoka Sky/Del Air. The microlights take two people: one pilot, one passenger. Because the passenger sits next to the propeller, cameras cannot be carried. However, you can arrange to be photographed, or even pictured on video, above the Falls from a camera fixed to the wing. This is the closest you can come to soaring like a bird over the Falls.

The microlights are affected by the slightest turbulence so, when you book a flight in advance, it's best to specify the early morning or late afternoon. Transport between their Maramba Aerodrome (about a five-minute drive from the border) and Livingstone or Victoria Falls hotels is provided.

Rates: US$70 per person for 15 minutes including circuits over the Falls and a flight over the game park; US$105 for 30 minutes, including mini-safari up-river

Helicopter

This is the most expensive way to see the Falls, but it is tremendous fun. Del Air use a five-seat Squirrel helicopter, based at their Maramba Aerodrome, which is designed to give all passengers a good view. The front seats are on a 'first come, first served' basis. The Zambezi Helicopter Company, based at Elephant Hills, offer similar trips from the Zimbabwe side.

Rates: typically US$70 per person for 15 minutes, US$130 per person for 30 minutes. Prices include all transfers, from either Livingstone or Victoria Falls

Ultra-lights

Another way to get a bird's eye view of the Falls is with an ultra-light (which feels like a cross between a microlight and small plane). As with the microlight, you are completely exposed with the wind in your hair and they take only one passenger at a time. The craft flies more like a small plane and you can carry your camera with you, making for good photographic opportunities without the confines of a small plane. It is also much quieter than a small plane.

These trips are based out of the Victoria Falls main airport (look for them on the tarmac if you fly in here) and run by Bush Birds Flying Safaris. Being so far out of town does make them slightly inconvenient, but they are the closest option to a microlight on the Zimbabwean side. On balance, the microlight is more fun, though you do get a nice view of the gorges as you fly up to the Falls.

Rates: US$100 per person for 35 minutes, US$150 per person for 55 minutes

Upper Zambezi canoeing

Canoeing down the upper Zambezi is a cool occupation on hot days, and the best way to explore the upper river, its islands and channels. The silence of canoes make them ideal for floating up to antelope drinking, elephants feeding, or crocodiles basking. Hippos provide the excitement, and are treated with respect and given lots of space.

There are a variety of options available, from half-day excursions to full days ending with a game drive in the Mosi-oa-Tunya National Park, and even overnight camping trips. You'll find any of them generally relaxing, although paddling becomes a bit more strenuous if it's windy. All canoe trips must be accompanied by a qualified river guide. Canoes range from two-seater open-decked kayaks to inflatable 'crocodiles'.

There are some sections of choppy water if you'd like a little more excitement, though it's possible to avoid most of these easily if you wish. Trips concentrating on these are sometimes sold as white-water kayaking – which shouldn't be confused with the white-water rafting mentioned below.

Once you are used to the water, the better guides will encourage you to concentrate on the wildlife. Trips on the Zambian side have long been run by Makora Quest and Chundukwa Adventure Trails – both are owner-operated and run by very experience guides.

Newer (and more commercial) entrants on the Zambian side include Raft Extreme, Bundu and Safari Par Excellence, whilst on the Zimbabwean side the main operators are both very large: Shearwater and Kandahar.

Zambian rates: around US$75 for a half day, including lunch, or US$85 for a full day. Two-day fully-inclusive camping trips are about US$235 per person. Zimbabwean rates are around US$70 for a half day or US90 for a full day.

Jet-boats

There is a new company on the Zimbabwean side running jet-boats up the upper Zambezi. These have been widely criticised as very noisy and damaging the river's tranquil ambience as well as frightening its wildlife. Readers should think twice about these allegations before embarking on such a trip.

Bungee-jumping

There's only one company organising bungee-jumping – African Extreme, an offshoot of the original pioneers from New Zealand, Kiwi Extreme. You jump from the middle of the main bridge between Zambia and Zimbabwe, where the Zambezi is around 111m below you. It is the highest commercial bungee-jump in the world, and not for the nervous.

Masochists can do a 'gruesome twosome' where they jump and are then lowered

A MATTER OF PERSPECTIVE
Judi Helmholz

Spanning the border between Zambia and Zimbabwe is the dramatic Victoria Falls Bridge. Built close to the mighty Falls so railroad carriages could be doused in spray, this famous bridge is becoming renowned for another attraction – the highest bungee-jump in the world: a daunting 110m. It is not unusual for hordes of spectators to gather at the jump site to watch daring individuals test their courage on the elastic line.

Over the course of a week, the Jump Master noticed the same two Zambian men at the bridge each day, closely observing the jump activities. This was unusual. Following each jump, the gentlemen engaged in seemingly heated discussion, gesturing and shaking their heads. After eight straight days of this, the two Zambians approached the Jump Master. 'We have been here many days trying to get up our courage. Although we are very scared, we have no jobs and need money. How much will you pay us to jump?'

When the Jump Master delicately informed them that in actual fact one must pay for the privilege of jumping, the men were confounded. Surely, no one in his or her right mind would actually pay to jump. There must be some misunderstanding. 'Ah, you have failed to understand. We are prepared to jump... FOR MONEY!' the men exclaimed in unison. Further clarification by the Jump Master left the two Zambians incredulously shaking their heads and seeking alternative means of employment. They were last seen heading toward one of the rafting companies.

directly on to a white-water rafting trip rather than being brought back up on to the bridge. Alternatively, 'tandem' bungee-jumps are possible for two people.

You can book in advance, through any of the agencies, or simply turn up at the bridge and pay there. Pictures and videos of your jump are available at extra charge. *Rates: US$90 for one jump (no refunds if you change your mind)*

White-water rafting

The Zambezi below the Falls is one of the world's most renowned stretches of white water. It was the venue for the 1995 World Rafting Championships, and rafting is now very big business here with keen competition for tourist dollars. (About 50,000 people now go down the river every year, paying about US$80–100 each. You can do the sums.)

Experienced rafters grade rivers from I to VI, according to difficulty. Elsewhere in the world, a normal view of this scale would be:

- Class I   No rapids, flat water.
- Class II   Easy rapids, a float trip. No rafting experience required.
- Class III   Intermediate to advanced rapids. No rafting experience required.
- Class IV   Very difficult rapids. Prior rafting experience highly recommended. No children.
- Class V   For experts only. High chance of flips or swims. No children or beginners.
- Class VI   Impossible to run.

The rapids below the Falls are mostly graded IV and V. This isn't surprising when you realise that all the water coming slowly up the Zambezi's 1.7km width is being squeezed through a number of rocky gorges that are often just 50–60m wide.

Fortunately for the rafting companies, most of the rapids here may be very large, but the vast majority of them are not 'technical' to run. This means that they don't need skill to manoeuvre the boat whilst it is *within* the rapids, they just require the rafts to be positioned properly *before* entering each rapid. Hence, despite the grading of these rapids, they allow absolute beginners into virtually all of the rafts.

High or low water, and which side of the river?

Rafting is offered from both sides of the river by a wide range of companies. Some operate on both sides, like Safari Par Excellence. The Zambian side offers a far more spectacular entry, just at the base of the Falls; whereas on the Zimbabwean side you miss this entirely and start off at Rapid Number Four.

During high water this might be partially obscured by spray, but you should try to go from the Zambian side during low-water months (roughly from August to January) so as not to miss such a stunning place to start below the Falls. These low-water months are probably the best time to experience the Zambezi's full glory, as then its waves and troughs (or 'drops') are more pronounced.

In high-water months (February to July), only half-day trips are offered. These start below Rapid Number 9 on both sides. Note that when the river is highest its rapids may seem less dramatic, but it is probably more dangerous – due to the strong whirlpools and undercurrents. At that time, the water is sometimes too high and rafting should then be stopped until it recedes to a safer level.

The trips

A typical rafting trip will start with a briefing, covering safety/health issues, giving the plan for the day and answering any questions. Once you reach the 'put-in' at the river, you will be given a short safety/practice session to familiarise yourself with the raft and techniques that will be used to run the rapids. Half-day trips will run about half of the rapids, but a full day is needed to get through all the rapids from one to twenty-three. Lunch and cool drinks are included. Note that the climb up and out of the gorge at the end can be steep and tiring.

A trained river guide pilots every raft, but you need to decide whether you want to go in an oar boat or in a paddle boat. In an **oar boat** expect to cling on for dear life, and throw your weight around the raft on demand – but nothing more. Oar boats are generally easier and safer because you rely on the skills of the oarsmen to negotiate the rapids, and you can hang on to the raft at all times. Only occasionally will you have to 'highside' (throw your weight forward) when punching through a big wave.

In a **paddle boat** the participants provide the power by paddling, while a trained rafting guide positions the boat and yells out commands instructing you what to do. You'll have to listen, and also paddle like crazy through the rapids, remembering when and if you are supposed to be paddling. You can't just hang on! In paddle boats you are an active participant and thus are largely responsible for how successfully you run the rapids. The rafting guide calls commands and positions the boat, but then it's up to you. If your fellow paddlers are not up to it, then expect a difficult ride. Paddle boats have a higher tendency to flip and/or have 'swimmers' (someone thrown out of the boat).

Originally, only oar boats were run on the Zambezi. However in recent years paddleboats have become more popular as rafting companies compete to outdo each other in offering the most exciting rides. There is, of course, a very fine line between striving to be more exciting, and actually becoming more dangerous.

With either option, remember that people often fall out and rafts do capsize. Despite this, safety records are usually cited as excellent. Serious injuries are said to be uncommon and fatalities rare. (Curiously for an industry that claims such a good safety record, none of the larger companies seem to keep transparent records of injuries or fatalities.)

The operators

All rafting companies offer broadly similar experiences at prices that are invariably identical. Videos and photos of your trip are offered at additional cost. The rapids are numbered starting from the boiling pot, from one to twenty-three, so it's easy to make a rough comparison of the trips on offer.

In addition to day trips, there are four-day expeditions that go as far as the Batoka Gorge, while seven-day expeditions reach the mouth of the Matetsi River. These offer more than the adrenaline of white water, and are the best way of seeing the remote Batoka Gorge. Adrift and Shearwater offer these longer trips out of the Zimbabwean Side. A new company, Zambezi Elite, also from the Zimbabwean side, offers smaller, more personalised and upmarket trips at a higher cost (US$150 per person).

Rates: half-day trips are around US$85, full day trips around US$95 per person. Both include transfers as well as breakfast and snacks or lunch and cool drinks.

River-boarding

For a more up-close and personal encounter with the Zambezi rapids, adrenaline junkies can try their hand at river-boarding (also known as boogie-boarding). Serious Fun and Safari Par Excellence both offer daily trips down the Zambezi from Zambia.

After donning your flippers, life jacket and helmet, you and your foam board (the size of a small surfboard) will have an opportunity to 'surf' the big waves of the Zambezi, after being taught basic skills in a calmer section of the river. A raft accompanies each trip and takes you downstream to the best surfing spots of the day. Here you can try your hand at finding the best 'standing waves' where you can stay still and surf as the water rushes beneath you. Experts can stand, but most will surf on their stomachs.

Thrilling for the fit who swim strongly, but not for the faint of heart. Trips are fully inclusive of transfers, a light breakfast, lunch and sundowners.
Rates: US$95–125 per person, fully inclusive

Abseiling and swinging
The newest additions to the adventure menu are a highwire, a cable slide, abseiling, and 'Rap' jumps (rappelling forwards) down the side of the gorge from the Zambian side. These are currently only offered by Abseil Africa. It's a full day's activity starting with a light breakfast and a basic abseiling course. It continues with a day of highwiring, abseiling and cable sliding to your heart's content. Lunch and cool drinks are included and sundowners are offered. The site is a short drive from the Falls, in a scenic spot on the edge of the Gorge.
Rates: US$95 per person for a full day fully inclusive of transfers and meals

Tandem parachuting
For an adrenaline rush 8,000 feet high, try tandem parachuting. Here you will be securely strapped to an instructor and free-fall at 200km/per hour for 30 seconds before safely drifting back to earth, some four minutes later, underneath a parachute.

This is currently being offered by Tandemania in Victoria Falls, and is being started by Batoka Sky/Del Air in Livingstone as this goes to press.
Rates: US$160–180 per person inclusive of transfers

Horse-riding
There are two operators offering horse-back safaris in the Falls area: in Zambia, Chundukwa Adventure Trails, and in Zimbabwe, Zambezi Horse Trails. Both can offer day trips for novices in search of game, as well as longer sojourns with overnight camps for more experienced riders.
Rates: US$45–65 per person

Elephant-riding
For an elephant encounter, The Elephant Company in Victoria Falls offer morning, lunchtime or afternoon elephant-back safaris. They are only 15 minutes' drive from Victoria Falls, at the Nakavango Estate adjacent to Zambezi National Park. Here you and your 'Nduna' (the elephant pilot) will have an opportunity to ride African elephants through the bush accompanied by the professional guide on foot.

There is game in the area – including kudu, buffalo, bushbuck and impala – which are sometimes seen. All the elephants were originally orphaned and raised on family farms, and so are comfortable being around people. You will have a chance to interact with them close up – a memorable and moving experience. You will also hear about elephant issues and conservation efforts in Africa. Breakfast, lunch or sundowners and all transfers are included from Victoria Falls. It's a worthwhile experience, especially if you can't afford to stay at the Elephant Camp, just outside the Falls.
Rates: US$118 per person

Booze cruises
These used to be strictly at sundown, and the drinks were free. Now, sadly, the river is full of booze cruise boats operating round the clock (you can now choose

from breakfast, lunch, sunset or dinner cruises!), and they are often less generous – with drinks bought from a bar on board. Nostalgia aside, floating on the upper Zambezi with a glass in one hand, and a pair of binoculars in the other, is still a pleasant way to watch the sun go down. Meanwhile you take a gentle look around the Zambezi's islands, surrounded by national parks on both sides of the river. You may even spot the odd hippo, crocodile, or elephant.

On the Zambian side these are organised by Safari Par Excellence, Bwaato Adventures and Taonga Safaris. (Saf Par and Bwaato also have offices on the Zimbabwean side.)

In Zimbabwe, boats leave from several different jetties and there is a wider range of trips to choose from – from upmarket cruises to more basic ones. Book in advance through one of the agents in town, who can advise what best suits you, and will also arrange for you to be picked up about half an hour before the cruise. *Rates: US$20–40 per person inclusive of drinks and perhaps a meal*

Livingstone Island lunch

Livingstone Island stands in the middle of the great waterfall, and is the island from which Dr Livingstone first viewed the falls. Only Tongabezi (see page 161) runs these trips and you will be transferred over to the island by banana boat (a long, almost cylindrical design of motorboat) from a launch site fairly near to the waterfall. There you'll spend a few hours gazing over the edge, perhaps bathing in a few small pools, and having a delicious gourmet lunch, usually complete with sparkling wine (French champagne at considerable extra cost). It's a lovely spot and makes an amazing experience.

During the months of very highest water the spray is too intense, so these trips don't operate. When the water's at its lowest, around October and November, you can sometimes walk to the island – and so it loses some of its appeal. But for the rest of the year it's a great trip and well worth the cost.

These can be arranged by tour operators and travel agents as well as directly with Tongabezi, and you must book in advance. *Rates: about US$65 per person*

Safaris around the Falls area
Mosi-oa-Tunya National Park

Study a map and you'll see that much of the Zambian area around the Falls is protected within a national park. (This is also variously spelt as Mosi-Oa-Tunya or Mosi-O-Tunya, with or without the hyphens and/or capitals. Hence for ease I'll refer to it here as the MOT National Park.)

All of this is a protected area, but only a small section is fenced off into a game park, with a low entry fee. This small sanctuary is well worth a visit, and not just because it protects what are probably Zambia's only remaining rhino (five white ones). In a few hours' driving you'll probably see most of the common antelope, including some fine giraffe, and have the chance to visit the old cemetery at Old Drift. You can drive yourself around easily, or go with one of the many operators who run these trips. Shungu Mufu and Makora Quest are highly recommended.

Victoria Falls National Park

Like the northern side of the river, a good section of Zimbabwe's land around the falls is protected – though only the rainforest area, criss-crossed by footpaths to viewing points, is actually fenced off. If you are feeling adventurous, then follow the riverbank upstream from Livingstone's statue. (If the gate is closed beyond the statue, then retrace your steps out of the entrance to the rainforest; and turn right, then right again, down Zambezi Drive, to reach the outside of that gate.)

This path runs next to Zambezi Drive for a while. After almost 2km Zambezi Drive leaves the river and turns back towards town, passing a famous baobab tree called the Big Tree. From there the path continues for about 8km upstream until it reaches A'Zambezi River Lodge, just outside the gate to the Zambezi National Park. This is a very beautiful, wild walk but, despite its innocent air, you are as likely to meet hippo, elephant or buffalo here as in any other National Park. So take great care as you admire the view across the river.

Zambezi National Park

This park borders the Zambezi River, starting about 6km from Victoria Falls and extending about 40km upstream. You cannot walk here (without a professional guide), so you need a vehicle, but there are several Zimbabwean operators running morning and afternoon drives through the park who will collect you from any of the main hotels.

The park is actually bisected by the main road from Victoria Falls to Kazungula/Kasane (which has long been an unlikely, but favourite, spot for sightings of wild dogs). Better game viewing is to be had from the roads designed for it: the Zambezi River Drive, or the Chamabondo Drive.

The former is easily reached by driving out of town along Park Way, past the Elephant Hills Hotel and the Victoria Falls Safari Lodge. This road follows the river's course almost to the end of the park, and there are plenty of loop roads to explore away from the river.

The Chamabondo Drive has a separate entrance on the road to Bulawayo. Take a right turn just before the road crosses the Massive River, about 7km out of town. This leads past several pans and hides until it terminates at Nook Pan, from where you must retrace your steps as there are no loop roads.

The park has good populations of elephant, buffalo and antelope – especially notable are the graceful sable which thrive here. The riverfront is beautiful, lined with classic stands of tall winterthorn trees, *Acacia albida*. Note that when wet this park is often impossible to drive through in a 2WD, and when dry some of the roads remain in poor condition.

Excursions from the Falls area

If you are seeking an excursion for four or five days from the Falls area, then there are a number of superb game parks within easy reach:

Kafue National Park, Zambia

The southern side of Kafue is actually quite close to the Falls, though the area is undeveloped. You will need either several fully-kitted 4WDs in convoy, or the help of a local operator. Game viewing in this part of the park is by vehicle and foot from one of a handful of camps; see *Chapter 16* for more details. You are unlikely to meet anyone else in this remote area. The obvious choice of operator is Chundukwa Adventure Trails, who run Chundukwa River Camp here, and have two small camps in the southern Kafue.

Batoka Sky/Del Air offer a day trip here by private plane, including flights, a game drive, breakfast in the bush, a short walk to lunch in the bush, and a game drive back to Ngoma airstrip. This costs US$195 per person, for a minimum of four.

Chobe National Park, Botswana

This is often suggested as a day trip from the Falls, but is too far to be worthwhile. (You end up arriving after the best of the morning's game viewing is finished, and leaving before the afternoon cools down sufficiently for the game to re-appear!)

However, the Chobe riverfront, around Serondella, probably has higher wildlife densities than any of the other parks mentioned here. So if you can cope with the sheer number of vehicles there, it may be worth a trip for a few days. Its luxurious lodges (and high park fees) mean that northern Chobe is always expensive. So do avoid the dismal day trips; visit for a few days or don't bother.

There are regular transfers between Victoria Falls and Kasane (in Botswana, beside the park) which take around two hours. Then stay at either Chobe Game Lodge or Chobe Chilwero – the only two lodges in that section of the park. Either can easily be arranged by a good tour operator before you arrive, or by a travel agent in the Falls. The lodges in Kasane, outside the park, don't compare. (Though Impalila Island Lodge or Ichingo Chobe River Camp are little-known options on the opposite bank of the river. Both are excellent value, and far cheaper.)

Alternatively, if you have a good 4WD then you can drive yourself around and (advance reservations essential) camp at the basic, unfenced site at Serondella. Take all your food and equipment with you, and watch for the baboons, which are very bad here.

Hwange National Park, Zimbabwe

Zimbabwe's flagship national park has four established public camps that provide excellent value, basic accommodation and camping. It also has several more basic camping spots at picnic sites.

Alternatively there are a bewildering choice of more expensive, all-inclusive private lodges clustered around its borders (and even dotted inside the park). The cheapest serious safari option from Victoria Falls is probably to rent a vehicle from Victoria Falls, and stay at the national park's camps. (Ideally perhaps Main Camp, then Sinamatella and perhaps Nantwich.)

Note that the roads around most of these are very rough, and most Zimbabwean car hire companies won't allow their 2WD vehicles near to Sinematella, Robins or Nantwich camps.

If your budget is less limited, then take the advice of a good tour operator before you leave, and organise a trip to one of the better private lodges. Note that price is not always a good guide in this area to what is good and what's not.

Chizarira National Park, Zimbabwe

One of Zimbabwe's wildest and least visited parks, Chizarira requires patience, lots of driving skill, and preferably a 4WD – and that's just to get there. Most visitors fly in, or are taken by an operator, and because the land is rugged and remote much of the game viewing is on foot. You won't see the quantities of game this way that you see elsewhere, but the wilderness experience is excellent.

One main lodge operates, Chizarira Wilderness Lodge, and also a tented camp, Jedson's Safari Camp. Both are excellent. Alternatively Leon Varley and his team run walking safaris here and have been doing so for years. They're another first-class operation.

Kasuma Pan National Park, Zimbabwe

This small, little-visited national park borders on to Botswana between the Zambezi and Hwange National Parks. Like Chizarira, it is used for walking safaris more than for driving, though the environment is very different. It consists of a huge, almost flat depression – a grass-covered pan surrounded by forests that are dominated by the familiar mopane and teak trees.

Only a few groups are allowed into the park at any time, each requiring a fully-licensed walking guide – which effectively limits access to organised operators.

Backpackers' overland trips
Like cut-down overland trips, there are usually several operators running buses or trucks to Windhoek, Maun or even Harare. These often stop at parks on the way, and typical examples at the moment are:

Okavango Mama
If you like groups then Wild Side Tours & Safaris have a 30-seater German-built bus which makes regular trips between Victoria Falls and Windhoek. It takes five days, with a mokoro trip and two-night stay on one of the Okavango Delta's islands. Cost is US$350 per person sharing, including meals but not drinks. Bring your own sleeping bags, sleeping mats, insect repellent and torch.

The Botswana Bus
Operated by *African Horizons* (owners of Fawlty Towers), the Botswana Bus offers seven-day trips from Livingstone and Victoria Falls to the Okavango Delta. Trips costs US$345 and are fully inclusive of four nights on an island in the Okavango Delta reached by mokoros. The route takes you through Mahango National Park, in Namibia, and a small section of Botswana's Chobe National Park (the fast road from Ngoma to Kasane).

USEFUL INFORMATION
Telephones
By a convenient arrangement, callers in Livingstone or Victoria Falls can telephone the other side using a local, rather than an international, telephone code. From Zambia just dial '6' before a Victoria Falls number; from Victoria Falls dial '8' before a Livingstone number. This makes huge savings on international call charges, but the few lines available are often busy. Just keep re-dialling – you will get through.

Tourist information
Both Livingstone and Victoria Falls have tourist information offices. You can expect pleasant, friendly staff with little useful information.

Livingstone's is situated next to the main Museum, where Mosi-oa-Tunya Road bends into the centre of town. The Victoria Falls office is a small bungalow opposite the Wimpy on Park Way.

Important note on visas
In recent years both Zambia and Zimbabwe have started to change their rules on visas, requiring more payments for crossing the borders. Zambia's visas proved the major problem, seeming excessive to the operators in the Falls area, who relied for their livelihood on a free-flow of people across the border. (Visitors may stay on one side, but would want to take part in activities on both sides.)

Now a deal has been reached whereby you can legally pop across the border, from Zimbabwe to Zambia, to do an activity or even to stay, without buying a visa – provided that the operator you are going to gives at least 24 hours' notice to the immigration authorities. They basically just need to put your name on a list down at the border post, and you pass through free.

So don't be put off by the cost of a Zambian visa, just remember to book your Zambian accommodation or activity in advance by a few days, and you generally won't need to pay.

Zambian operators with a base in Livingstone

By the time you read this, this list won't be exhaustive – new operators are starting up all the time. However, I hope that it proves a useful reference for you to work out who does what. Note that virtually all the operators will book virtually anything (as they receive a commission). Here I've tried to list companies that actually run the specified activities, and don't merely act as booking agents:

Across Africa Overland PO Box 60420. Tel: 03 320823; fax: 320277 or 320732; email: aaover@zamnet.zm

Across Africa Overland is run by Di and John Tolmay and used to be based at Thorn Tree Lodge. This operation has two very large trucks, and several 4WDs, which are deployed as one unit for large, self-contained expeditions around Southern Africa. These cost around US$1,800 per day for a group of up to eight people, and are usually chartered for long safaris or hunting trips.

Abseil Africa PO Box 61023, Livingstone. Tel: 03 323454; email: abseil@outpost.co.zm

Located in the Livingstone Adventure Centre, they are the first company to operate abseiling, high-wire trips, and a cable slide out over the gorges.

African Horizons (see also Fawlty Towers) Tel/fax: 03 323432; email: ahorizon@zamnet.zm or Zimbabwe cell: 011 708 184

Their offices are in Fawlty Towers, and they run the Botswana Bus.

Bundu Adventures PO Box 60773, Livingstone. Tel: 03 324407; fax: 324406; email: zambezi@zamnet.zm

Their main office and headquarters is off Mosi-oa-Tunya Road, on the Industrial Road, near the railway crossing – look for the sign. They are one of Zambia's larger companies which operate rafting and canoeing trips. Many of their rafting guides have a good level of experience.

Bwaato Adventures PO Box 60672, Livingstone. Tel: 03 324227; fax: 321490

Several offices, one in Livingstone's town centre in the post office complex, another in the New Fairmount Hotel, and a third upstairs in Soper's Arcade, in Victoria Falls.

Bwaato operates the full range of river cruises – breakfast, barbecue lunch, sunset booze and dinner – from their jetty near the Boat Club in Livingstone. They also conduct day tours through the MOT National Park and excursions to Chobe.

Most useful are the Euro-Africa coaches which depart daily for Lusaka, at about 07.30–08.00. These are modern, fast coaches that can be booked and paid for in advance, and run on time. They take about six hours to arrive in Lusaka, where their office is behind Findeco House. One-way costs about US$15.

Chundukwa Adventure Trails PO Box 61160. Tel: 03 324006; fax: 324006; tlx: ZA 24043

Owned and run by Doug Evans, this has its base at Chundukwa River Camp (see page 160). Doug is an experienced old Africa hand, with professional hunting and guiding licences in both Zambia and Zimbabwe: just the kind of chap to have on your side when the going gets tough. He organises and guides safaris from horseback, canoe and foot. When canoeing he concentrates on two- or three-day trips (covering about 90km) on the upper Zambezi, usually ending at Chundukwa. Horse-riding is usually just one or two days in the region around Chundukwa, though longer trails are possible for experienced riders.

If you're looking for a trip into the southern part of Kafue, then Chundukwa runs a couple of tented camps on the Nanzhila Plains in the southern part of Kafue National Park (see pages 329–36). Chundukwa's walking and vehicle safaris are probably the best way of seeing this remote area. Itineraries are flexible, but eight days in total is popular: three canoeing, one riding, three walking in Kafue, and one relaxing.

Del Air/Batoka Sky Ltd Maramba Aerodome, off Sichango Road, PO Box 60971, Livingstone. Tel/fax: 03 320058; email: reservations@batokasky.co.za

Del Air is signposted from the Mosi-oa-Tunya Road (turn at Tunya Lodge) and operates flights over the Falls in microlights, helicopters and fixed-wing aircraft. Also offers flight charters, air transfers, and is starting tandem parachuting.

Kalai Safaris Beside Livingstone Adventure Centre, 215 Mosi-oa-Tunya Road, PO Box 61075, Livingstone. Tel: 03 321103; email: safaris@kalai.co.zw or PO Box 112, Victoria Falls. Tel: (26313) 5842; fax: 5843

Operates a variety of full- and half-day trips in Livingstone and Victoria Falls including village tours, game parks and scenic tours. Also runs transfers and offers extended trips to Zimbabwe's Hwange National Park.

Livingstone Safaris PO Box 60007. Tel/fax: 03 322267; email: gecko@zamnet.zm

Run by Dave Lewis, Livingstone Safaris is based at Gecko's Guesthouse on Limulunga Road. Dave runs three-hour tours of the Mosi-oa-Tunya National Park or the Mokuni Village and Zambian side of the Falls. Both cost US$25 per person, minimum of two people.

He will also run much longer impromptu trips anywhere else in Zambia (in the dry season), on request for small groups of people. He's been in Zambia for five years and spent ten months of that in the Bangweulu Wetlands area.

Makora Quest Office in the Livingstone Adventure Centre, PO Box 60420, Livingstone. Tel: 03 324253/321679; fax: 302732; email: quest@zamnet.zm

Run by Colin Lowe, Makora Quest was started in 1985 and has a base just downstream from Kubu Cabins. He was the first canoe operator on the Upper Zambezi, and still runs by far the best guided half- and full-day canoe trips there. Compare Colin's knowledge and experience with that of some of the newer guides; the difference is stark.

Makora Quest also conducts excellent tours of the MOT National Park and the local area, as well as organising reliable transfers.

Raft Extreme PO Box 61105, Livingstone. Tel: 03 324024; tel/fax: 322370; email: grotto@zamnet.zm

Run from a base at Grubby's Grotto (see page 155), Raft Extreme caters almost exclusively for white-water rafting groups on overland trucks, most of whom stay at the Grotto. Only if there's a truck group already scheduled will they take bookings from individuals.

They also operate canoe trips, and have a combination trip including full English breakfast, followed by a half-day canoe trip to the MOT National Park, an hour's game drive with snacks and drinks, and a booze cruise with barbecue dinner and free drinks (cost US$95 per person).

Grubby claims passionately that his guides are the most professional on the river, and is a founder member of AZRO (Association of Zambezi River Operators).

Taonga Safaris Tel/fax: 03 324081

Run by Andrew Simpson, Taonga is based on the riverbank next to the boat club, on Sichanga Road (turn off Mosi-oa-Tunya Road at the Tunya Lodge). They offer breakfast, lunch and sunset cruises; game drives in the MOT National Park; and canoeing on the Upper Zambezi using three-person Canadian-style canoes.

Serious Fun office is in the Livingstone Adventure Centre, 216 Mosi-oa-Tunya Road. Tel: 03 323912; fax: 321850; Zimbabwe cell: 011 210 422; email: tloxton@zamnet.zm

This company pioneered river-boarding trips on the Zambezi, and that's what they do. For a full day they will collect you at 08.30, go as far as rapid 13, and charge S$95. Half-day trips run from 06.00 to 13.30 and cost US$90.

Shungu Mufu Tours Office at Pilgrim's Tea Room, PO Box 60403, Livingstone. Tel: 03 322692; (home) fax: 324094

Run by Cilla and Graham Young, Shungu Mufu are probably the best, and certainly the most established, operators of day trips on the Livingstone side.

They run an excellent full-day trip encompassing the Falls, a local village, lunch and a game drive around the MOT National Park – costing around US$80 per person (US$50 for a half day).

These tours have been run for years, and part of their beauty is that a small percentage of their cost is automatically paid to the Nakatindi village. Thus the villagers are happy to see strangers strolling around, accompanied by a local guide, and you will not encounter any begging or hassle.

Wild Side Tours & Safaris Liso House (in Livingstone centre), tel: 03 323726; fax: 323765; email: wild@zamnet.zm or in Victoria Falls at PO Box CT 450, Victoria Falls. Zimbabwe cell: 011 211 103
This owner-operated company, run by Peter and Karin Kermer (who speak English, Dutch and German), offers a wide range of camping safaris to Zambian and regional National Parks – all tailor-made to suit each client. They also operate the Okavango Mama bus which runs between Victoria Falls and Windhoek.

Zimbabwean operators with a base in Victoria Falls

There are a *huge* number of operators in Victoria Falls – probably many more than are in Livingstone. Therefore this list isn't exhaustive. It contains just a few of those who are most notable (for better or worse – I make no quality judgements here), and doubtless will leave out many excellent companies.

Backpackers' Africa PO Box 44, Victoria Falls. Fax: (26313) 2189; cell: 011 406 584; email: ziabmgll@ibmmail.com
This is a long-established Zimbabwe-based safari operation running organised walking safaris around Zimbabwe – with a special emphasis on Chizarira National Park. Normally a vehicle takes your luggage ahead, and so you are free to walk with just your camera and binoculars.

Backpackers' Bazaar Shop 5, Victoria Falls Centre, PO Box 44, Victoria Falls. Tel: (26313) 2189/5828; fax: (26313) 2189; email: zaibmgll@ibmmail.com
Convenient and efficient booking facilities for backpackers and independent travellers. Accommodation, excursions, overland trips, transfers etc.

Bush Birds Flying Safaris PO Box 157, Victoria Falls. Tel: (26313) 3398; fax: (26313) 2411; email: ulazim@samara.co.zw
Operates scenic ultra-light flights over the Falls, leaving from Victoria Falls Main Airport.

The Elephant Company PO Box 125, Victoria Falls. Zimbabwe cell: 011 406 997; fax: (26313) 4341; email shearmpd@zol.co.zw
Book through Shearwater office. Operate elephant-riding trips.

Frontiers 3 Parkway, Pumula Arcade, Victoria Falls. Tel: (26313) 5800/1; fax: (26313) 5801
Operate white-water rafting, river boarding and canoe trips.

Shearwater Adventures Victoria Falls Centre, PO Box 125. Tel: 4471–3; fax: 4341; email: shearad@zol.co.zw
Shearwater is probably the largest Zimbabwe-based safari operator, with extensive operations in most of the adrenaline activities. Their head office is in Harare, but you'd have great difficulty avoiding the publicity generated by their office (near the Wimpy) in Victoria Falls.

Safari Par Excellence Corner Livingstone Way & Parkway, Victoria Falls. Tel: (26313) 2051, fax: (26313) 4510
Another very large operator which runs Thorntree Lodge and The Waterfront in Livingstone, as well as operating rafting, river-boarding and canoeing trips amongst many others.

Tandemania Shop 20B, Second Floor, Soper's Arcade, PO Box Ct 383, Victoria Falls. Zimbabwe cell (tel/fax): 011 211 092
A small operator that pioneered tandem sky dives in the area. Also runs introductory sky-diving courses and rental of equipment for certified sky divers.

Zambezi Elite PO Box 107, Elephant Walk Shopping Complex, Victoria Falls. Zimbabwe cell: 011 601 408; email: squash@id.co.zw
Operates smaller and more upmarket white-water rafting trips on the Zambezi than the larger, more mainstream operators.

Zambezi Helicopter Company PO Box 125, Victoria Falls. Tel/fax: (26313) 4513; email: heli@id.co.zw
Based at Elephant Hills Hotel (where there is a convenient heli-pad) they offer the Flight of Angels by helicopter, and other helicopter charters.

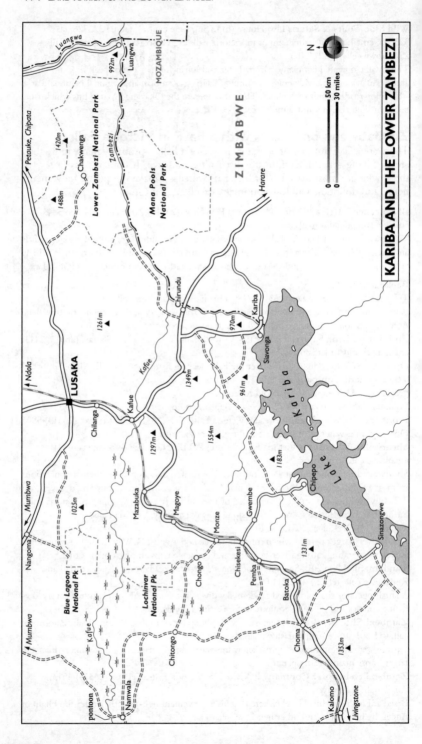

KARIBA AND THE LOWER ZAMBEZI

Lake Kariba
& the Lower Zambezi

Zambia's border with Zimbabwe is defined by the course of
the Zambezi, as it slowly meanders towards the Indian
Ocean. Below the Victoria Falls, it flows east, sometimes
northeast, and today's biggest features of this
river are artificial: Lake Kariba, between Zambia
and Zimbabwe, and Lake Cabora Bassa, in
Mozambique.

Zambia's attractions on Lake Kariba are limited to a
few islands in the lake, accessed from Sinazongwe, and
perhaps Siavonga, which is a pleasant enough place to relax. Access to the islands
is relatively new, and Cheté's Island is certainly large enough to be a credible
wilderness destination with some good wildlife on it. Meanwhile, Chikana Island
offers access to the lake for a much lower cost, and may become a promising spot
for more affluent backpackers.

Below the wall of Kariba Dam, the Zambezi continues through the hot, low-
lying Lower Zambezi Valley and some of the best game viewing in the country. On
both sides of the river – Zambian and Zimbabwean – are important national parks.
The game viewing is excellent, and this is the place to canoe down one of the
world's great rivers, whilst game-spotting and avoiding the hippos. It should be on
every visitor's list of things to do in Zambia.

FROM LIVINGSTONE TO LUSAKA

Whichever way you drive, this main tar road is only 473km, but it seems longer.
Despite its many sections which are faultlessly smooth, many others are dotted
with dangerous potholes. Speeding on the smooth surface will certainly lead to
problems with the potholes, so allow about six or seven hours for the journey if
you're driving yourself, then stick to a safe 80kph or so. Better still, stop along the
way and explore – making Choma's museum top of your list. If you've more time,
then detour to Sinazongwe and on to one of Kariba's islands.

Those brave few hitchhikers will find it one of the easiest roads in the country:
lots of towns, regularly spaced, and lots of traffic. The buses are frequent if you
get stuck.

Here I've arranged a few brief comments on what you'll find if you're heading
towards Lusaka from Livingstone.

Where to stay

Mabula Farm Campsite Tel: 324332

About halfway between Livingstone and Zimba, perhaps 38km from each, there's a camping
site signposted to the east. Run by Mokika Botha, this has just four showers and two toilets
and is 200m from the road. Barbecue packs are available, as are simple meals if you give the
staff a little bit of notice. If you're driving north and need to stop, this makes for a more

peaceful night than one spent in Livingstone.

Rates: US$5 per person for camping

Zimba

Zimba is the first town reached from Livingstone, after about 76km. It's about 397km to Lusaka and really only notable for having a large local market beside the main road. There's little else to detain you here, except perhaps the Mobil fuel station. Otherwise there's just a church and a small shop.

Kalomo

Kalomo is a small town about 126km from Livingstone and 347km from Lusaka. It has a general hospital that serves the whole district, a BP petrol station and an Anglican church. On the Livingstone side of town you'll find Toppers Nightclub, Chris's Guesthouse (no connection with the author), and the main police station. Nearer to the centre, the Kalomo Hotel is a rather run-down old-style place.

If you want to drive into the southern section of Kafue, and have your own 4WD, then the Kalomo Hotel marks where you turn off the main road. See *Chapter 16*, page 342, for details of this route which passes through the Dumdumwenze Gate.

News has come in of a game farm near Kalomo, run by Tony Middleton, which is set in 'beautiful woodlands' and has self-catering accommodation for self-drive visitors, but I have no further details at the moment.

Administrator's House

Between the centre of Kalomo and its main suburb/township is a national monument, the Administrator's House. This was built around 1903–4 for the Administrator of Northwestern Rhodesia, as appointed by the British South African Company. Then Kalomo was the 'capital' of the territory, and the house is said to be the first non-traditional brick house built in Northern Rhodesia. It is now occupied and so not open to the public. As you pass though Kalomo there's a small monument by the roadside to record this history.

Kalundu Mound

About 3km north of Kalomo, basically on the main road, is a slightly raised mound (a matter of just a few metres) of earth through which the road passes. This marks the site of an iron-age village, and the mound is the accumulated debris of many centuries of occupation.

It was excavated in the late fifties and early sixties when the road was being built, and the archaeologists estimated that it might have been occupied as early as the fourth century AD, although it was certainly full of people from about AD 800–1300. (Note that the occupants during this latter period are sometimes referred to by Zambian archaeologists as following the 'Kalomo Tradition'.)

Choma

Choma is another small, friendly town, about 285km from Lusaka and 188km from Livingstone. The main road between the two, here called Livingstone Road, runs through the centre of the town, and on (or just off) it you'll find the main shops, central post office, the Choma Hotel, a market and a super little museum.

Choma's largest supermarket is aptly called Superstore and has a good variety of fresh and frozen food. The in-store bakery/confectionery counter is quite an attraction – the ginger cake and freshly-baked bread come highly recommended – and you'll also find chips, pies and roasted chicken pieces for take-away snacks.

Where to stay

There are a couple of very ordinary hotels on the main road in town, a guesthouse in the suburbs and a couple of excellent spots on farms just outside of town.

Choma Hotel (20 rooms) Livingstone Road, PO Box 630805, Choma. Tel: 032 20189
In the heart of town, on the main road, this looks like the old, original town hotel. Now it's rather run down, so can't be recommended.

New Kalundo Motel (40 rooms) Livingstone Road. Tel: 032 20028 or 20655
On the southwest side of town, behind whitewashed walls, lies the New Kalundo (unsurprisingly, it used to be the Kalundo Motel). It's a typical small-town motel with space for cars beside the rooms.

Hot Springs Gue\sthouse PO Box 630717, Choma. Tel: 032 20064
On the northeast side of town, just beyond the museum, this is clearly signposted across the railway line.

Nkanga River Conservation Area (lodge and camping) PO Box 630025, Choma.
Tel/fax: 032 20592; email: nansai@zamnet.zm
About 5km before Choma, as you approach from Lusaka, there's a signpost on the road to Nkanga, 20km away. There you'll find a conservation area that's been set up covering a large area and a number of local farms. It now protects antelope including sable, eland, puku, hartebeest, wildebeest, kudu, waterbuck (both the normal and Defassa sub-species), tsessebe and many other species.

Within the area is a lodge with en-suite facilities. Game drives are available (maximum 8 people – US$48 per vehicle), as are guided bush walks for game and birdwatching (US$5 per person). It's a notably good area for Zambia's only true endemic species, Chaplin's barbet, which is perhaps most easily seen in the fig trees around Muckleneuk House.

There's also a basic campsite on the riverbank, with cooking facilities provided. This has cold showers, toilet and electric lights, as well as firewood and the facility for barbecues. Note that it can become cold here down by the river, and do bring your own mosquito protection if you're staying here.

Other activities available include fishing for bream and barbel (US$12 per group), for which basic equipment is provided, and riding (experienced riders only) for US$12 per person per hour.

One of the main focuses for the area is valuable education work, as Nkanga runs bush-camps for groups of 8–24 children aged 5 to 18 years old. These run from April to October and include bush knowledge, skills and outdoor activities.

As it's a conservation area that sustainably manages its populations of native game, some trophy hunting is also conducted, though this never interferes with the photographic visitors. *Rates: lodges are US$60 per person (US$35 for children under 12), including all meals and laundry. Camping is US$6 per person. Note that advanced booking are essential here; you cannot just drop in.*

Mambushi Chalets c/o Gwembe Safaris, PO Box 630067, Choma. Tel: 032 20169 or 20021 or 20119; fax: 032 20054 or 20570
About 3km southwest of Choma a sign points to **Gwembe Safaris**, which is 1.5km off the road on the west side. This is a working crocodile farm (transgressors beware) run by the Brooks family. It has four brick chalets with thatched roofs built around a quadrangle in landscaped gardens. Two of these sleep four people, and have ceiling fans, en-suite showers and toilets; the others have twin beds and share communal showers and toilets. All have solid wooden beds, built on the farm, cane chairs, curtains and reed mats on the floor. Each of the rooms has a fridge, and is decorated with local art and baskets made by the Tonga people. If you prefer to be outside, then there's also a campsite under lovely shady trees adjacent to the chalets.

There's an open-sided dining room, with reed mats thast roll down to keep in some of the heat when it's cold. Sometimes the staff will put burning braziers inside to keep everyone warm or light them on the patio outside, which makes a good place to relax after dinner.

Activities include riding, walking and birdwatching on the farm. Ox-cart rides, floodlit tennis courts, volleyball and swimming are also possible for the more energetic. Breakfast is supplied, but dinner is by prior arrangement (drinks available with dinner) and a laundry service is available.

Rates: US$35 per person sharing, US$50 single, for en-suite chalets. US$28 sharing, US$35 single, for the twin chalets. Breakfast US$5, dinner US$10. Camping US$5 per person.

Pemba

Another small town, Pemba, is about 251km from Livingstone and 222km from Lusaka. There's really very little here indeed – it's scarcely more than a dot on the map.

Monze

Again, Monze is another small town with little of note, though 16km to the west of the town is the site of Fort Monze, which was one of the first police posts established in Zambia by the colonial powers. (Access is now only possible in the dry season, and the track is in very poor condition. It's signposted from town.) This post was founded in 1898 by the British South Africa police, led by Major Harding. He was subsequently buried in the cemetery here.

The post was demolished soon after, in 1903, by which time the colonial authorities had a much firmer grip on the country. Now all that's left is a rather neglected graveyard and a monument in the shape of a cross.

Excursions from Monze
Lochinvar National Park
Lochinvar National Park, northeast of Monze, has been designated by the WWF as a 'Wetland of International Importance' for its very special environment. It's about 48km from Monze, and if you have an equipped 4WD and some time to explore, then it's well worth a visit. See pages 347–50 for details.

Mazabuka

This large town, 349km from Livingstone and 124km from Lusaka, is at the centre of a very prosperous commercial farming community. The huge Nakambala Sugar Estates dominate it, and you'll see their fields of mono-culture sugarcane lining the main road either side of town.

It's certainly the largest and most developed of the towns between Livingstone and Lusaka, with a major branch of Shoprite supermarket and a Barclays Bank and police station, as well as numerous smaller shops, several 24-hour fuel stations and the odd small café.

Tastebuds Restaurant is one such café with a good reputation, and they have recently opened a small guesthouse with half a dozen rooms called 40 Winks (tel: 032 30643). This is comfortable but simple, and costs US$20 per person, including a full breakfast. To reach it, follow the signs to Tastebuds and ask them for directions. The best practical alternative is:

Mazabuka Garden Motel (6 chalets) Livingstone Road, PO Box 22, Mazabuka. Tel: 032 30284

Run by the Garden Group of hotels, based in Lusaka, this is a small and quite acceptable stop-over, but not at all plush.

Rates: about Kw40-60,000/US$16–24 per room, including breakfast

LAKE KARIBA

Lake Kariba was created by the construction of a huge dam, started in November 1956 and completed in June 1959. It was the largest dam of its time – 579m wide at its crest, 128m high, 13–26m thick – and designed to provide copious hydro-electric power for both Zimbabwe and Zambia. It was a huge undertaking that turned some 280km of the river into around 5,200km^2 of lake. It has six 100,000kW generators on the Zimbabwean side, and was designed to have another set on the Zambian side. The total construction cost was £78 million.

In human terms it immediately displaced thousands of BaTonga villagers, on both sides of the border, and took the lives of 86 workers in the process – around 18 of whom are entombed within the dam's million cubic metres of cement. It has opened up new industries relying on the lake, just as it closed off many possibilities for exploiting the existing rich game areas in that section of the Zambezi Valley.

It inevitably drowned much wildlife, despite the efforts of Operation Noah to save and relocate some of the animals as the floodwaters rose. However, the lake is now home to rich fish and aquatic life, and several game reserves (and lodges) are thriving on its southern shores.

For the visitor, Zambia's side of the lake is less well developed than Zimbabwe's and lacks a National Park. Only on its islands, Cheté and Chikana, will you find much game. However, the fishing is very good and the small resorts of Siavonga or Sinazongwe make pleasant places to relax, or to base yourself for outings on to the Lake.

Health and safety around the lake
Bilharzia

Bilharzia is found in Lake Kariba, but only in certain areas. Unfortunately, it isn't possible to pinpoint its whereabouts exactly; but shallow, weedy areas that suit the host snail are likely to harbour the parasites, and you're unlikely to contract bilharzia whilst in deep water in the middle of the lake.

See *Chapter 6* for more detailed comments on this disease. Local people who engage in watersports consider it as an occupational hazard, and are regularly treated to expel the parasites from their bodies (those who can afford the treatment, that is).

Animal dangers

The lake contains good populations of crocodiles, and also a few hippos. Both conspire to make bathing and swimming near the shore unsafe. However, it is generally considered to be safe to take quick dips in the middle of the lake – often tempting, given Lake Kariba's high temperatures and humidity. The crocodiles have apparently not yet learned how to catch water-skiers.

Siavonga

The road to Siavonga leaves the main Lusaka-Chirundu road a few kilometres west of the Chirundu bridge over the Zambezi. From that turn-off, it is just over 65km of rolling road (excellent tarmac) to Siavonga, mostly through areas of subsistence farming. There are lots of small villages, and hence animals wandering over the road, so drive slowly. This is a marvellous area for baobab trees, and an excellent one for roadside stalls – selling a range of baskets from small decorative ones to large linen-baskets.

During a visit at the end of the dry season, the problems of erosion and overgrazing seemed especially bad. Numerous gullies cut through the powdery, red soil, there was little green grazing to be seen anywhere, and even the goats were looking thin.

ZAMBIA MEANS GEMSTONES
Judi Helmholz

'Zambia means Gemstones' heralds the cover of Zambia's tourist magazine, *The Visitor*. A full-sized photograph of a large, rough emerald graces the cover, courtesy of the Gemological Institute of America. It tells us that Zambia is internationally recognised as a major supplier of gemstones – emeralds, aquamarines, amethyst and tourmaline. Apparently, Zambian emeralds are of a high quality and in much demand.

One source of Zambian gemstones lies in the hills and valleys neighbouring Lake Kariba, approximately 200km from Lusaka, Zambia's capital. While en route to Lake Kariba, my husband, Arthur, encountered some local villagers displaying beautiful pieces of raw amethyst for sale along the highway. Never one to pass up a good opportunity, Arthur stopped and negotiated to purchase the best specimen. The amethyst, a bargain at the original asking price of Kw5,000 (U$5), was a steal at the final negotiated price of Kw1,000 or U$1. What luck!

As Arthur was leaving, an old man rushed to him clutching a little plastic bag. 'Ah, Bwana, perhaps some of these,' he said in hushed tones, glancing cautiously around. Intrigued, Arthur examined the small, tightly sealed plastic bag containing some remarkable green stones. Emeralds? Perhaps! The old man had only given him the local tribal name for these stones.

'Only 5,000Kw, special price for you,' whispered the old man. Arthur offered 1,000Kw for the bag. The old man hesitated and then agreed, stipulating that Arthur must buy two bags for such a low price. So he did. What a bargain! Obviously, the local villagers had absolutely no idea of the value of these gemstones, knowing only that travellers seemed keen to purchase the colourful stones they had found in the hills.

In Kariba, Arthur proudly recounted the tale of his extraordinary gemstone purchase to a business associate from Lusaka. 'Funny thing,' the man commented, 'as soon as those green stones began appearing for sale along the road, all the green traffic lights in Lusaka were smashed, their green glass stolen.'

Ripping open one of the tightly sealed plastic bags, Arthur examined the stones. Sure enough! You could even see the little bumps and ridges from the traffic light. Obviously, the local villagers did know the value of what they were selling. Arthur had just paid U$2, the equivalent of two days' wages for the average Zambian worker, for smashed traffic-light glass from Lusaka.

Do you know anyone who collects gemstones and is interested in adding some Zambian specimens to their collection? Special price – just for you!

Approaching Siavonga, the road winds its way around the hills in steep spirals before finally dropping down into the town, on the edge of Lake Kariba. Like Kariba, its Zimbabwean neighbour over the dam, Siavonga has an artificial layout as the result of being built on the upper sections of three or four hills – the lake's recently created shore.

Where to stay
Siavonga has a surprising amount of accommodation considering its small size and relatively few attractions. The reason is its proximity to Lusaka – just two and a half hours' drive away – encouraging conferences to come here: the stock trade for all

of Siavonga's hotels. On a quiet night, you can find a good bed at a reasonable price. Because the town is used to the conference trade, check the rates for dinner, bed and breakfast, and full board – these are often good value, and there are no sparkling local restaurants to compete. Campers have less choice, and will probably head to the Eagle's Rest.

Zambezi Lodge (30 rooms) PO Box 30, Siavonga. Tel: 01 511148/511200; fax: 511103 (also contact at PO Box 31701, Lusaka)
This pleasant hotel perches slightly above the lake, with its rooms spread out between its main building and the slipway into the water. For the energetic, the Lodge has an excellent swimming pool and good facilities for watersports: two cabin cruisers, two speedboats, and the kit for water-skiing, windsurfing and paragliding. Inside the bar is open most of the time, and popular with locals. Try playing on the 'winner stays on' pool table: an evening's fun for Kw1,000, if you are good with a cue. The kitchen serves good, inexpensive food until late.

The twin rooms are large, though not modern, with en-suite bath/shower and toilet, and a ceiling fan. This is a good-value choice for a few days by the lake.
Rates: US$50 double, US$33 single, bed & breakfast

Lake Kariba Inn (35 rooms) PO Box 177, Siavonga. Tel: 01 511358/500; fax: 511249 or via Lusaka office tel: 01 252518; fax: 252859
Built about nine years ago, Lake Kariba Inn has recently been repainted and is now looking good. The rooms have a small entrance hall, space for two children's beds if needed, and a veranda. There's a ceiling fan, and an en-suite shower (with instant water-heater) and toilet.

The main building has a large bar, buffet restaurant, and the requisite pool. A steep set of stairs leads down to the water, many metres below, where the inn's boats – *Chipembere* and *Matusadonna* – are usually moored. See page 203 for details of their operations and costs.
Rates: US$78 per double/twin, US$53 single, full board basis

Manchinchi Bay Lodge (30 rooms) PO Box 115, Siavonga. Tel: 01 511299/399; fax: 511218; tlx: ZA 70903
This hotel changed hands in late 1995 for US$1million, making it the most valuable of Siavonga's hotels, as well as the plushest. The gardens are certainly the best in town, with extensive manicured lawns, shrubby borders, and a main swimming pool with an adjacent shallow one for children. Non-residents can use these, and their nearby changing rooms, for Kw3,000 each, and there is a convenient public phone just beyond.

A few yards below, the hotel has a private sandy cove with thatched umbrellas and sun-loungers, if you must fry yourself. Inside, the small lounge has a well-stocked bar and a darts board. The rooms all have en-suite facilities (shower only), air conditioning, CNN/M-Net colour TV, and private verandas. They are comfortable rather than plush, as their fittings are too old.
Rates: US$70 per double/twin, US$55 per single, bed & breakfast

Leisure Bay Lodge (14 rooms) PO Box 92, Siavonga. Tel: 01 511135/6 or via Lusaka office tel: 01 252779
Set in a small cove with sandy beach and thatched umbrellas, the lodge has a large patio area and adjacent bar (with TV) which is often busy with locals – and a good place to meet people. Most of the small twin rooms overlook the lake, and all have air conditioning and en-suite toilet and shower. Though very clean, they still manage to appear rather dingy.
Rates: US$40 double, US$25 single bed & breakfast

Eagle's Rest Chalets (18 chalets) PO Box 1, Siavonga. Tel/fax: 01 511168
If Eagle's Rest is still poorly signposted, then turn left at the gate to Manchinchi Lodge, and follow the winding road for about 1km. It may be worth the trip, as Eagle's Rest is the first place in Siavonga that tries to appeal more to tourists than to conferences.

Here 18 self-catering chalets have been built, each big enough to take four beds in one room with a ceiling fan, and an en-suite shower and toilet. Outside each is a useful sheltered area for preparing food, including a fridge, sink, simple gas cooker, and basic cutlery and crockery. There's also a small restaurant/bar for breakfast, snacks and evening meals.

Activities can be arranged here including canoeing trips, overnight camping on islands, and house-boat cruises.

Rates: US$23.50 per person. Breakfast US$6.50, dinner US$12.50

Eagle's Rest Camping PO Box 1, Siavonga. Tel/fax: 01 511168
Immediately next to the chalets is a small camp-ground with ablutions block and points for electricity and water. Campers are free to use the restaurant/bar area.

Rates: US$6.50 per person camping

Lake View Guest House
This government resthouse is used by visiting officials, and not available for casual visitors.

Mundulundulu Campsite Gwena Rd. Box 79, Siavonga. Tel: 01 750686 (ask for Panos); email: cic@pmb.lia.net
Mundulundulu is signposted near town and very rustic indeed. It has three thatched shelters, under which you can pitch a tent if you wish, and just one longdrop toilet. Water and firewood can be provided on request, and the owners advise that their water has been tested as bilharzia-free. The owners' money ran out before they could develop this further, but campers are still welcome provided that they pay the staff for any service.

Sandy Beach Camping & Chalets Siavonga Road, Siavonga. Tel: 01 511353; fax: 273865
This is another simple campsite on a picturesque beach, and again it's signposted from town.

Getting around
Siavonga is small, but is not easy to get around without your own vehicle. The roads curve incessantly, sticking to the sides of the hills on which the town is built. Each of the hotels is tucked away in a different little cove or inlet, and to get from one to another usually involves several kilometres of up-and-down, winding roads.

By ringing well in advance you may be able to arrange a lift here from Lusaka or Kariba, in Zimbabwe. Then you could ask around for lifts going out of town, and perhaps even hitch from the outskirts. Alternatively, you could get a bus in and walk around everywhere, which would be practical – but you'll find it much easier with your own transport.

Getting organised
Siavonga is quite a sleepy, relaxed place but it does have a bank (Zambia National Commercial Bank), a Caltex petrol station, a post office and a few shops. These, together with the civic centre (which includes a police station and a courtroom), form the 'town centre' which is perched high on one of the hills.

The main (only) supermarket, Zefa Trading Ltd, has large stocks of an eclectically selected and very limited range of goods. Expect to find dry goods and various cold drinks, but few foodstuffs and lots of biscuits. Before you complain too loudly about anything, you should know that it is run by the area's MP. Next door, the Kool Centre Restaurant & Take-away serves cold soft drinks and the local *chibuku* alcoholic brew.

What to see and do
Most of the activities in Siavonga revolve around the lake: boating, fishing and watersports – note the comments on safety on pages 75–7.

Watersports

For windsurfing, paragliding or waterskiing, try the Zambezi Lodge and Manchinchi Bay first, as both have equipment.

Houseboats/fishing trips

There are several options for hiring boats or pontoons (essentially floating platforms):

Matusadonna is a proper houseboat, on which a 4-day, 3-night cruise will cost a total of US$1,500 (including food, drink and fishing tackle). This begins to sound good value when it is split between up to six passengers. Accommodation is in two private cabins with bunks and one double cabin. There's a kitchen, bar and shower/toilet on board, and a shaded upper deck you can sleep on to keep cool. A small crew will normally accompany you, including a chef, and a tender boat is brought along to allow forays to the shore. Book this via Lake Kariba Inn, or their agent in Lusaka (tel: 01 252518; fax: 252859).

Chipembere is a much simpler affair, little more than a pontoon about 5m x 7m in size, with an engine at the back. Fortunately there's a cool box, braai stand, and flush toilet on board. A 4-day, 3-night trip, bringing all your own food, costs US$500 split between up to ten people (though six would be more comfortable).

NYAMINYAMI STRIKES BACK

We now expect large projects with huge environmental impacts like the Kariba Dam to have equally big effects on local communities in their vicinity. Plans for dams frequently create political strife. Proponents argue the benefit to the whole country or region, and opponents cite the damage to the environment and the local communities which will be sacrificed for the project. Recent projects in Tasmania and China, to name but two, have resulted in similar arguments.

In the late 1950s, when construction on the dam was started, the world's environmental lobby was less influential than it is now. There was little effective resistance to the removal of thousands of the BaTonga people from the valley on to higher ground around the new lake. The BaTonga were amongst the least developed ethnic groups in the region, so their physical resistance to their relocation was easily overcome. However, the BaTonga had inhabited the valley for centuries, treating the river with reverence as home to Nyaminyami – guardian of the river. Their elders were certain that the project would stir up Nyaminyami's anger, and he would then destroy the dam.

Work started in November 1956 and July 1957 saw a rare dry-season storm raise the river's level by a massive 30m to smash through the coffer dam and destroy months of work. The following year, 1958, saw another momentous flood, as unusually heavy local rains combined with the flow from distant deluges in its catchment area to produce one of the greatest flows that the river had ever seen. Again, Nyaminyami's attempt to defeat the dam was only narrowly beaten.

At last, the dam was officially opened by the Queen Mother in May 1960, and has been producing power ever since. Nyaminyami may still have the last word, though, as there are concerns over cracks found in the dam's concrete.

There's virtually no privacy aboard – so make sure you charter with very good friends.

Hooligan is a catamaran houseboat that is usually booked from Lusaka. It's a popular option for a small group to use for a weekend on the lake. It is an 18m x 8m three-deck boat, with three crew and facilities broadly similar to the *Matusadonna*, described above. Contact Michelle in Lusaka, on tel: 01 989281, for more details.

A final avenue worth exploring would be Manchinchi Bay, which has a 17m cruiser (used sometimes for booze cruises) for rent at about US$140 per evening.

Visiting the dam

Whilst you're here, take a walk over the dam wall (despite the border controls on each side), and perhaps even up to the Observation Point on the Zimbabwean side. There's an excellent little craft shop here, well known for its Nyaminyami sticks on which the river guardian is represented as a snake with its head at the top of the stick. The local carvers have become adept at carving intricate, interlinked rings and cages containing balls out of just one piece of wood. They're not cheap, but make great souvenirs. See box on page 194.

Note that both Zimbabwe and Zambia are acutely aware of the vulnerability of the dam to damage or terrorist attack. So don't appear 'suspicious', and always ask before taking photographs – it may be just a wall to you, but it's of vital importance to them. There used to be tours available in the morning of the underground hydro-electric power station, so ask at the dam if these are still running.

Kapenta rig tour

Kapenta are small sardine-like fish introduced into Kariba in the 1960s from Lake Tanganyika. Fishing for them has become an important new industry around the lake, in both Zimbabwe and Zambia. When dried, Kapenta is tasty, high in protein, and very easy to transport: an ideal food in a country where poorer people often suffer from protein deficiency.

Look out over the lake at night and watch the fishing rigs use powerful spotlights to attract the fish into their deep nets. These are then brought back to shore in the early morning, sun-dried on open racks (easily smelt and seen), and packaged for sale.

Short tours lasting a couple of hours in the early evening can be arranged to one of these rigs, and you'll bring back fresh kapenta to eat.

Rates: around US$15 for a group, usually arranged by the hotel

Crocodile Farm

There's a genuine, commercial crocodile farm near town, which welcomes visitors and charges only a few dollars entrance.

Sinazongwe

Zambia's second small town on the lakeside is roughly equidistant between Livingstone and Siavonga. It is a typical small Zambian town, originally built as the fishing and administrative centre for the southern lakeshore area, and is used mainly as an outpost for kapenta fishing. When the lake was first flooded Sinazongwe was a much busier harbour, and even had the only lighthouse on the lake.

Now its prosperity has faded somewhat, though it is well placed to become the hub of operations for Zambian tourism to Lake Kariba, and there is already a small campsite here.

Getting there and away

There's a good tar road from Batoka, signposted to Maamba Mines, on the main Lusaka–Livingstone road (about 30km east of Choma), to within 15km of Sinazongwe, and then the rest is a reasonable, all-weather gravel road. Hitching is certainly a possibility, and shouldn't be that difficult. If you're heading for Chikana Island then you may be able to stop at Mambushi Chalets, in Choma (see page 197), and find a lift from the owners.

By road, transfers serving visitors to Cheté Island run from Livingstone daily, departing at 08.00, on request. These cost US$75 per person per transfer, for a minimum of two people. Similar transfers from Lusaka cost US$100 per person and take four and a half hours. Those from Livingstone usually stop at Choma's craft museum on the way, and take about three and a half hours to reach Sinazongwe. Either way, from Sinazongwe you'll continue to the island by trimaran.

By air, light aircraft charters from Livingstone would cost around US$520 for a six-seater plane (five passengers), one way. However, Sinazongwe lies almost directly beneath the flight-path between Livingstone and the Lower Zambezi National Park. Both Tongabezi and Safari Par Excellence have operations in both areas, and both run regular flights between them. Organising these may be tricky, so you must book this with a knowledgeable tour operator.

Day-trips from Livingstone to Cheté Island are possible for around US$210 per person (minimum of four people), including return flights (small chartered aircraft) and meals and activities on the island.

Where to stay

Sinazongwe Campsite Westlake Islands Group, PO Box 88, Sinazongwe. Tel: 01 483144; tel/fax: 483045; email: westisl@id.co.zw

This is a new campsite, with very basic facilities – just follow the signs to the Westlake Island base. You'll find a house with a bathroom and a kitchen. Booking ahead is advisable, and you should bring all your own food as the shop in Sinazongwe is small, and the local market limited in scope.

Lake View Campsite Gwembe Safaris, PO Box 630067, Choma. Tel: 032 20169 or 20021 or 20119; fax: 20054 or 20570

Gwembe Safaris, who own Chikana Island, are just putting the final touches to three thatched chalets and a campsite here, mainly for travellers on their way to Chikana Island. Contact them for the latest information.

Cheté Island

Cheté is the largest island in the lake, and after a quick glance at the map you'll realise that it's much nearer to the Zimbabwean mainland (150m) than it is to Zambia (15km). This is because the border is defined as the deepest part of the Zambezi's old river course, not a line through the middle of the lake. A glance at Zimbabwe's map shows that it's just offshore from Zimbabwe's Cheté Safari Area – so it's no surprise to learn that it's become recognised under the national parks system as a private wildlife reserve and bird sanctuary.

Cheté is in a very remote corner of the lake, which feels very isolated except for the occasional twinkle from the nocturnal fishing of kapenta rigs in the distance. It's a wilderness experience, and the game on Cheté isn't tame, nor as dense as you'll find in the Luangwa or the better areas of the Kafue. But there is a sense of isolation and wilderness as only a wild island like this can give. Its closest point of contact is really Sinazongwe, 17km away across Lake Kariba.

Much of the bigger game migrates to and fro between Zimbabwe and the island.

This is especially true of the elephant bulls, but typically there's a resident breeding herd of about 40 elephants on the island. There's also normally a pride of lion around, perhaps half a dozen leopard, a herd of eland, and plenty of waterbuck, bushbuck, impala and some magnificent kudu. Not forgetting the many crocodile and hippo around the shores.

Cheté's landscape is very varied, similar in parts to both Zimbabwe's Chizarira and Matusadonna National Parks. There are areas of dense cover, and also open floodplains beside the shore and rugged interior woodlands and gorges. There are no roads here, as it's very much a wilderness area, and there's just one small camp by the lake.

Where to stay

Cheté Island Luxury Tented Camp (8 twin tents) Westlake Islands, PO Box CH570, Chisipite, Harare. Tel: (2634) 499783; tel/fax: 499060; email: westisl@id.co.zw
Started in 1998 by Rob Fynn – the founder of the excellent Fothergill and Chikwenya safari camps in Zimbabwe (on Lake Kariba and in Mana Pools, respectively) – this small camp has been 'out on a limb' from Zambian tourism. It's off the normal routes and so ignored by most operators, and omitted from their brochures. Perhaps that's fortunate, as it's a lovely quiet camp in a remote location.

The simple Meru-style tents are widely spread out along the brow of a low hill, facing the shoreline, with good views over a classic Kariba scene of skeletal trees and islands beyond. Inside each are twin beds, and decorations using various local African fabrics. The solid furniture is also locally made from cane and woods. The en-suite bathroom, at the back, has a white canvas roof and reed walls, flushing toilet and shower (hot and cold). All very rustic and simple; don't expect the height of luxury.

There's a central thatched, L-shaped bar/dining area with comfy cane furniture and paraffin lamps (the camp has no electricity). This has no walls, so the views are uninterrupted, though in bad weather canvas sides appear as windbreaks. After three courses of simple, wholesome food eaten from large Mukwa dining tables, you'll often retire outside to sit around the fire. Activities include walking safaris (with armed game scout), boating safaris around the islands (using motor boats and/or canoes), and also fishing, for both tiger and bream. The canoes are two-person Canadian-style canoes, with a 30m sailing trimaran also available.
Rates: US$200 per person, including all meals, safaris, laundry and most drinks. No single supplements. Open: all year

Island Canoe Safaris contact via Cheté Island, above
If you're staying for 4–5 days then consider taking a few of these to canoe around the islands in this part of the lake, camping under the stars as you go. With all the game around, this is an exciting option, but not for those of nervous disposition. All the kit is provided, including 3m x 3m walk-in tents and a field kitchen. The lead canoe is equipped with a motor, in case a strong head wind is unavoidable, and groups are limited to a maximum of eight people.
Rates: around US$150 per person per night, including all meals, equipment and most drinks

Getting there

This can be tricky, as it is not accessible directly over the water from Zimbabwe. If you can get yourself to Sinazongwe (see above) then the rest is easy, as transfers by the island's trimaran (or motor boat) are free and available on request. These are very much part of the trip; sailing into the wind and the wilderness is the stuff of dreams in good weather, but take a raincoat just in case. (There's always a dry cabin if life on deck becomes too challenging!)

Chikana Island

Chikana Island covers 240ha (2.4km^2) and is privately owned by the Brooks family of Gwembe Safaris (see page 197). It lies about 8km from the Zambian mainland; 10km west-southwest of Cheté and 18km southwest of Sinazongwe. It's smaller than Cheté, and has recently become an archipelago of three islands due to the high level of the lake.

There are three chalets on the island, booked through Gwembe Safaris: PO Box 630067, Choma. Tel: 032 20169 or 20021 or 20119; fax: 20054 or 20570.

Getting there

Transfers from Sinazongwe cost US$10 per person (minimum four people) on a local kapenta rig and take a few hours.

Where to stay
Chalets

There are three twin-bedded chalets. Each is completely gauzed to deter insects (mosquito nets are also provided) and has en-suite flush toilets, showers and solar lighting. These stand on a cliff, facing Zimbabwe over the lake.

Nearby is a large thatched dining room, sundeck and a small paddling pool. At present this is only a self-catering facility. Drinking water is supplied from the mainland and a fully equipped kitchen (including gas fridge and freezer) and a cook are provided, but you must bring your own food and drinks.

Rates: US$55 for twin chalet, US$35 single, US$5 for an extra bed

Camping

There used to be a campsite here, but it didn't exist easily next to the chalets. Gwembe plan to build another, on a separate section of the island, but for now there may be no camping here at all.

What to see and do

If you wanted to find an unspoilt bit of bush in which to wander, look no further. Activities are low-key, and it's up to you to make them happen. There's a game guard to accompany you, a rowing boat if you feel like a spot of fishing and a large island full of trees, birds and game.

FROM LUSAKA TO CHIRUNDU

The tar road from Lusaka to Harare, via Chirundu, is an important commercial artery and so it is kept in good repair. Leaving Lusaka, you soon pass the town of Kafue and, shortly before the busy turning to Livingstone, cross over the wide and slow Kafue River that is also heading to join the Zambezi. Then the road, gradually, consistently and occasionally spectacularly, descends. It leaves the higher, cooler escarpment for the hot floor of the Zambezi valley, before crossing the busy bridge at Chirundu into Zimbabwe.

Kafue

This small town is close to the Norwegian-built hydro-electric dam on the Kafue River. Tours of the plant are possible if arranged with ZESCO (Zambia Electricity Supply Corporation Ltd), which even has its own small lodge for accommodating visitors. Otherwise, there is little of interest here, though the town does have large concrete and textile factories. Outside town is the impressive Lechwe Lodge, and if you are stuck for somewhere to stay then the River Motel is always a possibility.

River Motel (52 rooms and 30 chalets) PO Box 373, Kafue. Tel: 032 30992
In the heart of the small town of Kafue, this motel is large and surprisingly good for a small-town hotel in Zambia. To get there you just follow the main road through Kafue, heading south. The motel is on the main road, about 5km from the town, with a stone lion guarding each side of the big white gates.

The hotel's twin rooms have a double bed with simple pine furniture: a bedside table, dressing table, desk and wardrobe. A few have air-conditioning units (none was working when visited) and all have en-suite shower and toilet.

Alternatively, the slightly decrepit chalets have small kitchen (a sink and cupboard) for which cooking equipment can be supplied if you're staying for a few days. They also have a small lounge with comfy chairs and a bath as well as a shower and toilet. Several have TVs (there's satellite dish outside), but none is yet connected.

Facilities include a small gym, a tennis court, a hairdressing salon, two television rooms, two swimming pools and a cocktail bar called 'Surf and Turf.' There are also two conference rooms, and this trade in local conferences probably explains the motel's relative prosperity. Its restaurant adopts a simple café style, with blue-and-white checked tablecloths and buffet meals. The hotel's staff are friendly, and the atmosphere pleasant and relaxed. If you need to stop, do so without fear!

Rates: Kw35,000 for a twin room, Kw40,000 for a chalet, excluding breakfast

Lechwe Lodge (6 rondavels) PO Box 37940, Lusaka. Tel: 032 30128; fax: 30707; cell: 01 704803; email: kflechwe@zamnet.zm
On a working farm just west of Kafue Town, this small lodge was started in 1990 by Di Flynn, who still runs it. To get there, turn west off the main road just north of Kafue Town, which passes the Nitrogen Chemicals factory immediately on the left, and later Kafue Textiles, before bending right. Take the next left turn, and stay on a gravel road for about 3.2km. Then take the left turn signposted to Brunelli and Lechwe Lodge, which is 6.5km from the turning.

The lodge's rondavels are spread around almost manicured lawns and are very well kept. All are roomy with solid wooden furniture standing on expanses of cool polished floor. Two are family units, with four beds in two rooms. The others have twin beds or lovely wooden-framed double beds. All the beds are covered with mossie nets and each rondavel has an en-suite shower and toilet. The food is good, fresh and plentiful, richly deserving the cliché 'wholesome farm fare' in its best possible sense.

Lechwe's farm covers about 13km^2, which varies from *brachystegia* and *acacia* woodlands through a 'termitaria' zone to open floodplains and the river itself. The game includes giraffe, eland, Lichtenstein's hartebeest, Kafue lechwe, oribi and sitatunga, as well as the more common antelope of the region. None of the large predators are here (except for crocodiles in the river), though serval are plentiful, apparently due to the prevalence of cane rats in the reeds. In and around the river you'll find Cape clawless and spotted-necked otters, hippos and crocodiles.

The birdlife is very good, with more than 420 species recorded. Lechwe was the base for a local birding guru, Peter Leonard, for many years. You should see wide ranges of waterfowl, kingfishers, herons, egrets and perhaps even a rare visiting osprey. Boat trips along the river are possible most of the year, a super way to watch birds, and tackle is always available if you prefer to fish.

Riding is possible, with the farm's own horses, though the lodge insists that only experienced riders should partake (you must be comfortable with a rising trot for 15–20 minutes at a time). A guide takes two visitors out for as long as they wish; hard hats are provided and must be worn. If you prefer to walk, with or without a guide, then that's easily arranged, as are short game drives for the less energetic. The four (6m high) viewing platforms overlooking the Kafue are always good spots at which to stop and just watch.

Finally if you're interested in farming, then ask for a farm tour; it's fascinating. Pigsties are situated near to large ponds. Their manure promotes the growth of infusoria, which feed the small organisms on which fish feed. Thus the farm produces commercial quantities of pork and fish, in a very eco-friendly way.

The lodge's activities are tailored to the guests, and arranged by Joshua Chizuwa, a super guide with wide experience. Lechwe is a very gentle, civilised and relaxing place, perfect for your first (or last) few nights in the country. It's also excellent value and open all year. It's just a shame that it is too far from Lusaka for one night.

Rates: US$120 per person, including all activities, meals, drinks and laundry. Road transfers to/from Lusaka are US$40 per vehicle (max 4 people) per journey. Air transfers to the lodge are also possible at around US$150 per plane (max 5 people) per trip.

Camp Pretorius PO Box 30093, Lusaka
About halfway between Chirundu and Lusaka, Camp Pretorius has a simple campsite with showers, a bar and barbecue facilities. To get there, head south from Lusaka, past Kafue town and the river. About 10km after the Livingstone turn off, and take the left turn signposted for the Kafue Gorge Power Station. Continue on this for about 20km, following the signposts to the camp. If you miss the final turn to the camp then you'll end up at the main gates to the power station, and the staff there will re-direct you to the camp.

Pretorius Haloba, a Zambian, owns the camp, which is run by Mr Jones. Currently there is no phone here. It is right on the waterfront – beautiful but in need of development. Boat hire (with driver) is US$30 per hour, plus fuel. Hikes and sightseeing walks cost US$10 per person. A kitchen is being constructed, and it seems likely that the facilities here will gradually improve over time.

Rates: US$5 per person per night camping

Chirundu border area
A few kilometres before Chirundu, just after the turn-off to Siavonga and Kariba, keep a look out for a roadside plaque indicating the Chirundu Forest Reserve – a small area around the road where the remnants of petrified trees can be seen strewn on the ground.

The border post at Chirundu always seems to be busy with a constant stream of trucks going through, or at least waiting to go through. There's a BP garage here, an office for the Manica Freight Company, and the Nyambandwe Hotel. This is a promising place to look for a lift if you are hitchhiking, but otherwise there is the slightly seedy, unsafe feel typical of a town where many people come and go, but few ever stay.

About 2–300m north of the border at Chirundu is a road signposted northeast to Chiawa and Masstock Farms; this is the road to both Gwabi Lodge and the Lower Zambezi National Park.

Where to stay
Nyambandwe Motel PO Box 37160, Lusaka. Tel: 01 515084/515088
This is convenient if you are unexpectedly stuck in town: the rooms are small (with frilly pink fabrics) and have tiny en-suite shower/toilets. In Chirundu's heat, you will probably appreciate the electric fan on a stand, though perhaps not the noisy local disco that is held here on Friday and Saturday nights. There is often a live band – which could be fun, but if you want any sleep get a room as far from the bar as possible. It seems likely that some of the rooms are hired by the hour, as well as the night.

Rates: US$20 double, US$15 single, bed and breakfast

Gwabi Lodge (6 rooms and camping) PO Box 30813, Lusaka. Tel: 01 515078
This small lodge is set in impressively green lawns about 12km from Chirundu, and 3km up from the Kafue River's confluence with the Zambezi. It is used extensively by overland

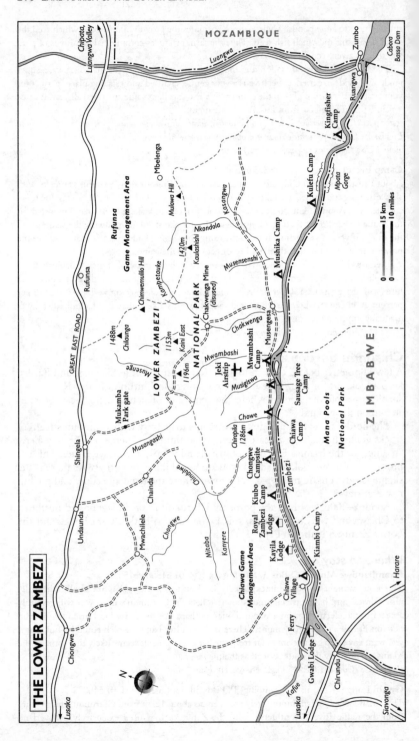

trucks, making it quite a busy place that is well prepared for campers and budget travellers. You'll find everything has its price here, from a bag of drinking-water ice to overnight use of the car park for non-residents – but these prices are generally reasonable.

The thatched chalets are comfortable: solidly built with stone floors, mains electricity, en-suite showers/toilets and fans. There's a great pool here, overlooking the Kafue River some distance below, and a cool thatched bar area next to it serving sensibly priced drinks. Whilst game activities are offered here, you are nowhere near the National Park, so game densities are much lower than further down the river. So this is a good place to stop, but it's too far from the park to use as a safari lodge.

Rates: US$65 per person per night, for dinner, bed & breakfast. Camping US$6 per person.

St Nectarios Lodge (6 rooms) PO Box 30815, Lusaka. Tel: 01 251734; fax: 01 233264
About 1km from the Kafue's confluence with the Zambezi, beside the Zambezi, this is run by the Garden Group of hotels, based in Lusaka. It's a very simple hotel.

Rates: about Kw50–75,000/US$20–25 per room, including breakfast

LOWER ZAMBEZI NATIONAL PARK

The Lower Zambezi valley, from the Kariba dam to the Mozambique border, has a formidable reputation for big game – leading UNESCO to designate part of the Zimbabwean side as a World Heritage Site. The Lower Zambezi National Park protects a large section of the Zambian side. Across the river, much of the Zimbabwean side is protected by either Mana Pools National Park or various safari areas. This makes for a very large area of the valley devoted to wildlife, and a terrific amount of game actually crosses the river regularly, notably elephants and buffalo.

However, take a look at a map of the Zambian bank and you'll realise that the land up to 55km east from the Kafue River (from Gwabi Lodge) is not in the National Park at all. Going past the Kafue, the first land that you arrive at is privately owned, then it becomes Chiawa Game Management Area, which is leased from the chieftainess in the area. Finally, east of the Chongwe River, is the National Park.

As you might expect, the game densities increase as you travel east, with the best game in the National Park, and fewer animals on the privately owned land nearer to Chirundu. The situation is similar on the other bank of the river, in Zimbabwe, so if you want good game viewing then do get into the park if you can, or at least near to it.

Geography

From Chirundu to the Mozambique border, the Zambezi descends 42m, from 371m to 329m above sea-level, over a distance of over 150km. That very gentle gradient (about 1:3,500) explains why the Zambezi flows so slowly and spreads out across the wide valley, making such a gentle course for canoeing.

From the river, look either side of you into Zambia and Zimbabwe. In the distance you will spot the escarpment, if the heat haze doesn't obscure it. At around 1,200m high, it marks the confines of the Lower Zambezi Valley and the start of the higher, cooler territory beyond which is known as the 'highveld' in Zimbabwe.

The valley is a rift valley, similar to the Great Rift Valley of East Africa (though probably older), and it shares its genesis with the adjoining Luangwa valley. The original sedimentary strata covering the whole area are part of the karoo system, sedimentary rocks laid down from about 300 to 175 million years ago. During this time, faulting occurred and volcanic material was injected into rifts in the existing sediments.

One of these faults, the wide Zambezi valley, can still be seen. In geologically recent times, the Zambezi has meandered across the wide valley floor, eroding the mineral-rich rocks into volcanic soils and depositing silts which have helped to make the valley so rich in vegetation and hence wildlife. These meanders have also left old watercourses and ox-bow pools, which add to the area's attraction for game.

So look again from one side of the valley to the other. What you see is not a huge river valley: it is a rift in the earth's crust through which a huge river happens to be flowing.

Flora and fauna

Most of the park, made up of higher ground on the sides and top of the escarpment, is thick bush – where game viewing is difficult. This is broad-leafed miombo woodland, dominated by *brachystegia*, *julbernardia*, *combretum* and *terminalia* species. Fortunately, there's little permanent water here, so during the dry season the game concentrates on the flat alluvial plain by the river.

Acacia species and mopane dominate the vegetation on the richer soils of the valley floor, complemented by typical riverine trees like leadwood (*Combretum imberbe*), ebony (*Diospyros mespiliformis*), and various figs (*ficus* species). Here the riverine landscape and vegetation are very distinctive: similar to the Luangwa Valley, but quite different from other parks in the subcontinent.

Perhaps it is the richness of the soils which allows the trees to grow so tall and strong, forming woodlands with carpets of grasses, and only limited thickets of shrubs to obscure the viewing of game. The acacia species include some superb specimens of the winterthorn, *Acacia albida*, and the flat-topped umbrella thorn, *Acacia tortilis,* (the latter being a huge favourite with the game, as its tightly spiralled seedpods are very nutritious: 19% protein, 26% carbohydrate, 5% minerals). It all results in a beautiful, lush landscape that can support a lot of game, and is excellent for the ease of viewing which it allows.

Mammals

The Lower Zambezi has all the big game that you'd expect, with the exceptions of rhino (due to poaching), giraffe and cheetah. Buffalo and elephant are very common, and can often be seen grazing on the islands in the middle of the river, or swimming between Zimbabwe and Zambia. It is normally safe to get quite close by drifting quietly past these giants as they graze.

The antelope in the valley are dominated by large herds of impala, but good populations of kudu, eland, waterbuck, bushbuck, zebra, wildebeest and the odd duiker or grysbok also occur. Giraffe are notable for their absence.

Lion, leopard and spotted hyena are the major predators. There have long been plans to reintroduce cheetah (obtained from the Africat project in Namibia) but these have not yet come to fruition. On my first visit, back in 1995, lion were very visible, with one marvellous pride having an excess of thirty animals. Many of the larger trees have branches that seem made-to-measure for leopards – these are sometimes seen on night drives, but rarely during the day.

In the river crocodile and hippo are always present, but look also for the entertaining Cape clawless otter and the large water monitor lizard, or *leguvaan,* which both occur frequently though are seldom seen.

Birds

Around 350 species of birds have been recorded in the valley. By the river you will find many varieties of water-loving birds like kingfishers: pied, giant, woodland, malachite and brown-hooded kingfishers, to name the more common ones. Similarly, darters, cormorants, egrets and storks are common, and fish eagles are always to be found perching on high branches that overlook the river. Less common residents include ospreys, spoonbills and African skimmers.

Poaching

The original inhabitants of the valley, the Nsenga people, were moved out of the area during the colonial era. It was declared a national park in 1983. Poaching from the park was a major problem, initially because the surrounding peoples had always hunted for food in the valley, so they were not happy to stop. However in the 1980s commercial poaching for ivory and rhino horn completely wiped out the park's black rhino population, and threatened to do the same to the elephants.

The world ivory trade ban did much to stop this, and the elephant population in the park is now good. There now seems to be no difference between the populations on the two sides of the river, and the herds are not nervous of vehicles (a good sign). However, poaching occurs occasionally and there are game scouts, stationed at Chilanga and in the park, who monitor it very closely.

Several honorary wildlife rangers are involved with safari camps in the valley, so supporting these camps helps to stop the poaching – both by supporting the livelihoods of these rangers, and by keeping a presence of people in the park that makes it more difficult for poachers to operate.

Where to stay

There are three ways of getting into this area. Visitors can stay at one of the private camps as a base, and go for game-viewing drives, walks and trips on the river from there. This will involve being transferred from Lusaka by road or private plane.

Alternatively they can take part in one of the popular canoe safaris which run along both sides of the river, usually using sparse temporary 'fly' camps each night. These generally start at either Kariba or Chirundu, and you'll be driven out of the valley at the end by road.

The last option is for the adventurous and well-equipped – to drive in with their own vehicles, and all their own supplies and camping equipment. For safety's sake, in case of a breakdown, two 4WD vehicles would be a sensible minimum for such a trip.

Private camps and lodges

There are three main lodges in the valley; all are good and have different styles of operating. With advance notice and a 4WD, you can drive yourself into any of these. However, most people will probably arrange for a transfer by road or charter flight. Looking at the lodges from west to east:

Kiambi Camp (8 twin-bed tents) Karibu Safaris, PO Box 35196, Northway 4065, Durban, South Africa. Tel: (2731) 563 9774; fax: 563 1957
New for '99, Kiambi is only used by Karibu as part of one of their six-night group lodge trips, which include boat transfers between camps. A minimum of four people, maximum of 16, are needed to guarantee a trip. These depart from Kariba by vehicle and spend two nights at each of Kiambi, Kiubo and Kulefu camps, returning by vehicle.

The camp's accommodation is in furnished Meru tents on wooden platforms, looking out on to the river. Each has green netting to shade it from the sun and a large veranda with chairs and table at the front, overlooking the river. Inside are twin beds and at the back, under the tented roof, is an en-suite shower, toilet and washbasin. Unlike its sister-camps, Kiambi has mains electricity, and so electric lights in the camp.

The lounge/bar is high over the river, next to a young baobab tree, and next to that is a thatched dining area surrounded by reed walls. There's a small plunge pool nearby, and a little thatched curio shop.

Activities from camp include boat trips in flat-bottomed motorboats with canopies. These hold up to 12 people, plus a driver at the back. Canoeing is also possible; the camp uses three-man fibreglass Canadian-style canoes, and there is always a river guide at the back of the lead canoe. Half-day or whole-day canoe trips are also possible, as are 4WD game drives (though Kiambi is outside the national park).

Rates: currently only possible as a 6-night trip, see above, which costs US$1,500 per person sharing.
Open: March to end-December

Kayila Lodge (6 chalets) Safari Par Excellence, Harare, Zimbabwe. Tel: (2634) 700911/2
For many years until Mwambashi was built, this was Saf Par's main camp in the area, and it is about 45km from Chirundu in the Chiawa GMA. It's about an hour's drive into the national park from here.

Kayila is solidly built with furniture carved from heavy railway-sleepers, and has an air of permanence. Its central thatched lounge/dining area is built with open sides, and set in a small group of baobabs on a small rise next to the river. The inside of one of those great trees has been converted into a small toilet (complete with wash basin and mirror) for the bar, accessed by a small door in its trunk.

The rooms are all different and very comfortable. The Tree House is a favourite, built quite high in a sausage tree overlooking the river. There are two large single beds upstairs, covered by mosquito nets, and a private bathroom/toilet built solidly in stone at the bottom of the tree. The honeymoon suite is much larger, and has its king-size bed and large bath set in stone. It is open to the river on one side, which lends a feeling of space. There are also four stone-and-thatch chalets, also with en-suite facilities, one with a double bed. All the chalets have their own verandas overlooking the river, with deck chairs.

Activities include day and night game drives in the area around Kayila, boat trips, fishing (bring your own rods and tackle), canoeing and even hiking in the mountains on the edge of the escarpment.

Rates: US$240 per person (US$195 before 15 June) including all meals and activities.
Open: 1 April to end November.

Royal Zambezi Lodge (6 twin-bed tents) PO Box 31455, Lusaka. Tel: 01 223952 or 224334; fax: 223504; cell: 752304
Situated quite a few kilometres west of the National Park, in the Chiawa GMA, Royal Zambezi is a beautiful lodge that has been well designed, though it feels quite formal. The rooms are very comfortable Meru-style tents; all have en-suite facilities and are protected from the sun under a thatched roof. They look out on to well-watered green lawns, and the river beyond.

The 'Kigelia Bar' is built around the trunk of a large sausage tree, *Kigelia africana*, and there's a small plunge pool for occasional cooling dips. Most of your activities here will be drives into the park, including night drives, but there are also opportunities to canoe, take short walking trips around the area, or go tiger-fishing on the river.

To get here the camp will arrange road-and-boat transfers for you from Lusaka; about US$160 per person return, for two people. Alternatively you can fly in for US$220 one way, landing at a strip near the lodge.

Rates: US$185 per person sharing, including full board and all activities. Open: March to December

Royal Zambezi Self-catering Camp (5 twin tents) contact via Royal Zambezi Lodge
As well as their main camp, Royal Zambezi run a small self-catering camp a few kilometres down-river from their main camp. This has five tents accommodating up to ten people. All share ablutions which have hot and cold running water, flush toilets and hot showers. There is refrigeration supplied and staff are around; just bring your own food, drink and towels.

With advanced notice, they can usually arrange fishing, boat excursions, day and night game drives and walking safaris at an extra cost. Transfers are also possible via air/road and boat, and there are plans for a campsite here by July 2000.

Rates: US$36 per person sharing. Open: March to December

Kiubo Camp (8 twin-bed tents) Contact via Kiambi and Karibu, above
The second of Karibu's permanent camps in the Lower Zambezi, Kiubo has eight large Meru tents on platforms overlooking the river – and is basically very like Kiambi Camp. All tents have a veranda with chairs, en-suite facilities and netting to shade them from the sun. The camp has a lounge/bar and an adjacent dining area and small plunge pool. There is no mains electricity – it relies on solar power.

It is perhaps most notable for being at a point on the river bank where the great escarpment comes very close to the river, which makes a lovely scenic backdrop to the camp. Its activities/facilities are otherwise similar to Kiambi's, and it is usually visited as part of Karibu's six-night trip split equally between the three camps.

Rates: only possible as a 6-night trip, which costs US$1,500 per person sharing. See Kiambi Camp description for details, page 213. Open: July to December

Chiawa Camp (8 twin/double tents) G&G Safaris, PO Box 30972, Lusaka. Tel: 01 261588; fax: 262683; email: chiacamp@zamnet.zm
Chiawa is a small, friendly camp set beneath a grove of mahogany trees, about 8km (30 minutes' drive) within the National Park. Its rooms are insect-proof, Meru-style tents on raised timber decks, with solar lighting and en-suite facilities (flush toilets and hot showers). Several have double beds, the rest twin. Being in the park, Chiawa is a seasonal camp used only during the dry season, so is mostly built of wood and reeds, giving it a pleasantly rustic air.

A full range of activities is offered here, from walking safaris and 4WD trips (including night drives), to motorboat trips, fishing excursions and short canoe trips along the river. Chiawa has maintained a good reputation for serious fishing trips for tiger fish, though only a few of its visitors just want to fish.

There are two ways of getting to the camp from Lusaka: by road transfer (two hours) and then motor boat (a further one and a half hours) which is fun, or by flying (40 minutes) into the Lower Zambezi's bush airstrip at Jeki. Private flights from elsewhere, including the Luangwa, can also be organised.

In 1998 the camp logged its sightings, and out of about 200 game-viewing days, they had 249 separate sightings of lion and 51 of leopard (including two of a *very* unusual black leopard). This is a good record, but fairly typical of what a small private camp in Zambia can achieve with good guides. Chiawa is run by a family team and has carved out a reputation as one of Zambia's top camps.

Rates: US$295/415 per person sharing/single (US$265/375 before 1 June), including full board, all activities, drinks, laundry and park fees. Open: 15 April to 15 November

Sausage Tree (5 twin and 2 double tents) Tongabezi, P. Bag 31, Livingstone.
Tel: 03 323235, fax: 323224, email: tonga@zamnet.zm
Sausage Tree is set in a beautiful position inside the Lower Zambezi National Park, and it is usually accessed by a short flight to Jeki airstrip. Its tents are large and unusual, being of an oval marquee design in cream canvas. They have the customary en-suite bathrooms, and can be left open all the time if you wish. Local reed furniture is used throughout, as are first-class fabrics and linen sheets.

Jeki offers the full range of day and night drives, canoeing, walking, boating and fishing trips on the river. One of its main assets is the proximity of a lovely backwater, the Chifungulu Channel, which runs the parallel to main river for about 10km and makes a lovely area for a gentle paddle about.

(As an aside, chifungulu is said to be the local name for *Combretum microphyllum,* the 'flame creeper' with blood-red flowers that grows up winterthorn trees here. Smith's book on the Luangwa's flora, see *Further Reading,* observes that some local people used to grind up the roots of this creeper, mix them with dog turds, and then burn the mixture – using the ashes as a cure for lunacy. It's uncertain if anyone at the camp has ever tried this.)

Rates: US$315/440 per person sharing/single, including full board, drinks, all activities and park fees, but excluding flight transfers. Open: April to November

Mushika Camp (8 twin-bed tents) Safari Expeditions (Zambia) Ltd, PO Box 71542, Lusaka. Tel/fax: 02 640542/617552; email: safex@zamnet.zm

This brand new camp, within the national park, is being built and run by Safari Expeditions – a company with powerful backers best known for its hunting safaris. Mushika will, of course, be strictly a camp for photographic visitors.

Mwambashi River Lodge (6 twin- and 2 double-bed tents) Safari Par Excellence, Harare, Zimbabwe. Tel: (2634) 700911/2

This is a sister-camp to Kayila and is now Saf Par's flagship in the Lower Zambezi, one of their two permanent camps. It is usually reached by short flights into the area. Its large walk-in tents are all built on wooden platforms overlooking the river. Each has twin beds with mosquito nets and en-suite toilet, shower and washbasin at the back. The central dining area is on a raised platform, with a thatched roof and an open balcony, and a bar (and toilet) on the ground level underneath.

Activities involve day and night game drives, walking safaris, canoeing and boat trips. Fishing is possible, but the lodge doesn't have any equipment so you must bring your own.

Rates: US$240 per person (US$195 before 15 June) including all meals and activities, but excluding US$20 per person per night park entry fees. Open: 1 April to end November

Kulefu Camp (8 twin-bed tents) Contact via Kiambi and Karibu

This is the third of Karibu's permanent camps in the Lower Zambezi area, and the only one within the Lower Zambezi National Park. Like the others, Kulefu has eight large Meru tents on platforms, with verandas, en-suite facilities and shade. It has a lounge/bar though no pool.

The lounge/bar and separate dining area are marquee-type tents, with open walls, under *Acacia albida* and *Acacia robusta* trees. The camp doesn't have mains electricity, but relies on solar power. Its activities/facilities are otherwise similar to Kiambi's, and it is usually visited as part of Karibu's six-night trip split equally between the three camps.

Rates: only possible as a 6-night trip, which costs US$1,500 per person sharing. See Kiambi Camp description for details, page 213. Open: July to December

Kingfisher Camp (8 twin chalets) Contact via African Tour Designers, PO Box 36600, Lusaka, Zambia. Tel: 01 273864; fax: 273865

Between the Lower Zambezi National Park and the Luangwa River, which forms the border with Mozambique, lies a narrow neck of land barely 10–15km wide. Within this, Kingfisher Camp was set up beside the Zambezi, close to the dramatic scenery of the Mpata Gorge.

Its current status is unknown, as is that of its bushcamp in the Lower Zambezi National Park, called Flycatcher Camp. Kingfisher has sadly closed in the last year or so. If it reopens then it may be one to watch, as it's got a very unique position.

Kingfisher was just 30 minutes by boat from the small town of Luangwa, which can be reached fairly easily by road from the Great East Road (turn south on the west side of the bridge over the Luangwa), or by charter flight from Lusaka.

Visiting independently

The roads into the park need a 4WD vehicle (ideally two) but are not difficult driving in the dry season. Get detailed maps of the whole valley before you leave Lusaka, and pack a compass. It would be wise to get a permit before you arrive, from the National Parks office in Lusaka or Chilanga, though you may be able to get one at the scout's camp in the park itself.

To find the right track, take the turning off the main road just before Chirundu and follow the signs to Gwabi Lodge. Where the sign points left, indicating the lodge is 2km ahead, continue straight ahead to reach the pontoon which crosses the

Kafue River. Then it's a simple case of sticking close to the river, and following the main track.

Masochists might like to know that there's a much more difficult approach possible via the Great East Road. You'll certainly need permission from the National Parks office in Chilanga to attempt this route, and it would be wise to take a guide for most of the way. The road starts just beyond the National Park's boundary (as indicated by a tsetse-fly barrier) and after about 22km leads to the park gate, and nearby scout's camp. You'll need to collect a guide from here if you wish to continue. The road soon heads for Chakwenga (a disused old mine), about 60km inside the park, and then drops over the escarpment. It then becomes steep, little-used and very overgrown. This isn't an easy option at all, but the track does eventually lead down into the main game-viewing area on the valley's floor.

Canoeing on the river

Canoeing down the Zambezi is a terrific way to relax in the open air and see the river, whilst doing some gentle exercise and game-viewing at the same time.

Physically, you will feel tired at the end of a day, but canoeing down-river is not too strenuous (unless you meet a strong headwind) and no previous experience is demanded. All the operators use very stable Canadian-style fibreglass canoes about 5.7m long. These are large enough for two people plus their equipment, and very difficult to capsize.

Psychologically, it's great to view game from outside of a vehicle, and whilst moving under your own propulsion: it makes you feel in charge of your own trip, and an active participant rather than a passive passenger. However, there is normally only one guide to a party of four to eight canoes, so on occasions you will be much closer to a pod of hippos than to your trusty guide.

Which section to canoe?

Canoe safaris are run from the Kariba Dam wall right to the confluence of the Luangwa and Zambezi rivers – where Zambia and Zimbabwe end, and Mozambique begins. This whole trip is normally a 10-day/9-night canoe trip. However, most people are limited by either time, or money, or both, and so choose to do just a part of this.

Kariba to Chirundu is the easiest, shortest section, normally taking around 3 days/2 nights and costing around US$300. The first few hours of this, through the Kariba Gorge, are the best part. After that there are no great attractions and still very little game around. Because both Kariba and Chirundu are easily reached by road, the transfers to and from these trips will be very cheap.

Going from Chirundu to the Lower Zambezi (or Mana Pools, if you're with a Zimbabwean operator) is the most popular section. Typically this also takes 4 days/3 nights, costs around US$450, and gradually the game viewing gets better and better as you go along. Obviously the more time afforded in the National Park areas, the more animals you're likely to see, so quiz your chosen operator on *precisely* where the trip starts and finishes, and where the final camp is in relation to the National Park boundary and the rivers in the area.

The final section, through the Lower Zambezi National Park and on to the Luangwa River confluence, is the wildest, with the best game and the fewest other canoes. Eventually the river passes through the spectacular Mpata (sometimes called Mupata) Gorge, before reaching the border. As you would expect, the transfers into and (especially) out of this section are expensive: this trip costs around US$700 for 5 days/4 nights.

These costs include transfers to and from the river from Kariba, but note that they do vary seasonally: prices in July, August, September and October could be about 30% higher than this.

Canoeing operators

With canoeing operators leading groups down both sides of the river, the Lower Zambezi can seem almost busy. But the river is wide, with many islands in the middle, so though you may spot people in the distance on the other side, you won't be within chatting distance. The southern side (Zimbabwe) has noticeably more visitors than the north (Zambia), which is quieter, and there is a greater choice of trips in Zimbabwe than Zambia.

As a limit on numbers (for the sake of maintaining some semblance of a wilderness atmosphere), the Zimbabweans do not allow more than one party of canoeists on each section of their side of the river at a time. This is an excellent policy to avoid groups meeting each other, and spoiling the isolated atmosphere. Fortunately the Zambian side is much less busy than this, and the main operator is:

Safari Par Excellence

Sold extensively through outlets in Zimbabwe, Saf Par (as it is universally known) has several different trips, mostly concentrating on the section from Chirundu to the Chongwe tributary, which is the western boundary of the Lower Zambezi National Park. They use a combination of Saf Par's two lodges, Kayila and Mwambashi, and two established fly camps, Mtondo Camp and Chongwe Camp.

They have two different styles of trips, using different camps. Their 'participation safaris' have basic fly-camps and ensure that visitors get involved with the cooking and camp chores. All the camping equipment is supplied, including tents, mosquito nets, mattresses, sleeping bags (each with liner and pillow), cooler boxes, tables and chairs, gas cookers, cooking utensils and cutlery.

Typical of these is their 'Kariba Gorge Canoe Trail' that starts in Kariba and covers the 60km to Chirundu, spending two nights camping beside the river and costing around US$295 per person. On a similar basis, Saf Par's 'Island Canoe Trail' goes from the Kafue River to the Chongwe River and costs US$395 per person. Neither penetrates the Lower Zambezi National Park.

By contrast, their 'Great Zambezi Trail' includes fully-serviced camps and starts with a 45-minute motorboat ride downstream from the Kafue River. This is basically so that the paddling doesn't become a chore, and yet you can get into an area of good game. Your first night is then spent in Mtondo Camp, just 30km from the park, your second at Chongwe Camp, on the park's border, and your third at Mwambashi Lodge, another 30km downstream right inside the park. These require no cooking or help from the guests, and are more comfortable than the participation camps – but they are also more expensive. They operate from 15 March to 15 November and cost about US$795 per person for 4 days/3 nights.

Africa Archipelago
Specialist Zambia operators
Please contact us for detailed quotes and itineraries
Or visit us in London for a presentation
Tel   44 (0) 208 788 5838
Fax   44 (0) 207 384 9549
Email worldarc@compuserve.com

AFRICA
ARCHIPELAGO

The Luangwa Valley

This lush rift valley, enclosed by steep escarpment walls, is one of the continent's finest areas for wildlife. Four national parks protect parts of this area: South Luangwa, North Luangwa, Luambe and Lukusuzi. Separating these are Game Management Areas (GMAs) – which also contain good populations of game. This entire valley is remote but, for the enthusiast, the wildlife is well worth the effort made to get here.

For most visitors, South Luangwa National Park is by far the most practical park to visit in the valley. This is the largest of the parks, with superb wildlife and many excellent camps to choose from. Organising a trip to South Luangwa is not difficult, and its infrastructure is easily the best. However, it is still a very remote park, and so most visitors arrive on trips organised outside Zambia. Few arrive independently and, though this is possible, it does limit their choices.

The more intrepid might organise a safari from there into North Luangwa, which is even more remote and exclusive. Its wildlife is now flourishing, thanks to some intensive conservation efforts over the past decade, and the few safaris that run concentrate on taking small groups for walking trips. Luambe National Park is much smaller than either the South or the North park, and there are no longer any camps there. The birdwatching is good, as with the other parks, though there is less game.

Finally Lukusuzi National Park is something of an unknown quantity, as there are no facilities or camps there at the moment; few people have even visited this park.

FROM LUSAKA TO THE LUANGWA

Chipata is about 570km from Lusaka along a road which is good tar in places, and potholed in others. It's a long drive. Hitchhiking is possible, though even leaving Lusaka early in the morning might not get you to Chipata by evening. Buses leave Lusaka for Chipata frequently, from early morning through to late afternoon, and take 10–12 hours. Expect them to cost around Kw13,000.

Petauke

Little more than a dot on the map, this small town does have a campsite and a simple motel.

Nyika Motel Tel: 71002
This comes recommended as a clean and safe place to stay, and as serving a decent meal of chicken and rice if requested.
Rates: Kw30,000 per person

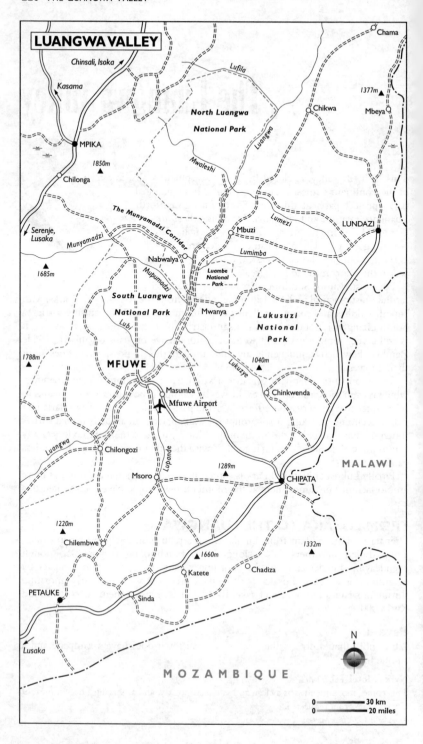

Zulu's Kraal Campsite PO Box 560198
I recently received news of a new campsite here, from its manageress, Nellars Tambo. She wrote that the camp offers campsites and a couple of simple A-frame chalets, each sleeping four people, as well as hot showers and a fully-equipped kitchen for campers to use. Perhaps this is just the place for breaking the long journey from Lusaka to the Luangwa Valley or Malawi.
Rates: US$3 per person for camping, US$7 per person for a chalet

Chipata

This tidy, busy town is more than just a gateway to South Luangwa; it is also a border town just 19km from Malawi. As you fly into the town, Chipata is on a flat valley surrounded by low bush-covered hills. Between the hills is quite a fertile area of subsistence farms.

As you arrive by road from Lusaka, there is a useful AGIP petrol station on your right, just after the welcome arch, which also has a little supermarket attached to it. The police station is about 1.5km after this on your left, after which there is a left turning that leads down to the main township – from which all the local buses depart. The road then bends to the right, and shortly after that the main post office is on your left. Continuing, there is a Barclays Bank and a BP petrol station on the left, and further on the right you'll find a small garage (Engine Reconditioning Services) owned by a chap called Musadaya. He supplies Toyota spares and is the best local mechanic if repairs are needed.

Shortly after the garage is a large branch of Shoprite, the town's largest and best supermarket. Then, as you leave for Malawi, there's a good private medical centre on your right (just after Shoprite). Chipata is not a large town but, because of its position near Malawi, it has easy access to supplies from there which may be unobtainable elsewhere in Zambia.

Getting there and away
By air
By far the easiest way to get there is by air, as Chipata has a good all-weather gravel airstrip. There are regular flights to and from Lusaka, sometime via Mfuwe, with Zambian Airways (formerly Roan Air) and Eastern Air, though these are more frequent during the height of the safari season from June to the end of October. See page 114 for details. Expect a one-way Lusaka–Chipata flight to cost US$130, and Chipata–Mfuwe to be US$30.

Where to stay
Most visitors will continue down to the Mfuwe area and the national park if they can, but if you arrive late then staying in Chipata is a wise move. If you are hitchhiking, then a night or two here may be a necessity due to lack of lifts. There are several places to lay your head:

Chipata Motel Mfuwe Road, PO Box 510020, Chipata. Tel: 22340
Just on the left as you turn off the main Lusaka road on the way to Mfuwe, this is a very basic motel used mainly by low-budget local business-people. If you are hitchhiking then it is convenient. The bar will sell you Cokes, and you can sleep here if traffic is scarce (around US$15 per person).

Wildlife Campsite
Has a bar and simple campsite with simple ablution blocks. Camping US$5 per person.

Sunny Side Farm
Equidistant from Chipata and the Malawi border, about 14km from each, this has a black signpost for 'camping' pointing to the north of the road. Nicci Donken has a simple thatched

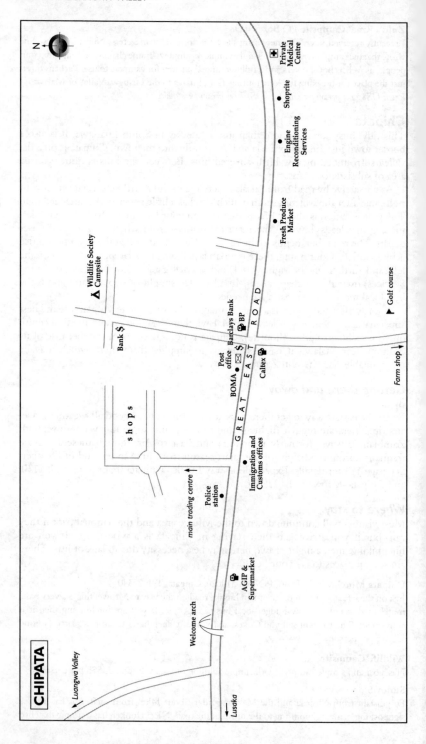

CHIPATA

Luangwa Valley

N

Wildlife Society
Campsite

shops

Bank $

Post
office
BOMA
Barclays Bank
BP

GREAT EAST ROAD

main trading centre

Welcome arch

Police
station

Immigration and
Customs offices

Caltex

Farm shop

AGIP &
Supermarket

Lusoka

Fresh Produce
Market

Engine
Reconditioning
Services

Shoprite

Private
Medical
Centre

Golf course

area there with a sitting area, camp site and ablution blocks – all about 1.5km from the road. Fresh eggs, milk and chickens are available on the farm. Firewood and charcoal can also be bought for a few kwacha. In an emergency, the farm may be able to help with vehicle repairs. Their campsite is on the side of a dam, and it's a favourite site for overlanders.
Rates: US$2.50 per person camping

Lundazi

About 180km north of Chipata, well off any obvious route for travellers, lies the small, pleasant town of Lundazi. It's perched high above the eastern side of the Luangwa Valley, and close to a quiet border crossing to Malawi.

Lundazi has no huge supermarkets, but plenty of small, local shops where you can buy most essentials. It's a friendly place and there are a lot of farming areas around it, so fresh produce is available. It also has a few banks, a post office, a police station, an airstrip, assorted places of worship (Christian and Moslem), a mission station, a convent – and a fairytale Norman castle with a dungeon, turrets and battlements.

Getting there

The easiest way to reach Lundazi is from Chipata. Then it's just 180km of (very potholed) tar, accessible in a sturdy 2WD if you've got the patience. This drive will take about five hours in a strong high-clearance 4WD; longer if you need to be gentle with your vehicle.

From the north reaching Lundazi is trickier, requiring a 4WD and even more time and patience. Approaching Isoka on the main road from Mpika, you pass the turning to Isoka, on the left. Shortly afterwards is a turning to the right, signposted to the 'airport bar', which you take. This will lead you through Ntendere and up into the mountains. After about 75km, there's a fork and you turn right, heading almost south to reach Muyombe 50km later. It's a rocky road on the escarpment with many gullies, but the scenery is beautiful. A high-clearance 4WD is essential.

From Muyombe, continue south towards Nyika Plateau and the border with Malawi, dropping down from the mountains as you do so. After around 25km, just before the Malawi border, turn right (southwest) on to a dirt road. This is generally good, though sandy in parts. After shadowing the border for some 70km, there's a fork and Lundazi is signposted to the left, whilst Chama is about 35km away if you take the right turn. Lundazi is now about 110km south of you; making the whole journey a very full day's drive from Isoka.

From the Luangwa Valley there are two roads. Both are impassable during the rains, and require hours of hard 4WD travel in the dry season. The better of them leaves the main road on the east side of the valley about 20–25km north of Luambe National Park. It then climbs up the escarpment directly to Lundazi, about 130km away. It's a five-hour drive.

The second turns eastwards around the northern boundary of South Luangwa National Park and then cuts up the escarpment through Lukusuzi National Park. It then joins the Chipata–Lundazi road some 60km south of Lundazi (120km north of Chipata).

Where to stay

There's only one place of choice, but if the castle's full then the town has several other small, basic resthouses.

Lundazi Castle Hotel (12 rooms) PO Box 530100, Lundazi. Tel: 064 80173
Dick Hobson's excellent *Tales of Zambia* (see *Further Reading*) tells of how the district commissioner in the late 1940s, Errol Button, needed to build a resthouse here. Tourism was then taking off and visitors needed to stop between Nyika Plateau and the Luangwa Valley

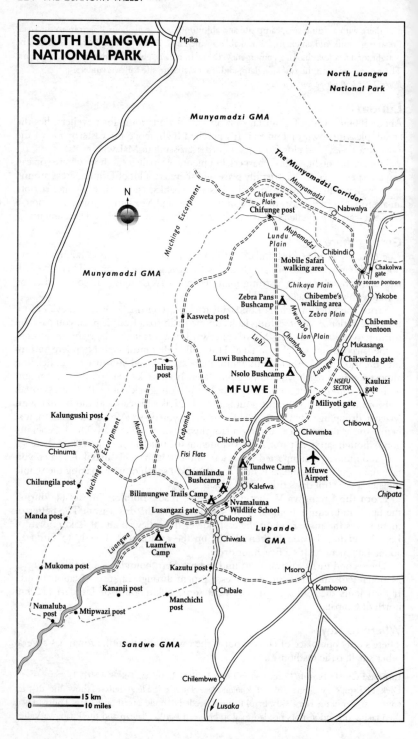

SOUTH LUANGWA
NATIONAL PARK

(the same could be said today!).

Thus he designed and had built a small castle in Norman style, with thick walls and narrow slits for archers, overlooking a lake. It has a dungeon, high turrets at each corner and battlements all around. It was christened 'Rumpelstiltskin' after a fairytale character suggested by his daughter, and cost a mere £500 at the time. The castle quickly became very popular, and was extended in 1952 to accommodate more visitors.

Now the castle remains a small hotel and is often fully booked. It has 14 rooms, sharing four bathrooms with hot and cold running water. There is electricity here after 17.00, but not usually earlier in the day. Very simple traditional meals are served, normally a choice of meats with nshima (beef and nshima is Kw4,500, chicken and nshima Kw5,800), for both lunch and dinner. It's the best place around, but like any castle can be very cold in the winter.

Rates: US$10/Kw25,000 per room. Continental breakfast is Kw4,500, full breakfast Kw5,800

SOUTH LUANGWA NATIONAL PARK

Park fees: US$20 per person (Kw10,080 for Zambian residents), plus US$15 per vehicle, per day

There are many contenders for the title of Africa's best game park. The Serengeti, Amboseli, Ngorongoro Crater, Etosha, Kruger, Moremi and Mana Pools would certainly be high on the list. South Luangwa has a better claim than most. Some of these other areas will match its phenomenally high game densities. Many others – the lesser known of Africa's parks – will have equally few visitors. One or two also allow night drives, which open up a different, nocturnal world to view, allowing leopards to be commonly seen and even watched whilst hunting.

However, few have South Luangwa's high quality of guiding together with its remarkable wildlife spectacles, day and night, amidst the isolation of a true wilderness. These elements, perhaps, are how the contenders ought to be judged, and on these the Luangwa comes out around the top of the list.

Background information
History
In the 19th century the area was crossed by many European explorers who came to hunt, trade, or bring the gospel; or simply out of curiosity. Around 1810 to 1820, a trading post was opened at Malambo, some 100km north of Mfuwe. This was on the main trade route from Tete to Lake Mweru which had first been established by Lacerda as early as 1798.

In his last book, *Kakuli*, Norman Carr quotes a Portuguese captain, Antonio Gamitto, as writing of the Luangwa in around 1832:

> 'Game of all kinds is very abundant at this season of drought; great numbers of wild animals collect here, leaving dry areas in search of water... we can only say that this district appears to be the richest in animal life of any we have seen.'

Later, in December 1866, when Livingstone crossed the Luangwa at Perekani (a place north of Tafika and south of Chibembe), he was just one of many Europeans exploring the continent.

In 1904 a Luangwa Game Park was declared on the eastern bank of the river. However, this was not maintained, hunting licences were given out to control allegedly marauding elephants, and the park came to mean little. Then on May 27 1938 three parks were defined in the valley: the North Luangwa Game Reserve, the Lukusuzi Game Reserve, and the South Luangwa Game Reserve – which corresponded roughly to the present park, though without the Chifungwe Plain or the Nsefu Sector.

In the following year, Norman Carr and Bert Schultz were appointed as game rangers and villages within the reserves were moved outside its boundaries. Initially Norman Carr recommended hunting safaris be started, but over the coming decade he realised that visitors would also come for what we now call 'photographic safaris'.

In 1949 the Senior Chief Nsefu, prompted by Norman Carr, established a private game reserve on the Luangwa's eastern bank, between the Mwasauke and Kauluzi Rivers. A safari camp was started here which sent some of its income directly back to the local community. (Norman Carr was ahead of his time!) This soon moved to the site of the present-day Nsefu Camp. The chief's reserve became the Nsefu Sector, which was absorbed into the boundaries of the present park – along with the Chifungwe Plain, north of the Mupamadzi River – when new legislation turned all game reserves into national parks on 15 February 1972.

Norman Carr himself lived at Kapani Safari Lodge until he died, having played a pivotal role in the history of the valley by pioneering commercial walking safaris, upon which South Luangwa has founded its reputation. He remained an important and highly outspoken figure to the end, and devoted much energy in his latter years to development projects helping the surrounding local communities to benefit from the park. He was especially involved with projects involving local schools: encouraging the next generation of Zambians to value their wildlife heritage. The private operators in South Luangwa have not, with one or two notable exceptions, been over-zealous in instigating similar forward-thinking development projects – so once again Norman Carr was ahead of his time.

Geography

The South Luangwa National Park (known locally as simply 'the South Park') now covers about 9,050km² of the Luangwa valley's floor, which varies from about 500m to 800m above sea level. On its western side the park is bounded by the Muchinga Escarpment, and from there it generally slopes down to the eastern side of the park, where it is bounded by the wide meanders of the Luangwa River.

Near the banks of the Luangwa the land is fairly flat, and mostly covered with mature woodlands. These are few dense shrubberies here, but many open areas where beautiful tall trees stand perhaps 10–20m apart, shading a mixture of small bushes and grassland. Occasionally there are wide, open grassland plains. The largest are Mtanda Plain in Nsefu, Lion Plain just opposite Nsefu, Chikaya Plain north of there, Ntanta around the Mupamadzi's confluence with the Luangwa, the huge Chifungwe Plain in the far north of the park, and the little-known Lundu Plain, south of the Mupumadzi River. These are not the Serengeti-type plains with short grass: they usually have tall species of grasses and often bushes. It is their lack of trees that makes them open.

Understandably, the highest density of animals (and hence camps) is around the Luangwa River. However, increasingly camps are being set up elsewhere in the park. Norman Carr's trio of bush camps are located along the Lubi River, one of the Luangwa's smaller tributaries, while walking camps run by Robin Pope Safaris and Chilongozi are dotted around the Mupamadzi River rather than the Luangwa.

Geology

The Luangwa Valley is a rift valley, similar to the Great Rift Valley of East Africa, though probably older, and it shares its genesis with the adjoining Lower Zambezi Valley. The original sedimentary strata covering the whole area is part of the karoo system, sedimentary rocks laid down from 175 to 300 million years ago.

During this time, faulting occurred and volcanic material was injected into rifts in the existing sediments. One of these faults is the wide valley that the Luangwa now occupies. In geologically recent times, the Luangwa has meandered extensively across the wide valley floor, eroding the volcanic rocks and depositing mineral-rich silts. These meanders also left behind them old watercourses and ox-bow pools. The most recent of these can still be seen, and they are an important feature of the landscape near the present river.

Flora and fauna
Vegetation
To understand the Luangwa Valley's vegetation, the base of its productive ecosystem, consider the elements that combine to nurture its plants: the water, light, heat and nutrients. The rainfall in the valley is typically 800 to 1,100mm per annum – which is moderate, but easily sufficient for strong vegetation growth. Occupying a position between 12° and 14° south of the equator, the valley lacks neither light nor heat. (Visit in October and you will probably feel that it has too much of both.)

However the key to its vegetation lies in the nutrients. The Luangwa's soils, being volcanic in origin, are rich in minerals, and the sediments laid down by the river are fine, making excellent soils. Thus with abundant water, light, heat and nutrient-rich soils, the valley's vegetation has thrived: it is both lush and diverse.

Unlike many parks, the 'bush' in the Luangwa is very variable, and as you drive or walk you'll pass through a patchwork of different vegetation zones. See *Flora and Fauna*, in *Chapter 4*, for more detail, but the more obvious include some beautiful mature forests of 'cathedral mopane'. Just outside the national park on the way to the salt pans (south of Mfuwe) is one area where the mopane are very tall.

Along the Luangwa's tributaries, which are just rivers of sand for most of the year, you'll find lush riverine vegetation dominated by giant red mahogany trees, *Khaya nyasica* (now known as *Khaya anthotheca*) and *Adina microsephela*. Sometimes you'll also find Natal mahoganies, *Trichilia emetica*, and African ebony trees, *Diospyros mespiliformis*. There are several locations in the park where the latter form dense groves, casting a heavy shade on the sparse undergrowth. Look for such groves where the tributaries meet the Luangwa; there's one beside Mchenja Camp.

Elsewhere are large, open grassland plains. Chief amongst these are probably the plains in the Nsefu Sector. These surround some natural salt springs, which attract crowned cranes in their thousands.

Antelope and other herbivores
Because of its rich vegetation, the Luangwa supports large numbers of a wide variety of animals. Each species has its own niche in the food chain, which avoids direct competition with any other species. Each herbivore has its favourite food plants, and even species that utilise the same food plants will feed on different parts of those plants. This efficient use of the available vegetation – refined over the last few millennia – makes the wildlife far more productive than any domestic stock would be if given the same land. It also leads to the high densities of game that the valley supports.

The game includes huge herds of elephant and buffalo, commonly hundreds of animals strong, which are particularly spectacular if encountered whilst you are on foot. Despite the Zambia's past poaching problems, South Luangwa's elephants are generally neither scarce nor excessively skittish in the presence of people. Just north of Mfuwe Lodge, you'll find an open plain with few trees, just the skeletal trunks of an old cathedral mopane forest. This is the legacy of elephant damage from the 1970s, before ivory poaching became a problem, when there were around

100,000 elephants in the park.

The park's dominant antelope species are impala and puku. Whilst impala are dominant in much of Southern Africa, puku are rare south of the Zambezi. They stand a maximum of 0.8m high at the shoulder and weigh in at up to about 75kg. These form the small breeding groups which are exceedingly common in their favourite habitat – well-watered riverine areas – dominated by a territorial male adorned with the characteristic lyre-shaped horns. Impala do occur here but are not the most numerous antelope, as they are in the Zambezi Valley and throughout Zimbabwe.

Luangwa has a number of 'specialities' including the beautiful Thornicroft's giraffe, *Giraffa camelopardalis thornicroftii*. This rare subspecies differs from the much more common southern giraffe, found throughout Southern Africa, in having a different (and more striking) colouration. When compared with the normal southern species of giraffe found in Kafue and south of the Zambezi, Thornicroft's have dark body patches and lighter neck patches; their colour patches don't normally extend below the knees, leaving their lower legs almost white; and their faces are light or white.

Fortunately, around the Mfuwe area there is a widespread traditional belief that people who eat giraffe meat will get spots like they do. Hence giraffe are rarely hunted by the local people, and are very common to the east of the river, in the GMA (game management area) outside the national park.

Cookson's wildebeest, *Connochaetes taurinus cooksoni*, are endemic to the valley and a subspecies of the blue wildebeest, which are found throughout the subcontinent. They are more common in more northerly areas of the valley (like North Luangwa); and Norman Carr's wildlife guide (see *Further Reading*) maintains that they also seem to favour the east side of the river, rather than the west. The Nsefu sector is perhaps the only place in South Luangwa where you are likely to spot them. They differ from the blue wildebeest in having cleaner colours including slightly reddish bands, and being a little smaller and more compact.

Another special of the Luangwa valley is Crawshay's Zebra, *Equus burchelli crawshaii*, a subspecies of the more common Burchell's Plains Zebra, which is found in much of the subcontinent. Crawshay's occur west of the Muchinga Escarpment – in the Luangwa Valley and on Nyika Plateau – and lack the brown shadow-stripe that Burchell's usually have between their black stripes.

In contrast to these examples, the common waterbuck (*Kobus ellipsiprymnus*) is found in the valley. Its rarer subspecies, the defassa waterbuck (*K. e. crawshayi*), is found over most of the rest of Zambia. This has a white circular patch on its rump, rather than the common waterbuck's characteristic white 'toilet seat' ring.

Other antelope in the park include bushbuck, eland and kudu. The delicate oribi occur occasionally in the grassland areas (especially Chifungwe Plain), while the small grysbok are often encountered on night drives. Reedbuck and Lichtenstein's hartebeest also occur, but not usually near the river, whilst sable are occasionally seen in the hills near the escarpment and roan antelope seem to be most frequently seen south of Chichele Lodge.

A special mention must go to the hippopotami (and crocodiles) found in the rivers, and especially in the Luangwa: their numbers are remarkable. Look over the main bridge crossing the Luangwa at Mfuwe – sometimes there are hundreds of hippo there. Towards the end of the dry season, when the rivers are at their lowest, is the best time to observe such dense congregations of hippo. Then these semi-aquatic mammals are forced into smaller and smaller pools, and you'll appreciate their sheer numbers.

Predators

The main predators in the Luangwa Valley are typical of subSaharan Africa: lion, leopard, spotted hyena and wild dog. During the day, the visitor is most likely to see lion, *Panthera leo*, which are the park's most common large predator. Their large prides are relatively easily spotted, and their hunting trips make gripping spectacles.

South Luangwa seems to have made a name for itself amongst the safari community as an excellent park for leopard, *Panthera pardus*. This is largely because leopard hunt nocturnally, and South Luangwa is one of Africa's few National Parks which allows operators to go on spotlit game drives at night.

However, estimates made whilst filming a BBC documentary about leopards in the park suggest an average leopard density of one animal per $2.5km^2$ – roughly twice the density recorded in South Africa's Kruger National Park. So perhaps the reputation is justified. In the author's experience, night drives in Luangwa with experienced guides do consistently yield excellent sightings of these cats – at a frequency that is difficult to match elsewhere on the continent.

In contrast to this, cheetah do occur here but are very uncommon. Typically sightings are only recorded every few years. There seem to have been a few cheetah sightings in the early '80s, but I'm not aware of any since 1985.

Wild dog are also uncommon, though their population seems to oscillate over a period of years. A study of wild dogs in Zambia by Kenneth Buk in 1995 (see *Further Reading*) suggested that the Luangwa holds Zambia's second largest wild dog population, even though this had been badly depleted by an outbreak of anthrax in 1987. Recently more sightings have been reported, with one pack in the park near Nkwali pontoon in May 1999, which seems to have remained near the river in the south side of the park as I write. Numbers seem to be building again, with sightings occurring most frequently in the earlier months of the year.

Birds

The Luangwa has the rich tropical birdlife that you would expect in such a fertile valley. This includes species that prefer a dry habitat of plains and forests, and those that live close to water. It is difficult to mention more than a few of the Luangwa's 400 species, but note that in *Further Reading*, page 398, are books which cover the region's birds.

Because the Luangwa is situated between southern and east Africa, keen birdwatchers may want to arrive with two field guides, each describing birds from one region, so that between them they will cover the full range of species encountered in the valley.

Better, bring a good guide to Southern Africa's birds, like Newmann's guide, and buy Aspinwall and Beel's Zambian guide locally. See *Further Reading* to explain the logic of this.

Species of note include flocks of crowned cranes occurring on the marshes of the Nsefu Sector; the colonies of iridescent carmine bee-eaters which nest in sandy river banks in September and October; the African skimmers found along the Luangwa; and the giant eagle owls which are sometimes picked out by the spotlight on night drives.

The best time for birds is the summer: the rainy season. The birds' food supply is then at its most abundant, and the summer migrants are around. Just drive into the park during the rains and it becomes immediately apparent that both the vegetation and the birdlife are running riot. Dry plains have sprouted thick, green vegetation mirrored all around by shallow water. Flocks of egrets, herons and storks wade through this, around feeding geese and ducks.

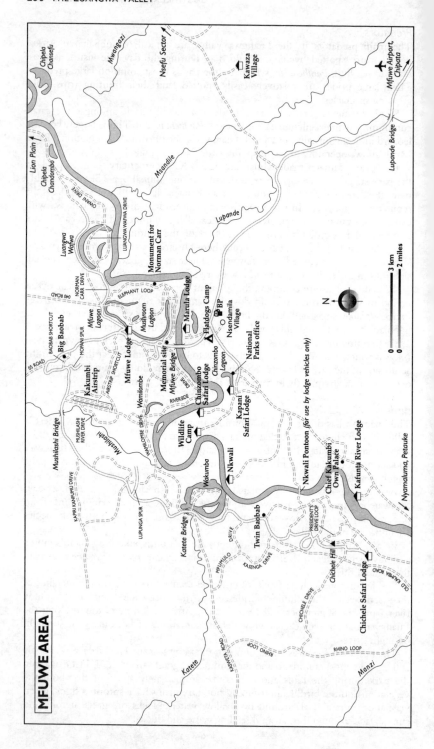

MFUWE AREA

Many species breed here, including storks that often form impressive colonies. There are several sites of tall trees in the Nsefu Sector which, when surrounded by shallow water, regularly become breeding colonies. The most amazing of these has half a dozen huge trees filled with nests of yellow-billed storks in their spectacular pink breeding plumage. It's one of the Luangwa's most remarkable sights.

Hunting and poaching

South Luangwa has always been Zambia's 'most favoured park'. Over the years it has been given a disproportionately large share of the resources allotted to all of the country's National Parks. Many would argue that this has been to the detriment of the other parks, though it did enable it to fight the plague of commercial poaching, which hit the country in the 1980s, with some success. The poachers came for rhino horn – which is sold to make dagger-handles in the Middle East and Chinese medicines for the Far East – and of course ivory.

Sadly the valley's thriving black rhino population was wiped out, as it was throughout Zambia. The last confirmed sightings in the Luangwa were in 1987. (One or two sources suggest that there are a couple of individual animals left in the country, but this is probably just wishful thinking.) Fortunately, the elephant populations were only reduced; and in recent years, thanks in part to the CITES ban on the ivory trade, they have bounced back.

Today there is minimal poaching in the park, as demonstrated by the size of the animal populations, and certainly no lack of game. Only in the nervous elephant populations of North Luangwa does one get a feeling for the poaching problems of the past.

Conservation and development in Lupande GMA

South Luangwa has always been protected from poaching in a way that Zambia's other parks were not. This wasn't always 100% effective, but it was a lot better than elsewhere. Several years ago a project was started in sections of the Lupande GMA, which is immediately adjacent to the national park, to distribute direct cash benefits from the park to the local people.

This has worked very well beside the river (ie: beside the park), where the animals are plentiful and the hunting income has been very good. Certainly one of the local chiefs has a very nice brick-built palace with satellite TV and an impressively new twin-cab land cruiser parked in front.

However, further from the park the hunting isn't so good, and the fees have certainly been less. Locals comment that the influx of people into the Mfuwe Bridge area over the last decade has been very noticeable: there are now far more people around.

Much of the cause of this may well be simply the employment prospects generated directly (and indirectly), by the lodges. However, this influx means that the GMA's revenues are being effectively divided between more people. It also puts more strain on the area's agriculture, to increase cultivated land in the area. But with more people and more cultivation… will come a reduction in the game.

Thus there's another Gordian knot for those working on conservation and development in the area to tackle. See the section on *Conservation* in *Chapter 4* for a more general discussion of these issues.

Getting organised
Orientation

If you're arriving on an organised trip, then you can relax. A vehicle will be waiting to take you to camp, and there's no need to think ahead. However, if you are driving or hitching here, then you may be aiming for a dot on the map marked 'Mfuwe'. Forget it. Mfuwe is more of an area than a place. In spirit, its centre is probably the airport and adjacent Moondogs Café and Magenge Crafts (see below). This is the terminus from which most of the valley's visitors arrive and depart – and so it is a hub frequented by vehicles from most of the valley's camps.

About 25km northwest of this is the main Mfuwe Bridge over the Luangwa. This lies at the heart of the park's all-weather road network, and many visitors entering the national park pass this way. Between the airport and the bridge is a stretch of road where you will pass the occasional farm stalls selling vegetables, a BP fuel station, a school, small shops, church and clinic – but don't look for a small town here, as there isn't one. (Yet.)

As you approach the bridge there's a left turn to Kapani, Nkwali, Chinzombo and the camps on the southern side of Mfuwe, then immediately on the left is the new site for Flatdogs, which has moved from its old spot on the right of the road. And just over the bridge, inside the park, is the grand, new Mfuwe Lodge itself.

Mfuwe Airport

Mfuwe Airport is technically an international airport, with customs and immigration, but it feels very much like a small, local airport. There's one small terminal building containing a handful of shops, and if you're on one of the smaller flights in and out of the valley, then you're quite likely to have the pilot coming to find you before embarking on your flight.

Inside the terminal are toilets, a few small shops, a very small bank and a rather flashy curio shop selling glossy picture books and expensive carvings and curios. Just outside you'll find the labelled parking spaces where 4WDs from the lodges wait for their pre-booked incoming passengers. A few yards away are two gems, well worth investigating:

Moondog Café PO Box 100, Mfuwe. Tel: 062 45068; fax: 45025; email: moondog@super-hub.com
Beside the airport, and the camps, there's one essential place to know about – and that's the invaluable little Moondog Café. It's situated beside the airport and run by Jake and his team from Flatdogs Camp. It's a relaxed place to have a drink as you arrive, or before you leave, or even a tasty snack or bite to eat. It's also got a useful notice board and fair bit of local wit. (Ask about 'Coppinger's Corner', amongst other local legends.)

However, in an emergency Moondog is valuable as a communications hub – for its radio links to the Valley's camps. So if you have problems near the airport, or want to contact someone, then sit down, order a drink, and ask for their help.

Tequila is served all day, without an eyebrow being raised, and the menu includes home-made pasta, pizzas, nachos, tacos, quesadillas and chilli, burgers, toasted sandwiches, meat pies and samosas. Expect a full meal for around US$8.
Open: May–December, but closes January–April for the rains

Magenge Crafts PO Box 97, Mfuwe. Tel: 062 45094; email: tonyg@zamnet.zm
Beside the Moondog Café, outside the main airport building, is a small and stylish shop selling craftwork and various books on Zambia and the Luangwa in particular. It's owned by Ali Shenton, who also owns the African Visions shop in Livingstone.

The crafts include textiles, baskets, wirework, wooden carvings, Elephant-dung greetings cards (much nicer than they sound!), papier-mâché animal heads, embroidered T-shirts and various artefacts – many of which make super souvenirs. Virtually all are locally made, providing a valuable income for the local people who produce them. Look out especially for items by

Mango Tree Crafts, which is a community project recently initiated by Gillie Lightfoot (Tribal Textiles), using local materials to make mobiles, table mats, wooden animals and, using old snares collected by National Parks, wire flowers and animals. Magenge is one of the valley's few outlets for such crafts, and it is run with these development aims in mind. ('Magenge' is the local name for termites – noted for the impact of their co-operative schemes despite their small size.)

This is also a good place to buy natural history guides to Zambia, and probably has the best selection of books on the Luangwa Valley's natural history that you'll find anywhere. See *Further Reading* for notes on some of the Zambian-published books, and consider emailing the shop to see if they have a copy for you before you arrive.

Open: late-March to early-January, and only closes during the height of the rains

Getting there
By air
During the main safari season, from June to the end of October, Mfuwe is one of the easiest places in Zambia to reach by air. Currently it is regularly serviced by Zambian Airways (formerly Roan Air), Eastern Air and Proflight. Expect a one-way trip between Lusaka and Mfuwe to cost around US$160 per person; double that for a return.

By road
Arriving cross-country **from Mpika**, via Luambe National Park, is possible in the dry season as there are tracks – see page 255 for directions. However, without at least two well-equipped 4WD vehicles, and a very high degree of self-reliance, this route is neither safe nor practical.

Approaching **from Chipata** is by far the easiest way to reach the park if you are driving. As you enter Chipata from Lusaka, you pass under a 'Welcome to Chipata' arch over the road (the independence memorial archway). Instead of going under this, turn left before it. The turn-off is marked with many small signs for local companies, but there are probably still none to Mfuwe or South Luangwa.

This road winds down from the high escarpment and into the valley. The views are spectacular, and you will pass many local villages on the way. Keep the windows open and you will feel both the temperature and the humidity rise as you descend.

This road continues for about 67km to the Chisengu turn-off where the right-hand road becomes a rough track leading (if passable) to Chibembe. The left leads to Jumbe after about 16km, then forks left over a bridge. After this there's a short stretch of tar over Mpata Hill, and some 15km further on, after passing a small catholic church, the road forks – keep left. At the tarmac T-junction turn left to get to Mfuwe Airport (about 3–4km), or right for Mfuwe Bridge and the park. From Chipata by this route it's about 95km to Mfuwe airport, or about 115km to the main bridge into the park over the Luangwa River.

4WD vehicles coming from Lusaka could take an earlier turn off the great East Road, and approach the south by the road **from Petauke**. This beautiful road is slower and more difficult, taking about 150km to reach the park's southern gate at Chilongozi, then a further 40km to Mfuwe.

Hitchhiking
With plenty of water and stamina, getting to Mfuwe from Chipata is possible. Start hitching early at the turn-off, or outside the Chipata Motel. (You can always sleep there if necessary.) Don't accept local lifts going just a few kilometres, there's no point – better to wait for a vehicle going at least to Mfuwe airport. Some of the camps have trucks doing supply-runs to Chipata, there are occasional tourists (though fewer with space to spare), and there is a small amount of local traffic. As

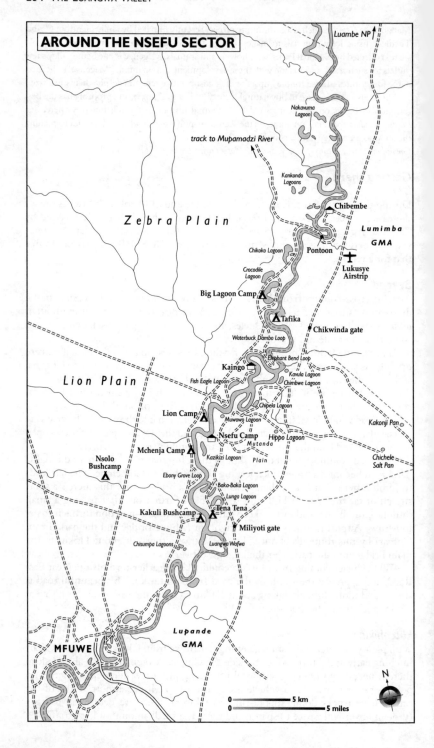

AROUND THE NSEFU SECTOR

Luambe NP

Nakavuma Lagoon

track to Mupamadzi River

Kankondo Lagoons

Zebra Plain

Chibembe

Lumimba GMA

Chikoko Lagoon

Pontoon

Crocodile Lagoon

Lukusye Airstrip

Big Lagoon Camp

Tafika

Chikwinda gate

Waterbuck Dambo Loop

Elephant Bend Loop

Kaingo

Kavula Lagoon

Chimbwe Lagoon

Lion Plain

Fish Eagle Lagoon

Chipela Lagoon

Lion Camp

Muwowo Lagoon

Kakonji Pan

Nsefu Camp

Hippo Lagoon

Mchenja Camp

Mutanda

Chichele Salt Pan

Nsolo Bushcamp

Kazikizi Lagoon

Plain

Ebony Grove Loop

Baka-Baka Lagoon

Lunga Lagoon

Kakuli Bushcamp

Tena Tena

Miliyoti gate

Chisumpa Lagoons

Luangwa Wafwa

Lupande GMA

MFUWE

N

0 — 5 km
0 — 5 miles

far as I know, there are no regular bus services. I took five hours to get a lift from here one October morning, so expect a *long* wait.

Getting around
In your own vehicle
South Luangwa's network of roads is not as extensive as you might expect. A few all-weather roads (mostly graded gravel) have been built in the park around the Mfuwe area – accessible over the main bridge into the park. These are the only roads that can be relied upon during the wet season.

Elsewhere, the park has seasonally passable roads that are (optimistically) marked on some of the maps. Such tracks follow both banks of the Luangwa, north and south of Mfuwe, and a few penetrate westwards into the park. In the areas near camps, there are numerous 'loop' roads, which leave these main tracks and return to them. These are just side roads for game viewing, and trying to be precise about their position is pointless – they are usually made simply by the passage of a few vehicles, and will disappear again very swiftly once the vehicles stop.

Note that if you are driving your own vehicle around the park then you are limited to being in the park from dawn to dusk. You are not allowed to stay in and drive around after dark, as only the local safari companies have licences to conduct night drives. (Note also that the Nkwali pontoon marked on many maps opens 1 June to 31 October and is *not* for use by private vehicles.)

Without a vehicle
If you do not have a vehicle of your own, then you should organise your camps or lodges before you arrive. If you haven't done so before you arrive, then you may be limited to the Wildlife Camp or Flatdogs. If your budget is higher, then you might consider stopping at Moondogs Café (by the airport) and asking them to radio a few of the more upmarket camps to see if any have space left. This is unusual, and don't expect bargains (as you won't find any), but it is a real waste to get all the way here and then not make the most of the park. So if you can, splash out on the best place that you can afford.

Maps
Two different maps of the South Luangwa National Park are available in Lusaka. One showing South Luangwa and Luambe National Parks was compiled for the National Tourist Board, and is useful in giving the general scheme of the area's roads. Otherwise the information on its reverse side is fairly dated, and so not very valuable.

A second very different map concentrates on just the South Luangwa National Park. This was produced in 1989 using aid donations and shows the landscape and vegetation in considerable scientific detail. Its reverse side details the various land systems in the area: the different combinations of land form, rock, soil and vegetation in the park. This is a fascinating map which has some of the camps marked, but only a few of the existing roads.

In the unlikely event that you need to navigate yourself at all, get both of these and consider also buying more detailed Ordnance Survey-style maps available from the Surveyor General's office in Lusaka. Such detailed maps would be essential for visits to Luambe or Lukusuzi.

Where to stay
Upmarket camps and lodges
Most of South Luangwa's camps aim at upmarket visitors from overseas. Given the park's remote location, this is not surprising. They incur great difficulties (and

costs) in communicating, organising supplies, and actually getting clients into the valley. Then remember that many of them can only operate for six months of the year, after which they pack up, returning to re-build their camps after every rainy season. Thus, they do have some plausible reasons to be expensive.

The rates at these camps generally include your meals and activities for around US$250–350 per person per day. Some will also include your bar bill and park fees in this.

Most offer a special 'safari rate', typically about 5–10% cheaper than the normal rate, if you stay in camps run by just one operator for seven nights or more. This can be very convenient and is certainly recommended. It will provide a welcome continuity whilst you visit totally different camps. Such combinations include Kapani and its bushcamps; Nkwali, Tena Tena and Nsefu; Tafika and Mwaleshi; Mfuwe and its bushcamps.

A few offer discounts if you are a resident of Zambia, especially when they're desperate for trade. In the busier parts of the season (August to October) when they're likely to be full, these are often 'unavailable'.

Note that although many of the camps cost about the same, their atmospheres and styles differ greatly – so choose carefully.

For a complete trip to the valley, using smaller camps of a high standard, the author can personally recommend Norman Carr Safaris, Robin Pope Safaris and Remote Africa Safaris. All offer several camps that have been consistently excellent over the last four years. Kaingo and the new Kafunta should also be mentioned, as good individual camps. Mfuwe Lodge is new, very luxurious and must also be considered; it promises something totally different to the rest. Doubtless in the next edition of this guide this list of my favourites will change – and I look forward to readers advising me of their own favourites after visiting.

The valley's camps, in alphabetical order, include:

Big Lagoon Camp Contact via Lion Camp, via Naturelink
Planned in the same mould as Lion Camp (see page 241), Big Lagoon Camp is another old safari site, long disused. If Lion camp goes well, then Big Lagoon is planned to open in 2001. Expect around 8 tents built on raised wooden platforms.

Bilimungwe Trails Camp (4 twin-bed chalets) Contact via Ulendo Safaris (see page 257) About 46km (as the eagle flies) southeast of Mfuwe, Bilimungwe stands about a hundred metres from the Luangwa, slightly upstream of its confluence with the Kampamba River. Its central bar/dining area has been originally and beautifully designed as a thatched roof suspended between the trunks and branches of some tall old trees (mostly Natal mahoganies, *Trecilia emetica*). Underneath is a platform of wooden decking with a bar one end and tables at the other. A fascinating design with open sides – allowing a cool breeze through in the heat.

Accommodation is in very comfortable chalets, and the camp overlooks a vlei. Chalets have tall thatched roofs, and walls made of cane and reeds at the bottom, and mosquito gauze at the top. Each has two double beds, with separate mosquito nets, and an en-suite shower, a toilet and two wash basins. This is the height of luxury for a Luangwa bushcamp – hence they've called it a 'trails camp'! Activities concentrate on walking safaris, though sometimes there are short drives in the late afternoon and into the evening.

Transfers here from Mfuwe take about three hours, and the drive down is mainly through miombo woodlands, across a series of the escarpment's foothills. It's quite different from much of the rest of the valley and, although the game on the way isn't dense, it does feel very remote and there is chance of spotting roan, sable and hartebeest which all frequent the area. A stay at Bilimungwe is often followed by a few nights at Chendani Trails Camp.
Rates: US$275/345 per person sharing/single, including full board, bar, laundry and activities. Open: 1 June to 31 October

Chamilandu Bushcamp (3 twin and one double chalets) Contact via Chinzombo Safaris (see page 256)
About two hours' drive southwest of Mfuwe, Chamilandu was originally set up in 1988 as a bush camp for walking safaris. For '99 it has been rebuilt on a new site, again on the banks of the river, and totally refurbished and upgraded – and I've not seen it yet.

The chalets in the new camp are still made of thatch and reeds, have en-suite showers and flush toilets, and have been built with a view out over the nearby Chendani Hills. The twin or double beds have mosquito nets and small solar-powered reading lights, and game drives are offered as an alternative to the usual walks.

One very attractive option is the chance to walk between this and Kuyenda bushcamp and spend the night at a temporary tented fly-camp in the middle. Chamilandu and Kuyenda are about 16km apart, and the fly-camp in the middle is completely set up before you arrive – with toilets, shower and cold drinks already on ice. It is dismantled when you leave and your luggage is carried for you to the next bushcamp, to be waiting when you arrive there.
Rates: July to October US$260 per person including full board, bar, activities and park fees. Open: June to late October. Note: minimum of two guests in the camp at any time.

Chendani Trails Camp (4 twin-bed tents) Contact via Ulendo Safaris (see page 257)
About 7km further upstream than Bilimungwe, Chendani is about three hours' drive south of Mfuwe. It stands on the banks of a large, permanent ox-bow lagoon, which stretches away from it on both sides. The main river is about 1km away, and in the near distance rise the Chendani Hills, overlooking the park's eastern boundary.

Chendani's tents are each tucked into the vegetation beside the lagoon, and raised up on hardwood decks. Each has a shaded veranda with chairs at the front, and an en-suite (hot and cold) shower, flush toilet and pair of wash basins at the back. These are really very well furnished for such a small camp – with large writing desks and deck chairs and great attention to detail. The central dining room/bar area is also on wooden decking, in the centre of the four tents, and underneath ebony and tamarind trees.

It's usual to spend a few days here as well as time at Bilimungwe, and the camp is only about 2km from the Nyamaluma Pontoon (which the lodge has helped to put back into good working order). Crossing the river there, the drive back to Mfuwe area is fairly rugged as the road passes the National Parks Training Centre at Nyamaluma, before heading through a very rugged section of the Chendani Hills, all within the Lupande GMA. It finally approaches Mfuwe after passing Kafunta and Kapani. This is a quicker than heading south through the park, but there's usually less game to be seen.

Chendani is primarily a walking camp, though short drives can also be arranged. On a promising note, in the first half of 1999 both camps reported regular sightings of wild dog in the Kapamba River area; it seems that a pack of nine dogs were frequenting the area.
Rates: US$275/345 per person sharing/single, including full board, bar, laundry and activities. Open: 1 June to 31 October

Chibembe (4 twin and 2 double tents) Contact via Chilongozi (see page 256)
In the northwest of the park, Chibembe was a large and busy camp. Wilderness Trails (its owners) sold it in 1998 as they pulled out of Zambia. This was convenient for a new company, Chilongozi, who were looking to start a camp in the valley at the time.

Chibembe has always had a super location, the farthest north of any of the permanent camps in the South Park. There was a hunting camp recorded here as long ago as 1932, but more recently (around 1974) a larger camp was built with wood-and-brick rooms. Its old rooms stood on a high river bank. Each rainy season the river ate further into the soft sand beneath it, and the camp moved closer to the edge. Every time one returned to the bar, which sat in the shade of a magnificent Natal mahogany (*Trichilia emetica*), there was a closer view of the river!

Now the camp faces the mouth of the Chibembe Channel, as it joins the main Luangwa, in a shady spot under a mix of acacia and mahogany trees. The old buildings have gone, and in their place is a smaller, upmarket tented camp – which started operation in '99. Its stylish green tents have cream linings and en-suite toilet, wash basin and shower with hot and cold running water. Each tent has comfortable cane furniture and the style is slightly Arabic.

Central to the camp is a large tented lounge/dining room/bar with comfy chairs looking out over the river. Chibembe's activities centre on day and night game drives, and there are plans to add two tents (making a total of 8) to the camp for the year 2000.

Rates: US$250 per person per night, full board, bar, laundry, activities and park fees
Open: 1 May to 31 October

Chibembe's walking camps (3 twin chalets) Contact via Chilongozi (see page 256)
Chibembe has always been the hub of operations for five small (maximum six guests each) satellite bushcamps, all situated in a private walking area within the park to the west of Chibembe. This is a super area, long renowned as an area for walking safaris. These are small, simple camps built afresh every season and used exclusively for walking safaris. Each is in quite a different location and there are no roads in the area. Hence when you stay at these, your luggage is carried for you in advance, by porters.

Each bushcamp is made from reeds and thatched; they usually need rebuilding for each season. For '99, Chilongozi's first year of operation, only two are formally open: Mumbulu and Kasansanya. These both have four chalets, and toilets are longdrop, not en suite. **Mumbulu** is close to Chibembe, about 30 minutes' walk, and means 'wild dog', though it's not an area noted for its sightings of them. (This was called 'Mbulu' for a while, meaning 'monitor lizard', but perhaps this doesn't have quite the same crowd-pulling potential?) **Kasansanya** is about an hour's drive further on, on a big bend in the Luangwa.

For the year 2000, they plan to open a third of the bushcamps, possibly **Chunga**, and also to install en-suite flushing loos in all three. If all goes to plan, then the following year they'll finally open the last two, Nakaloya and Makavuma.

Rates: US$250 per person per night, full board, bar, laundry, activities and park fees
Open: 1 June to 31 October

Chichele Safari Lodge (30 rooms) Star of Africa, P. Bag 6, Hillside, Zimbabwe. Tel: (2639) 41225 or 41715 or 41837; fax: (2639) 229909
About 15km southwest of Mfuwe Lodge, Chichele was another large and decaying lodge, once owned by the parastatal 'National Hotels', which has recently been put out to private management. It stands in a hilly area where the river starts to come much closer to the escarpment. Around it are a variety of environments including miombo woodland and mopane glades, on soil that varies from patches of gravel/sand to patches of black-cotton soil. The lodge itself is high up, atop a hill named President Hill, as Chichele was the president's private lodge in the Luangwa during KK's reign.

It has now been taken on by a new company: Star of Africa, owned and run by Allan and Scotty Elliot. They come to Zambia with a long history of operating good – if slightly mass-market and formulaic – lodges in Zimbabwe under the 'Touch the Wild' banner. (Irreverently known by local wits as 'Touch the Wallet'.)

They were just starting the building work in June '99, and are selling rooms for Christmas '99. It seems likely that they will use some form of tented accommodation on the site (perhaps on a spot known as Puku Ridge) until the gargantuan task of renovation and rebuilding is completed.

If and when completed, it seems that Star of Africa have been forced to keep many of Chichele's present buildings for their alleged historical value. Given that many of these cut the skyline and are in an advanced state of disrepair, that's no easy task. The company's stated plan of development involved splitting the lodge, with 20 rooms in the section on top of the hill, and another ten in a smaller section down the hill. If you book Chichele in advance, do make very sure that it is open and operational *before* you do so; ask to speak to someone who has actually seen the lodge themselves.

Chinzombo Safari Lodge (9 twin-bed chalets) Contact via Chinzombo Safaris (see page 256)

Coming from Mfuwe Airport, turn left just before the bridge to reach several of the camps including the old Chinzombo. About 4km beyond the main road there's a fork, right for about 1km to Chinzombo and left (a similar distance) to the Wildlife Camp.

Chinzombo is a large, shady camp that is dwarfed by the beautiful stand of huge Natal mahogany (*Trichilia emetica*) and ebony trees in which it stands. It's also an old camp, with a respected history as one of the valley's first safari camps. However, in recent years it's lost a lot of its original ground due to the river's continual erosion of its bank (3–5m of bank *per year* would be typical here). When last visited by the author (at the end of '98), its facilities were extensive – a swimming pool was shimmering, and a Mongolian Barbecue was planned – but the camp was looking tired. Its thatched, brick-built rooms were an old design and a little grubby. Inside each were two twin beds (with single mosquito nets), a few rugs to brighen up the concrete floors, and an old-style tiled bathroom with a shower. Meshed windows looked out into the camp.

Since then, I've heard more news. I'm assured that two chalets have been enlarged and completely refurbished with lots of space, comfortable furniture and balconies overlooking the river. All have been re-thatched, there's a new bar and swimming pool in operation, and more renovations are in the pipeline (including a new fleet of game-viewing vehicles for the rest of 1999). It is hoped that these are the first of a total revamp that will see Chinzombo catch up with the innovative improvements that other camps have made, so that once again it's one of the valley's best.

Game drives (and night drives) in the park are the main activities here, and walks are also possible. A stay here is often combined with Chamilandu or Kuyenda bushcamps. The land on which Chinzombo stands is controlled by the Save the Rhino Trust, to which the camp's management pay rent. Thus the camp's rates are sometimes marketed as including a 'donation' to this charity.

Rates: July to October US$260 per person (US$180 in April or May) including full board, bar, activities and park fees. Open: April to early January

Kafunta River Lodge (8 wooden chalets) PO Box 83, Mfuwe, Zambia. Tel/fax: 062 45026; email: miles@super-hub.com

Kafunta is about 9km from the main road between Mfuwe Airport and the bridge. To get there take a left turn before the bridge, signposted to Kafunta, Kapani, Chinzombo and other lodges. Then around where the tar ends (just before Kapani) you'll see a left turn signposted to Kafunta. Believe it or not, this is the main road that runs southwest outside the park and follows the river downstream. You'll pass a road to Nkwali on the right, and another that leads to Nkwali Pontoon. One of the right turns from this road leads to Chief Kakumbi's palace (notable for a large satellite dish and 4WD rather than more regal accoutrements), about 2km before you turn right to Kafunta. The lodge is well signposted, beside the river.

Kafunta was built from scratch by the team that owns the Wildlife Camp and opened in 1998. Its central dining/bar area under a huge thatched roof is very impressive – built around a wild mango tree and closer in scope to a grand Zimbabwean lodge than a traditional Luangwa bushcamp. Half is a bar-cum-lounge, the other is dotted with tables for dining, and both sides overlook the river beyond a floodplain. There's lots of space and beside the bar is a swimming pool.

Kafunta's rooms are, as yet, unique in the Luangwa. They're thatched, square wooden chalets built about a metre off the ground on stilts. Reed mats are dotted around the wooden floor and in the corner of each is an en-suite tiled bathroom, containing a shower (hot and cold), wash basin and flushing toilet. Under a walk-in mosquito net lie two three-quarter beds. All the rooms have mini-bar/fridges, coffee makers and ceiling fans – powered by mains electricity. Their windows have an insect-proof gauze and each chalet has a veranda overlooking the river. All are comfortable, spacious and airy, though their steps made me feel somehow 'separated' from the land around.

Activities from Kafunta centre around 4WD game drives (day and night) and walking safaris. Kafunta is only about 1.5km from the Nkwali Pontoon (an entrance to the park for safari operators' vehicles only), which makes access to the area south of Mfuwe very swift, but it's further from the Mfuwe Bridge. Kafunta's run by a very friendly, welcoming team headed by Georgina and Anke.

Kafunta also offers walking trips from bushcamps in the park, usually using bushcamps controlled by Chinzombo or Chibembe and supplying their own guides and staff.

Rates: US$280/370 per person sharing/single, including full board, activities, drinks and park fees. (This reduces to US$240/330 before 1 June.) Open: all year

Kaingo (5 twin-bed chalets) Shenton Safaris, PO Box 810064, Kapiri Mposhi. Tel/fax: 05 362188; email: shensaf@satmail.bt.com

Where the seasonal Mwamba River meets the main Luangwa River, the small camp of Kaingo looks over the water towards the Nsefu sector from beneath an old grove of mahogany and ebony trees. The dining room is a large brick and thatch building, with an amazing bar made from an old leadwood tree-trunk. Four of Kaingo's chalets are brick with a thatched roof, and inside are twin beds with mosquito nets, and an en-suite shower/toilet.

The fifth is a honeymoon suite in a shady spot on the river bank a little further up-stream. It is reed and thatch, with en-suite shower, toilet and basin. A skylight has been cut from the roof above the double bed; outside is a bath beside the river.

Kaingo's owner, Derek Shenton, is quiet and unassuming, which has perhaps helped the lodge to attain a solid, established and yet very calm air. The camp has been open since 1993 and its guides include Deb Tittle, one of the valley's best women guides. The usual walks and day and night drives are offered, plus picnics in the bush and fishing in the river by camp. Drives lasting the whole day are also possible if you book in for longer than the usual 3–4 nights. Note that the Shentons also run Forest Inn, near Mkushi (see page 259).

Rates: US$285/370 per person sharing/single, including full board, drinks and activities. Open: 21 May to 5 November

Kakuli Bushcamp (4 twin-bed tents) Contact via Norman Carr Safaris (see page 257)
There has long been a camp here (formerly one run by Savannah Trails) overlooking a wide bend in the Luangwa, but Kakuli was reopened by Norman Carr Safaris in 1996. Kakuli is the local word for an old buffalo bull which has left the main herd, and by association was also Norman Carr's nickname amongst the local people before he died.

Kakuli bushcamp is linked to Nsolo camp (10km away) and Luwi camp (20 km away) by the seasonal Lubi River, which makes three-day walks between these three sister-camps a very interesting option. The bushcamp was re-designed in 1998 and its reed chalets replaced with large, walk-in tents provided with simple solar lights. These have an open-roofed, enclosed area at the back, with a toilet, shower and washbasin under the stars. Each also has a veranda at the front, complete with canvas chairs and table, and is shaded by a high thatched roof.

The dining-room bar area is small, simple and comfortable: a thatched, reed-walled structure with one open side, a sprinkling of cushioned chairs and a good bookshelf. The camp seldom takes more than six guests, and it concentrates firmly on walking, though night-drives are possible in the area. A stay here is usually combined with the main Kapani Lodge and sister-bushcamps, Luwi and Nsolo.

Rates: US$290/375 per person sharing/single, including full board, activities, drinks and park fees. Open: 1 June to 31 October

Kapani Safari Lodge (8 twin-bed rooms) Contact via Norman Carr Safaris (see page 257)
To get to Kapani turn left just before the Mfuwe Bridge, and it's well signposted on the right about 3km after that junction. The lodge overlooks a beautiful old lagoon, within Lupande

Game Management Area, just south of the main Luangwa River – thus ensuring that changes in the river's course won't wash away its bank.

Founded by the late, legendary Norman Carr, the present camp was built as recently as 1986, though Kapani's solid, quality accommodation feels as if it has been here forever. The rooms are brick-built, with thatched roofs, heavy wooden furniture and cool tiles on the floor. Mains electricity powers efficient (and quiet) ceiling fans, sensibly placed within the walk-in mosquito nets surrounding the beds. The rooms are spacious, and each includes a separate sitting area with large, mosquito-netted windows overlooking a lagoon, and its own small drinks fridge. They are amongst the most spacious and comfortable of the Valley's smaller camps.

Central to Kapani is its lounge and bar area, containing a bookshelf of local interest surrounded by pictures of the area in former times, including some of Norman and his children when young. (Norman's children, Adrian, Pam and Judy, and even grandchildren, Miranda and Alistair, are still involved with the safari operation.) There's a dining room under thatch by the lagoon and a wooden deck over it, often used as a venue for breakfast. The food's consistently good.

Activities from here involve game drives into the park or occasionally walks if requested. The guiding is well up to the Valley's excellent standards; Kapani is notable for having several excellent and long-serving Zambian guides from the local community who were originally trained by Norman Carr. It also acts as base camp for three small, satellite walking camps – Luwi, Nsolo and Kakuli. Together the four make a fine combination: ideally staying at Kapani for the first few nights (and possibly also for the last night) and then a combination of the walking camps.

Rates: US$290/375 per person sharing/single, including full board, activities, drinks and park fees. Reduced to US$215/270 before 1 June. Open: all year

Kuyenda (4 twin-bed chalets) Contact via Chinzombo Safaris (see page 256)
This is a small bush camp overlooking a sand-river tributary to the main Luangwa, concentrating on walking safaris, and has always been similar to its sister, Chamilandu. It's about 75 minutes' drive from Chinzombo.

The guiding here is usually done by Phil Berry – arguably the valley's most experienced guide with a legendary reputation for his knowledge of leopards. The round chalets, made of thatch and reeds, have en-suite showers and en-suite toilets. The twin beds have mosquito nets and small solar-powered reading lights, and drives are offered as an alternative to walks.

Rates: July to October US$260 per person including full board, bar, activities and park fees. Open: June to late October. Note: minimum of two guests in the camp at any time.

Lion Camp (8 twin-bed tents) Contact via Naturelink at PO Box 15585, Sinoville 0129, South Africa. Tel: (2712) 543 3448/9; fax: 543 9110
Situated inside the park and to the north of the Mfuwe area, Lion Camp stands on an old site. It is being built using tents (with en-suite facilities) on raised wooden platforms, and its designers have a good pedigree in building good safari camps. It's another venture into Zambia for the owners of Kasaba Bay, on Lake Tanganyika (see page 299), and is being promoted by Naturelink in South Africa as part of a circuit of camps across the subcontinent.

It's another new camp, due to open in September 1999. Its 4WDs will have canvas sun-shades and the camp plans a swimming pool. (Quite how the elephants are to be kept out of this was unclear at time of writing!) Watch this space.

Luwi Bushcamp (4 twin-bed reed chalets) Contact via Norman Carr Safaris (see page 257)
A further 10km up the Lubi River from Nsolo, Luwi Camp is equally rustic camp set under a group of tall shady trees (*vitex, breonadia* and *khaya nyusica*), looking out over a small plain.

The chalets are similarly reed and thatch, with grass matting covering their earth floors, mosquito nets, storm lanterns, solar lights and a small veranda. Three chalets have twin beds, while the fourth has a double (it's a particularly lovely room). All have en-suite facilities. Two of the twins have these under thatch, the other two chalets have their toilet, shower and wash-basin under the sky.

A very short walk leads to a small lagoon at a bend in the river (much frequented by hippos). This is purely a camp for walking: either for day walks based here, or for walks linking with Nsolo and Kakuli Camps. It's not a camp for taking drives and seldom takes more than seven guests. Time at Luwi is often combined with its sister bushcamps and/or a few nights at Kapani.

Rates: *US$290/375 per person sharing/single, including full board, activities, drinks and park fees. Open: 1 June to 31 October*

Mchenja Camp (5 twin-bed wooden huts) Savannah Trails, PO Box 37783, Lusaka. Tel: 01 224457; fax: 01 224427; tlx: ZA 40257

Owned by Taj Wixted and run by his daughter, Nulal, Mchenja has a potentially superb position beside the Luangwa River. What really makes this is that the camp stands in deep shade at the end of a serenely beautiful grove of African ebony trees, *Diospyros mespiliformis*. (Which, incidentally, are known as Muchenja in the local dialect of ChiNyanja.)

The accommodation consists of six wooden chalets, a Swiss-style A-frame in design, built on brick plinths. These are not large, and have wooden walls and a thatched ceiling with windows at the front. Inside are twin beds, each with its own mosquito net, solar powered lights, and en-suite shower and toilet. Though I haven't slept inside, they seem ideal if you need to keep warm and wish to be isolated from what's outside your door.

About 30km from Mfuwe, Mchenja stands opposite the Nsefu sector, between Nsefu Camp and Tena Tena. It's not a well-known camp, but in the past was very popular with Italian visitors.

Rates: *US$230 per person sharing, US$260 single, including full board, laundry, drinks, all activities and park fees. Open: 1 July to 31 October*

Mfuwe Lodge (18 twin-bed chalets) Contact via Ulendo Safaris (see page 257)

Mfuwe Lodge has always stood in a prime location at the heart of the South Luangwa National Park. It overlooked the picturesque Mfuwe Lagoon in the centre of the park's all-weather road network. The game in this area has always been prolific and relaxed.

In the '80s and early '90s the lodge degenerated, until it was bought by Ulendo Safaris, the owners of Club Makokola (a successful lodge in neighbouring Malawi). They demolished and rebuilt it, starting from scratch: a huge project. Now complete, this has made Mfuwe Lodge the grandest safari lodge in Zambia but it is big by local standards, accommodating up to 36 guests.

Mfuwe has 18 beautiful split-level, timber-and-thatch chalets. Each overlooks the lagoon and has double or twin beds, encased in a walk-in mosquito net and cooled by a fan; plus a writing desk, mini-bar/fridge, tea/coffee maker, comfy chairs and rugs. The wide expanse of polished wooden flooring (dotted with rugs) opens, through sets of double-doors, on to a broad veranda. In the bathroom there's a separate toilet, a bath/shower with a view, and dual wash-basins. Each chalet is beautifully designed, down to the individual fabrics and pottery used.

Mfuwe's dining/bar area shelters under a vast thatched roof, surrounded by the now-familiar wooden decking. The food is good and the bar well-stocked. Morning and afternoon/night drives are either on high Mercedes 4WDs, which are good for spotting but the driver/guides are further from the eight passengers than is ideal, or on more normal Toyota landcruisers. Walks are also possible, though serious walkers should also stay at one of Mfuwe's satellite trails camps: Bilimungwe (see page 236) and Chendani (see page 237). There's no doubt that this lodge is a tremendously impressive place, and a match for many of Africa's more grand establishments. If luxury is your top priority, look no further

Rates: *US$220 per person (no single supplements) including full board, laundry and activities. Open: all year*

Mwamba (3 twin-bed chalets) Contact via Shenton Safaris at Kaingo (see page 240)
About 7km north of Kaingo along the sand river lies its smaller sibling, Mwamba bushcamp, which is due to open in June 2000. It stands at the confluence of East Mwamba and main Mwamba rivers. Although both are full of sand when the camp operates, there is a small waterhole in the riverbed near the camp. Activities centre on walking safaris, and there's an area of mopane forest close, as well as ebony groves and grasslands.

The three chalets here are shaded underneath an ebony grove. They are planned to have the unusual design of metal frames with reed matting for the walls and ceilings. Thus it should be possible to roll back the ceiling at night and sleep under the stars. The en-suite showers will be cut into the riverbank and eating is alfresco, under the trees.

Rates: US$285/370 per person sharing/single, including full board, drinks and activities.
Open: 1 June to 30 September (note that Mwamba closes earlier than most camps)

Nkwali (5 twins and 1 double room) Contact via Robin Pope Safaris (see page 257)
As you turn left just before the main bridge at Mfuwe, Nkwali is well signposted. Take the road for about 5km before turning left just before the end of the tarmac. Take this for about 2km before you turn right for about 4km more. Nkwali overlooks the Luangwa and the park beyond from the Lupande GMA that includes some beautiful tall acacia and ebony woodlands, a favourite haunt for giraffe and elephant.

Each of Nkwali's comfortable, airy rooms has a thatched roof resting on creamy-white bamboo walls, with a double bed (or two twin beds) surrounded by a large walk-in mosquito net. At the back of each chalet the en-suite shower is open to the sky, while the toilet is enclosed in a small thatched hut. All the chalets have solar-powered battery lights and the camp has a generator for recharging video batteries.

The bar is spectacularly built around an ebony tree, and there's a small waterhole behind the dining room that often attracts game very close to the camp. Nkwali's food is predictably good and the camp feels rustic, but very stylishly so. It's usual to combine time here with time at Tena Tena and/or Nsefu Camps, further north.

Most trips from Nkwali will be drives into the park, which is accessed over the main Mfuwe Bridge, via the convenient nearby Nkwali Pontoon, or occasionally by boat. Walks are led into the park and in the surrounding GMA. Often you'll just cross the river by boat and walk from there. The camp has permission to run walking safaris throughout the year.

Rates: US$250/325 per person sharing/single, including full board, drinks, activities and park fees.
Reduces to US$175 sharing/single for April, May, Nov and Dec (children are welcome during these months for US$85 per child sharing). Open: April until early January

Nsefu Camp (6 twins and 1 double chalet) Contact via Robin Pope Safaris (see page 257)
Nsefu is superbly situated on the Luangwa River, in the middle of the Nsefu Sector. It was first opened in the late 1940s by Norman Carr – Zambia's oldest safari camp – and moved to its present location in 1953. Then the camp consisted of raised brick rondavels that were entered via a few steps.

In recent years these deteriorated until, in late '98, the camp was bought by Robin Pope Safaris, who completely rebuilt and refurbished it for 1999. (Robin himself had guided there for many years before starting up his own company, and so had always been closely connected with Nsefu.) Now it is once again one of the best camps in the valley.

Nsefu's original round rondavels have been retained, but each now has a shady wooden veranda at the front. Inside are twin beds surrounded by a walk-in mosquito net. Soft colours and quality fabrics are used throughout. Large windows look out over the river, stylishly curtained (and animal-proofed). At the back, each rondavel has had an en-suite shower and toilet added – complete with old-style bath taps (but efficient hot water) – which are open to the stars.

The camp has been furnished with taste and elegance, in the style of the 1950s – complete with wind-up gramophone and old silver service. The whole effect is impressive and, despite the camp's creature comforts, it has retained an old, solid feel of history.

Nsefu's thatched bar stands beside a huge termite mound, overlooking a small lagoon and a sweeping bend in the river. In a separate dining area, under thatch, the food very good, and the atmosphere relaxed. A stay here is often combined with Nkwali, Tena Tena, or one of Robin Pope's walking safaris.

Rates: US$300/390 per person sharing/single, including full board, bar, activities and park fees. Open: June until end October

Nsolo Bushcamp (4 twin-bed reed chalets) Contact via Norman Carr Safaris (see page 257)
Nsolo is a small, reed and thatch camp overlooking a bend in the seasonal Lubi River. The chalets are built on wooden decks with reed walls and canvas roofs, twin beds under mosquito netting, and en-suite showers and flush toilets. Solar lights are used in the evenings. The central bar/dining area is open to the surrounding bush, and the camp has a very relaxed, rustic feel about it. It doesn't usually take more than six guests.

Nsolo is nine or ten kilometres inside the park from the main Luangwa River, directly west of the Nsefu sector in a sandy area dominated by mopane trees. Though short game drives during the day and evening are possible, walking is the major attraction. On my first visit to Nsolo the ranger accompanying our walks was Rice Time, a sprightly Zambian hunter who strode through the bush with the speed and confidence of a youth – despite being over 70 years of age. A stay here is usually combined with the main Kapani Lodge and sister-bushcamps, Luwi and Kakuli.

Rates: US$290/375 per person sharing/single, including full board, activities, drinks and park fees. Open: 1 June to 31 October

Tafika (5 twins and 1 larger chalet) Contact via Remote Africa Safaris (see page 257)
Tafika stands on the bank of the Luangwa, overlooking the national park. It is perhaps the smallest of the valley's main camps, with just five reed-and-thatch chalets. Four of these have a double bed and a three-quarter-size bed with two mosquito nets. The fifth has two rooms, with a king-size double in one room, and two singles in the other, all built around the trunk of a stunning sausage tree, *Kigelia africana*. This is usually the honeymoon suite, though is sometimes used by family groups. All have en-suite facilities – including a flush toilet, wash basin, and excellent shower that is open to the skies. Lighting is by solar-powered storm lanterns.

It was founded by John and Carol Coppinger, who managed Chibembe for years before about 1995, when they branched off on their own to start Tafika. John's years of experience in the valley are augmented by the experience of the two other top guides here, Bryan Jackson and Rod Tether. Thus Tafika's guiding is amongst the best in the valley. Game activities include day and night drives, as well as walking trips.

The bar/dining area has some comfy chairs and a large, circular dining table, though dinner is a relaxed affair, often eaten together outside. Tafika is not luxurious, but the food is excellent, the atmosphere very friendly and unpretentious, and the guiding truly expert.

John (who had a commercial pilot's licence at one stage) keeps a microlight aircraft nearby, which can take a passenger. If he's in camp flights can be arranged for about US$60 per 20 minutes, so if you stay at Tafika then don't miss seeing the park from an eagle's point of view.

During the dry season, Tafika works closely with its sister-bushcamp in the North Luangwa National Park, Mwaleshi Camp (see page 254). This is in an even more remote location than Tafika. There are plans for a small satellite bushcamp, Chikoko, slightly north of Tafika on a superb site, but these may take a while to materialise.

Tafika is also open for river safaris in the wet season, around February and March. It's the only camp outside Mfuwe's all-weather road network that opens during the rains, and it's marvellous. See *River safaris* on page 248 for more comments.

Rates: US$300/370 per person sharing/single, including full board, bar, activities and park fees. Reduces to US$260/330 before 1 June. Open:1 May to 30 November (plus around mid-February to mid-April for river safaris)

Tena Tena (3 twins and one double tent) Contact via Robin Pope Safaris (see page 257)
Tena Tena overlooks the Luangwa River at the southern end of the Nsefu sector of the park, about 20km northeast of the bridge at Mfuwe. Tena Tena is not only a widely recognised name in safari circles, it's also one of the park's best camps. Accommodation is (unusually for Luangwa) in large tents – each set on a solid base with twin beds inside, and en-suite shower and toilet at the rear. These tents are very comfortable and insect-proof, and have recently been moved further apart to allow more privacy. There has also been an electric wire installed around camp, to discourage elephants from wandering through.

Tena has a separate dining area and also a well-stocked bar and small library of books, lit by a generator in the evening. (This is usually switched off as the last person goes to bed.) It's been built on a lovely sweeping bend in the river, and there's even a comfortable couch set into the bank so that you can relax and watch the river's wildlife just on the edge of camp.

Tena's activities concentrate on morning and afternoon walks and game drives (including night drives). The guiding, like everything else at Tena, is first-class – it ranks with the best on the continent. A stay here is often combined with Nkwali, Nsefu, or one of Robin Pope's walking safaris.

Rates: US$325/420 per person sharing/single, including full board, bar, activities and park fees. Open: June until end October

Zebra Pans Bushcamp

This small bushcamp lies deep in the north of the park, about 30km from either the Luangwa River to the southeast or the Mupamadzi River to the north. It is situated on the edge of the Kabvumbu Pans, in a low, undulating landscape covered in miombo woodland. As the park's only camp in this type of environment, and the only one not near a river, it was an original choice of site and provided visitors with a contrasting range of plants and trees.

It was started and run by Robin Pope Safaris for several years, almost exclusively as a walking camp. The area had good numbers of uncommon antelope species like hartebeest, roan, reedbuck and eland. However it closed in 1998, due to difficult logistics and generally low game densities of the more common species of game. As the areas around the Luangwa River gradually become more popular, watch out for news of this small, rustic bushcamp being reopened.

Budget camps

South Luangwa National Park is not an ideal safari destination for the impecunious backpacker. Hitchhiking into the park from Chipata is difficult (flying is the best way to arrive 'independently'), and there are no touts selling cheap safaris; just a few budget camps and a lot of small, exclusive ones (with all-inclusive rates) which don't cater well for unexpected visitors.

If you want to be independent, then the best way to arrive is in your own fully-equipped 4WD – as then you can see the park for yourself. Make sure that you bring supplies of food (fresh vegetables and limited tinned foods can be bought locally), and the best maps that you can buy in Lusaka.

Most budget travellers who come to the Luangwa arrive in overland trucks. These travel between Malawi and Zimbabwe, stopping here and in Lusaka. They usually stay, together with the odd backpackers and independent travellers, at one of Luangwa's less-expensive camps:

Flatdogs Camp (camp-site) Chibuli Guides and Tours, PO Box 100, Mfuwe. Tel: 062 45068; fax: 45025; email: Moondog@super-hub.com
'Flatdog' is a local nickname for a crocodile, hence when a campsite opened at the location of the old crocodile camp (just on the right of the main Mfuwe Bridge) in 1992, the choice of name was no surprise. A few years later they offered self-catering chalets as well and gradually Flatdogs (and its maverick owner-manager, Jake da Motta) were becoming better known.

However, as this book goes to press Jake and his team have outgrown that original site and bought about 100 hectares of land beside the river across the road, just to the left of the main Mfuwe Bridge.

It's a lovely site, with lots of shade from winterthorn, *Acacia albida*, and mahogany, *Trichelia emetica*, beside the river. A lot of game currently wanders through the area, including a good population of giraffe (attracted by the acacia trees). It is hoped that these will still be around even after the new camp has been built.

Plans for the new Flatdogs are for an extensive camp, including a 'Dog and Cat' bar with pub food and barbecues; a games room with pool, darts, table football and satellite TV; a swimming pool; a shop for crafts, bush clothes, toiletries and foodstuffs; and a restaurant serving breakfast, lunch, dinner and snacks throughout the day (catering for up to 60 diners at once – with overland trucks in mind). How much of this materialises remains to be seen, but it should be operational by the end of this millennium. Jake's aiming for a lively and 'sociable' atmosphere, including good facilities for children and even a nanny service.

The campsite will be split, one section for overland trucks and another for backpackers and those with their own vehicles. Plans are for both areas to have barbecues and washing-up stands, and an ablution block with eight hot showers and flush toilets. Water is from boreholes; there are plans for lights and mains electric points; firewood and laundry services will be available. Overland truck drivers and tour leaders will get free use of simple thatched cottages.

Flatdogs also plans to build four two-storey chalets, with groups and families in mind. Each will have two furnished rooms with a communal kitchenette/dining area (self-catering equipment provided) and en-suite bathroom. Downstairs is surrounded by a veranda; upstairs will have a tented roof and view of the river.

Activities organised by the camp include day and night drives in the park, walking trips, and also 'nature walks' outside the park – for which you won't need to pay park entry fees. Flatdogs' 4WD vehicles are usually full, with far more people per vehicle than those of the smaller safari camps. The new Flatdogs is expected to offer a different experience from that offered by the upmarket camps, and to charge a different price for it.

Rates: camping US$5 per person, chalets US$20 per person, drive or walk US$25 for the first activity, US$20 for subsequent activities (excluding park entry fees and game drive levies)

Kapamba

This basic camp does not usually accept overseas visitors. It is run by, and for, some of the more affluent members of Chipata's business community and does not have a very good reputation in the local area.

Luamfwa Camp

Well away from any other camp, in the south of the park, Luamfwa Camp overlooks the Luangwa River. It is currently under the care of a helpful chap, Pascal, who is really just looking after it and helping any ad hoc visitors (who arrive with their own transport, equipment and supplies).

Despite many years of building, and a superb site beside the river, Luamfwa is still effectively closed. Given its remote position, it seems likely that guests will arrive direct by light aircraft, and hence it would only be viable as an upmarket, expensive camp.

Marula Lodge (7 chalets: one twin and 6 with four beds each) Contact Salim Mitha, PO Box 510237, Chipata. Tel: 062 21472; fax: 21584.

In a classic position just upstream from the main Mfuwe Bridge, Marula is reached by turning right towards the Croc Farm (and the old Flatdogs site), just before entering the park over the bridge. Despite its beautiful position, this camp is not well known, perhaps because it caters mainly for local visitors from the surrounding Zambian provinces.

Marula's seven chalets are dotted out over well-kept lawns and built like conventional rooms. Asbestos sheets have been used under thatch, with low ceilings and concrete floors. Most chalets are family rooms, sharing a shower and toilet between two twin-bedded rooms.

Previous page Sunset over the Upper Zambezi near Tiger Camp in western Zambia (PD)

Above Open-bill stork on a tributary of the Kafue (PM)

Right Fish eagles are common throughout Zambia (PM)

Below Male masked weaver bird under its nest (PM)

Above Yellow-billed stork in breeding plumage, Nsefu Sector of South Luangwa (CM)

Below One of the colonies of mainly yellow-billed storks in the Nsefu Sector during the green season (CM)

Above Victoria Falls and its gorges seen
from a microlight (CM)

Below Ngonye Falls on the Upper
Zambezi – as seen by Livingstone (CM)

Each has small, louvered windows that contribute to a slight feeling of claustrophobia.

There is also one twin-bed chalet, a pleasant airy bar and a dining area. The camp's focal point is a large double-storey building that contains a comfy lounge for guests, with TV and video on the ground floor, and a simple dormitory with ten mattresses and a fan upstairs.

Guests at Marula usually arrive with their own food, which can be cooked by themselves or by one of the camp's chefs. Fridges and freezers are provided. Game drives and walks are usually available. This is a very simple camp, used more by local businesspeople than anyone from overseas.

Rates: US$100 per person per night, including full board and activities. Open: 1 May to 31 October

Tundwe Camp (6 chalets, each with 4 beds) Contact Steve Blagus Travel, PO Box 37538, Lusaka. Tel: 01 221681

At time of writing, Tundwe is not operational, despite its beautiful situation on the banks of the Luangwa, about 25km southwest of Mfuwe. It used to be run by Sobek Adventures, then was taken over by a group associated with the Busanga Trails team in Kafue.

However, it has not really run on a normal basis, accepting regular paying clients from overseas, for many years. When last seen, its chalets were on two levels, with two smaller beds on an upper level and two down below. All had en-suite shower/toilets, mosquito nets, and electricity for a few hours in the evening. There was a separate dining/lounge area, self-service tea and coffee, and an area for quiet reading with reference books on the area's flora and fauna. Perhaps now that the Nyamaluma Pontoon is back in action, Tundwe will wake up again.

Wildlife Camp (32 beds in chalets and family rooms plus camping) Miles Safaris, PO Box 53, Mfuwe. Tel/fax: 062 45026; email: Miles@super-hub.com

Coming from Mfuwe Airport, turn left just before the main Mfuwe Bridge, following the signs to Kapani, Nwali, the Wildlife Camp, and others. Past the entrance to Kapani, about 4km beyond the main road, this forks – left for about 1km to the Wildlife Camp, and right (a similar distance) to Chinzombo.

The camp has four self-catering family rooms, each with four beds and a separate (outside) bathroom. The self-catering facilities include the use of kitchen equipment (fridges and freezers, electric stove, crockery, cutlery, etc) and also the staff, who will prepare food for you. There are also four en-suite chalets, each with three beds, as well as one new double chalet which has two double rooms sharing a bathroom and sitting room. All the rooms and chalets are clean and pleasant, but none is luxurious.

If you prefer to camp, then there's a campsite here also, set in a large grove of mopane trees, and thatched roofs (without walls) are dotted around if you want to pitch your tent under one.

The Wildlife Camp is run in association with the Wildlife and Environmental Conservation Society of Zambia (WECSZ); see page 104 for more details of that. Sixty per cent of what the camp is paid for accommodation goes straight to the Chipata branch of the WECSZ, to be used for their conservation/development projects. So if you can afford to have a chalet rather than camp here, much of your extra money is going to a very good cause.

The bar/restaurant area is often busy and always relaxed. It overlooks the main Luangwa River and serves à la carte meals and snacks. The camp runs activities including exceedingly popular day and night game drives, and walking safaris. If you have your own vehicle then you can drive yourself into the park (Note, though, that you can't drive at night in your own vehicle in the park.)

The Wildlife Camp makes a good base if you have your own vehicle. Zambians, Malawi residents, and members of the WECSZ qualify for discounts off the rates below.

Rates: US$5 per person camping, US$15 per person for a family room (4 beds), US$20 per person for a 2–3-bed chalet. Game drives US$20 per person, night drives US$25 per person, walks (June to October only) US$25 per person. You must also pay park fees on top of these. Open: 1 May to 31 October

Mobile safaris

There's a lot of hype about mobile walking safaris. Perhaps images of Livingstone or Stanley striding through deepest Africa with an entourage of trusty porters and guides are to blame. I don't know. But these days, let's be honest, it is somewhat different. The term 'mobile safari' is overused.

It used to mean that you set off with all your kit on the backs of porters and camp where you stop. Think, for a moment, of the costs of this. You'll realise that it resulted in either very basic camping stops with few facilities, or more comfortable camps requiring a safari of enormous cost. It also required total freedom to camp where you like, which is now limited and controlled by the National Parks Board for very good reasons.

Although the term 'mobile safari' is often abused, there is one operation in the Luangwa that really does run a proper mobile operation:

Robin Pope Safaris (see page 257 for contact details)
Between late June and late September, Robin Pope Safaris (RPS) organises about twelve mobile walking safaris into the far north of the park, along the Mupamadzi River. The trip itself lasts six days and five nights, and participants also spend at least two nights prior to the trip at Nkwali, and two more at the end at Tena Tena or Nsefu – though a few more either side would be ideal.

The walks are about 10km per day and a truly mobile camp is used, and moved by the back-up vehicle to meet you. The camp has comfortable walk-in tents (each with twin beds), shared hot and cold showers, shared longdrop toilets, and a staff of eight or nine. Typically they'll use three different sites for the five nights, and the choice depends on the game and the walkers' interests.

These trips are organised on fixed dates each year, and take a minimum of four people or a maximum of six. They are *always* oversubscribed, and sometimes booked up a year or two in advance. There's usually a premium charged for walks that Robin leads himself (currently US$100 per person per night).

The real attraction of these trips is, firstly, that they are just walking in a wilderness area. There's no driving, and you are away from everything but the bush. Secondly, you're in a small group that stays together with just one guide. Thus you get to know each other and have a lot of time with one of the valley's best guides. They're very relaxing. (As there is no single supplement whilst walking, these trips are popular amongst single people.)

On a similar note, RPS also runs what it terms 'Mupamadzi Trails' and 'Nsefu Trails'. These are run on a similar basis, for up to six people, using one guide for the whole trip. They also use RPS's permanent camps for a few days either side of the walking camps, and have fixed dates. Typically the Mupamadzi Trail use Luwi bushcamp for two nights, and then one mobile camp on the Mupamadzi for three nights, whereas the Nsefu Trails have a shorter duration and use Chibembe's bushcamps, Kasansanya and Mumbulu, for a total of three nights. All Robin Pope mobiles should be booked as far in advance as possible.
Rates: US$370 per person per night (sharing or single) whilst at the walking camps, US$300 at Mupamadzi, plus costs at Nkwali and Tena Tena

River safaris

River safaris are only possible around February to April, depending on the water level in the river. Then this is the only way to get around most of the park. See *When to go*, in *Chapter 5*, for more comment on the wet season – but if you've only seen the Luangwa (or Southern Africa) in the dry season then you should try to make a trip during the rains. The place comes alive and the birdlife is phenomenal. Only one operation runs river trips at the moment:

Remote Africa Safaris (see page 257 for contact details)
Remote Africa Safaris operate the park's only river safaris, which take place during February and March using Tafika as a base. They are a fraction more adventurous than your average dry-season trip as they utilise dinghies and canoes during the Luangwa's flood.

A typical trip would start with a couple of nights on arrival at Kapani, or one of the (few!) other lodges open in the Mfuwe area. This gives you a chance to acclimatise, and go on some game drives around the park's limited network of all-weather roads. Then you'll be collected for a journey up-river on a six-man inflatable dinghy, which takes about four hours (including stops for game viewing and birdwatching).

Tafika then becomes the base for about four or five days of exploration on the river and its tributaries. You'll usually use three-person canoes, always with a guide or paddler at the back of each, to explore the main river and its larger tributaries. This is typically 100m wide and the hippos in it are safely dispersed. Crocodiles are numerous, and not a threat, leaving you free to watch the birdlife and the game on the river's banks.

Then you'll used motorised dinghies to explore the side-channels and lagoons, which are often stunningly beautiful. For ten months of the year most of these are sand-rivers, but for just a few months they fill with water. Often they are lined by tall old hardwood trees. (I had my best sighting ever of the much-hyped Pel's fishing owl in such a grove during the rains.)

In a few areas the trees open out on to wide, shallow floodplains, usually dotted with egrets, waders or geese. In the middle of two such floodplains, in the Nsefu sector of the park, are a couple of nesting colonies for storks and herons. These rely on a high water-level, and the birds won't nest unless the area is flooded. (This is probably a protection mechanism against nest raiders who would be deterred by the water at the foot of the trees.) The main one of these is a huge colony for yellow-billed storks. These take on a beautiful, delicate pink hue when breeding and the colony is an amazing sight.

When possible, a microlight flight with John is included as part of the 'activities', and doesn't cost extra. These not only add a different dimension to your view of the park, but also allow you to spot game in areas of otherwise impenetrable vegetation.

Finally the trip draws to a close with a boat ride back to the Mfuwe area and a night at Kapani before departing. Such a trip is the only way to take a good look at the park during the rainy season, when the heronries and other bird colonies are at their most spectacular.
Rates: around US$260/330 per person sharing/single, including full board, bar, all activities and park fees.

Cultural tourism
Though wildlife is often the main draw of the Luangwa Valley, increasing numbers of visitors are enjoying meeting the local people and learning more of their traditional lifestyles. Cultural tourism is gradually taking off. Currently this has two main points of focus:

Nsendamila Cultural Village
Very close to the hub of the Mfuwe area, Nsendamila Village is easily found by turning left towards Kapani and Nkwali just before the Mfuwe Bridge. Then it is off the road, shortly on the left.

This has been built by the local communities with traditional rondavels to demonstrate a local village's way of life. It includes a traditional healer, a blacksmith, and examples of traditional food and drink and how these are prepared. A local person will show you around.

Exhibitions of traditional dancing are performed at 14.00–16.00, currently on Monday, Tuesday, Thursday and Saturday, though these can be organised at other times on request. It is also a crafts centre where local people display their wares. You can be sure of finding interesting local crafts here and also that your money goes direct to the local community.

Kawaza Village Tourism Project Contact via Robin Pope Safaris (see page 257)
This is very different from Nsendamila, and involves visitors staying overnight with the village,

to spend time with people from this Kunda community and learn more of their daily ways of living, traditions and culture. It was started as an effort to end the villagers' feeling of exclusion. Some of the communities around Mfuwe feel that a lot of overseas visitors arrive and leave… but without ever having any form of real cultural exchange or even social contact with them.

They also wished to get involved in tourism to raise funds for the local school, and to support vulnerable members of their community (orphans and the elderly). Kawaza is a real village and visitors are encouraged to participate in its normal everyday life – to help the women cook *nshima* and relish, to visit the local traditional healer, to fish with nets, to visit the local school, church or clinic. Villagers will tailor-make an agenda to suit your interests.

Kawaza Village has long had an association with Robin Pope Safaris, not least because the headman of Kawaza is the father of Webby Njobvu, who is the foreman of RPS's mobile team and has been with the company for about 11 years. Eventually, after many discussions, the villagers put up a handful of rondavels built just for visitors. These are small, clean, round huts of traditional design with thatched roofs. Then, with help from Jo Pope, a Danish aid fund and others, the village bought a few utensils for visitors. An advanced booking of a group of Scandinavian visitors (paid in advance) helped them to buy items like mattresses and mosquito nets.

Now there are nine huts for visitors, some with beds raised off the ground and mattresses, others without. All have spotlessly clean sheets and mosquito nets. There are several separate longdrop toilets and rondavels for bathing (using a large tin bath and a scoop for the water). The food is grown locally and prepared in the village – including tasty cassava eaten for breakfast, with coffee, tea and milk.

Now a committee of villagers runs the scheme. David Mwewa, the deputy head of the adjacent school, is secretary of the project. He explained to me that the village's objectives were 'to provide an authentic Zambian experience and raise money for the community'. For the visitor, this means that the village's earnings from their stay is helping David's village. However, it also means that Kawaza offers a fascinating and genuinely moving insight into another culture.

Activities are really just taking part in whatever is going on when you are there, and whatever you are interested in. That might mean going into the bush to tend the crops, fishing, collecting local plants and herbs, preparing the food, or even going to help teach a class at the school. Depending on the time of year, you will even be allowed to see some (though not all) of the initiation ceremonies for the young people. Men attend only the men's ceremonies and women only the women's, as you'd expect.

Of special interest, usually arranged on request, would be a visit to a traditional healer, a local clinic, or a meeting with the area's senior chief Nsefu – the paramount chief of the six local chiefs. In the evening the community's elders tell traditional stories or sing songs around the campfire.

The effects of this on the community are gradually showing. Some of the villagers are learning more English in order to communicate better with visitors. David commented, 'When the visitors first came the villagers could not imagine dancing together with a white person or eating together. But when guests come to the village they are instructed to join in all the activities… when they see the villagers putting up a roof they join them… it's fantastic. The visitors like it that way.'

Further, the school is benefiting very directly, as a proportion of the money paid automatically goes straight into school funds. The school's five-year plan now includes building more staff housing and making sports facilities for the children, as well as getting solar lighting units and buying a few radio-cassette machines.

If you've never really tried to put yourself in a totally different culture, then you *must* spend a night here. It'll make you think about your own culture as much as Kawaza's, and you'll remember it long after you've forgotten the animals.

Rates: US$100 per person per night, including a US$35 donation for the school

NORTH LUANGWA NATIONAL PARK

Park fees: US$20 per person (Kw10,080 for Zambian residents)
North Luangwa National Park (known usually as 'the North Park') covers about 4,636km² of the Luangwa Valley; half the size of the South Park. It shares the same origin as South Luangwa, being part of the same rift valley. Like the South Park its western boundary is the steep Muchinga Escarpment, and its eastern boundary is the Luangwa River. It has the same geology, soil types and vegetation as South Luangwa, and so its landscapes are very similar.

For the visitor, this is strictly an area for walking safaris; there's very little driving done here. Perhaps the park's most important natural feature is the Mwaleshi River – which is unlike the Luangwa or any of its tributaries in the South Park (except, possibly, stretches of the Mupamadzi). It's a permanent river that flows even in the heat of the dry season and yet it's generally very clear and shallow.

All three of the park's bushcamps stand on the banks of this, and it's one of the few sources of water for the game, which thus gravitates to it. It is shallow enough to be easily crossed on foot, allowing you to follow game back and forth across the river. That's not usually an option beside the main Luangwa, but is easy here. Certainly in the heat of October I relished the cool of paddling across it and even the chance to just sit down in the middle with a drink at sundown. Having such a convenient, cool stream next to camp does make a big difference to both your comfort in the heat and your game viewing.

Recent history

Without the conservation efforts and funds that were devoted to South Luangwa, the country's premier game park, the North Luangwa National Park has until recently been a 'poor relation'. Poachers hunting rhino and elephant met less resistance there, and local people crossed its boundaries freely in search of food. The impact on the game was inevitable.

North Luangwa remained a wilderness area for many years, officially accessible only to the Game Department, until 1984 when Major John Harvey and his wife Lorna (daughter of Sir Stewart Gore-Browne, of Shiwa N'gandu) started to run walking safaris here. They were the first safari operators here and their son, Mark Harvey, is still involved with safaris to the North Park as part of Shiwa Safaris/Zambian Safari Company.

In 1986 a couple of American zoologists – Mark and Delia Owens – visited the park in search of an African wilderness in which to base their animal research, and returned in October '87 to base themselves here. They came from a project in Botswana's Central Kalahari Game Reserve, with an uncompromising reputation for defending the wildlife against powerful vested interests. They also had behind them an international best-selling book about their experiences – *The Cry of the Kalahari*. This had brought conservation issues in Botswana to a popular audience, which earned them considerable financial backing for high-profile conservation efforts.

Their presence here was to have a profound impact upon the park, which continues to the present day. In the early 1980s, elephant poaching was estimated at about 1,000 animals per year. Their second best-seller, the highly readable *Survivor's Song* (called *The Eye of the Elephant* in the US, see *Further Reading*), relates their struggles to protect this park from the poachers, and their efforts to find alternatives for the local people so that they would support the anti-poaching work.

Read it before you arrive, but don't be alarmed: the place is much safer now. Also be aware that their book has been written to sell. It's an excellent story, but does describe events as if they were a personal campaign. It doesn't mention any

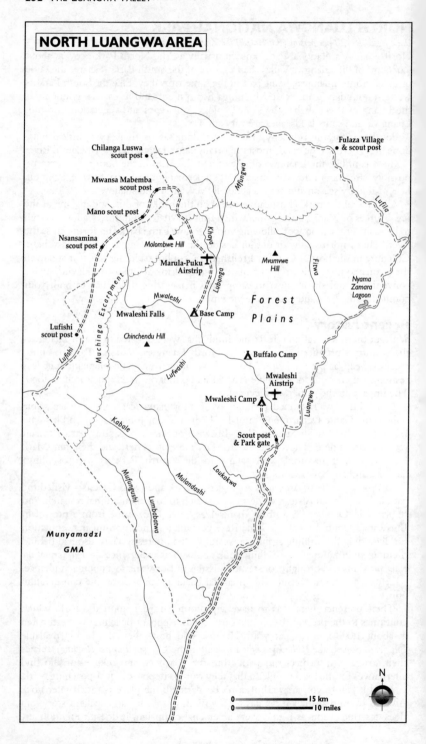

NORTH LUANGWA AREA

Chilanga Luswa
scout post •

Mwansa Mabemba
scout post

Mano scout post

Nsansamina
scout post

Molombwe Hill

Marula-Puku
Airstrip

Mwaleshi

Mwaleshi Falls

Chinchendu Hill

Base Camp

Lufishi
scout post •

Muchinga Escarpment

Lufishi

Kabole

Mufungushi

Lumbabatwa

Mulandashi

Lufwashi

Fulaza Village
• & scout post

Mfuwe

Lufila

Mvumwe
Hill

Khoyo

Lubuonga

Fitwa

Nyama
Zamara
Lagoon

Forest
Plains

Buffalo Camp

Mwaleshi
Airstrip

Mwaleshi Camp

Scout post
& Park gate

Loukokwa

Luangwa

Munyamadzi
GMA

| 0 | 15 km |
| 0 | 10 miles |

N

real contribution to education, development or anti-poaching from anyone apart from Mark and Delia. Others involved with the park have long maintained that this was not a true picture, and that the Owens simply didn't write about any of the 'bigger picture' which was going on at the time. Whatever the truth, it's worth reading.

Present situation
With the dedication of the Owens, amongst others, and the financial assistance that they could direct, poaching has been virtually eliminated. The park's game scouts are now well paid and properly housed, and so have become amongst the most zealous and effective in the country. More importantly, a series of local education and development programmes have been initiated in the local villages around the park. These aim to raise awareness about conservation and to provide alternatives for people who relied upon poaching for food.

Mark and Delia left Zambia in 1996. It has been alleged that they left swiftly, following an incident in which forceful anti-poaching actions went too far. They have yet to return to Zambia. The North Luangwa Conservation Project continued under their direction until 1997, and it is now funded by the Frankfurt Zoological Society, of Germany.

Flora and fauna
In general, the flora and fauna of the North Park are the same as those found in South Luangwa. See pages 227–31. The native game species found in the two parks, and their ecosystems, were originally virtually identical. Perhaps the North Park has some East African bird species that don't occur further south – like the chestnut-mantled sparrow weaver, the white-winged starling, and especially the yellow-throated longclaw – but the differences in species are minor.

However, several differences are apparent when you visit. You're more likely to see Cookson's wildebeest, *Connochaetes taurinus cooksoni*, one of the valley's endemic subspecies. The population seems much larger in the north of the valley than in the south. However, you won't find any giraffes here, as they don't seem to occur much north of the Mupamadzi River. (John Coppinger comments that in his nine years operating to the North Park, he's only ever seen one giraffe there… and it was probably lost!)

Eland, the largest of the antelope, are more common here, and hartebeest are also seen more often than in the South Park. Because of their long lifespan, and hence slow regeneration after poaching, elephant are scarce and skittish in the North Park. This is changing, and the population is growing, but it'll take a long time before they are as numerous, or as relaxed, as they are around Mfuwe.

Lion and especially buffalo seem to be very numerous. The buffalo herds are perhaps even larger than those in the South Park, and form the staple diet for the lion. Hyena are also common, and those in the North Park seem to hunt more than those in the South, and have developed a tactic of chasing puku into the Mwaleshi River in order to catch them. Those in the south tend perhaps to do a little more scavenging, and less hunting.

On my last visit I was lucky enough to spot the dark, angular shape of a bathawk, swooping low across the Mwaleshi in the last sun of the day. I remain unsure if they are well-distributed in the area, or I was lucky.

Where to stay
At present, only a couple of safari operators are allowed into the park, all of whom run small, specialist trips, concentrating on walking rather than driving. Two

(detailed below) have semi-permanent camps in the park. No private visitors, however self-sufficient, are allowed. North Luangwa offers an experience that is even more remote and isolated than the rest of the valley: you can guarantee that you won't be disturbed by anyone else whilst walking here.

Base Camp (5 twin-bed chalets) Shiwa Safaris/Zambian Safari Company, Farmers House, Cairo Rd, Lusaka. Tel: 01 228682; fax: 222906
Situated at a bend in the Mwaleshi River, this small camp is set under some beautiful Natal mahogany trees, *Trichilia emetica*, which provide welcome shade. It is surrounded by plains areas, and all the chalets have basic private facilities. Hammocks are available for relaxing during the heat of the day, and when it is cooler game viewing is done on foot – with only the occasional drive. A minimum stay of four nights here is required in Base/Buffalo camps, with one night before, and one after, spent in South Luangwa or Shiwa N'gandu.
Rates: US$250 per person per night, full board, excluding park fees and drinks. Open: mid-June to 31 October. Transfers from Shiwa or South Luangwa possible

Buffalo Camp (6 twin-bed chalets) Contact Shiwa Safaris/Zambian Safari Company, Farmers House, Cairo Rd, Lusaka. Tel: 01 228682; fax: 222906
Similar to Base Camp, Buffalo is set under trees and all its chalets have basic private facilities. Game viewing is on foot, with only the occasional drive. A minimum stay of four nights here is required in Base/Buffalo camps, with one night before, and one after, spent in South Luangwa or Shiwa N'gandu.
Rates: US$250 per person per night, full board, excluding park fees and drinks. Open: mid-June to 31 October

Mwaleshi Camp (4 twin-bed chalets) Contact via Remote Africa Safaris (see page 257)
John Coppinger set up Mwaleshi Camp for Wilderness Trails (who have now left the valley) some years ago, and so retained control of it when he set up his own operation: Remote Africa Safaris. Transfers from Tafika, in South Luangwa, to Mwaleshi take about six hours by road, and so most people fly between North and South Luangwa National Park. However you arrive, a minimum stay of about four nights at Mwaleshi is sensible.

There is now a good bush airstrip just 15 minutes' drive from Mwaleshi. (The alternatives are Waka Waka, three hours away by road, and Luelo, about two hours' drive.) If you drive, then the road passes through Luambe National Park.

Mwaleshi is a simple bush camp, with four chalets constructed from reeds and grasses, set on a very scenic stretch of the Mwaleshi River. There are two communal toilets (both now flush!) and each chalet has a hand basin. The two showers are also shared, and each has a view across the river. There's a small, thatched dining and bar area, also overlooking the river.

Because the North Park is so remote, in the past the camps here have had a permanent staff for each season – but not usually a permanent manager. In 1999, for the first time, a resident couple, Rod Tether and Guz Thieme, will run Mwaleshi. They've been part of the Remote Africa Safaris team for many years and Rod's a super guide who spent several years running mobile trips into the North Park, and the last few seasons guiding from Mwaleshi and Tafika. Guz's speciality is conjuring faultless cuisine from minute grass huts with open fires – remarkable! They're likely to reinforce my feeling that Mwaleshi is one of my favourite bushcamps in Africa.

Walking really is the main activity here (very convenient, given the amount you'll be tempted to eat), and the first time you get on a vehicle from camp may well be when you're leaving. The wildlife in the camp's vicinity is abundant and there is a particularly good population of buffalo and lion.
Rates: US$300/370 per person sharing/single, including full board, bar, activities and park fees. Flight transfers from South Luangwa cost about US$150 each way. Open: mid-June to 31 October

LUAMBE NATIONAL PARK

Park fees: US$20 per person (Kw10,080 for Zambian residents)
This small park, just 247km^2, is situated between North and South Luangwa national parks and only reachable between about May and October. The first serious rains turn the area's powdery black-cotton soil into an impassable quagmire – impossible even for the best 4WD. Even in the dry season the roads are bad, as the black-cotton soil seems to set into bumps with the onset of the dry season.

Getting there

You'd be foolish to drive to Luambe with fewer than two 4WD vehicles, with spares, and plenty of food and water. Some form of reliable emergency back-up is vital in case of accident or breakdown.

From South Luangwa

The entrance to the park is about 80km north of Mfuwe. Just take the track north that passes Chibembe heading towards Chama and continue driving – there's a small scout camp and a boom across the road at the entrance to the park. This road continually deteriorates beyond South Luangwa, and little traffic gets this far. Perhaps one vehicle passing per day would be normal.

From Mpika

Take the Lusaka road southwest from Mpika, and then take a left on to a track after about 40km. After 26km, this track passes the Bateleur Farm where camping is possible (arranged in advance with Mr and Mrs Stone at Northern Meat Products in Mpika, see page 276). About 46km from the main road you reach the Ntunta Escarpment, with its breathtaking view over the whole Luangwa Valley.

The road now becomes very rough as it descends down the escarpment, and after about 11km (it feels longer) you will reach the Mutinonondo River. Cross this, and after 8km there's a turning to the left which would take you to the Nabwalya Village in the middle of the Munyamadzi Game Management Area. In the dry season there's a pontoon across the Luangwa just south of Nabwalya village (near Nyamphala Hunting Camp), and once across you can join the 'main' road linking Chibembe and South Luangwa with Luambe.

If you continue straight on and don't turn left to Nabwalya, then after about 15km you will reach the Chifungwe Game Scouts' Camp on the Mupamadzi River – the boundary to South Luangwa National Park. Crossing the Mupamadzi and heading due south will take you right across the heart of the park, skirting around the western side of Zebra Pans. About 55km after the Mupamadzi you will reach the Lubi River (usually just deep sand) and then some 10km after that you will join one of the all-weather roads in the Mfuwe area.

Flora and fauna

Luambe is mostly mopane woodland, and some of this is beautiful, tall cathedral mopane with lots of space between the trees and very little undergrowth. There are also areas of miombo woodlands and grasslands.

Luambe is a small park in the middle of a large Game Management Area, where hunting is allowed. Thus, although the ecosystem is virtually identical to that of the North and South Luangwa parks, the game densities are lower. There is game left, but a trip here is worthwhile for the birdwatching, which is excellent, and the sense of isolation.

Where to stay

There is currently nowhere in the park to stay. Although older guidebooks may imply that a camp will soon open here, it seems highly unlikely.

LUKUSUZI NATIONAL PARK

This remote park is on the eastern side of the Luangwa Valley, slightly higher in altitude than the other parks in the valley. There are no facilities here at all – just a game scouts' camp at the gate, and an exceedingly poor track leading through the park. Equally, it is uncertain how much wildlife has survived the poaching here, though it is thought that the dominant predator here is the spotted hyena, rather than the lion. The vegetation is mostly miombo woodland, dotted with grassland. Visiting the park requires a small expedition.

Getting there

There is a track that turns east from the 'main' Chibembe–Luambe track, and then continues through Lukusuzi National Park until it reaches the Great East Road. This is in very poor repair and impassable during the rains. The easiest approach to the park would be to take the Great East Road to Chipata, then turn north towards Lundazi. About 110km beyond Chipata there is a track on the left to Lukusuzi. There is a game scouts' camp at the park's entrance, so stop and ask them for advice about the park before you go any further.

LUANGWA VALLEY SAFARI OPERATORS

When choosing a camp or local operator, it's important that you pick a good and reliable one. You're in such a remote area that you can't afford to have problems. One safeguard is to seek advice from a good, independent overseas tour operator – who would rather not send you than send you to a place that you won't enjoy. They should keep up to date with the latest developments and can plan your whole trip for you. Perhaps also check out Sunvil Discovery's website, www.sunvil.co.uk (even if you're not arranging a trip with Sunvil Discovery), as I hope to post updates there for all to see.

Meanwhile, selected snippets of background information on a few of the main safari operators are included here, in alphabetical order:

Chilongozi, P Bag 286x, Ridgeway, Lusaka. Tel: 01 265814; fax: 262291; email: info@chilongozi.com

Chilongozi is a relatively new company, owned and run by Tim Came, Justin Matterson and Henry Hallward. They originally had strong links with Tongabezi, and especially with the old 'Tongabezi Expeditions' company. Now they are totally separate, with a new name and most of the Zambian operations of the old Wilderness Trails (sold to them in 1998).

Their main lodge is Chibembe, which they have essentially rebuilt for the 1999 season. They also have five walking camps in a lovely area near the Mupamadzi, plus a small tented camp in Kafue (see page 338), a plan to re-build Ntemwa there, and an interest in operations on Livingstone Island, beside the Victoria Falls.

Chinzombo Safaris PO Box: 30106, Lusaka. Tel: 062 211644; fax: 226736; email: chincamp@zamnet.zm or chinzsaf@zamnet.zm

Chinzombo Safaris operates Chinzombo Safari Lodge, as well as two smaller bush camps, Kuyenda and Chamilandu, which are designed mainly for small parties going on walking safaris. Pivotal to the company is the tall, brusque Phil Berry, who is renowned for his knowledge of leopards and has been widely regarded as the most senior guide in the valley since Norman Carr died.

Norman Carr Safaris PO Box 100, Mfuwe. Tel: 062 45015, fax: 45025;
email: kapani@super-hub.com
Norman Carr himself lived at Kapani until he died, and his children and grandchildren are
still involved with the company. Operations encompass Kapani Safari Lodge and three
bushcamps used for walking trips – Nsolo, Luwi and Kakuli – and all are now run by a
capable team including Nick Aslin, Craig Doria and Miranda Carr. All are excellent camps
and Norman Carr Safaris rightly retains one of the best reputations of any company in the
valley.

Remote Africa Safaris PO Box 5, Mfuwe. Tel: 062 45018; fax: 45059;
email: Remote.Africa@satmail.bt.com
Founded by John and Carol Coppinger, Remote Africa Safaris is a small but high-quality
operator with two excellent camps and truly innovative ideas. John used to run Wilderness
Trails in the valley, and is regarded as one of the most experienced guides there. Remote
Africa's camps are Tafika in South Luangwa and Mwaleshi in the North Park, and its guides
include Rod Tether and Bryan Jackson, who are experts on the area in their own right.

Remote Africa is the only company to run river safaris (during February and March) and
John pilots the valley's only microlight aircraft, which is based at Tafika. John's one of the
very few people to have canoed the length of the Mwaleshi and Luangwa Rivers, and Remote
Africa is another of the valley's very best operators.

Robin Pope Safaris PO Box 80, Mfuwe. Tel: 062 45090; fax: 45051;
email: rps@super-hub.com
Robin Pope was raised in Zambia, trained by Norman Carr, and is another of the top wildlife
guides in the valley. His English wife, Jo, was the first woman to qualify as a walking guide
in the valley – but it is her efficiency with the marketing and business side of the operation
which make her legendary. Together with a very good team they run what is probably the
valley's most complex set of camps and trips, including Tena Tena, Nkwali, Nsefu, a range
of different walking safaris (including some true mobiles), and even custom-requested
mobiles throughout Zambia. RPS is an excellent and highly reliable company.

Ulendo Safaris PO Box: 91, Mfuwe. Tel/fax: 062 45041; email: mfuweloj@zamnet.zm.
Alternatively contact via Malawi office at PO Box 30728, Capital City, Lilongwe 3, Malawi.
Tel: (265) 743 501/507; fax: 743 492; email: rob@ulendo.malawi.net
Owned and run by Andrea Bizzaro and his family, Ulendo Safaris was a newcomer to the
valley in 1998. So far, it has had a large and lasting effect. With a successful resort on Lake
Malawi, and considerable financial backing, Ulendo won the bid for a plum site just inside
the park over the Mfuwe Bridge: the old government-owned Mfuwe Lodge.

This was gradually demolished, and in its place Ulendo built a lodge on a scale that the
valley simply hadn't seen before. Initially this drew criticism for its size, as 36 beds was held
to be far too large for the valley's normal small-and-intimate style of lodges. However, when
built it also drew gasps of appreciation, as it has been beautifully done on a scale, and to a
standard, that none of the existing lodges could match. The following year Mfuwe's two
bushcamps were built – Bilimungwe and Chendani – which again were far more comfortable
than bushcamps had ever been.

Having made a large investment in both money and time, Ulendo is very committed to
the valley and to the success of Mfuwe Lodge. They are already pioneering some innovative
ways of linking flights into the valley from Lilongwe in Malawi. The Lodge seems destined
for success, but perhaps it has already done the valley a favour. It has already woken up some
of the older operators to the possibilities of more modern camp design, and set them real
targets against which to judge their efforts.

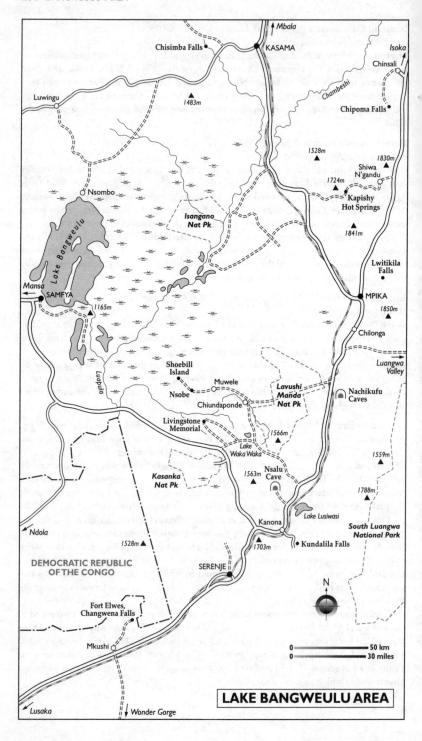

LAKE BANGWEULU AREA

Bangweulu Area

The spectacular Bangweulu Wetlands are, after the rains, a fascinating water-wilderness of a similar size to Botswana's Okavango Delta. A huge wetland area with its own endemic species of antelope, it is also a breeding place for one of Africa's strangest and rarest birds: the shoebill stork.

Nearby Kasanka National Park is a jewel of a reserve, proving beyond doubt that small can be beautiful, while the manor house and estate at Shiwa N'gandu are a must for anyone seeking an insight into Zambia's colonial history. Aside from these three main attractions there are numerous fascinating stops around here – from waterfalls to caves and old colonial monuments – in this area where David Livingstone, literally, left his heart.

MKUSHI

On the way from Kapiri Mposhi up the Great North Road, Mkushi is not just another stop on the TAZARA line, it is also the centre for a prosperous farming area, with a number of large commercial farms in the vicinity keeping cattle and cultivating cash crops. There are shops, fuel, a post office, Barclays Bank and a police post, as you'd expect in a small town this size.

Where to stay

Just outside Mkushi, two farms have lovely small guesthouses for passing travellers:

Forest Inn (9 chalets) Shenton Safaris, PO Box 810064, Kapiri Mposhi. Tel: 05 362003; fax: 362188

Forest Inn is just beside the Great North Road, about 30km south of Mkushi. It is clearly marked. Approaching from Kapiri Mposhi, the inn is on the right side of the road, about 7km past the small bridge over the Lunsemfwa River. About 2km beyond the Inn is the main farm.

This is a small camp run by the Shentons, owners of Kaingo Lodge in the South Luangwa (see page 240). Here there are nine very comfortable thatch-on-brick chalets with simple wooden furniture, electric lights and en-suite (hot) showers and toilets. The farm's fresh produce is available, and there is a restaurant and a bar and lounge area – complete with a very cosy real fire for the cooler winter evenings. Outside are barbecue facilities and a campsite. If you're not just passing through, then the Inn has mountain bikes which can be hired, a grass badminton court, and signposted walking trails for short walks.

Rates: US$32 single, US$45 for two sharing, and US$60 for three sharing. Full breakfast is US$8 per person, 3-course dinners are US$10. Camping is US$5 per person

Sweetwater Guesthouse (7 rooms) PO Box 840041, Mkushi. Tel/fax: 05 362245; evenings tel: 05 362271; email: sweetwtr@zamnet.zm

Run by Vernon and Michelle Cantley on a working farm situated on the Mkushi River, this small guesthouse is signposted about 123km northeast of Kapiri Mposhi, on the road to Mpika. After passing Mkushi, the turning is left from the road, and the guesthouse is about a kilometre up the hill from there. Approaching from the north, this is about 90km from Serenje, just after you cross the Mkushi River.

Sweetwater has seven rooms, in a row, all with en-suite shower and toilet. One is a family room and sleeps four, the others are all doubles. The furniture is simply made, using local timber, and furnishings are basic. Electricity is from an enterprising combination of the farm's own small hydro-electric system, solar power and a small generator.

Behind the rooms a bar/dining room doubles as a lounge. Everyone normally eats together, but at separate tables. The food is copious and fresh, with home grown vegetables and beef. Real coffee on request!

Most people use this as an overnight stop, but if you have more time then there are some interesting walks (with good birding) in the local area, and you are within reach of Kundalila Falls (see page 262), Nsalu Cave (page 261) and Changwena Falls (see below).

Rates: Kw80,000 for a double/twin, Kw60,000 single, including full breakfast. Dinner is US$7 per person. Camping is US$3 per person

Excursions from Mkushi

There are two very interesting sites to the north of Mkushi, and one to the south, though you'll need a self-sufficient 4WD to reach any of them. If heading north, note the proximity of the sites to the border with DRC (ex Zaire), and check the security situation locally before you go. Make sure that you don't inadvertently drive too far, which would be surprisingly easy to do. Explaining an illegal entry into DRC might not be fun.

Changwena Falls

This is a very pretty waterfall, near to Fort Elwes and Mount Mumpu. It's about two hours north of Mkushi, accessible using a bush track road through a forest reserve. These tracks are highly seasonal, so do ask local directions from Mkushi before you set off.

The falls themselves are where a small stream leaves its dambo and cascades through a series of three rock pools. The rocks around are a very attractive copper colour, helping to make this a beautiful and remote spot. Camping is allowed, and from there you can climb Mumpu and easily visit Fort Elwes (see below).

Fort Elwes

Almost on the border with the DRC, Fort Elwes lies about 40km northeast of Mkushi at an altitude of 1,600m. The tracks to get there are in poor condition; ask local directions before you embark upon this trip.

The fort was built around 1896–7 by Europeans who came to seek gold in the area west of the Luangwa Valley. They feared reprisals from the local Ngoni people, if (as planned) the British attacked them near Chipata and the Ngoni were forced west.

It's an impressive structure, with superb views of the hills in the surrounding area. Four huge dry-stone walls, some 2m thick and 3m high, form a rectangular structure, which was originally entered by a single entrance under one of them. Today it's disintegrating, but a few remnants of the original wooden structures still survive. *The National Monuments of Zambia* booklet (see *Bibliography*) attributes the building to Frank Smitheman.

Wonder Gorge

This is a spectacular and steep gorge marking where the Mkushi River meets the Lunsemfwa, as both flow through deep (300m) gorges cut into the sedimentary rocks of the Muchinga Escarpment. It is east of Kabwe, and about 130km south of Mkushi, further south than what is known as Old Mkushi.

The best vantage point is known as Bell Point (apparently after a Miss Grace Bell, who was a friend of the first European to see the gorge, in 1913). It's technically a National Monument but entry is free and there are places you can camp. It's in a very rural, remote area so you'll need a reliable and sturdy 4WD, good maps of the area, and someone to come and look for you if you get stuck.

SERENJE

Northeast of Mkushi, Serenje town itself is about 3km from the main Great North Road (to get there, turn at the BP garage). It has a TAZARA station, a (noisy and busy) bus station, a bank, a Catholic mission, a teacher training college, a fuel station, a post office, a police station, a small hospital, and three basic guesthouses (not a lot to choose between them).

Where to stay

There's the **Sige Siga Resthouse** (tel: 05 382362) at the turn-off from the main road, and also the **Golden Valley Guesthouse**, near the market and bus station. However, the best is probably the **Malcolm Moffatt College Guesthouse** (tel: 05 382151), although this only has four rooms and is 2km from the centre of town – beyond the market at the college.

A useful point of contact, good food and local information is **Mapontela Enterprises** (tel: 05 382026), on the left as you enter the town. They may even open their own guesthouse soon.

Excursions around Serenje

There are several sites of interest around Serenje, though you'll need local help and/or a self-contained 4WD to reach any of them.

Nsalu Cave

This semi-circular cave, cut into Nsalu Hill, is about 8m high, 20m wide, and 10m deep. It stands about 50m above the level of the surrounding plateau, perhaps halfway up the hill and contains some excellent San/bushmen rock paintings. Sadly a few years back the caves were vandalised and a protecting fence erected. Now the graffiti are fading much faster than the paintings themselves, and the fence is no more, so once again many of the paintings can still be seen.

Archaeological investigations have demonstrated occupation by Middle and Late Stone-Age people, and later by Iron-Age settlers.

The oldest paintings are in yellow and include parallel lines, circles and loops. Later drawings were executed in rust-coloured paint, and later ones still using red and white paints together. The last paints applied appear as grey-white pigments and have been applied rather clumsily. They contain animal fats and are thought to have been the work of Iron-Age settlers within the last 2,000 years.

When you've finished looking at the paintings, the view from the cave's mouth over the surrounding countryside is stupendous.

Getting there

Head north on the Great North Road and take a left turn at the sign post for Nsalu Cave, 30km north of Kanona (where there's a small post office, a shop and occasionally a roadblock), between Serenje and Mpika. This is about 15km north of Chitambo Mission Hospital.

Follow this road for about 15km and then turn left at the sign. After a further 8km this track ends and the caves are visible about halfway up the hill, on which a walking trail is marked. The caretaker's house is about halfway along the track, and he may charge a small entry fee to the caves – though is frequently not around to collect it.

The Livingstone Memorial

This plain stone monument, under a simple cross, marks the place where David Livingstone's heart was buried in 1873. He died from dysentery and malaria in the village of Chitambo, where his followers removed his heart and internal organs, and buried them under a mupundu tree that once stood where this monument is now.

In an amazing tribute, his two closest followers, Susi and Chuma, salted and dried his body before carrying it over 1,000 miles to Bagamoyo (now on Tanzania's coast). This journey took them about nine months. From there they took Livingstone by ship to London, and he was finally buried with full honours in Westminster Abbey on April 18 1874.

In 1899, after fears that the mupundu tree was diseased, it was cut down and a section of its trunk which had been engraved with Livingstone's name, and the names of three of his party, was shipped to the Royal Geographical Society in London. There it remains to this day. The village has since moved, but a memorial now stands to mark the spot where Livingstone's heart was buried.

The present Chief Chitambo, Freddy Chisenga, is the great grandson of the Chief who received Livingstone, and if you are lucky he will guide you from his home in Chalilo village to the memorial at Chipundu. (A gift or tip would normally be expected for this.) He is also involved with the community's participation in the Kasanka National Park.

You should also stop at the clinic on the way to the memorial to sign the visitor's book, where you may also have to pay a small entry fee.

Getting there

The monument is clearly marked (if sometimes vaguely positioned) on most maps. The easiest route is to take the Great North Road 36km from Serenje, and turn left on to the 'Chinese' road to Mansa and Samfya. Then turn right about 10km after the sign for Kasanka National Park. This is about 65km after you turned off the Great North Road. There is a small market, a signpost and sometimes a roadblock at this turning.

Follow the main track here for 1km, turning left at Chalilo School (there's a sign to the chief's palace). After 500m bear right to avoid the chief's palace, or left if you want to visit the chief. Then continue straight for about a further 25km and the memorial is signposted near Chipundu School.

On your return, it's best to avoid forking left along the old road which is marked on many maps, as this takes a very long time to get back to the tarmac road. It is, however, a useful short cut if you're heading towards Lake Waka Waka, Shoebill Island or Nsobe Camp.

Kundalila (Nkundalila) Falls

Kundalila means 'cooing dove', and this is one of Zambia's most beautiful waterfalls, set in an area of scenic meadows and forests on the edge of the Muchinga escarpment. The clear stream drops 65m into a crystal pool below, and makes a great place for a picnic and a cooling dip. Look out for blue monkeys that are said to inhabit the forests here.

Note that the falls are in an area of military sensitivity, where camping was not allowed in years past. Now it is common, but make sure that the caretaker is clear about how much this costs. Pay in advance, and obtain a full receipt, as misunderstandings are often said to arise here.

Rates: entry Kw1,000 per person, camping Kw1,000 per person per night

Getting there

Drive to Kanona on the Great North Road, about 20km north of the turn-off to Mansa, and 180km southwest of Mpika. A track turning southeast is clearly signposted as 'Kundalila Falls National Monument', so follow this for about 13km (15 minutes) to a grassy car park and campsite. You should sign in with the caretaker before you enter. The altitude here is about 1,400m so it's frequently cold and windy (and pleasantly devoid of mosquitoes).

At the bottom of the site there is an old bridge across the Kaombe River. The path then splits and the right branch leads you to the top of the gorge – with no safety fences. The left takes you to the bottom, where there's a beautiful pool for swimming, if you can bear the water's chill.

Lake Waka Waka

If you're looking for some relatively untouched bush and a quiet setting, where you're very unlikely to encounter anyone else, then this lake is a lovely tranquil spot. It's good for walking, and makes a convenient camping stop on the way to Bangweulu Wetlands, or even simply a lunch spot if you're not staying. The views from the surrounding hilltops are panoramic. There is game around – including sitatunga and roan antelope – though it's very skittish and scarce.

Getting there

Take the road to Mansa and Samfya for about 65 km, turning right 10km after the sign to Kasanka National Park. (See the directions to the Livingstone Memorial.) Continue past Chalilo School for about 30km, before turning left at a sign for Lake Waka Waka. Note that you'll need a 4WD for this road at any time of year.

Where to stay

There's a basic campsite here, with longdrop toilets and hot showers (bucket variety). Short boat trips on the lake are also available. Camping costs US$5 per person per night, which goes to maintaining the camp and protecting the surrounding area. For more information, ask at Kasanka National Park.

KASANKA NATIONAL PARK

Park fees: US$5 per person, US$10 per vehicle, per day

This small park is the first privately managed national park in Zambia. It is run by a charity, the Kasanka Trust, and the proceeds from tourism go directly into conservation and development in the park and surrounding communities. It is only 420km² in area, but encompasses a wide variety of vegetation zones from dry evergreen forests to various types of moist forest and permanent papyrus swamps. The park and its camps are so well kept that it really is a delightful place to spend a relaxing few days, and keen bird-watchers will find many more pressing reasons to visit.

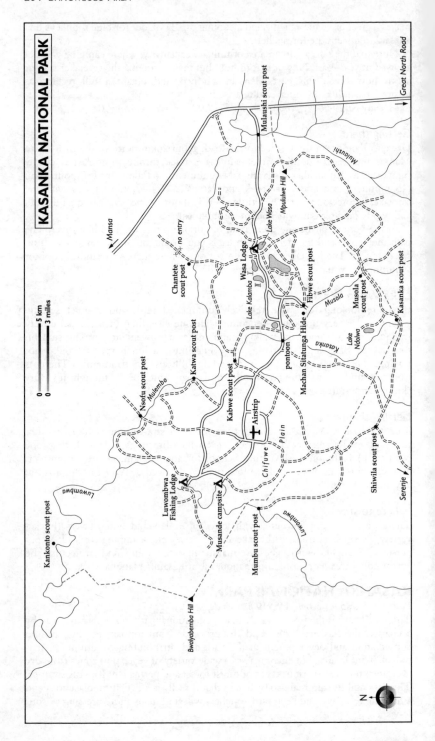

KASANKA NATIONAL PARK

History

Kasanka was made a national park in 1972, but it was poorly maintained and poaching was rife until the late 1980s. Then an initiative was started by David Lloyd, a former district officer, and Gareth Williams, a local commercial farmer. With the approval of the National Parks and Wildlife Department and the local community, they started to put private money into revitalising the park.

In 1990 the National Parks Department signed a management contract with the Kasanka Trust, giving the latter the right to manage the park and develop it for tourism in partnership with the local community. The trust, which is linked to a registered charity based in London (contact Dr T Ashworth at 22 Limehouse Cut, London E14 6NQ. Tel: 020 7515 2826; email kasanka@online.rednet.co.uk), which appears to be trailblazing a model for the successful private management of a Zambian national park. It has been fortunate in gaining the financial backing of the European Union, through the British Council, though this is now coming to an end and the park will increasingly rely on tourism and private donations to finance it.

The Kasanka Trust aims to manage the area's natural resources for the benefit of both the wildlife and the local people. Thus the local chief, Chief Chitambo IV, who rules over the communities in the park's immediate area, is represented on the committee that runs the park.

Geography, flora and fauna

Kasanka is on the southern fringes of the Bangweulu Swamps, and just 30km from the border with DRC. It is almost completely flat and, lying at an altitude of about 1,200m, it gets a high rainfall during the wet season (about 1,200mm) which results in a lush cover of vegetation.

Although there are several small rivers flowing through the park, the evenness of the land has caused an extensive marsh area known as the Kapabi Swamp. There are eight lakes in the park, though seven of these are really just small permanently flooded dambos.

The park's natural flora is dominated by miombo woodland, in which *brachystegia* species figure heavily. The local people use fire as part of their cultivation and hunting/gathering activities, which can spread into areas of the park, so some of this is less tall than it might be – perhaps reaching only 5m rather than its normal 20m. The park operates a programme of limited, controlled burning to reduce the damage caused by hotter fires later in the dry season.

There are also sections of much taller dry evergreen forest, where the tallest trees have an interlocking canopy, and the *mateshi* undergrowth is dense and woody. A good area for this is near the Kasanka River around the Katwa guard post.

Elsewhere you will find evergreen swamp forest, with some superb tall specimens of waterberry and mululu trees (*Syzygium cordatum* and *Khaya nyasica*). Around the Fibwe guard post is one such area, and the Machan Sitatunga Hide is perched in a huge mululu tree. Similar species also occur in the areas of riparian forest found by Kasanka's small rivers. Interspersed in these forested areas are open grasslands and swamps. The latter include large areas of permanent beds of papyrus and phragmites, often with very little open water to be seen. The wild date palm, *Phoenix reclinata*, is one of the most common species of tree found here.

Mammals

Poaching in the 1970s and '80s caused drastic reductions in the numbers of animals in the park, but seems to have had only a few long-term effects on the species present. Many of these move into and out of the park quite freely and, as they gradually learn that the park is a safe haven, they are staying longer or becoming resident, and seem less shy.

The puku is the most common antelope here, and other relatively common residents include bushbuck, reedbuck, defassa waterbuck, Sharp's grysbok and the common duiker. Lichtenstein's hartebeest, sable and roan occur in good numbers, while oribi, zebra and buffalo are more scarce. A small herd of elephant is now resident in the park.

Of particular interest are the shy sitatunga antelope, which can almost always be seen in the very early morning from the Machan Sitatunga Hide, near Fibwe guard post. This offers one of the subcontinent's best opportunities for viewing these beautiful creatures in an undisturbed state – far superior to simply getting a fleeting glance of the back of one as it flees from the speedboat in which you are travelling. On occasions 70 different animals have been spotted in a morning from here. It's excellent.

The smaller carnivores are well represented in Kasanka, and caracal, jackal, civet, genet and cape clawless otter are all regularly recorded. Others, including lion, leopard, serval, spotted hyena, honey badgers, and the african wild cat are more rarely seen.

Mongooses are well represented: the water (or marsh), slender, white-tailed, banded, dwarf and large grey mongoose are all found here.

In the lakes, rivers and swamps, hippo and crocodiles are common. The slender-snouted crocodile, a typical resident of DRC's tropical rainforest rivers, occurs here – though it is less common than the 'normal' Nile crocodile. Because of the park's proximity to DRC, other species, which are typical of those equatorial rainforests (but rare for Southern Africa), can be spotted in Kasanka. For example, the blue monkey is often sighted on the western side of the park, occurring with the area's more common primates: baboons and vervet monkeys.

Probably the most spectacular sight occurs only around the start of the rains (in November and December) when an enormous colony of fruit-bats roosts in the Mushitu Forest near Fibwe Hide. Each night they pour out of their resting-place just after sunset, filling the sky as they fly in search of food. The bats have wingspans of up to 1m, making a grand spectacle that is best observed from the area of the Machan Sitatunga Hide.

Birds

With lush vegetation and a wide range of habitats, Kasanka is an excellent place for quiet, undisturbed birdwatching. A list of over 400 species recorded here is available in the park. The rivers and wetland areas have excellent populations of ibis, storks, herons, kingfishers and bee-eaters as well as many waterfowl. The larger birds include wattled cranes and saddle-billed storks, and occasionally the rare shoebill stork, which breeds in the Bangweulu Swamps to the north. Reed cormorants and African darters are common on the more open stretches of water.

Many species common in East or Central Africa occur here, on the edges of their ranges, like the grey apalis, green sunbird, the red and blue sunbird, green lourie or Boehm's flycatcher. Equally, it is a good area in which to seek generally uncommon birds, like Lady Ross's touraco (also known, more prosaically, as Ross's lourie), the African finfoot and the half-collared kingfisher. The park was the site for a recent study of hornbill species by a team organised jointly by the universities of Manchester (in the UK) and Lusaka.

The more common raptors in the area are the bateleur, martial, crowned, and steppe eagles, plus the snake eagles (black-breasted, western-banded and brown) and the chanting goshawks (pale and dark). Kasanka's fish eagles are often seen, and there is a good population of Pel's fishing owls.

Getting there

The entrance to Kasanka, on its eastern border, is marked with a large sign. Coming from Kapiri Mposhi, do refuel in Serenje, as there is no fuel available in the park. Then 36km further, take the main left turning signposted to Samfya and Mansa – often referred to as the 'Chinese Road' because, like TAZARA, the Chinese built it. After about 55km (the milestones on the left of the road are no longer readable!) turn left, where you will find the Mulaushi guard post at the entrance to the park. You may need to register and pay an entrance fee here, but if the post is unmanned then just proceed to Wasa Lodge. If you're flying around, then the park has a good 1,000m airstrip for light aircraft.

For small groups, the Kasanka Trust can organise 4WD trips to visit nearby attractions including the Livingstone memorial, Nsalu caves, Kundalila Falls, Lake Waka Waka and Shoebill Island, including catering and transport. They can also do road transfers to/from as far away as Lusaka, Shiwa N'gandu and North and South Luangwa National Parks (via the escarpment road and Munyamadzi corridor).

Camps

The Kasanka Trust runs all the camps in the park. They can be booked in advance by contacting PO Box 850370, Serenje; satellite tel: 00 873 762067957; email: kasanka@aol.com. Kasanka can accommodate 'drop-in' visitors who want to stay in the chalets, but campers must make an advance booking to camp here.

Wasa Lodge (4 twin-bed rondavels and 2 three-bed chalets)
This delightful spot on the shore of Lake Wasa is the park's main camp; it's about 20 minutes' drive from the main road. Wherever you are going in the park, you should first report in here. Wasa's thatched rondavels are very well maintained, and the shared toilets and bucket-showers are among Zambia's best. It has small solar lights and no generator.

The camp is well staffed and equipped, so if you bring your own supplies the camp's staff will cook them for you. If you don't have food then they'll usually try to help, but if you want meals then you should really let the camp know in advance. They will also prepare hot water for showers, and are generally around for any reasonable help that you might need. A bar is always available.

Rates: US$20 per person per night self-catering. US110 per person per night full board and activities – which is best pre-arranged. Open: all year – but requires high-clearance vehicle in the wet season

Luwombwa Fishing Lodge (6 twin-bed rondavels)
This sits on the bank of the Luwombwa River in the western half of the park. Its accommodation is equally good, with simple thatched huts, three separate showers and both longdrop and flushing toilets. There is a bar and dining area made of reeds and thatch. The camp works on a similar basis to Wasa – you bring your supplies and the camp's staff will look after you. Note that no supplies are kept at Luwombwa, so make sure you arrive here with all your food and drinks, or that you have made arrangements for meals and drinks with the camp in advance.

To reach Luwombwa before dark, make sure that you get to Wasa before 17.00, or it will be too late to continue here. Motor boats (5 seats) with guides are available for hire here, as are canoes (3 seats).

Rates: US$20 per person per night self-catering. US110 per person per night full board and activities – which must be pre-arranged. Open: all year – but requires high-clearance vehicle in the wet season

Musande Campsite
Just a few kilometres south of Luwombwa, Musande is also on the bank of the Luwombwa River. It's normally used for groups who pre-book and stay at least two or three nights, as there are no staff based here permanently. The site has a shower, a longdrop toilet and a shelter. Firewood is provided, and note that you must reach the main gate before 16.30 in order to have time to get here by 18.00.
Rates: US$10 per person per night camping.

Guided walking safari
Led by expert, armed game scouts, these last three to five days and offer a real bush experience: the chance to see the many different vegetation types, insects, birds and animals, and discuss the bush, the project, and anything else at leisure! It usually also includes some time canoeing. The fly camps are simple, but supplies are delivered ahead by vehicle and so you don't need to carry a heavy pack.
Rates: US$110 per person per night full board and activities, including fly-camping equipment and supplies delivered in advance by vehicle. Open: only possible May to December – though you may have rain in Nov–Dec

Special note on camps
The Kasanka Trust has recently received a grant to upgrade the accommodation facilities at Wasa and Luwombwa, and plans to add en-suite chalets during the year 2000. These are likely to cost $30 per person self catering, but visitors booking in on the all-inclusive rate will have priority for them.

What to see and do
During the dry season Kasanka's roads are generally good, and accessible with a high-clearance 2WD. There is a manually operated pontoon for crossing the Kasanka River in the centre of the park, with staff stationed nearby who can assist. Activities organised by the Kasanka Trust include escorted walks, game drives (including night drives), canoeing, motorboat trips and fishing (bream and tigerfish). There's also the chance to see the workings of Kasanka's community-based conservation project and meet its participants.

One such project was initiated in the nearby Kafinda area in 1997, aiming to raise awareness of the importance and benefits of conservation, and to provide alternatives to poaching for the community. Requested in advance, it is often possible for visitors to see some aspects of this project.

Alternatively driving yourself around is easy, though it's a shame to go by yourself when good guides are around and their community relies on their income. A few places within the park are worth specific mentions:

Machan sitatunga hide
A magnificent mululu tree, *Khaya nyasica*, near to the Fibwe guard post, can be climbed, using a basic ladder, to reach two platforms almost 18m above the ground. The views over a section of the Kapabi swamp are excellent, and if you reach this in the early morning and climb silently then your chances of seeing sitatunga are excellent. (Leisurely risers can take heart, I have seen sitatunga from here as late as midday.) Failing that, late afternoon is also good for sitatunga here. This must be one of the best tree-hides on the continent!

Lake Ndolwa
Shoebill storks have been spotted here at a quiet place on the southern side of the park. A small bench on an anthill affords good views over the lake, which has a resident population of sitatunga, and some excellent birdlife.

Chikufwe Plain

This is a large open area of seasonally flooded grassland, which is a favourite place to spot sable, hartebeest and reedbuck. There is a good grass airstrip here, and a loop road around the southern side of the plain.

Fishing

Fishing is allowed within the park (get a permit in advance from Wasa), and the best waters are normally the Luwombwa River, so head for the Luwombwa or Musande camps if you want to do much fishing. The camp's cooks will prepare your catch for dinner, if you wish. The main angling species found here are tigerfish; largemouth, small-mouth and yellow-belly bream; and vundu catfish. There are strict rules that allow only large fish to be removed for eating.

Further information

Finally, if possible, get hold of a copy of *Kasanka – A Visitor's Guide to the Kasanka National Park* before you arrive. It is a delightful and generally comprehensive little guidebook which covers the park in detail (see *Further Reading*, page 397), though one expert on the area described its main map of the camps and roads as 'dangerously inaccurate'. Good maps are available at Wasa.

LAVUSHI MANDA NATIONAL PARK

This park is potentially interesting for its hilly and very pleasant landscape, though sadly it has lost some of its animals to poachers over the last few decades. Until tourism picks up in Zambia, there will probably be little incentive for anyone to try to rejuvenate its fortunes by restocking it with game, and its rocky, undulating land would be difficult to farm.

Geography

Lavushi Manda is over three times the size of Kasanka, and covers 1,500km^2 of the Lavushi hills. It is easily reached from the Great North Road, almost equidistant from Serenje and Mpika, and the landscape is attractive and undulating. To the north the land slopes away, and the park's streams all drain into the Lukulu or Lumbatwa Rivers and thence ultimately into Lake Bangweulu.

Miombo woodland covers most of the park, with some areas of riparian forest nearer the larger streams and many grassy dambos. Though this is very pleasant and attractive and the scouts report that there are still populations of game left, the area has no accessible roads.

Getting there

The turning off the main Mpika–Serenje road is about 141km beyond the turn to Mansa (also the Kasanka turn-off), and about 65km from Mpika. This road goes across the railway line, and 12km later enters the park via a checkpoint. It leads directly east–west through the park, and on the western side of the park it intersects an ungraded road just before a big village called Chiundaponde. This ungraded road runs roughly northwest to Muwele, Ngungwa and Chikuni (and also Nsobe Camp) in the Bangweulu GMA. Continue to Chiundaponde, and you can easily head from there to Lake Waka Waka and eventually Kasanka (via a possible detour to the Livingstone Memorial).

Alternatively, the Kasanka Trust (see page 267) have recently been given permission to bring visitors here, and have in mind to organise some long walking treks in the area. Anyone interested should contact them.

Where to stay/what to see and do

There are no camps, and much doubt over whether camping is allowed or not. If you want to camp, then drop by the regional NPWS office in Mpika and enquire there. If the answer is yes, you'll need all your food, water, and equipment. If you are planning on venturing off the main road, then you'd probably want to arrange for one of the scouts from the gate to accompany you.

Driving through the park makes an interesting diversion; it is a convenient route into the Bangweulu Game Management Area and few regard it as a destination in itself, although it might make a good area for exploration if you are a very dedicated hiker.

LAKE BANGWEULU AND SWAMPS

This area is often described, in clichéd terms, as one of Africa's last great wilderness areas – which might be overstating its case a little, but it is certainly a very large and very wild area, which very few people really know and understand.

Under the RAMSAR Convention of 1991 it was designated as a Wetland of International Importance, and since then the WWF has been involved in trying to help the local communities in the GMA to sustainably manage it as their own natural resource.

Though most visitors' image of a wilderness area is an unpopulated, barren tract of land, this GMA area does have small villages. It remains as home to many local people, who still hunt and fish here, as their ancestors have done for centuries. The old way of conserving an area by displacing the people and proclaiming a National Park clearly hasn't worked in much of Zambia: witness the minimal game left in many of the lesser-known parks. This more enlightened approach of leaving the people on the land, and encouraging them to develop through sustainable management of their natural resources, is a more modern way to attempt to preserve as much of the wildlife as possible.

Sadly, this area has a growing population of poor, rural people. Many rely, at least partially, on hunting and fishing for their survival. Locals involved with conservation express strong fears for the wildlife's future if no national park is declared here. They comment that it is changing fast, and the wildlife scouts do little to prevent or stop illegal hunting. They doubt that the area's wildlife will live long enough to see a sustainable solution to the problem of co-existence. This would be a shame, as then Zambia will have lost one of its most precious ecosystems, and the local people will have lost a great resource for their future.

Geography

The low-lying basin containing Lake Bangweulu and its swamps receives one of the highest rainfalls in the country – over 1,400mm per annum. On the northwestern edge of the basin is Lake Bangweulu itself, about 50km long and 25km wide at its widest point. This is probably the largest body of water within Zambia's borders, and an excellent spot for watching the local fishermen, but is of little interest to most visitors beside the lake's remarkable white, sandy beaches. See also *Chapter 14*, page 301. It is easily reached at Samfya, a small town on the main road from Serenje to Mansa.

The more fascinating area is the seasonal swamp to the southeast of the lake, which covers an area two to three times the size of the lake. Here is a wild area with few roads and lots of wildlife. This is one of the few areas in the country where the local communities are beginning to use the wildlife in their GMAs as a really sustainable source of income. There is little development here, just a small, tented lodge and a simple community-run camp for visitors who arrive on their own. The area still has many residents who continue to fish and eke out a living directly from the environment, but gradually the community development schemes are beginning to tap into tourism as a way to fund sustainable development.

Flora and fauna

Towards the end of the rains, and for a short time after them, this area becomes a water-wilderness of low islands, reed-beds, floodplains and shallow lagoons. From March through to about June/July, the birdlife can be amazing and the animals impressive. This is the best time to visit, because towards the end of the dry season the southern side of the swamps dries out. Then the waters recede towards the lake, and the wildlife gradually moves north after them.

Animals

The speciality here is the black lechwe, an attractive dark race of the lechwe said to be endemic to the Bangweulu area. The only other places where they have been recorded are the swamps beside Lake Mweru, where their status is now uncertain, and the Nashinga Swamps near Chinsali, where they have been re-introduced. They are much darker than the red lechwe found throughout Southern Africa, or the race known as the Kafue lechwe which occur in the Lochinvar area.

Their current population in this area is estimated at 30,000 animals, and herds measured in their thousands are not uncommon. As well as these huge herds of black lechwe you'll find other animals including sitatunga, tsessebe, reedbuck, common duiker and oribi. Some zebra have been translocated here and are now doing well. Elephant and buffalo are frequently seen; predators are uncommon but hyena, leopard and jackal are sometimes observed.

Birds

The big attraction here is the chance to see the unusual and rare shoebill stork (sometimes known as the whale-headed stork). This massive, grey bird, whose looks are often compared to a dodo, breeds in the papyrus beds here and nowhere else in Southern Africa. Its population is estimated at about 1,500 individual birds, and Bangweulu is a vital refuge for this very threatened species. (The nearest alternative spot to see shoebills is probably Uganda.)

Aside from the elusive shoebill, the birdlife after the rains is amazing. Migrants that stop here while the floodwaters are high include flamingos, pelicans, spoonbills, cranes, storks, ibises, ducks and geese. Bangweulu is also an important reserve for wattled cranes, which occur in large flocks here. (There are greater numbers here than almost anywhere else, with the possible exception of the Kafue Flats.) The swamp's shallow waters are ideal for smaller waders, like sandpipers, godwits and avocets. The whole area is remarkable, and worth the effort required getting here.

When to go

Assuming that you're coming for the birdlife, and the shoebills in particular, then the earlier in the dry season you visit, the better. As the season wears on the water levels drop and the wetland areas recede further north, nearer the lake. With these go the birds, and especially the shy shoebills. So ideally visit in March or April … but do realise that Shoebill Island may not be accessible until around that time.

Note that during some of the year lechwe flies and other insects can become a nuisance; the wet season from November through to March is especially difficult. Bring insect repellent here: it is vital. Arriving with a head-net, covering your face and neck below your hat, would certainly not be going too far. Both camps supply mosquito nets, and guests are advised to take all possible anti-malaria precautions.

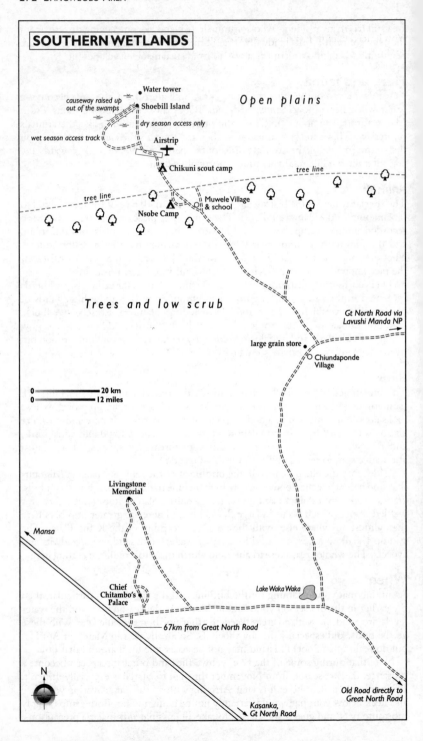

SOUTHERN WETLANDS

Water tower

causeway raised up
out of the swamps

Shoebill Island

dry season access only

wet season access track

Open plains

Airstrip

Chikuni scout camp

tree line

tree line

Muwele Village
& school

Nsobe Camp

Trees and low scrub

Gt North Road via
Lavushi Manda NP

large grain store

Chiundaponde
Village

0 ——— 20 km
0 ——— 12 miles

Livingstone
Memorial

Mansa

Chief
Chitambo's
Palace

Lake Waka Waka

67km from Great North Road

N

Old Road directly to
Great North Road

Kasanka,
Gt North Road

Getting there

You'll need to either organise a special trip here, or fly in, or have your own vehicle and drive in. None of these options is simple – but you wouldn't expect such a remote part of Africa to be easy, would you?

Organised trips

Two operators regularly run trips here: Shiwa Safaris/The Zambian Safari Company (see page 144) and the Kasanka Trust (see page 267). Both know the area well. They usually visit as part of a 6–10-day guided 4WD trip. These often are designed between Lusaka and Shiwa N'gandu, stopping around Mkushi, at Kasanka, here in Bangweulu and at Shiwa. From Shiwa it's easy then to charter flights into the Luangwa.

Fly-in trips

You can simply fly into Shoebill, as there is an airstrip (called Chimbwe) at Chikuni, just 3km from Shoebill. However, the charter cost could be high and the camp currently isn't up to the standard of the camps, say, found in the Luangwa. Further, there is no vehicle usually based at either of the camps here – so just collecting you from the airstrip could be tricky. Hence having a vehicle, a reliable guide (and possibly food) at your disposal would be wise, even if you are staying at Shoebill.

Driving yourself

Best attempted out of the rainy season, or at least after March/April. Note that the road through Lavushi Manda (ie: the second route described here) is probably the better road to Chiundaponde – though there's not a huge difference.

From the southwest via Kasanka to Muwele

Take the road to Mansa and Samfya for about 67km, turning right 10km after the sign to Kasanka National Park. There is a small market, a signpost and sometimes a roadblock at this turning.

Follow the main track here for 1km, where a left turn at Chalilo School is signposted to Chief Chitambo's palace. Ignoring that turn, continue past the school for about 30km, before turning left at a sign for Lake Waka Waka. (The lake makes a good rest/lunch spot.) Note that you'll need a 4WD for this area at any time of year.

To get to Shoebill or Nsobe Camp, bear left after the camp at Waka Waka and continue 40km to Chief Chiundaponde village. About 1km after a large, new grain store, turn left towards Muwele School and Chikuni. Continue along this road and keep left at any forks (including a major left fork on a causeway) to reach Muwele.

From the northeast via Mpika to Muwele

Approaching from Mpika, leave the Great North Road about 35km south of Chilonga. This is about 65km from Mpika, and the road goes across the main TAZARA railway line and 12km later reaches the park gate. You may need to sign in before driving across the park.

About 68km later, after passing through Lavushi Manda National Park, there is a turning to the right a few kilometres before the village of Chiundaponde. Take this turning; if you reach the village you have missed it. Recognise it by noting that the soil colour on the road is light brown, while you are turning on to a track with a grey substrate. If you need to ask directions, the local people know this as the road to Muwele and Chikuni. From here it is about 40km to Muwele Village.

After Muwele village

Muwele village is about 30km after Chiundaponde. About a kilometre after Muwele village and school is a left turn signposted to the Nsobe Safari Camp.

Alternatively continue straight on without taking the turn to Nsobe and you will emerge from low scrub into a plain of open grass, stretching for as far as you can see. Here there is a long causeway leading to Chikuni, but it is in poor condition and rarely used. Instead, look for vehicle tracks which have continued parallel to the causeway, and then left it on the right. After about 4km, you will reach Chikuni. Here you will probably be asked to sign the register.

If you arrive late then it's always possible to camp here, and there may also be a few very simple chalets for rent if you need one.

Shoebill Island is about 10km from here. If you are heading there then continue through Chikuni. Follow the airstrip a little, and then hit out at 30° to your right, following the tracks of other vehicles to the Shoebill Island causeway. If in doubt, try scanning the flat horizon for Shoebill's distinctive rectangular water tower amongst a patch of small trees.

Facing the camp, you will need to bear slightly to the left in order to join the beginning of the causeway (or later on depending on the water levels). If the levels are high, as is typical from March to around June, then you may even have to leave your vehicle with the scouts at Chikuni and continue to Shoebill by boat. Ask the scouts for their advice when you get to Chikuni.

Do allow *plenty* of time for this journey. It takes at least five hours from the Serenje–Mansa or Great North Road to get here. Most visitors spend a night in Kasanka (which can also provide better directions, a map and can check on Shoebill bookings by radio for you).

Camps

There are two main camps in the area: Shoebill and Nsobe. If you're on an organised trip then you'll probably be staying at Shoebill. If you're driving yourself in to see the swamps, then bring all your supplies and consider staying at Nsobe, which is more used to independent visitors – and much more Zambian in feel. It will cost you less, and more of the money will go directly to supporting the local community. Failing that perhaps it would be best to spend one or two nights at each, to get the best of what they both offer.

Shoebill Island Camp (4 twin-bed tents) Contact via Gary and Sue Williams, in Mkushi. Tel: 05 362164 or 362174. Alternatively book via Kasanka.

Accessed down a causeway, Shoebill Island Camp is built just outside the woodland, with a fine view over the swamps. There are large mosquito-proofed walk-in tents and two separate bucket showers, a longdrop toilet and a bar/dining area. During your stay do make the effort to see the camp's best view over the swamps – by climbing the water tower.

If there isn't enough water to travel through the swamps by canoe, the usual form of water transport, then the guides will take you walking over the floating reed-bed in search of shoebills and other wildlife. Alternatively the camp will organise drives on to the drier areas of the plains, and into the surrounding woodlands.

The tents are now getting to look a little old here, and the staff are sometimes sleepy and not brimming with enthusiasm – so don't expect a posh safari camp when you arrive here. However, the boat trips which run into the swamps (possible around February to August) are excellent don't miss them.

Rates: US$40 per person per night, including use of boats, local guides and the RAMSAR levy. (Fully-inclusive rate around US$150.) Camping US$10 per person, boating and guides cost extra. Open: all year when accessible – often March to end-December

Nsobe Safari Camp (5 twin-bed chalets) Contact Sanford C Kangwa, Lavushimanda Safai Company, Nsobe Camp, PO Box 450141, Chiundaponde, Mpika. Or via WWF Wetlands Project, National Parks & Wildlife, P Bag 1, Chilanga. Tel: 01 278231

Nsobe is the local name for the sitatunga, and Nsobe Camp is billed as Zambia's only safari camp that is wholly owned by the community. The community developed, maintains and runs the camp with the help of the WWF, who are closely involved in the efforts to preserve these wetlands. Nsobe is built in mandamanta woodlands on the edge of the floodplain, and its five chalets have shared ablutions. Supplies must be brought with you, but there is a kitchen with a deep-freeze available. Booking would be wise, but you may find space if you just turn up.

Each of Nsobe's chalets is clean and tidy, with twin beds, mosquito nets, and rugs on the floor. Each also has a private longdrop toilet and simple bucket shower. There are also two flushing toilets shared between the five chalets.

Game viewing is possible on foot, by boat or by vehicle, and boats (with two boatmen) can be hired here for about Kw2,000 per hour. For walking safaris, very experienced trackers are also available for around Kw4,000 per hour, and for the less energetic there are secluded hides nearby. Note that the camp is used extensively by hunters, with whom some visitors may feel uncomfortable.

Sanford Kangwa is currently managing the camp, having previously worked at Kaingo Camp in the Luangwa and also in Kasanka National Park. Nsobe doesn't have as good a position as Shoebill, as you feel less as if you're in the middle of the wetlands. However, it does have a friendlier atmosphere, thanks to Sanford and his keen team.

Rates: US$20 per person; US$5 per person for campers. Open: 1 June to 31 December

What to see and do

Driving, walking, boating and canoeing are the activities here, and all are better done with guides. While the black lechwe are spectacular, the birdlife is Bangweulu's main attraction, and the ungainly shoebill is a particular favourite among visitors.

As you might expect from an area which is seasonally flooded, and whose name translates as 'where the water meets the sky', Bangweulu is a largely trackless wilderness. It is easy to get lost if you simply head into it yourself, and indiscriminate driving does much damage to both the soil structure and the ground-nesting birds. It is strongly recommended on safety and conservation grounds that 4WD owners use one of the camps as a base for their explorations, and take the local advice that they are given about where to go and how to minimise their environmental impact.

Isangano National Park

East of Lake Bangweulu, Isangano National Park covers 840km^2 of flat, well-watered grassland. The western side of the park forms part of the Bangweulu Wetlands, which are seasonally flooded.

The park's ecosystem is apparently the same as that of the Bangweulu GMA's. However, it is reported that the game in Isangano has mostly disappeared because of poaching, and there is no internal road network within the park at all.

Thus visitors are generally advised to look toward Bangweulu GMA if they want to visit this type of area. At least there is some infrastructure, and the local communities will derive some positive benefit from a visit.

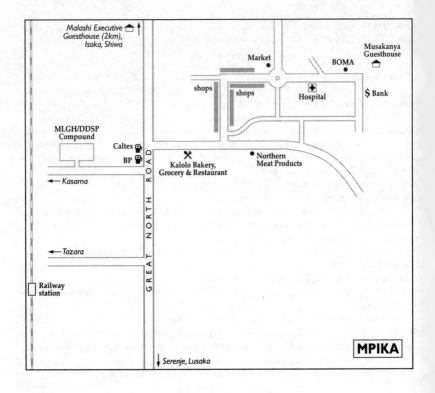

MPIKA

Though not much bigger than Mkushi or Serenje, Mpika is a busy crossroads of a place which seems to have an importance outweighing its size. Here the Great North Road forks: one branch going to Kasama, Mbala, and Mpulungu on Lake Tanganyika, the other heading directly for the Tanzanian border at Nakonde. It is also about a day's travel from Lusaka, Mpulungu or the Tanzanian border, which perhaps explains why one often ends up stopping here overnight.

Getting there

Getting to Mpika is easy; it is getting away that always seems to be tricky. Fortunately there is a choice of public transport if you are not driving:

By bus

Daily local bus services link Mpika with Lusaka, Mbala and (to a lesser extent) Isoka. These all pass by the main central *boma* of town (the central, circular meeting place), so if you wait there you shouldn't miss any of them. Sometimes, the same buses will pick you up if you wave them down whilst hitchhiking, but not always.

By train

The TAZARA station is about 5–6km out of town, almost on the road to Kasama, and private pick-up trucks operate shuttle runs between there and the central boma in Mpika, fitting as many people on to the vehicles as they can carry. If you arrive by train in the early hours of the morning then your options are to get one of these shuttles quickly, or sleep rough on the station until daybreak and then try to get one. At times like this, the station is crowded but fairly clean and safe.

The TAZARA train connects Kapiri Mposhi with Dar es Salaam in Tanzania, and Mpika is one of the stops between. Mpika to Kapiri Mposhi costs around Kw43,200 for first class, Kw28,800 for second and Kw16,000 for third.

Hitchhiking
With clear roads and a reasonable amount of traffic, hitching is a very practical form of transport to and from Mpika. There is probably more traffic going towards Mbala than Nakonde, but if you're heading towards Lusaka hitch around the BP station where both roads join.

If you're going towards Kasama and Mbala, then hitch on the turn-off by the BP station. Alternatively, and especially if it is late in the day, walk a further 2–3km down that tarred turn-off road, until you reach a smart, fenced compound on your right. This is known as the DDSP compound, or the MLGH (Ministry of Local Government and Housing) compound – it houses offices for various aid and semi-governmental groups, small businesses, and a nice resthouse with a simple bar and restaurant. You may pick up a lift from one of its workers, who travel widely in the district. You'll certainly see them come and go in a variety of plush 4WDs, and if the worst happens and no lift appears then you can wander across the road and sleep comfortably.

Where to stay
The best place to stay by far is the **DDSP compound** mentioned above. The sign outside details many of the offices here, including the Development Organisation for People's Empowerment – more usually known by its acronym. (You may also see this called the MLGH or MAFF compound, but they all mean the same place.)

The communal rooms at DDSP are the cheapest: two separate bedrooms which share a single toilet/washbasin/shower are Kw17,000 per bed. These rooms are clean and the beds are OK, though the shower/toilet area is less sparkling. Self-contained rooms with their own shower/toilet are Kw20,000. There are houses available, each with a comfortable sitting room, kitchen, and two bedrooms which sleep four people easily for a total of Kw32,000 each.

Breakfast, lunch and dinner are prepared here, at Kw5,000 per meal – just let them know. If you are likely to arrive after about 21.30 then reserve a room in advance by telephoning Mpika (04) 370118 during the day. The key to your room will then be left at the gatehouse.

The alternatives to the DDSP are the **Musakanya Resthouse** and the **Government Resthouse**, both of which are on the side of the boma away from the main road. Rooms at these are about Kw15,000 each, but are much less pleasant. Rather better than these, the last alternative is the **Malashi Executive Guesthouse**, which is about 2km north of town on the west side of the main road to Kasama. This is small and friendly, and has double rooms for Kw20,000.

What to see and do
For supplies, GM Trading/Retail & General Dealers is worth a glance. It has a good range of supplies – from curry powder and canned foods, to South African wine, chocolates, and a fine selection of beautiful *chitenjes*. However, the Kalolo Bakery, Grocery and Restaurant is probably the best store in town at the moment. .

Southwest of there, just a few hundred yards, is the Northern Meat Products butchery (tel: 04 370599), which sells the area's best fresh meat and sausages. The managers of this also own Bateleur Farm, where you can camp if you are taking the bush route from Mpika into the Luangwa Valley described on page 255.

If you need to change any money then the only bank in town able to do this is the TAZARA bank, which is off on the right as you head towards the TAZARA station – ask for local directions, and watch for the 'Zamtel' sign.

Excursions around Mpika

There are a few interesting caves and waterfalls around Mpika, and Shiwa N'gandu is worthy of a section on its own. To go anywhere away from the main roads you'd be very wise to have a 4WD even in the dry season.

Nachikufu Caves

This cave complex contains excellent San/bushmen rock paintings: when excavated in the 1940s it was estimated to have been occupied intermittently for about the last 15,000 years.

There is a cave here, and also a rock shelter. Both look north over a wide plateau, and are formed from a ridge of quartzite rock – perfect for stone tools. There's also a perennial stream about 500m away from the cave. The paintings inside are fairly simple: various figures silhouetted in black, including a couple of elephants and human figures.

Getting there

About 20km south of Mpika, before the Lavushi Manda turn-off, is the signposted turning to Nachikufu going west from the main road.

Chipoma Falls

The Lubu River drops 40m over a distance of 500m at this large set of rapids and cascades, southwest of Chinsali.

Getting there

Heading for Chinsali and Isoka from Mpika, turn left about 24km before you reach the turn-off for Chinsali (that's about 57km past the turning to Shiwa N'gandu). Follow this road for around 6km, taking left turns at all the forks and junctions encountered, until you reach the caretaker's house by the falls.

Lwitikila Falls

This small waterfall is a good place for a dip and lunch, though don't expect to have it all to yourself as it lies in a local community area.

Getting there

Take the road to Chinsali and Isoka from Mpika for about 15km, until you see a right turn signed to the Lwitikila Girls' Secondary School. Continue along this track, which bends round slowly to the left and then goes uphill, until you see some houses on the right. In front of the first house a smaller track goes off to the right – this leads directly to the falls.

Shiwa N'gandu

Shiwa N'gandu was founded by Stewart Gore-Browne, who was born in England in 1883, and first came to Africa in 1911 as a member of the military commission. Whilst surveying the boundary between Northern Rhodesia and the Belgian Congo, he saw Shiwa N'gandu: the 'Lake of the Royal Crocodiles'. After World War I, Gore-Browne returned to buy the lake and surrounding land, using his inherited income and with help from his aunt. Then it was 70 miles on foot or horseback from Ndola to the Luapula River, followed by ten days in a canoe across the Bangweulu Swamps, followed by another 70-mile march.

Having spent time in South Africa, after the Boer war, Gore-Browne knew the attitude of white South Africans to blacks – and it appalled him. He based his views, especially with regard to Africa and the Africans, soundly on his own experiences, and refused to accept the prejudices of the resident white community. His vision for a utopian mini-state in the heart of Africa translated into an estate run with benevolent paternalism, and by 1925 Shiwa N'gandu was employing 1,800 local people.

Gore-Browne passed on skills to them, and with their help built neat workers' cottages with slate roofs, bridges, workshops, a school, a dispensary, and finally a magnificent manor house, set on a hill above the lake. All that could not be made locally was transported on the heads and backs of porters along the arduous route from Ndola. Simply look at all the heavy English furniture, the paintings, ornaments, and the walls of books to appreciate the determination with which Gore-Browne pursued his vision.

He also built a distillery for the essential oils that he hoped to make into a profitable local industry. Given Shiwa's remote location, Gore-Browne knew that the estate's produce had to be easily transportable: a non-perishable, valuable commodity of low bulk. He had several failures, trying roses, geraniums, eucalyptus, peppermint and lemon grass with no success. Eventually, he found success with citrus fruit, which flourished and at last brought a good income into the estate.

In 1927, when he was 44, he married Lorna – a 'ravishing' young lady from England who was just eighteen years old.

She came to Shiwa, threw herself into her husband's projects, and the estate and its inhabitants prospered. Then, in the 1950s, a *tristezia* virus killed off the fruit trees, hitting the estate hard and forcing it to turn to more conventional, less profitable, agriculture – possible because the main road which passes near the estate had then been completed.

Gore-Browne had become a rare, political figure in Northern Rhodesia, an aristocratic Englishman with excellent connections in London who commanded respect both in the colonial administration and with black Zambians. He was elected to Northern Rhodesia's Legislative Council as early as 1935, and was the first member of it to argue that real concessions were needed to African demands for more autonomy. He was impatient with the rule of the Colonial Office, and resented the loss of huge amounts of revenue through taxation paid to Britain, and 'royalties' paid to the British South Africa Company.

Stewart Gore-Browne was knighted by George VI of England, but also trusted by Zambia's first president, Kenneth Kaunda. When he died, an octogenarian, in 1967, he was given a full state funeral and allowed to be buried on a hill overlooking the lake at Shiwa – an honour only bestowed on the Bemba chiefs. In the words of Kaunda, 'He was born an Englishman and died a Zambian'. Perhaps if Africa had had more like him, the transition from colonial rule to independence would have been less traumatic.

On his death, the estate at Shiwa passed to his daughter Lorna and her husband, John Harvey, a farmer from near Lusaka. However, with just the income of the farm and without the lucrative essential oils, both the manor house and the estate proved difficult to maintain. John and his wife Lorna were both murdered in the early 1990s, allegedly because of what they knew of a high-ranking official's misdeeds. The incident has never had a satisfactory investigation.

Lady Lorna Gore-Browne returned to England and now lives in Highgate,

London – she never returned to Shiwa after her husband's death. The estate is now run by David Harvey, Sir Stewart Gore-Browne's grandson.

A highly readable historical account of the life and times of Stewart Gore-Browne and Shiwa N'gandu has recently been written called *The Africa House*. See *Further Reading* for more details.

Shiwa N'gandu manor house

Today the estate is a monument to Gore-Browne's utopian vision for this verdant corner of Africa. As you approach from the main road, the rectangular cottages built for farm workers come into view first, their white-washed walls and tiled roofs saying more of England than Africa. Then a red-brick gate-house appears, perhaps of Italian design. An old clock-tower rises above its tiled roof, and through its main arch is a long straight avenue, bordered by eucalyptus, leading to the stately manor house.

Climbing up, the avenue leads through the very English gardens – designed on several levels with bougainvillaea, frangipani, jacaranda and neatly arranged cypresses. Above the front door is a small carving of a black rhino's head: a reminder that Gore-Browne had earned the local nickname of Chipembele, black rhino.

At the centre of the manor is the square tiled Tuscan courtyard, surrounded by arches, overlooking windows and a red tiled roof. Climbing one of the cold, stone-slab staircases brings you into an English manor house, lined with wooden panelling and rugs hung on the walls, and furnished with sturdy chests, muskets, and all manner of memorabilia, including pictures of old relatives and regiments. Two frames with certificates face each other. One is from King George VI, granting 'our trusty and well-beloved Stewart Gore-Browne, esq' the degree, title, honour and dignity of Knight Bachelor. Opposite President Kaunda appoints 'my trusted, well-beloved Sir Stewart Gore-Browne' as a Grand Officer of the Companion Order of Freedom, second division – it is dated 1966.

The library remains the manor's heart, with two huge walls of books, floor-to-ceiling, which tell of Gore-Browne's interests – Frouede's *History of England* in at least a dozen volumes, *Policy and Arms* by Colonel Repington and *The Genesis of War* by the Right Honourable H H Asquith. His wife was very keen on poetry: there is a classic collection of works by Byron, Shelley, Coleridge, Eliot and others. Central to the room is a grand fireplace, surmounted by the Latin inscription: *Ille terrarum mihi super omnes anculus ridet* – this corner of the earth, above all others, smiles on me.

Shiwa today

Today the estate's greenery is luxuriant, even at the height of the dry season, which is seldom the case elsewhere in Zambia. David Harvey studied agriculture in England and returned to manage the estate, which now farms both animals and crops. Despite success in updating production methods, and diversifying into chickens, pigs, groundnuts, and dairy produce, there isn't the income from such a farm to maintain the manor house to Gore-Browne's original standards.

As you walk around, the peaceful atmosphere is one of an ancient country estate that is gradually slipping back into the African bush. It is almost as if Africa's rampant vegetation were accelerating the manor's decline, having aged it by centuries in a mere 70 years. The working farm now at its core will survive into the next millennium, though much of Gore-Browne's vision will not.

Getting there

Shiwa N'gandu is reasonably well signposted off the main road to Isoka and Nakonde, about 87km northeast of Mpika. The main Shiwa N'gandu house is about 13km from this turn-off. The road then continues to Kapishya Hot Springs and on to the Mpika–Kasama road.

Alternatively it can be reached directly from the Mpika–Kasama road; again turn off about 87km from Mpika, and pass Kapishya Hot Springs before finally reaching the house.

With a post office at Shiwa, the estate is due to be linked to Mpika by a post bus. Inquire at Mpika about the latest situation.

Where to stay

There's only one choice in the area, also run by the Harveys:

Kapishya Hot Springs (6 twin chalets and a campsite) P Bag E395, Lusaka. Tel: 04 370064; fax: 04 370040

About 20km from Shiwa N'gandu, the Harveys have built a small camp beside some natural hot springs. This is the best place to stay in the region, though you will need your own transport in order to reach it. There's a pool of hot spring water, and a cool rocky river, both of which make great sites for bathing. All is surrounded by *combretum* bushes and gently curving raffia palms. It's a very relaxing spot.

The solid thatched chalets have mosquito-netted windows and are furnished inside with reed mats, comfortable beds and shelves. They have en-suite flush toilets and nice large showers and wash basins – plus individual mosquito nets for the beds. Nearby the grassy campsite has soft earth that's easy on tent pegs, bucket showers and longdrop toilets. If you just turn up here then bring your own food, otherwise meals can be provided if you request them in advance.

Rates: US$30/40 per person sharing/single self-catering, US$80/110 per person sharing/single full board, camping: US$5 per person. Open: all year

What to see and do

If you come to stay at Kapishya Springs, which are an attraction in their own right, then ask there to arrange a tour of the house – which normally includes afternoon tea and costs a few dollars per person.

Other than that, a stay here can easily be combined with a visit to North Luangwa National Park, as the Harveys run Shiwa Safaris (contact via the Zambian Safari Company, page 144) who own Main and Buffalo camps there (page 254), and know the park and its wildlife well.

If you've time to spare then take a slow wander around the estate, and perhaps down to the lake. As ever, you will find the local people very welcoming and friendly, and usually happy to talk about what they are doing.

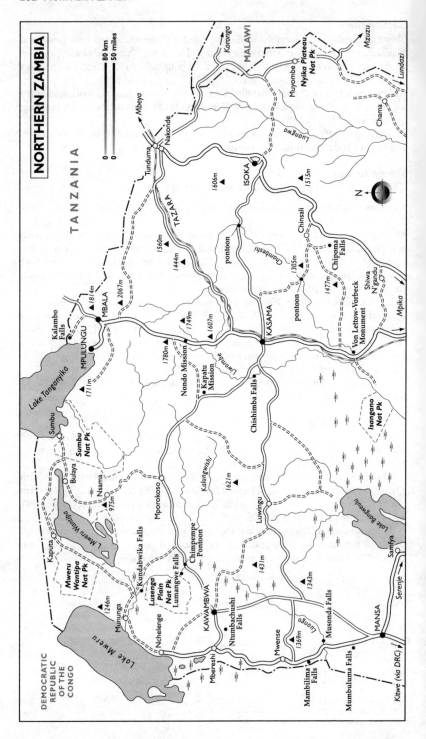

Northern Zambia

To explore northern Zambia properly, and to visit the national parks here, requires some determination, or at least advance planning. All of the area's three main national parks have suffered from neglect over the years. However one, Sumbu, is really starting to rejuvenate with a handful of excellent small lodges and a very promising future. This large reserve is bounded by GMAs and Lake Tanganyika, and promises fishing and diving as well as more traditional safari pursuits. It is probably the most obvious park to become Zambia's next big safari destination.

Tanganyika is one of the largest lakes in East Africa's Great Rift Valley, and has a rich aquatic life found nowhere else. Even outside the park small lodges are springing up for casual visitors – the snorkelling and fishing are good and it's a pleasant place to relax.

The north's other two parks, Mweru Wantipa and Lusenga Plain, may take more to put them back on the map, as neither has organised facilities for visitors, or good roads within it. Years of poaching have reduced the populations of game animals within them, and what animals are left remain shy and understandably wary of mankind.

Outside of the national parks, this part of northern Zambia is a fascinating area, and there are numerous sights and waterfalls at which to stop and wonder.

Finally, a word about Nyika, a high plateau that straddles the Malawi border and provides the Luangwa with many of its early tributaries. There are national parks on both sides of the border. Nyika Plateau National Park, on the Zambian side, is unlike anywhere else in the country: high mountains clothed in rolling heathlands and often draped with mist. It's a great walking destination, a cool respite after the heat of the Luangwa Valley and home to numerous endemic species. However, it's easiest to access from the east, from Malawi, and so it's often forgotten when talking of Zambian national parks.

THE GREAT NORTH ROAD

The Great North Road stretches from Lusaka through Kapiri Mposhi to Mpika, Kasama and Mbala to Mpulungu – about 1,150km. It's all tar, and so despite its variable state of repair, this is the region's main artery.

In mid-'99 the road from Lusaka to Serenje was basically good tar, then there were a few difficult sections between Serenje and Mpika, and the road from Mpika to Kasama was fine except for the last 50km which was appalling. Kasama to Mbala is also basically OK.

In fact work on rebuilding the road completely, from the Kapiri turn-off to Nakonde on the Tanzanian border, started in 1998. By July '99 it had reached Mkushi, and was projected to reach Nakonde by the end of 2000. This is not just repair work, but complete re-construction to very high standard up to Serenje, with full resurfacing from Serenje to Nakonde.

Kasama

Kasama is centrally located, about 860km from Lusaka. Visitors to northern Zambia will invariably end up spending some time here, even if only to refuel and buy a few soft drinks. It is a busy little town, with lots going on. As it acts as a supply centre for much of the north of the country, there are some well-stocked stores, and a relatively large amount of traffic coming into, and leaving, town.

If you are driving between Lake Tanganyika and Lusaka, then Kasama's small guesthouses, and perhaps one of the small lodges near Mkushi, provide essential respites from long hours of pothole dodging on the main road.

Getting there
By air
Currently there are two flights a week to Kasama with Eastern Air, which run a route Lusaka–Ndola–Kasama–Kasaba Bay–Kasama–Ndola–Lusaka on Monday and Thursday. Check the timetable and the latest status of these before you set out. Lusaka–Kasaba Bay costs US$185 one-way, and Kasama–Kasaba Bay costs US$60 one way.

Travel International Air Charters (see *Chingola*, page 327) also fly to Kasama every Tuesday and Friday.

By train
The TAZARA station is a few kilometres from the centre of town, on the right as you enter from Mpika. This is your last chance to disembark at a major town before the railroad turns east, and away from Lake Tanganyika.

The express train from Kapiri Mposhi to Dar-es-Salaam passes through Kasama on Wednesday and Saturday at about 02.00. A return ticket to Dar costs about US$40 in first class (compartments sleep four) or US$30 in second class (compartments sleep six).

By bus
The bus services are generally good. A post bus makes the trip from Lusaka and Ndola (ask at the post office) and costs about US$10 one way. It is not usually overcrowded, and so fairly comfortable. Numerous normal buses come this way, usually rather more full. They link Kasama to Luwingu, Mbala and Mpulungu – though hitching may be faster than taking a bus if you're heading past Mbala for the lake.

If you're heading west then there is a bus station on the road out to the airport, a little way up from the House of Kasama store.

Going east is probably trickier. Last reports confirmed that both pontoons across the Chambeshi River, on the roads to Isoka and Chinsali, were out of action. Thus to go west, travellers had to head back down to Mpika, and then take the main road northeast. (With a 4WD you can cut a corner off this by going past Shiwa N'Gandu.) Alternatively, take the TAZARA to Nakonde, at the border, and then take the road south.

If any of the pontoons on the roads out of town are out of action, then there's usually a sign on the way out of town saying so. This can be a frequent occurrence in the second half of the rainy season.

Hitchhiking
Kasama is a good place for hitching. If you want to go north, to Mbala or Mpulungu, walk on past the Zambia National Commercial Bank and the BP

garage, to beyond the roundabout, and start hitching – there is a convenient lay-by.

If you're heading south towards Mpika then you need to walk out past the TAZARA station, or perhaps a little further, hitching as you walk. There are four memorable speed humps on this road, which should slow down even the most ardent of speed-kings to a crawl.

Heading west or east is more difficult, as there is much less traffic. However, a traveller going in that direction is something of a rarity, so novelty value will encourage potential lifts. Most drivers will not have a clue where you're heading for.

Where to stay

The New Kwacha Relax Hotel (tel: 04 221124) seems to have gone downhill a lot and is often closed due to a lack of basics. It costs US$10 per person, and no food is available. Fortunately there are now several good, small places to stay in Kasama. Of these, Thorn Tree and Kasembo stand clearly above the rest.

Thorn Tree Guesthouse (5 rooms plus a cottage) PO Box 410694, Kasama. Tel/fax: 04 221615; email: kansato@zamnet.zm
Hazel and Ewart Powell came to this area of Zambia to teach in 1969... and stayed here to run this. Consequently they've a fund of knowledge on the local area and its people, and can help you get the best out of the region.

You'll find Thorn Tree about 1km from town, on the edge of an escarpment with a great view. To get there, turn left at the main crossroads as you enter Kasama from Lusaka, and continue for about 300m. Pass the police station and government offices on the left, and a park on the right. Then take the right hand fork and carry on for a further 300m to where Thorntree is signposted on the left hand side of the road. This is only two minutes drive from the centre or a ten-minute walk.

In their own house they have three double bedrooms which share a bathroom and the use of the main lounge (with TV, video and library). There's also a bedroom in an extension to this that would sleep four, again sharing a bathroom in the main house. All have mosquito nets and fans.

In the grounds there's a cottage on the hillside (stunning view) which has one bedroom which sleeps two people (an extra bed could be added) plus a bathroom, a fully-equipped kitchen and a lounge with its own TV and video. It's been built from local materials, including an attractive 'pink stone' local to the area, and furnished with pine furniture from their own workshop. Also away from the main house are four purpose-built rooms with en-suite showers and toilets and great views. These share one lounge/bar of their own.

Hazel will arrange meals for you whenever you'd like them, and most of the ingredients are produced here on the farm – from oranges and limes to egg and bacon, coffee and tea, and even the jams and peanut butter at breakfast. For drinks, the lodge has a fully licensed small bar. You can arrange for Ewart to collect you from the airport, station, or buses. Similarly, if you want to play tennis, golf, or swim, or if you need transport to get out to Chishimba Falls (or wherever), then they can make a plan for you to do so. They are also closely in touch with what's happening up by the lake and in the general area, so can help you with your travel arrangements if you're heading further north.

Thorn Tree also has a few small swimming pools in the grounds, and it's suitable for children – a very homely place where you can easily feel part of the family.

Rates: rooms in house are US$17.50, in the extension US$15, and those in the cottage or the en-suite rooms US$25. All rates are per person, and include a full breakfast.

Cinci's Nest Guest House (6 rooms) PO Box 410761, Kasama. Tel/fax: 04 221441
Owned by a Mr Mugala, and situated opposite Kasama Girls' School, which is on the Isoka road about 4km out of town. There's no sign post for this, just ask for Cinci's. It has several clean rooms and meals can be cooked on request. Cinci's rooms are pleasant, with TV and

small fridge, but on the smallish side. Parking space is available within its wall-fence, and it is said to be popular with Zambian politicians on tour in the north. So you never know whom you'll meet over breakfast.

Rates: US$32 per person, including continental breakfast. Full breakfast is US$2 extra, and evening meals cost US$6 and should be booked in advance

Kasembo Guesthouse (7 rooms) PO Box 410040, Kasama. Office tel: 04 221158 (ask for the guesthouse manager); evening tel: 04 221380 (ask for Father Ivo); fax: 221369 (office hours only); email: bshone@zamnet.zm

This guesthouse is 8km from the centre of town, on Kasembo Farms, opposite the airport. To get there leave town for the airport and, about 150m after the end of the tar road, take a left turn down a farm road, signposted to Kasembo. The guesthouse is about 1.5km from that turn-off.

Kasembo Farms was founded 50 years ago and is now owned and run by the Missionaries of Marianhill. It stretches for about 1,000 acres, and keeps around 175 Friesian cows (40 are milked), 150 pigs, 150 sheep, 2,000 hens for egg laying, and a few thousand chickens for the pot. The priests say that they leave things as natural as possible. 'Our vegetable-garden has never seen a grain of fertiliser in its existence,' commented one. With most of the basic ingredients grown on the farm, it's no surprise that meals are a highlight here.

The accommodation for visitors (of any creed) consists of two houses, standing about 80m apart in a clearing within an old section of indigenous forest. The buildings are about 15–20 years old and were originally the family homes of two sons of the former owner. Since then, they were extensively renovated in early '99, in order to take guests.

One house has four twin rooms (two are en suite, and two share a shower and a toilet), and highly-polished red cement floors. It has the warmer atmosphere of the two and has a small pool and a lovely view over the escarpment. The second is perhaps a little more stylish, floored with flagstones of local stone. It has three en-suite rooms. All the rooms in both houses have mosquito nets, electric fans, duvets, blankets and linen. Both are furnished with new pine furniture, made locally in a carpentry workshop in Kasama, and each has its own kitchen, dining room, lounge, a big veranda and ample parking space.

The missionaries make a point of ensuring that the service is attentive and discussions with them can give you an interesting insight into the area. Several types of local beers and a few spirits are on offer during meals. If you arrive in town and want to stay then ask at the Kasembo Farms shop, which is right across the central market in town, at the back of PEP-Stores.

Rates: US$17.50/25 single, US$30/45 double, for rooms without/with private facilities including full English breakfast. Dinner is US$5, on request. Lunch is by 'special arrangement' only.

Kapolonga Resthouse

This old government resthouse is situated halfway between the TAZARA station and town. Its rooms should have fans and hot water, but are *very* basic. It's best avoided if at all possible.

Rates: US$5 per person, excluding breakfast

Bush-camping

If you just want a quiet place in the bush to camp 'rough' around Kasama, then one very experienced old Zambian hand recommended the old (defunct) Kalungwishi State Ranch to me, a few two hours drive from town. He comments that it's a fantastic place to explore and is enormous with very few local people about and lots of nice habitat for birds, including good miombo woodlands and large dambos.

To get there take the Luwingu Road, then turn north before you reach Luwingu (about 20km). Drive past Chitoshi and aim for the headwaters of the Kalungwishi River. (You'll need a good map of the area!) Pass the trig-point tower (from which there is a good view, if you climb it) and take a left into the old ranch. There are two entrance roads to Kalungwishi, and at least one still has a sign.

Where to eat

Shoprite has come to Kasama, and with it a vast array of foodstuffs and commodities are now obtainable that were very difficult to find previously. For a bite to eat there are lots of small cafés. The **Tropicana Restaurant** set back from the main crossroads serves typical nshima and chicken/meat/fish; it is very basic, but friendly. The **Golden Tulip** (tel: 04 221642), found behind the Bata shoeshop, is small, quaint and serves tasty Zambian food (rice with everything!).

Leah's Snackshop is on the main road, opposite the central market in town, is small and serves well-prepared snacks. Then there's the **Hungry Lion**, part of Shoprite (which itself is the largest bakery in town), and lots of smaller places will also sell bread and filled rolls.

Excursions around Kasama

Von Lettow-Vorbeck Monument

At the north end of the bridge over the Chambeshi River, about 85km south of Kasama, is a monument beside the road. It marks the place where General von Lettow-Vorbeck, Commander of the German forces in East Africa during the First World War, surrendered to Hector Croad, the British District Commissioner, on 14 November 1918.

Von Lettow-Vorbeck and his forces had marched south from German East Africa (now Tanzania). They didn't realise that the war in Europe had been over for three days until told by Croad. Upon hearing the news from the British the Germans agreed to march back to Abercorn (now called Mbala) and there hand over their prisoners to the British. It seems as if it was all very civilised.

Part of the monument is a breach-loading field gun, made in 1890, which was the type that the German forces used during the First World War.

Chishimba Falls

To get to Chishimba, go through Kasama and head west past the airport and towards Luwingu. After about 30km, take a right turn on to the wide gravel road to Mporokoso. Follow this for about 5km, before turning left on to the road towards the power station. About 2km down this, turn right down a small track to reach the falls. There you should find a sheltered picnic place and probably also a guard, who is usually willing to act as a guide. If the guard's around then it is generally safe to leave vehicles at the top here. There are a few thatched observation points along the falls and paths leading down to the bottom of them.

These falls are used partially to run an unobtrusive hydro-electric station, but the water that is left makes for a super waterfall. The Falls are actually three falls, the first artificial and the next two natural.

The first, Mutumuna, has a drop of about 20 metres where it descends on to a rocky riverbed, and it's probably the prettiest of the three. The second falls, Kevala, is protected by a weir. This has created a large pool, and nearby is a camping and picnic site laid out among the trees. (If you're camping, leave about US$2 extra per person for the guide.) You can camp where you like; there are no facilities.

The third, actually called Chishimba, is a short walk through a dambo. Water spouts over huge cliffs into a dark canyon and legend has it that spirits live here. If you walk right down to the bottom you can stand behind the curtain of water with the rock-face at your back and the water in front of you.

Mbala

This is a small town just off the road from Kasama to Mpulungu. There is a BP station, a few shops, several banks and a fairly cool, relaxed air. The road to

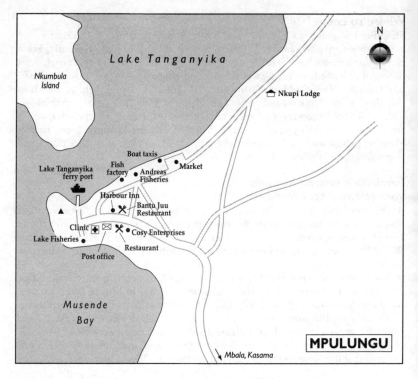

Mpulungu descends into the merciless heat of the rift valley beyond here – so enjoy the relative cool whilst you can.

Mbala is notable for the Moto Moto museum, described below, which is one of the country's best museums and well worth stopping for.

Where to stay

Aside from an old government resthouse, there are three options here. Christy Inn is new and has been recommended, but I have no other information about it! The town's two older places are:

Arms Hotel (10 twin rooms and 2 single rooms) PO Box 420161, Mbala. Tel: 04 450585
This used to be called the Abercorn Arms, but changed its name when the town became Mbala instead of Abercorn. It is in the centre of town on the main road, on the right just after the BP fuel station. If you stay here then watch your belongings very carefully, as I have had a report that it is not safe.

The facilities are very basic indeed, and note that the telephone number above also covers for the 'bar and bottle stall' … so at least you're assured of a drink here. Lunches and dinners are served. They're very simple Zambian fare – Kw3,500 for nshima and chicken, Kw3,000 for nshima and meat, Kw2,000 for nshima and fish.
Rates: Kw11,500 for a double, Kw8,500 single. Breakfast is Kw3,000 extra

New Grasshopper Inn (14 rooms) PO Box 420093, Mbala. Tel: 04 450589, 450075 or 450403
Not to be outdone in name-changes by the Arms Hotel, the New Grasshopper used to be merely the Grasshopper Inn. It has recently had its bar area enlarged and more rooms built for conference delegates, and so is recommended as the best option in town.

Moto Moto Museum

This museum opened in 1974 and has an excellent reputation as perhaps the best place in the country for Bemba history and artefacts. It was originally assembled by a missionary stationed here, Father Corbell, who amassed a very extensive collection of tools, craft instruments, and exhibits connected to traditional ceremonies and witchcraft. These have been housed with the help of some aid money, and the museum is now well signposted just outside Mbala on the north side. The locals know it very well.

Open: 09.00–16.45 every day except Christmas. Entry: US$10 per person

Mpulungu

Sitting in the heat of the rift valley, about 40km from Mbala, Mpulungu is Zambia's largest port. It's a busy place and visited by many travellers, most of whom are Africans but with the odd backpacker mixed in too. The atmosphere is very international, a mix of various Southern, Central and East African influences all stirred together by the ferries which circle the lake from port to port.

There is a strong local fishing community and a small but thriving business community, complete with a small contingent of white Africans, expats and even aid workers. So though Mpulungu might seem like the end of the earth when you get off a bus in the pitch-black evening, it isn't.

Getting there

By bus

As Mpulungu is the end of the route, most of the buses from Mbala tend to arrive in the afternoon and evening, and those departing tend to leave in the morning. The 'terminus' is on the main road, beside the market area – you cannot fail to go through it.

Hitchhiking

Hitching here from Mbala in the afternoon is very easy, with lots of lifts. However, getting out again in the morning is virtually impossible. Everybody who has a little space in their vehicle goes to the area for buses and fills up with paying passengers, so few are at all interested in a stray hitchhiker walking away from the main station. So, if you want to get out of here then go with the crowd and hang around the main market area quizzing any likely buses or vehicles. Because of the steep, twisting road out of the valley, heavy or under-powered vehicles can be painfully slow, so get a lighter, more powerful lift if you can.

By ferry

There are two large international Tanganyika ferries each of which calls at Mpulungu once every week. Both arrive in the morning and leave in the afternoon: the *Liemba* on Fridays and the *Mongosa* on Mondays.

From Mpulungu they sail over the Tanzanian border to Kasanga, then to Kigoma in the north of Tanzania, and then on to Burundi. (This last stop was omitted whilst the country was in turmoil.) The ferries stop at countless places in between these more major ports.

In mid-'99 the *Mongosa* was out of the water and undergoing repairs, leaving just the *Liemba* as a once-weekly service on a Friday. However it's likely that *Mongosa* will be back in service by the time you're reading this.

First class is comfortable with videos for entertainment and meals of rice and fish or chicken, while second class is considerably more basic.

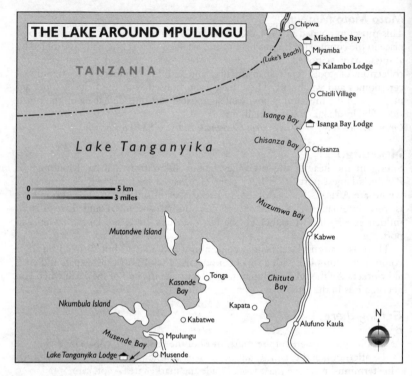

THE LAKE AROUND MPULUNGU

TANZANIA

Lake Tanganyika

Chipwa
Mishembe Bay
(Luke's Beach) Miyamba
Kalambo Lodge
Chitili Village
Isanga Bay
Isanga Bay Lodge
Chisanza Bay
Chisanza

0 — 5 km
0 — 3 miles

Muzumwa Bay

Mutondwe Island
Kabwe

Kasonde Bay
Tonga
Chituta Bay

Nkumbula Island
Kapata
N
Kabatwe
Alufuno Kaula
Musende Bay
Mpulungu
Lake Tanganyika Lodge
Musende

By boat-taxi

If you need a short trip out to one of the lodges on the lake then hire a boat-taxi from the beach-side market, next to Andreas Fisheries Ltd. You will need to make sure that the driver knows the lodge that you want, and exactly where it is, and you may want to bargain over the rate a little.

It's essential that you have a crystal-clear deal over the price for the trip, including you and all your baggage, before you set off from Mpulungu – as disagreements on arrival (or worse still, on the lake) are bad news for you and the person running the boat.

Where to stay

If you are backpacking through, or have arrived late in the day, then staying in Mpulungu for a night or two is probably your best option. Without wishing to denigrate the attractions of Nkupi Lodge, and its venerable owner Denish, I recommend the Harbour Inn as a very good value alternative. If both are full, then Mpulungu does have a District Resthouse – but it wouldn't be top of my list to visit.

Nkupi Lodge Tel: 04 455166

This relaxed backpackers' retreat has become something of a legend with overlanders, largely because of its total lack of competition in Mpulungu and its laid-back owner, Denish. There are very basic clean chalets here, and campsites. Both showers and toilets are shared and separate. Beer is available, as is scrupulously boiled water. Food must be ordered well in advance if required (when Denish is around, so is the food – but when he's not there don't expect any!).

To find it, either ask one of the locals, or follow the tar road past the main bus/market area. The road climbs a hill, and you should follow one of the paths to your right which goes up and over to the other side of the hill, to around Andreas Fisheries Ltd and the beach-side market. Then turn right and follow the road parallel to the lakeshore, keeping the water on your left and reasonably close. You'll find Nkupi Lodge on your right in a few hundred yards, surrounded by a good fence. Food is now usually available here; expect a simple one-dish meal to cost around Kw10,000.

Rates: Camping is KwUS$2.50/Kw6,500 per night. A bed with a mosquito net in a basic curtained chalet costs US$10/Kw25,000

Harbour Inn Tel: 04 455041

This is a new place in the heart of Mpulungu. It's on the right of the road as you get near to the ferry port, just before the post office and on the left of the Bantu Juu Restaurant. It's run by Martin Pierce and isn't anything fancy, but has double rooms with en-suite facilities which are clean and very good value. Martin also has a boat for hire, if you want to go fishing or out to Kalambo Falls.

Rates: US$10/Kw25,000 per double room

Lodges on the lake near Mpulungu

If you have more time, and want to explore the lake a little, then it's worth organising transport out to one of the lakeside lodges. To do this, I'd first call Mrs Neilson, who runs Mpulungu's Caltex fuel station (PO Box 71, Mpulungu. Tel: 04 455185; fax: 455112). Coming from Mbala, you pass this on your left about 1km before you reach the main bus station/market area of town.

Mrs Neilson has radio contact with most of the lodges, and acts as a *de facto* agent for them in town. She'll usually be able to advise what is open, how much it is, and how to get there. She'll probably also be able to contact them on the radio, given a little time. Others who can often help about the various options in the area include Jeanne and Chris Blignaut, who run a small harbour at Samaki Fishing (tel: 04 455103; fax: 455008; email: ckachese@zamnet.zm), and also Hazel at Thorn Tree Lodge in Kasama (see page 285)

Do remember that this area is fairly new to tourism, and so details of these lodges and their operations will almost certainly change before you read this.

Lake Tanganyika Lodge

Reached by a short boat-taxi ride, this is a basic lodge right beside the lake on a lovely pebbly beach. It's only about 5km west of Mpulungu. If driving then you can reach it by a poor 4WD road. Just turn off the main tar road from Mbala about 5km before Mpulungu town centre (before the police check – if you go too far the police will direct you back!). It aims at backpackers, who can get a shared boat-taxi from the market to the lodge for Kw1,500 each, or charter their own boat for around Kw20,000.

There are eight simple chalets available and also some thatched shelters under which you can camp. All share clean toilets and showers. There's plenty of scope for swimming (blissful) in the lake around the area of the lodge, and the management are friendly and will help you arrange boats for fishing, snorkelling, trips to Kalambo Falls and similar excursions. Food is available on request – breakfast for Kw4,500, lunch Kw8,500, and dinner around Kw 8,500. (The barbecued fish here is excellent.)

Rates: US$10/25,000 per person for the chalets, US$3/Kw8,000 per person camping

Kalambo Lodge (6 twin chalets) PO Box 34065, Lusaka. Tel: 01 235382; fax: 235381

This was run by Toby Veall (it was often referred to simply as Toby's Lodge) and was Zambia's first upmarket lodge on the lake. It originally started as Toby's base for catching aquarium fish for export – a business he's still involved with. At first curious aquarists arrived for trips, and then the lodge gradually developed to having six twin-bed thatch-on-stone chalets, each with its own flush toilet, shower and solar-powered lighting. The main activities here were fishing and snorkelling, and the underwater visibility in the lodge's area is excellent. Walks from the lodge to the Kalambo Falls (about 90 minutes away) were also popular. The lodge is 16km from Mpulungu, close to the Kalambo River, and is reached by a short boat transfer or water-taxi.

Sadly, the lodge has recently been closed. However, Toby is still up on the lake, catching fish for aquaria, and is reported as trying to sell it. If you were flying in with a small group of aquatic enthusiasts, and paying handsomely for the privilege, then Toby might even be persuaded to open the lodge up for a few days. But if you're just passing through then ask Mrs Neilson at the Caltex station for the latest news. If/when it reopens properly it may again be a super place to stay.

Mishembe Bay – Luke's Beach (2 tents and stone cottages) contact via Thorn Tree Lodge, Kasama. Tel/fax: 04 221615; email: kansato@zamnet.zm
Run by Luke Powell, son of Ewart Powell (who owns Thorn Tree Lodge in Kasama), this occupies the last bay on the Zambian side of the shore. It's really Robinson-Crusoe stuff – just a pure white sandy beach sheltered in its own bay. Mishembe is usually accessed by a 30-minute water-taxi from Mpulungu.

There's a stone chalet hidden on the hillside, two simple safari tents on wooden platforms overlooking the lake, and space for campers. Just you, the baboons, monkeys and birds. (No chefs, so bring all your food!) It's a magical beach and very good value.

The bay is ideally situated for walks up to Kalambo Falls, which is about 60 minutes each way, and there is very good snorkelling right in the bay – the visibility is about 10m.
Rates: US$15 per person in the chalet or tent, including a guided walk to Kalambo Falls. Camping US$5/Kw12,500 per person

Isanga Bay Lodge (3 thatched chalets)
Originally built by Hugh Smith, who sadly died recently, this was due to be a smart lodge about halfway between Mpulungu and the Tanzanian border. It consists of three thatched chalets on stilts on a beautiful sandy beach, surrounded by coconut palms – and despite Hugh's death it is slowly being finished. The water in front of its beach is shallow, and so safe for swimming. However, its status is now very uncertain. Ask at Samaki, the Caltex garage, or even Thorn Tree Lodge (Kasama) for the latest information on this lodge.

What to see
Niamkolo Church
Just a few kilometres east of Mpulungu, beside the lake, you may see a tall, rectangular turret rising above the shoreline as you head to Kalambo Falls or one of the lodges in a water-taxi. This isn't a fort, but the remains of one of Zambia's oldest churches.

It was originally built by the London Missionary Society around 1893–6, but abandoned in 1902 because of health problems suffered by the missionaries. The original buildings were burned, but in 1962 the walls were restored to their former height and cemented into place. Now they're all there is to see. At 80cm thick in places, they may last for another century yet.

LAKE TANGANYIKA
Lake Tanganyika is one of a series of geologically old lakes that have filled areas of the main East African Rift Valley. Look at a map of Africa and you will see many of these in a 'string' down the continent: Lakes Malawi, Tanganyika, Kivu, Edward and Albert are some of the larger ones. Zambia just has a small tip of Tanganyika within its borders, but it is of importance to the country. Access to Tanganyika

grants Zambia a real port with transport links to a whole side of Tanzania and direct access to Burundi.

It also makes this one corner of Zambia totally different from the rest of the country, with a mix of peoples and a 'tropical Central Africa' feel. There are some well-established lakeside lodges, most within striking distance of Kalambo Falls, and two of the old lodges in the vicinity of Sumbu National Park are already emerging as the area's rising stars.

Geography

Lake Tanganyika is the deepest of the Rift Valley Lakes of Central/East Africa, with a maximum depth of about 1,470m. It has an area of around 34,000km² and is estimated to be about 10–15 million years old. The surface layers of water are a tropical 24–28°C and support virtually all of the known life in the lake.

Well below these, where it is too deep for the sun's light to reach, are separate, colder waters. Below about 200m, these are deprived of oxygen and hardly mix with the upper layers. They are currently the subject of much scientific study.

The lake has a variety of habitats around its 3,000km-or-so of shoreline, ranging from flat sands to marshy areas and boulder-strewn shores. Most of the fish species live within about 30m of the surface, where the water is generally very clean and clear, with a visibility as high as 10–20m in places.

Flora and fauna

The geology of the rocks around the lake has led to the water being unusually hard (between 7° and 11° dH), alkaline (average 8.4 pH) and rich in minerals for a freshwater lake. It is not an ideal environment for normal aquatic plants, and so these are generally found near the entry of rivers into the lake but not elsewhere. Various species of algae have adapted to fill this ecological niche, and extensive 'lawns' of grass-like algae cover many of the lake's submerged rocks.

Animals

The water's excellent clarity, the lack of cover and the rocky shores do not encourage either hippo or crocodiles, though both become more common around the relatively undisturbed shores of Sumbu. They are also seen regularly near the mouths of rivers, and must always be remembered before you swim. The lake is a reliable source of water for the game, which often come to drink during the dry season.

Birds

The birdlife on the shoreline is generally good, and the species found here also tend to represent many more of the typical East African birds than can be found elsewhere in Zambia. The area's more unusual residents include purple-throated cuckoo-shrikes, white-headed saw-wings, stout cisticolas, and Oustalet's white-bellied sunbird.

Fish

Lake Tanganyika and the other lakes in the rift valley continue to fascinate both zoologists and aquarists as they have evolved their own endemic species of fish. So far, around 450 have been identified in Tanganyika, mostly from the *Cichlidae* family – cichlids (pronounced sick-lids) as they are known. Many of these are small, colourful fish that live close to the surface and the shoreline. Here they inhabit crevices in the rocks and other natural cavities, avoiding the attention of larger, predatory fishes that patrol the deeper, more open, waters.

These are generally easy to keep in home aquaria being small, colourful, and fairly undemanding; several operations have sprung up in recent years to catch specimens for the pet trade, and fly them out to Europe and America. One of the lake's lodges makes most of its living out of this, and tourism is really just an emerging side-line for them.

For anglers, who will find most of the cichlids too small to be of interest, the lake is the furthest south that the goliath tigerfish or Nile perch can be found, and an excellent place for the *nkupi*, which are the largest cichlids in the world. All are eagerly sought by fishermen, with the best time for fishing between November and March. This is taken very seriously as Nile perch can reach an impressive 80kg in weight.

Safety in Lake Tanganyika

Tanganyika is a marvellous lake in which to go snorkelling, or even scuba diving, as the numerous fish are beautifully coloured and there is seldom any need to dive deeply. That said, you must be aware of the risks – from crocodiles and hippos to bilharzia. Both animals can be very localised and, if bilharzia exists here, then it will also be patchy in its distribution. (There is some doubt about this, but see page 73 for general guidelines.)

There is also an endemic fish-eating snake, the Tanganyika cobra, which usually avoids swimmers like terrestrial snakes avoid walkers... but watch out for them anyhow. The locals obviously know the area, so if you are considering taking a swim then ask their advice about the precise place that you have in mind. They may not be infallible, but will give you a good idea of where is likely to be safe, and where is not.

KALAMBO FALLS

For a short distance the Kalambo River marks the boundary between Zambia and Tanzania. At the Kalambo Falls, it ceases to flow on a high plateau and plunges over the side of the Great Rift Valley in one vertical drop of about 221m. This is the second highest waterfall in Africa, about double the height of the Victoria Falls, and about the twelfth highest in the world.

On either side of the falls there are sheer rock walls, and a large colony of marabou storks breed in the cliffs during the dry season. The falls themselves will be at their most spectacular towards the end of the wet season, in February or March, though are worth visiting in any month.
Rates: entry Kw1,500/camping Kw3,000 – per person per day/night

Archaeology

Though few visitors realise it, the Kalambo Falls are also one of the most important archaeological sites in Southern Africa. Just above the falls, by the side of the river, is a site that appears to have been occupied throughout much of the Stone Age and early Iron Age. The earliest tools discovered there may be over 100,000 years old, a semi-circle of stones suggests some form of wind-break, and three hollows lined with grass were probably where the inhabitants slept.

It seems that the earlier sites of occupation were regularly flooded by the river, and each time this deposited a fine layer of sand – thus preserving each layer of remains, tools and artefacts in a neat chronological sequence. Much later, the river cut into these original layers of sand and revealed the full sequence of human occupation to modern archaeologists.

Kalambo's main claim to fame is that the earliest evidence of fire in subSaharan Africa was found here – charred logs, ash and charcoal have been discovered amongst the lowest levels of remains. This was a tremendously important step for stone-age man as it enabled him to keep warm and cook food, as well as use fire to scare off aggressive animals. Burning areas of grass may even have helped him to hunt.

The site is also noted for evidence of much later settlement, from the early Iron Age. Archaeologists even speak of a 'Kalambo tradition' of pottery, for which they can find evidence in various sites in Northern Zambia. The Kalambo site is unusual, and thus important, because it is a place which has had a number of settlements throughout the centuries. Thus the remains of each can be found on top of the last, and a reliable time-scale can easily be established.

It seems that the early iron-age farmers displaced the area's stone-age people around the 8th century BC: no further stone-age remains are found after that date. After that there is evidence of at least four different iron-age settlements between the 5th and 11th centuries AD.

Getting there
By boat-taxi
The river's mouth is around 17km from Mpulungu, so adventurous backpackers can get private water-taxis to take them upstream to near the base of the falls, and then ask to be collected the following day. From there it is a strenuous climb to the top of the falls, where camping is allowed. You will need to bring all your own food and equipment.

A better option by far is to bring all your provisions and stay at one of the lodges nearer the Falls – Mishembe Bay or (if either is open) Kalambo or Isanga Bay. Then you can make a day-trip to the falls, perhaps even walking there.

Alternatively, small boats that ply between Mpulungu and Kasanga, in Tanzania, may drop you off one day, and pick you up on the next.

Driving
To get to Kalambo take the road to Zombe and the Tanzanian border from Mbala, then a few kilometres out of town the falls are clearly signposted to your left. The falls are about 33km from Mbala, and this track deteriorates towards the end. It's possible to get through with a 2WD vehicle, but only just.

Because of Kalambo's border position, policing it is difficult. Vehicles left unattended are likely targets for theft, so consider taking extra safety precautions, like having someone with you to look after the vehicle.

SUMBU NATIONAL PARK
Sumbu National Park covers about 2,020km², and borders on Lake Tanganyika. To the west the park is mostly surrounded by the Tondwa Game Management Area, which has been leased out to a small professional hunting operator since 1996. This has enabled it to act as a very effective buffer for the park, keeping the local subsistence hunters/poachers out whilst the game numbers had a chance to increase. This, combined with the resurgence of three lodges in this area, has made Sumbu's future look very promising indeed.

On another promising note, Sumbu is one of several parks in Zambia that have been designated as being 'viable game parks' under a recent study funded by the EU. Plans are afoot to change the way the parks are run, and EU money is set to help the less developed parks to become self-sustaining. Eventually, each of Zambia's parks should have greater autonomy, which will allow them to use their own funds for community development schemes as well as anti-poaching operations. This is vital if the wildlife of parks like Sumbu is to recover and tourism is to become a worthwhile source of revenue.

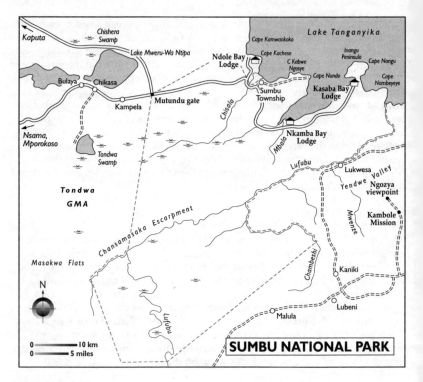

Flora and fauna

Sumbu protects populations of elephant, and a range of antelope including blue and yellow-backed duiker, Lichtenstein's hartebeest, roan, sable, bushbuck, waterbuck, sitatunga, a few zebra and a large number of puku. Buffalo herds range up to about 400 individuals, and move around between Sumbu and the neighbouring GMA. The park's main natural predators are lion and leopard. Although poachers continue to kill occasionally, the animal populations are increasing.

A study in 1993–4 concluded that there were still wild dogs in the park, and its surrounding GMAs, though their continued long-term survival was in doubt. I don't know of reports of wild dog since then.

Although Sumbu cannot yet boast huge herds of the larger antelope, elephant or buffalo, there is sufficient game to make a trip to the park worthwhile. Its vegetation and environment are, on the whole, in pristine condition and offer a real Zambian wilderness experience.

The birding is good, and a number of East African species occur here that you won't find in the rest of Southern Africa. Look out especially for the bare-faced go-away bird, common on the open floodplain areas; also a waxbill known as the redcheeked cordon bleu, occasional ospreys, palmnut vultures and redfaced crombecs. Pel's fishing owl and bat hawks also occur, though not more commonly than elsewhere.

In the lake itself, there are plenty of hippos and a very healthy population of crocodile. Some are sufficiently large to dissuade you from even thinking of dipping your toe in the water.

Sumbu Township

On the edge of Sumbu National Park, Sumbu Township has grown considerably over the last few years and now has about 10,000 residents. Most of the employed population either work for various government bodies – the national parks, police, immigration or council – or are involved in commercial fishing on the lake, mostly for kapenta. There are lots of small shops and bars, an open-air market for vegetables, dried fish and second-hand clothing, but no places to stay. There is also a government-run clinic, with a doctor available (but seldom any drugs), and normally petrol and diesel here too.

Sumbu isn't nearly as cosmopolitan as Mpulungu (!) but can be fairly lively. It doesn't yet have electricity (although there have been plans for several years now to connect it to the grid). Most of the water-taxis from Mpulungu end up at Sumbu.

Getting there
By air

There is a fully tarred airstrip (1,500m long) at Kasaba Bay, which is currently used by all the lodges for visitors arriving by air. Limited amounts of AV-Gas are usually available, but there are no customs or immigration facilities. Ndole Bay and Nkamba Bay collect their passengers from this strip by boat, which takes about 30 minutes to each of the lodges.

Eastern Air (see page 95) is probably the best way here, as they run two scheduled flights per week, on Mondays and Thursdays, to Kasaba Bay from Lusaka, usually flying via Ndola and Kasama. As passenger numbers increase, so should the frequency of these flights.

Several charter companies in Zambia will provide charters at other times, and one company in Chingola, Travel International Air Charters (see page 327), has even made a speciality out of weekend breaks from the Copperbelt to the lake, departing Friday and returning Sunday evening! These typically use small planes taking five or seven passengers, and might cost around US$500 per person for the weekend (including all meals, accommodation and activities) if you fill the plane.

In addition to these, the South African parent company of Kasaba Bay, Naturelink, runs scheduled tours, including charter flights, which link Kasaba with Lion Camp in the Luangwa, Marlin Lodge in Mozambique, Impalila Island Lodge on Namibia's Caprivi Strip, Deception Valley in Botswana's Kalahari, and Wonderboom Airport in South Africa. They are designed for people taking a few weeks away from South Africa, and wanting a whole, organised package trip. Naturelink can be contacted at PO Box 15585, Sinoville 0129, South Africa. Tel: (2712) 543 3448/9; fax: 543 9110; email: naturelink@mweb.co.za.

Driving

By road, Sumbu can be approached relatively easily in a 4WD via Kaputa or Mporokoso. There is also a very difficult track from Mbala to the park's eastern boundary – but it's not for the faint-hearted or ill-equipped.

From Mporokoso

The easiest approach to the park is from Mporokoso, from where you head north. This road continues roughly northwest. Keen birdwatchers should note that just north of Nsama there's a patch of miombo woodland where the relatively uncommon white-winged starling is easily spotted.

Eventually the road turns northeast and passes close to the eastern shores of Lake Mweru Wantipa, before turning to the right, to go southeast. The map shows that you pass through Bulaya, which is nothing more than a dot on the map. Don't expect a town here.

About 140km from Mporokoso and 45km before Sumbu, you'll reach a game check point called the Mutundu Gate. This marks the beginning of the national park, and also where the road from Kaputa (the area's administrative centre) joins the road from Mporokoso to Sumbu.

From there the road runs along the northwestern edge of the park, deteriorating as it goes. It deteriorates as it enters the park and continues to Sumbu Township. Past this there are no local villages, and Sumbu finally feels like a game park! Here you'll find the Sumbu Gate entrance, where you'll have to pay park fees if you want to continue into the park. This road then continues to Nkamba Bay and Kasaba Bay.

About 5km before Sumbu Township (see page 297), 39km after the Mutondo Gate, there's a left turn to Ndole Bay Lodge. The lodge is 7km down this road.

From Nchelenge via Kaputa
Taking the Chinese Road turn-off and then going via Mansa, Mwense and Mbereshi, you'll reach Nchelenge about 584km after turning off the Great North Road. About 3km beyond Nchelenge the tar runs into gravel at a place called Kashikishi and the road turns more northeast as it shadows the edge of Lake Mweru towards the small town of Mununga. There you take a right and later a left to Kaputa, driving through Mweru Wantipa National Park. On reaching Kaputa, head straight through to join the road from Mporokoso to Sumbu.

Note that on some maps this road passes through a place called Bulaya, which is sometimes credited with having a ferry or pontoon over an arm of the lake. Years ago there was a ferry here, which took people over the eastern portion of Mweru Wantipa. It was the only way to get through to Kaputa. However, now there is a road that passes along the edge of this lake, and no ferry. As noted above, Bulaya is simply a dot on a map rather than a town.

Similarly, be aware that the road shown on many maps which runs from Mununga beside the south side of Lake Mweru Wantipa to Nsama is very bad and becoming impassable.

Cross-country from Mbala
Strictly for adventurers, there is a very poor track (on some maps it's a veritable highway, confirming that the cartographers have never been here!) from Mbala to Nkamba Bay Lodge. To find the start of this, look for a left turn about 5km after the Mbala/Mpulungu T-junction. There may be a sign to the Lufubu River there. The presence of the Lufubu River, which marks the park's southeastern boundary, helps to ensure that this is totally fictional during or just after the rains.

Even in the height of the dry season, you're going to need a 4WD with lots of spare wheels, a winch and a lot of patience. Gerard, from Ndole Bay, commented that 'intrepid drivers may want to do the journey for the sheer experience – as the countryside is wonderful and the drop from the escarpment into the Yendwe Valley is breathtakingly beautiful – but it is no short cut. The track is about 90km long, but it takes at least six hours in a good vehicle.' This road is allegedly used regularly by poachers, and there is no access to the western side of the Lufubu River.

By boat
Though a long way away, the lodges in Sumbu are easily and commonly reached by boat from Mpulungu. All three lodges use the harbour facilities of Samaki

Fishing. To get there turn left down the gravel road opposite BP's North Wind service station, which is about 500m before the Caltex Station. (Samaki is run by the friendly and helpful Jeanne and Chris Blignaut, who can be reached on tel: 04 455103; fax: 4555008; email: ckachese@zamnet.zm.)

You need to arrange the transfers in advance with the lodges. Each lodge has different speeds and sizes of boat available, at different costs. A 'banana boat' (a long, thin chug-chug motor boat) will take about six hours to Sumbu, whilst a speedboat will arrive in less than two hours. If you arrive with your own vehicle, or even towing your own boat, then you can usually park your vehicle and trailer/boat safely at Samaki whilst you go to Sumbu. A launching ramp is available, and there's usually no charge for this, though you must ask permission from Samaki's staff and security guards. They're usually very helpful, and it's strongly recommended that you tip them for this very useful service.

Transport boats
If you don't want to hire a boat for the trip, then transport boats do ply up and down, but they're very crowded. Ask around at Samaki, and expect to pay about US$5/Kw12,000 per person for the trip, which takes about ten hours. If you want to hire your own, then ask water taxis at the main market, and expect to pay around US$130–140/Kw320–350,000 one way. (You can always check the current rates with the Samaki staff, and then bargain from a position of knowledge at the market.)

Getting around
With the growth of the new privatised lodges in the area, the network of roads in the park has been extended and improved vastly in the last few years. Kasaba Bay Lodge have put in good roads around the Inangu Peninsula, Nkamba Bay Lodge have improved the roads in the Nkamba Valley, and Ndole Bay Lodge (and a helpful local couple who live here, the Blignauts) have developed those around the Chisala River, putting in various game-drive loops. Plans are even afoot to develop further roads within the Nundu Headland area. However, note that many of these areas still cannot be accessed during the rains.

Camps and lodges
There are two lodges actually within the park, Nkamba Bay and Kasaba Bay. A third lodge, Ndole Bay, lies on the shoreline just outside the park's northwestern boundary.

Both of the lodges in the park were run by the government, and both were in terminal decline by the early 1990s. They were expensive yet poorly maintained. Eventually they were put up for tender in late 1995 and snapped up by private operators. Ndole Bay Lodge was originally privately owned, but was taken by the government in 1989... only to be closed down in the early 1990s when its trade disappeared. Recently Ndole Bay reverted to its previous owners and is thriving once again.

All three lodges are now in private hands, and all have been regenerated with extensive refurbishment and investment in the past few years. They have good facilities to cater to upmarket visitors in search of somewhere special. Sumbu's future for tourism is looking brighter than ever!

Kasaba Bay Lodge (13 chalets) Contact via Naturelink at PO Box 15585, Sinoville 0129, South Africa. Tel: (2712) 543 3448/9; fax: 543 9110; email: naturelink@mweb.co.za
Kasaba Bay Lodge is within the park, and the nearest of the three lodges to Mpulungu. Its chalets all overlook the lake, most of them standing separately. They are spacious, brick

structures with thatched roofs and, inside, polished stone floors. Originally this was built as one of the 'presidential lodges' for Kenneth Kaunda. All the chalets have en-suite showers and toilets. Mossie nets hang over the beds, and colourful fabrics lighten the mood. None have air-conditioning or fans yet, but there are plans to change this.

The main lodge has a deck overlooking the lake, and space to eat inside or out (under a large tree). The wooden-panelled bar occupies a corner of the dining room, complete with a few photos of the lodge as it was and some local carvings. Historians will note that it was here that Mozambique's president Samora Machel met regional leaders before he caught his fatal flight in 1986.

Boats are available for hire, from US$30–150 per day. Game drives or boat cruises are US$10 per person, walks US$5 per person, all based on a minimum of four people.

Finally one spot well worth an excursion is the balancing rocks (one large rock balancing on three small ones) which stand on the Nundo Head Peninsula – it's a favourite trail destination shrouded in local mystery.

Rates: US$200 per person sharing, US$300 single, including all meals, tea and coffee

Nkamba Bay Lodge (9 thatched chalets) Contact via Gametrackers' Safaris, PO Box 33772, Lusaka. Tel: 01 288044/287291; fax: 287677/288884; email: nkamba@zamnet.zm
Nkamba Bay is currently owned by a Gametrackers', who cater largely for local hunters on fishing expeditions and have few overseas visitors. Nkamba has nine thatched chalets, each of which has its own private veranda, overlooking the lake, and an en-suite bathroom. I haven't visited it, but it's said to have been renovated well: keeping the rustic atmosphere whilst introducing more comfort and bringing the place up to more modern standards.

Currently activities include boat hire at US$24/90 per hour/day plus fuel (US$30/120 if 'luxury' boat is used). They have five speedboats, and this is the lodge's main focus. Game drives are US$12 per person; game walks are US$30 per person for a full day (including lunch) or US$24 for a half-day including snacks. Nkamba have set up special hides overlooking reedbeds near the lodge to look for sitatunga. Trips here cost US$12 per person. Note that none of Nkamba's rates quoted here include VAT, service, or national park fees.

Rates: US$65 per person sharing, US$85 single, room only. Meals are US$15 per person per meal, transfers to/from Kasaba Bay Airport are US$10 per person

Ndole Bay Lodge (13 chalets and a campsite) PO Box 21033, Kitwe. Tel: 02 711150; fax: 711390; cell: 01 780196; email: ndolebay@coppernet.zm
Owned and run by Gerard and Barbara Zytkow, Ndole Bay Lodge stands beside Lake Tanganyika in Cameron Bay, just to the northwest of the Sumbu National Park boundary. Being outside the park gives it a little more autonomy, allowing it, for example, to operate a small campsite here.

It has its own private beachfront on the lake, and the chalets and main lodge area are set back from this, spaced out within the dense foliage surrounding the beach. It's a lovely wild spot and, despite its many creature comforts, still feels deep within the African bush.

The chalets are generally very spacious with thatched roofs on stone walls, and en-suite showers and toilets. All are well decorated and comfortably furnished. (Some are large enough for a few extra beds if required – and one even has three separate double rooms with a large lounge area.)

The main area of the lodge has a dining room linked to its bar, both under a marvellously large thatched roof, with a low wall (of natural stone) around it. It's a very practical design – cool and airy, with a space for a welcome breeze. Down beside the beach is another thatched lounge with low walls and open sides leading out on to a wooden sundeck with loungers. Both are comfortably furnished with comfy seats and plenty of space.

Beside the main lodge is a separate campsite which has running water and barbecue stands, and a nice clean ablution block with toilets and hot showers. Campers can book into the lodge for meals, and are usually allowed to use its facilities – provided they are careful not to disturb the other guests.

Activites at Ndole Bay include angling, game drives, nature walks, birding trips, lake cruises, snorkelling and water skiing. It's really the only one of the Sumbu lodges where it is safe to swim and snorkel from the beach in front of the lodge (hence also the water-skiing). Excursions further afield include trips to local hot springs, kapenta fishing rigs (a night trip to watch local fishermen catching fish using bright lights) and Kalambo Falls. You can hire various types of boats here (ranging from US$40 to 180 per day!), snorkelling equipment and basic fishing tackle. Scuba diving trips can also be organised by special arrangement.

The lodge also has a small swimming pool, for magical cooling dips, and a shop for essential toiletries, local crafts and curios and fishing lures! This is an excellent place with exceptionally helpful owners – it's well worth a visit.

Rates: US$125 per person sharing, US$140 single, including all meals. US$75 for children under 12 if sharing; infants stay free. Camping US$15 per person

What to see and do

Angling has always been a huge draw for coming to Sumbu, because of the huge variety of fish that can be caught on rod and line. Lake Tanganyika (and especially the Sumbu area) has a first-class reputation in freshwater angling circles, and it is not unusual for visitors to catch a dozen different species in a single visit.

As the lodges extend their influence and the numbers of animals increases, game-viewing is once again becoming another reason to venture up here. Apart from the ubiquitous puku, most antelope species are still re-establishing their populations; so although you won't see huge herds, you should see some good game here. The lodges have all worked to increase the road network for game drives, and the animals themselves are becoming much more relaxed as a result. Fortunately, with a large area and only a few lodges the roads are very quiet and other vehicles are a pleasant rarity. The birdwatching here has always been excellent.

Each of the lodges organises its own activities, but you can expect game drives and birding walks, as well as cruises on the lake, fishing trips, and excursions which include trips to Mpulungu (if you like) and Kalambo Falls.

THE ROAD TO MWERU WANTIPA

Coming from Kapiri Mposhi, it's always wise to refuel at Serenje. Then, about 36km further along the Great North Road, there's a main left turning signposted to Samfya and Mansa. This is the artery that runs over 580km of tar to Nchelenge, in the far northwest corner of the country.

The section of this up to the T-junction (just west of Samfya) is usually referred to as the 'Chinese Road' because, like TAZARA, the Chinese built it. After about 55km you'll pass the entrance on your left to Kasanka National Park, and then 10km later the right turn which leads to the Livingstone Memorial and Bangweulu.

Continuing, the first town of note is Samfya…

Samfya

About 260km after turning on to the Chinese Road from the Great North Road, you'll reach a T-junction. Turn right and after about 9km you'll reach Samfya, a small town beside the remarkable white, sandy beaches of Lake Bangweulu. However, there's really nowhere to stay here and do remember that the lake is full of crocodiles – however tempting the beach looks.

Note that Lake Bangweulu has regular postboats on it, similar to the postbuses, which collect and deliver mail to the island communities in the lake. Like the buses, these will happily take paying passengers. So if you have your camping kit and food, and feel like a few days' adventure, perhaps this is the perfect place for you to start.

Mansa

About 73km from the T-junction, or 81km from Samfya, Mansa is a larger place with a BP station, a Barclays Bank, and a couple of places to stay. Of these, the Mansa Hotel is by far the best.

The Mansa Hotel (30 rooms) PO Box 710008, Mansa. Tel: 02 821606; fax: 821407

The Mansa Hotel is in town immediately next to Barclays Bank, just down the road from the main Catholic church. It has thirty rooms, all simply furnished but very clean and pleasant. Each has an en-suite bathroom, with toilet and bath.

It also has a lively and well-stocked bar, and a small restaurant serving breakfast, lunch (Kw8,500) and dinner (Kw8,500). The staff is also friendly and very helpful, making this the obvious place to stop if you're not planning to camp. It's a cut above the average of Zambia's town hotels.

Rates: Kw61,000 per room, including continental breakfast

Getting there and away

Driving north from Mansa, after about 9km the road splits and there appears to be a choice. The left turn is to Mwense, Mbereshi and Nchelenge, whilst the road straight ahead is for Kawambwa. The Kawambwa road looks as if it's beautifully tarred. And it is. But only for the first 25km, after which it rapidly deteriorates into a very bad dirt road, which is well worth avoiding.

If you're heading towards Kawambwa take the road to Mbereshi via Mwense, and then turn right at Mbereshi for Kawambwa. It's much easier and quicker.

The Luapula Waterfalls

The Chinese Road from south of Kasanka to Nchelenge skirts the Bangweulu area, and then runs north. It follows the valley of the Luapula River, which flows north into Lake Mweru. Frequently rivers cross it, flowing from Zambia's higher ground to the east, down towards the Luapula River (the border with DRC). Along this route there are numerous lovely waterfalls, many virtually unmarked, including the following:

Mumbuluma Falls

About 34km north of Mansa (167km from Mbereshi) there's a poorly signposted turning left. After about 15km of rather bad track you'll reach the falls. The water goes over a two-stage drop, about 30m across. There are attractive rapids in between and a deep pool at the bottom – but no facilities at all.

Musonda Falls

About 60km north of Mansa (141km south of Mbereshi) you cross the Mwense Bridge over the Luongo River. There is a lovely set of falls near here, but you first need to get permission to view them from the nearby hydro-electric power station. This can be time-consuming, although locals who have seen the falls say that the view is well worth the effort.

Mambilima Falls

About 90km north of Mansa, and 161m south of Nchelenge (111km from Mbereshi), there's a set of lovely rapids on the Luapula River, about 12km from the main road. Turn off west, as indicated by a signpost, and gaze over at DRC on the other side of the river. These used to be called the Johnstone Falls, and they make a very pleasant spot to stop for lunch.

From Mbereshi to Kawambwa and Mporokoso

Turning east at Mbereshi, towards Mporokoso, you turn off the tar and on to a good gravel road. Note that after about 86km from Mporokoso there is a pontoon – the Chimpembe Pontoon – across the Kalungwishi River. This only operates from 06.00 to 18.00, though you'd be very unwise to be travelling on these roads outside these hours. Some interesting detours off this road include:

Mbereshi church

Just after you turn off the main road at Mbereshi, there's a church beside the road that is one of Zambia's earliest. It was built in the early 1900s by the London Missionary Society.

Ntumbachushi Falls

These falls are very clearly signposted about 23km east of Mbereshi and 20km west of Kawambwa. The track to them is good, and they are only about 3km south of the road.

These make a good spot to camp, and an ideal base from which to visit the many other waterfalls in the area. The main falls drop about 40m into a dark pool, with a second cataract alongside. Don't swim in the main pool, as there are strong currents and undertows that can pull you under the falls themselves. However, both the second cataract and the area above the first falls are ideal for a cooling dip or a proper swim. All around here you'll find some beautiful thick *mishitu* forest.

Falls on the Kalungwishi River

Here the Kalungwishi River forms the boundary between Luapula and Northern provinces of Zambia, and also the eastern boundary of Lusenga Plain National Park. This has three major waterfalls in a relatively close succession – Lumangwe, Kabweluma and Kundabwika.

If you've time to spend here then there are miles of pleasant walking upstream, and a small self-contained cottage here, Cascade Cottage. Perhaps consider staying here and using a day to explore the other falls further downstream.

Where to stay

You can camp at Lumangwe or Kundabwika Falls, or very nearby there's a small cottage:

Cascade Cottage

There are two ways to reach the cottage. One is off the road to the Lumangwe Falls from the main road. However, the easiest way is to follow a clear sign to 'Cascade Cottage Tourist Accommodation' which is about 300m from the Chimpempe pontoon on the road between Kawambwa and Mporokoso. The cottage is about 2km from the sign; just follow the tracks.

The cottage is simply furnished, though has more home comforts than you would expect in such an isolated area. It has four beds and two sofa-beds (which can be used separately or joined to make a double bed). Linen and mosquito nets are provided if requested, and the kitchen has cooking utensils, crockery and cutlery.

There's a solar-powered system of lights and the cottage has running water which is powered ingeniously by a paddle wheel driven by the Kalungwishi River. There are plans to set up a simple methane generator for the kitchen, making the cottage completely environmentally self-contained.

There is a small cascade in the river nearby, Chimpempe Falls. The main Lumangwe Falls are 5km away, Kabweluma Falls 10km. A caretaker, called Happy, usually looks after the cottage. He will guide you around if you want to walk down to Kabweluma (for which he appreciates a tip).

The cottage is owned by an Australian couple, Ron and Lyn Ringrose, who now live mostly in Lusaka (mobile tel: 01 772052; email: 101663,2471@compuserve. com). They came out to Zambia on an aid project in 1992, and were offered the land near the waterfalls by the local chief, in return for their help for the local community. Despite being due back in Australia in 1995, they've stayed in Zambia ever since.

Rates: US$10 per person per night for the cottage

Lumangwe Falls

To reach these, turn off the Kawambwa to Mporokoso road about 2km east of the Chimpempe pontoon – which crosses the Kalungwishi River about 65km from Kawambwa and 86km from Mporokoso. Note that this only operates from 06.00 to 18.00.

The falls are clearly signposted on the north side of the road, and the outside of a bend. The track bends left and continues for about 9km to the falls themselves. There's a caretaker here and you may have to sign in. It is possible to camp here and quite safe.

Lumangwe is a solid white-and-green wall of water, 100m across and 40m high. The noise is deafening and the air is filled with fine mist. The energetic might want to climb to the bottom of the falls in order to reach the bottom of the rainbow that's seen on most days. (There are no pots of gold here though…) It's perhaps the most spectacular of the waterfalls in this region and bears comparison with Victoria Falls.

Kabweluma Falls

These falls are 5km downstream from Lumangwe, which makes a pleasant walk for two or three hours through the forest. Ask for precise directions at Lumangwa. The vegetation is quite lush and thick, and you'll emerge to see a most magnificent waterfall – a curving curtain of water 20m high and 75m across. Below is a deep pool, which itself flows over a second fall of 20m. On the left are two cataracts falling the whole 40m; on the right water pours down the cliff face. Look about you and this makes 180° of water – with the cataract, the main waterfall, and the waterspout. It's a lovely spot.

Kundabwika Falls

Though on the same river, these are accessed from a different road. The normal route starts about 63km from Mporokoso and 88km from Kawambwa, where there is a junction. Most maps mark this as a place called Mukunsa. To reach Kundabwika take the road northwest that doesn't lead to either Kawambwa or Mporokoso.

This passes through villages for about 30km, and then descends into less populous woodlands. After about 45km from Mukunsa there is a left turning with two small signs saying 'Hydro' fixed to trees either side of a track. This leads down to the river, where there are plenty of places to camp.

However, this road was washed out in about February 1999, and has not yet been repaired. Now the best route to these falls is to drive 65km north of Nchelenge to the town of Mununga, on the banks of Lake Mweru. Then turn east on to the Kaputa road. After 30km this road splits: the left branch heads through Mweru Wantipa National Park to Kaputa, while the one going straight ahead continues to join the Kawambwa–Mporokoso road. After about 5km you reach a small right turn with two small signs saying 'Hydro', as above. Continuing further would bring you to the place where the road is washed out.

To get the best view of the falls, walk to the top of the rock outcrop. It's not possible to get very close to the falls, but there are good long-distance views from here. Kundabwika is a geometrical waterfall, a 25m-wide rectangular block of green and white water

Lusenga Plain National Park

Lusenga Plain was originally designated as a park to protect a large open plain, fringed by swamp and dry evergreen forest and surrounded by ridges of hills, but without enough support it is now a park in name only. Poaching has reduced the game considerably and, with no internal roads in the park, there are few reasons to visit.

On its northeastern side the park is bordered by the Kalungwishi River, which passes over three beautiful waterfalls, described above.

Getting there

Recent visitors have had success in reaching the park by getting a game scout for a guide from the National Parks and Wildlife Office in Kawambwa. Otherwise the park is hard to enter. It is usually approached from the Kawambwa–Mporokoso road, and you should be very well equipped for any attempt to reach it.

Nchelenge

This is a small town near the shores of Lake Mweru, which is the base for a thrice-weekly ferry service out to the two populated islands in the lake: Kilwa and Isokwe.

There are two places to stay here. The Lake Mweru Water Transport Guest House (tel: 02 972029/64) is down by the waterfront and its clean rooms have en-suite facilities. No meals are provided, so look to eat out at one of the cafés – *nshima* and fish is the normal dish. This is also the place to organise boat trips out to Isokwe and Kilwa.

The nearby Nchelenge Resthouse (tel: 02 972045/10) is a slightly less attractive alternative, run by the Nchelenge District Council. This area by Lake Mweru will seem just like a continuous series of lakeside fishing villages. The fishing is (apparently) excellent, but there's also an abundance of crocodiles.

Birdwatchers might like to take a detour, using the track to the shore next to Chabilikila Primary School, which is just south of Nchelenge. This will lead you to some areas of papyrus near the mouth of the Luapula – a promising spot for finding swamp-dwelling species.

Mweru Wantipa National Park

This is another large tract ($3,134km^2$) of Zambia that was once a thriving national park. It was renowned for having large elephant and crocodile populations. Now poaching has much reduced these, though reports suggest that some big game still lives here. The lake shores are dense papyrus beds, and claims are even made that sitatunga can still be found here.

The main road from Nchelenge to Kaputa goes straight through the park, on the side of Lake Mweru Wantipa, so look out for animals. If you anticipate camping here, or even exploring, then try to find some local national park scouts (perhaps at Kawambwa or Kaputa) and ask for one of them to accompany you.

Mporokoso

Mporokoso is a useful small town in the heart of northern Zambia. In early 1999, following problems with the war in DRC, a number of refugees and loyalist

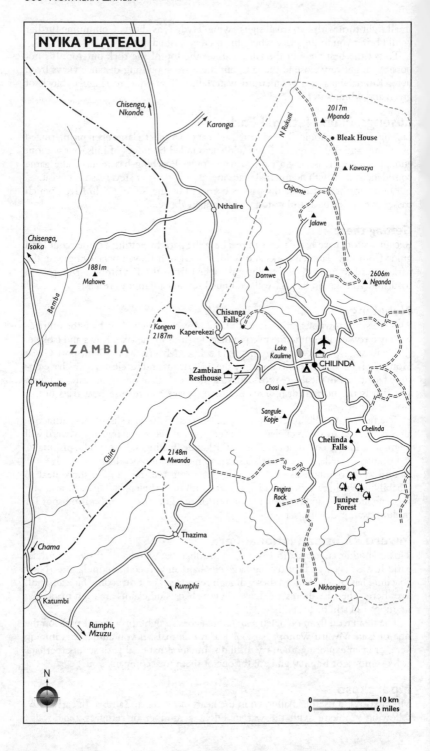

NYIKA PLATEAU

Chisenga,
Nkonde

Karonga

N Rukuru

2017m
▲ Mpanda

● Bleak House

▲ Kawozya

Chipome

Nthalire

▲ Jalawe

Chisenga,
Isoka

1881m
▲
Mahowe

Domwe ▲

2606m
▲ Nganda

Bemba

Chisanga
Falls

▲ Kongera
2187m   Kaperekezi

Lake
Kaulime

✈

ZAMBIA

△

■ CHILINDA

Muyombe ●

Zambian
Resthouse □

Chosi ▲

Sangule
Kopje ▲

▲ Chelinda

Chelinda ●
Falls

Chire

2148m
▲
Mwanda

Fingira
Rock
▲

Juniper
Forest

Chama

Thazima

Rumphi

▲ Nkhonjera

Katumbi

Rumphi,
Mzuzu

N

0 ———————— 10 km
0 ———————— 6 miles

Congolese troops fled across the border to Zambia, crossing around Kaputa and Sumbu. The refugees (currently around 12,000 people) are being looked after by the UNHCR, the Red Cross, Oxfam and other agencies in a new camp. This is about 60km outside Mporokoso on the way to Kawambwa.

There have, to date, been no problems caused by their presence and no reports of danger posed by either the troops or refugees. However, you should check with reliable local sources that this is still the case before coming up to this area.

There's also a fairly large government hospital here (with doctors but generally poor medicines and equipment), serving a large area of the country.

Getting there and away

If you're approaching Mporokoso from Mpulungu or Mbala, then about halfway to Mbala from Kasama you'll pass the Nondo Mission. Continue for a further 18km towards Kasama and you'll find a turn-off right, to the west. This road is about 60km long and will take you through to the Kasama–Mporokoso road, joining it about 8km northeast of Kapatu Mission (70km from Mporokoso). This is a very rough road; 4WD is essential, and it's difficult in the wet season.

A further 15km along this Kasama–Mporokoso road (about 23km from Kaputa Mission and 55km from Mporokoso) is a left turn, heading southwest. This short cut joins the Kasama–Luwingu road. It's not in superb condition, but is just passable in a normal car during the dry season, though you would certainly need a 4WD when it's wet.

NYIKA PLATEAU NATIONAL PARK

Nyika Plateau is a marvellous area for hiking, and has some unusual wildlife. It lies mostly in Malawi, with just a slim Zambian national park hugging the border, and is best approached from the Malawian side. For this reason, below is a description of the plateau as a whole, and how to see it, including directions within Malawi.

Geography

Nyika Plateau National Park is a tiny Zambian national park of only 80km^2. However, it adjoins Malawi's Nyika National Park, which is the country's largest national park. This was established in 1965 and extended to its present size of 3,134km^2 in 1978. At the heart of both parks lies the gently undulating Nyika Plateau, which averages over 2,000m in altitude.

In addition to the main plateau, the Malawian National Park also protects part of the eastern slopes of the Nyika range, where grassland and forest are replaced by thick miombo woodland.

Flora and fauna

Nyika is notable for its wonderful montane scenery, and as being an ideal hiking destination. The lower slopes harbour miombo woodland, which is replaced by more open grassland at the higher altitudes.

Of particular interest to botanists are the roughly 200 orchid species recorded in the park, of which 11 species are endemic to Nyika.

Mammals

Nyika protects a rich diversity of mammals – almost 100 species have been recorded – including an endemic race of Burchell's zebra, *Equus burchelli crawshaii*, and a very high density of leopard.

Game viewing is good all year round, and the open nature of the plateau ensures excellent visibility. In the area around Chilinda, the main camp, visitors are practically guaranteed to see roan antelope, scrub hare, zebra, reedbuck, bushbuck and (in the rainy season only) eland. Your chances of seeing leopard around Chilinda are good.

The lower slopes of miombo woodland support good populations of buffalo and elephant, though these animals only rarely move up to the grassland of the plateau. Lion and cheetah are also infrequent visitors to the plateau.

Birds

With well over 400 species recorded, Nyika supports a great diversity of birdlife. However, this figure is rather deceptive as many of the species included on the checklist are found only in the inaccessible miombo woodland of the lower slopes, and are thus unlikely to be seen by visitors who stick to the plateau.

Nevertheless, the grassland around Chilinda Camp is inhabited by several tantalising birds. Foremost are the wattled crane, Denham's bustard and the exquisite scarlet-tufted malachite sunbird (distinguished from the commoner malachite sunbird by its much longer tail). More rewarding than the grassland for general birding are the forests, particularly the large Chowo forest near the Zambian Resthouse, where localised species such as Sharpe's akalat, bar-tailed trogon, olive-flanked robin, white-breasted alethe and a variety of other robins and bulbuls may be seen.

Four birds found at Nyika (yellow mountain warbler, churring cisticola, crackling cloud cisticola and mountain marsh widow) have been recorded nowhere else in Malawi, while the Nyika races of red-winged francolin, rufous-naped lark, greater double-collared sunbird and Baglafecht weaver are all endemic to the plateau. There are also three butterfly species endemic to the plateau, and one species each of chameleon, frog and toad which are found nowhere else.

The rivers and dams on the Nyika Plateau are stocked with rainbow trout, and are thus popular with anglers.

An entrance fee of US$5 per person per day is charged for visiting the Malawian side of Nyika.

Getting there and away
By air

By far the easiest way to Nyika is by air. Since early 1998, Air Malawi has been running scheduled flights to the Chilinda airstrip via Mzuzu. This makes sense even for those on a budget, as the cost of a return ticket to Chilinda from Mzuzu is only about US$60. The views from the aircraft are stunning, if you've picked a clear day with few clouds, and you can clearly see the foothills, the patches of natural forest, the plantations in Linnaean symmetry and the open expanses of rolling heathland.

There are currently two flights per week, but it's not at all unknown for the schedules to change, even at very short notice, so it's best to book a seat far in advance, and then check that the schedule is still the same a week or so before you fly.

By road

Coming from Malawi, Chilinda Camp lies roughly 100km from Rumphi, and is reached along roads which shouldn't present any problem to a 2WD in the dry season but which will require a 4WD vehicle after heavy rains. The route is clearly signposted: from Rumphi you need to follow the S85 westwards for roughly 50km, then turn right into the S10 to Chitipa. Thazima entrance gate is 8km along the S10. About 45km past the entrance gate, a signposted left turn-off leads to the

Zambian Resthouse, which lies about 2km from the S10. Perhaps 500m further towards Chitipa, you'll see the turn-off to the right signposted for Chilinda Camp. Chilinda lies about 16km from this turn-off.

The best place to stock up on food before you reach Nyika is Mzuzu, and the last place where you can buy fuel is Rumphi. The drive between Lilongwe and Nyika cannot be done in a day during the rains, and it's a very long slog even in the dry season.

Hitchhiking

There is no public transport all the way through to Chilinda. In the dry season, a twice-weekly bus between Rumphi and Chitipa can drop you at the turn-off from where you'll have to either walk the last 30km to Chilinda – it's reasonably flat – or else try to hitch. In the rainy season there is no bus but you can get easily get a lift from Rumphi along the S85 (ask for a vehicle heading to Katumbi). Then walk the 8km from where you will be dropped to the entrance gate – where, provided you have a tent, you can camp. Facilities there are very basic.

If you want to hitch, you'd be wiser trying to do so from Rumphi all the way to Chilinda, and be sure of not getting stuck halfway. The best days to hitch are Fridays and Saturdays, which is when Malawian residents tend to head to the park (but also when accommodation is most likely to be fully booked – not a problem, of course, if you have a tent).

Another option is to ask the National Parks and Wildlife Office Service in Mzuzu (next to the bus station) whether they have any vehicles heading to Chilinda, bearing in mind that such vehicles are infrequent and very often too loaded with park staff for tourists to be offered a lift.

One of the options for backpackers leaving the park is to hike to Livingstonia over two or three days.

Where to stay

There's currently only one viable place to stay in the area – **Chilinda Camp**. This overlooks a beautiful small dam, and is encircled by extensive pine plantations. Its bar is open to all and will serve anyone staying around Chilinda, which means that it's normally very quiet indeed. The camp is very good and run by a first-class team from the Nyika Safari Company. Contact them via PO Box 2338, Lilongwe, Malawi; tel/fax: (265) 740848; fax: 740579; email: nyika-safaries@malawi.net.

In the main camp are six double **rooms**, each having an en-suite bathroom with toilet and bath. These are simple and solid, with a huge fireplace in the bedroom that really comes into its own in the winter – roaring log fires are exactly what you need. The baths are large and old, and the hot-water system good. These cost about US$182/280 single/double, including full board and all activities.

Alongside the rooms are four private **chalets**, each of which costs US$100 for up to four people. These have a large lounge, a bathroom with toilet and bath, two bedrooms, and a fully equipped kitchen. There's a resident chef who will prepare your food for you if you wish, but you must bring it all with you. Realistically, this is only an option if you are driving up here. Although there is a shop here, it's not at all reliable and its range of goods is exceedingly limited.

About 2km from the main Chilinda Camp is a **campsite**, where you can pitch your own tent. It's in a lovely spot in the forest and has a large, clean ablutions block that should soon have hot water. If you wish to eat in the main camp then you can, provided that you book in advance – US$10 for breakfast or lunch, and US$15 for dinner. Note that there are now no permanent tents here; you must bring your own.

On the Zambian side of the plateau there is a **resthouse**, which used to be run by Robin

Pope Safaris (see page 257) from the Luangwa. It was situated near some extensive patches of indigenous forest, making it very popular with birdwatchers. It had four double bedrooms, hot showers and an equipped kitchen with resident cook... but has sadly been shut down and fallen into disuse – so forget staying here.

Thanks to a large grant of aid money, there's a 16-bed upmarket **lodge** being constructed near Chilinda. It's now almost finished and will be the place to stay in the area when completed – large and luxurious log cabins, on the edge of the forest and overlooking the expanses of the plateau. Contact the Nyika Safari Company for more details of this, as they will be running it. Staying here will cost about US$260/400 single/double, including full board and all activities (but not park fees or drinks).

What to see and do

Nyika National Park has many very scenic spots, archaeological sites, and an extensive network of roads and trails. There are many different hiking and driving options. The following synopsis of major attractions serves as a taster only:

Walks around Chilinda

Plenty of roads radiate from Chilinda Camp, and it would be quite possible to spend four or five days in the area without repeating a walk. A good short walk for visitors with limited time is to the two dams near Chilinda. The road here follows a dambo and the area offers good game viewing (reedbuck and roan antelope), as well as frequent sightings of wattled crane. The round trip covers 8km and takes two hours. The dams offer good trout fishing in season.

Another good short walk (about an hour) is from behind Chalet Four to the Kasaramba turn-off and then left along Forest Drive through the pine plantation back to Chalet Four. At dusk there is a fair chance of seeing leopards along this walk.

A longer walk is to Lake Kaulime, which lies 8km west of Chilinda. This is the only natural lake on the plateau and is traditionally said to be the home of a serpent that acts as the guardian to Nyika's animals. More certain attractions than legendary serpents are migratory waterfowl (in summer) and large mammals coming to drink. I spent a fascinating hour here once lying silent amidst the undergrowth, watching as a small group of roan antelope waded around in the deeper sections drinking their fill, and then munching the succulent waterplants under the surface.

Walks and drives further afield

Many of the more interesting points in Nyika are too far from Chilinda to be reached on a day walk, though they are accessible to visitors with vehicles.

Jalawe Rock is about 1km on foot from a car park 34km north of Chilinda. The views here are spectacular, stretching across Lake Malawi to the mountainous Tanzanian shore. With binoculars, it is often possible to see buffaloes and elephants in the miombo woodland of the Mpanda Ridge below. A variety of raptors, as well as klipspringer, are frequently seen around the rock, and the surrounding vegetation includes many proteas.

Nganda Peak is, at 2,605m, the highest peak on the plateau. It lies about 30km northeast of Chilinda, and can be reached by following the Jalawe Rock road for about 25km then turning left on to a 4km-long motorable track. It's a 1.5km walk from the end of the track to the peak.

Kasaramba Viewpoint lies 43km southeast of Chilinda. You can drive to within 1.5km of the viewpoint and then walk the final stretch. When it isn't covered in mist, the views to the lake are excellent, and you can also see remnants of the terraced slopes built by the early Livingstonia missionaries. The most extensive rainforest in Nyika lies on the slopes below Kasaramba, and visitors frequently see the localised crowned eagle and mountain buzzard in flight. From Kasaramba, a 3km road leads to the top of the pretty 30m-high Nchenachena Falls.

Further along the road to Kasaramba, also 43km from Chilinda, is a large juniper forest, the most southerly stand of *Juniperus procera* in Africa. There is a rustic cabin on the edge of the forest, from where a short trail offers the opportunity of sighting forest animals such as leopard, elephant shrew, red duiker, bushpig and a variety of forest birds. The forest can also be explored from the firebreaks that surround it.

Zovo Chipola Forest, near the Zambian Resthouse, is of special interest to birdwatchers, and also harbours several mammal species, the most commonly seen of which are bushbuck, blue monkey and elephant shrew. The larger Chowo Forest lies in the Zambian part of the park, and is also easily visited from the Zambian Resthouse. A 4km trail runs through Chowo.

Fingira Rock is a large granite dome lying 22km south of Chilinda. On the eastern side of the rock, a cave 11m deep and 18m long was used as a shelter by humans around 3,000 years ago – excavations in 1965 unearthed a complete human skeleton and a large number of stone tools. Several schematic rock paintings can be seen on the walls of the cave. A reasonable track runs to the base of the rock, 500m from the cave. The miombo woodland around Thazima entrance gate is rich in birds and noted for unusual species.

Horseback trails
A stable of around 20 horses is kept at Chilinda, with animals suitable for both novice and experienced riders. Visitors can do anything from a short morning's ride to a ten-night luxury riding trail. Shorter rides can be arranged at minimal notice, and are an excellent way of getting around, and getting closer to the game. Both eland and roan can be approached far more closely on horseback than on foot or by vehicle. Riding costs around US$10 per hour, or US$50 for a full day.

Longer riding safaris, using mobile tented camps, can be arranged given as much notice as possible (at least weeks and preferably months). These cost around US$200 per person per night, and include everything except park fees and drinks. Again, contact the Nyika Safari Company for more information.

Wilderness trails
Six wilderness trails have been designated within Nyika National Park, ranging from one to five nights in duration. Visitors wishing to use these trails must supply their own camping equipment and food, and are required to hike in the company of a National Park guide. Porters can be arranged on request, for a small extra charge. All the trails must be booked in advance through the Nyika Safari Company.

The most popular of Nyika's wilderness trails leads from Chilinda all the way to Livingstonia on the Rift Valley escarpment east of the national park. Depending on which route you select, the hike can take between one and four days (though the one-day route is, at 42km, only a realistic option if you're exceptionally fit). Note that it is not permitted to hike this route in reverse, as a guide and park fees cannot be organised at Livingstonia.

Of particular interest for wildlife viewing is the four-night Jalawe and Chipome River Trail, which passes through the miombo woodland in the northern part of the park. It offers the opportunity to see elephant, buffalo, greater kudu and a variety of other mammals that are generally absent from the plateau.

Most of the trails cost US$30 per person for the first night and an additional US$20 per night thereafter for the first two people. Additional people are charged US$5 per person per night. The Livingstone Trail commands a one-off payment of US$50 extra, above this.

Note on guidebooks

If you have the opportunity, buy a copy of Sigrid Anna Johnson's book: *A Visitor's Guide to Nyika National Park, Malawi*. It is often available at the park reception at Chilinda, and is an excellent guide to the plateau. See *Further reading* for more details. A small booklet containing a detailed map of the Chilinda area is also sold at the park reception for a nominal charge.

The above description of Nyika Plateau has been edited from an original section in the excellent *Malawi: The Bradt Travel Guide* by Philip Briggs. If you plan an extended visit to Malawi, then get hold of a copy of this before you travel – it's the standard reference on travel in Malawi.

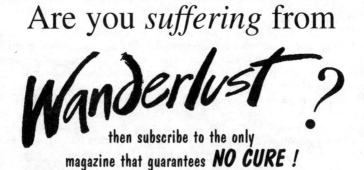

The Copperbelt

The Copperbelt is Zambia's industrial base, a prosperous area
around Ndola, Kitwe and Chingola dotted with mines –
the area's production of copper and cobalt are of global
importance. The population density here is high, and
the environmental impact of so many people can
clearly be seen. Despite this, the centres of the
Copperbelt's cities are pleasant and not the sprawling
industrial wastes that might be expected.

For the normal visitor, these areas have very few
attractions and so this chapter is deliberately concise. For simplicity's sake, this text
also aims to cover three of the main towns around the Copperbelt – Kabwe and
Kapiri Mposhi to the south, and Solwezi to the west – even though these are not
strictly part of the Copperbelt.

The history of the copper

Zambia's rich copper deposits have been exploited since around the 6th or 7th
century AD. There is evidence that the early iron-age inhabitants of Zambia mined,
smelted and even traded copper with their neighbours – bracelets and bangles have
been found at several sites.

However, large-scale exploitation of these reserves waited until the 20th
century. Around the turn of the century, the old sites where native Africans had
mined copper for centuries, like Bwana Mkubwa southeast of Ndola, were being
examined by European and American prospectors. The demand for metals was
stimulated from 1914 to 1918 by World War I, and small mines opened up to
satisfy this need. They worked well, but these small-scale productions were only
viable whilst the price of the raw materials remained high. Copper, zinc, lead and
vanadium were among the most important of the minerals being mined.

Given Zambia's location, and the high costs of transporting any produce out of
this land-locked country, it made economic sense to process the mineral ores
there, and then export the pure metal ingots. However, this would require
considerable investment and large-scale operations.

After the war, demand for copper continued to increase, fuelled by the
expansion in the worldwide electrical and automotive industries. Large-scale
mining became a more feasible option. In 1922 the British South Africa Company,
who claimed to have bought all of the country's mining concessions in various
tribal agreements, started to allocate large prospecting areas for foreign companies.
Exploration skills from overseas flowed into the country, locating several large
deposits of copper – well beneath the levels of the existing mining operations.

By the early 1930s, four large new mines were coming on stream: Nkana,
Nchanga, Roan Antelope and Mufulira. These were to change Northern
Rhodesia's economy permanently. Despite a collapse of the prices for copper in

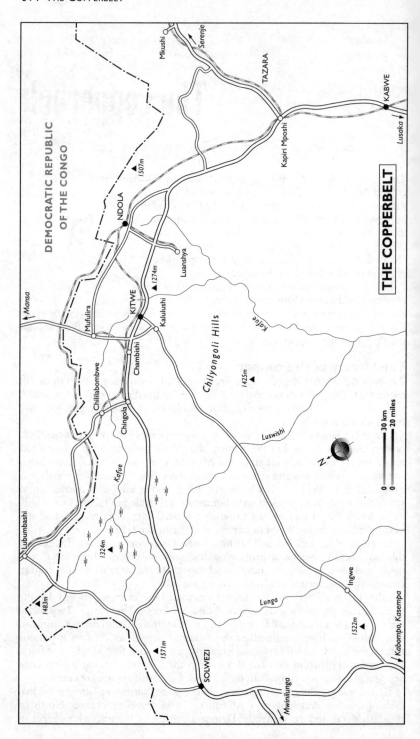

THE COPPERBELT

1931, the value of the country's exports increased by 400% between 1930 and 1933 – leaving copper accounting for 90% of the country's exports by value. Thus began the mining industry which still accounts for about 7% of Zambia's GDP and 68% of Zambia's export earnings, and employs about 11% of the workforce.

KAPIRI MPOSHI
Kapiri Mposhi's main claim to fame is that it stands at one end of the TAZARA railway. There is a constant flow of people, buses and trucks through town which makes it lively, but not safe. Kapiri is a town which visitors often pass through, but where they seldom linger. Expect people around at all times of the day and night, and be on your guard against opportunist thieves.

Getting there
Kapiri Mposhi is hard to avoid if you're travelling northwards from Lusaka. Its links to the rest of the country are excellent.

By bus
Kapiri Mposhi is very easily reached by bus, as it stands on the main routes between Lusaka and both Northern Zambia and the Copperbelt. There are very frequent arrivals and departures, especially to/from Lusaka and the Copperbelt. If you enter the town travelling north, then the bus terminus is in the centre, on your left behind a variety of market stalls.

By train
If you continue along the road going north, it will soon cross a railway line. Turn right just before this and follow the road for about 1km to reach the bustling and quite imposing TAZARA terminus.

If you did not buy one in Lusaka, then this is the place to buy your ticket to Dar es Salaam, or to find an easy way to get as far north as Kasama. It becomes exceedingly busy around train departure times, and foreigners will encounter considerable hassle. To avoid this, arrive well before the train is due to depart and take great care of your belongings. If you need to buy a ticket, then allow at least an extra hour.

Express trains run all the way to Dar, and leave at 14.27 on Tuesdays and Fridays. Ordinary trains run only to the Zambia/Tanzania border – where Nakonde and Tunduma are on opposite sides. They depart at 13.00 on Mondays, Thursdays and Saturdays. All of these services have an excellent reputation for time-keeping, which is almost unrivalled in Africa. As a guide, the express trains cost, in kwacha:

From Kapiri	1st class	2nd class	3rd class
To: Mkushi	9,500	5,600	3,000
Mpika	43,200	28,800	16,000
Kasama	51,300	31,200	19,000
Border (Nakonde/Tunduma)	67,500	45,000	25,000
Dar es Salaam	148,500	99,000	55,000

An ordinary train costs only a little less than an express, about Kw55,000 for a first-class ticket to Nakonde – instead of Kw67,000 for the express.

Hitchhiking
Alternatively, hitching there is fairly easy. Trying to hitch from within town would be difficult, so walk out a kilometre or so until you find space. Alternatively ask

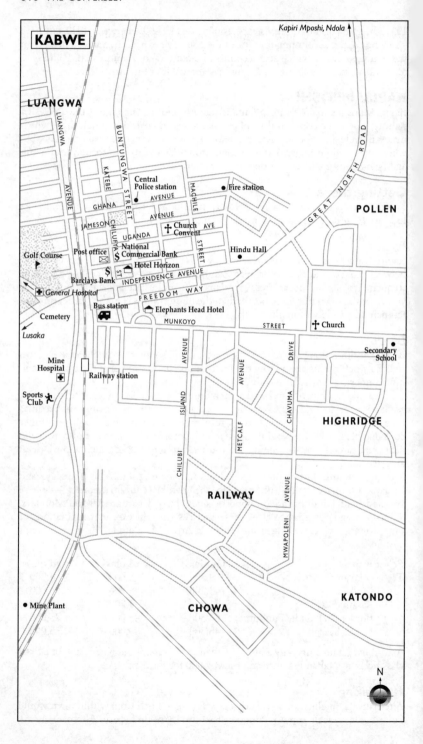

around the truckers in town for a lift. If you are going north, then get a short lift or taxi to take you the 3km to where the road to the Copperbelt proper splits off the Great North Road which continues on up to Mpika and beyond. This is an excellent hitching spot.

Where to stay

There are a few small hotels here, including the **Unity Motel** and the **Kapiri Motel**. All are basic and noisy, and rooms are rented by the hour as well as the night. Kapiri is not a town to stay in unless you have to.

Where to eat

There are lots of take-aways, though relatively little fresh food seems to be available at the market. Several stand out by virtue of their names. The **Try Again Restaurant** must surely be an invitation to unhappy customers, whilst the **Combahari Steak House and Clinic** is one to watch.

The **Malila Restaurant**, which is on the left if you are travelling north, just after the bus station, is not much of a restaurant but is probably the best shop for food supplies – tins, packets and the like.

If you are driving then look out for the bakery and Coke-shop just to the south of where the roads split, about 2–3km north of Kapiri. It also sells a good selection of pirate videos and cassette tapes. Better than this is the Agip fuel station in the centre of Kapiri, on the left as you drive north. This is cleaner and has more variety than the one above.

KABWE

This pleasant town is situated little more than 60km south of Kapiri Mposhi and about 130km north of Lusaka. It is built on the old colonial model of a perpendicular road-grid central business area, surrounded by pretty, spacious suburbs and with 'satellite' townships containing lots of high-density housing for poorer people.

These divisions have now melted a little, but the centre still has pleasantly wide streets lined with a variety of busy-looking shops. The town's economy has always been closely linked with mining, which recently has been for zinc and lead (with very high quality silver as a by-product).

The mine, which was only about 2km south of the centre, has now been closed for a few years although a consortium of locals (management buy-out) with some foreign capital have bought the rights to re-cycle its dumps. They may also be considering some further extraction here, although it's unlikely to match the mine's previous scale.

History

Kabwe, when under colonial rule, was known as Broken Hill. In 1921 an almost complete human skull was unearthed here during mining operations, at a depth of about 20m. Together with a few other human bones nearby, it's estimated to be over 125,000 years old – making these the oldest human remains that have come to light in Southern/Central Africa to date. Scientists christened the specimen *Homo rhodesiensis,* but it has always been called 'Broken Hill Man'.

Where to stay

Elephant's Head Hotel (35 rooms) PO Box 80410, Kabwe. Tel: 02 222521/2/3
On the corner of Freedom Way and Buntungwa Street, on the southern side of town, this is Kabwe's main hotel. It's not an exciting place to stay, but the rooms are clean, the TVs work,

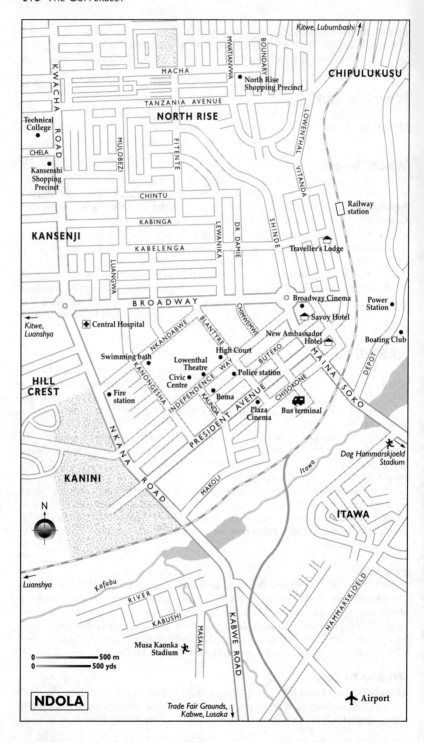

NDOLA

and there's a basic restaurant.
Rates: Kw100,000 per twin, including breakfast

Hotel Horizon Tel: 02 223398; fax: 221019
On the corner of Independence Avenue and Buntungwa Street, this is less impressive than the Elephant's Head Hotel, but also a bit cheaper.
Rates: Kw70,000 per twin, including breakfast

NDOLA

About 320km north of Lusaka, Ndola is Zambia's second largest city and the heart of the Copperbelt. Considering its strong industrial base, it is a pleasant city with broad, leafy streets and little to indicate its industry apart from a certain air of prosperity.

Getting there
By air

Ndola's airport is on the southern side of the centre of town, and well signposted off to the right as you enter town from the south. It used to be well-served by Zambia Airways, and it is now a major hub for the private airlines, with excellent links to Lusaka. A few more distant flights are gradually appearing, to/from places like Mfuwe, Livingstone and Lake Tanganyika, but it remains to be seen if these will be economic to maintain.

Inter Air is also reported to be linking Ndola with Johannesburg and Kampala, with about three flights a week. But with any of these flights, don't trust anything except the latest airline schedules as they are likely to change often.

By bus

Ndola's main bus terminus is at the southern end of Chimwemwe Road, less than a kilometre south of the Savoy Hotel – though some buses can be caught around the back of the Savoy. There are very frequent links to the other towns of the Copperbelt, and also Lusaka. To reach Northern Zambia (accessed via the road through Mkushi and Serenje) then first get a southbound (probably Lusaka) bus and change at Kapiri Mposhi.

By train

There are regular departures from Ndola to Livingstone, and back, stopping at all stations – but these are too slow to be of use to many travellers.

Hitchhiking

Ndola is quite a big town, so good hitch spots are a long walk from the centre – so consider getting a taxi for a few kilometres.

If you want to get to northern Zambia, via Mansa, then resist the temptation to 'cut the corner' by crossing into and out of DRC – it's far too dangerous.

Where to stay

There is a small choice of hotels here, but they aim at visiting business-people and prices are correspondingly high.

Savoy Hotel (145 rooms) PO Box 71800, Ndola. Tel: 02 611097/8; fax: 614001; telex ZA 30020
This has always tried to maintain its image as the most lavish hotel in Ndola, and prides itself on its casino and 'suspended swimming pool situated on the mezzanine floor'. It stands on Buteko Avenue, just off Maina Soko Road, near the eastern end of Broadway, in the heart of

Ndola. There is a secure car park here and its rooms boast CNN and 24-hour video on demand. They are comfortable and functional, but lack originality.

The Savoy was bought by its management and some private investors, a few years ago. In the past year there have clearly been some problems with it, and allegedly some disagreements amongst the partners. So it's looking pretty shabby at the moment, and may even close. (Along with the small restaurant at the airport, which the Savoy also runs.) Check on its current state before you book in here.

Rates: US$80 single, US$90 double, including breakfast

Mukuba Hotel (52 rooms plus suites) PO Box 72126, Ndola. Tel: 02 655545/ or 655738 or 655763; fax: 655729

This reasonable hotel is inconveniently located about 6km from the centre, on the southern side of town adjacent to the grounds used for the annual Trade Fair. To get there head south towards Kabwe, then take a right into the industrial area, on to Arkwright Road, then Crompton Road.

If you have transport, then it is worth the trip. The rooms all have tea/coffee makers, two telephones and a fridge. The televisions in the rooms are very well served with video channels, CNN, M-Net and various other TV stations, whilst outside there is a 9-hole golf course, with a small resident herd of impala. For a drink there is a choice of three bars, and for dining the excellent Chondwe Restaurant. If you can live with the ten-minute drive from the centre of town, this is better value than the more flashy Savoy.

Rates: US$75 single, US$80 double, including full breakfast

Travellers' Lodge (52 rooms) PO Box 240040, Ndola. Telephone: 02 621840; fax: 614476; email: travell@zamnet.zm

On the corner of Vitanda Street and Kabelenga Avenue, the Travellers' Lodge is under the same progressive management as the Edinburgh Hotel in Kitwe. It's also quite an old hotel, having opened in the mid-1940s, at the heart of Ndola's business district. (Back then it had several different names, including the Coppersmith Arms and the Naaznina Hotel.)

Its rooms all have en-suite facilities, as well as satellite TV, direct-dial telephones, mini-bar/fridges and tea/coffee machines. Downstairs there's a restaurant, a bar and secure parking.

Rates: all are charged per room, US$30–75 depending on the facilities, excluding breakfast.

The New Ambassador (30 rooms) PO Box 71198, Ndola. Tel: 02 617071

The New Ambassador is found on President Avenue, fairly near the Plaza Cinema, and is more basic than either the Savoy or the Mukuba.

Rates: Kw80,000 per twin, including a basic breakfast

Where to eat

There are plenty of take-aways around town, but for evening meals the main hotels are best. The **Mukuba**'s restaurant is good, though not cheap, and there is a choice of three bars if you feel in need of a drink.

Recently the South African 'Steers' chain has opened one of its usual steak-or-burger restaurants in the **Broadway Centre** here. Its decor is no better than the rest of that chain, but its food is reliably good – if you fancy steaks, burgers and salads. Alternatively consider one of the following:

Arabian Nights Ground Floor, Development House, PO Box 71692. Tel/fax: 02 621086
Sister restaurant to the ones in Lusaka and Kitwe, Arabian Nights serves Pakistani cuisine with a sprinkling of other dishes and a few special vegetarian options. Starters around Kw5,000–6,500, main courses Kw15,000–19,000

Hong Kong Restaurant President Av North, PO Box 72048. Tel: 02 614014; fax: 614658
A super Chinese restaurant with starters around Kw5–7,000 and main dishes Kw11–15,000 – the spring rolls and sweet and sour dishes come highly recommended.

What to see and do

Ndola doesn't have many sights as such. However, one worth looking for is the old Slave Tree on Makoli Avenue. This is a very old pod mahogany tree, *Afzelia quanzensis* (known locally as a mupapa tree), on which two species of figs are parasitic. In 1880 the Swahili slave-traders frequented this area. They built a stockade around here, using the shade of this tree as a meeting place. It was also a place where slaves were sold and traded between the various traders.

This trade was abolished here in the early 1900s, as the British established a colonial administration. Ndola was founded in 1904 and now just a representation of the tree features on its coat of arms, and a plaque at the foot of the tree reads:

> 'This plate has been placed on this mupapa tree to commemorate the passing of the days when, under its shade, the last of the Swahili traders, who warred upon and enslaved the people of the surrounding country, used to celebrate their victories and share out their spoils.'

Useful addresses

If you're in town and need help with local arrangements then contact one of the following:

Voyagers Travel Agency at Ndola Airport, PO Box 70023. Tel: 02 617062 or 620604/5; fax: 620605. Generally highly regarded.
Steve Blagus Travel 32b President Ave, PO Box 71474. Tel: 02 610993/4; fax: 619072

KITWE

Situated a few kilometres southwest of the large Nkana Mine, Kitwe is another large town which relies for its prosperity on a nearby copper mine. Getting to or from Kitwe is easiest by bus, and it's only about 65km from Ndola.

Like most of the Copperbelt towns, Kitwe has been in the doldrums for the past few years with a steady decline in amenities, activities and general infrastructure. However, recently it has also seen new shops and businesses opening regularly in anticipation of the Nkana Mine being privatised. The town centre, especially, has undergone a fairly dramatic change. If/when the full privatisation of the Nkana Mine takes place, a steady boom is anticipated and it is expected that Kitwe will expand considerably.

Getting there
By air

Kitwe has an airport – Southdowns Airport. It is about 25km west of the town on the Kalulushi and then Kalengwa roads. It is mostly local traffic and there are daily connections to Lusaka (usually with Zambian Airways, formerly Roan Air). However, Ndola is a much better airport for longer, regional flights.

By bus

Kitwe's main bus terminus is in Martindale (shown on some maps as the 'second class trading area') next to the main town centre. Here you'll find many departures for Ndola, plus daily minibus connections to Solwezi and Lusaka. There are also regular buses to the Luapula area and Northern Provinces, although buses on these long-distance routes will hang around until they fill, even if this takes a day or two.

By train

Kitwe is the end of the line from Livingstone that passes through Ndola and Lusaka, so slow trains connect it to Livingstone and Lusaka daily.

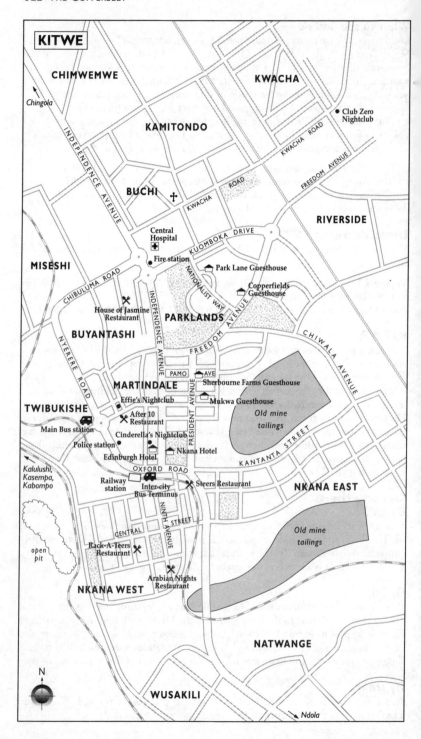

Hitchhiking

Like Ndola, Kitwe is a large town, so good hitch spots are a long walk from the centre. It is best to get a taxi for a few kilometres.

Where to stay
In Kitwe

There was a time (eg: when the last edition of this book was written) when there was little choice of accommodation in Kitwe, and that which existed was poor value. However, that's all changed as small guesthouses seem to have sprung up everywhere, leaving the large old hotels like the Edinburgh with no choice but to radically reform or go out of business.

The most recent rumour (from an impeccable source) is that the Anglo-American Corporation intends to build a US$12m shopping complex including a Holiday Inn in Kitwe, starting in July 2000. They've apparently located a site already, and the feasibility studies and plans are under way. Watch this space. Meanwhile, the current choices (which mostly accept Visa and MasterCard credit cards), in alphabetical order, are:

Arabian Nights (5 rooms) 17, 9th Av, Nkana West. Tel/fax: 226842, 221097 or 705050
As well as being one of the town's best restaurants, Arabian Nights also has five rooms for guests. They are all a reasonable size, comfortably furnished and have en-suite bathroom and toilet. Like those above their Lusaka restaurant, these rooms are better suited to longer stays, as they are an afterthought when compared with the restaurant.

Arabian Nights have four more double rooms in their 'Heer' guesthouse (20 Kanyanta Av, off Independence). This is booked through the main Arabian Nights complex, above, and room service from the restaurant can be delivered to the guesthouse.
Rates: US$35 single, US$50 double, including a full breakfast

Copperfields Executive Guesthouse (7 rooms) 48 Freedom Av, Parklands, Kitwe. Tel: 02 230709/10; fax: 231027; email: cfields@zamnet.zm
Copperfields is a double-storey Tuscan-style building that has the guesthouse and also the Copper Pot Restaurant below. The rooms are all a good standard, with en-suite showers and toilets, satellite TV, direct-dial telephones, tea/coffee machines and each even has a private safe. Laundry can be turned around rapidly and there's a facility for room service if you don't feel that social.

Note that because this is used a lot by visiting business-people during the week, it does usually offer special weekend rates.
Rates: US$53 per person sharing, US$75 single, including full breakfast

Edinburgh Hotel (78 rooms) PO Box 21800, Kitwe. Tel: 02 222444, fax: 225036; email: edin@zamnet.zm
This has always been the main hotel in Kitwe and as of 1998 is under new ownership/management. It is situated on the corner of Independence and Obote Avenues, a few blocks north of the Oxford/Kantanta Road. Within the hotel, on its ground floor, are some useful service agencies – like a travel agent, Mercury Mail and secretarial services. Just behind the hotel is a small shopping mall, the Edinburgh Arcade, which has a wider variety of small shops.

In the last two years the Edinburgh has been completely refurbished, and there are now a range of different rooms at different prices. There are executive suites, mini-suites, superior rooms, deluxe rooms, and a whole floor of budget rooms – all of which have en-suite facilities, telephones and satellite TVs. It's all very impressive.

For all the guests there's the Highlander Restaurant, several bars, a casino, a swimming pool and secure parking. If you want somewhere efficient and central, this could be for you.
Rates: budget US$30, standard US$50, superior US$60, executive suite US$100 – all rates are per room and include full breakfast

House of Jasmine (15 chalets and 3 rooms) Buyantanshi, PO Box 8029, Parklands, Kitwe. Tel: 02 215124 or 210134; fax: 211142; email: jasmin@coppernet.zm
To reach Jasmine from Independence Avenue, take a left turn at the roundabout by the fire station into Chibuluma Road. Take the first left turn into Poinsettia Road, and Jasmin Close is then the second road on the left.

Jasmine has a variety of different rooms. It has 12 double rondavels with en-suite facilities; three 'family units' with four beds and a shower toilet; and also three twin rooms within its main house, which share bathrooms. All the rondavels and rooms have satellite TV and telephones. Outside is an open area, a swimming pool and bar.
Rates: rondavels US$55 per person sharing, US$65 single. Rooms US$50 per person sharing, US$60 single

Mukwa Guest House (10 double rooms) 26 / 28 Mpezeni Av (off President Ave), PO Box 21216, Kitwe. Tel: 02 224266; fax: 224266; email: trekafrica@coppernet.zm
Mukwa (the name of a colourful local wood) is an old colonial-style building surrounded by attractive gardens and with a swimming pool. It's also the base for a local travel agent (Trek Africa Tour & Travel, tel: 02 227217/224350) and even has Kitwe's Avis car hire agency on the premises (tel: 02 227217).

Each of the rooms has satellite TV, a direct-dial telephone, a small fridge, complementary fruit basket and a facility for making tea and coffee. There's also a 'pool bar' here for relaxing, or the smart Indian/continental restaurant mentioned below.
Rates: US$53 per person sharing, US$65 single, including full breakfast

Nkana Hotel (49 singles, 9 doubles, 5 family rooms) PO Box 20664, Kitwe. Tel/fax: 02 230767
Standing opposite the Edinburgh on Independence Avenue, the Nkana attracts more Zambians than the Edinburgh, and its bar can become very lively at times.
Rates: from Kw25,000 to Kw45,000 including continental breakfast

Park Lane Guest House (9 double rooms) P O Box 20516, 672 Mabumbu Crescent, Parklands, Kitwe. Tel: 02 226855; fax: 226855; cell: 780855
Park Lane is easily found off Nationalist Way (turn right as you are going towards Kuomboka Drive). It has nine double rooms, seven have en-suite facilities, the other two share a bathroom. All have telephones and satellite TV.

You'll also find a couple of lounges, a swimming pool and jacuzzi outside amidst delightful gardens. There's a small restaurant that opens every day apart from Sundays.
Rates: en suite US$60 per person sharing, US$85 single. Others US$40 per person sharing, US$55 single. Including continental breakfast (US$4.50 extra for full!).

Sherbourne Farms Guesthouse (10 plus 4 rooms) PO Box 21058, Kitwe. Tel: 02 222168 or 230548 or 230549; fax; 02 226477 or 214870; email: sherbo@zamnet.zm
This is actually split into two, with the main guesthouse at 20 Pamo Avenue, and an annexe at 14 Mpezeni Avenue.

The main location has ten double rooms, whilst the annex has four at the moment, and five being built. (There's also a conference room and business centre being added.) All the rooms have satellite TV, mini-bar/fridges and telephones (though those in the annexe cannot make outgoing calls).

The site already has a swimming pool, jumping castle and even water slides for kids, set in attractive, established gardens. Airport transfers to/from Ndola, Chingola and Kitwe can be organised for around Kw50,000 per person. Lunch and dinner are available: starters around Kw4–6,000, main courses Kw12–15,000 and sweets Kw4–6,000.
Rates: Pamo Avenue costs US$35 per person sharing, US$55 single. Mpezeni Avenue costs US$30 per person sharing, US$45 single, including breakfast

Outside Kitwe

About 15km north of Kitwe is a place worth a special mention. Taking the road to Chingola for about 12km, you reach a right turn to Itimpi. Then about 3km down the road, you'll come to a small guesthouse:

Shamabinga Retreat (7 rooms) Plot 174, Wolfram Av, PO Box 9088, Itimpi, Kitwe. Tel 02 711448; fax 711329 or 212726.
Shamabinga has a main house with three rooms and two adjacent chalets. In the house there is a lounge with satellite TV, a kitchen, a dining room, a bar, and also facilities for guests to use the telephone and fax machine.

The larger chalet, called Shamabinga, has two rooms, each with en-suite facilities, which share a lounge, dining room and kitchen. The second chalet, Savanna, has just two rooms with their own showers and toilets, but no communal rooms. All are comfortably furnished and use local Zambian curios and crafts.

The interest in Shamabinga lies in its surroundings. This is a place containing a number of small-holdings, which in colonial days was developed as a sort of market garden to feed the towns of the Copperbelt.
Rates: Shamabinga US$75 double, US$59 single. Savanna US$65 double and US$47 single, including breakfast

Where to eat

Like Ndola, there are plenty of take-aways around Kitwe, with reliably hygienic standards – if not haute cuisine. The most notable include the **Hungry Lion** (in the centre of town) for hamburgers and pies; the new **Steers** (at the entrance to town coming from Ndola) for steaks and hamburgers; and **After 10** (in Martindale – the 'second class trading area') for snacks, sandwiches, pizzas, curries, Chinese and even Arabian dishes. The latter, predictably given its name, stays open late. Prices range around Kw4–10,000 for all these places.

For a good evening meal you need to look more carefully. Of course, if a new, large shopping centre along the lines of Lusaka's Manda Hill complex ever comes off the drawing board, and on to Kitwe's streets – as is planned – then you're likely to have even more choice. However until then try the following (and note that in addition to the restaurants listed here, the Park Lane and House of Jasmine guesthouses, mentioned above, will accept non-residents for meals).

Arabian Nights 17, 9th Av, Nkana West. Tel/fax: 02 226842/221097/705050
Sister restaurant to the ones in Ndola and Lusaka, Arabian Nights serves Pakistani cuisine with a sprinkling of other dishes and a few special vegetarian options. Starters around Kw5,000–6,500, main courses Kw15,000–19,000.

Mukwa Restaurant 26/28 Mpezeni Av (off President Av), PO Box 21216, Kitwe. Tel: 02 224266
Part of the guesthouse of the same name, Mukwa is an elegantly stylish little restaurant serving a good variety of Indian food, as well as more usual continental fare. (It could seat about 40 diners.) Expect a three-course meal to cost around Kw35–40,000 each, including a few drinks.

Acropolis Taverna Old Greek Club Premises, Wenye Way, P O Box 21416, Kitwe. Tel: 02 220703; fax: 02 229329
You'll find the Acropolis by heading towards Chingola on Independence Avenue and then taking the first right after the bridge. Keep going round a bend, and then take the first right again.

This is a big restaurant – it could seat over 200 – but has been rated as one of the country's best. A congenial host, George, runs it. He's the jovial chap who normally talks through the daily specials with you when you arrive.

Its decor is stylish and it specialises in very high quality Greek cuisine. 'Meze' is a real speciality here. The menus change regularly, but at about Kw50–60,000 for a normal three-course meal, it's not cheap.

Rack-A-Teers Restaurant 7th Av, Ek Park, Nkana West, Kitwe. Tel: 02 227800
Rack-A-Teers, which is within Nkana Squash Club's premises, opened in July 1996 as a steakhouse. It gradually expanded to cover a wider range of food and has carved out a good niche for itself. The portions are substantial and children are welcome. Expect a three-course meal including service to work out at about Kw25–30,000.

Copper Pot Restaurant 48 Freedom Av, Parklands, Kitwe. Tel: 02 230709/10; fax: 231027; email: cfields@zamnet.zm
Downstairs at Copperfields Guesthouse, this is a small restaurant that isn't only for the use of the guests.

Jubilee Restaurant Tel: 02 230610; fax: 227033; email: cacss@zamnet.zm (also during office hours tel: 02 225008 or 230611)
In the Showgrounds, this has a full à la carte menu offering well prepared continental cuisine. The decor is rustic, and it seats about 120. Expect to pay about Kw25–30,000 for a three-course meal.

Nightlife
There are several nightclubs in Kitwe – though do take local advice as the current 'in' places change regularly. The three most popular are probably Effie's, Cinderella's and Club Zero. All have pool tables, dance floors and disco music. Effie's plays a wide mix of different music, the others tend to stick more to rhumba and Rhythm and Blues.

All are frequented almost exclusively by black Zambians, and they open until very late. Overseas visitors have no problems here and the owners of the clubs are generally quite good at sorting trouble out if/when it develops. Normally these clubs have a very lively and friendly atmosphere. You should, of course, take the standard precautions that apply in any such busy places, to avoid the attention of thieves and pickpockets – by dressing down and not carrying valuables.

Entrance to Effie's is free, whilst the others charge about Kw3,000 per person. Effie's is on Blantyre Road in the 'second class trading area'. Cinderella's is on Obote Ave, in the town centre (just down from the Edinburgh Hotel). Club Zero is in Kwacha East township (turn right at traffic lights for Buchi on Independence Avenue, and this is about 3km down the road).

Emergencies
If you get ill in or near Kitwe, then there is an excellent mine hospital: Nkana Mine Hospital, PO Box 21900. (Tel: 02 243555/249555; fax: 228917/225082.) As you enter Kitwe from Ndola take a left at the first set of traffic lights, and go past the mine. The hospital is opposite Nkana's main offices.

For situations that are more serious, and may require immediate evacuation, consider also contacting one of the following two specialist services:
Speciality Emergency Services in the Garneton suburb. PO Box 20324, Kitwe.
Tel: 02 231409; fax: 231410; email ttmkemp@zamnet.zm
Health International 1 Kalemba Drive (cnr Freedom Av), Parklands, PO Box 8006, Kitwe.
Tel: 02 230715/230716; fax: 230722; email: hlthcmc@coppernet.zm

Both of the above offer ambulances and in-patient care, as well as emergency cover. They also offer short-term insurance cover for visitors, which can be arranged prior to arriving in Zambia or at their local offices after arrival.

CHINGOLA

Chingola is the end of the Copperbelt, beyond which you either proceed north towards Lubumbashi in DRC, or head west towards Solwezi and Mwinilunga.

Where to stay

There are two basic hotels in town. Both are adequate, though most visitors try to get out to the Chimfunshi Orphanage, below.

Musunshya Hotel (19 rooms) Katanga Rd, Box 10021, Chingola. Tel: 02 311115 or 311115
The Musunshya makes a point of being the cheapest hotel in town, and has 19 rooms, all fairly simple with en-suite facilities.

Lima Motel (35 rooms) PO Box 10497. Tel: 02 311894

Useful addresses

Travel International Air Charters (TIAC) PO Box, 10724, Chingola. Tel: 02 311773 or 312812 or 311212; fax: 313521; email: tiac@zamnet.zm
An expanding air charter company based in Chingola, which has even been known to take people on weekend breaks from the Copperbelt to Lake Tanganyika, departing Friday and returning Sunday evening! These typically use small planes taking five or seven passengers, and might cost around US$1,300 for the five-seater and US$1,800 for the seven-seater for the return journey.

They are now looking at scheduled services – which may include connections to Kitwe, Ndola, Mansa, Kasama and Mbala – as well as their usual charter fare. (For those with a technical bent, TIAC recently acquired a Turbo Prop Kingair B90.)

Chimfunshi Wildlife Orphanage

This haven for some of Africa's great apes is one of Zambia's gems – certainly the highlight of the Copperbelt for most visitors. Despite this, it remains firmly off the track for most visitors from overseas and not at all well known outside Zambia and South Africa. This may be changing as you read this, as there are ambitious plans to use future visitors as one source of funding for improving the facilities at the orphanage.

Background

Run by David and Sheila Siddle, Chimfunshi has started off as part of the Siddles' 10,000-acre farm. Their involvement with chimps began in October 1983 when they received an orphaned chimpanzee, named Pal, who was confiscated from Zairian poachers. Pal was very sick, having been malnourished and physically abused, and was expected to die. Sheila nursed him back to health.

Up until then, it was known that Zambia was a conduit for the (illegal) export of chimps from Zaire (now DRC). However, with nowhere practical to release any confiscated animals, the authorities had not been over-zealous in trying to stop the trade. Gradually more chimps were confiscated, and by the middle of 1988 the Siddles had 19 chimps at Chimfunshi. All were kept in cages, but taken out for regular forest walks – this was the best that could be done at the time.

Chimps are not indigenous to Zambia, and sending them back to Zaire wasn't a safe option, and so it was decided to build them a large enclosure at Chimfunshi. With minimal backing, the Siddles sectioned off seven acres of their own forest land, and built a 4m-high wall around it. Then they gradually introduced a group of chimps into it which, contrary to expectations, eventually melded into a coherent family-type group. Clearly this was a great success.

By this time orphaned chimps were being sent here from many corners of the globe. In 1991 a second enclosure was constructed to accommodate another group of chimps, this time covering 14 acres and using a solar powered electric fence. But still the numbers are growing. Now there are 69 chimps on the property, 12 of which have been born here.

The future

The Chimfunshi Trust now has title to a 13,500-acre stretch of land adjacent to Chimfunshi. The northern boundary of this is formed by the Kafue River, which surrounds a large 2,500-acre area of dense forest suitable for chimpanzees. Most of this is covered with thick bush forest, but there are also large grassy areas of river floodplain and several small tributaries of the Kafue River. There is also a patch of tropical forest, which follows a narrow gorge and is particularly beautiful.

The plan is to build a weir downstream of the new sanctuary, to raise the Kafue's water level during the dry season – thus making an effective barrier that runs around much of the perimeter of the reserve. The rest would be secured by a solar-powered electric fence. It's also planned to restock the area with indigenous animals – kudu, waterbuck, sitatunga, lechwe, zebra, hippo and the like. This would then be not only the world's largest chimpanzee sanctuary, but also a wildlife reserve in its own right. It's envisaged that there will be a conservation education centre, as well as opportunities for study by zoology students.

It's also suggested that there could be a visitors' lodge within the game area here, with the potential to provide a valuable income for the running of the sanctuary in the future.

Chimfunshi Wildlife Orphanage Trust

The orphanage is supported by a trust, based in South Africa. If you would like to help, contact them via Brenda Santon at PO Box 3555, Kempton Park 1620, South Africa. Tel: (2711) 394 0465; fax: 606 2403; email: adoption@mweb.co.za.

Getting there

Take the tar road from Chingola towards Solwezi for about 52km until there's a sign pointing right to the orphanage. From there it's about 18km of track to the sanctuary, which takes about 30 minutes to drive.

Where to stay

At present, facilities for visitors are very limited. The Siddles do take occasional paying guests, and the money raised goes to support the chimps. Their daughter and son-in-law, Lorraine and Ian Forbes, have also set up a small campsite and a few basic chalets on a nearby farm, and can arrange visits for you to see the chimps. Camping here is around US$5 per person, and Lorraine and Ian can arrange a visit to the orphanage. It's best to contact them in advance if you're coming, on tel: 02 311845, 311100 or 311293 (also a fax).

The Kafue River Basin

16

Southwest of the Copperbelt, the Kafue River Basin covers a large swathe of central Zambia stretching from almost DRC to the west of Lusaka. It encompasses large areas of very sparsely populated bush as well as the Kafue, Blue Lagoon and Lochinvar National Parks.

Much of this region of the Zambia is difficult to visit, consisting of endless seasonal bush tracks which link occasional farming settlements. At its heart lies the huge Kafue National Park, which has some superb game viewing areas within its boundaries. The best of these, the Busanga Plains, take time to reach, but at times rank with the subcontinent's most impressive game areas.

Elsewhere, there are seasonal floodplains that sustain game and attract a rich variety of birdlife – like the Lukanga Swamps and the Kafue Flats. Part of the latter is protected by two small national parks – Blue Lagoon and Lochinvar – but most such areas remain outside the parks. The Kafue River Basin is a wild area, with some excellent game and endless possibilities for exploring, but very little development.

MUMBWA

After about three hours' drive from Lusaka (148km), on the Great West Road to Mongu, a large modern factory looms next to the road. Orderly warehouses stand behind well-watered lawns. This hive of activity at Mumbwa is perhaps the country's biggest cotton ginnery.

A few kilometres west is a turning off the road to the north, which leads to the thriving township of Mumbwa, about 5km north of the ginnery. This busy little centre is a place with petrol stations, a Barclays Bank, a 'medi-test' laboratory – and lots of small local shops.

Getting there

On the far side of the shops, in the township, is the local bus station. All the buses passing through Mumbwa – heading west to Mongu or east to Lusaka – will stop here. Being a relatively busy route, there are arrivals and departures at all times of day, though the highest frequency is the middle of the day, when buses that left from Lusaka or Mongu in the morning will pass through Mumbwa.

Where to stay

La Hacienda Hotel is the only place here. It is fairly clean though very uninspiring.

KAFUE NATIONAL PARK

Park fees: US$10 per person per day. US$5 per vehicle per day

Kafue is a huge national park: two and a half times the size of South Luangwa.

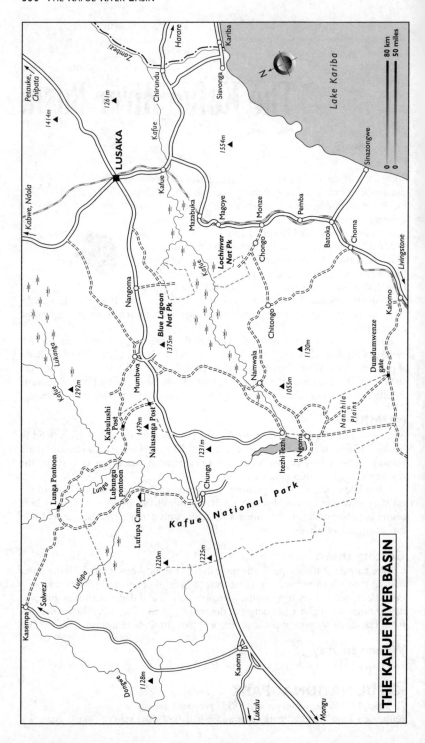

THE KAFUE RIVER BASIN

Sadly, in the '80s and early '90s, few resources were devoted to its upkeep and anti-poaching efforts were left to a couple of dedicated souls from the few safari lodges that remained in the park.

Now the situation is much better. Although many of the camps named here are not fully operational, those that are bring a steady trickle of visitors into the park – which help add weight (and finance) to the ongoing effort to build the park back up to its former glory. Even the park's elephants are visibly recovering (both in number and in terms of losing some of their shyness), although it will be a while before they return to their former strength. It is very heartening to see that the rest of the game is thriving, and occurring in numbers that deny any problems have ever existed here.

The camps here are not all as plush or well-oiled as the better camps in the Luangwa, but the game is at least as good. Game viewing in the Busanga and Nanzhila Plains can be stunning, so don't visit without at least a side-trip into one of these remarkable areas.

Geography, flora and fauna
Established in 1924, the Kafue National Park covers about 22,400km^2 (about the size of Wales, or Massachusetts) of very varied terrain and is one of the world's largest parks. Naturally, its geography varies considerably.

The map clearly shows that the park is bisected by the tarred Great West Road between Lusaka and Mongu. This provides the easiest route into the park, and also a convenient split that allows me to refer to 'northern' and 'southern' Kafue as simply meaning the areas to the north and the south of the road. These have slightly different habitats and species, and also very different access routes – in many ways they could be two separate parks.

Surrounding the whole are no fewer than eight Game Management Areas (GMAs), which do provide some element of a buffer zone for the park's wildlife.

Animals
Covering such a large area, with a variety of habitats, Kafue is rich in wildlife and many of its species seem to exhibit strong local variations in their distribution. This is a reflection of the wide variety of habitats in such a large park.

Antelope
Kafue has a superb range of antelope, but you will have to travel throughout the park if you wish to see them all. In the park's far north the permanent waters of the Busanga Swamps are home to the secretive sitatunga, which is uniquely adapted to swamp life. These powerful swimmers will bound off with a series of leaps and plunges when disturbed, aided by their enlarged hooves which have evolved for walking around on floating reed islands. They will then stand motionless until the danger passes, or even submerge themselves leaving just their nostrils above the water for breathing.

A little further south the Busanga Plains have large herds of red lechwe and puku, with smaller groups of zebra and blue wildebeest. Oribi are locally common here, as they are on the Nanzhila Plains, and you also have a good chance of seeing roan and the beautiful sable antelope.

In the main body of the park, kudu, bushbuck, eland, Lichtenstein's hartebeest, reedbuck, common duiker, grysbok and defassa waterbuck (a subspecies without the distinctive white ring on the rump) are all frequently seen. Numerically, puku dominate most of the northern side of the park, though they gradually cede to impala as you move further south.

Predators

Lion are widespread all over the park, and are easily spotted on the plains. On the Busanga Plains, where large prides stalk through nervous herds of puku and lechwe nightly, using the natural drainage ditches for cover with deadly efficiency. There are currently at least five different prides in this area, and they seem to be thriving. Elsewhere they are probably equally common, though less easily seen.

Leopard are very common throughout the main forested areas of park, though they are seldom seen on the open plains. They are most easily observed on night drives, and continue with their activities completely unperturbed by the presence of a spotlight trained upon them. They appear particularly common in the area around Lufupa – though this is probably due to the success of Lufupa Lodge's guides in locating these elusive cats. This is one of the best places in Africa for seeing leopard in the wild.

Spotted hyena are seen regularly, though not often, throughout the park. They appear to occur in smaller numbers than either lions or leopards.

Cheetah are not common anywhere, but are most frequently spotted on the Nanzhila and Busanga Plains where they seem to be thriving. Sightings have certainly become more frequent over the last few years, with some first-class instances of very relaxed cats being watched by visitors.

Occasional sightings of wild dog occur all over the park (though fewer around the road on the east side), and Kafue is Zambia's best stronghold for them. The park's huge size suits their wide-ranging nomadic habits and I have had a number of reports of them being seen on the north side of the park in the last few years. They remain uncommon in any locale, but a possibility all over the park.

Other animals

Elephants occur in Kafue, though their numbers are still recovering from intensive poaching. On the northern side of the park small herds are becoming more commonly seen, though some are still wary of humans. In 1995 they were seen often around Lufupa – the first time that this had happened in eight years. Now family groups are more common there, and becoming more relaxed. The situation is a little more advanced in the south, where elephants are now commonly seen around the Kafue River, in the Chunga and Ngoma areas.

Buffalo are widely distributed throughout the park, but seem not to be common, though herds do frequent the Busanga and Nanzhila Plains. Sadly, black rhino appear to be extinct throughout the park after sustained poaching.

The Kafue River, and its larger tributaries like the Lunga, are fascinating tropical rivers – full of life – and infested with hippo and crocodile, which occur in numbers to rival the teeming waters of the Luangwa.

Hunting and poaching

For many years ('80s and early '90s) there were few efforts or government resources devoted to protecting Kafue, and poaching was rife. This ensured the extermination of black rhino, and a sharp reduction in elephant numbers at the hands of organised commercial poachers. Fortunately the park is massive, surrounded by GMAs, and not easily accessible. So although the smaller game was hunted for meat, this was not generally on a large enough scale to threaten the population of the smaller game. Nor did it adversely affect the environment.

Organised commercial poaching is now virtually unknown, and the remaining incidence of smaller scale poaching by locals (for food) is being tackled by a number of initiatives.

Some concentrate on increasing the physical policing of the park, the most obvious being the KANTIPO anti-poaching patrols, which have been partially funded by some of the lodges. Others try to tackle the underlying reason for this poaching, and attempt to offer practical alternatives for the local people of the surrounding areas that are more attractive than shooting the game. For example, one such project allows local people in neighbouring areas to come into the park to collect natural honey. Both types of initiatives work with the help and support of some of the more enlightened local safari operators.

With the exceptions of elephant and rhino, the park's game densities appear to have been restored to normal levels in most areas, and the situation is continuing to improve.

Birds

The birding in Kafue is very good, and about 450 species have been reliably recorded here. Near the Kafue and the larger rivers expect the full range of water-birds, from fish eagles through to darters and cormorants. Even for a casual observer, many species are common and an afternoon's observation by the river would probably include several species of kingfishers, bee-eaters, geese, ducks, cranes, storks, ibises, and vultures. The brochures are fond of mentioning the existence of Pel's fishing owl – though these are resident in Kafue, they are neither common nor easily spotted wherever they occur in Southern Africa.

Specialities worth noting are the skimmers which nest on sandy beaches of islands in the middle of the river, and the shy African finfoot, which frequents the shady fringes of the slower rivers, swimming under the overhanging trees with part of its body submerged.

On the drier, southern side of the Busanga Plains you'll often find wattled cranes and the uncommon Stanley's bustard, as well as the kori bustard – the world's heaviest flying bird.

Northern Kafue

The northern section of the park is a slightly undulating plateau, veined by rivers – the Lufupa, the Lunga, the Ntemwa, the Mukombo, the Mukunashi, and the Lubuji – which are all tributaries to the main Kafue, whose basin extends to the border with DRC. The main Kafue River is already mature by the time it reaches this park, though it has over 400km further to flow before discharging into the Zambezi.

Thus in the park its permanent waters are wide, deep and slow-flowing, to the obvious pleasure of large numbers of hippo and crocodile. Its gently curving banks are overhung by tall, shady hardwoods, and the occasional islands in the stream are favourite feeding places for elephant and buffalo. In short, it is a typically beautiful large African river.

Occasionally it changes, as at Kafwala. Here there is a stretch of gentle rapids for about 7km. The river is about 1,000m wide and dotted with numerous islands, all supporting dense riverine vegetation – making a particularly good spot for birdwatching.

Most of the park's northern section, between the rivers, is a mosaic of miombo and mopane woodlands, with occasional open grassy pans known as dambos. The edges of the main rivers are lined with tall hardwood trees: raintrees *(Lonchocarpus capassa)*; knobthorn *(Acacia nigrescens)*; jackal berry *(Diospyros mespiliformis)*; leadwoods *(Combretum imberbe)*; and especially sausage trees *(Kigelia africana)* are all very common.

The Kafue's tributaries are smaller, but the larger ones are still wide and permanent. The Lufupa is probably the most important of these. It enters the park

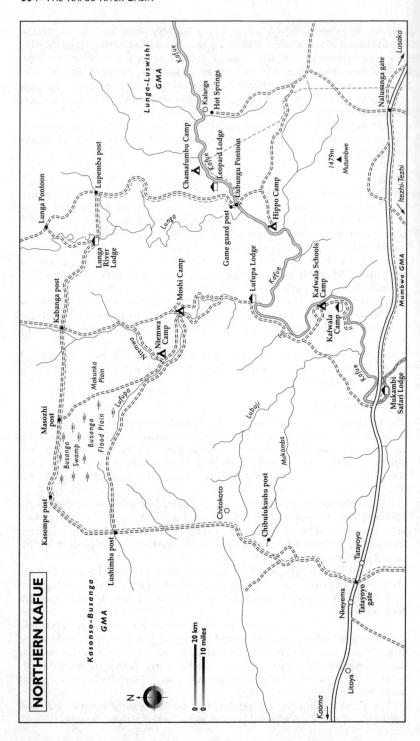

NORTHERN KAFUE

Lunga-Luswishi GMA

Lusaka

Kalanga
Hot Springs

Chamafumbu Camp

Leopard Lodge

Lubungu Pontoon

Nalusanga gate

1479m
Mutumbwe

Lupemba post

Lunga Pontoon

Lunga River Lodge

Hippo Camp

Itezhi-Tezhi

Game guard post

Kabanga post

Moshi Camp

Lufupa Lodge

Kafwala Schools Camp

Mumbwa GMA

Ntemwa Camp

Kafwala Camp

Masozhi post

Busanga Swamp

Busanga Flood Plain

Mokunka Plain

Lubuji

Mukambi Safari Lodge

Kasompe post

Lushimba post

Kasonso-Busanga GMA

Chitokoto

Chibulukushu post

Mukombo

Tatayoyo

Nkeyema

Tatayoyo gate

Litoya

Kaoma

0 20 km
0 10 miles

N

from the Kasonso-Busanga GMA in the north, and immediately feeds into a permanent wetland in the far north of the park: the Busanga Swamps. In the wet season these waters flood out over a much larger area, the Busanga Plains, before finally draining back into the river which then continues its journey on the south side of the plains.

The swamp and seasonal floodplain together cover about 750km², and are a superb area for game. The seasonal floodwaters on the plains are shallow, but enough to sustain a healthy growth of grasses throughout the year on the mineral-rich black-cotton soil. These open plains are dotted with numerous small 'islands' of wild date palms, *Phoenix reclinata*, and wild fig trees (various *Ficus* species).

The area is perfect for huge herds of water-loving lechwe and puku, which are joined by large numbers of zebra, wildebeest, and other plains grazers, as the waters recede at the end of the wet season.

However, the Busanga Plains are very remote, and normally impossible to reach by vehicle until about June/July. Thus few people (even in the safari business) have heard about them, let alone visited them, and so this remarkable area continues to go largely unknown and unrecognised.

Getting there
With a couple of 4WDs and experienced drivers, Kafue is a magical wilderness with lots of empty space and a few decent tracks through it. But for most conventional visitors, driving is generally impractical and you'll either be driven, or have an air transfer into the park arranged for you when you book. Unless you're bringing your own camping kit, you should book in advance for any of the better camps.

By air
There are various airstrips dotted around the park, some in good repair, others being quietly reclaimed by the surrounding bush. There are no scheduled flights into the park, but Lunga River Lodge does run an extensive programme of charter flights between the lodge and Lusaka, Livingstone and Mfuwe (for South Luangwa). Other destinations are also possible on request.

Visitors to Chilongozi's Busanga camp also normally arrive by air, whilst those visiting Lufupa and Shumba are generally driven in from Lusaka.

Driving from Kasempa in the north
There are reasonable gravel roads from either Kitwe (via Ingwe) in the Copperbelt, or Solwezi (via Mwelemu) in the north, to Kasempa – which is just 50km north of the park. From here gravel roads lead southwest towards Kaoma and southeast towards Mumbwa. No fuel and only minimal supplies are available at Kasempa.

Take the Mumbwa road that leads southeast from Kasempa for about 82km until a track turns right from the road. This smaller track will lead, after about 19km, to the National Park's Kabanga Post – from where a road proceeds southwards into the park keeping on the east bank of the Ntemwa River until around Ntemwa Camp. This is the easiest way to enter the park from the north.

Alternatively, if you ignore the right turning and continue, then you will reach the Lunga pontoon (across the Lunga River) after about 16km. If you turn right just before the pontoon, then keep left (near the river) as the track divides, this will lead eventually to Lunga River Lodge.

Crossing the Lunga pontoon it is then an 80km drive to Lubungu pontoon, along a route which skirts the eastern boundary of the National Park. Hippo Camp is just inside the park from here, Leopard Lodge is about 3km upstream from this pontoon (keep on the north side of the river) and Chamafumbu Camp about 8km beyond that. See the route described below, from Mumbwa, for the tracks south of this.

Driving from the main Lusaka-Mongu road

From Lusaka, Mumbwa has the last fuel station before you reach the park. If you are driving into the north of the park, then you're probably heading to either Lufupa or Kafwala. In this case the route is very easy: simply turn north off the main road at the scout gate beside the west bank of the Kafue River.

This dirt road heads northeast through the heart of the park for about 44km, where a right turn leads east to Kafwala Camp. Continuing roughly northeast for about a further 26km will lead you to Lufupa. In the dry season it's basically a good track, fine for a 2WD with high clearance, though designed more for game viewing than speed. In the wet it is impassable due to the toffee-like consistency of the black-cotton soil. Apart from possibly the river, it is the main artery in the north of the park. If you are looking to reach one of the camps on the eastern side of the park – Hippo, Leopard, Chamafumbu or Lunga – then a better option would be to leave the main road further east.

The standard route (4WD only) on the park's eastern side has always been to strike north at Mumbwa. For this, turn north into Mumbwa Township, then left at the Total garage. At the top of the next rise is a right turn, marked by an old sign to Hippo Mine. This track continues for 30km, then forks. Keep left, and battle on for another 30km until you reach the park's Kabulushi Post.

This is 20km from the Lubungu pontoon. If the Lubungu's waters are very low, then the pontoon will not be in operation and you will have to ford the river a few kilometres upstream – ask at the village for a guide to help you find this. Leopard Lodge is a kilometre or two further upstream, on the north bank of the river. This trip, from Mumbwa to Lubungu pontoon, will currently take you about four and a half hours, as the road is in very poor condition. (Do check locally to see if anything's improved recently!)

However, a better route than this at the moment is probably to use a new road (also 4WD only), which skirts the eastern boundary of Kafue National Park. This starts from Nalusanga Gate – which is beside the Great Western Road just inside the eastern edge of the park, around 40–45km west of Mumbwa. There you turn north and head directly to the Kabulushi Gate of the park, and on to Lubungu pontoon. This road is very new and in better condition.

But do remember that it's vital to take local advice before setting out on either of these routes.

Where to stay

Though there are a range of camps listed here, most non-Zambian visitors are probably best to choose between a combination of Lufupa and Shumba, or alternatively a combination of Lunga's River Lodge and its Busanga Bushcamp. Both of these operators are true specialists in northern Kafue; neither has other interests or lodges. Both have been in the park for many years and are closely involved with its conservation. Both are also very reliable – and yet they are totally different. Read on…

Camps in the north of Kafue

Lufupa Lodge (10 rondavels, 12 houses) Busanga Trails, PO Box 37538, Lusaka. Local residents contact via Steve Blagus (see page 321). Overseas contact Sunvil Discovery in the UK, tel: 020 8232 9777; fax: 020 8568 8330; email: africa@sunvil.co.uk
This large lodge overlooks the confluence of the Lufupa and Kafue Rivers. It is the centre of

activity in the northern Kafue, and the base for Busanga Trails. Access is easy, though not quick. If you're coming from overseas then Busanga Trails normally runs a shuttle service between the lodge and Lusaka on one or two days every week – designed to connect with some of the BA flights from London. This takes about five hours, including a break for a packed lunch.

Alternatively, if you're driving then enter the park by turning north from the tar road on the western side of the main bridge, past a game scouts' check-point. Follow that dirt road about 44km northeast, ignore the right turn to Kafwala, and continue for about 26km more to Lufupa.

Lufupa's accommodation is in simple, thatched, brick rondavels. These are large (having 3–5 beds), clean and comfortable, with en-suite (hot and cold) showers, toilets and wash basins. The lodge prides itself generally on a 'no frills' approach, so you won't be waited on hand and foot (it's just not that kind of place), but there's always someone to help when you need it.

The dining room serves buffet-style meals and whilst there is little choice, the food is good. Tea and coffee are always available (help yourself) and there is a good, comfortable bar near to the small swimming pool. The lodge's atmosphere is friendly, casual and very unpretentious.

Activities are mostly by 4WD and boat, though walks can also be organised when requested. The lodge is large enough to run several activities at once, and an afternoon boat trip up either the Lufupa or Kafue rivers is excellent.

For those with a 4WD there is a campsite here. Wood is supplied and there is a slipway for launching boats.

The guides are first class and have proven adept at locating leopards in the area, so exciting night drives are the lodge's chief attraction. (I have had consistently good reports of these since I last wrote about the lodge three years ago.) Watching a leopard stalk by night is unforgettable, and Lufupa offers visitors one of the best chances in Africa of spotting these cats.

Lufupa is an unusual lodge. It attracts an international clientele, whilst having fairly simple accommodation and facilities. Its secret lies in sensible pricing, access that is easy to arrange, and a remarkable reputation for leopards.

Rates: £905/US$1,450 per person for seven nights, full board, including transfers to and from Lusaka, all meals, all game activities and two nights at Shumba Bushcamp. No single person supplements. Camping: US$5 per person per night. Open: June to around early November. All rates above exclude park fees.

Shumba Bushcamp (4 twin-bed chalets) Book as part of a trip to Lufupa Lodge.
Shumba is the permanent bush-camp of Busanga Trails on the Busanga Plains. It is set on a picturesque 'island' of large fig trees, in the middle of the plains about 75km (2 hours' drive) north of Lufupa, and some 15–20 minutes drive south of the base of the permanent swamps.

Accommodation is in one of four thatched, reed-walled chalets, each of which has twin beds, a shelf and a mirror. (These are gradually being replaced by large tents on wooden platforms.) Shared showers and flush toilets are nearby. There is a two-storey look-out lounge, with excellent views across the floodplain and a waterhole nearby. Below this is a dining area where buffet meals are served.

Activities here revolve around driving: little game is seen if you walk around an area this open. As with Lufupa, the highlights are the night drives, and Shumba's guides are also expert at locating the Busanga Plain's resident prides of lions.

Rates: Shumba can only be visited as part of a trip including Lufupa, see above

Lunga River Lodge (6 twin-bed cabins) African Experience, PO Box 30106, Lusaka. Satphone: 873 762 093 985; email: safariafrica@experience.co.za
Standing on the bank of the Lunga River, just outside Kafue's northern boundary, in the

GMA, Lunga is a very comfortable lodge. It's not a place that anyone drives to normally; guests usually arrive by light aircraft. (Lunga can organise charter flights to nearby regional destinations.)

Accommodation is in well decorated, solid thatched cabins with en-suite showers and toilets. These have a 12V lighting system powered by solar cells and a back-up generator. Facilities include a thatched dining area, a bar with a sundeck that extends over the river, a small pool and even a steam bath. Activities include walking safaris, day and night 4WD trips, and river excursions using motor boats and canoes. There's also the option (advise them in advance) to spend a night out in the bush at a small fly-camp, as part of a guided canoe trip down the river.

A stay here is often combined with time at their Busanga Bushcamp, and/or a day or two on the river canoeing. A slightly reduced rate is offered if you book into these for a total of seven nights or more, and there are plans for some 'set departure' seven-night packages including canoeing and walking.

Rates: US$280/390 per person per night sharing/single (reduces to US$220/310 before 15 June). Canoeing US$260/365 per person sharing/single. Includes all meals, activities, laundry and park fees. Open: 1 June to end of November.

Busanga Bushcamp (4 twin chalets) Contact via Lunga River Lodge
This is a small satellite camp of Lunga River Lodge, which stands on the Busanga Plains about three hours' drive from Lunga. Accommodation is simple, in one of four small reed-and-thatch chalets, each with en-suite shower (hot and cold water) and longdrop toilet (the ones that don't flush!). These are dotted around a small fig-tree island in the middle of the flat, open plains.

The trees also shade the comfortable central 'mess tent' where you'll dine and drink. Meals are often prepared over an open fire – so this is a close-to-nature experience, with plenty of super game around you. Activities are mostly drives, both day and night – the terrain is too flat and open for walking close to game on foot – though short bird-spotting walks are easily arranged.

Rates: US$320/450 per person per night sharing/single (reduces to US$260/370 after 15 October). Includes all meals, activities, laundry and park fees. Open: mid-June to around mid-November

Busanga Plains Tented Camp (4 twin and 1 double tents) Contact via Chilongozi, see page 256.
This is a small, seasonal bushcamp used by Chilongozi Safaris for their guests who fly directly into the Busanga Plains. Each tent has en-suite facilities with running cold water (hot water for bucket showers is brought on request). Activities include walks, drives (day and night) and day trips west to the Lushimba springs and south to the Ntemwa and Lufupa rivers.

Rates: US$250 per person sharing per night, including meals, activities, laundry and park fees. Open: 1 July to end of November

Hippo Camp (6 twin-bed tents and 2 rondavels) Lubungu Wildlife Safaris, PO Box 30796, Lusaka. Tel: 01 242083/244285; fax: 01 243032
Sited on an anomalous patch of private land within the national park, Hippo is an old camp (once known as Lubungu Camp) which was closed in 1992. Since then it had only been used privately by its owners, the Younger family, until Chris and Charlotte MacBride arrived, in March '99. Professional naturalists who have moved here to research the park's carnivores, they plan to accept a limited number of visitors to fund their research.

Hippo has six twin tents and two brick-and-thatch rondavels, all with en-suite facilities, and a central thatched dining and lounge area. It's comfortable rather than luxurious, and very informal. Most visitors are Zambian residents who arrive in their own 4WDs (see page 336 for directions from Mumbwa), complete with fuel and supplies. It's about 110km from Mumbwa, which is a good six hours' drive. However, there is a good airstrip nearby, so charters from Lusaka are possible.

Hippo is about 15km from the Lubungu pontoon, and 25km upstream from Lufupa Lodge. This is an isolated area, with few roads, dominated by miombo woodlands and dambos. As yet, the MacBrides don't have guests on a regular basis but if you give them advance notice that you will be passing, then you can stay on a self-catering basis. In the future it's likely that game drives, walks and boating will be available.

Rates: US$40 per person sharing, self-catering. This does not include activities, food, or transfer to/from Lusaka

Leopard Lodge

Outside the national park's northeast boundary, Leopard Lodge is a few kilometres north of the Lubungu pontoon, which crosses the Kafue River just on the edge of the park. Although it is marked on many maps, it's currently closed (and hasn't been fully operational for years).

Chamafumbu Camp Contact via Pioneer Campsite, Lusaka. (See page 130.)
On the north bank of the Kafue River, about 8km east of Leopard Lodge, after the river leaves the park, this is a small and very simple fishing camp. (It's marked as Mbizi on some maps.) It's not really set up for visitors, but if you're driving around Zambia in self-contained 4WDs and want to stop for a few nights fishing, then it might be worth giving them a call. It's owned by Chris Wienand, who also runs Pioneer campsite in Lusaka and a large game ranch in the Luangwa Valley.

Treetops Conservation School Camp

This camp was very run-down, but has now been renovated a little by a group of schools in Lusaka, including Baobab School. It accepts small groups of school children for short stays to learn more about the park, its flora and fauna. Educating Zambia's next generation about the country's remaining wildlife is vital if it is to be conserved throughout the next century, so initiatives like these are essential to the park's future.

Ntemwa Camp (about 8 tents) Contact via Chilongozi; see page 256.
105km north of the main bridge over the Kafue, Ntemwa has a beautiful situation overlooking a watercourse just south of the Busanga Plains. Originally it had four concrete rooms with tin roofs and two thatched cottages, which all slid into various stages of dereliction.

This camp was offered for private tender as early as 1995, but it wasn't until March '99, after two years of negotiations, that Chilongozi finally signed a 25-year lease to build and run a camp here. Currently they intend to open a small tented camp here for the 2000 season, and they will need tenacity to develop and run a camp as remote as Ntemwa.

Moshi Camp contact Star of Africa, P Bag 6, Hillside, Zimbabwe. Tel: (2639) 41225, 41715 or 41837; fax: 229909
This is slightly south of Ntemwa, about 90km north of the bridge, and in a similar situation in many ways. It also has been derelict for several years. Like Ntemwa, it was offered for tender in 1995, and also snapped up by an unknown quantity: Star of Africa. They intend to develop it in the future, and have even quoted rates for April 2000 (about US$360 per person sharing, including meals and activities) to go with 'photographs' of the camp (which were poorly disguised photo-fit pictures from other locations).

Given that the camp is cut off by road until around June, quite how they're going to bring in their first guests remains a puzzle. They are also developing Chichele in South Luangwa and sites in Lochinvar and Livingstone. Many comment that reopening just one of these sites at a time would be more than enough for anyone to cope with.

Kafwala Camp (4 two/three bed huts) Wildlife and Environmental Conservation Society of Zambia. Book through the WECSZ branch in Kabwe – PO Box 80623, Kabwe. Tel: 05 223467 or 224600; fax: 224859 – or via their head office in Lusaka, see page 104.
This camp is built on the bank of the Kafue about 700m below the start of the Kafwala

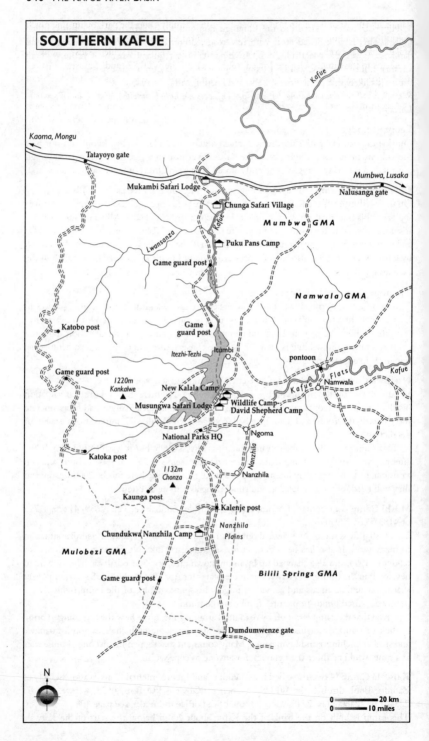

SOUTHERN KAFUE

Kaoma, Mongu

Tatayoyo gate

Mukambi Safari Lodge

Chunga Safari Village

Kafue

Mumbwa, Lusaka

Nalusanga gate

Mumbwa GMA

Lwansonza

Puku Pans Camp

Game guard post

Namwala GMA

Katobo post

Game guard post

Itezhi-Tezhi

Itumbi

pontoon

Flats

Kafue

Game guard post

1220m
Kankalwe

New Kalala Camp

Kafue

Namwala

Musungwa Safari Lodge

Wildlife Camp
David Shepherd Camp

National Parks HQ

Ngoma

Katoka post

Nanzhila

1132m
Chonza

Nanzhila

Kaunga post

Kalenje post

Chundukwa Nanzhila Camp

Nanzhila
Plains

Mulobezi GMA

Bilili Springs GMA

Game guard post

Dumdumwenze gate

N

0   20 km
0   10 miles

Rapids, northeast of the main bridge over the Kafue. Simply enter the park by turning north from the tar road on the western side of the main bridge, past the game scouts' checkpoint. Follow that dirt road about 44km northeast, then take the right turn which leads to Kafwala.

Access to the camp itself is restricted to members of the WECSZ, and it must be booked in advance. If you're thinking of staying here then join the society in Lusaka: it does a lot of good and needs more support. See page 104.

Accommodation is in basic huts, with a total of eleven beds: huts 1 and 2 have three beds each; hut 3 has two beds; hut 4 has just one bed; and there's a semi-open 'Breezeway' with two beds and limited privacy. Toilets, shower and bathroom are communal, as are the lounge and barbecue area.

Deep freezes, fridges, lamps, crockery, cutlery and bedding are all provided – but you must bring all your own food and drink. The camp's staff will cook for you, so don't forget to bring flour and yeast if you'd like some fresh bread. If you bring light fishing tackle then the cook will fillet and prepare your catch for dinner. The staff will also service the rooms, do the washing, and help with anything else that is reasonable. (You should tip them at the end of your stay.)

Rates: around US$15–20 per person per day. Open: all year

Kafwala Schools Camp (Schools Camp) contact via Busanga Trails at Lufupa
Near to the Wildlife Society camp, this is derelict and has been taken over by Busanga Trails, who intend to redevelop it at some point.

Before this happens, it is possible (with permission from Busanga Trails) to camp on the riverbank. This is a stunning location, but only suitable for the self-sufficient, as there are no facilities. Note that the hippos in this area have not read the textbooks, and seem to be living happily in and around the fast running water of the rapids. The bank is well scent-marked by them, and you should plan to be well out of the way before their nightly forage begins after sunset.

Camping
Camping in the park is easily arranged at Lufupa, and Kafwala is only a little more expensive than a campsite. It may be possible to camp up at Treetops; ask the scouts for the latest information on this, and possibly for permission. Note – there are no campsites on the Busanga Plains, and you are not allowed to just camp anywhere. This rule is both wise and effectively enforced.

Southern Kafue
South of the main road, the park is long and thin; and stretches about 190km southwards, although is only about 85km wide at its broadest point. On the park's eastern boundary is the Itezhi-Tezhi Dam: 370km^2 of water. It differs from many dams as, apparently, it is not made of continuous concrete but instead is filled with earth in order to render it less vulnerable to tremors and minor earthquakes.

The vegetation and geography of the southern side are similar to the north – mostly a mosaic of miombo and tall mopane woodlands – although stands of teak are increasingly common. Underfoot, much of southern Kafue, especially towards the western side, stands on Kalahari sand. Open grassy dambos retain the moisture of small streams and so sustain green grass throughout the year.

In the far south of the park, the Nanzhila Plains are a fascinating area. Wide expanses of grassland are dotted with islands of vegetation and large termitaria – often with baobabs, *Adansonia digitata*, or jackal berry trees, *Diospyros mespiliformis*, growing out of them.

Getting there
Chunga and Mukambi are very near the main road, and so are clearly signposted around the main bridge over the Kafue in the centre of the park. To reach the heart

of the southern section of the park you must either take the road through the GMA, which leaves the Great West Road about 65–70km west of Mumbwa, or alternatively approach from the southeast from Monze, Choma or Kalomo on the Lusaka–Livingstone road.

Only the first of these approaches is practical in the wet season, and all require a 4WD throughout the year. There are no easy approaches to any of the camps from the west.

From the Lusaka–Mongu road

Despite a fiction perpetrated by cartographers, the 'road' south from Chunga to the Itezhi-Tezhi Dam which follows the western bank of the Kafue southwards is not navigable any more – even with the best 4WD. Thus the only way into this most southern section of the park is by taking the turning which runs south-southwest from the main Lusaka–Mongu road.

Heading west from Lusaka, Mumbwa is almost 150km away. Continue through Mumbwa for about 35–40km until you reach Nalusanga Gate Post, the entry to the Kafue National Park.

The road into the south of the park leaves this Lusaka–Mongu road about 66km from Mumbwa (and 59km from the main bridge over the Kafue if you're approaching from the west). It is signposted to Itezhi-Tezhi; take this turning. About 6km after turning, you will pass the Lukomeshi Post (a game scout checkpoint which isn't always manned).

The road here isn't good, and you will really need a 4WD, but it is definitely the best road into the southern half of Kafue. It's about 120km of poor, potholed road before you reach the Itezhi-Tezhi Dam, which will take about 5–6 hours in a good 4WD at any time of the year. Do take drinks and some food when driving here, as there's nowhere to buy snacks along the way. Sections of the road have lots of tsetse flies; if you have air conditioning you will be grateful to close the windows and use it. About halfway you'll see a signposted turning right, to the west, to Puku Pans. This is about 30–40km away.

When you finally reach Itezhi-Tezhi, continue past the police station and towards the lake and the dam wall. Once over the dam wall it is just a few kilometres to New Kalala, the David Shepherd Camp and also Musungwa. All are well-signposted on the right-hand side of the road. It is just a couple of kilometres further to the Musa Gate into Kafue National Park itself.

From Kalomo on the Lusaka–Livingstone Road

There's a BP station in Kalomo, and you should fill up there. From Kalomo (which is about 126km from Livingstone on the way to Lusaka), there is an old sign to Kafue and Musungwa pointing roughly north. You will drive past the Kalomo Hotel and turn left at the next T-junction. Within 20 metres the road becomes a dirt track. Continue on this to another T-junction, turn right and follow the road as it curves left (ignoring right-hand turn-off).

Continue over a railway bridge, and shortly afterwards a river bridge, and then take the next left turn. Continue following the main track, ignoring any turnings and keeping left at forks. After a few kilometres you should be travelling northwest. About 40km after the main road you will start leaving the rural villages behind you and climb through some hills. Eventually, after about 74km, you drop down gradually to Dumdumwenze Gate, where the game scouts will sign you into the park. (Note that Dumdum*wezi* is local spelling and pronunciation.)

From here, keep right as the road forks if you are heading for Ngoma, which is about 100km away, or Nanzhila, which is about 56km from the gate.

This approach is impassable in the wet season, so from Dumdumwenze Gate ask the scouts for the best route. You will probably be directed almost due west, skirting the southern side of the park, until you meet the cordon road which crosses yours. Turn right on this road and it will lead you in a north-northeasterly direction straight to Ngoma. Given the prevalence of black-cotton soil in the area, travelling alone in the wet season would be very inadvisable.

From Monze on the Lusaka-Livingstone Road

From Monze take a turning on the north side of town towards Chongo, heading northwest towards Lochinvar National Park. You may need to ask local directions to get on the right track. After 7–8km you will pass Chongo – keep left there as the track divides after the village. (The right fork, about 8km after Chongo, leads to Lochinvar National Park.) About 35km later you will reach Chitongo, and a T-junction. Take the right turn and then about 18km later keep left as the track gradually turns from heading slightly west of north, to heading due west. The track forking right here, heading northwest, is less reliable but goes the same way. About 50km after Chitongo you will reach the larger village of Namwala, on the southern edge of the Kafue's floodplain, from where the track leads west into the park, entering past the site of the old Nkala Mission, and about 2km north of Ngoma.

Ngoma

Ngoma is the national park's headquarters in the south side of the park, about 20km from the Itezhi-Tezhi Dam wall. There's also an all-weather airstrip about 5km south of here. (If you buzz Musungwa lodge three times from the air, then they'll come out to collect you.)

Where to stay

If you're just passing through the park on the main Lusaka–Mongu road, then perhaps Mukambi and Chunga are the places to stop for a night or two. However, with more time it is better to probe deeper and get at least to the accessible Itezhi-Tezhi area and, preferably, to the Nanzhila Plains.

If you're driving and taking camping kit then you can probably afford to turn up at the lodges in the Itezhi-Tezhi area and find somewhere that suits you. If you're pre-arranging a trip, and have a flexible budget, then Chundukwa's camps in Nanzhila Plains are probably your best option.

Looking at southern Kafue's camps – starting with those near the road and going south:

Mukambi Safari Lodge (10 twin-bed chalets) P. Bag E523, Lusaka. Tel: 01 228185; fax: 228184

The turn-off to Mukambi is signposted on the main Lusaka–Mongu tar road, about 5km east of the main bridge over the Kafue. The camp is very close to the main road, and easily accessed in a normal 2WD vehicle. The thatch-on-brick chalets are solidly built using beautifully carved wooden doors. Inside, the windows are effectively mosquito-netted, and the decor is consciously ethnic with the odd carving or *object d'art*, and murals on the walls. The clean tiled bathrooms have showers heated by gas geysers.

The central dining/bar area is also well designed, though quite formal – almost like a hotel. It overlooks the Kafue River, and there's an open pool on the terrace outside, overlooking the river. A range of walking, boating and 4WD game-viewing trips are available – and a conference room for work trips!

Aside from the main camp, Mukambi has the facility to set up a tented fly-camp on the Busanga Plains, about five hours' drive to the north.

Mukambi is a well-built lodge that appears to have concentrated its efforts, successfully, on being comfortable. However, it's close to neither the Busanga nor Nanzhila Plains, which are Kafue's best areas for wildlife. It would make a very pleasant stopover, as you pass through on the Great West Road, but if you have longer to spend then I'd go further into either north or south Kafue.

Rates: US$90 per person sharing, including full board. Open: all year. Excursions: walking US$30, boating US$25, driving US$20 – all prices per person.

Chunga Safari Village (6 twin-bed rondavels) Njovu Safaris, PO Box 35058, Lusaka. Tel/fax: 01 221681

Turn south off the main road a few kilometres west of the main bridge over the Kafue, and after about 22km you will reach this camp, next to the National Parks and Wildlife Service Headquarters at Chunga. It has plenty of space on a bend in the river, and accommodation is in basic thatch-on-brick rondavels, with shared showers and toilets. The cost includes use of linen, cutlery, crockery, etc, and the help of a chef – but you must bring all your own food and drink. Campers are welcomed here, and the camp staff are generally friendly and helpful.

Rates: Kw20,000 per person per night, less for camping. Open: all year

Puku Pans Camp (6 chalets) contact via ATD on tel: 01 224616, 223641 or 225386; fax: 224915

Puku Pans is an attractive lodge that overlooks the park from the GMA beside the Kafue River, north of Itezhi-Tezhi Dam. As the fish eagle flies, it's about 35km south of the main Lusaka–Mongu road. (See above for directions.) Many visitors drive themselves here, though it's also possible to use a short charter flight, as Puku Pans has its own airstrip nearby.

Its chalets are built of wood and some stand on stilts above the riverbank. All have en-suite facilities. Four of them have twin or double beds, one is large enough for six beds, and one has eight. Each has a veranda overlooking the river, and the separate, open-plan dining room and bar area also gives a good river view. Puku Pans is owned and is currently being run by Rob Buske, although at time of writing it seems to be up for sale. It's vital to book in advance, and not just to turn up here.

Rates: US$180 per person per night including full board and all activities. (The self-drive rate is US$85 including all meals but no activities.)

New Kalala Camp

New Kalala is just north of the dam wall, overlooking the lake, and run by the same group as Andrews Motel in Lusaka (see page 124). Its thatched chalets and rondavels all have en-suite facilities and camping is also available here. You can either bring food to cook for yourselves, or order meals at the lodge. The camp is built around large granite rocks where you'll see the odd rock dassie scurry, and it has a swimming pool that is sometimes filled with water.

Wildlife Camp – David Shepherd Camp (3 four-bed chalets) contact via the Wildlife and Environmental Conservation Society of Zambia (see *Zambia Today*, page 104) or Musungwa Safari Lodge (see below)

A little less than a kilometre north of Musungwa Safari Lodge, the Wildlife Camp stands between large granite boulders on the shores of Lake Itezhi-Tezhi Dam about 20km from Ngoma. It was originally built for members of the Wildlife Conservation Society of Zambia (the WCSZ – the forerunner of the present Wildlife and Environmental Conservation Society of Zambia), though is now open to all. The team from Musungwa now manages it, although the WECSZ still benefit by receiving a percentage of the monies that it earns.

Accommodation is in three basic four-bedded chalets, all of which have en-suite toilet and shower. The camp provides deep freezes, fridges, a cooker, a barbecue, lamps, crockery, cutlery and bedding. The staff here will cook for you, service the rooms, do the washing, and help with anything else that is reasonable. (You should tip them at the end of your stay.) You must bring all your own food and drink, and book in advance. It's worth joining the WECSZ before you book.

Because Musungwa Safari Lodge is so close, visitors staying here can usually use Musungwa's facilities and excursions, provided they give the lodge advance notice of meals and activities required.

Rates: US$15 per person sharing for members of WECSZ, US$25 for non-members.

Open: all year

Musungwa Safari Lodge (23 chalets) P.O. Box 31808, Lusaka. Tel: 01 273493; Tel/fax: 274233; email: zamker@zamnet.zm

Sitting on the eastern shore of Itezhi-Tezhi dam, Musungwa is about 5km south of the dam wall. It's a long-standing lodge with three large rondavels for the reception, bar and restaurant. Nearby are eleven twin-bed chalets and twelve chalets with four beds. All have en-suite shower and toilet, and their own private verandas overlooking the lake.

Musungwa has a swimming pool, tennis court, squash court and sauna. Activities offered include boat cruises on the lake and up the Kafue River as well as morning, afternoon and night game drives inside the park. Day-trips further into into southern Kafue are also possible (mid-June to mid-Oct).

Barbecues and cultural dancing are a feature of the weekends at Musungwa, while the lodge is large enough to cater for conferences of up to 80 people, and at Christmas it usually hosts themed fancy dress competitions. Fuel is available for sale between 07.30 and 08.30 for residents.

Rates: US$200 per person per night, including full board and all activities – minimum of four people for the activities. (US$120 per person for full board but no activities.) Children 3–12 pay half price. Open: all year

Musungwa Campsite contact via Musungwa Safari Lodge

About 350m from the main Musungwa Lodge, this grassy campsite has shady trees around it and two showers (hot and cold), two toilets, and two wash basins. There is often an overland truck staying here, sometimes with 40–60 people, and then campers can use some of the lodge's facilities provided the main lodge isn't full. There is also an area for food preparation, a barbecue, two sinks for washing up cooking equipment and a dining area with seating for seven.

Campers may use the bar, swimming pool, safaris and (with a day's advance reservation) order meals in the restaurant.

Rates: US$10 per person per night camping

Chundukwa Nanzhila Camp (4 thatched A-frame chalets) Contact via Chundukwa Adventure Trails – PO Box 61160, Livingstone. Tel/fax: 324452 or 324006. See page 191 for more details.

This is the slightly plusher of the two camps run by Chundukwa in the south of Kafue. Both are about five hours' drive from Livingstone, and their activities focus on walking safaris, though day and night game drives are also possible.

Chundukwa Nanzhila Camp is sited in a great position in the centre of the Nanzhila Plains, where the main National Parks Camp used to be. It stands beside a permanent pan that is covered in lilies and frequented by Africa jacanas. A vast number of birds come to drink at this pool. It has four wooden, thatched A-frame chalets, each of which has twin or a double bed upstairs and a shower and flush toilet below. The design is unusual and rustic, but works well.

A typical day here would probably involve an early start with coffee and rusks before a walk in the cool. Then back to camp in the late morning for brunch, followed by time at leisure for a siesta. Tea is usually served at four o'clock, which might be followed with a game drive and a walk around sundown. Then back to camp for a hearty dinner and sleep.

Road transfers here from Livingstone are included in the cost, though those with less time may want to charter a small plane and fly in. There's an airstrip at Ngoma, 45 minutes' drive from camp, and the rates from Livingstone are fairly economic. Together with its sister-camp, this offers probably the best and most reliable way to see the southern Kafue's Nanzhila Plains.

Rates: US$225 per person sharing, US$280 single, per night full board, including transfers and park fees.
Open: around April to the end of October, depending on the rains.

Chundukwa's Nanzhila Tented Camp (4 tents) contact via Chundukwa Adventure Trails, Livingstone. See above and page 191 for details.
This simple tented camp is a comfortable day's walk from its thatched sister-camp. Accommodation is in one of four large, Meru-style tents, each of which is protected from the sun by a thatched shade and has its own en-suite toilet and shower.

Activities centre around walking safaris, though can include game drives as well. Doug Evans, or one of his guides, escorts all these safaris and knows the area very well. So come for a few days at each camp for a really good view of the area.

Rates: US$225 per person sharing, US$280 single, per night full board, including transfers and park fees.
Open: around April to the end of October, depending on the rains.

Getting around Kafue independently

If you are not seeing Kafue as part of an all-inclusive trip, then you will need two good 4WD vehicles, the most detailed maps you can buy, and all your provisions for the duration of your stay. Camping is possible, but proper facilities are few and far between. If you have problems, you must be able to solve them yourself, as you can expect little help. Despite the fact that there are many camps listed in Kafue, only a handful would be capable (and willing) to offer any help in an emergency.

However, if you come well equipped then the park is wonderful. Camps like Musungwa, Chunga Safari Village and Lufupa will be happy to help you with advice on the area and, if they have them to spare, will usually sell you a bed and a cold beer. If you do come, then you can be assured of seeing very few other vehicles during your stay in this stunning area.

Mobile operators in Kafue

A couple of safari operators run trips into Kafue without having a permanent base there. Some do this with permission from the National Parks Board, others without. Some work well, though without a long-term presence in the park, they clearly don't know the ground as well as the established camps. Further, if they encounter serious difficulties, they seldom have the logistical support to solve their own problems. (There are tales of one inexperienced company which recently came up into the Busanga Plains too early, and ended up with its vehicle stuck in mud for two days.)

Perhaps more importantly, most of the established camps work hard to maintain the park's roads and minimise poaching. Few, if any, of the mobile operators contribute to this vital work.

As Kafue starts to receive a few more visitors, the Busanga Plains (especially) is becoming better known and the focus for more attention from many small mobile operators. If you want to get the very best from it, and also to support operators who work to preserve the area, then I recommend that you support the area's permanent operators.

LOCHINVAR AND BLUE LAGOON NATIONAL PARKS

Rates: US$5 per person per night, plus US$5 per vehicle per night.
Further down the Kafue's course, about 120km east of Ngoma, are two small national parks that encompass opposite sides of the Kafue River's floodplain. Their geography and ecosystems are very similar, although Lochinvar's wildlife has probably fared better over the past few decades than that of Blue Lagoon.

Neither receives many visitors, and those who do visit should arrive with a 4WD and their own supplies, prepared to camp.

Geography, flora and fauna

Both parks are very flat, and the sections nearer the river are seasonally flooded. The resulting level grassy plain reflects the sky like a mirror, for as far as you can see. It is quite a sight, and a remarkable environment for both animals and waterfowl.

The parks are home to huge herds of Kafue lechwe – a little-known subspecies of the red lechwe, endemic to the Kafue's floodplain – and a sprinkling of buffalo, zebra, wildebeest and other antelope.

The landscapes in both parks change with proximity to the river, and as you move further from the river, above the 'high flood' line, the environment becomes different. The grassland here does not receive an annual flooding, so termitaria can exist – their occupants safe from drowning. These sometimes form areas known as 'termite cities' where many termitaria rise up from the plain, often with nothing else in sight, but sometimes accompanied by a distinctively shaped *Euphorbia candelabra*, or even the odd baobab. This open grassland is typical habitat for the delightful, diminutive oribi antelope, as well as the larger grazers – zebra, wildebeest and buffalo.

Further from the water, the plains gradually merge into woodland, where *albizia* species of trees occur with typical species from munga woodlands like *acacia* and *combretum*. Here you may find kudu, baboon, or buffalo hiding in the thickets.

Birds

The best season for birds on the Kafue's floodplain is during the summer rains. Then the river floods and the resulting lagoons attract a great variety of migrant birds – from flamingos and pelicans to large flocks of cranes, storks and ibises. Species that are otherwise uncommon can often be seen here in fairly large numbers, like spoonbills and wattled cranes.

Because of their shallow depth, these floodwaters also prove a great attraction for the smaller waders – sandpipers, godwits and avocets – and many species of ducks and geese can be found here in large numbers.

Lochinvar National Park

Lochinvar's northern boundary is the Kafue River. This area was a cattle ranch from 1913 until 1965 when the government, helped by the World Wide Fund for Nature, purchased it to make it a National Park.

Subsequently the park has been designated by the WWF as a 'Wetland of International Importance', and a WWF team has been working with the local people on a project to manage the park on a sustainable basis for the benefit of both the people and the wildlife. Details of the project are available within the park – though there are a lot of settlements in the area, and conservation here is not proving to be an easy task.

Getting there

Lochinvar is easiest to approach from Monze, on the Livingstone–Lusaka Road – about 287km from Livingstone and 186km from Lusaka. The road that heads northwest from Monze, signposted for Namwala, is just north of the grain silos on the Lusaka side of town.

It passes Chongo village and forks about 8km afterwards – perhaps 25km from Monze. Ask local advice to find this junction if necessary. Take the right fork, or

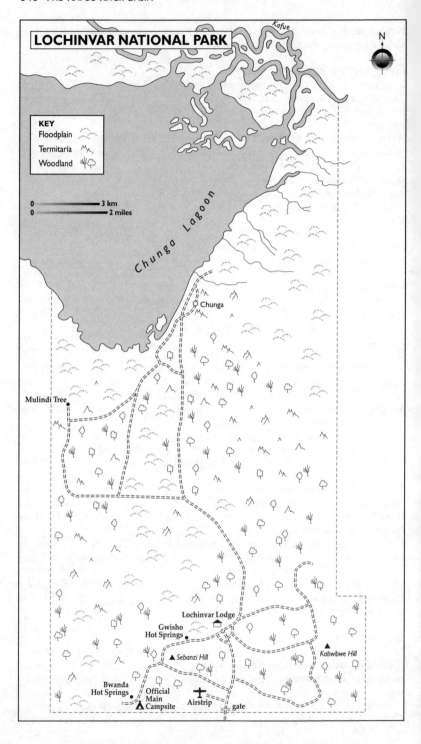

LOCHINVAR NATIONAL PARK

N

KEY
Floodplain
Termitaria
Woodland

0 ———— 3 km
0 ———— 2 miles

Kafue

Chunga Lagoon

○ Chunga

Mulindi Tree •

Lochinvar Lodge
Gwisho
Hot Springs •
▲ *Sebanzi Hill*
Bwanda
Hot Springs •
Official
Main
Campsite
✝
Airstrip
gate

▲ *Kabwibwe Hill*

you will end up in Kafue. Follow this road for about 10km and then turn left at another sign. It is then about 15km to the park gate. This last section of the track twists and turns, but all the tracks that split off eventually rejoin each other and lead to the park. There are also a few more signs so, if you become unsure, ask a local person and they'll show you the way. The gate to Lochinvar is about 48km from Monze.

Maps
An excellent (albeit very out-of-date) 1:50,000 visitors' map to Lochinvar was published by the Surveyor General in 1986, and is still available at their main office in Lusaka. It indicates the vegetation types and also gives photographs and short descriptions of some of the park's interesting features and wildlife. Most of the 'camps' depicted are now disused, and some of the roads now seem as if they were figments of a cartographer's imagination.

Where to stay
The original state-run Lochinvar Lodge was put up for tender to private safari operators in 1996. No buyers were found until recently, when 'Star of Africa' bravely took on the task. They plan a floating lodge here, along the lines of Water Wilderness on Zimbabwe's Lake Kariba. However, they are also planning to build Chichele in South Luangwa, Moshi in northern Kafue, and a new property in Livingstone. Clearly they are going to be very busy people.

Until this lodge materialises, your only option is to camp, for which you must bring all your supplies. There were three or four small campsites here, but only one is really open. Otherwise they receive so few visitors that the scouts are generally fairly relaxed and if you are self-contained then you can camp anywhere.

To reach the **official campsite**, drive about 2km past the gate into the park, and take the second left turning. Continue for about 5km. This site has water, a longdrop toilet and a simple cold shower. Firewood and a barbecue are provided. This is very close to the hot springs at Bwanda, near what used to be Lupanda Wildlife Camp. If you wish to pick up a scout from the gate to guide you, then it's probably best to arrange this in advance.

What to see and do
The birds and animals are the main attraction here, and the best birding is probably close to the water, on the floodplain. For this it's probably best to walk north and east from Mulindi Tree or north of Chunga towards Hippo Corner. It's vital to avoid driving anywhere that's even vaguely damp on the floodplain as your vehicle will just slip through the crust and into the black-cotton soil – which will probably spoil and extend your stay in equal measure. A few sites to note include:

Gwisho Hot Springs
Gwisho Hot Springs is near the southern edge of the park. To get here from the campsite, drive north out of the camp and turn right towards Sebanzi Hill, following the edge of the plain. After about 2.5km turn left at a stone cairn and palms. The springs are signposted, and just a few kilometres further on, about 2km west of the old lodge.

They occur because of a geological fault, which has an associated deposit of gypsum – the mineral used to make plaster of Paris. This was mined here from 1973 to 1978.

The spring's hot waters vary from about 60°C to 94°C, and have a high concentration of sodium, chlorine, calcium and sulphates in their water. It is surrounded by a picturesque stand of real fan palms, *Hyphaene petersiana*, which have small fruits – when opened, these are seen to have a hard kernel known as 'vegetable ivory'.

Sebanzi Hill

This is a National Monument marking the position of an iron-age village which archaeologists say has been inhabited for most of the last millennium. Looking out from it you have an excellent view over the park and the springs. Notice the low mounds around the hot spring, where excavations have found evidence of human settlement dating as far back as the first few centuries BC.

Drum Rocks

Close to the lodge, in the south of the park, is an outcrop of rocks that echo when tapped, producing a curious, resonant sound. Ask the scouts to direct you to these: they are fascinating. (Similar rocks, on the farm called Immenhof, in Namibia, were originally discovered by San/bushmen and are now known locally as the 'singing rocks'.) Nearby is a large baobab with a completely hollow trunk that can be entered from a crack in the side (which is the size of a small doorway).

Chunga

This group of large winterthorn trees, *Acacia albida*, is roughly where the main track meets the lagoon. It's the site of the old wildlife camp, and a good spot to camp provided you don't mind being disturbed by the odd vehicle.

Blue Lagoon National Park

Blue Lagoon is on the north side of the river. A farming couple turned conservationists, the Critchleys, originally owned it. In years past, during KK's reign, the Ministry of Defence restricted access to this 'park' to the military, plus a few privileged politicians and generals who used the old farmhouse intermittently as a retreat. Now it's much more relaxed and you can usually sign in with the game scouts and explore where you like.

Getting there

Blue Lagoon is not well signposted, and there are several ways to reach it. From Lusaka, the easiest is probably to take the Great West Road then turn left about 28km after leaving Cairo Road, opposite a small shop called Bancroft Supermarket.

This track will lead you to the National Park's scout camp at the gate. After signing in with them, you will then need to be guided by a scout on to another road to actually get into the park.

If coming from the west, then pass through Mumbwa and look for an Agip garage near Nangoma, around 81km east of Kafue's Nalusanga Gate. Fill up here. Then continue towards Lusaka, taking the first right turn after this filling station. In less than a kilometre, turn right at the crossroads. (This junction is on a local bus route, so if you ask directions you will end up with a guide and their luggage. A fair deal for you and them!) Continuing for 9km brings you to Myooye village, where you should take the left fork that passes the clinic on the right-hand side.

Follow this track for 31km to a T-junction, ignoring smaller side-tracks. (If the group of huts on the left, halfway along this road, has a flag flying, it means that the Tonga chief who lives here is in residence.) At this T-junction turn right. To reach the park entrance, continue straight on for 22km, first ignoring a right-hand turn, then passing the first gate and finally reaching the scout post.

At the post sign in, paying the park and camping fees, and check the current camping rules with the scouts. You may end up turning around to retrace your tracks for 11km, before passing through the gate and turning right at the road signposted to 'Nakeenda Wildlife Police Unit'. This road quickly passes a derelict entry and after 7km reaches the Critchley Farm, near the edge of the lagoon.

Where to stay

There is no organised camp here so bring all your supplies with you, and ask the scouts if you can camp somewhere inside the park itself. There is no shortage of spectacular sites, and a large fig tree by the water's edge near the Critchley Farm is proving a popular spot.

This is close to some derelict cottages and a small ranger camp consisting of about three rangers and their families. You will need to be completely self-sufficient. There are no facilities for tourists.

What to see and do

This park is dominated by the Kafue Flats, which are flooded in the rainy season. That is the best time for birdwatching here; then the park is at its best. In the dry season the view is not so stunning but still worth a visit.

The Critchleys did build a causeway here which extends for about 5km over the marshy flats, enabling a 4WD with a tight turning circle to drive out on to the flats, giving a wonderful view of the stunning birdlife. There are several memorial stones along this causeway and one reads:

> Erica Critchley 1910-1976.
> To the memory of the
> one who loved Zambia
> So much she cared for
> human and natural resources.
> Let what she stood for
> not be forgotten by Zambians
> especially by its youth.
>
> Kenneth Kaunda
> President of Zambia
> 30 March 1976

In the dry season the end of the causeway doesn't usually reach the water so you need a ranger from the scout post, who will take you on walks around the flats. While walking you can see Kafue lechwe, reedbuck, eland, roan antelope and hyena, together with a myriad of birds: herons, storks, cranes, kingfishers, korhanns, eagles (especially fish eagles), ducks, martins and lots of LBJs ('little brown jobbies' – which means any small, inconspicuous birds that the observer can't name).

Aside from the wildlife, ask to be shown around the old farmhouse that used to be owned by the Critchleys. The interior has been very well preserved for years – complete with the family's furniture – and if it's still in good condition, it's fascinating to see.

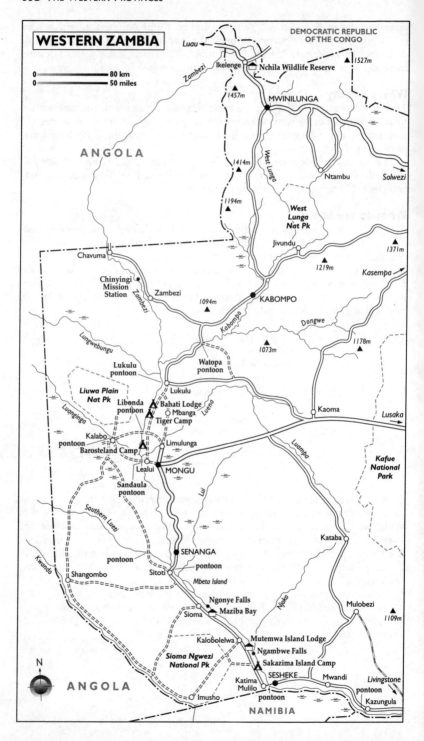

17

The Western Provinces

This remote area of western Zambia is difficult to visit but can reward intrepid travellers with some of the country's most interesting experiences. The Barotseland floodplains, near Mongu, offer a glimpse of rural Zambian life that is still largely untouched by the 20th century, while the Liuwa Plain National Park has excellent game and few visitors. It may be the venue for one of Africa's last great wildlife migrations, which has remained largely unknown because of the difficulty of getting into the area. Other parks, Sioma Ngwezi and West Lunga, do not have the same reputation for wildlife, but are still very wild places to explore with a well-prepared group of 4WD vehicles.

Common to the whole region are the related problems of supplies and transport. Much of the region stands on deep Kalahari sand where vehicles need a high-clearance 4WD capability. If you are going off the main roads, then a small expedition is needed: consisting of several vehicles, in case one runs into problems. During the rainy season, many of the roads are impassable, and even the pontoons (as ferries are usually known here) across the rivers will often stop working. Being stranded is a very real possibility. Thus the area's paucity of visitors is largely explained by the sheer difficulty of getting around.

The missions have a very well established network here. On the whole, these do remarkable work for the communities in the area, being involved with schools, hospitals, churches, development projects and many other aspects of local life. The courteous traveller can learn a lot about the region from these missions, and they are also good places to find English-speaking guides to accompany you on your travels – who will prove invaluable for just a few dollars per day.

I've divided this chapter up into three sections: northwestern Zambia, Barotseland, and southwestern Zambia. These don't slavishly follow provincial divisions, rather they reflect the differences between the areas as I understand them and are a convenient way to organise this chapter.

NORTHWESTERN ZAMBIA

West of the Copperbelt, squeezed between Angola and DRC, this area is distant from most of Zambia. This is reflected in its flora and fauna which, in parts, are much more like those of the wet tropical forests which occur to the north than those of the drier areas of the Kalahari to the south.

Despite being out on a limb, the roads here generally work well, with a tar road from the Copperbelt to Mwinilunga and another being constructed over the top of the good gravel road known as the M8, which links Solwezi with Zambezi.

Mwinilunga

Mwinilunga is an outpost, the main town in the remote northwest corner of Zambia. In the town you'll find petrol, shops with basic supplies, a couple of banks, a few outposts for aid agencies, a small Franciscan mission, and two basic local resthouses – one council and one government. Beyond the tar, a good track leads north into DRC via Ikelenge. Alternatively head for Angola via Kalene Hill, and the border at Jimbe Bridge is just over 100km away.

Getting there

By far the easiest way to get to Mwinilunga is via the Copperbelt, Chingola and Solwezi. To reach it, travel through Chingola and then take the turn to Solwezi. This used to be tarmac, but it is currently in a poor state of repair. The first 40km or so are particularly rough.

Solwezi has a small motel, the **Changa Changa Motel** (PO Box 110249, Solwezi. Tel: 08 821572). This is very basic. A 'continental breakfast' consists of tea and a dry bread roll here, though its evening meals are a little better. Perhaps you'd do better to visit the in-store bakery in Solwezi's supermarket for meals.

About 28km after Solwezi there's a T-junction. Mwinilunga should be signposted to the right, but this is easy to miss, so be on the look out for it. From there it's about 298km of quite good tarmac to Mwinilunga. Eventually you'll descend a hill, cross the West Lunga River, and enter town.

Excursions from Mwinilunga

One small, private reserve stands out in this area as a very interesting spot to visit in its own right, and perhaps to use as a base for short trips around the area, possibly including an excursion to the source of the Zambezi.

Nchila Wildlife Reserve (3 chalets) PO Box 50, Ikelenge, North Western Province. Or c/o Wager, PO Box 20241, Kitwe. In evenings only – satphone: 871 682 345 486; fax: 871 682 345 488; email: Nchila@compuserve.com.

The Fisher family has lived in Zambia for generations and Peter and Lynn Fisher now live on a remote ranch near the source of the Zambezi, in the northwestern tip of Zambia. There they keep beef and dairy cows, and cultivate coffee and cereals. Nchila Wildlife Reserve is a 40km^2 area of virgin bush, within the boundaries of Hillwood Farm.

To reach here after arriving in Mwinilunga, continue through town on the main road, past the turn-off to the airport and on to a well-maintained gravel road. This will then cross a series of rivers, and you'll drive over four bridges. First comes the Luakela River, then the Chitunta River, next the Kaseki River and finally the Sakeji River. Then 11km after the Sakeji River there is a signpost to the right for Hillwood Farms and Nchila Wildlife Reserve. Follow this off the main road and up to the office. This is about 68km from Mwinilunga and will take a bit less than two hours. Alternatively, Nchila can be reached by a short (though not cheap) charter flight from Lusaka or even northern Kafue.

Within Nchila, a small bushcamp accommodating a maximum of about ten people has just been finished. It stands beside a dambo next to a stream, surrounded by riverine forest and miombo woodlands. There are two thatched chalets, both equipped with twin beds and mosquito nets. These share separate showers and toilets. There's also a larger family chalet, for four people (a double room and a twin), which has its own private toilet and shower. The camp's focus is its thatched dining area which has a lovely view over the dambo and makes a pleasant place to just sit and watch the wildlife.

Currently this camp is only for self-catering visitors, though fresh produce is always available from the farm – milk, eggs, butter, beef and pork products, as well as lamb and game on request. Meals can be provided, but only for special groups when booked well in advance. Similarly, local guides are available on request, and there's a 4WD and driver that can be hired with advance notice, making a fly-in trip a realistic possibility.

The larger wildlife here includes duikers (both common and blue), puku, reedbuck, impala, red lechwe, waterbuck, hartebeest, wildebeest, sable, roan, eland, zebra, warthog and sitatunga. This is beautiful area, made all the more interesting because of its location: sandwiched between Angola and DRC. It contains pockets of wet, evergreen forest (rainforest) which is typical of those neighbouring countries so you'll find species here which you can't see anywhere else – unless you're prepared to brave the instability of either Angola or DRC. Hence Nchila attracts a steady stream of ornithologists, herpetologists, zoologists, and other keen observers of the natural world.

For ornithologists some of the area's 'specials' are black-collared bulbul, Angola lark, honeyguide greenbull, various longclaws (rosy-breasted, Fülleborne's and Grimwood's), Bates' sunbird, Stanley's bustard, Forbes' plover, Anchieta's barbet, and Bocage's weaver – though this is not an exhaustive list by any means.

Rates: US$30 per person sharing, US$10 extra includes all fresh farm produce. Camping US$20 per person. 4WD hire – US$40 for self-drive within the reserve; US$80 for trips outside the reserve (this includes the services of a local driver/guide).

West Lunga National Park

150km northwest of Kafue, as the pied crow flies, West Lunga is another of Zambia's parks which is ideal for small expeditions to explore, although not practicable to visit casually. Check with the National Parks and Wildlife Service for the latest news about the park (there is an office at Solwezi if you are approaching from the north) and don't arrive without the backing of several vehicles for safety in the event of an emergency. There are no camps here, or commercial operators, or even scouts inside the park – so you must get around independently.

Geography, flora and fauna

West Lunga National Park covers 1,684km² of forests, dambos, open grasslands and papyrus swamps. It is bounded by the Kabompo River to the south (adjacent to which are most of the park's swamps) and by the West Lunga River to the west.

Despite persistent local poaching, Rob Munro reports that he saw buffalo, impala, puku and warthog in the park on a trip in mid-1999. It is also thought to harbour elephant, lion, leopard, hippopotamus and a wide range of antelope including sitatunga, blue, common and yellow-backed duiker, sable, bushbuck and defassa waterbuck. All the park's game is skittish and scarce.

Buk's 1993–4 survey (see *Further Reading*) reported two sightings of wild dog in West Lunga, although noted that poaching remained heavy and the species was probably declining here. Excluding local poachers, the park probably receives fewer than a dozen visitors a year at the moment.

Getting there

The easiest ways to get to West Lunga are to approach from the Copperbelt or by skirting Kafue National Park's eastern boundary and proceeding through Kasempa. Approaching from Mongu is very time-consuming and slow going – with a good 4WD essential even in the dry season.

From the Copperbelt

Take the tar road through Kitwe and Chingola to Solwezi, from where it turns south until crossing the Mutanda River at Mwelemu. On the other side of the river, there's a good tar road on the right, which heads west to Mwinilunga. The road continues south, towards Kabompo and Kasempa – so take this road. After almost 90km the road is joined from the east by a road coming from Kitwe (which would have made a shorter, but more time-consuming, approach), via the village of Ingwe.

About 16km later there is a road left to Kasempa, and one right to Kabompo. Take the road to the right. This is the section of the M8 where tarring has been started, and what's been completed is a super road. After 140km there is a signpost to turn right to the small village of Jivundu, which is on the south bank of the Kabompo River. The park is on the north bank and there is a pontoon that will take you across.

From Kafue
Follow the directions in *Chapter 16* to approach Kasempa from Mumbwa via the Lubungu and Lunga pontoons, then head north from Kasempa on to the road from Mwelemu to Kabompo. Alternatively, taking the tar road to Kitwe and Solwezi, and then cutting southwest, is likely to be easier and probably faster.

What to see and do
In mid-1999 the 'road' into the park was overgrown and required clearing to make it passable. A much better way would be to leave your vehicle at Jivundu and take a scout/guide from there to walk with you into the park for a few days. You'll certainly be able to penetrate deeper this way than with a vehicle.

Zambezi
The road from Kabompo, which is usually known as the M8, is a remarkably good gravel road (gradually being tarred), with relatively few villages and lots of thick teak forests along its route. In the dry season the smoke from occasional bush fires will be seen drifting in the sky, above areas of scorched and blackened ground.

Zambezi is a small town with a few very basic shops, a mission, a telecommunications centre (Zambia's PTC), and a small local market. There is one simple hotel here, the **Zambezi Motel** (tel: 08 371123), which costs around US$12 per night, and an even more basic government resthouse which charges US$5 per night. Note that the town, like many regional centres in Zambia, is referred to locally as 'the boma'.

Zambezi has just one fuel station, but this is unreliable and often empty. There are disturbing reports from this area of watered-down petrol from illicit sources – known as 'bush fuel' – being sold to unsuspecting travellers. This makes it even more essential, if heading west from Mongu or south from Mwinilunga, to do so with very large reserves of fuel.

Note on security
Because tourists are rare, and the border with Angola is a sensitive one, travellers going west or north from Zambezi should report to the local police – just to let them know that you're here. Perhaps going in to the police station to inquire 'if it is safe to proceed' is the easiest way to do this. It will allow them to ask you questions if they wish, and reassure them that you mean no harm and are not there to cause problems.

Getting there and away
From Lukulu
From Lukulu follow the road north towards Watopa pontoon, which is about 70km away (1½ hours' drive). It's on the left, just after you enter the two-shop town of Watopa. Look out for the 'God's Word Grocery' and note that the pontoon (or ferry) is incorrectly marked on the ITM map of Zambia.

The Kabompo is a major tributary of the Zambezi and the ferry consists of a manually operated cable pontoon, which is free. From here it is about 20km north to the junction with the road from Kabompo to Zambezi, and turning left it is a further 75km to Zambezi.

This good M8 road continues to the Angolan border, at Chavuma, and there are plans to tar it.

What to see and do
Traditional dancing
A few kilometres north of town are the palaces of the Lunda and the Luvale senior chiefs, on the east and west sides of the road respectively – as you might predict from the rough distribution of languages mapped out at the start of *Chapter 3*. The Luvale chief's palace is not only the venue for the Lykumbi Lya Mize (see page 29), but also for traditional dancing which is held here several times a week.

Chinyingi Mission
About a third of the way from Zambezi to Chavuma, just after the Makondu River, is a major track heading west and leading to the Chinyingi Mission. If you miss this turning then there is another better-signposted turning a few kilometres later.

The Mission is located on the east side of the river, and runs a school and a rural health centre. It is perhaps most famous for the Chinyingi suspension bridge – one of only four bridges to span the width of the Zambezi anywhere along its length. (The others are at Chirundu, Tete and the railway bridge near Livingstone.) The mission is run by Capuchin brothers. They are helpful and very jovial, and will happily tell you more about the area and the mission if you ask them.

Chavuma
Chavuma stands about 6km south of the Angolan border and the place where the Zambezi re-enters Zambia. The land around here is arid, and the soil mostly grey in colour, which makes villages in this area look dull compared with those further south.

As in Zambezi, paying your respects to the local police is a wise move, just so that they know who you are and what you are doing in their area.

The same goes for the Brethren Missionaries, who will also be able to help you

THE CHINYINGI BRIDGE
Judi Helmholz
The suspension bridge at Chinyingi was built in the mid-1970s by Brother Crispin Baleri of the mission after four people drowned whilst trying to ferry a sick person to the health centre. The tragedy happened in a *mekoro* (dugout canoe) on the river late at night, and brother Crispin was so determined that it would never happen again that he decided to build a bridge.

Despite his lack of technical training, Baleri read all he could find on bridge construction and elicited donations of cables from the mines of the Copperbelt. Locals worked for second-hand clothes to construct the bridge, which is still used today, bouncing and swaying as you walk across it. Below there is now a pontoon operated by cables which is capable of ferrying a vehicle across.

with advice on camping or accommodation. They are found in a large compound up on the hill by the town. They have their own camping spot by the river, which they may allow you to use, and they will certainly be able to direct you to any other suitable places.

Getting there
The M8 road here from Solwezi via Kabompo and Zambezi is very good gravel, and is gradually being tarred from the east – though this will take a few years to reach Chavuma. If you're approaching from the south via Lukulu then it's best to cross the Kabompo River at the Watopa pontoon, and then join this road from there.

What to see and do
Chavuma Falls
This is not nearly so spectacular as the Zambezi's later drops at Ngonye and Victoria Falls, but makes a good picnic site for an afternoon – the falls are found by taking the footpath near the pontoon.

No man's land
Every morning there is a small market here in no man's land, between the territories of Zambia and Angola. Both Zambians and Angolans come to barter for goods, under the watchful eyes of the armed border guards. As a foreigner, make sure you have very clear permission from the border guards before you even consider joining in, and don't take any photographs without permission. That said, it is a fascinating occurrence.

BAROTSELAND
The former British protectorate of Barotseland, now usually referred to as simply the Western Province (WP), covers the floodplains which surround some of the upper reaches of the Zambezi. It is the homeland of the Lozi king, the Litunga, and his people – a group who have retained much of their cultural heritage despite the ravages of the past century. They were granted more autonomy by the colonial authorities than most of the ethnic groups in Zambia's other regions, and perhaps this has helped them to preserve more of their culture. The Litunga has winter and summer palaces nearby, and a hunting lodge in Liuwa Plains.

Chapter 47 of John Reader's excellent *Africa: A Biography of the Continent* covers some of the history of this area in fascinating detail. See *Further Reading*, page 397, for details.

For the traveller this means that some aspects of life here have altered relatively little since pre-colonial times. Most of the local people still follow lifestyles of subsistence farming, hunting and gathering, and when rains are good they must still move to higher ground to escape the floodwaters.

Kaoma
Kaoma is a small district town beside the Great West Road between Lusaka and Mongu, about 76km from the west gate to Kafue National Park. Whilst only on the edge of the Western Province, it is very much a gateway to the area. It has a post office, a district council resthouse, some basic shops and local eateries, and a vital fuel station. Vital to anyone travelling west that is.

It's definitely wise to fill your fuel tank (and spare fuel drums) here, and if you have spare space in your vehicle, then you'll find no shortage of people wanting to share the journey. Given the shortage of transport, and the insight that hitchhikers can give to visitors, you'll appear very rude to the locals if you refuse them.

Getting there and away
From Kaoma to Lukulu
If you're heading to Lukulu then take the tar road towards Mongu for about 25km. Then there's a gravel road on the right, signpost as 195km to Lukulu. After 16km on this road it forks: keep to the right. Later there's a sign heralding a turn to the right, to the M8, which leads to the Watopa pontoon.

Lining this road are small villages, each consisting of thatched huts built in varying sizes. Ox-carts are also a frequent sight, straight out of a biblical scene.

From Kaoma to Kasempa
Turning off the Great West Road at Kaoma, there's a poor road which heads north and then northeast to Kasempa.

Mongu
On the edge of these floodplains, Mongu is the provincial centre for Western Zambia. It is linked to Lusaka by a tar road that starts by crossing a raised causeway across the Zambezi's floodplains. Because of this road, Mongu is easily reached from Lusaka and is the best place in the region to get fuel or supplies.

There is a Caltex fuel station on the main street, along with many small local shops and stalls. The Shoprite chain has reached here, and is by far the biggest and best store in town. There are several banks although Roger Marston reports that the Standard Chartered bank here charges US$25 to cash travellers' cheques.

At the northern end of the main street is the Nutritional Centre, which houses the town's best arts and craft shop (head north beyond the Caltex garage; it's on the left after the next crossroads) and has some good local weaving.

Mongu has a reputation for theft, so visitors should take great care of their belongings and vehicles here. The police appear to be vigilant, as there are often several roadblocks around the town where they will check your vehicle and its papers. Make sure that you're wearing your seat belts and driving slowly through town.

Geography
Mongu stands about 25km from the Zambezi, and is set on a ridge overlooking the north of the Barotse plains. The town is spread out over several kilometres in a giant arc, which follows the ridge. It has two petrol stations, a bakery, a few grocery stores, a garage, several small hotels, and a large local market. Government administration has a strong presence here, and most departments are represented in a rather ramshackle collection of offices.

The views north over the floodplain are spectacular: a myriad of waterways snaking through apparently endless flat plains. Small villages and cattle dot the dusty plains during the dry season, but when wet it is all transformed into a haze of green grass on a mirror of water that reflects the sky.

Getting there and away
By air
Mongu is served twice a week, on Tuesday and Sunday, by Eastern Air. Lusaka–Mongu flights cost around US$135 one way. Mongu–Livingstone is US$105 but only runs on a Tuesday.

By bus

Several buses link Lusaka to Mongu every day – expect a minibus to cost around Kw18,000/US$7.20 and a larger, slower bus to be about Kw13,500/US$5.40. There is also a postbus that serves this route, so ask at the post office for details. A very slow service also plies between Livingstone and Mongu, via Sesheke, during the dry season. Ask at the bus station for details.

Driving north – to Lukulu

By far the best route to Lukulu is from just after the Kaoma turn-off, on the Lusaka–Mongu road (see page 359). This is an all-weather road. However, if you are starting from Mongu and travelling late in the dry season, then there are two other more direct possibilities.

One starts by heading west from Mongu towards Kalabo. Several kilometres before the Sandaula pontoon over the Zambezi, at Lealui, a road turns off north. This passes the Barotseland Fishing Tours and Safaris Camp, then the Libonda pontoon, and continues towards Lukulu on the eastern bank of the Zambezi. Nearer to Lukulu it passes Tiger Camp and Bahati Lodge, before finally reaching Lukulu after about 120km.

The alternative, which is easier, is to go from Limulunga towards Mbanga. For this you should cross the dambo at the end of the Limulunga Road, and then ask for the road to Mbanga. This is a bush track through small villages across the floodplain, and even driving carefully you can expect scrawny multi-coloured chickens with chicks in tow to be scattered everywhere as you pass, and emaciated village dogs to bark wildly and show an unnatural interest in your tyres. If you are heading for Tiger Camp then pick up a guide at Mbanga, who will show you the camp. Otherwise continue through Mbanga in the same direction to reach Lukulu.

Driving west – to Kalabo

There are two obvious routes here and for both see the description of how to get to Kalabo on page 368. However, both basically start by heading west to Lealui, on the Zambezi.

This road begins by going past the Mongu post office (turning off near the Caltex garage), and dropping down on to the Barotse floodplain. Remember that Mongu is your last place to fill up with petrol. This road west used to be a raised causeway over the Zambezi floodplains though now it is broken down in several places and there are many tracks leading west. There are plenty of people to ask, so it's difficult to get lost. After some 30km the pontoon at Lealui is reached. This could easily take two or three hours.

Driving south – to Senanga

This is lovely wide tarmac and probably the easiest road in the region.

Hitchhiking

Hitching to Mongu on the Great West Road is possible for the determined. Hitching to get around the surrounding countryside is very slow and difficult – but it is how most of the local population travel.

Getting around

By boat

Boat transport is the best way to see the immediate area around Mongu, and it is the only way if the flood is high. For a few dollars you can hire a mokoro (dugout canoe) to take you out on the waterways, and perhaps down towards Lealui and the main channel. Spend a few hours like this, on the water, and you will appreciate how many of the locals transport themselves around. You will see everything from people to household goods, supplies, live animals and even the occasional bicycle loaded on to boats and paddled or poled (punted) from place to place.

By postboat
Given that boats are the only way to reach some settlements in this area during the wet season, there is a 'postboat' on the Zambezi that carries passengers, cargo, and even the mail. It is large enough to also take the odd vehicle, though this may need a special arrangement. Ask at the Mongu District Council offices, or telephone 07 221175, for more details.

Driving
Apart from the main roads from Lusaka to Mongu and Lukulu, most of the area's gravel roads degenerate into patches of deep sand occasionally. Thus they require a 4WD even in the dry season, and the worst of them will require almost constant low-range driving through long sections of Kalahari sand.

During the wet season, the whole area north of the Ngonye Falls is subject to flooding. Then the Barotse floodplain becomes a large, shallow lake – much of the population moves to higher ground to live, and boats are the only options for getting around. Don't even think about trying to drive through here then.

Where to stay
There are several small hotels in Mongu, and all are very basic. Because of the town's bad reputation for crime, especially theft, you should take maximum precautions against losing your belongings, even when staying in one of the hotels.

Ngulu Hotel (16 twin-bed rooms) PO Box 910308. Tel: 07 221028
The Ngulu (also known as the Ngulu-Ta-Utoya) is a few kilometres south of where the Lusaka road meets the main street. It's probably the best place in town, and all the rooms have en-suite bathrooms.
Rates: US$25/Kw62,500 per person

Lyamba Hotel (17 twin-bed rooms) PO Box 910193. Tel: 07 221271/138
This is the town's largest hotel, near the boat terminal. There is little to choose between this and the Ngulu, as all of its rooms have en-suite bathrooms.
Rates: US$20/Kw50,000 per person sharing

Mongu Lodge PO Box 26, Mongu. Tel: 07 221501/221606
This is one of the town's more basic places. The rooms do have their own en-suite bathrooms, though these are not very sparkling.
Rates: US$15/Kw37,500 per person sharing

Aside from these, there are a couple of very dingy resthouses for a few dollars a night, or you can camp. Given the problems of theft around Mongu, any campsite should be chosen with care. Consider the compound at Limulunga as a possibility. There is also a small guesthouse there that sometimes operates.

Where to eat
The hotels will sometimes serve food if requested but for the town's best food try the Bisiku Restaurant, in the centre of town near the main market. With an afternoon's notice they will serve up an excellent dish of bream. Otherwise the grocery stores and the main local market are your best source of ingredients, though the variety is often limited.

Fishing camps

In the early 1990s several fishing camps started up between Mongu and Lukulu, focusing on the superb tiger fishing in the area. However, it's at least a whole day's drive to Lusaka and proved a difficult and expensive place to run a camp.

Only one really managed to carve out an overseas market for itself: Tiger Camp. That was due to the skill and determination of its owners, Bernie and Adrienne Esterhuyse – and the fact that they made superb hosts. Now with their departure the camp is up for sale. So there remain three camps in this area, though it's essential to check the current status of any which you intend to visit.

Tiger Camp (6 twin-bed tents) Tiger Fishing Tours, PO Box 31730, Lusaka. Tel/fax: 01 262810; email: tiger@zamnet.zm or tigercamp@aol.com
This upmarket fishing camp is on the eastern side of the Zambezi, about 32km from Lukulu. It's a beautiful and remote section of the river. Accommodation at Tiger is in large tents with en-suite (hot and cold) showers, flush toilets, and protection from the sun by individual thatched roofs. Each has a view of the river. The meals are extensive, and the three-course dinner is usually served with wine.

Boats, with skippers, and tackle are included in the rates, as are laundry and fishing licences – though you will have to pay for any fishing lures that you lose. At the beginning of 1999, this camp held 14 world records for fishing (three for fly-fishing).

Ideally, you should book in advance to stay here, and there is an airstrip for charter planes. The camp is in daily radio contact with its Lusaka offices. When run by Bernie and Adrienne, Tiger could be recommended without hesitation for not just fishing, but also outstanding hospitality, helpfulness, personal attention and friendliness – even if you never picked up a rod there. They also operated mobile trips up to Liuwa Plains, and could use their vehicle to guide and accompany anyone going up there.

In early '99, Bernie & Adrienne moved to Camp Moremi, in Botswana. Tiger is awaiting a serious buyer. The staff are maintaining the camp, and will assist you if you want to camp there – but the camp's accommodation and all its facilities are not operational.
Rates: When running again, expect about US$200/250 per person sharing/single, including full board and activities. Open: May to November

Barotseland Fishing Tours and Safaris PO Box 30172, Lusaka. Tel: 01 261768; fax: 01 263557
This company has a camp between Lealui and the Libonda pontoon, on the bank of the Zambezi. It's run by Barry Myers and a few friends who are very keen fishermen – and opened specifically for fishing trips when requested, so these should be booked in advance. It's not a place to just drop in on. In the past they have also offered special trips to see the spectacular Ku'omboka Ceremony (see page 28 for more details).
Rates: about US$200 per night, including meals and activities. Open: May to November

Bahati Lodge (5 twin-bed tents) PO Box 10122, Chingola. Tel: 02 311454; fax: 312396
30km downstream from Lukulu and 60km north of Mongu, Bahati Lodge is the most northern of the fishing camps on the Upper Zambezi. It is owned by Harry Randall and operated from 1994 to 1996. Unfortunately it's been closed since then because of sickness – and flattened by the rains over three successive years. Keep your eyes open, as it may reopen in the future.

What to see and do

Aside from wandering around the local market, in the town centre, there are no specific sights in Mongu. The two obvious attractions are both excursions from the town:

The Litunga's summer palace at Lealui

About an hour from Mongu, on the floodplains, the summer palace is set in a large grove of trees, which is easily seen from the escarpment on which Mongu stands. Driving takes about an hour, or it is possible to hire a *mekoro* to bring you out here from Mongu.

Don't expect a western-style palace, as the Litunga's will appear to be a normal small African village with thatched huts. However, this is not only the King's summer residence, but also the main Lozi administration centre. Visitors are warmly welcomed, though are strongly advised to show the utmost courtesy and respect to their hosts.

Museum at Limulunga

Just outside Mongu, near the Litunga's summer palace, is a small museum housing some interesting exhibits on the history and culture of the Lozi people. There is also a small craft shop which sells some really beautiful basketwork from the area, typically at around US$2–3/Kw5,000–7,500 per piece.

The Ku-omboka

If the rains have been good, and the floodwaters are rising, then around February or March, often on a Thursday, just before full moon, the greatest of Zambia's cultural festivals will take place. The Ku-omboka is the tradition of moving the Litunga, the Lozi king, plus his court and his people, away from the floodwaters and on to higher ground.

This spectacular ceremony is described in detail in *Chapter 3*, page 28, and it involves a flotilla of boats for most of the day, plus an impromptu orchestra of local musicians and much celebration. Don't miss it if you are travelling in western Zambia at the time.

Lukulu

Lukulu is the main town of the district, hence it has a collection of government offices and local council offices in the 'boma' (the central area, see map). There is also a district hospital, which includes two doctors from the Netherlands (as do many such hospitals in the Western Province, which is being helped by a Dutch aid programme). However, medical facilities and supplies here are very limited.

Lukulu is a typical rural town. It has a ZESCO plant (Zambia's electricity supply company), and hence has erratic supplies of electricity. It also has a public water pumping and distribution system, which means running water some of the time. It's also sufficiently rural to make visitors – especially ones with fair skins – something of a novelty.

Getting there and away
From Kaoma to Lukulu

This is a reasonable, all-weather gravel road, and the most reliable way to reach Lukulu. When the Barotse Plains are flooded, then travellers from Mongu will reach Lukulu either by boat, or by driving east to Kaoma and then northwest to Lukulu.

If you are backpacking then there are buses that ply between Kaoma and Lukulu. However, they don't run to a fixed schedule, rather the driver waits (possibly for several days) for the bus to fill up enough to make the trip worthwhile. Karun Thanjavuvr (a VSO volunteer working in Lukulu) described the road as 'an axle breaker ... the buses creak and groan from abuse'. She advises travellers coming this way on public transport to travel with a good stock of food and water (at least

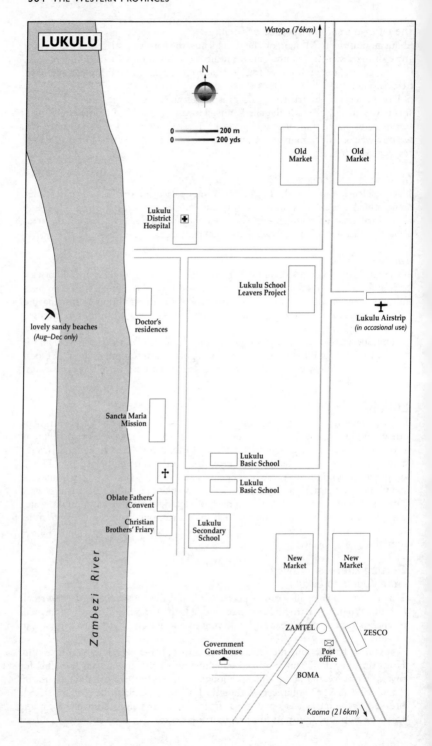

for two days), and a sleeping bag (with mosquito net/coils) etc – just in case the bus breaks down. Most people will hitch a ride on any vehicle rather than wait for a bus, and van drivers charge about US$2–4/Kw5,000–10,000 for the trip.

From Lukulu to Watopa

Without your own vehicle, the only means of public transport here are private local 4WDs (often simply called 'Hi Luxes') and assorted lorries and vans. The charge varies (depending whether you wish to ride in the cab or in the open back braving the elements) but you can get to Watopa or Kabompo for US$4/Kw10,000. Karun reports that some drivers will charge much more if you are fair skinned, as you are perceived to be a wealthy '*makuwa*' (white person). On average, it's probably a fair assumption – so pay and don't complain!

This road is in a very bad condition, which worsens after the rains. Fortunately the M8 (the Solwezi–Zambezi–Chavuma road) to the north of the Watopa pontoon is rather better.

From Mongu

By far the best route to Lukulu is from just after the Kaoma turn-off, on the Lusaka–Mongu road. However, if it is dry then there are two other possibilities: a road shadowing the Zambezi to the west, and a more direct route via Mbanga. See the section on Mongu, page 359, for more details of both.

West from Lukulu

There is a pontoon crossing here, but no real roads on the other side – just a series of paths that link the small villages there. Crossing here and then driving south to Kalabo would be possible in the dry season, but a local guide (preferably backed up by a GPS!) would be essential. Kalabo would normally be easier to reach by crossing the river further south.

If you do want to use the pontoon at Lukulu, then Sue Grainger commented: 'The pontoon at Lukulu is an adventure. The pontoon is owned by the hospital, the engine by the veterinary service and fuel is a matter of local negotiation. Therefore time, patience and the services of a guide are much appreciated. [She had expert assistance from Tiger Camp.] It is a one-car pontoon and the steep sandy east bank of the Zambezi is perceived to be better than the west bank. It is best to get off the pontoon on the west bank in a forward gear. You therefore back on to the pontoon – which can be quite daunting when you are looking at a 1-in-3 slope of sand on the east bank!'

Where to stay

Lukulu has a government guesthouse, reached by turning southwest off the main road, just west of the post office and Zamtel office, and then taking the first right turn. There's also a private hotel, near the old market on the right of the road as you head north to Watopa. A room at either will cost around US$4–8/Kw10–20,000; both are very simple and basic.

There are no campsites, but in the dry season there are many lovely spots along the river (especially just across from Lukulu on the far bank) where a well equipped traveller can camp in peace.

Where to eat

There are several basic restaurants here, mostly in the old and new markets. All usually offer rather meagre fare of nshima and some form of relish for around Kw3–5,000. Fernando's Butchery, in the old market, can serve slightly more elaborate meals for around Kw7,000, if you give them a few hours notice.

The shops in the old and the new markets have only the most basic essentials. The chances of finding even canned food here are slim. Both soft drinks and beer depend on a truck supplying them from Lusaka; news of its arrival spreads like wildfire through the town.

The local people live by subsistence farming and fishing; each eating just what s/he cultivates or catches. Hence, not much fresh produce reaches the market. You'll probably find just one or two varieties of seasonal fresh fruits and vegetables, dried fish, roller meal for nshima, etc. Visitors should arrive with a good stock of food and drink – and the locals will probably be grateful for anything that you leave behind.

What to see and do

Lukulu doesn't have many obvious attractions, though the nearby Zambezi is very scenic. As with many of the area's smaller places, privacy can be a problem as an outsider is regarded as a source of free entertainment by some of the local community. Karun, a VSO volunteer living here, commented: 'If the visitor is willing to offer to the local people the same right to watch that s/he has assumed, then we have a happy relationship; if not, we have an unhappy visitor but content

MAKISHI DANCERS
Judi Helmholz

Sometimes in Mongu, or whilst travelling in the north of the Western Provinces, you will encounter colourfully clad characters adorned with fearsome costumes – Makishi dancers. To the uninitiated (defined as women and children in Luvale society), these are traditionally believed to be female spirits from the dead, and most will talk in high voices and even have 'breasts' made of wire.

The creative and artistic skills of the Luvale people are reflected in the wide variety of mask styles worn by the Makishi. These are huge constructions, often made of bark and wood and frequently coloured with red, white and black. Even helicopter blades are sometimes spotted in the designs – a memory of the war in Angola.

Each Likishi (the singular of Makishi) dancer is distinctive and plays a specific role within the various ceremonies and festivals. For example, the Mungali, or hyena, depicts menacing villains, whilst the Chikishikishi, a monster with a boiling pot, represents discipline – and will consume mischievous members of society.

Apart from their occasional appearances throughout the land, the Makishi dancers play central roles during two of the most important ceremonies of Luvale culture: the Mukanda and the Wali. These are the initiation rites for boys and girls respectively.

The Mukanda, also known as circumcision camps, are traditional 'schools' for local boys, aged from 12 to 17, where they are introduced to adult life and circumcised. The dancer known as 'Chileya cha Mukanda', which literally means 'the fool of the school', serves as a jester by mimicking the participants so as to relieve tension and anxiety before the circumcision ceremony. The girls attend a similar ceremony, though there is no physical clitoridectomy operation, as occurs in other cultures.

locals. Except for an occasional visit by a group of Makishi dancers, there are no other festivals that take place in Lukulu.'

Perhaps, for sanctuary, you might like to stop at one of the country's loveliest mission stations:

Sancta Maria Mission
This Catholic mission near Lukulu was founded in the 1930s and has a stunning setting high on one bank of the Zambezi, overlooking palm-fringed woodlands opposite. It is a beautiful place from which to watch the sunset. The mission is run by the Sisters of the Holy Cross whose projects include community education and a leprosy clinic.

There is a Sunday service in Lozi that offers a fascinating blend of Catholicism and Lozi culture – with lots of singing and dancing. Being just over the river from Liuwa Plains, the sisters tell of one day, in the 1950s, when the bell in the tower started ringing wildly. On investigation the bellringer proved to be a spotted hyena which had seized the raw-hide rope in its jaws, and was trying to pull it off and eat it.

Kalabo
This small town by the Luanginga River is the gateway to Liuwa Plain National Park. Kalabo is a rambling group of dwellings. Coming from Mongu, one of the first to be reached is the Sunday School, from where the staff will give directions down a series of sandy roads to the small pontoon over the Luanginga. The fare is Kw1,000, reflecting the 'Heath Robinson' state of this one-car pontoon. Alternatively, later in the dry season, the river can be forded (with a little local guidance on where to cross).

Kalabo has a few small shops and a National Park office, which can issue permits for the park and a scout to accompany you. However, note there is no fuel available here – you must bring all you need from Mongu. Kalabo also has a mission and a basic government resthouse. The former is a good source of information on the whole area, and can direct you to the resthouse if you need it.

Getting there and away
Kalabo is not easy to reach, and anywhere west of the Zambezi is really expedition territory. The roads are usually just tracks in the Kalahari sand, which need days of low-range driving. This not only requires a 4WD (preferably several, in case of emergency), but also large quantities of fuel. Fuel cannot be replenished outside of Mongu, so long-range extra fuel tanks and lots of jerry cans are the normal solution. Note also that if there is any risk of the ferries going out of operation, then your only way back out is to keep west of the river, and drive south via Sitoti, south of Senanga. If you were forced to do this, it would take *much* more time and fuel than going straight from Kalabo to Mongu, but you need to bear the possibility in mind.

Water is also a problem, as it tends to seep through the Kalahari sand rather than forming pans on the surface. Hence no potable water can be relied upon outside Kalabo, so take some good containers and fill up at Mongu and Kalabo.

In the wet season the town is cut off, and the only way to reach here is using the postboat from Mongu. This can take one vehicle at a time: enquire locally to find out how it can be arranged. During the rest of the year, several approaches are possible:

From Mongu via Lealui

From Mongu, the best route for most of the year is to start by crossing the Zambezi using the Sandaula pontoon, at Lealui.

This is about 30km west of Mongu, a journey that can easily take two or three hours. The pontoon here is large enough for three cars and costs around US$6/Kw15,000 per vehicle. After this the tracks diverge as they cross the floodplains – which can be confusing. However, if you pick up any local hitchhiker going to Kalabo, then s/he should be able to direct you on to a navigable track.

It is about 82km from the pontoon over the Zambezi at Lealui, which is around three hours' drive. One main track initially veers away from the river and then runs parallel to it before passing through a village and setting out across mostly open terrain. This track alternates between soft sand and hard bumps, making progress hot and slow. There are many sidetracks, so taking a guide is a good idea. Whichever route you take, you are likely to encounter lots of semi-naked herdboys waving sticks furiously at cattle to move them out of the vehicle's path.

From Mongu via the Libonda pontoon

If the pontoon at Lealui has problems, then the one at Libonda, higher up the river, may be working. This is reached by driving upstream from Lealui for about two hours (35km).

After crossing on the Libonda pontoon, there is a direct track to Kalabo but it is difficult to locate. Again, taking a local guide (hitchhiker) is the best way to travel – and you will see plenty of these throughout the area. You will pass men, women and children carrying everything from luggage to mattresses and supplies on their heads. Given the area's lack of transport, it you have room in your vehicle then you should offer lifts whenever possible.

From Sitoti to Kalabo

From the Sitoti pontoon, just south of Senanga, there is a track on the western side of the river, but the difficulties of over 150km of low-range driving, with no access to fuel, should not be underestimated. Approaching from Mongu is certainly easier if it is possible to cross the river. However, if the river is high and the pontoons are not operating, then this may be your only option.

Liuwa Plain National Park

'Liuwa' means 'walking stick' in the local language, and a legend relates how one Litunga (Lozi king) planted his walking stick here on the plain, where it grew into a large *mutata* tree. The tree in question can still be seen from the track which leads from Minde to Luula: after leaving the first tree belt, look in the distance on your left side when you are halfway to the next tree belt. Liuwa Plain is certainly the most fascinating park in the region, but getting here requires an expedition. There isn't another way.

Getting there
From Kalabo

From Kalabo it is only about 40km to the game-scout post at Minde, the entry to Liuwa Plain National Park. You'll normally be travelling with a game scout, so once s/he's found the track, it is just a case of following the tyre tracks in the soft sand. It is an attractive but slow drive initially through woodland, which becomes more and more sparse as the plain is reached. There are a few villages, but little game along the early part of this drive. The route is frequented by many lilac-breasted rollers, which brighten up the top of trees along the roadside, giving dazzling flashes of blue as they fly.

The plain itself is are deep into the park, so anticipate another two or three hours of rough, sandy driving after you leave the scout post.

Geography

Except for the sandy track leading through the park, passing the game-scout camps of Minde and Luula (which is on the northern boundary of the park), there are no roads at all in the national park. That, however, is part of the park's attraction: around 3,660km² of untouched Africa. Most of this is a vast honey-coloured sea of grass, with just the occasional pan, island of raffia palms, or small tree-belt interrupting the flatness. You won't see the pans until you are almost driving into them. The environment is unlike any other park in Zambia, and the game is prolific.

Unfortunately Angola's civil war has ensured that guns are available in Angola, and the park's proximity to the border means that armed poachers are occasionally encountered in Liuwa. Provided that you travel with an armed game scout, they will try to avoid you and should not be a problem.

The best time to visit Liuwa is certainly August to December, with November being the ideal month. Then the land is dry, and the game is at its most prolific.

Flora and fauna
Mammals

Liuwa's attraction lies mainly in the great herds of blue wildebeest that amass here at the start of the rainy season, around November and December. Thousands of wildebeest group together, with zebra, tsessebe and buffalo amongst them. Though widely regarded as a 'migration', some suggest that it may in fact just be a gathering on the plain of all the game that has previously been in the surrounding bush, rather than an actual migration from, say, Angola. Regardless, if you can catch it at the right time, it's a stunning sight: flat, open plain with animals as far as the eye can see.

At any time of year the open plain is also frequented by oribi, a diminutive and very beautiful antelope, as well as resident populations of roan antelope, red lechwe and reedbuck.

Predators are also well-represented in Liuwa. Lion and hyena are relatively common. Liuwa's prides of lion, which blend superbly into the golden grass, have a reputation for aggression and even for charging vehicles, so be careful. It may simply be that they are unfamiliar with humans – although if this were the case excessive timidity might be a more normal reaction.

Wild dogs occur here and are sometimes seen. Buk's survey (see *Further Reading*) suggested that in 1993–4 the size of the packs was larger than average, though poaching was a problem and they were persecuted by the local people. Leopard occur within the national park, though the surrounding forest is a better habitat for them than the plain itself.

Birds

Liuwa boasts a total of about 300 bird species. The groups of crowned cranes are spectacular, often numbering several hundred birds. Wattled cranes, so endangered in many places, also thrive here although their groups seldom extend above 50–60 individuals. Slaty egrets are found in Liuwa in groups, a rare occurrence elsewhere. Pelicans, open-billed storks, and many water birds arrive here when the pans contain water. The plain is a great area for raptors, which include resident marshall eagles, fish eagles, palmnut vultures and even Pel's fishing owl (in the south of the park).

For serious twitchers, there's a (sub-?) species of pink-billed lark that occurs in Liuwa that some claim is endemic. Others view it as simply a race of the pink-billed lark that also occurs south of Zambia.

Camps and lodges

Though several operators have tried to set up permanent camps in Liuwa, all have failed so far. It's just too remote. The only option now is to drive yourself in a small expedition, or to find a competent mobile operator who can bring you.

Tukuluho Wildlife, from Maziba Bay (see page 372), has had plans for a camp here for years, but these have yet to materialise. Robin Pope Safaris (see page 257) based in the South Luangwa used to run one mobile trip per year up here, around November. Robin usually came along himself on this. However, the cost of a mobile rig and the hassle involved finally outweighed any benefit for RPS, and they no longer do such trips.

Chilongozi (see page 256) have a mobile rig and some of the team have at least been here before (when they were known as Tongabezi Expeditions, or 'TEX'). However, their trips were not without problems – and I could not recommend their services in Liuwa until they have built up a stronger track record for reliability.

Until recently, the best option was to drive up to Tiger Camp (see page 362) by yourself, and then go to Liuwa in convoy with a vehicle from Tiger, with a guide (and usually a cook also). Bernie knows the plain better than most, and has a track record second to none in the area. Unfortunately, he has now left – though it's possible that his successors at Tiger will pick up the baton and run with the idea.

I would not venture here with a mobile operation which has less than three or fours years experience in the area. If you find such an operator, expect to pay about US$3-400 per person per day for the trip. Even professionals would be very stupid to come here with less than two sturdy, reliable vehicles.

Getting around independently

Venturing into Liuwa Plain National Park should really be left to the experts. However, if you have several vehicles and the equipment, and insist on your own trip, then you can go in with an armed National Park scout from Kalabo. You will need to supply all of his provisions (cigarettes and other extras are greatly appreciated). It is wise to contact in advance the head office of the National Parks and Wildlife Service in Chilanga (see page 103), or the office in Mongu, to arrange for the permits and a guide. They will also be able to advise you of the costs in advance.

The park is approached from the National Park office in Kalabo by crossing the Luanginga River on a pontoon. This crossing can be tricky if your vehicle is heavily loaded, when recruiting some strong local help to get your vehicle on and off the pontoon is a good idea.

From there the park is about 30km of soft-sand driving. Some cut wooden poles mark the entrance, and there are no tracks in the park other than the one leading to the Minde and Luula scout villages. The only reliable water in the park is at Minde; it is red-brown in colour and fine for washing, but unappealing to drink.

SOUTHWESTERN ZAMBIA

The southwest of the country has almost been neglected, with few roads (which are generally poor) and no major towns. This does mean that its sights, like the marvellous Ngonye Falls, are very quiet.

Senanga

Approaching from Lusaka, Senanga is beside the Zambezi and right at the end of a very long stretch of tar. It's a pleasant place with a fuel station (sometimes this even has fuel), a clinic, a post office and a handful of shops and small bottle stores – but you can't shake off the feeling that it's out on a limb. Of course if you're coming from the south, then this is the first 'proper' town since Sesheke, *and* you're now back on tarmac. Bliss!

Getting there and away

Heading north to Mongu is tarmac all the way – about 110km which has been tarred in the last few years and so is now one of the best roads in the country. Travelling south is a little trickier.

The Sitoti pontoon

The pontoon across the Zambezi is about 30km (40 minutes) south of Senanga. It's similar to the Sesheke pontoon, costing US$25 or Kw27,000. (The lesser price, in kwacha, appears to be the price for locals, while the higher, in US dollars, is applied to foreign-registered vehicles. But this rule doesn't seem to be strictly adhered to.) Whatever you pay, it's available from 06.00 to 18.00, and crosses when necessary. There's no set schedule.

Senanga to Ngonye Falls

There's no navigable road on the east side of the Zambezi south of the Sitoti pontoon, so you've got to cross to the west bank to head further south. From the pontoon it's about 70km southeast to the Ngonye Falls and Maziba Bay.

A RUDE AWAKENING
Judi Helmholz

Owners of a lodge in western Zambia were dismayed when a nearby village got a rooster. The rooster's loud pre-dawn cock-a-doodle-do was marring the remote, bush-like atmosphere of the lodge. After considering various alternatives, they decided to buy the rooster from the village and then quietly dispose of it, solving their problem for good.

First, they sent one of their staff to go buy it, claiming it was for himself. They figured that the price would be increased if the village knew it was being purchased by the lodge. He returned without the rooster. Apparently, it was not for sale.

Next, the lodge owners ventured to the village – a two-mile hike through the bush and across the Zambezi. The chief told them that the village valued its rooster and it was not for sale. After all, it was their only one.

By now, price was no longer an issue – the lodge owners wanted that rooster gone! Finally they persuaded the village to part with their single rooster, at a cost of three times the normal price. The lodge owners were relieved, the rooster was dispatched, and the tranquillity of the lodge was restored. No more pre-dawn wake-up calls.

The village was even happier. The proceeds from the sale of that one rooster enabled them to buy three new ones – which is exactly what they did.

Where to stay

Senanga Safaris (PO Box 920077, Senanga. Tel/fax: 07 230156) runs a passable small hotel, where a room costs around US$15/Kw37,500. Ask nicely and they may allow camping here, otherwise there are a few very basic resthouses in town.

The Ngonye Falls area

The main reason for visiting this area of southwest Zambia is for the Ngonye Falls (often referred to as the Sioma Falls) and the Sioma Ngwezi National Park. The falls are spectacular, and the park is interesting, so the nearby camps on the Zambezi have a wider range of activities than just fishing. With travel in the area often taking much time, these are also good places at which to rest for a few days if you are travelling between Sesheke and Mongu.

Livingstone passed this way, having come north through what is now Botswana. He noted:

> '30th November, 1853. – At Gonye Falls. No rain has fallen here, so it is excessively hot. The trees have put on their gayest dress, and many flowers adorn the landscape, yet the heat makes all the leaves droop at mid-day and look languid for want of rain. If the country increases as much in beauty in front, as it has done within the last four degrees of latitude, it will indeed be a lovely land.
>
> … For many miles below, the river is confined in a narrow space of not more than one hundred yards wide. The water goes boiling along, and gives the idea of great masses of it rolling over and over, so that even the most expert swimmer would find it difficult to keep on the surface. Here it is that the river when in flood rises fifty or sixty feet in perpendicular height. The islands above the falls are covered with foliage as beautiful as can be seen anywhere. Viewed from the mass of rock which overhangs the fall, the scenery was the loveliest I had seen.'

This was about two years before Livingstone journeyed further down the Zambezi and saw the Victoria Falls for the first time.

Getting there and away

The Ngonye Falls, and Maziba Bay, lie adjacent to a good all-weather gravel road that links Katima Mulilo with the pontoon at Sitoti. It's 122km (three hours' drive) from Katima, and about 70km from Sitoti. This should be navigable with a high-clearance 2WD all year, although sections do get washed away sometimes and there's very little traffic on the road – so I'd feel happier travelling this way with at least a 4WD, if not two.

Camps and lodges

There are just three camps on this stretch of the Zambezi, and two are much further south, nearer Sesheke. If Sioma Ngwezi is ever regenerated, and its game has chance to recover, then this would be a superb area for more camps.

Maziba Bay (6 chalets & camping) c/o Tukuluho Wildlife Ltd, PO Box 1120, Ngwezi, Katima Mulilo. Book through Namibia Mirages, Windhoek; tel: (26461) 214744; fax: 214746
A few kilometres south of the Zambia's spectacular Ngonye Falls, Maziba Bay is on the western bank of the Zambezi River. It is about 110km north of Sesheke – about three hours' driving along a graded gravel road – and is run by David and André Van de Merwe.

The main lodge is rustic and wooden, with a bar and deck area, overlooking a huge beach of fine white sand which stretches down to the Zambezi. It squeaks when you walk on it and is marvellously fine – just don't be tempted to join the crocodiles in the river for a swim.

Maziba has six stunning thatched chalets, three on each of the promontories that surround its bay. These are large, rustic, and beautifully designed. There is a small swimming pool, a lounge/bar area, and an outdoor *boma* for barbecues.

Unlike many of the other river camps here, Maziba Bay isn't just for fishing. It offers an impressive range of activities including white-water rafting, kayaking and canoe safaris on the river, as well as game drives into the wild Sioma Ngwezi National Park, and tiger-fishing trips.

If you are not driving yourself, then access here can be tricky or expensive. Flying by private plane from Livingstone would be one way, and the camp will organise vehicle transfers from Katima Mulilo (in Namibia) on request.

Despite being impressed when I visited here, I've had less positive reports about Maziba Bay in recent months. Several travellers have made negative comments about the owners' dealings in the region. Be aware of this if you visit, and keep an open mind to the possibility that Maziba may not have as great an atmosphere now as it had when I stayed here.

Rates: US$225 single, US$175 per person sharing, including activities. Camping US$10

National Parks campsite
Though this isn't really a campsite run by the national park's staff, if you stop at the National Parks and Wildlife Service office near the falls, then they'll point you to a basic campsite nearby. They'll also give you advice on the best way to see the falls.
Rates: Camping US$10

What to see and do

Although not as impressive as Victoria Falls, the Ngonye Falls are spectacular, and if the former didn't exist then they would certainly draw visitors. The geology of the area is the same as that of Victoria Falls, and these falls are formed in a similar process with erosion taking advantage of cracks in the area's basalt rock.

Ngonye's main falls form a rather spectacular semicircle of water, with lots of smaller streams around the edges. Some of these form little pools, ideal for bathing, though be careful to remain here as the main river has too many crocodiles to be safe. They are at their most spectacular when full, from January to around July.

Viewing access is difficult, as the main falls cannot be seen from the bank; you must cross on to the island in the river in front of them for a good view. There are two ways to do this. The first possibility is to venture downstream a little and cross on to one of the islands using a small metal boat/ferry – which was made by Brother Hugh at the Sioma Mission. The track leading to this isn't easy to locate, though a local guide can usually be found to help you. Using this you will still need to cross a small side-stream before reaching the island nearest the falls.

The other way to see them is to take a boat. Maziba Bay, for example, offers half-day trips to the falls by canoe or raft for US$15 per person, including lunch. Other activities in the area include:

White-water rafting

The rapids below the falls are graded as a class III white-water run (see page 184 for an explanation of these gradings), and Maziba Bay takes rafting trips here which run them in a couple of hours. Usually such trips will include a visit to the main falls themselves, and the cost is US$20 per person. It's not really very serious rafting, especially after a trip below Victoria Falls, but is fun and makes a lovely afternoon activity.

Microlighting

Maziba Bay has a microlight that you can hire to take you over the falls, and also west to see some of Sioma Ngwezi National Park. Wherever you go, this costs about US$25 for 15 minutes in the air.

Fishing

The *raison d'être* of coming to the Upper Zambezi always used to be fishing – for bream and tiger fish. Now more activities are offered, but still many visitors are attracted here by the excellent fishing.

Sioma Ngwezi National Park

Of all of Zambia's remote and seldom-visited parks, Sioma Ngwezi would probably be one of the easiest to regenerate. It is really very close to the Victoria Falls/Livingstone area, which has a huge reservoir of visitors keen to do short safari trips. Tourism to Namibia's Caprivi Strip is rapidly taking off, and with the Golden Highway (which runs across the Strip) being almost completely tarred, access to the vicinity of the park is very good. Also mooted has been its inclusion in a trans-frontier conservation area, or 'peace park' as they're widely known.

However, despite all this, the park remains largely unvisited, whilst its game is persecuted and the local communities around it subsist in poverty.

Geography, flora and fauna

Positioned in the far southwestern corner of Zambia, Sioma Ngwezi National Park shares a long border with Angola, along the Kwando River, and also a short border with Namibia in the south. This corner is less than 50km from northern Botswana, and its vegetation and landscape owes much to the Kalahari sand that lies beneath it.

Most of the park is flat, dry and quite densely wooded – covered with a mosaic of miombo and acacia woodland, with the occasional area of teak forest and a few open dambos surrounding rare pools in the bush.

Sioma Ngwezi is the only Zambian park, outside the Luangwa valley and the Mosi-oa-Tunya park, where giraffe are found. They are certainly not of the same subspecies as those in Luangwa, Thornicroft's giraffe. It is claimed that they are an 'Angolan' subspecies, which is different again from the normal 'southern' variety found throughout the subcontinent.

The park's other antelope include roan, sable, tsessebe, blue wildebeest, zebra, and possibly lechwe on the Kwando River. The major predators are lion, leopard and spotted hyena. In Bak's report on the status of wild dog (see *Further Reading*), he observes that there had been several sightings of wild dog there in 1993–4.

Poaching is common, especially on the eastern side where there are a number of villages beside the Zambezi and the wildlife is generally very shy. However, the park is large and remote, so considerable wildlife probably still exists in this dense bush. Water is a big problem for the game, as many of the pools in the park's interior dry up by around June–July. This might make the end of the rains the best time to visit Sioma Ngwezi, as you'd find the game in the heart of the park.

After around July the nearest water is in either the Zambezi or the Kwando and both are lined by settlements. Hence much of the game (certainly the remaining elephants) seems to spend the day away from the river feeding, and then run the gauntlet of the riverside villages at night to drink. After a recent visit in June '99 one visitor, Rob Munroe, commented: 'We spent a couple of days here, and saw lots of evidence of game: lion, giraffe, eland, sable and hyena among others.'

Getting there

This is difficult and requires the backing of a couple of 4WDs. The Kalahari sand can be slow going, and there is only one decent road through the park. The driving is also very heavy on fuel – so remember that this is only available at Sesheke or Katima Mulilo in the south, or Senanga or Mongu to the north.

If you intend to explore this area independently, then get a guide from the National Parks and Wildlife Service office at Sioma (which is signposted from the main road). They probably won't know the park that well, but will make exploring much safer and more productive. Access to the park from Sioma is via the tsetse-fly control barrier (a dirt track), which bisects the Maziba Bay airstrip.

The main route through the park is the track that comes from the northwest, keeping close to the Kwando from Shangombo. A little short of the Namibian border, this turns sharply left and heads northeast through the middle of the park. Around the park's eastern boundary, at Ngwezi Pools, there is a poor track southeast to the Zambezi, via Cholola, and another track leading northwest, roughly along the park's boundary – as well as the continuation of the original track which leads directly to the Zambezi at Kalobolelwa. You may need local help to find these, but there are villagers in the area who can help.

Note that on the Kwando River there is a lot of local cross-border movement of local people. Villagers on the Kwando recently suggested to one party of visitors driving here (in '99) that that they could go across the river into Angola, to stay in a hunting camp – as there was nowhere quite as comfortable on the Zambian side of the Kwando. The camp's owners were described as very friendly. The same helpful Zambian later mentioned that this camp's owners were 'usually armed with AK47s'. Whilst they would probably have been very helpful and courteous, travellers with expensive 4WD vehicles and equipment should ponder the wisdom of taking these so close to the border, given Angola's present state of turmoil.

None of the lodges in the area drive into Sioma Ngwezi much (despite what is often claimed in their literature).

Sesheke

Sesheke actually consists of two small towns located on opposite sides of the Zambezi. The bigger town is on the east side, reached by driving from Livingstone, or taking the pontoon over the river. There are a few stores here, a simple hospital, a police station (listen for their marching songs at 04.30 if sleeping here!) and a small government resthouse.

The smaller western section, located next to the border with Namibia, has a police post and a small local store. Across the border in Namibia's Katima Mulilo fuel is cheaper and supplies more plentiful, so Sesheke can be very quiet.

Sesheke pontoon
The pontoon at Sesheke usually costs US$25 for foreign-registered vehicles, or US$10/Kw25,000 for Zambian vehicles, although (like the Sitoti pontoon) this rule does seem to be applied flexibly sometimes. It operates 06.00–18.00 with no fixed schedule, carrying three vehicles at a time and just going across when it's needed.

Camps around Sesheke
Sesheke might not be a centre of attraction in which to linger, but north of it, in Zambia, there are two fishing camps on islands in the river. Both are clearly signposted from the road:

Mutemwa Island Lodge (6 twin tents) c/o Safari Par Excellence, PO Box 1395, Randburg 2125, South Africa; tel: (2711) 888 3500/2431; fax: 888 4942
On the Upper Zambezi about 60km north of Katima Mulilo, this is a small camp with a mainly South African clientele. Its tents are all built on individual teak decks, with en-suite shower and toilet at the back, and a small sitting area at the front overlooking the Zambezi.

One interesting option based here is the possibility to be driven up to the Ngonye Falls, about 70km upstream, and then have two nights camping on islands in the river as you paddle back to the lodge.

As an aside, the lodge is well known in South African sporting circles because it was developed by a team including Gavin Johnson, the Springbok rugby player. Mutemwa has a central bar, a thatched dining area and a swimming pool. Its activities include fishing, sundowner cruises and canoeing. Note that its prices depend on where you live. It's accessed by a transfer from Katima Mulilo, or a charter flight from Livingstone.

Rates: US$105 per person sharing for Zimbabwe residents, R595 for other residents of the region, US$200 for international visitors, including activities and road transfers from Katima. Closed during heavy rains – January and February.

Sakazima Island Camp
About 26km north of Katima Mulilo, and 96km south of Maziba Bay, on the Upper Zambezi, this is another small fishing camp on one of the islands in the stream. Though the signs to the camp still stand beside the road, the camp appears closed and I can find no information about it.

Meanwhile, east of Sesheke on the road from Livingstone, about 130km from Livingstone and 60km from Sesheke, there's a small, rustic bushcamp. It might make a convenient camping stop on the way to Livingstone:

Soka Camp (3 chalets) c/o Gwembe Safaris, PO Box 630067, Choma. Tel: 032 20169, 20021 or 20119; fax: 20054 or 20570
It's run by the Brooks family, of Gwembe Safaris (see page 197), and has three spartan thatched chalets, each with its own showers and toilets. Beds and mattresses are provided, but not linen. There's a gas fridge, a wood stove and some basic kitchen equipment for cooking, but you must bring your own food. If you want to go on the river then there's a camp attendant who will paddle you about (in a banana boat) in the immediate area. This is very basic, and latest news suggested that Gwembe safaris might be selling Soka Camp.
Rates: US$10 per person

Getting there and away
Sesheke is most easily reached from Katima Mulilo in Namibia, which has excellent roads (easily navigable by 2WD vehicles) linking it to the rest of Namibia and also to Kasane in Botswana. If you're coming from Livingstone to Sesheke then read *Driving west* in *Chapter 10* for a discussion of the alternative routes – and consider driving via Zimbabwe and Botswana rather than using the direct road.

North from Sesheke
The route from Sesheke to Mongu is fairly straightforward, following the western bank of the river for about the first 190km, to Sitoti. After about 60km you pass through Kalobolelwa, where a track leads off left into Sioma Ngwezi National Park. Later, at about 120km, there is a sign for the camp at Maziba Bay (see page 372) before the Ngonye Falls are reached.

Appendix 1

WILDLIFE GUIDE

This wildlife guide is designed in a manner that should allow you to name most large mammals that you see in Zambia. Less common species are featured under the heading *Similar species* beneath the animal to which they are most closely allied, or bear the strongest resemblance.

Cats and dogs

Lion *Panthera leo* Shoulder height 100–120cm. Weight 150–220kg.

Africa's largest predator, the lion is the animal that everybody hopes to see on safari. It is a sociable creature, living in prides of five to ten animals and defending a territory of between 20 and 200km². Lions often hunt at night, and their favoured prey is large or medium antelope such as wildebeest and impala. Most of the hunting is done by females, but dominant males normally feed first after a kill. Rivalry between males is intense and takeover battles are frequently fought to the death, so two or more males often form a coalition. Young males are forced out of their home pride at three years of age, and cubs are usually killed after a successful takeover.

When not feeding or fighting, lions are remarkably indolent – they spend up to 23 hours of any given day at rest – so the anticipation of a lion sighting is often more exciting than the real thing. Lions naturally occur in any habitat, except desert or rainforest. They once ranged across much of the Old World, but these days they are all but restricted to the larger conservation areas in subSaharan Africa (one residual population exists in India).

Lions occur throughout Zambia, and are very common in the larger parks with better game densities – Luangwa (North and South), Kafue, and Lower Zambezi. Spend a week in any of these with a good guide and you'd be unlucky not to see at least some lion! They occur in smaller numbers in the more marginal parks and GMAs, and more sparsely in areas with more population.

Leopard *Panthera pardus* Shoulder height 70cm. Weight 60–80kg.

The powerful leopard is the most solitary and secretive of Africa's big cats. It hunts at night, using stealth and power, often getting to within 5m of its intended prey before pouncing. If there are hyenas and lions around then leopards habitually move their kills up into trees to safeguard them. The leopard can be distinguished from the cheetah by its rosette-like spots, lack of black 'tearmarks' and more compact, low-slung, powerful build.

The leopard is the most common of Africa's large felines. Zambia's bush is perfect for leopard, which are common throughout the country, as they favour habitats with plenty of cover, like riverine woodlands. Despite this, a good sighting in the wild during the day is unusual. In fact there are many records of individuals living for years, undetected, in close proximity to humans. Sightings at night are a different story and, because Zambia's national parks allow night drives, it's probably Africa's best country for seeking leopard.

South Luangwa National Park was recently chosen by the BBC for the filming of their remarkable documentary, *Night of the Leopard*. Leopard sightings often become the main goal of night drives there. Your chances of spotting them are equally good in the Lower Zambezi, whilst consistently first-class sightings are also reported from Lufupa Lodge in Kafue. Remarkably they usually seem unperturbed by the presence of a vehicle and spotlight, and will often continue whatever they are doing regardless of an audience. Watching a leopard stalk is captivating viewing.

Cheetah *Acynonix jubatus* Shoulder height 70–80cm. Weight 50–60kg.

This remarkable spotted cat has a greyhound-like build, and is capable of running at 70km per hour in bursts, making it the world's fastest land animal. Despite superficial similarities, you can easily tell a cheetah from a leopard by the former's simple spots, disproportionately small head, streamlined build, diagnostic black tearmarks, and preference for relatively open habitats. It is often seen pacing the plains restlessly, either on its own or in a small family group consisting of a mother and her offspring. Diurnal hunters, cheetah favour the cooler hours of the day to hunt smaller antelope, like steenbok and duiker, and small mammals like scrub hares.

Zambia has a small but growing population of cheetah, centred on Kafue National Park. They're very rare in the Luangwa, and have recently been reintroduced into the Lower Zambezi (though with mixed success).

Similar species: The **serval** (*Felis serval*) is smaller than a cheetah (shoulder height 55cm) but has a similar build and black-on-gold spots giving way to streaking near the head. Seldom seen, it is widespread and quite common in moist grassland, reedbeds and riverine habitats throughout Africa, including Zambia. It does particularly well in some of the swampier areas, and Lechwe Lodge reports a particularly high number of them, attracted by the prevalence of cane rats in the Kafue River. Servals prey on mice, rats and small mammals, but will sometimes take the young of small antelope.

Caracal (*Felis caracal*) Shoulder height 40cm. Weight 15–20kg.

The caracal resembles the European lynx with its uniform tan coat and tufted ears. It is a solitary and mainly nocturnal hunter, feeding on birds, small antelope and young livestock. Found throughout the subcontinent, it easily adapts to a variety of environments and even occurs in some of Zambia's populated areas. Despite this, being nocturnal it is rarely seen. Caracals normally stalk their prey as closely as possible, before springing with surprise.

Similar species: The smaller **African wild cat** (*Felis sylvestris*) is found from the Mediterranean to the Cape of Good Hope, and is similar in appearance to the domestic tabby cat and a little larger. It has an unspotted torso, a ringed tail and a reddish-brown tinge to the back of its ears. Wild cats are generally solitary and nocturnal, often utilising burrows or termite mounds as daytime shelters. They prey upon reptiles, amphibians and birds as well as small mammals.

African wild dog *Lycaon pictus* Shoulder height 70cm. Weight 25kg.
Also known as the painted hunting dog, the wild dog is distinguished from other African dogs by its large size and mottled black, brown and cream coat. Highly sociable, living in packs of up to 20 animals, wild dogs are ferocious hunters that literally tear apart their prey on the run. They are now threatened with extinction; the most endangered of Africa's great predators. This is the result of relentless persecution by farmers, who often view the dogs as dangerous vermin, and their susceptibility to diseases spread by domestic dogs. Wild dogs are now extinct in many areas where they were formerly abundant, like the Serengeti, and they are common nowhere. The global population of fewer than 3,000 is concentrated in southern Tanzania, Zambia, Zimbabwe, Botswana, South Africa and Namibia.

Wild dogs prefer open savannah with only sparse tree cover, if any, and packs have enormous territories, typically covering 400km² or more. They travel huge distances in search of prey and so few parks are large enough to contain them. In Zambia wild dogs have their strongest base in Kafue, closely followed by the Luangwa, though even in these parks they are regarded as an uncommon sight. They are sometimes seen in Luiwa, Lower Zambezi and Sumbu areas. Elsewhere their existence is less certain.

Side-striped jackal *Canis adustus* Shoulder height 35–40cm. Weight 8–12kg.
Despite its prevalence in other areas of Africa, the side-striped jackal is common nowhere in Zambia although occurring throughout the country. It is greyish in colour and has an indistinct pale horizontal stripe on each flank and often a white-tipped tail. These jackals are most often seen singly or in pairs at dusk or dawn. They are opportunistic feeders, taking rats, mice, birds, insects, wild fruits and even termites. The side-striped jackal is Zambia's only species of jackal.

Spotted hyena *Crocuta crocuta* Shoulder height 85cm. Weight 70kg.
Hyenas are characterised by their bulky build, sloping back, rough brownish coat, powerful jaws and dog-like expression. Contrary to popular myth, spotted hyenas are not exclusively scavengers; they are also adept hunters, which hunt in groups and kill animals as large as wildebeests. Nor are they hermaphroditic, an ancient belief that stems from the false scrotum and penis covering the female hyena's vagina. Sociable animals, hyenas live in loosely structured clans of about ten animals, led by females who are stronger and larger than males, based in a communal den.

Hyenas utilise their kills far better than most predators, digesting the bones, skin and even teeth of antelope. This results in the distinctive white colour of their faeces – which is an easily identified sign of them living in an area.

The spotted hyena is the largest hyena, identified by its light-brown, blotchily spotted coat. It is found throughout Zambia, though is increasingly restricted to the national parks and GMAs. Although mainly nocturnal, spotted hyenas can often be seen around dusk and dawn in the Luangwa, Kafue and Lower Zambezi. Their distinctive, whooping calls are a spine-chilling sound of the African night. Note that neither of the spotted hyena's close relatives, the brown hyena and aardwolf, are thought to occur in Zambia.

Common baboon *Papio cynocaphalus cynocaphalus* Shoulder height 50–75cm. Weight 25–45kg.

This powerful terrestrial primate, distinguished from any other monkey by its much larger size, inverted 'U'-shaped tail and distinctive dog-like head, is fascinating to watch from a behavioural perspective. It lives in large troops that boast a complex, rigid social structure characterised by a matriarchal lineage and plenty of inter-troop movement by males seeking social dominance. Omnivorous and at home in almost any habitat, the baboon is the most widespread primate in Africa, frequently seen in most game reserves. With their highly organised defence system, the only predators that seriously affect baboons are leopard, which will try to pick them off at night, whilst they are roosting in trees.

There are three African races, regarded by some authorities as full species. The chacma baboon (*P. c. ursinus*) is grey and confined largely to areas south of the Zambezi. The yellow baboon (*P. c. cynocephalus*) is the yellow-brown race occurring in Zambia, northern Mozambique, Malawi, southern and eastern Tanzania and eastern Kenya. The olive or anubis baboon (*P. c. anubis*) is a hairy green-to-brown baboon found in Ethiopia, Uganda, northern Tanzania and Kenya.

Vervet monkey *Cercopithecus aethiops* Length (excluding tail) 40–55cm. Weight 4–6kg.

Also known as the green or grivet monkey, the vervet is probably the world's most numerous monkey and certainly the most common and widespread representative of the *Cercopithecus* guenons, a taxonomically controversial genus associated with African forests. An atypical guenon in that it inhabits savannah and woodland rather than true forest, the vervet spends a high proportion of its time on the ground. It occurs throughout Zambia, preferring belts of tall trees and thicker vegetation within easy reach of water.

The vervet's light grey coat, black face and white forehead band are distinctive – as are the male's garish blue genitals. Vervets live in troops averaging about 25 animals; they are active during the day and roost in trees at night. They eat mainly fruit and vegetables, though are opportunistic and will take insects and young birds, and even raid tents at campsites (usually where ill-informed visitors have previously tempted them into human contact by offering food).

Blue monkey *Cercopithecus mitis* Length (excluding tail) 50–60cm. Weight 5–8kg.

Known also as moloney's monkey in Zambia, the samango monkey throughout

Southern Africa, as the golden monkey in southwest Uganda, as Sakes monkey in Kenya and as the diademed or white-throated guenon in some field guides. This most variable monkey is divided by some authorities into several species. It is unlikely to be confused with the vervet monkey, as blue monkeys have a dark blue-grey coat, which becomes reddish towards its tail. Its underside is lighter, especially its throat. These monkeys live in troops of up to ten animals and associate with other primates where their ranges overlap. They live in evergreen forests, and so are most likely to be seen around the Copperbelt and North-Western Provinces, or north of Kasanka. However, they occur as far south as the Lower Zambezi National Park and are resident along the Luangwa's Muchinga Escarpment.

Angola black-and-white colobus monkey *Colobus angolensis* Length (excluding tail) 65cm. Weight 12kg.

This beautiful jet black monkey has bold white facial markings, a long white tail and white sides and shoulders. Almost exclusively arboreal, it is capable of jumping up to 30m, a spectacular sight with its white tail streaming behind. Several races have been described, and most authorities recognise this Angolan variety as a distinct species. In Zambia they are very rare, but have been reported from the forests north of Mwinilunga.

Bushbaby *Galago crassicaudatus* Length (without tail) 35cm. Weight 1–1.5kg.

The bushbaby is Zambia's commonest member of a group of small and generally indistinguishable nocturnal primates, distantly related to the lemurs of Madagascar. In Zambia they occur throughout the country, though are very seldom seen during the day. At night their wide, endearing eyes are often caught in the spotlight during night drives,

Bushbabies are nocturnal and even around safari camps they can sometimes be seen by tracing a cry to a tree and shining a torch into the branches; their eyes reflect as two red dots. These eyes are designed to function in what we would describe as total darkness, and they feed on insects – some of which are caught in the air by jumping – and also by eating sap from trees, especially acacia gum.

They inhabit wooded areas, and prefer acacia trees or riverine forests. I remember once being startled, whilst lighting a barbecue, by a small family of bushbabies. They raced through the trees above us, bouncing from branch to branch whilst chattering and screaming out of all proportion to their modest size.

Similar species: **Lesser bushbaby** *Galago senegalensis* Length (without tail) 17cm. Weight 150g.

The lesser bushbaby, or night ape, is half the size of the bushbaby and seems to be less common than its larger cousin. Where it is found, it is often amongst acacia or terminalia vegetation, rather than mopane or miombo bush.

Large antelope

Sable antelope *Hippotragus niger* Shoulder height 135cm. Weight 230kg.
The striking male sable is jet black with a distinct white face, underbelly and rump, and long decurved horns – a strong contender for the title of Africa's most beautiful antelope. The female is chestnut brown and has shorter horns, whilst the young are a lighter red-brown colour. Sable are found throughout the wetter areas of Southern and East Africa.

They are not common in Zambia. However, Kafue is probably the best park for sable, with Kasanka also worthy of note. They're confined to the foothills of the Muchinga Escarpment in the Luangwa, and so very rarely seen by visitors. Sumbu has a small population, as is reported from Sioma Ngwezi and West Lunga.

Sable are normally seen in small herds: either bachelor herds of males, or breeding herds of females and young which are often accompanied by the dominant male in that territory. The breeding females give birth around February or March; the calves remain hidden, away from the herd, for their first few weeks. Sable are mostly grazers, though will browse, especially when food is scarce. They need to drink at least every other day, and seem especially fond of low-lying dewy vleis in wetter areas.

Roan antelope *Hippotragus equinus* Shoulder height 120–150cm. Weight 250–300kg.
This handsome horse-like antelope is uniform fawn-grey with a pale belly, short decurved horns and a light mane. It could be mistaken for the female sable antelope, but this has a well-defined white belly, and lacks the roan's distinctive black-and-white facial markings. The roan is a relatively rare antelope; common almost nowhere in Africa (the Nyika Plateau being one obvious exception to this rule). In Zambia small groups of roan are found in South Luangwa, Kafue, Kasanka, Sumbu, Liuwa Plains and (probably) Sioma Ngwezi.

Roan need lots of space if they are to thrive and breed; they don't generally do well where game densities are high. Game farms prize them as one of the most valuable antelope (hence expensive to buy). They need access to drinking water, but are adapted to subsist on relatively high plateaux with poor soils.

Waterbuck *Kobus ellipsiprymnus* Shoulder height 130cm. Weight 250-270kg.
The waterbuck is easily recognised by its shaggy brown coat and the male's large lyre-shaped horns. The common race of Southern Africa (*K. e. ellipsiprymnus*) and areas east of the Rift Valley has a distinctive white ring around its rump, seen on the left of the sketch. The defassa race (known as *K. e. defassa* or *K. e. crawshayi*) of the Rift Valley and areas further west has a full white rump, as indicated on the right.

In Zambia, the common waterbuck populates the Luangwa and Lower Zambezi valleys, whilst the defassa race occurs throughout most of the rest of the country, including Kafue National Park. They need to drink very regularly, so usually stay within a few kilometres of water, where they like to graze on short, nutritious grasses. At night they may take cover in adjacent woodlands. It is often asserted that waterbuck flesh is oily and smelly, which may discourage predators.

Blue wildebeest *Connochaetes taurinus* Shoulder height 130–150cm.
Weight 180–250kg.
This ungainly antelope, also called the brindled gnu, is easily identified by its dark coat and bovine appearance. The superficially similar buffalo is far more heavily built. When they have enough space, blue wildebeest can form immense herds – as perhaps a million do for their annual migration from Tanzania's Serengeti Plains into Kenya's Masai Mara. One such gathering occurs on the Liuwa Plains around November, when tens of thousands of animals gather here as the rains arrive.

In Zambia wildebeest naturally occur from around the Kafue National Park area westwards, to Angola. There's also a sub-species, Cookson's wildebeest, *Connochaetes taurinus cooksoni*, which is endemic to the Luangwa Valley. It's found commonly on the north side, in North Luangwa, but only rarely further south. It differs from the main species by having cleaner colours including slightly reddish bands and being a little smaller and more compact.

Lichtenstein's hartebeest *Alcelaphus lichtensteini* Shoulder height 125cm.
Weight 120–150kg.

Hartebeests are awkward antelopes, readily identified by the combination of large shoulders, a sloping back, a smooth coat and smallish horns in both sexes. Numerous subspecies are recognised, all of which are generally seen in small family groups in reasonably open country. Though once hartebeest were found from the Mediterranean to the Cape, only isolated populations still survive. Hartebeests are almost exclusively grazers and they like access to water.

The only one native to Zambia is Lichtenstein's hartebeest, which used to be found throughout the country, except for the extreme south and west. They are seen frequently in Kafue, and also occur in Sumbu and Kasanka. The Luangwa has a good population, but they generally stay away from the river, and so remain out of view for most visitors.

Similar species: The **tsessebe** *Damaliscus lunatus* is basically a darker version of the hartebeest with striking yellow lower legs. (A closely related subspecies is known as *topi* in East Africa.) These are very sparsely distributed in Zambia, occurring in the Kasanka–Bangweulu area, and to the far west of the Zambezi, in Liuwa and Sioma Ngwezi. Its favourite habitat is open grassland, where it is a selective grazer, eating the younger, more nutritious grasses. The tsessebe is one of the fastest antelope species, and jumps very well.

Kudu *Tragelaphus strepsiceros* Shoulder height 140–155cm.
Weight 180–250kg.
The kudu (or, more properly, the greater kudu) is the most frequently observed member of the genus tragelaphus. These medium-sized to large antelopes are characterised by their grey-brown coats and up to ten stripes on each side. The male has magnificent double-spiralled corkscrew horns. Occurring

throughout Mozambique, Zimbabwe, Zambia, Botswana and Namibia, kudu are widespread and common, though not in dense forests or open grasslands. They are normally associated with well-wooded habitats. These browsers thrive in areas with mixed tree savannah and thickets, and the males will sometimes use their horns to pull down the lower branches of trees to eat, with mahogany, *Trichelia emetica*, being a particular favourite.

In Zambia they occur throughout the country except for the far northern areas. Normally they're seen in small herds, consisting of a couple of females and their offspring, sometimes accompanied by a male. Otherwise the males occur either singly, or in small bachelor groups.

Sitatunga *Tragelaphus spekei* Shoulder height 85–90cm. Weight 105–115kg.
The semi-aquatic antelope is a widespread but infrequently observed inhabitant of west and central African papyrus swamps from the Okavango in Botswana to the Sudd in Sudan. In Zambia sitatunga are very widespread. Good populations are found in Bangweulu, the Busanga Swamps, Sumbu and Kasanka.

Because of its preferred habitat, the sitatunga is very elusive and seldom seen, even in areas where it is relatively common. They are also less easy to hunt/poach than many other species, although they are exceedingly vulnerable to habitat destruction. Kasanka National Park's tree hide is commended, at least to the more agile of visitors, as one of Africa's very best places to see these antelope. It provides a superb vantage point above a small section of papyrus swamp, and sightings are virtually guaranteed in the early morning or late afternoon. Sitatunga are noted for an ability to submerse themselves completely, with just their nostrils showing, when pursued by a predator.

Eland *Taurotragus oryx* Shoulder height 150–175cm. Weight 450–900kg.
Africa's largest antelope, the eland is light brown in colour, sometimes with a few faint white vertical stripes. Relatively short horns and a large dewlap accentuate its somewhat bovine appearance. It was once widely distributed in East and Southern Africa, though the population has now been severely depleted. Small herds of eland frequent grasslands and light woodlands, often fleeing at the slightest provocation. (They have long been hunted for their excellent meat, so perhaps this is not surprising.)

Eland are opportunist browsers and grazers, eating fruit, berries, seed pods and leaves as well as green grass after the rains, and roots and tubers when times are lean. They run slowly, though can trot for great distances and jump exceedingly well. In Zambia they occur widely but sparsely, and are largely confined to the country's protected areas.

Medium and small antelope
Bushbuck *Tragelaphus scriptus* Shoulder height 70–80cm. Weight 30–45kg.
This attractive antelope, a member of the same genus as the kudu, is widespread throughout Africa and shows great regional variation in its colouring. It occurs in forest and riverine woodland, where it is normally seen singly or in pairs. The male is dark brown or chestnut, while the much smaller female is generally a pale reddish brown. The male has relatively small, straight horns and both sexes are

marked with white spots and sometimes stripes, though the stripes are often indistinct.

Bushbuck tend to be secretive and very skittish, except when used to people. They depend on cover and camouflage to avoid predators, and are often found in the thick, herby vegetation around rivers. They will freeze if disturbed, before dashing off into the undergrowth. Bushbuck are both browsers and grazers, choosing the more succulent grass shoots, fruit and flowers. In Zambia they are very widely distributed and fairly common.

Impala *Aepeceros melampus* Shoulder height 90cm. Weight 45kg.

This slender, handsome antelope is superficially similar to the springbok, but in fact belongs to its own separate family. Chestnut in colour, and lighter underneath than above, the impala has diagnostic black-and-white stripes running down its rump and tail, and the male has large lyre-shaped horns. One of the most widespread and successful antelope species in East and Southern Africa, the impala is normally seen in large herds in wooded savannah habitats. It is the most common antelope in the Luangwa Valley, and throughout much of the central and southern areas of Zambia. However, in more northerly areas, puku are sometimes more common. As expected of such a successful species, it both grazes and browses, depending on what fodder is available.

Reedbuck *Redunca arundinum* Shoulder height 80–90cm. Weight 45–65kg.
Sometimes referred to as the southern reedbuck (as distinct from mountain and Bohor reedbucks, found further east), these delicate antelope are uniformly fawn or grey in colour, and lighter below than above. They are generally found in reedbeds and tall grasslands, often beside rivers, and are easily identified by their loud, whistling alarm call and distinctive bounding running style. In Zambia they occur widely, though seem absent from the very bottom of the Zambezi and Luangwa valley floors. (They do occur in both Luangwa and Lower Zambezi national parks, but usually on slightly higher ground, away from the rivers.)

Klipspringer *Oreotragus oreotragus* Shoulder height 60cm. Weight 13kg.
The klipspringer is a strongly built little antelope, normally seen in pairs, and easily identified by its dark, bristly grey-yellow coat, slightly speckled appearance and unique habitat preference. Klipspringer means 'rockjumper' in Afrikaans and it is an apt name for an antelope which occurs exclusively in mountainous areas and rocky outcrops from Cape Town to the Red Sea.

They occur throughout most of Zambia, except for the extreme western areas, but only where rocky hills or kopjes are found. Given Zambia's generally rolling topography, this means only the odd isolated population exists. They are seen occasionally on the escarpments of the main valleys, but usually away from the main game areas. Klipspringers are mainly browsers, though they do eat a little new grass. When spotted they will freeze, or bound at great speed across the steepest of slopes.

Lechwe *Kobus leche* Shoulder height 90–100cm. Weight 80–100kg.

Lechwe are sturdy, shaggy antelope with beautiful lyre-shaped horns, adapted to favour the seasonal floodplains that border lakes and rivers. They need dry land on which to rest, but otherwise will spend much of their time grazing on grasses and sedges, standing in water if necessary. Their hooves are splayed, adapted to bounding through their muddy environment when fleeing from the lion, hyena and wild dog that hunt them, making them the most aquatic of antelope after sitatunga.

Lechwe are found in DRC, Angola, northern Botswana and Namibia's Caprivi Strip, but their stronghold is Zambia. Wherever they occur, the males are generally larger and darker than the females, and in Zambia there are three subspecies. (Though none occurs in the Luangwa or Lower Zambezi valleys.)

The **red lechwe** (*K. l. leche*) is the most widespread subspecies. It's the only one found outside Zambia and has a chestnut-reddish coat, darker on the back and much lighter (almost white) underneath. Its legs have black markings, as does the tip of its tail. Inside Zambia red lechwe are found in large numbers (about 5,000 probably) on the Busanga Plains, with smaller populations in the Western Province and the Lukanga Swamps.

The **Kafue lechwe** (*K. l. kafuensis*) are slightly larger animals, with bigger horns, and are restricted to the Kafue Flats area, between Lake Itezhi-Tezhi and Lusaka. This race is more light brown than red, with black patches on their shoulders that run into the black on their legs. Most of the 40–50,000 that remain are confined to the Lochinvar and Blue Lagoon national parks.

The **black lechwe** (*K. l. smithemani*) used to occur in huge numbers, perhaps as many as half a million animals, centred on the plains to the south of the Bangweulu Swamps. They are now restricted to about 30–40,000 animals in the same area, and a small population have been reintroduced into the Nashinga Swamps to the west of Chinsali. Black lechwe are much darker and the older males have almost black backs and brownish undersides.

Steenbok *Raphicerus cempestris* Shoulder height 50cm. Weight 11kg.

This rather nondescript small antelope has red-brown upper parts and clear white underparts, and the male has short straight horns. It is very common south of the Zambezi, but only occurs in southwestern Zambia (Mazabuka seems to be about the limit of their distribution). They like grasslands and open country with a scattering of cover, and seem to do very well in the drier areas. Like most other small antelopes, the steenbok is normally encountered singly or in pairs and tends to 'freeze' when disturbed, before taking flight.

Similar species: **Sharpe's grysbok** (*Raphicerus sharpei*) is similar in size and appearance, though it has a distinctive white-flecked coat. It occurs widely throughout Zambia, and appears to be absent only from the far northwest (Liuwa/Mwinilunga area). It is almost entirely nocturnal in its habits and so very seldom seen.

The **Oribi** (*Ourebia ourebi*) is also a widespread but generally uncommon antelope. It is usually found only in large, open stretches of dry grassland, with the termitaria zones of the Busanga Plains, Lochinvar and Bangweulu area standing out as good places to spot them. It looks much like a steenbok but stands about 10cm higher at the shoulder and has an altogether more upright bearing.

Common duiker *Sylvicapra grimmia* Shoulder height 50cm. Weight 20kg.
This anomalous duiker holds itself more like a
steenbok or grysbok and is the only member of its
(large) family to occur outside of forests. Generally grey
in colour, the common duiker can most easily be
separated from other small antelopes by the black tuft of
hair that sticks up between its horns. They occur throughout
Zambia, and tolerate most habitats except for true forest and
very open country. They are even found near human
settlements, where shooting and trapping is a problem, and
are usually mainly nocturnal. Duikers are opportunist feeders, taking fruit, seeds,
and leaves, as well as crops, small reptiles and amphibians.

Other large herbivores

African elephant *Loxodonta africana* Shoulder height 2.3–3.4m. Weight up to
6,000kg.
The world's largest land animal, the African elephant is intelligent, social and often
very entertaining to watch. Female elephants live in closely-knit clans in which the
eldest female plays matriarch over her sisters, daughters and granddaughters. Their
life spans are comparable with those of humans, and mother-daughter bonds are
strong and may last for up to 50 years. Males generally leave the family group at
around 12 years to roam singly or form bachelor herds. Under normal
circumstances, elephants range widely in search of food and water, but when
concentrated populations are forced to live in conservation areas their habit of
uprooting trees can cause serious environmental damage.

Elephants are widespread and common in habitats ranging from desert to
rainforest. In Zambia they were common everywhere except for the Upper
Zambezi's floodplains, but have now become more restricted by human
expansion. However, individuals often wander widely, turning up in locations
from which they have been absent for years.

Zambia's strongest population is in the Luangwa, where there are now about
15,000. As recently as 1973 estimates put the Luangwa's population at more than
100,000, but the late 1970s and '80s saw huge commercial poaching for ivory,
which wiped out a large proportion of this. Outside of a small, protected area in
South Luangwa National Park, Zambia's elephants fared even worse. The
populations in Kafue and even North Luangwa are still small, and the individuals
are very nervous and skittish near people. (The exception here is possibly the
Lower Zambezi, where the elephants regularly swim between Zimbabwe and
Zambia, because the Zimbabwean parks were, on the whole, better protected from
poaching than the Zambian parks. Hence the Lower Zambezi's elephant
population is also fairly relaxed and numerous.)

Black rhinoceros *Diceros bicornis* Shoulder height 160cm. Weight 1,000kg.
This is the more widespread of Africa's two rhino species, an imposing and rather
temperamental creature. (White rhino are not thought to have been
native to Zambia.) In the 1960s, the black rhino was recorded in the
Kafue, Luangwa, Lower Zambezi and in the far north around
Sumbu and Mweru Wantipa. However, it is now thought to
have been poached to extinction in Zambia, whilst becoming
highly endangered in many of the other countries within its
range. (There are a handful of reports of isolated individual
animals existing in very remote areas; none has been confirmed.)

Black rhinos exploit a wide range of habitats from dense woodlands and bush, and are generally solitary animals. They can survive without drinking for 4–5 days. However, their territorial behaviour and regular patterns of movement make them an easy target for poachers. Black rhinos can be very aggressive when disturbed and will charge with minimal provocation. Their hearing and sense of smell are acute, whilst their eyesight is poor (so they often miss if you keep a low profile and don't move).

Hippopotamus *Hippopotamus amphibius* Shoulder height 150cm. Weight 2,000kg. Characteristic of Africa's large rivers and lakes, this large, lumbering animal spends most of the day submerged but emerges at night to graze. Strongly territorial, herds of ten or more animals are presided over by a dominant male who will readily defend his patriarchy to the death. Hippos are abundant in most protected rivers and water bodies and are still quite common outside of reserves.

Hippos are widely credited with killing more people than any other African mammal, but I know of no statistics to support this. John Coppinger (one of the Luangwa Valley's most experienced guides) suggests that crocodile, elephant and lion all account for more deaths in that area than hippos – despite the valley having one of Africa's highest concentrations of hippos. So whilst undoubtedly dangerous; perhaps they don't quite deserve their reputation.

In Zambia they are exceptionally common in most of the larger rivers, where hunting is not a problem. The Kafue, the Luangwa and the Zambezi all have large hippo populations.

Buffalo *Syncerus caffer* Shoulder height 140cm. Weight 700kg.
Frequently and erroneously referred to as a water buffalo (an Asian species), the

African, or Cape, buffalo is a distinctive, highly social ox-like animal that lives as part of a herd. It prefers well-watered savannah, though also occurs in forested areas. Common and widespread in sub-Saharan Africa, in Zambia it is widely distributed. The Luangwa, and especially the north park, seems to have some particularly large herds, hundreds of animals strong. Buffalo are primarily grazers and need regular access to water, where they swim readily. They smell and hear well, and it's often claimed that they have poor eyesight. This isn't true, though when encountered during a walking safari, they won't be able to discern your presence if you keep still and the wind is right.

Huge herds are generally fairly peaceful, and experienced guides will often walk straight through them on walking safaris. However, small bachelor herds, or even single old bulls (known in the Luangwa as 'kakuli'), can be very nervous and aggressive. They have a reputation for charging at the slightest provocation, often in the midst of thick bush, and are exceedingly dangerous if wounded. Lion often follow herds of buffalo, their favourite prey.

Giraffe *Giraffa camelopardis* Shoulder height 250–350cm. Weight 1,000–1,400kg.
The world's tallest and longest-necked land animal, a fully grown giraffe can measure up to 5.5m high. Quite unmistakable, giraffe live in loosely structured herds of up to 15 head, though herd members often disperse, when they may be seen singly or in smaller groups. Formerly distributed throughout East and

Southern Africa, these great browsers are now found only in the southern side of the Luangwa Valley and the far southwest of Zambia.

About eight subspecies of giraffe have been identified in Africa, and the Luangwa valley contains one such distinct population, **Thornicroft's giraffe** (*G. c. thornicroftii*). These are generally regarded as having dark body patches and lighter neck patches than the normal 'southern' race of giraffe, and their colour patches don't normally extend below the knees, leaving their lower legs almost white. Their faces are also light or white. The vast majority of these live on the east side of the Luangwa River, in the GMA outside the park. They have been protected from hunting by a local taboo.

Much further west, the pocket of giraffe which are thought to still survive around the Sioma Ngwezi National Park are **Angolan giraffe** (*G. c. angolensis*), although so little is known of what survives in Sioma Ngwezi that their current status there is uncertain.

Burchell's zebra *Equus burchelli* Shoulder height 130cm. Weight 300–340kg. Also known as common or plains zebra, this attractive striped horse is common and widespread throughout most of East and Southern Africa, where it is often seen in large herds alongside wildebeest. It is common in most conservation areas from northern South Africa all the way up to the southeast of Ethiopia.

Most southern races, although not those found in Zambia, have paler brownish 'shadow stripes' between their bold black stripes. In Zambia, the subspecies in the Luangwa Valley is **Crawshay's zebra** (*E. b. crawshaii*), which also occurs on Nyika Plateau and possibly in Malawi's Vwaza Marsh. Norman Carr comments in his book on the Luangwa's wildlife (see *Further Reading*) that the zebra found to the west of the Muchinga escarpment belong to the *E. b. zambeziensis* subspecies.

Regardless of these minor taxonomic differences, zebra are widely distributed throughout Zambia, though they tend to be restricted by human activity to the more remote or protected areas. They lack the brown shadow-stripes of their cousins further south, but otherwise are very similar.

Warthog *Phacochoerus aethiopicus* Shoulder height 60–70cm. Weight up to 100kg. This widespread and often conspicuously abundant resident of the African savannah is grey in colour with a thin covering of hairs, wart-like bumps on its face, and rather large upward curving tusks. Africa's only diurnal swine, the warthog is often seen in family groups, trotting around with its tail raised stiffly (a diagnostic trait) and a determinedly nonchalant air. They occur in most areas of Zambia, except in the extreme northwest, and are very common in most of the national parks. They don't usually fare well near settlements, as they are very susceptible to subsistence hunting/poaching. Wherever they occur, you'll often see them grazing beside the road, on bended knee, with their tails held high in the air as soon as they trot away.

Similar species: Bulkier, hairier and browner, the **bushpig** (*Potomochoerus larvatus*) is known to occur throughout Zambia, and even in the vicinity of cultivated land where it can do considerable damage to crops. However, it is very rarely seen due to its nocturnal habits and preference for dense vegetation.

Small mammals

African civet *Civettictis civetta* Shoulder height 40cm. Weight 10–15kg.
This bulky, long-haired, rather feline creature of the African night is primarily carnivorous, feeding on small animals and carrion, but will also eat fruit. It has a similar-coloured coat to a leopard: densely blotched with large black spots becoming stripes towards the head. Civets are widespread and common throughout Zambia in many habitats, and make frequent cameo appearances on night drives. Though occasionally called 'civet cats', this is misleading because they are far more closely related to the mongooses than the felines.

Similar species: The smaller, more slender **tree civet** (*Nandinia binotata*) is an arboreal forest animal with a dark brown coat marked with black spots. It really a resident of the equatorial forests, although is found in a few mountain areas on Zambia's Malawi border (including Nyika) as well as north of Mwinilunga. It is nocturnal, solitary, and largely arboreal – and so is very seldom seen.

The **small-spotted genet** (*Genetta genetta*), **large-spotted genet** (*Genetta tigrina*) and **rusty-spotted genet** (*Genetta rubignosa*) are the most widespread members in Zambia of a large group of similar small predators (which even the experts often can't tell apart without examining their skins by hand). All the genets are slender and rather feline in appearance (though they are *not* cats), with a grey to gold-brown coat marked with black spots (perhaps combining into short bars) and a long ringed tail.

You're most likely to see them on nocturnal game drives or occasionally scavenging around game reserve lodges. They are found all over Zambia, even in urban areas if there is a plentiful supply of rodents. They are excellent climbers and opportunists, eating fruit, small birds, termites and even scorpions.

Banded mongoose *Mungos mungo* Shoulder height 20cm. Weight around 1kg.
The banded mongoose is probably the most commonly observed member of a group of small, slender, terrestrial carnivores. Uniform dark grey-brown except for a dozen black stripes across its back, it is a diurnal mongoose occurring in playful family groups, or troops, in most habitats throughout Zambia. It feeds on insects, scorpions, amphibians, reptiles and even carrion and bird's eggs, and can move through the bush at quite a pace.

Similar species: Another eight or so mongoose species occur in Zambia; some are social and gather in troops, others are solitary. Several are too scarce and nocturnal to be seen by casual visitors. Of the rest, the water or **marsh mongoose** (*Atilax paludinosus*) is large, normally solitary and has a very scruffy brown coat; it's widespread in the wetter areas. The **white-tailed mongoose** (*Ichneumia albicauda*), or white-tailed ichneumon, is a solitary, large brown mongoose with long, coarse, woolly hair. It is nocturnal and easily identified by its bushy white tail if seen crossing roads at night. It's not uncommon in cattle-ranching areas, where it eats the beetle-grubs found in the manure.

The **slender mongoose** (*Galerella sanguinea*) is as widespread and also solitary, but it is very much smaller (shoulder height 10cm) and has a uniform brown or reddish coat and blackish tail tip. Its tail is held up when it runs, and it is common throughout Zambia where there is lots of cover for it.

Finally, **the dwarf mongoose** (*Helogate parvula*) is a diminutive (shoulder height 7cm), highly sociable light brown mongoose often seen in the vicinity of the termite mounds where it nests. This is Africa's smallest carnivore, occurring in a higher density than any other, and is widespread throughout Zambia. Groups of 20–30 are not unknown, consisting of a breeding pair and subordinate others. These inquisitive little animals can be very entertaining to watch.

The **large grey mongoose** (*Herpestes ichneumon*), also called the Egyptian mongoose, is a large mongoose with course, grey-speckled body hair, black lower legs and feet, and a black tip to its tail. It's found all over Zambia, but is common nowhere, is generally diurnal and is solitary or lives in pairs. It eats small rodents, reptiles, birds and also snakes – generally killing rather than scavenging.

The **bushy-tailed mongoose** (*Bdeogale crassicaude*) is a small, mainly nocturnal species that looks mainly black, especially its legs and tail. It is found throughout Zambia, though appears relatively uncommon south of the Zambezi.

Meller's mongoose (*Rhynchogale melleri*) is a variable shaggy, grey colour with dark legs and a large muzzle. Its distribution is patchy and somewhat uncertain, but it is thought to occur throughout western Zambia and the Luangwa, but not north of the Serenje–Mbala road. It is solitary and nocturnal, eating a large proportion of termites as well as reptiles, amphibians and fruit.

Selous's mongoose (*Paracynictis selousi*) is smaller, with fine, speckled grey fur, and a white tip at the end of its tail. It likes open country and woodlands, occurring in many areas of southern and western Zambia, even including the Luangwa. It is nocturnal and solitary, eating mainly insects, grubs, small reptiles and amphibians – it seems especially fond of the larvae of dung beetles, and so is sometime found in cattle country.

Honey badger *Mellivora capensis* Shoulder height 30cm. Weight 12kg.
Also known as the ratel, the honey badger is black with a puppyish face and grey-white back. It is an opportunistic feeder best known
for its allegedly symbiotic relationship with a bird
called the honeyguide which leads it to a bee hive,
waits for it to tear it open, then feeds on the scraps. The
honey badger is among the most widespread of African
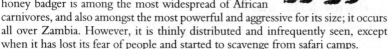
carnivores, and also amongst the most powerful and aggressive for its size; it occurs all over Zambia. However, it is thinly distributed and infrequently seen, except when it has lost its fear of people and started to scavenge from safari camps.

Similar species: Several other mustelids occur in the region, including the **striped polecat** (*Ictonyx striatus*), a widely distributed but rarely seen nocturnal creature with black underparts and a bushy white back, and the similar but much scarcer striped weasel (*Poecilogale albincha*). This has been reported from several locations in Zambia, but only rarely.

The **Cape clawless otter** (*Aonyx capensis*) is a brown freshwater mustelid with a white collar, whilst the smaller **spotted-necked otter** (*Lutra maculicollis*) is darker with light white spots on its throat. Both occur fairly commonly throughout the rivers, swamps and lakes of Zambia.

Aardvark (*Orycteropus afer*) Shoulder height 60cm. Weight up to 70kg.
This singularly bizarre nocturnal insectivore is unmistakable with its long snout, huge ears and powerful legs, adapted to dig up the nests of termites, on which it feeds. Aardvarks occur throughout Southern Africa, except the driest western areas of the Namib. Though their distinctive three-toed tracks are often seen, and they

are not uncommon animals, sightings of them are rare.
Aardvarks prefer areas of grassland and sparse scrub, rather than dense woodlands. They are absent from Zambia's floodplains and marshes, but otherwise occur throughout the country where termites are found.

Pangolin *Manis temmincki* Total length 70–100cm. Weight 8–15kg.
Sharing the aardvaak's diet of termites and ants, the pangolin is another very unusual nocturnal insectivore — with distinctive armour plating and a tendency to roll up in a ball when disturbed. (Then it can swipe its tail from side to side – inflicting serious damage on its aggressor.) Sometimes known as Temminck's pangolins, or scaly anteaters, these strange animals walk on their hindlegs, using their tail and front legs for balance. They are both nocturnal and rare – so sightings are exceedingly unusual and their distribution is uncertain. However, they are thought to occur in Kafue National Park and southern Zambia, as well as in the Luangwa Valley. (Evidence of their occurrence in the Luangwa is limited to about two sightings over the last few decades.)

In some areas further south, particularly Zimbabwe, local custom is to make a present of any pangolin found to the paramount chief (often taken to mean the president). This has caused great damage to their population.

Porcupine *Hystrix africaeaustralis* Total length 80–100cm. Weight 15–25kg.
This is the largest rodent found in the region, and occurs throughout Zambia and all over Southern Africa. It easily identified by its black-and-white striped quills, generally black hair, and shambling gait. If heard in the dark, then the slight rattle of its quills augments the rustle of its foraging. These quills drop off fairly regularly, and are often found in the bush.

The porcupine's diet is varied, and they are fairly opportunistic when it comes to food. Roots and tubers are favourites, as is the bark of certain trees; they will also eat meat and small reptiles or birds if they have the chance.

Similar species: Also spiky, the **Southern African hedgehog** (*Erinaceus frontalis*) has been recorded in a few locations in Zambia, including the Lusaka, Mumbwa and Chipata areas. It's likely to occur elsewhere, though is small and nocturnal, so rarely seen even where it does occur. Hedgehogs are about 20cm long (much smaller than porcupines), omnivorous and uncommon.

Yellow-spotted rock hyrax *Heterohyrax brucei* Length 35–50cm. Weight 2.5–3.5kg.
Rodent-like in appearance, hyraxes (also known as dassies) are claimed to be the closest living relative of elephants. Yellow-spotted rock hyraxes are often seen sunning themselves in rocky habitats, and become tame when used to people.
They are social animals, living in large groups, and largely herbivores, eating leaves, grasses and fruits. Where you see lots of dassies, watch out for black eagles and other raptors which prey extensively on them.

Similar species: Very similar, the **tree hyrax** (*Dendrohyrax arboreus*) has been recorded in a few locations on the eastern side of the country, including South Luangwa.

Scrub hare *Lepus saxatilis* Shoulder height 45–60cm. Weight 1–4.5kg.
This is the largest and commonest African hare, occurring throughout Zambia. In some areas a short walk, or drive, at dusk or after nightfall might reveal three or four scrub hares. They tend to freeze when disturbed.

Tree squirrel *Paraxerus cepapi* Total length 35cm. Weight 100–250g.
This common rodent is a uniform grey or buff colour, with a long tail that is furry but not bushy. It's widely distributed all over Southern and East Africa, and occurs throughout Zambia in most woodland habitats, although not wet evergreen or montane forests. It's often so common in mopane woodlands that it can be difficult to avoid seeing it, hence its other common name – the mopane squirrel.

Tree squirrels can live alone, in pairs or in small family groups, usually nesting in a drey of dry leaves, in a hole in a tree. They are diurnal and venture down to the ground to feed on seeds, fruit, nuts, vegetable matter and small insects. When alarmed they will usually bolt up the nearest tree, keeping on the side of the trunk away from the threat and so out of sight as much as possible. If they can attain a safe vantage point with a view of the threat, then they'll sometimes make a loud clicking alarm call.

Similar species: The **sun squirrel** (*Heliosciurus rufobrachium*) is the largest of Zambia's squirrels, and is found everywhere north of a rough line between Kabwe and Lukulu. It has similar habits to those of the more common tree squirrel, though will lie in the sun more often. Its colour varies considerably between individuals, and seasons, from light fawn to greyish brown, though its long bushy tail is consistently crossed by numerous whitish, longitudinal stripes.

The **red and black squirrel** (*Heliosciurus lucifer*) is a very pretty species with flame-red upper parts, a black patch in the middle of its back, and whitish underside. It occurs only in montane forest and in Zambia is thought to be restricted to the Nyika Plateau.

The **Boehm's squirrel** (*Paraxerus boehmi*) has a similar size, shape, and greyish colouring to the tree squirrel. However, it has two very distinct white stripes, bordered by black, down the side of its back from nape to tail. It inhabits riverine evergreen forest, and has a limited distribution in Zambia, restricted to the country's far north, around the Sumbu and Lusenga Plain areas.

The **flying squirrel** (*Anomalurus derbianus*) is quite unmistakable as there's a membrane of skin linking the fore and hind legs, and also the base of the tail. It uses this to glide with, when jumping from a higher branch to a lower one. It's a solitary, arboreal species that prefers miombo woodlands. It occurs from the Liuwa area east across Mwinilunga and the Copperbelt, and into the western side of northern Zambia, but is seldom seen.

Appendix 2

LANGUAGES

Zambia's main language groups are briefly outlined in *Chapter 3*. This section will try to note down just a few useful phrases, and give their local translations in six of the most frequently encountered languages: Nyanja, Lozi, Luvale, Lunda, Tonga and Bemba. The visitor will probably find Nyanja the most useful of these. However, in the more remote areas – like the Western Province – where Nyanja is not spoken, the other languages will prove invaluable.

Space is too short here, and my knowledge too limited, to give a detailed pronunciation guide to these six languages. However all are basically phonetic and by far the best way to learn the finer nuances of pronouncing these phrases is to find some Zambians to help you as soon as you arrive. Asking a Zambian to help you with a local language is also an excellent way to break the ice with a new local acquaintance, as it involves them talking about a subject that they know well, and in which they are usually confident.

As noted in *Cultural guidelines*, pages 30–31, learning a few simple phrases in the local language will go a long way towards helping the independent traveller to have an easy and enjoyable time in Zambia. Just remember to laugh at yourself, and have fun. Most Zambians will be very impressed and applaud your efforts to speak their language, no matter how hard they may laugh!

	Nyanja	**Lozi**	**Bemba**
how are you?	*muli bwanji?*	*muzuhile cwani?*	*mwashibukeni?*
I am fine	*good bwino*	*lu zuhile hande*	*eyamukwayi*
yes	*inde*	*kimona*	*eya ye*
no	*iyayi*	*baatili*	*awe*
thank you	*zikomo*	*nitumezi*	*twa to te la*
hey you!	*iwe!*	*wena!*	*iwe!*
I want	*ndifuna*	*nabata*	*ndefwaya*
there	*kunja*	*kwale*	*kulya*
here	*apa*	*faa*	*Hapa*
stop	*imilira*	*yema*	*iminina*
let's go	*tiyeni or tye*	*aluye*	*natuleya*
help me	*niyetizipita*	*nituse kwteni*	*ngafweniko*
how much?	*zingati?*	*kibukayi?*	*shinga?*
it is too much!	*yadula!*	*kihahulu!*	*fingi!*
where can I find...?	*alikuti...?*	*uinzi kai...?*	*kwisa...?*
the doctor	*sing'ang'a doctoro*	*mualafi*	*shinganga*
the police	*kapokola*	*mupokola*	*kapokela*
the market	*kumusika*	*kwamusika*	*ekobashita fyakulya*
drinking water	*mazi akumwa*	*mezi a kunwa*	*amenshi ayakunwa*
some food	*chakudya*	*sakuca*	*ichakulya*

	Lunda	Tonga	Luvale
how are you?	*mudi nahi?*	*mwabuka buti?*	*ngacili?*
I am fine	*cha chiwahi*	*kabotu*	*kanawa*
yes	*ena*	*inzya*	*eawa*
no	*inehi*	*pepe*	*kagute*
thank you	*kusakililaku*	*twalumba*	*gunasakulila*
hey you!	*enu!*	*yebo!*	*enu!*
I want	*nakukena*	*ndiyanda*	*gikutonda*
there	*kuna*	*okuya*	*haaze*
here	*kunu*	*aano or awa*	*kuno*
stop	*imanaku*	*koyima or ima*	*imana*
let's go	*tuyena*	*atwende*	*tuyenga*
help me	*kwashiku*	*ndigwashe*	*gukafweko*
how much?	*anahi?*	*ongaye?*	*jingayi?*
it is too much!	*yayivulu!*	*chadula! or zinji!*	*yayivulu!*
where can I find...?	*kudihi...?*	*ulikuli...?*	*ali kuli...?*
the doctor	*ndotolu*	*mun'g'anga*	*ndotolo*
the police	*kapokola*	*kappokola*	*kapokola*
the market	*chisakanu*	*musika*	*mushika*
drinking water	*meji akunwa*	*maanzi akunywa*	*meya a kunwa*
some food	*chakuda*	*chakulya*	*kulya*

NAMES
Judi Helmholz

During your travels you may have the good fortune to meet a Wireless, a Handbrake or an Engine. If you are really lucky, you may encounter a Cabbage. These are names of people I have met in Zambia.

Looking for Fame and Fortune? Look no further than twin boys living in the Western Province. Beware of Temptation though, he is a money-changer known for calculating exchanges solely to his advantage.

Working with Sunday and Friday got rather amusing, 'Sunday, can you work on Saturday with Friday?' Working with Trouble was another matter entirely, as we had frequently to enquire, 'Where can I find Trouble?' Gift, true to his namesake, felt compelled to ask for one, while Lunch took on a whole new meaning and Clever is a friend who is true to his name.

Unusual names aren't limited solely to English. For example, there is Mwana Uta which literally means 'son of a gun', and Saka Tutu meaning 'father of an insect'. Pity the local man named Mwana Ngombe or 'child of a cow'!

Appendix 3

FURTHER READING
Historical

Africa: A Biography of the Continent by John Reader. 1997. Penguin Books Ltd, 27 Wrights Lane, London W8 5TZ, England. ISBN 0-241-13047-6. Over 700 pages of highly readable history, interwoven with facts and statistics, to make a remarkable overview of Africa's past. Given that Zambia's boundaries were imposed from Europe, its history *must* be looked at from a pan-African context to be understood. This book can show you that wider view; it is compelling and essential reading. Chapter 47 is largely devoted to the Lozi people.

A History of Zambia by Andrew Roberts. 1976. Africana Publishing Company, a division of Holmes & Meier Publishers, 30 Irving Place, New York, NY 10003. ISBN 0-8419-0291-7. A detailed and complete history of Zambia, from prehistory to 1974.

Black Heart – Gore-Browne & the Politics of Multiracial Zambia by Robert I Rotberg. 1977. University of California Press, Berkley. ISBN 0-520-03164-4

David Livingstone and the Victorian Encounter with Africa. 1996. National Portrait Gallery, London. ISBN 1-85514-185-X. Six essays on Livingstone's life, concentrating on not only what he did, but also on how he was perceived in the UK.

Tales of Zambia by Dick Hobson. 1996. Zambia Society Trust, London. ISBN 0-952-7092-5-2. This is a lovely book, cataloguing big moments in Zambia's history, as well as some of its quirkier incidents and characters. It has sections on legends, mining, and the country's flora and fauna and is very readable. Dick Hobson's knowledge and love of Zambia shine through.

The Africa House by Christine Lamb. 1999. Viking. ISBN 0-670-87727-1. This is a fascinating book, piecing together the life and times of Sir Stewart Gore-Browne from diaries, correspondence and memories. It's a spellbinding tale, told eloquently. If this can't convey the fascination of Shiwa, and make you want to see it, then nothing can.

The Lake of the Royal Crocodiles by Eileen Bigland. Hodder and Stoughton, 1939.

Travels and Researches in Southern Africa by David Livingstone. 1857. This classic is fascinating reading, over a century after it was written.

Guidebooks

A Visitor's Guide to Nyika National Park, Malawi by Sigrid Anna Johnson. Mbabazi Book Trust, Blantyre. Length 150 pages; costs around US$4. It is available at most good bookshops in Blantyre and Lilongwe, and at the park reception at Chilinda. The book provides a detailed historical and ecological background to Nyika, 20 pages of special-interest sites and notes on recommended walks and hikes, as well as complete checklists of all mammals, birds, butterflies and orchids which are known to occur in the park. In short, an essential purchase.

Kasanka – A Visitor's Guide to Kasanka National Park by Lucy Farmer. First published July 1992 by the Kasanka Trust. A superb little 36-page guide, which includes comprehensive sections on the geography, vegetation, wildlife, birdlife, and facilities for visitors at Kasanka. Get hold of a copy if you can – try the Kasanka Trust in the UK, the Wildlife Shop in Lusaka, or the main Wasa Lodge in the park. Note that its map of the park's roads is now inaccurate.

National Monuments of Zambia by D W Phillipson, revised by NM Katanekwa. First published in Zambia by the National Heritage Conservation Commission in 1972 (4th printing 1992). Look for this small, green paperback around Lusaka, and buy it if you see one as they're quite scarce. It describes all of Zambia's national monuments, including many historical monuments, archaeological sites, and even places of great scenic beauty – with some great old black-and-white photos.

Travelogues

Pole to Pole by Michael Palin. 1999. BBC Consumer Publishing, UK. ISBN: 0563551062. This has an excellent section on Zambia, and Shiwa N'gandu in particular is covered well.

Survivor's Song: Life and Death in an African Wilderness by Mark & Delia Owens. First published in the UK by HarperCollins in 1993. Published as *The Eye of the Elephant* in the USA. ISBN 0-00-638096-4. This relates the authors' struggles to protect the wildlife of North Luangwa National Park from poachers, and their efforts to develop viable alternatives to poaching for the local people. It is excellent reading, though insiders complain of sensationalism, and that it ignores valuable contributions made by others.

Kakuli: A Story about Wild Animals by Norman Carr. 1996. CBC Publishing. ISBN 0797-415785. A collection of Norman Carr's tales from his time in the Luangwa Valley. Excellent light reading whilst on safari.

General reference

An Explorer's Handbook – Travel, Survival and Bush Cookery by Christina Dodwell. 1984. Hodder and Stoughton, 47 Bedford Square, London, WC1B 3DP. ISBN 0-340-34937-9. 170+ pages of both practical and amusing anecdotes, including chapters on 'unusual eatables', 'building an open fire', and 'tested exits from tight corners'. Practical advice for both plausible and most unlikely eventualities – and it's a great read.

Bugs, Bites & Bowels by Dr Jane Wilson-Howarth. Published in the UK by Cadogan Books Plc, London House, Parkgate Road, London SW11 4NQ. Distributed in the US by Globe Pequot Press. ISBN 0-86011-045-2. An amusing and erudite overview of the hazards of tropical travel which is small enough to take with you.

Zambia – Debt & Poverty by John Clark. 1989. Oxfam, 274 Banbury Road, Oxford, OX2 7DZ. This slim volume looks with clarity at Zambia's international debt, its causes and its consequences.

Wildlife reference

A Field Guide to Zambian Birds not found in Southern Africa by Dylan Aspinwall and Carl Beel. 1998. Zambian Ornithological Society. ISBN 9982-811-00-1. This excellent small guide is designed to complement a book covering Africa south of the Zambezi, like Newman's guide, by describing only the birds occurring in Zambia which aren't included in Newman's guide. It's widely available in Zambia, but difficult to find elsewhere.

African Wild Dog Survey in Zambia by Kenneth Buk of the Zoological Museum, PO Box 60086, University of Copenhagen. This piece of academic research looked at the distribution of wild dogs in Zambia in 1994, the reasons for their decline, and their possibilities for long-term survival.

A Guide to Common Wild Mammals of Zambia. 1991. Wildlife and Environmental Conservation Society of Zambia. ISBN 9982-05-000-1. A small field guide to the more common species, obtainable from the Wildlife Shop in Lusaka, or direct from the WECSZ.

A Guide to Reptiles, Amphibians & Fishes of Zambia. 1993. Wildlife Conservation Society of Zambia. ISBN 9982-05-001-X. Another good guide to the more common species, obtainable from the Wildlife Shop in Lusaka, or direct from the WECSZ.

A Guide to the Common Wild Flowers of Zambia and Neighbouring Regions. 1995. Macmillan Educational Ltd, London. ISBN 0-333-64038-1. This is a good small field guide to the more

common species, obtainable from the Wildlife Shop in Lusaka, or direct from the WECSZ.
A Guide to the Wildlife of the Luangwa Valley by Norman Carr. Montford Press, Limbe, Malawi.
First edition 1985, revised and reprinted '87 and '97. This small paperback (70 pages) was
written by the valley's most famous guide and conservationist. It's not comprehensive, but is
fascinating for the author's personal insights into the Luangwa area and its wildlife.
Common Birds of Zambia. Revised 1993. Zambian Ornithological Society. ISBN 9982-9901-0-1.
A good small field guide to the more common species, obtainable from the Wildlife Shop in
Lusaka, or direct from the WECSZ.
Common Trees, Shrubs and Grasses of the Luangwa Valley by PP Smith. 1995. Trendrine Press,
Zennor, St. Ives, Cornwall. ISBN 0-9512562-3-8. This small, practical field guide has
pictures to aid identification at the back, and includes a small section on the value to wildlife
of the various plants.
Newman's Birds of Southern Africa by Kenneth Newman. Southern Book Publishers, PO Box
3103, Halfway House 1685, South Africa. ISBN 1-86812-623-4. This has been re-published
numerous times since its first edition in 1988 and has become the standard field guide to
birds in southern Africa, south of the Kunene and Zambezi Rivers. It also covers most species
found in Zambia.

Websites

Website addresses seem to change frequently, especially in Zambia, but some of the more
interesting include:

expert.cc.purdue.edu/~warrier/addresse.htm An address book of Zambiophiles – many seem to be
young Zambians keeping up with their classmates.
www.africa-insites.com/zambia/ This is large Zambian resource has been well put together. It
includes extensive general information, plus numerous useful advertisements.
www.eurekanet.com/~sid/consulates/zca.shtml Lists the contact details of Zambian
consulates in other countries, whilst foreign consulates in Zambia are on
www.eurekanet.com/~sid/consulates/fciz.shtml. Good guides, but not infallible.
www.lowdown.co.zm/index.html An electronic version of *Lusaka Lowdown*'s monthly magazine
(see page 144). It's topical, informative and fun.
www.ftzambia.co.zm/ The *Financial Times of Zambia*, with up-to-date finance news and views
on the country.
www.sunvil.co.uk/africa/ Sunvil Discovery Africa's home page, including an on-line version of
virtually all of the information in this guide, and other guides I write, such as Bradt's *Namibia*
guide. Watch for regular updates, articles and info here, order a brochure if you're thinking
of travelling, and subscribe to the newsletter to get the latest special offers on trips to Zambia.
www.zamnet.zm/zamnet/times/times.html The extensive side of the *Times of Zambia*. Featuring
the main stories of the day, plus a searchable (but not listed) archive containing selected
stories from August 1996 to the present day.
www.zamnet.zm/zamnet/post/news/fpstory.html For a more independent view, look at this site
from *The Post* newspaper. It usually takes a more objective, critical and questioning approach.
Full archives of back copies from October 1995 to the present day. A first-class resource for
researchers.

THE PRICE OF LOVE
Judi Helmholz

People who say you cannot put a price on love have obviously never been to Zambia. Like many African countries, Zambia maintains its tradition of *lobola* or bride price, which must be negotiated and paid to the bride's parents before two people are permitted to marry. Lobola is paid in cows or cash or a combination thereof. Some entrepreneurial new in-laws might consider a 'pay as you earn' scheme, but often it is a case of no money, no marriage.

When we planned a trip to the Western Province, Victor, a friend, asked if he could come. He wanted to find a wife from his home village to bring back to Livingstone. Could we also loan him some money with which to pay the *lobola*? We agreed.

We dropped Victor off at his village, leaving him to initiate his search for a prospective wife. Two hours later we returned to find him with a huge smile on his face. 'I have found one!' he exclaimed. He had found two, as it turned out. 'Come and see,' he said excitedly, grabbing our hands and dragging us through the village to meet his prospective brides. 'OK!' he commanded, pointing to two young woman, neither of whom he had met before this morning. 'Choose one for me!' he said, smiling and pushing the women forward for our inspection. The girls looked at us blankly. 'Victor, we are merely loaning you the money. You must choose your own wife.'

A few hours later, we heard the wailing of women from the village. Victor must have made his decision. He came into camp with one of the girls in tow. 'This is Brona – my new wife!' he exclaimed. Brona was not smiling. She knew only that she would be leaving her village for a place she'd never been to, with a man she'd never met before, for possibly the rest of her life.

After some negotiation, Victor had paid Brona's father a deposit of Kw50,000 (about US$50) for his daughter. Driving back to Livingstone, Victor and Brona sat in the back seat holding hands. We hoped things might work out for the two of them.

Two British friends living in Zambia got a big surprise when they approached the council for a marriage licence. 'How much *lobola* did you pay?' the official asked. 'Nothing,' replied John. The official was aghast.

'You are telling me you paid nothing. You must have paid something!' Sue finally commented, 'John purchased my air ticket from the UK.' The official smiled, satisfied at last. 'Ah yes, you see, you did pay. What is the value of this?' 'Approximately US$1,000,' replied John. The official took John aside and whispered into his ear 'You paid too much!'

Arthur and I? We also got married in Zambia. *Lobola*? Of course! Arthur paid ten cows for me. My parents live in the USA, so Arthur arranged for a herd of ten small cows to be carved out of wood for my father. The herd sits on my father's mantelpiece at home and he proudly tells all visitors, 'That's what I got for my daughter.'

Index

Page numbers in **bold** indicate main entries, those in *italics* indicate maps.

abseiling 181, 186, 191
accommodation 6, 93, 98–9
adrenaline Sports 181
agriculture 20
AIDS 72
airlines 45, 94, 113–4, 149, 171, 327
alcohol 100
altitude 3, 35, 226
American Express (AMEX) 134
animal dangers 82, 87, 199
animals 36–40, 293, **377–93**,
arrest 76
Asian Zambians 27

Bahati Lodge 360, 362
Bangweulu GMA 269, 270, 275
Bangweulu Swamps 40, 44, 192, 259, 263, 266,
 270–5, 279
banks 94, 135, 166
Bantu 26
Barotseland 25, 26, 353, **358–70**
Barotseland Fishing Tours and Safaris Camp
 360, 362
Base Camp 254
Bateleur Farm 255, 277
Batoka 204
Batoka Gorge 149
bazaars 136
Bechuanaland 10
Bemba 24, 25
Big Lagoon Camp 236
bilharzia 73, 199, 292
Bilimungwe Trails Camp 236, 237, 257
binoculars 57, 59, 87
birdlife 40, 51, 179, 229, 266, 271, 293, 308, 333,
 347, 369
black market 55
black-cotton soil 81
Blue Lagoon National Park 329, **346–51**
boat-taxi 290
books 140, 167, **397–9**
borders 46, 195
bribery 77
British Council 141, 265
British South Africa Company 4, 11–12, 196,
 313
Broken Hill Man 7, 317
budgeting 55
buffalo 39, 50, 51, 88, 186, 188, 212, 227, 253,
 296, 308, 332, 333, 347, 369, 388
Buffalo Camp 254
Bulaya 298
bungee-jumping 181, 183
Busanga Plains 329, 332–2, 335, 346
Busanga Swamps 335
buses 96, 115, 152, 284, 289, 360

cameras 59, 87
campfires 83
camping **82–6**, 286, 395, 341
camping equipment 57, 84
canoeing **89–91**, 181, 182, 191, 192, 193, 217
Caprivi Strip 153, 374
car hire 60, 79, 142, 168, 177
Carr, Norman 41, 86, 225—6, 256, 257
carvings 120, 136, 138, 140, 141, 167, 168, 180,
 181
Central African Federation 4, 12
Chama 26, 223, 255
Chamafumbu Camp 336
Chamilandu Bushcamp 237, 256, 339
Chaminuka 98, 121
Changwena Falls 260
charities 33, 92
Chavuma 46, 357
Chavuma Falls 358
cheetah 39, 212, 332, 378
Chendani Trails Camp 236—7, 257
Cheté Island 195, 205
Chewa 9, 30
Chiawa Camp 215
Chiawa GMA 211
Chibembe 237, 255, 256
Chichele Safari Lodge 238
Chifungwe Game Scouts' Camp 255
Chifungwe Plain 225, 226, 228
Chikana Island 195, 207
Chikufwe Plain 269
Chilanga 103, 217, 370
Chilinda 309
Chilinda Camp 308–9
Chilongozi 237, 238, 256, 338, 339, 370
Chiluba, Frederick 5, 15, 16, 17
Chimfunshi Wildlife Orphanage 327–8
chimpanzees 327–8
Chingola 313, **327–8**, 355
Chinsali 278, 284
Chinyingi Mission 357
Chinzombo Safari Lodge 238, 256
Chipata 29, 116, 219, **221–3**, *222*, 233, 245, 260
Chipoma Falls 278
Chipundu 262
Chirundu 46, 199, 207, 209, 211, 213, 217
Chirundu Forest Reserve 209
Chisamba 98, 117
Chisamba Safari Lodge 122
Chisengu 233
Chishimba Falls 287
chitenje 167
Chitipa 47, 220
Chitongo 343
Chiundaponde 269, 273–4
Chizarira National Park 189, 193
Chobe National Park 188, 190, 191

cholera 56
Choma 195, **196–7**, 205, 342
Chongo 347
Chundukwa River Camp 160, 188, 191, 354
Chunga (in Kafue) 344, 346, 350
Chunga (in Lochinvar) 349, 350
cichlids 293–4
cigarettes 100
climate 3, 35
clothing 56, 87
coaches 96, 116, 152
coal 19
cobalt 19
conservation **40–4**, 231, 251
constitution 15
contraceptive pills 68
copper 11, 14, 19
Copperbelt 11, 12, 24, 46, **313—28**, *314*
Coppinger, John 89, 232, 244, 253, 254, 257
cost of living 93
cotton 8, 9, 10, 20, 56, 57, 134, 141, 329
coup 16
couriers 142, 169
crocodiles 51, 90, 137, 199, 204, 228, 249, 294, 297, 333
cultural guidelines 30
currency 5, 93

dambo 39, 269, 333, 373
David Shepherd Camp 104, 342, 344
De Beers 10
debt, national 13, 17, 18
Democratic Republic of Congo (DRC) 16, 25, 46, 266, 305, 315, 354
dentists 68, 109
development 41, 42, 231
diarrhoea 71
dress 30, 31
drinks 101, 140, 166
driving **79–82**, 91, 97, 361
drugs 76
Dumdumwenze Gate 196, 342

eclipse, solar *52*, 53–5
economy 4, **17–20**
education 32
elections 13, 15
electricity 107
elephant 39, 85, 88, 186, 212, 227, 231, 308, 332, 333, 374, 387
elephant-riding 186, 193
email 106
embassies
   Zambian abroad 48
   foreign in Zambia 107
emergencies 142, 169, 326
Enhanced Structural Adjustment Facility (ESAF) 18
entry requirements **47–9**
exchange rate 94
expatriates 27
exports 19

fax 106
Federation of African Societies 12
festivals 27, 357
film 60, 167
fish 293
Flatdogs 245, 246
Flight of Angels 181
flights 50
floodplain 39, 359, 361
food 69, **99–101**, 140, 166

footwear 57
forest 37–9
Fort Elwes 260
fuel 79, 291

Game Management Area (GMA) 43, 44, 331, 332
GDP 17, 18, 20
gemstones 5, 20
geology 35, 102, 226
getting to Zambia **45–7**
giraffe 3, 40, 123, 187, 208, 212, 228, 253, 374, 388
Gore-Browne, Stewart 12, 251, 278
government 5
GPS (global positioning system) 58
greetings 30
Gwabi Lodge 209, 211, 217
Gwisho Hot Springs 349

health **65–75**
heat exhaustion 69
hepatitis 72
hippo 89, 90, 195, 199, 228, 294, 297, 333, 336, 388
Hippo Camp 338
history 4, **7–17**
hitchhiking 97, 233, 245, 277, 284, 289, 309, 315, 360
horse-riding 186, 191, 311
hospitals 68, 109
houseboats 103
humanism 14
hunting 43, 231, 295, 332
Hwange National Park 189, 192
hyena, spotted 39, 86, 212, 229, 266, 332, 367, 374, 389
hygiene 91

Ikelenge 46, 354
Ila 29
impala 40, 41, 51, 331, 385
imports 14, 109
immunisations 66
Independence 12
inflation 17, 93, 94
Ingombe Ilede 8
Ingwe 335, 356
inoculations 66
insect bites 69
insect repellents 58, 68, 70, 74, 167, 190, 271
insurance 65
International Monetary Fund (IMF) 5, 14, 15, 18
internet 106, 143, 169
Iron Age 8, 261, 294, 313
Isanga Bay Lodge 292, 295
Isangano National Park 275
Isoka 26, 223, 278, 284
Isokwe 305
Itezhi-Tezhi Dam 342, 343, 344
itineraries 64

Jivundu 356
judicial system 5
Jumbe 233

Kabanga Post 335
Kabompo 355, 358
Kabompo River 355, 357, 358
Kabulushi Post 336
Kabwata Cultural Centre 101, 136
Kabwe 7, *316*, **317–19**

Kabweluma Falls 304
Kafue (town) 81, 207
Kafue Flats 7, 29, 329, 347
Kafue River 207, 211, 332, 346, 347
Kafue National Park 40, 103, 188, 191, **329–46**, 355, 358
Kafunta 237
Kafunta River Lodge 236, 237
Kafwala Camp 339
Kafwala 104, 333, 336
Kaingo 236, 240
Kakuli Bushcamp 240, 257
Kalabo 360–1, 365, 367, 368, 370
Kalambo Falls **291–5**, 301
Kalambo Lodge 291
Kalambo River 294
Kalene Hill 354
Kalimba Reptile Park 137
Kalobolelwa 375, 376
Kalomo 196, 342
Kalundu Mound 196
Kalungwishi River 303–5
Kanona 261, 263
Kaoma 358–9, 360, 363, 365
Kaonde 25, 30
Kapabi Swamp 265, 268
Kapamba 246
Kapani 237, 257
Kapani Safari Lodge 86, 226, 236, 240
Kapiri Mposhi 47, 96, 116, 259, 267, 263, 271, 283, 301, 313, **315**, 317
Kapishya Hot Springs 281
Kaputa 298, 305
Kariba 209, 213
Kariba Dam 46, 195, 199, 204, 217
Kariba Gorge *194*
Kasaba Bay 297, 299
Kasama 24, 115, 277, 283, 284, 287, 297
Kasane 188, 376
Kasanga 289, 295
Kasanka National Park 44, 93, 262, **263–69**, *264*, 273
Kasempa 25, 335, 355, 359
Kasonso-Busanga GMA 335
Kasuma Pan National Park 189, 276
Katete 47
Katima Mulilo 46, 372, 375
Kaunda, Kenneth 5, 13, 14, 15, 16, 279, 351
Kawambwa 131, 305, 307, 280, 300
Kawaza 249–50
kayaking 161, 182–3, 373
Kayila Lodge 214
Kazungula 46, 188
Khama 10
Kiambi Camp 213
Kigoma 289
Kilwa 305
Kingfisher Camp 216
Kitwe 225, 313, **321–7**, *322*, 335, 355
Kiubo Camp 215
Konkola Deep 19
Kubu Cabins 160, 164, 175
Kufukwila 30
Kulamba 30
Kulefu Camp
Kunda 30
Kundabikwa Falls 260, 304
Kundalila Falls 262, 267
Ku-omboka 25, 28, 363
Kuyenda 237, 241, 256
Kwacha 93
Kwando River 374, 375

Lake Bangweulu 96, *258*, 269, **270–6**, 301
Lake Kariba **26**, 195, **199–207**
Lake Mweru 9, 302, 305
Lake Ndolwa 268
Lake Tanganyika 49, 276, 283, **292–4**, 301
Lake Tanganyika Lodge 291
Lake Waka Waka 262, 263, 267, 267, 273
language groups 23–6
languages 4, *22*, 23, **395–6**
Lavushi Manda National Park 208, 273
Lealui 28, 363, 368
Lechwe 98, 117, 123, 208
  black 386
  Kafue **386**
leopard 39, 50, 89, 212, 229, 266, 296, 308
Leopard Lodge 339
Libonda pontoon 368
Likumbi Lya Mize 29
Lilayi 117
Lilayi Lodge 98, 123
Limulunga 28, 29, 363
lion 39, 50, 84, 88, 212, 229, 253, 266, 296, 332, 337, 369, 374, 377
Lion Camp 241, 297
Litunga 9, 28, 363
Liuwa Plain National Park 44, 353, 368
Livingstone 17, 25, 56, 116, *148*, **149–71**, *150*, 205
Livingstone, David 10, 145, 178, 262, 372
Livingstone Island 161, 187
Livingstone Memorial 187, 262, 263, 267, 269, 301
Lobengula 10
local buses **96**, 113
location 3
Lochinvar National Park 103, 198, 329, 343, **346–51**, *348*
Lower Zambezi 49, 50, 81, 89, 103, 195, 271, 277, 226
Lower Zambezi National Park 44, 205, **211–18**
Lozi 19, 25, 28, 159, 363, 367
Luambe National Park 219, 233, **254–6**
Luamfwa Camp 246
Luanginga River 367, 370
Luangwa River 89, 217, 226
Luangwa Valley 49, 50, 81, 86, 212, **219–58**, *220*
Luapula River 24, 279, 302
Lubi River 226, 240, 241, 244, 254
Lubumbashi 327
Lubungu Pontoon 335, 336, 356
Luchazi 25
Lufubu River 298
Lufupa Lodge 93, 335, 336, 346
Lufupa River 333
Lukanga Swamps 329
Lukulu 358–9, 360, 363–5, *364*
Lukuni Luzwa Buuka 30
Lukusuzi National Park 219, 223
Lumangwe Falls 304
Lunda 25, 357
Lundazi 223
Lunga River 332, 333, 335, 336
Lunga River Lodge 335, 337
Lupande GMA 231, 237
Lusaka 24, *112*, **113–143**, *118–19*, 263, 325, 329, 358
  Cairo Road *132*
Lusaka Lowdown 144
Lusenga Plain National Park 283, 305
Luula 368, 369, 370
Luvale 25, 29, 357
Luwi Bushcamp 241, 257
Luwingu 106, 284, 286, 287, 307

Luwombwa River 267, 268
Luyana 25
Lwiinda 30
Lwitikila Falls 278
Lykumbi Lya Mize 357

M8 353, 356, 357, 358, 365
Maala 30
Machan Sitatunga Hide 265, 266, **268**
Makishi dancers 29, 366, 367
Malaila 30
malaria 67, 72, 74
Mambilima Falls 302
Mambwe-Lungu 25
mammals 39, 212, 265, 307
Mana Pools National Park 211, 217
Mansa 262, 263, 270, 298, 301, 302
maps 58, 117, 349
Maramba Cultural Village 180
Marula Lodge 246
markets 135
Mashi 25
Mazabuka 198
Maziba Bay 370, 372
Mbala 276, 277, 283, 287, 298, 307
Mbanga 360, 365
Mbereshi 302, 303
Mbunda 26
Mbwela 26
Mchenja Camp 227, 242
medical kit 67
Mercury Mail 104, 142, 171
Mfuwe 95, 225, *230*, 232–3, 237, 253
Mfuwe Lodge 99, 227, 236, 242, 257
microlighting 182, 373
Minde 368, 369, 370
minerals 11, 37, 71, 227, 293, 313
Mineworkers' Union 12
mining 19
miombo 3, 37, 265, 269, 307, 333, 374
Mishembe Bay 292, 295
missionaries 10, 286, 292, 357, 367, 373
Mize 29
Mkushi **259–61**
mobile safaris 248
money **55–6**, 166
Mongu 96, 116, 329, 353, 355, 358–9, 360, 363, 367, 371, 376
Monze 198, 342, 343, 347
Moore Pottery Factory 137
mopane 36, 212, 227, 255, 333
Moshi Camp 339
Mosi-oa-Tunya 40, 145
Mosi-oa-Tunya National Park 147, 180, 181, 187, 191, 192
Movement for Multiparty Democracy (MMD) 5, 15, 16
Mpata Gorge 217
Mpika 24, 223, 232, 255, 261, 263, 269, **270–6**, *276*, 283
Mporokoso 297, 303, 305–7
Mpulungu 46, 276, 283, 287, *288*, 289, *290*, 295, 297, 298, 307
Muchinga Escarpment 226, 251
Mukambi Safari Lodge 343
Mukuni village 180
Mumbuluma Falls 302
Mumbwa 25, 335, 342, 350
Munda Wanga Zoo and Botanical Gardens 137
munga 37
Mununga 298
Munyamadzi GMA 255, 267
Mupamadzi River 226, 248, 251, 253, 255, 256

museums 179, 195, 289, 363
Mushika Camp 216
Muslim traders 8
Musonda Falls 302
Musungwa Safari Lodge 345, 346
Mutanda River 355
Mutemwa Island Lodge 342, 375
Mutinonondo River 255
Muwele 269, 373–4
Muyombe 223
Mwaleshi River 253
Mwaleshi Camp 236, 254, 257
Mwamba 243
Mwambashi River Lodge 216
Mwansabombwe 29
Mwata Kazemba 9
Mwelemu 355
Mwense 302
Mweru Wantipa National Park 283, 298, 301, 305
Mwinilunga 46, 353, 354
Mzuzu 308, 309

Nabwalya 255
Nachikufu Caves 278
Nakonde 276, 283, 284, 315
Namwala 29, 343, 347
Namwanda Art Gallery 138
Nangoma 350
Nanzhila Plains 331–2, 342, 345
National Archives 138
national parks 43, 44
National Parks and Wildlife Service (NPWS) 43, 103, 270, 357, 370, 375
navigation 58, 79
Nchanga 19, 313
Nchelenge 295, 301, 302, 305
Nchila Wildlife Reserve 354
Ndola 96, 279, 297, 313, *318*, **319–321**
Ndole Bay Lodge 277, 298, 299, 300
New Kalala Camp 342, 344
newspapers 106
N'gandu 9
Ngoma 342–3
Ng'ona River 29
Ngoni 260
Ngonye Falls 358, 361, 371–3, 376
ngwee 94
Ngweze Pools 375
Niamkolo Church 292
nightlife 326
Nkala Mission 343
Nkamba Bay 297, 299
Nkamba Bay Lodge 298, 300
Nkana 19, 313, 321
Nkanga River Conservation Area 197
Nkoya 26
Nkoya-Mbwela 26
Nkundalila Falls. see Kundalila Falls
Nkwali 236, 243, 245, 257
Nkwali Pontoon 235
North Luangwa *252*
North Luangwa National Park 44, 219, **251–5**, 267, 281
Nsefu 245
Nsefu Cave 260
Nsefu Camp 86, 236, 243, 257
Nsefu Sector 227, 231*234*
Nsendamila 249
Nsenga 26, 30, 213
Nshima 99
Nsobe Safari Camp 262, 269, 273, 274
Nsolo Bushcamp 244, 257

Ntemwa River 333, 335, 338
Ntemwa Camp 335, 339
Ntumbachushi Falls 303
Nyamaluma 237
Nyaminyami 203, 204
Nyanja 26
Nyasaland 4, 12
Nyerere, Julius 14
Nyika 26
Nyika Plateau 35, 47, 223, 283, *306*, 307
Nyika Plateau National Park 283, **307–12**

Old Drift 147, 187
operators *see* tour operators
Owens, Mark and Delia 251–3

pan 39
parachuting 186, 191, 193
parliament 138
park entry fees 103
Pemba 198
Petauke 26, 219, 233
photography 31, 51, 59, 178
poaching 44, 213, 231, 265, 295, 332, 374
police 76–7
politics 5
pontoons 82
Pope, Jo and Robin 91, 245, 257
population 4, 21
post 104, 143, 169
postboat 96, 301, 361
postbuses 96, 115
privatisation 18, 19
public holidays 103
puku 40, 228, 253, 266, 296, 301, 331, 332, 335, 385
Puku Pans Camp 344

rabies 73
radio 107
rainfall *38*, 270
religion 4
Remote Africa Safaris 89
resources 5
restaurants 176
rhino 39, 88, 212, 213, 231, 333
Rhodes, Cecil 4, 10
Rhodesia
    Northern 4, 11, 12, 13, 147, 313
    Southern 4, 11, 12, 13
Ridgeway 117
rift valley 35, 211, 219, 226, 251, 288, 289, 292, 293, 294
riparian forest 269
rivers, crossing 82
river-boarding 185, 192, 193
River Club 161
Roads 79–80
Royal Zambezi Lodge 214
rubber 10
rubbish 91
Rumphi 308, 309

safari, organising 61
safety **75–8**
Sakazima Island Camp 376
Samfya 96, 262, 263, 270, 273, 301
San/bushmen 8, 261, 350
Sancta Maria Mission 367
Sandaula pontoon 360, 368
Sausage Tree Camp 215
scorpions 70, 86
Sebanzi Hill 350

Senanga 360, 371
Serenje 261, 267, 269, 270, 283, 301
Sesheke 46, 371, 372, 375
sexually transmitted diseases 72
Shangombo 375
Shimungenga 29
Shiwa N'gandu 251, 267, 278
shoebill stork 259, 266, 271
Shoebill Island 262, 267, 271–3, 274
shopping **101–3**, 139, 166
Shoprite/Checkers 102, 198
Showgrounds 138
Shumba Bushcamp 335, 337
Siavonga 195, 199, 209
Sinazongwe 195, 205, 206
Sindabezi Island 161
Sioma 375
Sioma Falls *see* Ngonye Falls
Sioma Mission 373
Sioma Ngwezi National Park 353, 373–4
sitatunga 208, 263, 265, 266, 268, 270, 275, 296, 300, 305, 331, 355, **384**
Sitoti 368, 371, 372
size 3, 35, 331
slave trade 9, 321
sleeping sickness 70, 74
snakes 70, 86, 89
Solwezi 313, 328, 335, 353, 354, 355, 358
Songwe Point 163
South Luangwa 103, 251
South Luangwa National Park 219, *224*, **225–51**, 267
South West Africa 10, 13
souvenirs 141, 167
spiders 70, 86
Stone Age 7, 261, 294
Sumbu National Park 44, 103, 293, **295–301**, *296*
Sumbu Township 297
sunburn 68, 69
Sunvil Discovery 62
Surveyor General 79, 117, 349

Tafika 236, 244, 254, 257
Taita Falcon Lodge 163
taxis 96, 134, 166
TAZARA 46, 96, 116, 259, 167, 276, 284, 301, 315
teak forest 37, 374
telephones 105, 171
television 107
telex 106
Tena Tena 236, 245, 257
tent 84
termites 99
theft 75
Thorn Tree Lodge 162, 193
Tiger Camp 360–1, 362, 365, 380
tipping 101
Tondwa GMA 295
Tonga 26, 29
Tongabezi 161, 205, 215, 256, 370
topography *34*
topology 35
tour operators 45, 47, 62, 256
    canoeing 161, 191, 192, 193, 201, 213–6, 218
    worldwide 62–3
    Zambian 62–3, 143–4, 191–3
    Zimbabwean 193
tourism 6, 20, 42, 53
trade 8, 9, 10, 13–14, 18
trade, fair 31–3
trains 96, 116, 152, 284, 315

transport **94–8**
Treetops 339
tribes 21
trypanosomiasis 74
tsetse fly 70, 74
Tumbuka 26
Tunduma 46, 315
Tundwe Camp 247
Tuwimba 30

ultra-light aircraft 182
Umutomboko 29
Undi 9
United National Independence Party (UNIP)
    5, 15

vaccinations 66
van der Post, Laurens 174, 176
vegetation 36, 50, 227
Victoria Falls 56, 145, *148*, 149, *170*, **171–94**,
    195
Victoria Falls National Park 187
visas 47, 190
Von Lettow-Vorbeck Monument 286

walking safaris 53, **86–7**, 189, 193, 248
Wasa Lodge 267, 268
water purification 101
waterbuck 3, 123, 197, 206, 212, 228, 264, 296,
    331, 355, **382**
Waterfront, The 162, 175, 193
Watopa Pontoon 356, 358, 359, 365
weather 49
welfare associations 12

West Lunga National Park 353, 355
Western Province **353–76**
what to take 56–8
when to go **49–55**
White Zambians 27
white-water rafting 181, 184, 193, 373
wild dog 39, 188, 229, 237, 296, 332, 369, 374,
    378
Wildlife and Environmental Conservation
    Society of Zambia (WECSZ) 104, 344
Wildlife Camp (*see also* David Shepherd Camp)
    93, 104, 247
women travellers 75, 76, 98
Wonder Gorge 261
World War II 11

Zaire *see* Democratic Republic of the Congo
Zambezi (town) 29, 353, 355, 357, 358
Zambezi National Park 176, 188
Zambezi River 25, 28, 89–90, 149, 195, 357, 360,
    365, 368, 372, 375
    Lower *194, 210*
    Upper 182, 192
Zambezi Royal Chundu Lodge 159
Zambezi Valley 207
Zambia 196
Zambia African National Congress (ZANC) 13
Zambia Consolidated Copper Mines (ZCCM)
    14, 17, 19
Zambia National Tourist Board 49
Zambia Open Community Schools (ZOCS) 32
Zambia Wildlife Authority 43, 103
Zebra Pans Bushcamp 245, 255
Zimba 195